THE FORMATIVE YEARS

ALBION PUBLISHING COMPANY
SAN FRANCISCO
1974

EDITED BY

STANLEY COOPERSMITH

RONALD FELDMAN

UNIVERSITY OF CALIFORNIA, DAVIS

the formative years
principles of
early childhood
education

ALBION PUBLISHING COMPANY

1736 STOCKTON STREET
SAN FRANCISCO, CALIFORNIA 94133

COVER PHOTOGRAPH BY JOHN ARMS
DESIGNER, NANCY CLARK

74-10357

Library of Congress Catalog Card Number 73-88383

ISBN 0-87843-614-6

98765432

ACKNOWLEDGMENTS

The articles in this volume are reprinted by permission from the works in which they originally appeared. We wish to acknowledge the permissions received from the following authors and publishers of each article and indicate the sources of their contributions.

1 Platt, J. R. Changing human nature. From *The step to man.* New York: Wiley, 1966. Pp. 160–168.
2 Plumb, J. H. The great change in children. Children: The victims of time. From *In the light of history.* London: Penguin, 1972. Pp. 153–166. Copyright J. H. Plumb, 1971, 1972.
3 Akers, M. E. Prologue: The why of early childhood education. From I. J. Gordon, *Early Childhood Education: Seventy-first yearbook of the National Society for Study of Education,* Pt. 2. Chicago: University of Chicago Press, 1972.
4 Caldwell, B. M., & Richmond, J. B. The impact of theories of child development. *Children,* March–April, 1962, 9:73–78.
5 Ambrose, E., & Miel, A. A perspective on social learning. From *Children's social learning: Implications of research and expert study.* Washington, D.C.: Association for Supervision and Curriculum Development, 1958. Pp. 17–22.
6 Havighurst, R. J., & Neugarten, B. L. Society and education. From *Society and Education* (2nd ed.). Boston: Allyn and Bacon, 1962. Pp. 75–79, 102–104.
7 Bronfenbrenner, U. The split-level American family. *Saturday Review,* Oct. 7, 1967, 60–66.
8 Caldwell, B. M. Can young children have a quality life in day care? *Young Children,* 1973, 28(4):197–208.
9 Barth, R. S. On selecting materials for the classroom. *Childhood Education,* 1971, 47(6):311–314.
10 Beyer, E. Daily routines and group experiences. From *Teaching Young Children.* New York: Western, 1968. Pp. 115–127.
11 Fantini, M. D., & Weinstein, G. Toward a contact curriculum. From *Toward a contact curriculum.* New York: Anti-Defamation League of B'nai B'rith, 1969. Pp. 50–55.

12 Cole, L. Basic ideas of the Montessori method. From *A history of education: Socrates to Montessori.* New York: Holt, Rinehart, & Winston, 1950. Pp. 566–574.

13 Kagan, J. Preschool enrichment and learning. *Interchange,* 1971, 2(2).

14 Wann, K. D., Dorn, M. S., & Liddle, E. A. Children have ways of understanding their world. From *Fostering intellectual development in young children.* New York: Teachers College Press, Columbia University, 1962. Pp. 2–3, 24–37, 118–124.

15 Stendler-Lavatelli, C. B. Aspects of Piaget's theory that have implications for teacher education. *Journal of Teacher Education,* 1965, 16:329–339.

16 Copeland, R. W. Cognitive development and learning mathematics. From *Mathematics and the elementary teacher* (2nd ed.). Philadelphia: Saunders, 1972. Pp. 10–17.

17 Fennema, E. Manipulatives in the classroom. *The Arithmetic Teacher,* 1973, 20(5):350–352.

18 Shulman, L. S. Psychological controversies in the teaching of science and mathematics, *Science Teacher,* 1968, 35(6).

19 Heffernan, H. Concept development in science, *Science & Children,* 1966, 4(1):25–28.

20 Cazden, C. B., Baratz, J. C., Labov, W., & Palmer, F. H. Language development in daycare programs. From E. Grotberg (Ed.), *Day care: Resources for decisions.* Washington, D.C.: Office of Economic Opportunity, 1971. Pp. 153–171.

21 Pitcher, E. G. Values and issues in young children's literature. *Elementary English,* January–April 1969, 46(1):287–294.

22 Wanat, S. F. Language acquisition: Basic issues. *The Reading Teacher,* 1971, 25(2):142–147.

23 Durkin, D. Confusion and misconceptions in the controversy about kindergarten reading. From *Teaching them to read,* Boston: Allyn and Bacon, 1970. Pp. 68–76.

24 Galloway, C. S. Nonverbal communication. *The Instructor,* 1968, 27(8):37–42.

25 Elkind, D. Increasing and releasing human potentials. *Childhood Education,* 1971, 47(7):346–348.

26 Raths, J. A strategy for developing values. *Educational Leadership,* 1964, 21:509–514.

27 Kohlberg, L. Moral education in the schools: A developmental view. *The School Review,* 1966, 74:1–30.

28 Coopersmith, S. The antecedents of self-esteem. From *The Antecedents of self-esteem.* San Francisco: Freeman, 1967. Pp. 236–241.

29 Hartup, W. Early pressures in child development. *Young Children,* 1965, 20:270–283.

30 Fraiberg, S. H. The right to feel. From *The magic years.* New York: Scribners, 1959. Pp. 273–282.

31 Feldman, R. E. Aggression and timidity in young children. From Teaching self-control and self-expression via play. In S. Coopersmith (Ed.), *Developing Motivation in Children.* Columbus, Ohio: Merrill. 1974. Pp. 3–5, 21–24.

32 Barnow, E., & Swan, A. Disagreements between children. From *Adventures with children (in nursery school and kindergarten).* New York: Agathon, 1959. Pp. 66–95.

33 Frasher, R., & Walker, A. Sex roles in early reading textbooks. *The Reading Teacher,* 1972, 25(8):741–749.

34 Jackson, P. W. The student's world. *The Elementary School Journal,* April 1966, 345–357.

35 Vallett, R. E. A social reinforcement technique for the classroom management of behavior disorders. *Exceptional Children,* 1966, 33:185–189.

36 Coles, R. Like it is in the alley. *Daedalus,* Fall 1968, 97:1315–1330.

37 Goldberg, M. L. Issues in the education of the disadvantaged. New York: American Histadrut Cultural Exchange Institute, 1968.

38 Clark, K. B. Prejudice and your child. From *Prejudice and your child.* Boston: Beacon, 1963. Pp. 23–31, 58–59.

39 Miel, A., & Kiesler, E., Jr. The short-changed children of suburbia. From *The short-changed children of suburbia,* New York: Institute of Human Relations Press, 1967. Pp. 23–27, 44–45, 62–63.

40 Levin, E. Beginning reading: A personal affair. *Elementary School Journal,* November 1966, 67:67–71.

41 Havighurst, R. J. Requirements for a valid new criticism. *Phi Delta Kappan,* September 1968, 20–24.

42 Featherstone, J.   Open schools II: Tempering a fad. *New Republic*, 1971, 165:17–21.
Reprinted by permission of Citation Press, a division of Scholastic Magazines, Inc.
43 Borton, T.   Reach, touch, and teach. *Saturday Review*, Jan. 18, 1969.
44 Hess, R. D., Bloch, M., Costello, J., Knowles, R. T., & Largay, D.   Parent involvement
in early education. From E. Grotberg (Ed.), *Day care: Resources for decisions*. Washington,
D.C.: Office of Economic Opportunity, 1971. Pp. 265–285.
45 Lippitt, P.   Children can teach other children. *The Instructor*, 1969, 78(9):41–99.
46 Lee, D. M.   What is the teacher's role in diagnostic teaching? From *Diagnostic
Teaching*. Washington, D.C.: National Education Association, 1966. Pp. 16–27.
47 Anzalone, P., & Stahl, D.   Creative teaching. *The Instructor*, 1967, 76(9):17–18, 23–26.

contents

preface

The articles in this collection have been selected to fulfill four major objectives. First, we have focused on articles that deal with the principles and central issues of early childhood education. Second, we have attempted to place current views regarding early childhood in a broad perspective that transcends American society in the early 1970s. Third, we have emphasized the major trends in contemporary early childhood education, rather than more specific, limited studies. And fourth, we have supplemented those articles on more general issues with articles relating to specific practices and materials. Thus the work as a whole is intended to give the student both a broad perspective on early childhood education and specific information on practices and processes that would be useful in a teaching career. Some of the articles have been published within the last few months; others have become classics in the field. We have attempted to include as much recent information as possible, but in the last analysis the criteria for inclusion have been the quality of the material and its relevance to our objectives.

Several features of this collection warrant comment—indeed, it was because these features were lacking in other collections that we decided to prepare this work. One unique feature, as noted above, is the juxtaposition of theory and practice in each section. Another feature is that the articles are drawn from a number of fields, ranging from social history and psychiatry to the more traditional fields of education and psychology. Early childhood education is in a state of flux, and its boundaries have moved not only outward, but also in different directions. This state of flux is particularly apparent in the sections dealing with education of the disadvantaged (Section Seven) and recent innovations and appraisals in early childhood education (Section Eight). The issues and principles in these emerging areas of early education are given considered attention in this volume. Another feature, which reflects the growing concern for explicitly clarifying teaching goals, is exemplified by the behavioral objectives for each article. These objectives, which are listed at the end of each section introduction, afford an opportunity for both teacher and student to focus on the salient points. Finally, although the articles are authoritative, they are generally devoid of the technical language and the research report style that so often disconcerts students.

The first two sections of this volume provide a broad general perspective on the role and significance of early childhood, and the last two sections deal with recent trends, major emphases, and new directions in early childhood education. The articles in the middle four sections concern the traditional substantive concerns of early childhood education: cognitive skills, language abilities, personality development, and social behavior in young children.

Although the articles are organized in eight sections, for ease of reference they are numbered consecutively throughout and are referred to by number, rather than by author or by section. The source of each article is indicated in the acknowledgments section following the copyright page. The references for each article appear in a separate section at the end of the book.

We should like to extend our thanks to Nicolette LaSorella and to Nancy Clark, who aided in the numerous details involved in preparing this work.

As the editor of any collection knows, there are many articles deserving of inclusion that could not be included. We have followed our own judgments and preferences and can only trust that teachers and students will find this work as interesting and useful to read and discuss as we found it stimulating to develop.

STANLEY COOPERSMITH

RONALD FELDMAN

portrait of a changing field

At the 1970 White House Conference on Children the delegates were asked to vote on what they regarded as their overriding concerns and specific recommendations for America's children in the 1970s. The first recommendation and major concern of the delegates was that comprehensive family-oriented child development programs be established and that these programs include health services, day care, and early childhood education. This concern for young children reflected a growing recognition both of the importance of early experience for later achievement in life and of the increasing demands for preschool developmental opportunities for young children. The support expressed in 1970 differed in two major respects from the support expressed by the White House Conference convened twenty years earlier. First, between 1950 and 1970 our knowledge of early childhood and the conditions that would be most likely to enhance the development of young children had greatly expanded. Second, a significant financial commitment had been directed toward serving the needs of America's children for preprimary instruction. As such, it was a commitment to early childhood *education*, not merely to the provision of facilities, food, or basic custodial care for children. The changes since 1950 reflect the belief that stimulating and supportive early childhood experiences can be a significant factor in breaking the destructive cycles associated with unemployment, poverty, and social conflict. In the public world of attention, money, and social demand early childhood education is becoming an increasingly visible and important area of social concern.

The statistics of enrollment and need indicate some of the pressures underlying the calls for expanded educational services for young children. In 1950 only 52 percent of the nation's five-year-olds were enrolled in kindergarten, whereas in 1970 the enrollment was 78 percent. In terms of number of children, there was an increase from 906,000 in 1950 to 3,180,000 in 1970—a figure which also reflected the population increase over this twenty-year period. Since there are few states in which attendance in kindergarten is compulsory, however, the increase in percentage of children enrolled is a clear indication that parents have wanted or needed these services. This fact is even more apparent from the number of children enrolled in other preschool programs: in 1970 there were 11 million children under the age of six enrolled in various types of preprimary programs. At this point early childhood programs serve one-fifth of the nation's four-year-olds and 90 percent of all five-year-olds.

Part of the explanation for this increase lies in the rapid rise of employment among women, and especially among women with children. The number of working women is $2\frac{1}{2}$ times greater than in 1940, but the number of working mothers is more than 8 times greater. Altogether, there are some 33 million women working today, and 12 million of these women are working mothers. Half of these mothers have children between the ages of six and seventeen, and more than one-third—some $4\frac{1}{2}$ million—have children under six. In those families in which the mothers work approximately 40,000 young children receive no care at all (that is, they are left at home by themselves), and about twice that number are left in the care of brothers and sisters under sixteen. Fifteen percent of the children under six accompany their mothers to work.

It is apparent from these figures that one large and important group of children who need early developmental care are the children of working mothers who are unable to arrange responsible and stimulating care for their children at home. There is a great shortage of programs for these youngsters, and with the number of working mothers increasing at a much faster pace than the enrollment capacity, this shortage is becoming more acute daily. Another important group of children who would benefit from such programs are those in economically and educationally disadvantaged families who lack opportunities for the kinds of early developmental experiences that would give them an equal start. This group includes about 6 million children under the age of six, a large proportion of whose families have indicated that they would welcome part-time programs that provide health care and educational and developmental opportunities. In addition, there is a demand for early childhood programs for parents who are neither unavailable nor disadvantaged, but are eager to enhance the psychological and social development of their children. In many cases these mothers need some opportunity for social or intellectual outlets for themselves as well as for their children to offset the isolation that frequently marks urban and suburban living. Given the total number of children in the country between the ages of three and five, and the urgent requests for early childhood programs by various segments of society, the 700,000 openings for young children in our present programs will scarcely be adequate.

FROM CUSTODIAL CARE
TO DEVELOPMENTAL PROGRAMS

Despite the fact that young children are in their formative years, many early childhood programs have offered them little more than a place to wait for their parents. A recent survey of current facilities (Kayserling, 1972) indicates that about half are strictly custodial and provide little or no educational opportunities or other services beyond the meeting of basic physical needs. Another 14 percent rated as substandard included shocking examples of overcrowding (47 children and one mother), poor control (children tied to furniture or unsupervised at all), and lack of hygiene (stale food, unclean facilities). Of the 35 percent regarded as good, only 6 percent offered programs that were considered superior. These evaluations point to a dismal situation for many young children and are particularly distressing in light of all we have learned about the processes of child development and the conditions that foster social and intellectual growth. Although programs that provide these conditions represent a substantial cost, there is a growing conviction in many areas of society that such programs warrant public support. This conviction stems in part from a desire to reorder priorities so that children who are treasured in theory will also receive this attention in practice.

Another factor in the increasing support for high-level developmental care is that the criteria for such programs have become more clearly defined over the last two decades. Each society has found some means of caring for young children in the absence of their parents, but it is only recently that such care has been systematically examined in terms of its actual consequences. There are still gaps in our knowledge, and educators are not as effective as they would like to be. However, we now have an understanding of the conditions that facilitate or impede development which is based on extensive research rather than on folklore. For example, laboratory and field studies have generated the following kinds of information:

1 Physical, mental, and social contact are basic requirements for normal development. The failure to receive the necessary minimum levels of such contact can impair later social and intellectual functioning (Harlow & Harlow, 1962; Bowlby, 1952; Goldfarb, 1943).

2 Comparisons of primitive and advanced societies (such as the United States) show that advanced societies are in general more demanding of their children (Whiting & Child, 1953; Miller & Swanson, 1958).

3 Punishment is relatively ineffective as a means of changing unwanted behavior. On a long-range basis it tends to produce a boomerang effect in which the behavior that was punished is more likely to occur. Punishment of dependency in a child results in greater dependency when he is older; severe punishment of aggressive behavior produces greater aggression in the child (Sears, Maccoby, & Levin, 1953).

4 The less warmth or more punishment a child receives, the slower the development of his conscience. The more rejection he feels, the greater the likelihood that he will be dependent (Sears, Maccoby, & Levin, 1953).

5 There are critical periods in early life during which organisms learn and develop relationships at a rapid speed. Skills and experiences gained during these periods may be difficult to either replicate

or extinguish at later times. Animal studies reveal that failure to develop social contacts during the first year results in irreversible social and psychological damage (Scott, 1963; Harlow & Harlow, 1962). Observations of human infants strongly suggest that during certain periods, 18 months and 30 months to be precise, infants are particularly vulnerable to environmental influence (Spitz, 1945).

6 Early emotional support and environmental enrichment can produce significant improvements in children's intelligence and energy level. For example, children moved from impersonal orphanages to warmer and more personal institutions all registered increases in IQ (Skeels, 1966); and undernourished children given correct diet registered gains in intelligence and energy (Glass, 1968; Read, 1972).

7 There is a significant relationship between the child's early family and school experiences and his later learning ability and level of academic achievement (McVickers & Hunt, 1961; Bloom, 1964).

8 Significant short-term (and possibly long-term) improvement can be obtained from early childhood programs designed to raise academic achievement (Klaus & Gray, 1968). Such programs may also have a positive effect on the child's motivation and involvement in school activities.

9 Children derive an intrinsic reward from accomplishing tasks, from visual exploration, and from satisfying curiosity. Apparently members of the human species, as well as other primates, experience inner satisfaction both from attaining competence and from achieving material rewards from the external environment (White, 1959; Berlyne, 1966).

10 Educational programs that involve parents in guiding the program and facilitating the development of children's skills result in greater improvements than do those in which parents are not involved (Gordon, 1969; Weikart & Lambie, 1967).

As findings such as these continually expand our knowledge, the field of early childhood education is gradually changing from a service occupation to a profession based on highly developed theories and practices. The change is not merely one of title or status; it is one of increased competence. At one time a nursery school teacher had only to be caring, clean, and calm with children. Today we ask such teachers to have a working knowledge of developmental processes, an understanding of individual and group differences, and awareness of a wide range of other factors that relate to early childhood.

The age range for early childhood education is generally considered to be three to eight. According to the National Association for the Education of Young Children, this period "includes the nursery, kindergarten and primary years as a psychological entity." These boundaries are not absolute—some programs accept two-year-olds and some provide for older children—but they are the most common framework for programs of developmental education. Although some states, such as California, are considering the provision of educational programs for children younger than five, as a rule public education begins at six with the first grade. Only thirty-three states provide public kindergartens as an adjunct to their elementary systems, but since these are generally the most populous states, public kindergartens accommodate two-thirds of all five-year-olds. At this point no state education system provides a school program for all four-year-olds or all three-year-olds. However, federal, state, and local agencies finance programs for certain groups of children whose care falls within their areas of concern.

Day-care centers, for example, offer care for the children of working mothers. They accept children of two to sixteen and provide after-school facilities for older children as well as all-day care for infants and toddlers. In addition to the programs that are fully subsidized or operated on a nonprofit basis, there are many such centers operated on a private basis. Head Start and other compensatory programs are designed for children who are considered disadvantaged. These programs are supported by public funds and are generally half-day sessions for children of four to six, offered either year-round or during the summer. Nursery schools and preschools, which are usually privately operated, provide half-day sessions for children of two and one-half to five. Some are parent cooperatives, organized by parents who are interested in a professional program for their children. Many churches run nursery schools, operated either by the parents or by the church itself. Kindergarten programs—operated by the public school system, as private schools, or by the community—are designed to prepare children of five to six for the social and academic activities of first grade. The programs for the next two years of early childhood are provided by the first and second grades of elementary school.

With the expansion of early childhood education as a separate field, educators have proposed several different models for a basic approach to programs for the young (Grotberg, 1972). These models concern the overall function and source of responsibility for such programs, irrespective of the type of program or its source of support. One point of view, represented by the school model, is that state education systems should assume responsibility for all preschool and primary education. On the basis that education concerns the total welfare of the child, this responsibility would include the provision of clothing, meals, and health care. The coordinated-child-development model is based on coordination of all the different services that are now available to children, since many of the desired benefits could be obtained simply by organizing the various groups that already have expertise in dealing with young children. The advocacy model is based on the premise that children need not just services, but some agency set up specifically to represent their interests. This model proposes a government board that would develop and promote programs based on the needs of the child. The business model represents the view that day care and early education programs should be provided by members of the business community, either for a set fee or as an employee benefit.

It is clear from these models that educators hold widely varying views on the scope of early childhood education and the basis on which education programs should be organized. This issue may or may not affect the teacher in the classroom, but some fundamental issues concerning the purpose of education have direct bearing on the education process itself.

EDUCATION: CHILD AND TEACHER

Education is a complex enterprise, and educators differ on how it can best be carried out. One basic dimension of these differences relates to the center of focus of education. Adult-centered educators maintain that "certain social aims, meanings, values incarnate in the matured experience of the adult" should provide the substance and aims of the educational process (Dewey, 1902). Child-centered educators claim that the educational process should derive from and enlarge on the immediate interests, thought processes, and delights of the child. Interaction-oriented educators view education as a process of guiding the child via age-appropriate methods toward goals determined by the evolving goals of society. This view places the teacher in the challenging role of providing the child with the types of learning experiences which will produce genuine progress toward goals that represent the joint interests of child and adult.

In theory most teachers agree that education involves an interaction between the goals and interests of the child and those of adult society. When it comes to specific educational practices, however, they often hold convictions that place them in either the adult-centered or the child-centered camp. Eight common myths are especially prevalent in early childhood education (White House Conference on Children, 1970), six of which reflect extreme child-centered or adult-centered orientations.

MYTH 1: *Children really learn only in the context of schools.*
This adult-centered belief disregards the fact that children learn walking, talking, the rudiments of social interaction, and a number of other basic skills without formal instruction by teachers or parents. Teachers subscribing to this belief may negate the child's capacity for teaching himself; they may resist proposals for implementing guided teaching programs outside of the classroom setting.

MYTH 2: *Children cannot really learn in an organized school.*
This child-centered belief disregards the fact that children are not preprogrammed to learn from unguided experience the more complex traditions (reading, arithmetic, moral beliefs, and so on) that have been developed over the centuries by adult society. Teachers subscribing to this belief may negate the value of the learning experiences that teachers can array for the child; they may resist proposals for planning and limiting what activities take place in the classroom.

MYTH 3: *Adults understand and children do not.*
This adult-centered belief contradicts a deeply ingrained American tradition that individuals are to be taught and encouraged to make decisions for themselves. It also conflicts with research findings indicating that the influence of children over one another increases as they become older. Teachers subscribing to this belief may negate the value of cross-age tutoring programs, in which older children assist in the teaching of younger students; they may oppose curriculum programs in which the goals are determined in part by the concerns and needs of children.

MYTH 4: *Children understand and adults do not.*
This child-centered belief contradicts a deeply ingrained American tradition that in return for the freedoms granted by a democracy, individuals should consent to living by certain guidelines that apply to all citizens. It also conflicts with research findings indicating that children develop intellectual and social skills best when they receive a moderate level of *adult* guidance. Teachers subscribing to this belief may oppose curriculum programs in which the goals are determined in part by the concerns and values of adult society.

MYTH 5: *A best form of education exists and is applicable to all.*
This adult-centered belief denies the research-documented fact that children are very different from one another. It therefore obstructs

teaching procedures for children whose characteristics do not conform to the pattern on which a given so-called universal approach to education is based. Teachers subscribing to this belief may be inflexible in their approaches to teaching and may not realize that *they* can learn by observing their pupils.

MYTH 6: *The best form of education is entirely different for each child.*
This child-centered belief denies the research-documented fact that children have a number of common characteristics. It therefore obstructs the effective application of certain basic principles of learning that apply to all normal children. Teachers subscribing to this belief may lack consistency and structure in their approaches to teaching and may not realize that their pupils can benefit from the application of certain general teaching principles.

MYTH 7: *Schools today effectively prepare the child for future participation in the adult society.*
This belief presupposes that current educational practices prepare the child not only for functioning in the contemporary adult world, but also for confronting the stresses involved in adapting to a rapidly changing society. Actually, educators, whether adult- or child-oriented, have yet to develop *fully* adequate procedures for achieving this goal. Fully adequate procedures would assist the child in developing the capacity to build in new directions on the skills already acquired, the ability to make decisions and coping with stress in the face of uncertain outcomes, and the inner resources and enthusiasm to make productive use of the leisure time made available by technology.

MYTH 8: *The implementation of new educational procedures involves using children as guinea pigs and therefore is not a desirable course of action.*
This belief presupposes that "tried-and-true" procedures are preferable because the outcomes are known. It is based on a value judgment that taking risks with children is unethical and on factual evidence that innovations often are ineffective and may even have undesirable results. However, it disregards two considerations: (1) that the tried-and-true procedure may produce an outcome that is known, but not the outcome that is desired, and (2) that schools can reduce risk to an acceptable level by limiting innovations to those that have already been tested and refined by experienced educators. In the extreme form expressed above, this belief not only hinders schools in improving and in adapting to an ever-changing social environment; it also fails to take into account the fact that there is

generally more than one valid approach to the achievement of a given educational objective.

CHARACTERISTICS OF THE YOUNG CHILD

In order to understand the nature of the interaction between teacher and child it is necessary to understand the basic characteristics of the young child. Although children of two to five are immature and inexperienced, they have already become highly complex physical and social organisms. This is clearly illustrated by the following sketches of a typical child at the age of two and at the age of five.

> JILL AT AGE TWO: *Jill looks with obvious interest at a living-room staircase and then walks to the bedroom, where her mother is making pottery. Pulling her mother by the hand, Jill leads the way to the foot of the staircase and says, "See stair." As her mother looks on, Jill begins to climb the stairs, awkwardly but with determination. Every few stairs she looks back over her shoulder at her mother, smiling each time she catches her mother's eye. After a few minutes the mother briefly steps into the bedroom to retrieve her unfinished pot. As soon as Jill notices that her mother is not there, she sits down on a stair and squalls in distress.*

This incident demonstrates the central role played by adults in the life of the two-year-old. Jill enjoys her mother's attention, and through proximity to her mother she gains the confidence to undertake an otherwise frightening task. The incident also shows the normal two-year-old's developing capacity for autonomy and the pleasure taken in perfecting the skills that make autonomy possible. Additional characteristics of the two-year-old are heavy reliance on nonverbal language (in this case the pulling and the crying) for purposes of communication; the limitation of verbal language to very short phrases and to description of concrete desires, people, and objects; and a developing facility for using large muscles.

> JILL AT AGE TWO: *Jill is at home with her parents and her two-year-old cousin, Johnny. The children sit near each other, one playing with a truck and the other rolling a ball. Noticing a baby carriage, Jill gets up and pushes the carriage slowly across the room until she bumps it into a wall. She then tries to pull the carriage backward, but the handle is too high for her to apply enough leverage. Unwilling to accept defeat, Jill walks around to the front of the carriage and*

pushes it away from the wall. Excitedly, she begins to run and unwittingly slams the carriage into her peacefully playing cousin.

This is an example of the mental problem solving carried out by the two-year-old child. Without overtly attempting possible physical maneuvers, Jill discovers by reasoning (or accident) a solution to the problem of how to move the carriage away from the wall. The incident also illustrates the two-year-old's disinclination and inability to interact with age-mates—and also the fact that two-year-olds need guidance in learning to control and understand the consequences of their behavior.

By the age of five Jill has advanced considerably:

JILL AT AGE FIVE: *During the nursery school's indoor free-play period, Jill wanders among some actively involved children in an attempt to determine what to do with her time. She watches some girls playing in the dollhouse, some boys and girls making a mural, and her friend Georgia at work drawing triangles and circles. Noticing Jill peering over her shoulder, Georgia says, "This is fun." Jill asks a teacher for pencil and paper, sits down beside Georgia, and begins to draw the figures Georgia is drawing. She asks Georgia, "Is this how to do it?" When Georgia says yes, Jill exclaims in a delighted voice, "I can do it, too!"*

Peers have already assumed an important role by the time the child reaches five. In this instance Jill chooses an activity and models its style after that of an age-mate; the teacher serves as a resource person. This incident also illustrates the fact that the five-year-old child is developing a self-concept which encompasses abilities, characteristics, and personal traits. Jill shows a desire to define the range of her abilities and shows delight at discovering that she can carry out a new task to the satisfaction of her friend. Additional characteristics of the five-year-old are extensive use of verbal language for the purpose of communicating; the ability to form complete sentences that correspond to the grammatical conventions of the child's subculture and the capacity to express somewhat abstract concepts; a developing facility in using small muscles; and a preference for patterning behavior after that of members of one's own sex (sex typing).

JILL AT AGE FIVE: *Two of Jill's schoolmates are on the playground teeter-totter. Feeling friendly and eager to share in the fun, Jill climbs on and perches between one end and the center. As a result, the teeter-totter bangs heavily on the ground, and two agitated voices command Jill to go away. Feeling rejected and bewildered, Jill screams back that she has a right to stay and refuses to move. Eventually a teacher intervenes. The teacher lifts Jill from the teeter-totter, explains why the other children are angry with her, and suggests to Jill that she request the next turn.*

This incident illustrates the five-year-old's use of language in problem solving. In this particular case the children did not effectively solve the problem, and the teacher verbally provided a workable solution. Two further characteristics apparent here are the five-year-old's tendency to interact with age-mates, coupled with a frame of reference that is generally egocentric; at five children are typically unable to perceive a situation from the point of view of another person. This incident accurately depicts the five-year-old child as being in the process of developing patterns of moral behavior and judgment and shows the role of verbalized rules in identifying the characteristics of right and wrong conduct.

CHARACTERISTICS OF THE EFFECTIVE TEACHER

Teacher training programs usually place heavier emphasis on teaching techniques than on teachers as persons to whom children respond. Research has shown, however, that both factors are involved in a teacher's effectiveness. It is important, therefore, to consider the kind of person who is effective as a teacher as well as the elements that characterize effective teaching.

The effective teacher can be described in terms of certain personal characteristics, self-concepts, and attitudes that have been found to be related to student achievement and with favorable attitudes of students toward themselves, the teacher, and the classroom situation (Hamachek, 1969). The single characteristic most often found in effective teachers is flexibility. The flexible teacher is aware that students differ from each other and that no one style of teaching or interaction can be adopted with all students. Other traits that characterize effective teachers include:

Ability to perceive the world from the student's point of view
Ability to personalize their teaching
Ability to experiment, to try out new things
Skill in asking questions (as opposed to functioning as an answering service)
Knowledge of subject matter and related areas
Reflection of an appreciative attitude (evidenced by nods, smiles, or comments)
Use of conversational manner in teaching; informal, easy style

In addition to these behavioral characteristics, effective teachers also have favorable perceptions of themselves as persons; they consider themselves adequate, trustworthy, and wanted or worthy. This self-perception is reflected in a favorable perception of others, which generates a mutually positive response. The effective teacher, according to Hamachek, sees students not as "persons 'you do things to' but rather as individuals capable of doing for themselves once they feel trusted, respected, and valued."

The numerous studies on the specific strategies of effective teaching indicate that there is no one best way to teach. They do show, however, that effective teaching is characterized by some general underlying features. In a landmark study conducted with preschool children from economically disadvantaged backgrounds Weikart (1971) compared the results of three curriculum programs based on three entirely different theories of learning. The programs varied somewhat in the degree of freedom (choice of activities) and structure (limits in choice within a teaching context) presented to the children on a daily basis. They also varied considerably in the formality or informality of the learning setting and teaching approach (drill and practice versus real-world experience). In spite of all these differences, all three programs produced equally large gains in intellectual development, as measured on IQ and achievement tests.

This uniformity of effect in the face of such differences apparently is related to underlying factors shared by all three programs. Although the study did not isolate which shared features are critical to effective teaching, three possibilities appear likely:

1 Each program is formed within a framework that guides the teacher in selecting activities and in fitting the entire classroom as a learning setting into an overall scheme. There is structure rather than chaos, although (within limits) the range of choice for children varied.
2 The staff members are required to plan activities in advance (but are not rigid when implementing their plans), are given supportive supervision, are able to work with colleagues in daily teaching, are highly committed to their work, and are shown respect by being allowed some choice in program planning.
3 The program involved the mothers of the children, individual attention to each child in a home-teaching setting, and a focus on education as a goal.

Effective teaching, then, involves one or more of these factors: a framework for teaching, careful selection and sophisticated use of staff, and cooperative relationships and joint efforts with the home.

This discovery of the relative unimportance of any particular theoretical approach to teaching indicates what is truly important for effective teaching. There are many means of achieving that end and none appears to offer significantly greater benefits than others in terms of child achievement. In a real sense the human side of effective teaching involves the teacher's belief in what she is doing, an appreciation and use of the different strengths of different teachers, and joint and respectful interaction between the school and home.

the nature of the young child

There have been many revolutions in our time but I think that in the long run [the] psychological revolution . . . in the theory and practice of shaping behavior of the young will be the most important revolution of all for the success and happiness of man on this planet. . . . JOHN R. PLATT

The past two decades have seen a great change in our manner of thinking about children and childhood. The five articles in this section are concerned with several changes in our perceptions of children and the implications of current perceptions for the education and rearing of children. Through the work of historians we have learned that our modern ideas of childhood as a period of toys, fairy tales, and simple natural existence evolved in seventeenth-century Europe. Before that time children entered into the adult world of work, play, combat, and sexuality as soon as they could talk and walk. Although most students are aware of Sigmund Freud's views on infantile sexuality—that infants and young children are pleasure-seeking and self-centered—they are less likely to appreciate how drastically those views have influenced child-rearing and educational thinking and practices. We have learned that childhood has an inherent complexity of its own, that what we regard as "natural" to children is often determined by time and place, and that children live in a world of passions, change, and harsh judgments.

This new insight into the nature of childhood has broad social implications. These include such direct practical issues as using early childhood education as a means of breaking the poverty cycle, reducing prejudice and social unrest, and increasing the expression of talents and capacities. On a larger and more sober scale, early childhood education is regarded as one of the few remaining possibilities for developing a generation that will turn aside from conflict and create broader, more peaceful alternatives for living. Awareness of these practical implications of early childhood programs is apparent in the billions of dollars that are now expended on such agencies as Head Start, The Office of Child Development, The Office of Education's National Program on Early Childhood Education, and The National Institute of Child Health and Human Development. Surprisingly enough, none of these agencies existed as recently as 1960, which gives some idea of the impact of current concern with early childhood experiences.

Article 1, "Changing Human Nature," is an imaginative and thoughtful discussion by John R. Platt of how men can be shaped, changed, and damaged. Platt gives us a different way of perceiving that ephemeral topic "human nature" and attempts to liberate us from the view that each generation is destined to repeat the mistakes of its predecessors. Drawing on studies from psychological laboratories, he concludes that man's nature is not constant and can be influenced by well-designed early learning experiences.

This change in our thinking about human nature in general was accompanied by a more specific change in our thinking about children. Part of the current confusion about how to treat childhood is due to the great social and economic changes that have affected family living. In Article 2, "The Great Change in Children," J. H. Plumb indicates how the separate world of childhood has been created over the past four centuries. Since that separation divides the generations in ways that are neither natural nor desirable, Plumb's work gives us a broader perspective on the current trend toward including children as an integral part of society.

In Article 3 Milton Akers discusses "The Why of Early Childhood Education," including some of the social and political considerations that underlie the great recent interest in early childhood education. Evidence that at least half of the young adult's intellectual achievement is reached by age nine indicates that the young child has a remarkable capacity for learning. The net result is that parents are no longer content with child-care programs that do not stimulate and enrich the child's experiences in school and at home; rather, they are deeply interested in learning the most effective ways of enhancing the development of their children.

As Bettye Caldwell and Julius Richmond point out, "The Impact of Theories of Child Development" (Article 4) has been considerable for parents, teachers, and child-care specialists. Although behavioristic, maturational, and psychoanalytic theories have been taken as "objective" or gospel in the past, these writers suggest that there is a trend toward more careful and direct use of these and other theories.

One theory that has had particular impact on American psychologists and educators is described by Edna Ambrose and Alice Miel in Article 5, "A Perspective on Social Learning." This viewpoint represents a broadening of psychoanalytic theory to include the influence of social and cultural forces. Drawing upon the work of Erik Erikson and others, these authors discuss five components that they feel are requisite for healthy development: trust, independence, initiative, achievement, and identity. If the individual is to develop his potential, it is important that the family and school assist in the development of these components.

behavioral objectives   *To be able to discuss the following points*

1   CHANGING HUMAN NATURE
    The reason that the idea of a constant human nature is false
    Five studies showing how readily mammalian behavior can be changed or damaged

Two widespread fears regarding early education of young children
The significance of teaching children to deal with rapid change
Five ways in which the new vision of man differs from previous visions

2 THE GREAT CHANGE IN CHILDREN

Four social changes in the past fifty years that have affected attitudes toward children
The idea that today's youth is rebelling against four centuries of repression and exploitation
The pattern of attitudes toward children in most primitive cultures
The basis for evaluating social attitudes toward children at earlier periods of history
Two possible factors in the evolution of our present concepts of childhood
Three steps in the changes in the educational system which were associated with changing attitudes toward children
Differences between the life of a sixteenth-century child and a twentieth-century child

3 THE WHY OF EARLY CHILDHOOD EDUCATION

Four factors in the political and social climate of the 1960s that facilitated a national commitment to programs for young children
The orientation of programs for young children during the 1940s and 1950s
The significance of the works of Hunt, Bruner, Bloom, and Piaget in altering ideas of early childhood education
Two criticisms of early childhood programs that focus on increasing measurable IQ
Two concerns about projections for expanded programs of early childhood education

4 THE IMPACT OF THEORIES OF CHILD DEVELOPMENT

The meaning of the phrases "theories based on *a priori* assumptions" and "theologically toned"
The developmental theories known as social learning, maturational, and psychoanalytic
The meanings of "maturation," "conditioning," "fixation," "regression," and "oral period"
The distinction between ages and stages, between implicit and explicit theories, and between theory and practice

1

JOHN R. PLATT   CHANGING HUMAN NATURE

The comedians Mike Nichols and Elaine May have a funny dialogue which is supposed to be a long-distance telephone conversation between a New York mother and her son who is a space scientist at Cape Kennedy. The mother calls up her scientist-son; she begins to accuse him of neglecting her, and tells him all her neurotic troubles; finally, she gets so sorry for herself that she cries and will not hang up until he talks baby talk to her just like he used to do when he was a little boy.

Our view of human nature today is in many ways very much like this mother's view of her little boy. The boy has grown up into a spaceman, but we keep thinking of him as though he were still a baby. We are used to the idea that communications are changing, that the international political scene is changing, that science and technology are developing as never before, but for some reason we tend to go on believing that human nature remains the same and always will. Any debate over the cold war, or over social inequality, or over terrorism somewhere, is all too likely to be terminated by someone remarking rather smugly, "Well, after all, human nature never changes."

On sober reflection, probably none of us really believes this. Many of us spend time and money for political persuasion or social reform, hoping to convert other people to different ways of thinking and acting. And we all spend money to educate our children to new goals and abilities that will make them less like little savages. We are never quite sure it will work, but we have hope. This activity would be absurd if we actually thought there was no possibility of changing human nature. The time when we quote these false folk proverbs to ourselves is at that awful hour of five o'clock when we need to be reassured that there will not be any changes in our own status and attitudes.

Nevertheless, the idea that human nature is constant is expressed so often, by everyone from conservative politicians to drama critics, that it may be good now and then to remind ourselves of the extensive evidence—evidence from history as well as evidence from the laboratories today—that shows how easily human behavior can be formed and modified. I am not talking about changes in human knowledge or in the use of knowledge to control nature, which everyone knows about, but about changes in emotional reactions and social behavior that change the kind of friends we are and the kind of cities we make. I think we must conclude that the variability of human nature is much more remarkable than its constancy. It can be shaped by circumstances and culture into almost any form we wish. And today, like everything else, it is changing more rapidly than ever before.

It is perhaps only in the last century or two, since Rousseau and Pestalozzi and Montessori, that leaders have begun to think seriously about how they could change society systematically by changing the education of the children. In America, this notion was central in the minds of many early reformers. For example, George Ripley, who was the leader of the famous Brook Farm experiment in Massachusetts in the 1840's, was such an optimist that he thought he knew how to reform the worst savages. He said:

> Place the savage in a different situation; let the first words that fall upon his ear be those of Christian gentleness and peace; let him be surrounded by loving and generous hearts; another spirit will be manifested; and you would almost say that he had been endowed with another nature.

Somewhat romantic, of course. The colony foundered from an excess of romanticism in all directions. But the fundamental idea is certainly correct.

IN THE LABORATORY

But what is more important, these historical and philosophical conclusions are beginning to be supported now by laboratory experiments. The ease with which all our mammalian behavior can be shaped or demaged is one of the central features of the experimental psychology of the mid-twentieth century. The psychologist Hebb and his followers have shown that the sensory deprivation of young animals leads to disorganized perceptions and reactions for the rest of their lives. Harlow at Wisconsin has shown that monkeys who have been reared with artificial "mothers," made of cloth and wire and a baby bottle, become permanently psychotic and cannot even mate when they grow up; or if they are then impregnated artificially, they make no attempt to mother the babies they give birth to. Lorenz in Germany has shown that a duckling follows its mother because it has been "imprinted" to her shortly after hatching, but that it can be imprinted equally well to a mechanical toy or a graduate student. In another direction, Held, formerly at Brandeis and now at M.I.T., has shown how rapidly we human beings can adapt our behavior to compensate for systematic distortions of the external world. And Skinner at Harvard has shown that dogs and pigeons can be trained in a few minutes, by his "rapid-reinforcement" methods, without any punishment, to do tricks that dogs and pigeons never did in the history of the world before. And that human beings, with these rapid teaching methods and with the "programmed teaching" based on them, can likewise learn many things much faster and easier than was ever possible with older methods. Moore, now at Rutgers, has recently shown that with such methods children at ages two to four can learn to read and write on electric typewriters, and are soon typing out their own poems and stories.

There have been many revolutions in our time, but I think that in the long run this psychological revolution that we see beginning here in the theory and practice of shaping behavior of the young will be the most important revolution of all for the success and happiness of man on this planet.

Real teaching is *so* easy. The old ideas of severity and punishment are *so* irrelevant. "Efficient learning is never hard," says the psychologist, Kubie. The child is as eager to imitate us as the duckling is to follow the duck. He is instantly interested in what we are interested in. The girl learns the enjoyment of cooking—or the lack of enjoyment—from her mother as easily as the boy learns baseball and automobiles and war from his father. It is in the air they breathe. In fact, the reason our various theories of education have neither helped us nor hurt us very much is that each generation has succeeded so spontaneously and so closely in imitating the one before—all the way down to its theories of education. Our harassed schoolteachers and droning lecturers have simply created over and over again a new generation of bored students and harassed schoolteachers and droning lecturers. Nothing we do can make one generation very much better—or very much worse—than the one before, except, for the first time, an operationally effective theory of education.

I know that many thoughtful people are opposed to the use of these new methods. Brainwashing, they say; treating children as if they were pigeons. Deterministic and dangerous, they say; destroying the children's free will. (I once knew of a farm family that refused to have any books in the house, except the Bible, for very similar reasons. Powerful new reading and teaching devices have always been feared.)

But I think the issue in this case is not really one of the morality or determinism of more effective methods. Good teaching—and better teaching—has always been a most moral obligation, approved and commanded by the churches and the laws. And teaching has always been deterministic and dangerous. Harsh and stupid parents and schoolmasters have wrecked many a child's life—while society kept its hands off. Do we need to say what everyone knows—that this determinism of consequences is implicit in the nature of free will? The freedom of one moment, the choice and control of circumstances, is always used to determine the next. And the freedom of one generation, its choice and control of education, is always used to determine the next.

No; the issue here, I think, is that many of us do not trust our school boards and our teachers to use the new methods wisely. We fear that these easy and almost automatic techniques will be allowed to drive out human warmth and variety from the classroom; or will shape our children's learning into a frozen pattern, past some point of no return, where their behavior and their own eventual teaching will no longer be flexible or intelligent enough to meet new crises or to evolve further.

This would be fatal, of course. But a good automobile driver is helped, not harmed, by better technical devices, and a good driver will use all his intelligence not to destroy his later freedom or his children's freedom by driving into a ditch. Is not an intelligent society then helped by better technical devices, as well?

The cure for our fears is not resistance to the new teaching techniques, but insistence on trying them carefully, observing them, and then discussing and deciding how they can be fitted in to give children a faster and easier education in things that are best taught this way, while allowing teachers and parents not less but more time for the other education that we call variety and humanity and warmth and love.

TEACHING AS THE CHOICE OF CHANGE

Since caveman times, we must have known that human behavior is adaptable. We have always tried to teach our children what we wanted them to learn and what we wanted them to be. The only difference today is that it looks as though we may soon find out how to be successful at it. It seems to me that these changes in human nature and the possibilities and choices ahead form one of the most interesting subjects in the world for contemplative men. "We know what we are, we know not what we may become," said the Christian philosopher, thinking of heaven. But I would say, if we do not know what we may become, we cannot know what we are. The maturing child only begins to realize who he is when his imagination and his planning begin to turn toward the man he will become. It is the same with a maturing society.

Evidently the time is approaching when our whole society will begin to be self-conscious about what it may become, when we will begin to choose it deliberately instead of accidentally. We now realize that the society we can and will become is shaped by what we teach, by the kind of human nature we are producing day by day in our children. This means that there is a problem of choice in our teaching, a collective problem far larger than any single wise educator can solve for us. This old and yet remarkably new discovery of the plasticity of human nature means that all of us—natural and social scientists, psychologistis and teachers, historians and writers, students of economics and politics, government and university leaders, philosophers and citizens—all of us will be deciding and need to be deciding what kind of human nature and what kind of personal and social relationships we want to teach our children to have, so that they will be able to make a better society in turn for themselves.

We realize that we have to reexamine our attitudes—attitudes which are a primary part of what is taught—all the way down to the cradle. How do we want our children to learn to behave whenever they are frustrated by a mechanical toy or by a playmate? Do we want them to have perfect patience? Or to have patience for a little while? Or to stamp on the floor and strike out for their needs? Should we teach a child to say, "Mine!" at a certain age; or at another age to say, "You can have it"? Should we teach him to strive for leadership; or for group cooperation?

Different answers to these questions have been preferred over the course of history, and are preferred today in different families. One set of answers may produce conformists, while another set may produce maverick children who do not get along on teams and committees and who may be branded juvenile delinquents by the standards of their times. A dynamic society obviously needs a lot of this kind of independence—but not too much! What is the best mixture—and how do we train children both to fulfill their individual potentialities and yet to cooperate enough to keep their society functioning effectively?

Americans have one answer for such questions, Russians another, and Chinese another. No wonder we have different social structures. No wonder we are mystified and dismayed by each others' reactions! Will we have to reduce some of this variation in childhood training between nations, so that it will be easier to trust each other and easier not to get frightened into blowing each other up? Or will it be possible to keep some of the differences, so that the world will not be too dull?

In shaping our cultural inheritance, we have always made our children in almost our own cultural image. Their imitation is so spontaneous that we do it in spite of ourselves. There are variations and improvements in successive generations, but the parents' basic cultural image has been the only image, at a given moment in social time and space, that we knew would work together in all its parts.

But in a time like the present, of rapid changes and new demands, an intelligent conservatism that really *conserves* our society may come to demand rapid and intelligent change. When a man is about to be run over by an automobile, or when a world is about to be blown up, real conservatism may demand that he jump out of the way quickly. And collectively today, we may reach a point of no return by not changing fast enough, just as we may reach one by changing too fast. A radical and ill-considered plunge into Utopianism might destroy our culture, but it is also certain to be destroyed if we go on sticking to our old military belligerence or our old uncontrolled human fertility. Our only safety therefore lies in thinking about what is best to do, in which directions we should change and adapt rapidly and in which directions we should emphasize stability.

Our situation in this problem of social design is somewhat like that of those men who took such a bold step in designing a novel kind of government for the United States. In fact, we might paraphrase *The Federalist* papers by saying, "It seems to have been reserved to the people of this generation to decide the important question, whether societies of men are really capable or not, of establishing good *teaching* to shape a better society from reflection and choice, or whether they are forever destined to depend, for their social training and social structure, on imitation and accident." It is time to set up the best new design we can, with care but with confidence in what we are trying to do. As Washington said, "Let us raise a standard to which the wise and honest can repair. The event is in the hands of God."

It is not really going to be so hard to decide what we want to do in our teaching. Our problem, as we begin to come to the end of national wars and to move out into a still uneasy truce for the world, will resemble that of an ex-soldier who has finally got his discharge papers and has to decide what kind of life he wants next. Like him, we may be uncertain whether to take it easy for awhile, or to go on for more education, or to start a new job, or to do several of these at once. And we may try many new things, whether we are sure we want to go on with all of them or not. We may try to train the children for new artistic or scientific adventures, for space exploration or ocean exploration or experimental colonies. We will certainly try to use education to change some of the things we do not like about our present life, such as juvenile delinquency and unemployment. And we will be bored and restless unless we make some fairly magnificent plans for guiding our almost boundless energies in developing and unifying the world. But I think we cannot look too far into the future, but will simply have to trust our own developing culture—as an individual trusts his own developing body—to go on, with the useful and intelligent responses we have already developed, to deal with future problems as they come up.

NEW VIEWS OF THE NATURE OF MAN

These thoughts about the recent changes and the possible future changes in human nature take on additional significance if they are seen as part of our new picture of who and what man is, in the larger cosmic and evolutionary sense. Gauguin asked, in the title of one of his paintings, "Where do we come from? Who are we? Where are we going?" These are the central questions for the real understanding of human nature.

Inspiration and desperation, religion, myth, and poetry used to be the only source of answers to these questions. Today the answers can be based on more factual evidence, from a wide variety of different disciplines, and we find the story is quite different. The discovery of nuclear energy alone has changed our whole view of our past, our powers, and our prospects.

Astronomy, chemistry, and evolution now tell us that life is not a unique event dating from 4004 B.C., but something old and almost inevitable, with billions of years behind it and billions of years ahead, something perhaps repeated many times elsewhere in the universe. Biology tells us that, in this pattern, our complex brains with their manipulative and verbal intelligence have evolved rather suddenly and recently, and are evolving still.

In technology, we now realize we are not running out of energy as we had thought, but have fission and fusion power enough for millions of years. The earth is ours, we have reached its ends; and our satellites have begun to range the solar system and will take men to the moon. We have begun to acquire the biological keys of life and death, with the increasing elimination of disease and the potential control of our own population, and with the beginnings of the chemical manipulation of heredity.

And all over the globe, we have suddenly discovered we are one society, indivisible, for life or death. The nations all have a new intensity of interaction, with new levels of communication and involvement, new cooperation, new dangers, and new cooperative efforts at control.

Are not these all aspects of what man is? What may he become?

In many fields we can discern a new potentiality for shaping the future. This includes our new powers of genetic and biological manipulation, the new psychological shaping of behavior in the ways we have been discussing, powerful new systematic methods of problem solving in mathematics and the sciences, and new computer calculations and guidance for science, automation, communications, and management.

And I think mankind is showing a new level of will and purpose and design, a new feeling that he is the one responsible for himself. Around the world we are finally beginning to make thorough inventories and longer-range and more confident planning and endeavor, in industrial development and national and economic development and food supply and population control. Even at the very heart of the intellectual enterprise, there is a new self-reliance and personalism in philosophy and mathematics and the sciences. We now realize that in perception, it is we who map the world within ourselves. In discovering the nature of things, it is we who choose the problems and who must be convinced by the proofs. In decision, it is we who face the existential imperative to choose and act.

I believe this grand restructuring of our situation quite reverses the older philosophical views of man in several ways.

We used to think of ourselves as orphans in the world. Now we discover that we are children of the universe, that it has been creating and supporting us for a long time and can go on doing so. We were meant to be here, so to speak.

We thought we were insignificant. Now we discover that we are the most complicated thing in creation, as far as we know.

We thought we were disinherited. Now we discover that we have been given power and resources beyond imagining—the power of the sun itself—to do what we want with.

We thought we were helpless, bound by our animal inheritance, or by the darkness of our twisted subconscious, to irredeemable social organizations or to irrational follies and wars. Now we discover that it is culture that shapes our minds and actions, and that better education can lead to better actions, and that consequently we are free to make of ourselves and our children what we choose. There is an incredible amount of social engineering to be done, to make social structures that will give us freedom and yet keep us from killing each other; but it is now clear, on these and other grounds, that it can be done.

I think this revolution in philosophical attitudes that is coming out of the laboratories has not been widely appreciated but is even more important than the great technological revolutions of this century. This new position of intellectual man, in astronomy, in biology, and in psychology and the other sciences, opens the door to a new sense of human freedom. We have a new picture of man's place, his powers, his destiny, and his responsibility. Just as our perception of the external world transcends our internal accidents of construction, so our powers now begin to transcend our biological accidents of origin. It is time to stand up free, with awareness and confidence and choice, to shape, from now on, the further development of what we will become.

There are many ways to make an unstable society and to kill ourselves, but I think that there are also many different kinds of future that are possible and nonlethal and delightful. In fact, I believe it quite likely that we may evolve from one kind of future to another over the centuries, once we learn the basic social rules that will keep us from collective self-destruction. We will be able to try out several of the infinite number of possible social forms, as we go through our long life's day that extends ahead of us for millions or billions of years. Planning a good society as far ahead as we can see, does not mean that our adventures have ended; they have just begun. Human nature is growing up. As we put behind us the accidents and tears of childhood squabbles and the wooden swords and shields, and begin to try on our new space-pilot's uniform, so to speak, we begin to see what we can teach ourselves and what we can really become with new self-control over our new and adult powers.

2

J. H. PLUMB   THE GREAT CHANGE IN CHILDREN

Before World War I sixteen or seventeen was a not unusual age for a middle-class boy to leave school either in America or Europe. After World War II huge segments of the population, female as well as male, remained in the educational system to twenty-one and beyond, and the number increases every few years. Such a vast social change must necessarily have affected our attitudes toward childhood and youth, but there were other complex social forces at work as well. The great European powers lost their empires. Their need for conformity to a middle-class pattern weakened. America filled up, became urban, and its accepted social images of youth became blurred and confused at the same time. The whole purpose of education, other than the learning of crafts and skills, became entangled in debate. Add to this the psychoanalytical attacks on the Victorian concept of childish innocence, and the social confusion about how to treat childhood is easy to comprehend.

There were other muddying factors. The middle classes grew much richer, and the pressures on their children toward economic and social goals eased, too. They were pressurized neither to be Christian gentlemen nor Horatio Algers. And yet in spite of a myriad of warning signs that attitudes toward children needed to be changed, the attitudes belonging to an earlier and simpler world were still enforced. Children were not allowed to drink; parents and educators insisted on old patterns of overt deference and unquestioning obedience. Behavior, clothes, and hair styles had to conform to archaic standards; juvenile reading was still censored; sex was regarded as belonging to the adult world and certainly not to be practiced by those being educated. Repression, conformity, discipline, and exclusion were until lately the historically bred attitudes of most educationalists and parents.

Kept out of the adult world, the adolescents naturally created a world of their own choosing—one that incorporated their own music, their own morals, their own clothes, and their own literature. And they, of course, began naturally to capture the minds and imagination of the children who, though younger in age, nevertheless lived with them in the same basic educational territory. In consequence, during the past few years the period between infancy and adolescence has been sharply reduced, and may be reduced even further in the future.

Social movements and tensions in the adult world can be adjusted by politics, but adolescents and children have no such mechanism for their conflicts with the exclusive world of adults. And so the result has been, and must be, rebellion. That rebellion, however, is not due to the mistakes or difficulties of the last few years. Rarely do we look far enough into the past for the roots of our present problems. This revolution of youth has been building up for decades because we forced the growing child into a repressive and artificial world—a prison, indeed, that was the end product of four centuries of Western history, of that gradual exclusion of the maturing child from the world of adults. We can now look back with longing to the late medieval world, when, crude and simple as it was, men, women, and children lived their lives together, shared the same morals as well as the same games, the same excesses as well as the same austerities. In essence, youth today is rebelling against four centuries of repression and exploitation.

Within the family circle the affections binding parents and children seem so natural that one assumes these relationships are a part of our humanity. Certainly some aspects are. Mothers protect, look after, and feed children. One can see the biological urge of motherhood at work whenever one glances at animals or even birds. But once one moves away from this biological fact, one moves into a world of change, of varying social attitudes of remarkable diversity. And certainly our own attitudes toward children not only differ widely from our fathers' and grandfathers' but differ immensely once we push back into the early nineteenth century and beyond. The world that we think proper to children—fairy stories, games, toys, special books for learning, even the idea of childhood itself—is a European invention of the past four hundred years. The very words we use for young males—boy, *garçon*, *Knabe*—were until the seventeenth century used indiscriminately to mean a male in a dependent position and could refer to men of thirty, forty, or fifty. There was no special word for a young male between the ages of seven and sixteen; the word "child" expressed kinship, not an age state.

About the ancient world's attitude toward children we know next to nothing, though we are somewhat better informed about the training and education of youths in Greece, and especially in Sparta. For classical China the situation is similar: deep reverence for parents, particularly the father, was insisted upon, but we know very little of what was thought of childhood as a state. The common pattern of attitudes toward children among most primitive peoples, and there are discernible relics of this pattern in most advanced societies, is this: they are regarded as infants until seven years of age; little differentiation is made between the sexes, indeed, they are often dressed alike; at seven infancy goes and the boys begin to follow men's activities—herding cattle, hunting for food, working on the farm. Usually they are not men in two important aspects, the making of love and the making of war.

The entry into full manhood is customarily marked by intricate ritual, almost always painful. Spartan boys were viciously flogged, Arabian boys were circumcised without anesthetic. Nuer boys had their foreheads incised to the bone. The boys undergoing this operation were regarded as being of the same tribal age. They remained "classmates" for the rest of their lives, although their actual ages might vary by as much as four or five years. Most of them, however, would be unaware of their own precise age—indeed, this is true of the majority of men and women in medieval Europe. Often their ages would be associated with a village event, sometimes fairly decisively, but often in the vaguest way: a child of "about seven" could be any age from five to nine. Precision of age is a remarkably modern phenomenon; most societies until modern times simply grouped the young into blocks—infants, noninitiate boys or girls, and the like—in which age was irrelevant.

Again, it is very rare to find children depicted as children before the beginnings of the modern world, at the time of the Renaissance. In Chinese paintings, as in medieval manuscripts, they are usually shown as small adults, wearing the clothes, often having the expressions, of men and women. The Greeks paid little attention to childhood as a special state, and there are no Grecian statues of children. It is true that in the late Roman Empire there is the hint of a change. There are a few remarkable heads of young boys, ten or twelve years of age, very lifelike and obviously individual portraits; most of these seem to come from funerary monuments. They display a quite extraordinary sense of age, of the young and growing child, which was not to be found again in Western art until Renaissance times. And there was Cupid, who fluttered in and out of frescoes, who as Eros was sculptured again and again during Hellenistic times. He is the ancestor of the naked *putti* that flit through the pictures of so many European artists from the fifteenth to the nineteenth century, mischievous, impudent, and sentimental. But Eros was a stylized symbol, not a child. Similarly, toward the close of the Middle Ages, angels appear in illustrated manuscripts, singing and playing musical instruments, and they are quite obviously neither infants nor adults, but children. Yet they, too, like Cupid, fulfill a special function. And they do not lead to the portrayal of actual children. One has only to look at the church monuments of Elizabethan England to see how distant the concept was of childhood as a separate state. There, lined up behind the father are three or four little men, all dressed like himself in the formal clothes of the age, and behind his wife kneels a group of little girls wearing the habits of women. Only infants are clothed differently. They are shown either tightly bound in their swaddling clothes or dressed in the long robes worn by both girls and boys alike until they were "about seven."

Fortunately, enough records survive for us to be able to state with confidence that pictorial representation is but a reflection of a social attitude. And we can trace the slow evolution of our modern concepts of childhood over the past four hundred years. The journey, though slow, was immense—the development of a separate world of childhood. This seems so natural to us that it is difficult to conceive of any other.

First, we must remember that infants died more often than they lived. "All mine die," said Montaigne casually, as a gardener might speak of his cabbages. And until they had reached the end of infancy, between the ages of five and seven, they scarcely counted. A character in Molière, when talking of children, says, "I don't count the little one." Men and women of the sixteenth and seventeenth centuries would not have regarded the exposure of children by the Spartans, Romans, and Chinese as callous. Indeed, it is likely that the poor of Renaissance Europe treated unwanted infants with a similar brutality. Life was too harsh to bother overmuch about an infant who probably would not survive anyway. At that time the attitude was much nearer to the instinct of an animal—immense concern while the infant lived to feed it and protect it, indifference after it was dead, and death was expected.

A new sensitivity toward infant mortality can be discerned near the end of the sixteenth century, when dead children began to be represented on their parents' tombs. The fact that they were dead, not living, children is made grimly clear. They either have skulls in their hands, or kneel upon one, or have one hanging above their head, and even tiny infants are depicted, still in their swaddling clothes, which indicates that they were probably younger than two years of age. Children, even babies, were ceasing to be anonymous; yet if this was the beginning, the dawn of a new attitude toward childhood, its fulfillment was still far in the future.

Certainly there was no separate world of childhood. Children shared the same games with adults, the same toys, the same fairy stories. They lived their lives together, never apart. The coarse village festivals depicted by Bruegel, showing men and women besotted with drink, groping for each other with unbridled lust, have children eating and drinking with the adults. Even, in the soberer pictures of wedding feasts and dances the children are enjoying themselves alongside their elders, doing the same things. Nor need we rely on paintings, alone, for we have a wonderfully detailed record of the childhood of Louis XIII. His physician kept a diary, recording each day what the young dauphin did. From this, we can perceive how his father, Henry IV, and the court treated him. It gives one an insight into aristocratic attitudes toward childhood, and into middle-class attitudes as well, for we have corroborative sources, though none so rich, for this period just before some of the most momentous changes in adults' attitudes toward children were about to take place.

Like the peasant children painted by Bruegel, the young prince was involved in adult life to an outstanding degree. At four Louis was taking part in adult ballets, once stark-naked as Cupid; at five he enjoyed hugely a farce about adultery; at seven he began to go to the theatre often. He started gambling at the same age; indeed, he was playing crambo at three. By seven he was also learning to ride and shoot and hunt. He relished blue stories, as well as fairy stories, with a group of courtiers of all ages: fairy stories did not belong exclusively to children; courtiers, particularly the ladies, loved them. Similarly, the games he played—Hide-and-seek, Fiddle-de-dee, Blindman's Buff—were all played with adults and adolescents as well as with his child companions.

Although the adult and childhood worlds intermixed intimately, there were some differences, particularly before the age of seven. The dauphin when very young played with dolls, rode a hobbyhorse, and rushed about the palace with his toy windmill; these were specifically the activities of infants. Before he was breeched, he was often dressed up as a girl. More surprising, however, was the amount of open sexuality permitted. The dauphin and his sister were stripped and placed naked in the king's bed, and when the children played sexually with each other, Henry IV and the court were hugely amused. The queen, a pious and rather austere woman, thought nothing of seizing his genitals in the presence of the court, and the dauphin often displayed himself, to the amusement of his staid middle-aged governess. He acquired the facts of life as soon as he could talk. At seven, however, all was changed. He was severely reprimanded for playing sexually with a girl his own age, and the need for modesty was constantly impressed upon him. The importance of this very detailed evidence from the dauphin's doctor, who saw nothing odd in it, stresses that the world of children and the world of adults were deeply involved. Children, even infants, were not thought of as requiring a special environment, special entertainments, special clothes; nor was it considered necessary to keep them apart from the sophistications and ribaldries of adult life. There were, however, some distinctions: actions that could be permitted, even joked about, in very young children had to stop as soon as they left infancy and became young adults.

In some ways the court was old-fashioned, for by 1600 there was growing up a new conception of childhood. This has been developed by the Schoolmen of the fifteenth century, and adopted and adapted by the educationalists of the Renaissance, especially Erasmus, Vives, and Mosellanus. It became the stock in trade of the Jesuits, who were to dominate the education of the aristocracy and the richer middle class of seventeenth-century Europe. This new attitude was based on the concepts that childhood was innocent and that is was the duty of adults to preserve this innocence. The child, surely, was a prey to passion and to irrationality, but just as innocence could be preserved, so passions could be repressed. The protected child could be guided by remorseless effort into the world of rational behavior; innocence could be transmogrified into adult morality. So even while the dauphin was playing with his naked sister to the ribald amusement of the court, the Jesuits were purging schoolbooks of indecencies, and the religious at Port Royal were editing Terence so that he might be read at school. In many educational establishments discipline was becoming extremely stringent and the dangers of childish sexuality legislated against—boys were no longer put two or three to a bed, and there was a steady separation both of the sexes and of age groups. Parallel with this developed the cult of the Infant Jesus, which symbolized childish innocence. One of the most common devotional prints of the seventeenth century showed Christ summoning the little children to his knee. Increasingly, the child became an object of respect, a special creature with a different nature and different needs, which required separation and protection from the adult world. By 1700 for a child of middle-class family to be outwardly licentious would have been deeply shocking, to have been allowed to gamble for money at six would have appeared outrageous. By then, too, the child possessed his own literature, books carefully pruned of adult sophistication or broad humor, but also especially written for the young mind. The period between seven and adolescence was becoming a world of its own.

In the eighteenth century this new vision of childhood became the accepted social attitude of the affluent classes. Among the poor the old attitudes lingered on—poverty bred proximity, and so forced adults and children to share the same world. In villages and in slums children and adults still played games together, listened to the same stories, lived lives much more closely bound together, lives that could not be separated.

Nor was it only in the areas of manners and morals that changes took place in the lives of children between 1600 and 1800. This period also witnessed a revolution in the attitude toward the education of children—and many of the assumptions that we regard almost as belonging to human nature itself were adopted during this time. For example, everyone assumes that the processes of a literate education should develop with the developing child: reading should begin about four or five, writing follow, and then gradually, more sophisticated subjects should be added and become more complex as the child grows. Education now is tied almost inflexibly to the calendar age of children. In the modern world, at least in Europe and America, a class of children at a school will all be nearly the same age—a few months, perhaps, on either side of the average, but rarely as much as a year.

As with manners and morals, there were for a very long time two worlds of education: one belonging essentially to the Middle Ages, which persisted among backward people for a long time; and the other, basically our own, which took centuries to achieve its final organization and definition. The medieval child usually learned his letters with the local priest or a monk from a nearby monastery, more rarely in the singing schools attached to cathedrals, but the age at which he started his primary education would be dictated by his personal circumstances. Often, a boy would not start to learn Latin, without which all but the most basic learning was impossible, until he was in his teens, sometimes even twenty or older, simply because his economic situation prevented it. In the seventeenth century Girardon, the French sculptor, worked at home until he was sixteen; when his father, prosperous at last, sent him off to begin his studies. Still not unusual in Girardon's day, this practice had been customary in the fifteenth century, when old men, young men, adolescents, and children could all be found sitting in the same classroom, learning the same lessons. They turned up for classes, but no one cared about the rest of their lives. Sometimes, as we learn from Thomas Platter's story of his school days in the early sixteenth century, groups of students ranging in age from the early twenties to a mere ten, would wander in search of learning from France to Germany and back again. A young boy would be bound to an older boy, beg for him, be beaten by him, and might occasionally be taught by him, but always he would be fed and protected. Occasional jobs would enable them to attend classes and lectures; but usually they begged, and education proceeded by fits and starts. They lived like hippies and wandered like gypsies, begging, stealing, fighting; yet they were always hungry for books, for that learning that would open the doors of the professions. Platter was nineteen before he could read fluently, but within three years his hunger for learning led him to master Latin, Greek, and Hebrew. And in the end he became rector of Basel's most famous school.

Even in Platter's day, however, times were changing. The late Middle Ages witnessed the proliferation of colleges, particularly at Oxford and Cambridge and the University of Paris. Students entered the university at an early age—usually at fifteen, sometimes as young as twelve, though there was, of course, no bar to the very mature. Residence in colleges fixed them in one place, and parents could be certain that their sons would be subject to discipline, sent regularly to lectures and classes, and protected from the excesses of drink, the temptations of fornication, and the dangers of gambling. College rules became very strict; obedience was insisted upon, and whipping frequent for delinquency. Inexorably a world of learning, quite separate from the adult world, indeed, carefully protected from it, was created. In the sixteenth and seventeenth centuries all Etonians were taught in one large room. The boys were divided up into groups in accordance with the progress of their studies, and the usher and master would go from group to group. At this time few grammar schools or *lycées* had more than one master and one usher.

This system began to change at the end of the eighteenth century, and by the early part of the nineteenth century a new system had been established. Schoolrooms were divided up or added, boys of the same age were moved steadily from class to class, and as the numbers swelled, fees grew and so did the number of masters employed. Yet much of the adult world lingered on, even in the boarding schools, which were becoming increasingly popular in England. We know that at Eton, Harrow, Rugby, and elsewhere there was drinking, smoking, fighting with local boys, a great deal of gambling, and a considerable amount of surreptitious wenching. But reform went relentlessly on, creating a separate world of childhood and early youth. Even the leisure and amusements of schoolboys were differentiated. Organized team-games replaced casual, personal sporting activity; innocence was insisted upon and incessantly preached about; sex before entry into the adult world came to be regarded as a social crime; literature was even more carefully censored—the headmaster of Harrow in the mid-century would not allow the reading of any novel, for fear it would corrupt the reader; naturally gambling was forbidden and alcohol banned. Even food became different—far plainer than adult food and dominated by milk and suet puddings, which you may still hear an old-fashioned Englishman dismiss as nursery food. And school clothes changed, too. In the seventeenth century two ribbons at each shoulder marked a child's dress, otherwise it was the same as an adult's. In the eighteenth century children were frequently clothed in semifancy dress—sailor's costume, the kilt and bonnet of the Scottish Highlander, Vandyke dress for special occasions—rather as if society were searching for difference. Greater freedom was permitted to the child, and children were allowed trousers long before adults would wear them. But gradually, two basically separate forms of costume for children and adults evolved. By the early twentieth century boys between infancy and puberty wore short trousers, and their clothes were always far drabber than adults'—confined to grays and blues and blacks. At school children were clamped into uniforms as socially distinct as those of soldiers or prisoners.

In the European upper classes children in the nineteenth century were even excluded from adult society *in the home*. The children were forbidden most of the house and lived in day and night nurseries with nurses, governesses, or tutors, visiting the rest of the house and their parents only for very short periods. Indeed, the difference between the life of a sixteenth- and a late-nineteenth-century child is so vast as to be almost incomprehensible. Three centuries had created a private world for children.

Although this new attitude toward children developed in the middle classes, it seeped down into society as time passed. The pictures of working-class children of Victorian London or Paris show them still dressed as adults, usually in their parents' worn-out and cut-down clothes, and we now know that they participated in every form of adult life—indeed, they physically had no escape from it. But as affluence spread, the working class, too, was caught up in the system of mass education, and working-class children began to have a separate world forced upon them. Social legislation also took a hand. In the nineteenth and twentieth centuries children were excluded from public houses, forbidden to gamble or buy tobacco, and their sexual lives were regulated by the concept of the "age of consent"; for it was assumed that they would be innocent, and prefer innocence, unless a corrupt society forced sex upon them. So by World War I, speaking broadly, there were three ages—infancy, which had been shortened to the age of four or five; childhood, which ran from the end of infancy to late puberty for the lower classes and to early manhood for the rest; and adulthood. And no child anywhere in the Western world was expected to share the tastes, the appetites, the social life, of an adult.

And then the revolutionary change came. The change from medieval to modern had taken more than three centuries, but the revolution that frightens modern society is scarcely a decade old. To understand it, one must know why children had gradually been separated from the adult world, and their lives and education carefully regulated. The short answer is social need: after 1500 the Western world grew ever more complex, demanding more skilled and trained men for commerce and the professions. And for these activities boys rather than girls were needed, which is why attitudes toward the young male changed most of all. Also, the great empires—the French, the British, the Spanish, and the Dutch—required men with the habit of authority. The proconsuls of empire had to be stamped with the image of a gentleman, aware of obligations as well as privileges. Discipline, best enforced by regular schooling, proved the most efficacious mold for the colonial bureaucrat.

But society is never still, and even as the new attitudes toward childhood were becoming fully fledged, there were countermovements in social structure that were to make even profounder changes. Science and technology invaded more and more of economic and social life. From 1880 onward they increasingly dominated the activities of Western society. Their growth demanded a longer and longer education.

THE WHY OF EARLY CHILDHOOD EDUCATION 3 MILTON E. AKERS

By traditional White House standards it was a simple affair. On the morning of August 31, 1965, the President and Mrs. Johnson received approximately two hundred guests in the Rose Garden. The assembled guests, including directors of community-action programs, early childhood educators, psychologists, and pediatricians, were somewhat ill at ease, unaccustomed to such distinguished hosts and elegant settings. The president proudly reviewed the accomplishments made during the preceding summer in Project Head Start and announced that the program "which began as an experiment has been battle tested—and it has proved worthy." On the success of the project the president declared: "We have reached a landmark—not just in education but in the maturity of our democracy." With grim determination he proclaimed: "The success of this year's program and our plans for the years to come are symbols of this Nation's commitment to the goal that no American child shall be condemned to failure by the accident of his birth" [Johnson, 1965, pp. 953–954]. The president then elaborated a three-part extension of the project to include the development of year-round programs for children from three to five years of age, the expansion of summer programs, and a variety of "follow-through" efforts which would sustain the progress of the previous summer.

The president's words launched an unprecedented national awareness of the crucial importance of growth and learning in the early years. Perhaps of much greater significance, the president's pledge catapulted the young child into the political arena.

Most certainly the social and political climate was ripe for such a commitment. Minority groups were becoming increasingly aggressive in asserting their demands for a fair deal in this land of opportunity. The conscience of America as a nation was in the process of painful exposure through a bombardment of facts concerning the shocking existence of the millions of its citizens who were locked into lives of hopelessness and despair. Almost as if for the first time, we began to recognize the shocking plight of the people in Appalachia, the American Indian, the migrant population, and ghetto dwellers in the urban areas. The guilt of a prosperous nation was such as to cause it to seek relief through action programs designed to eliminate such "open sores" from the lovely American image of itself.

By a fortunate coincidence of timing, psychologists and researchers in child development and theorists in the learning process were ready to offer solidly based approaches to the correction of the situation. The work of J. McV. Hunt, which gave a new appraisal of the effect of the environment on the developing organism, that of Jerome S. Bruner, which suggested new instructional approaches, and that of Benjamin S. Bloom— all pointed in one direction. If the vicious cycle of apathy, lack of aspiration, and waste of human potential perpetuated by poverty was to be broken, then substantial energies and efforts must be directed toward the children of poverty at a very early age. It was in this context that Project Head Start was conceived, tested, and expanded. In spite of the ragged variations in the quality of programs developed and of the many questions raised as to its total effectiveness, Head Start stands today as the most significant and successful of all the efforts of the war against poverty. But Head Start was a simple beginning. In the years that immediately followed, millions of dollars funneled through the Elementary and Secondary Education Act and other legislation was directed into intensive research and development of a burgeoning array of compensatory programs which would intervene and redirect the lives of these children. The critical importance of a good start in life was "discovered."

A NEW LOOK AT CHILDHOOD

The recent concentration of investigation and study by psychologists, educators, pediatricians, psychiatrists, anthropologists, nutritionists, and others point clearly in one direction. The child's earliest years are the time of most rapid physical and mental growth. At no other period in his life is he so susceptible and responsive to positive environmental influences which enhance and expand his development. Environmental influences, if of a sterile or destructive nature, may have negative effects on his intelligence, his motivation and ability to learn, his concept of himself, his relationships with others, and on his later health.

The child is learning every moment of his life, sometimes actively and aggressively moving out, at other times assuming a more passive role. He is discovering who and what he is. He is discovering how other people feel about him and what they expect of him, as well as how he feels about them and what he can expect from them. He is continuously searching to understand the world of people and things which surround him and to determine what his own role is in this highly complex situation. There is little doubt that the optimal fulfillment of the potentials that are uniquely his and his emergence into greatest effectiveness as a socially competent adult are critically affected by what happens to him in infancy and childhood.

In the forties and fifties, concerns for the young child were essentially directed toward his psychosocial development—a healthy, well-adjusted personality. Heavily influenced by Freud and Erikson, early childhood educators and, perhaps to a slightly lesser degree, researchers were preoccupied with such aspects of development as trust, autonomy, and the acquisition of effective social skills. Attention to intellectual aspects of development were almost consciously avoided. Most early childhood educators were reluctant to organize programs for specific intellectual learnings but, rather, "supported the notion that young children should be left to learn only those things for which they have a particular bent as shown by their natural interest. Many nursery schools reflecting this point of view may have had elaborately inviting environments, but teachers were admonished to allow the child to set his own pace and make his own choices in activities and seldom interfere" [National Education Association, 1968, p. 9]. At the same time, constrained by a tenacious clinging to the myth that no child could or should learn to read before the age of six, the public schools were almost totally unconcerned with the younger child. Perceiving learning and reading as synonymous, public school personnel were content to leave the child to his own devices until he was ready for their formal learning program, i.e., reading. The kindergarten programs which were established were justified and generally characterized as programs of reading readiness.

The late fifties saw the beginnings of ferment in many quarters in a departure from exclusive emphasis on the child's affective and social development. From a vast range of persons showing emerging concerns for another aspect of development, the cognitive, it is perhaps unwise to attempt to pinpoint any particular person or group. One early and clear statement was articulated by Martin (1960), who pointed out that in our work with young children we had been overlooking "the one characteristic that once was thought to be unique in man, that is, the fact that he has a mind and he has capacity for thought" [p. 71]. The "rediscovery" of the child's mind was indeed an apt term as one recalls that much of the study and work in earlier decades dealt directly with the intellectual development of the young child, i.e., that of Montessori, Isaacs, Gesell, and many others. The earliest works of Piaget, recently discoverable through translation, make clear his lifelong concern with this aspect of development. The rediscovery of the child's mind, coinciding with the social and political climate of the times, brought a concentration of efforts and energies in this direction unprecedented in vigor and intensity.

THE ABILITY OF THE CHILD TO LEARN

To a nation still smarting from the humiliation of having been surpassed in the field of scientific endeavor by the Russian's successful launching of Sputnik, and, consequently, judging our own educational system to be lacking, the conclusions of Bloom and his associates offered both an explanation and a degree of hope. The obvious solution in the mind of the public was that we must begin our formal education at a much earlier age. Many early childhood educators, already deeply respectful of the ability and capacity of the young child to learn, were impressed by the implications of the Bloom study. According to Bloom (1964), "we may conclude from our results on general achievement, reading comprehension and vocabulary development that by age 9 (grade 3) at least 50% of the general achievement pattern at age 18 (grade 12) has been developed" [p. 105]. Bloom's thesis confronted us with new challenges and responsibilities. Quite clearly we had not been according the young child the respect he deserved.

This new awareness of the fact that the child has a tremendous capacity for learning and does learn an amazing amount through his own initiative meshed neatly with Hunt's dramatic challenging of the concept of the fixed level of intelligence (1961). Hunt's studies concerning the modifiability of development, including intelligence, presented exciting possibilities when related to Bloom's conclusions concerning significance of the first four years of life in the determination of the child's ultimate level of intellectual functioning. If, as Bloom suggests, these years offer a unique opportunity for exploiting the possible variation in the child's developing intellectual capacity, then the nature of his experiences and environment during these years becomes critically important. Our new view of the young child as a learner now expanded to include curiosity regarding the extent of his ability to learn and was strengthened by an intriguing awareness of the lifelong impact of these learning experiences. Bruner's proposition (1961) that "the foundations for any subject may be taught to anybody at any age in some form [p. 12]" added even another dimension. The early years were clearly spotlighted as the new frontier in education. We saw in it not only unlimited potential for breaking the cycle of poverty in working with the disadvantaged child, but also possibilities for revolutionary changes in the total educational system.

Child psychologists, early childhood educators, and pediatricians were ready and eager to respond to the challenge presented by President Johnson. The provision of unprecedented federal funds facilitated the "pioneering" movement. In addition to those moneys made available for Project Head Start, even greater funds for compensatory programs came from a variety of titles of the Elementary and Secondary Education Act. Throughout the country, research and development centers were established, as well as the National Laboratory on Early Childhood Education with its university-centered components. We were fully embarked on the task of finding out more about the nature of the learning process, what the young child could learn, and the most effective strategies for teaching him. The content of his learning, what the child needs to know, and the optimum timing for presentation of particular experiences received a full share of attention. We moved into the seventies *knowing* much more in each of these areas as the result of all such efforts. We have not progressed so well in the broad dissemination of this knowledge or in the development of methods for its application in the field. Many questions remain which are, as yet, unanswered or need further clarification.

Inspired by the studies of Hunt and Bloom, with their special emphasis on measurable IQ, it was inevitable that the goal of most of the programs focused on increasing the IQ. This emphasis was reinforced by the fact that evidence of increased IQ was the most significant criterion applied by the federal government in its decisions to fund experimental projects. A few insistent pleas that increased intellectual capacity as measured by the IQ did not guarantee more effective learning or performance were politely heard but, unfortunately in the eyes of some, not acted upon. Recently, some psychologists have been more aggressively questioning the possibility of misdirected efforts in many projects. From the vantage point of his deep involvement in a variety of projects, Miller (1969) cites McDavid as courageously and emphatically posing the issue:

> The most massive error ever made in educational research has been our commitment to IQ testing as a criteria for measuring the effectiveness of educational practice. For forty years psychologists and educators have interchanged the subject. The concept of intellect is an abstraction, an intangible quality of capacity or ability which as far as I am concerned has never been directly measured and never

will be. In contrast, an IQ is the result of measured performance. Performance and capacity are not identical [pp. 32–33].

Commenting on this same issue, Zigler (1970) has expressed concern for the overemphasis on cognitive ability and the measurement of achievement, which actually reflects the richness and extent of the child's experience, with too little consideration devoted to the motivational and emotional systems of the child. Zigler says:

By all means, let us continue to work on how and when particular experiences influence the development of specific cognitive processes. But my bet is that a considerably larger pay-off would result if we spent as much time in our Head Start centers getting children to use the ten points of intelligence that motivational factors cause to lie dormant as we do trying to add ten more IQ points to the child's potential. If we work directly on those motivational and emotional factors that often constitute the roots of a child's ineffectual behavior, the entire IQ issue falls into proper perspective [p. 7].

The American public seems always to seek "the" way, the panacea—if you will, the quick miracle. This pressure has contributed to competition among various exploratory and development projects, leading to pronouncements of superiority or greater effectiveness of this approach over that. The worker in the field has been left either in a position of confusion and dilemma or of unyielding commitment to a particular program. If such is, indeed, the state of mind of the most critically important individual, the one who works directly with children, then a valid question may be raised as to the positive impact on children of such projects. Three studies of the comparative effectiveness of various approaches, Seifert (1969), Karnes, and Weikart (both cited in Hunt, 1969), suggest that there may be little difference in the results or in the staying power of the results. The important conclusion is that of Seifert: "A child seems clearly better off in one of the programs rather than in none" [p. 557]. Perhaps children would be better served if the competition among researchers and program developers could be minimized and an open and cooperative search for more effective strategies be facilitated instead.

EDUCATION AS A COMPONENT OF A COMPREHENSIVE SERVICES PROGRAM FOR CHILDREN

A most significant trend in the forward movement of organized education is toward a closer coordination of the facilities of the home and of the school. If one were to inquire of any student of social progress, "What is the newest development in the educational world?" the answer would almost surely be, "Schools for infants and a constructive program of education for parents." [p. 7]

To a generation which feels that it has "discovered" the critical importance of educational provisions in earliest infancy and the need for programs which accomplish more effective parenting, it may come as a bit of a shock to learn that the above quotation comes not from this decade but from the 1929 yearbook of the National Society for the Study of Education, *Preschool and Parental Education.* Recognition of the need for programs which provide educational services for the child at an early age within the context of his family situation is certainly not new. What is new within the past few years is a clearer understanding of the complexity of the delivery of such a program and the extent of the mustering of forces striving to accomplish its fulfillment. The meshing of thought and energy from the broad variety of disciplines concerned with fostering the total well-being of young children, coupled with thoughtful actions from the federal government including both the administrative and legislative components, offers hope that at long last this nation is ready for a full commitment to maximize opportunities for the fullest development of the potential of each and every child in this nation.

The term *comprehensive services* gained popularity within Project Head Start. Such services, however, were viewed initially within that program as health services (Office of Economic Opportunity, 1967). As the project developed, the effectiveness of parent education programs, parent involvement opportunities which included significant roles in major policy decision-making, and community-action endeavors which set out to accomplish safe, attractive, and comfortable neighborhood environments lent both depth and breadth to our growing understanding of what an extensive program of comprehensive services for young children and their families might be. Legislation proposed in both the Ninety-first and Ninety-second Congresses included many references to comprehensive services.

It may be said at this moment that we have a fairly clear notion as to what many of the essential components of such a program should be. What appears still to be lacking is a truly imaginative expression of the concept, one which clearly articulates the need for and potential power of such a program along with a viable delivery system. "Comprehensive family-oriented child development programs, including health services, day care, and early childhood education" was the top-priority recommendation of the 1970 White House Conference on Children, but the supporting papers set forth a limited and unsatisfactory program. Perhaps at this particular moment in time we are limited rather than freed in our thinking by aggressive and articulate social forces at work in our society. The need and desire of women to enter into the labor field, the demands of some women that they be afforded the right to be personages in and of themselves in addition to their role as mothers, the vested interests of industry which narrowly and selfishly see services for children as a means of insuring fewer employee absences and a decrease in turnover of personnel—each force is commanding and will exert substantial influence toward the provision of services for the young child. Where, however, are those groups which will speak with comparable forcefulness of the need for relevant training for parenthood beginning in earliest adolescence, for immediate action based on our shocking new knowledge concerning the importance of prenatal diet and care for the mental as well as physical development of the young child, for action which will lead to a less embarrassing new ranking on the international scale of infant mortality? Will there be a convergence of concerns for job training and job opportunities which will afford lives of decency and dignity for all, for neighborhood and community institutions which "pull for" the young child rather than stand as situations with which he must learn to cope? Can we soon eliminate the destructive barrier which now exists in too many situations between the public school and the life of the child prior to his entry there—between the in-school and out-of-school life of the school-age child?

These are questions with which we are confronted realistically as we dream of a program of comprehensive services for young children. Tremendous progress has already been made in isolated situations—unfortunately few. One promising approach is that of Coordinated Community Child Care (Day Care and Child Development Council of America, 1969). The coordination, meshing, and sharing of all available resources at every level, as proposed under this approach, can only result in greater economic benefits for all in terms of most efficient utilization of personnel and physical resources and also result in more impactful benefits for children and their families.

There is reason for optimism. The sincere and informed concerns expressed in recent contacts of this writer with a number of governors, with legislators, and other key personnel at the federal and state levels lead to the belief that we are on the verge of a full commitment to such an all-out effort. Most certainly we have the knowledge and the vision to design and implement an effective program of comprehensive services. Adequate funding is one of the essential ingredients lacking. To speak of offering a broad program of services for young children without recognition of the fact that it will necessitate money—and lots of it—is not only an exercise in futility but sheer hypocrisy. We also must come to grips with the human problem of lerning how to share and coordinate funds and energies without the threat of loss of personal or institutional identity. When and only when this nation really understands the significance of offering the young child the best beginning in life that our knowledge can produce will we accomplish a real commitment expressed in terms of necessary funds. With such a commitment, possibly a brighter, more productive present may be expected for the young child, with boundless possibilities for his future functioning as a socially competent adult.

CONCLUSION AND SOME CAUTIONS

Efforts in the past decade have added immensely to our knowledge of the nature of child development and learning. Psychologists and educators together have demonstrated their ability to devise and implement programs for young children and their families which facilitate greater human effectiveness. Certainly the social and political climate is right for both the concentration and expansion of further energies in this direction. At this point in time, two cautions seem worthy of note. Because recent efforts have been to a substantial degree politically motivated, is there the possibility that "this too shall pass"? One recalls the excellent nursery schools created under the Works Progress Administration (WPA). This effort was forwarded, not because of a desire to serve children, but rather to afford job opportunities for the unemployed. Similarly, during World War II some superb day care centers were established which enabled many mothers to ease the manpower shortage. Supporters of the concept of Project Head Start have respectfully noted that even within the project "professional help has been pushed aside in an effort to give status and jobs to the needy [Omwake, 1969, p. 130]," thus compromising the potential benefits of that program. Based on such past experiences one may legitimately ask the question, Will the 1999 yearbook of the National Society for the Study of Education still be striving for the goals initially set forth in 1929 and reiterated and elaborated in this present issue?

A second and not inconsistent concern lies in the area of public expectations from programs for young children. Cognizant of this nation's persistent search for the simple and easy solution to any problem, may we at some point find ourselves guilty of having "oversold" the promise of early learning, oversold in the sense of having created unrealistic expectations? Most certainly a good beginning is essential, but of equal importance is providing the most effective educational opportunities we can develop for the ten-year-old, the fifteen-year-old, and even the adult. Programs for younger children must be viewed as a critically important segment to be integrated into the total educative process for America's children.

4

It is appropriate, on this 50th Anniversary of the Children's Bureau, to discuss the impact of child-development theories on child care in the United States, for no agency has had a greater influence on the gradual improvement of child health and the translation of child-development theory into practice than the Children's Bureau.

Direct improvements of the physical health of children are easier to assess than indirect benefits from educational programs. Yet in this area of indirect influence, the Children's Bureau has played a major role. The two pamphlets, "Prenatal Care" and "Infant Care," have over the years reached more American families than any comparable publications, thus serving as the major interpreters of child development theories. If one knew none of the direct research studies and none of the writings of the system makers, one could read successive editions of "Infant Care" and infer the prevailing theoretical approaches of each time period.

But even before the Children's Bureau, there were theories about the nature of the child and attempts to persuade parents to act toward their children in some particular way. Generally these theories were based on *a priori* assumptions rather than on any data and were theologically toned. An example is the doctrine of innate depravity which asserted that the child was inherently evil and that the main duty of parents and educators was to eradicate this depravity.

Probably each major theory which left any mark on the history of ideas had to be attuned to its era—a little bit, but not too far, ahead of its time. Thus intellectual prerevolutionary France was receptive to Rousseau's challenge of the doctrine of innate depravity with his assertion that the child is inherently good until corrupted by society. In postrevolutionary America, when rigid self-discipline and industry were required to subdue the frontier, theories which stressed obedience, discipline, and submission to adult authority found acceptance.

In every era there are two kinds of "experts" about child behavior—those who publish and those who do not. Every parent has his or her theory about how children develop. This theory may remain at the level of proverbs or cultural maxims ("Spare the rod and spoil the child"), may involve broad generalizations lacking behavioral referents ("Just give them love and security"), or may propose precise hypotheses about genetic influence on behavior or the relative efficacy of reward or punishment for inducing learning.

These implicit theories are important determinants of parental action and reaction. For example, "a spare the rod" theory makes it unnecessary for the parent to make a fresh decision about how to handle a particular type of behavior each time it occurs; it also insulates the parent from guilt about behaving punitively toward his child.

TWENTIETH CENTURY THEORIES

During the 20th century, three theoretical systems about child development have made major inroads into the personal learning theories of American parents: the behavioristic (or social learning); the maturational; and the psychoanalytic.

SOCIAL LEARNING THEORIES

While the work of several theorists could be cast into the framework of social learning theory, John B. Watson had the greatest influence in this direction. Watson's concept of infancy was essentially a Lockean *tabula rasa*—an amorphous bit of behavior potential to be shaped by the learning opportunities experienced by the infant. His psychological theories appeared at a time in the history of ideas when most complex types of emotional experience were attributed to the expression of instincts.

Convinced as he was that emotions were acquired throughout the learning process, Watson used naive subjects, infants, to test his hypotheses. He designed and executed a number of ingenious experiments which demonstrated that many fears could be acquired and subsequently eliminated through conditioning. From these experiments he concluded that most forms of complex behavior were the result of concatenations of reflexes and simple response systems associated through conditioning.

Such a view of the child places an awesome degree of power into the hands of parents and other "teachers." A completely malleable infant bespeaks an omnipotent training agent. Watson wasted no time in extrapolating from the laboratory to home and school and in communicating his ideas directly to parents. His widely read publications had considerable influence on recommendations made to parents about child care. The 1928 edition of "Infant Care," always the best statement of current professional ideas, relied heavily upon Watsonian suggestions about shaping behavior, such as developing habits of regularity, dependability, independence, and self-reliance.

Watson attempted to put to pasture many sacred cows of child development literature, including mother love and the importance of encouraging emotional dependency between parents and children. His language was too pungent to escape caricature. Witness this example (1928):

> *There is a sensible way of treating children. Treat them as though they were young adults. Let your behavior always be objective and*

kindly firm. Never hug and kiss them, never let them sit in your lap. If you must, kiss them once on the forehead when they say good night. Shake hands with them in the morning. Give them a pat on the head if they have made an extraordinarily good job of a difficult task. Try it out. In a week's time you will find how easy it is to be perfectly objective with your child and at the same time kindly. You will be utterly ashamed of the mawkish, sentimental way you have been handling it.

Unfortunately publishers have no standard code for reporting whether an author wrote a particular passage with tongue in cheek. Therefore, an author must expect to be taken literally and to live with the implications of his words as written. In recent years Watson and his theories of conditioning have been felled by the impact of just statements as the above. The reactions of his critics have ranged from vilification to mere ridicule, and feeling still runs high. Several modern theorists, however, notably Skinner (1953), Miller and Dollard (1953), and Rotter (1954), have significantly advanced social learning theory and have extended our knowledge about the limits of external manipulation and control of infant and child behavior.

MATURATIONAL THEORY

This system is represented by the writings of Arnold Gesell (1956; Gesell et al., 1940; Gesell & Ilg, 1943, 1946). A prolific and at times poetic writer, Gesell also recognized the journalistic principle that one picture is worth a thousand words and copiously illustrated his books with pictorial samples of child behavior. Although perhaps referred to more often for his methods of developmental diagnosis and cinema-analysis and for the norms of behavioral development which he and his students accumulated over the years, Gesell was nonetheless an important formulator of a theory of child behavior.

Gesell's theory of development is relatively simple yet, in some ways, more global than other more complex theories. The key concept is that of *maturation* or growth. It is a theory of intrinsic development, of an infant's maturation proceeding from both the human and the individual nature of the infant.

Implicit in the concept of maturation is self-regulation of growth. Gesell urged recognition of this principle in every aspect of development from the establishment of infant feeding schedules to the acquisition of moral values. Acceptance of the principle by parents calls for a certain considerateness, an "alert liberalism," to use Gesell's phrase. Infants, as well as older children, are entitled to certain courtesies, to being regarded as "people." A passionate regard for the individual was, Gesell maintained, crucial to a truly democratic orientation to life.

A corollary of this stress on the importance of the individual is the concept of individual differences. Yet, paradoxically, it is here that Gesell seems to have been most generally misinterpreted and, indeed, almost to have courted misinterpretation. This stems from the organization of most of his books in terms of ages and stages of behavior. Indeed, the books' typography—the capitalization of each age period as though personified—conduces to such misinterpretation. For example (Gesell & Ilg, 1943):

> THREE *is a kind of coming-of-age. . . . You can bargain with* THREE *and he can wait his turn. . . .* FOUR *(and half past) tends to go out of bounds. . . .* FIVE *is a* SUPER-THREE *with a socialized pride in clothes and accomplishments, a lover of praise.*

About this approach, Gesell and Ilg (1943) say:

> *We regard the formal concept of chronological age and the functional concept of maturity level as indispensable both for practical common sense and for the science of child development. In the guidance of children it is absolutely necessary to consider the age values of behavior and the behavior values of age. The reader is warned, in advance, however, that* the age norms are not set up as standards and are designed only for orientation and interpretive purposes. . . . *The prevalence and significance of individual variations are recognized at every turn [p. 17].*

Perhaps these occasional warnings do not carry enough weight to counterbalance the continued stress on ages and stages in development throughout childhood and adolescence.

With respect to the timing of the maximum impact of the three major theories we are discussing, Gesell followed Watson and preceded Freud. Nevertheless, many of Gesell's most popular publications came out during the period of popularization of psychoanalytic thought. Gesell did not seem to be a man for polemics, however, and he seldom bothered to take notice of other points of view. His books deal largely with the presentation of his own material. He quotes other researchers only when their studies relate to his interests. In the four Gesell books reviewed for this article, there are only two references to Freud. Gesell was more concerned with developmental congruences than interpersonal conflicts, with eye-hand coordination and prehension than emotional cathexes. Even in the volume "Youth" (1956), "sex" is indexed in terms of "differences" and not of preoccupations and problems.

Watson is quoted once in these four Gesell works, but anonymously as "a distinguished behaviorist" and the source of the quote is not in the reference list. However, in isolated articles, Gesell occasionally opposed certain points important in behavioristic doctrine, as he did when he suggested (1929) that the conditioned reflex theory promised too much and threatened too much, and that maturation protected the infant from certain chance conditionings.

In reflecting on the impact of Gesell's work one must not overlook the influence of distribution.

Until the appearance of the amazing Spock volume (1946), Gesell's writings were probably more widely disseminated than any other full-length book on child development. Furthermore, Gesell, like Watson, was persuaded of the obligation to present child development material directly for parental consumption. Knowledge about infants and young children, he said, "must extend into the homes of the people; for the household is the 'cultural workshop' where human relationships are first formed."

PSYCHOANALYTIC APPROACH

The theoretical formulations of psychoanalysis and the body of empirical data collected to test the hypotheses have provided perhaps the most significant and pervasive influence on child-development theories and child-rearing practices in recent decades. By clinically reconstructing the life history of the adult or child through therapeutic efforts, psychoanalysts have developed theoretical formulations concerning the meaning of interaction of the infant or young child with his environment. It is understandable that, in a scientific era, a theory explaining the develop-ment in all its subtleties (unconscious and conscious) would capture widespread attention.

The complexities of psychoanalytic theory are difficult to distill into a few paragraphs. Unlike the maturation theory, psychoanalytic theory has undergone many revisions and is continuously modified. Classical (or Freudian) psychoanalysis and the neo-Freudian formulations differ in many respects.

Psychoanalysis is generally referred to as a biological theory of personality; yet the biological drives are manifested entirely in a social context. From the standpoint of the developing child, this context is mainly the family group. Unless basic drives (instincts) are gratified during early interactions with the parents—primarily the mother—the child moves forward from infancy with some degree of fixation at this earlier stage and somewhat impaired in adaptability. Or, if gratification at succeeding stages of development is insufficient, the child falls back on earlier patterns of behavior (regression) for gratification.

The concepts of fixation and regression are based on a sequence of stages in development. Thus personality development progresses from oral to anal stages in early life and then to a sequence of genital stages—oedi-pal, latent, adolescent, and mature. Experiences during each period are conceived of as affecting character traits of later life.

During the "oral period" in infancy, for example, it is thought the child develops feelings about accepting things and the mother's manner of giving them. Erikson (1950) has postulated that from the totality of experiences in this period, the individual develops a basic sense of trust in people—or else a lack of trust which hampers his ensuing development. During the period of acquisition of bowel and bladder control when the child must integrate contradictory impulses of retention and elimination, traits related to orderliness, punctuality, and thrift are thought to develop.

The awareness of genital differences and feelings brings with it even more complex integrative tasks. Personality begins to take shape in more recognizable form, and characteristic modes of dealing with adaptive problems (mechanisms of defense) become evident. The relationship of the individual's later feelings and character traits to earlier experiences suggests that manipulation of these experiences in a "healthy" direction may favorably influence later development. This assumes agreement on a desirable mature model toward which to strive. Chronic failure of the parents to provide for the gratification of the basic drives is likely to result in permanent personality distortions remediable only through a kind of regrowth process via the therapeutic relationship.

These formulations have been theoretically enticing and have provided many hypotheses for investigation by workers in the field of child development as well as for child-care workers in various disciplines interested in the prevention of emotional disorders. Many psychoanalytic concepts have been embraced as guides to child rearing by parents concerned with raising "emotionally healthy" children. However, a review of the experimental literature (Richmond & Caldwell, in press) indicates that no specific relationships between early experiences and later development can be established at the present time.

There is growing recognition among psychoanalytic investigators that the application of knowledge gained from psychoanalysis in preventive efforts must be approached cautiously. The objective of psychoanalytic investigation as stated by Erikson (1950) a decade ago remains valid:

> Psychoanalysis today is implementing the study of the ego, the core of the individual. It is shifting its emphasis from the concentrated study of the conditions which blunt and distort the individual ego to the study of the ego's roots in social organization. This we try to understand not in order to offer a rash cure to a rashly diagnosed society, but in order to first complete the blueprint of our method.

To pursue these objectives, psychoanalytic research workers are departing from the predominant use of reconstructive interview or play techniques to the greater use of direct observation of development (as indicated by the current interest in research in mother-infant interaction), experimental approaches (animal and human), and cross-cultural studies. Also, more intensive and objective studies of psychoanalytically oriented interviews are being developed.

IMPLICATIONS FOR TODAY

The fact that different theories can flourish contemporaneously validates Knapp's observation (1960) that man is a "recalcitrant and reluctant experimental subject." Yet these theories of child development are not contradictory or mutually exclusive. All are concerned with learning, with the interaction of organism and environment. They all highlight different facets of behavior and use different conceptual systems. And, undoubtedly, they are all a little bit right.

From all of them one can infer that parents wield an awesome degree of power in shaping the lives of their children. Even maturational theory, with its emphasis upon the growth integrity of the young organism, its inherent potential for healthy development, implies that the parent can inhibit or distort this growth potential. With greater awareness of the implications of their caretaking activities, some parents have shown signs of what might be loosely termed a midcentury parental neurosis: an over-determination to seek suggestions for child rearing as insurance of healthy development for their children.

Professional workers in the field of child care (pediatricians and other health workers, psychologists and child welfare workers) have not been immune to these pressures. They have sometimes advocated as universally desirable such programs as "natural childbirth," rooming-in of the newborn with the mother at the hospital, breast feeding, and permissive or self-regulating patterns of child care. To their credit, psychoanalysts have not been in the forefront of these movements. Rather, these movements have often represented misinterpretation or premature application of psychoanalytic principles. Recently they have been placed in a more appropriate perspective, as doctrinaire approaches to "prevention" have been given up in favor of the more traditionally eclectic orientation of child-care professions—except perhaps by social work which has remained heavily committed to psychoanalytic theory.

Guidance in child rearing will probably become increasingly professionalized in the United States in the years to come. The child-care professions, therefore, must face up to the challenge of providing services for parents even with incomplete knowledge. If these services are to be provided for families, adequate professional personnel must be made available. The specific professions to provide this personnel, the appropriate distribution, and the organization of services are issues with which we as a nation have not yet come to terms. The current ferment about the "new pediatrics" and concern with the directions in which this profession should move educationally and in practice suggests the need for planning constructively for all kinds of child-care services.

Since the launching of Sputnik in 1957, we have awakened to our responsibilities to fulfill our potentialities as a democratic nation. The resultant emphasis on academic achievement has the same over-determined emphasis which other child-rearing formulae have had in previous years. While we must strive for full intellectual development of our children, this need not be at the expense of their social and emotional growth. If it is, we may inhibit the learning we seek to foster.

IMPLICATIONS FOR FUTURE THEORIES

What thoughts can now be projected about the child development theories of the future? Undoubtedly they will continue to be prevalent both at the scientific level and as part of each individual's general philosophy. The individual theories will change only as rapidly as cultural changes occur, and presumably those cultural changes will be at least in part a function of the rapidity of scientific change. However, we will make a few predictions about the characteristics of heuristic child development theories:

PREDICTION 1: *Extrapolation from research data will not be so extreme.*
The science of behavior has matured into a more conservative, slightly subdued stage. Professionals in the field have themselves matured somewhat. Also the interdisciplinary origin of many of the reasonably stable parts of child development knowledge is conducive to conservatism.

The young Watson, with little knowledge of genetics and its constitutional limitations upon adaptability of the organism, could assert that he could take any four healthy infants and make them whatever type of adult he wished. The somewhat provincial Freud, unaware of the nascent body of data from cultural anthropology, could assume that the memories and fantasies of individuals from a fairly narrow sociocultural context represented universal attributes. Today's theorists are no longer permitted the luxury of being uninformed about work in any area of knowledge which might limit the predictions from a given theoretical system. With greater availability of information which might make predictions hazardous, the theories themselves will become more cautious about specific predictions.

PREDICTION 2: *Future theories of child behavior will be concerned with a broader time spectrum.*
The view of the child as a miniature adult is outmoded. But in its place has come with too much finality a view of the child almost as an eternal child.

The child *is* a future adult, as he is a future adolescent and a future senescent. The 6-month-old baby who experiences a certain type of mothering will presumably carry some residual of that experience with him at age 3 or 13. Since each type of later experience may modify the nature of the residual, such differences need to be fully explored. Useful child development theories of the future will be concerned with predictions which span wide segments of the developmental curve, not just one narrow section.

PREDICTION 3: *Future theories of child behavior will be related to broader aspects of social theory and philosophy.*

A point already stressed in this paper is that each enduring or influential child development theory [is] related to powerful currents of social history. Within the past few decades even the seemingly remote physical sciences have had to face such a relationship. There is now less talk about a separation of science from values. Certainly in the field of child development no such separation is possible. We rear children to fit into a particular culture, on the basic premise that the culture is somehow "good" or at least acceptable.

The past two decades have seen considerable sniping at Watson for the naïveté of his theories, with an occasional implication that he was heartless and cruel for denouncing mother love and the child-rearing practices of most parents. Such criticism fails to recognize that Watson was far more explicit than most theorists about the behavioral attributes he wished to foster. He concludes one of his books (Watson, 1928) with a formal apologia to critics who have taken him to task for having no "ideals" for bringing up children, commenting perceptively that different programs of care fit different civilizations. Then he describes briefly the kind of child he had in mind when making his child-rearing suggestions, the kind he considered best adapted to the changing America of the late twenties:

> *We have tried to sketch in the foregoing chapters a child as free as possible of sensitivities to people and one who, almost from birth, is relatively independent of the family situation. . . . Above all, we have tried to create a problem-solving child. We believe that a problem-solving technique (which can be trained) plus boundless absorption in activity (which can also be trained) are behavioristic factors which have worked in many civilizations of the past and which, so far as we can judge, will work equally well in most types of civilizations that are likely to confront us in the future.*

Undoubtedly, many persons would not agree with Watson's goals, but it is to his credit that he attempted to relate his theory to the social milieu.

PREDICTION 4: *Future theories of child development will not attempt to answer (or predict) everything about child development for all time. They will modestly relate themselves to one sociocultural group—until something is proven to have universal relevance—and for a finite scientific era.*

New discoveries can outmode existing theories overnight. For example, future research on behavioral genetics might drastically modify many of the assumptions underlying research on the effects of specific parent practices on child behavior. Any heuristic theory will be quick to incorporate new data, thus building a more stately theoretical structure. Victor Hugo's tribute to the power of an idea whose time has come might well apply in reverse here, for nothing is more effete than a theory that has outlived its time.

5

A PERSPECTIVE ON SOCIAL LEARNING

EDNA AMBROSE
ALICE MIEL

The schools of the United States face no task more important and exacting than that of helping the young acquire the social learnings which enable them to function as responsible and effective members of a democratic society in a world of ever expanding horizons. Challenges to democracy, both at home and abroad, and changes wrought by advances in scientific and technological fields underscore the urgency of utilizing available knowledge to improve social education in the schools.

Fortunately, at the very time when these challenges confront educators with overwhelming responsibilities, there is an increasing flow of helpful information at their disposal. Research and thoughtful study of experts in such fields as biology, psychology, medicine, and psychiatry have produced a vast amount of knowledge about the human organism and its growth. The younger social sciences, such as social psychology, cultural anthropology, and sociology have revealed the impact of social phenomena upon human growth and learning. Psychiatry and psychoanalysis have emphasized the significance of interpersonal relations and the inner organization of experience upon the development of personality. As Giles (1954) avers in presenting his growth-belonging theory of human dynamics:

> It is possible that we now have, if we could put it into usable form, a large part of the knowledge needed to manage human affairs for

purposes of good, for a fuller life for all, rather than for purposes of evil, of destruction of the fullness of life for all. The young sciences of the past twenty-five years have given us research material which has the most powerful meaning, if it were but generally known and used. Slowly it is beginning to be known, yet development of its understanding, and still more its use, is painfully behind the need [p. 1].

A FRAMEWORK FOR VIEWING PERSONALITY DEVELOPMENT

A cursory overview of the process of personality development will highlight some factors which should be known by all who influence the social learnings of children. The meaning of personality in this discussion is that presented in the report of the Midcentury White House Conference on Children and Youth:

Personality is the thinking, feeling, acting human being who, for the most part, conceives of himself as an individual separate from other individuals and objects. This human being doesn't have a personality; he is a personality. . . . What we are really talking about in discussing health of personality is the concrete human being and the relative success of his endeavor to play his part in relation to other human beings and to the institutions through which social life is carried on [Witmer & Kotinsky, 1952, p. 364].

According to an analysis of personality development based upon psychological theory and knowledge from the fields of child development and cultural anthropology, the growing child is confronted with a succession of personal-social conflicts which must be resolved favorably in order for him to add needed components to his personality. If the conflict is resolved fortuitously, the child will move forward with good feelings and confidence in himself and others and in his ability to master the ways of the world. He will be *free* to *become* that which his potentialities and his surrounding environment permit. Interpersonal relations play a major role in determining the outcome of the child's struggles. What he needs from important adults are approval, support, encouragement and freedom to follow his laws of development. The point of view here advanced is the authors' interpretation of materials presented in Erikson (1950), Witmer & Kotinsky (1952), and Almy (1955).

The following table presents the conflicts which are part of growing up and the periods of a child's life at which each becomes dominant. In each case, the positive aspect is italicized:

Trust–mistrust	Infancy
Autonomy–shame or doubt	Toddlerhood
Initiative–guilt	Early Childhood
Industry–inferiority	Later childhood
Identity–role diffusion	Early adolescence

According to the theory, these problems are not faced and resolved, for better or worse, at just one period of life. They are always present. But the effort to develop one of these components of personality appears in clearest form during a certain period.

As the positive aspect is incorporated into the child's concept of self, it becomes a bulwark for future development. However, none is a permanent achievement; throughout life, experiences can either strengthen or shatter earlier victories. Nor is there any perfection in life, except by definition. No one, for instance, would trust everybody, or his own capacities, or the outer world wholly and unquestioningly. In fact, the realities of existence call for a certain amount of judicious mistrust. What is needed during each period is a balance on the positive side.

THE COMPONENT OF TRUST The first social achievement, *trust,* which starts in infancy, is believed to be the primary element in personality development and the seat of good feelings about self and others. The feelings are fostered by warm, accepting relationships and consistency in the behavior of those who care for the infant. Important also is the regulation of demands to what he is biologically prepared to do. The baby who receives the needed care and warm relationships has the groundwork to advance to the next struggle armed with good feelings about himself and others and a sense of regularity in the outer world.

THE COMPONENT OF INDEPENDENCE Throughout the second period in personality development the child will be striving to develop *a sense of autonomy.* He will struggle to assure himself and the important people in his life that he is an individual in his own right. What he must learn is exactly what he is trying to assure himself: that he can do things on his own, that he can make some choices that are truly his own. From the adults in his life he needs continued trust and affection in the midst of a change in relationships. The change entails allowing him to do for himself, to use his growing powers to explore a wider world. It also entails standing behind him in his efforts and helping him gradually to discriminate between what he can and cannot do. During this period he needs to learn to heed a clear, consistent and reasonable "no" used to prohibit those activities which he cannot sensibly be left free to do on his own.

When adults stand behind him and give approval for his efforts to use his new powers and make some choices of his own, the child experiences a sense of inner and outer goodness which adds mightily to his basic trust in himself, in others, and in his capacity to master the ways of the world. Now in the company of other children and adults he can find out what a person like himself can *do*.

THE COMPONENT OF INITIATIVE The push to develop a sense of *initiative* comes at a time when the child is, if all has gone well, a ready and avid learner, eager to use all his developing powers to become one with the world. Spurred on by an intense curiosity, aided by all his distance senders and receivers he eagerly tests his growing powers. By running and jumping and falling and rolling and doing all the wonderfully exciting things a person like himself can do, he learns. Those who can see and hear as they live with children have learned that the play and phantasy and work of young children cannot be nicely differentiated. All are the engrossing activities through which the child becomes at home in the world, learning its properties and building confidence in himself and others, as with these others he explores ways of dealing with the world and discovers what he can do. Erikson's proposal (1950) in this connection is particularly pertinent:

> The playing adult steps sideward into another reality; the playing child advances forward into new stages of mastery. I propose the theory that the child's play is the infantile form of the human ability to deal with experience by creating model situations and to master reality by experiment and planning. It is in certain phases of his work that the adult projects past experience into dimensions which seem manageable. . . . He anticipates the future from the point of view of a corrected and shared past. . . . No thinker can do more and no playing child less [p. 195].

Socialization moves on apace during this period. The child learns about his social world, its institutions and processes and finds out much about people by playing their roles. That is, from the point of view of the adult, children are playing roles. To young children, usually, this is in no sense the case. The small child is not, from his point of view, *playing* pilot—he *is* the pilot.

Other children enter importantly into his life, adding dimensions to his learning or creating threats to his own feelings of importance and power. This is a time when there must be on hand a trusted grown-up to whom the child can repair when the tensions created by the challenges of age-mates become too great.

Throughout, a child's learnings will be greatly affected by the family and cultural groups to which he belongs. The expectations of adults, the ways in which they attempt to control his behavior, the guidance and encouragement they give and the models they set for his imitation—all importantly influence his learning.

This is a period when the child has the beginnings of a conscience to guide him in his activities. It is likewise a period when an over-strict conscience can cause great distress and sometimes overwhelming feelings of guilt. The problem for the adults, while the child is striving to develop a sense of initiative, is one of exercising nice discrimination concerning freedom-restraint. The child has to build within himself a sense of his powers and the rightness of his ways of doing things. Without some choices and opportunities to carry through the tasks he initiates on his own, this cannot be done. On the other hand he has to be protected from too impulsive a use of his energies lest he run into danger or suffer feelings of guilt.

When helped to do what *he* can do and not held to some outer, adult-imposed standard, his meanings become clearer. They become more fully incorporated into the inner core of his being. He learns to look upon himself as a "can-doer," one who can venture forth on his own and not be shamed when, for instance, he's jumping four inches while someone else jumps a foot. In addition to plenty of opportunities to try things out on his own, he needs encouragement and support when he has been unsuccessful or has undertaken something beyond his capacities.

If he is fairly successful, he will have learned to initiate activities, set goals and persevere in achieving them. It is worth noting that these important social learnings are built within the child, not because someone on the outside told him this was a good way to behave, or read him a story about the desired behaviors. They are built because the child has lived through experiences in which he has felt within himself what it is like to try something on his own, to follow through and to achieve.

THE COMPONENT OF ACHIEVEMENT At about the age of six—earlier for some, later for others—and continuing throughout the years of the elementary school for most, children are busily engaged in establishing a sense of *industry* and accomplishment. Now is the time when the child welcomes real achievement—achievement which has meaning in his society. He is a great realist and wants to know if "it's really so" or it "really happened" or it "really worked." Small wonder that he turns to his peers. Who else can know the world as he knows it? Who else can master the world as he masters it? Peers are wonderful participants in the process of acquiring new knowledge and skills, in helping one feel secure in asserting increasing independence from adults, in helping one work out codes of cooperation, fair play and other rules of the social game.

As the child achieves more independence he needs more ability to make disciplined use of freedom. He needs a conscience which functions more flexibly than the young child's; that is, he needs a conscience which permits him to determine behavior according to the situation. If he has learned to follow instructions blindly, he may find himself unable to exercise any judgment as to which values are appropriate in the various situations in which he finds himself. Conversely, he must have accepted restrictions of his impulses to the extent that he can grant privileges to others. If he has known too inconsistent guidance or too few prohibitions, he may be in a worse position than the child who is hemmed in by an overstrict conscience. He may be "much more the creature of his impulses, much less able to channel, control, and direct them in a way increasingly satisfactory not only to himself and to his peers, but to the society of which he is a member (Almy, 1955, p. 345)."

Difficulties arise if he fails to see himself and his abilities as acceptable or if parents and teachers cannot accept the childish rebellion which is sure to come when, with his peers, he moves to affirm his independence from adults.

The problem throughout the period is how to become an achiever with his abilities and limitations. The way he sees things, the way he feels about himself, the way he believes people feel about a person like himself, are the reality with which he deals. They count far more than do objective facts in building his feelings about himself and others and in determining his orientation to the world.

THE COMPONENT OF IDENTITY Though most children in the elementary school will be in the period of later childhood, it is well, for purposes of continuity in the picture, to look briefly at the next phase of personality development.

As the growing child moves into puberty and adolescence, he is confronted with the task of establishing an *identity*, of determining just who and what he is and what his place in society is. He also has to learn to accept and live with a changing body. All these concerns cause some youngsters a great deal of anxiety and uncertainty. Young adolescents in our country seem to seek their assurance through being solidly "in" with a peer group.

According to Almy (1955, p. 457), those who have not established autonomy or initiative seem to have particular difficulty. She believes that much depends upon the nature of interpersonal relations, and how the youth has learned to live with himself. "If, as he grows up, he is able to keep in touch with his emotions, to know that he is angry and at whom, that he is afraid and of what, that he feels warmly and positively, then he is at adolescence in a better position to know his changing self and to make decisions that are 'right' for it."

RELATIONSHIP OF COMPONENTS TO
DEMOCRATIC SOCIALIZATION

Emerging insights on personal-social development reveal close affinity between the components of personality development and a successful orientation to democratic living. The four components of trust, independence, initiative, and industry, which are strengthened or developed during the years a child spends in the elementary school, are achievements highly prized by a democratic society.

Trust, the first social achievement, lays the groundwork for a life of friendliness and cooperation with others, as well as a belief in oneself and in regularity in the outer world. Autonomy brings a sense of personal dignity, as well as ability to control one's impulses and feel comfortable about oneself. These are indispensable attributes for a cooperative life which is dedicated to the enhancement of each individual. Initiative, the will to try things out on one's own, to make one's own choices, and learn by the consequences, is the very essence of democratic living. It is, in fact, the process through which democracy builds selves.

Industry and its accompaniments, a sense of duty and accomplishment, are achievements which give confidence that one can master the ways of the world and make things work for the betterment of people—essentials for a successful orientation to democratic living.

All of these components, which can best be developed in childhood, are crucially needed by the children who will be called upon to maintain and advance democracy during the last half of the twentieth century. But no child will automatically and necessarily build within himself these important elements of effective social living. He needs encouragement and guidance, opportunities to explore his environment of people, ideas and things, and help in interpreting his experience. He needs good sense and sound decision-making on the part of the important adults in his life. This requires that their expectations and means of control be geared to his particular timing and ways of growing. Then, in the midst of warm interpersonal relations, he can have a good chance to grow and learn without experiencing mistrust, overwhelming feelings of self-blame, guilt or inadequacy. He and he alone does the growing; he and he alone does the learning, but conditions in the environment must be propitious, else he cannot approximate his potential growth. Most significant of all in the environment will be the interpersonal relations he experiences and the pictures they give him of himself and others.

early experiences and early education

A child's development is a product of two influences: his heredity, that is, the characteristics transmitted to him biologically from his parents, and his environment, that is, the set of experiences to which he is exposed by others or to which he chooses to expose himself. This section focuses on the young child's environment.

The seven selections can be viewed in broad perspective if the reader is aware of certain considerations relating to an "optimally enriched" environment. The typical American child lives in an environment that provides the basic physical and psychological necessities of life. (Children whose environments are lacking in these basic necessities are termed "deprived" or "environmentally disadvantaged"; these children are discussed in Section Seven.) The typical American child does not, however, develop in an optimally enriched environment that incorporates the benefits of our current medical, educational, and psychological knowledge. The articles in this section concern the basic processes through which the developing child interacts with the environment, the ways in which the contemporary urban family setting provides an environment that is enriching in ways that are not traditional, and programmatic features that day-care and early school environments might incorporate to become more enriching.

In Article 6, "Society and Education," Robert Havighurst and Bernice Neugarten discuss the socialization process, the procedures and situations through which the child learns, for better or worse, patterns for interacting with the society about him. This article focuses on the family, peers, and the school, the function of "role expectations" in the socialization process, and the issue of why the family in particular exerts a profound influence on the infant and preschool child.

Urie Bronfenbrenner opens Article 7, "The Split-Level American Family," with some provocative sentences:

> Children used to be brought up by their parents. It may seem presumptuous to put that statement in the past tense. Yet it belongs in the past tense. Why?

He then goes into some of the reasons that contemporary urban American parents are much less important influences in the socialization of their children than were American parents of earlier generations. This theme of decreasing parental influence is interrelated with a discussion of the increasing influence of peers in the personality development of modern American children.

In Article 8, "Can Young Children Have a Quality Life in Day Care?", Bettye Caldwell proposes a practical solution to the situation described by Bronfenbrenner—that the number of day-care facilities with sophisticated and caring teachers be greatly increased. She presents research evidence in support of her contention that young children can "have a quality life in day care." As Caldwell notes, there is only limited evidence on many questions of care for young children, and most day-care centers that have been studied have well-developed programs and carefully selected staffs.

The articles by Barth and by Beyer consider environmentally enriching factors so basic to schooling that they are often overlooked in program planning. In article 9, "On Selecting Materials for the Classroom," Roland Barth presents guidelines for selecting educational materials tailored to a child's learning styles and interests as well as designed to allow active exploration and flexible, individual thinking patterns. Barth's article reflects his "open-classroom" value orientation. In Article 10, "Daily Routines and Group Experiences," Evelyn Beyer examines the routines that usually occupy a significant portion of the preschool and day-care schedule. She gives suggestions for using the routines to contribute to a general learning climate of informality within clearly defined limits, a climate characterized by moderation between the extremes of formality and chaos.

Article 11, Fantini and Weinstein's "Toward a Contact Curriculum," details four areas in which teaching can tie into the emotions of children and thereby become more relevant and effective. The authors propose a curriculum in which the affective (emotion-related) and cognitive (thought-related) components of learning are equally emphasized. They also attempt to dovetail the teaching of skills and information with reaching children "where they are." Although this material was written for teachers of economically disadvantaged children, it contains some generally applicable guidelines and examples.

Article 12, "Basic Ideas of the Montessori Method," concerns the theories and the teaching practices of Maria Montessori, the influential Italian educator whose work was the subject of much controversy in the first half of this century. Luella Cole's presentation is a balanced one. Emphasizing the validity and novelty of Montessori's ideas, she first discusses the ideas of individuality and freedom that constitute the "Montessori point of view" and the emphasis on training the senses that comprises the "Montessori technique." Then she considers the shortcomings of the Montessori method, indicating that many of these deficiencies result from the fact that some of Montessori's ideas are derived from theories no longer thought valid.

behavioral objectives   *To be able to discuss the following points*

6 SOCIETY AND EDUCATION

Reward and punishment and didactic teaching as methods of social training

The learning processes of imitation and identification and their relationship to each other

The meaning of social role and the function of roles in the development of the child

Three factors involved in the impact of the family on the developing child

7 THE SPLIT-LEVEL AMERICAN FAMILY

The positive and negative features of child-adult relationships a generation ago

The conditions of life that militate against urban parents' spending time with their children

The focus of Western studies of influences on personality

Coleman's findings regarding peer-group influences in American high schools

The role of the peer group in the United States and in the Soviet Union

Bandura's findings on the effects of aggressive models on child behavior

Sherif's findings with regard to the conditions that promote inter-group cooperation as opposed to intergroup hostility

The arguments for the care of young children as a superordinate goal in uniting various groups in the community

8 CAN YOUNG CHILDREN HAVE A QUALITY LIFE IN DAY CARE?

Previous attitudes toward the families who placed children in group day care

The social need filled by day-care centers

The cognitive gains by children in day care in relation to socioeconomic background

The relationship of day care to children's health

The influence of day care on child-mother attachments and on the child's relationship to other adults and to age-mates
The reasons the child should have a primary attachment bond before he goes to a day-care center

9 ON SELECTING MATERIALS FOR THE CLASSROOM
The general relationship between classroom materials and learning
The advantages of allowing children to supply their own materials for learning
The value of exploration of the world outside of school and class-room
The advantages of inexpensive learning materials
The value of ambiguity of use in learning materials and how this factor relates to structure of learning materials
The benefits that are possible with materials selected to induce active exploration

10 DAILY ROUTINES AND GROUP EXPERIENCES
The general features of the casual, middle-ground approach to routine in preschools today
The advantages of a casual, middle-ground approach to routines over both "rigid" and "anything goes" extremes
The relationship of routine to other features of the usual preschool program
The salient features of toileting, cleanup, rest, and snack and group periods

11 TOWARD A CONTACT CURRICULUM
How irrelevance results from a lack of match between teaching procedures and learning styles
How to reduce irrelevance in what is taught
The relationship of positive and negative feelings to the relevance of material
Why evoking negative feelings does not necessarily add to relevance in teaching
The difference between concerns and feelings and their relationship to each other

12 BASIC IDEAS OF THE MONTESSORI METHOD
What Montessori means by individuality
The relationship between Montessori's notion of freedom and the concept of self-discipline
Training the senses as a prelude for the development of the intellect

The major shortcomings of the Montessori system
Montessori's idea that schoolwork be based on what comes spontaneously from children

6

SOCIETY AND EDUCATION

ROBERT J. HAVIGHURST
BERNICE L. NEUGARTEN

The socialization of the individual is carried out by various agencies of society. The social groups within which the infant is changed into the socialized adult are the groups that take care of him, love him, reward and punish him, and teach him. The major socializing agencies in the life of the child are the family, the peer group, the school, the church, the youth-serving organizations, various political and economic institutions in the community, and the mass media such as radio and television. It is their variety that is to be emphasized; and the fact that in a complex society such as America there are both formal and informal agencies at work in influencing the behavior of the child and the adolescent. The school is an example of an agency formally organized for the purpose of inducting the child into his society; the peer group is an example of an agency that, although informal, plays an important role in the socialization process.

METHODS OF SOCIAL TRAINING

Not only are there various agencies at work in the socialization process, but there are also various *methods* of social training, various ways in which the child learns, and various ways people teach the child.

The first is the general method of *reward and punishment.* The young child who is scolded for messing with his food is being socialized by the use of punishment; when he is praised for eating with a fork, he is being socialized by the use of reward. Rewards and punishments become more subtle and more indirect with the increasing age of the child, but they continue to be of many types. A reward may, for instance, take the form of material goods, as when a young child is given a piece of candy, an older child is given a bicycle, or an adult is given a higher salary. A reward may take the form of social approval, as when the child is kissed by his mother, the adolescent is praised by a friend, or the adult is commended by his employer. Rewards often take the form of increased status and prestige for the individual, as when a child is told he is now "old enough" to cross a street alone, or when an adolescent finds a job and feels he has now become an adult.

In the same way, punishments are of various types. There are corporal punishments, as when a parent slaps a child for misbehaving, or when a playmate strikes out when the child has trespassed upon his property. Physical or social restrictions are potent forms of punishment, as when a parent confines the child to his room, a teacher keeps a child after school, an adolescent is told by others that he cannot join them at the lunch table, or when an adult is not invited to a party. Punishment often takes the form of withdrawal of something valued by the individual, as when a toy is removed from the child's hand, a parent threatens the withdrawal of love or approval, or an adult is fined for disobeying a traffic signal.

While certain forms of rewards and punishments are recognized as undesirable, still the method in general is a pervasive one and, in at least its subtler aspects, operates continually in everyday life to shape the behavior of individuals young and old and to teach them how to behave so as to meet social expectations.

A second form of social training takes the form of *didactic teaching*, when the individual is given a bit of information or is told what to do or how to do it. This is the method of telling and explaining, and, while it is the method most easily observed in the school room, it occurs in other social settings as well. Religious leaders as well as school teachers, parents as well as age-mates, Boy Scout leaders as well as television announcers, all use the didactic method over and over again. Thus a father teaches a boy how to hammer a nail by telling him, "Hold the hammer in your right hand and hold the nail in your left!" The minister explains verbally that it is wrong to steal. The teacher says, "The letter *l* is a longer letter than *e* and you must write it so that it doesn't look like *e*."

A third form of social training, often closely related to the second, is that of setting an example for the child so that he will learn by *imitation*. The father takes the hammer and says, "Watch how I do it!" and the teacher demonstrates on the blackboard how to write the letters *l* and *e*, then asks pupils to do the same. Imitation may be conscious, as in the examples just given, when the child deliberately copies what he sees; or it may be unconscious, as when a boy learns to walk just like the father walks, or when a girl uses the same vocal mannerisms as her teacher. Unconscious imitation is especially important in the learning of social behavior and social attitudes.

The child in his first years of life usually learns that life is more rewarding and more interesting if he follows in the footsteps, literally and figuratively, of the older and more experienced people whom he loves and respects, his parents or his older brothers and sisters. The young child forms the habit of imitating the people who have power and experience, and to whom he feels a close emotional bond. This habit is formed so early and repeated so often that it becomes unconscious; it operates without the child's awareness.

Imitation is closely related to the process of *identification*, in which the child tries to *be* another person. There are differing theories regarding the basis for early identification; some psychologists believe that the young child identifies first with the person who gratifies his needs; others believe the child identifies with the person whose status he envies and who withholds from him the things he wants (Kagan, 1958; Bronfenbrenner, 1960; Burton & Whiting, 1961). In any case the child imitates, consciously and unconsciously, the behavior of the person with whom he identifies; he takes on that person's attitudes, values, and ideals.

Usually identification begins with family members, where parents are taken as models. In time, the child takes other models for his behavior: teachers, ministers, scout leaders, and older children; then persons outside his immediate environment—imaginary as well as real, of the past as well as the present—such as movie idols, historical figures, and so on. In general, persons who are admired or who have status in the eyes of the child or adolescent are taken as models.

A large part of what the child learns occurs through unconscious imitation and identification. Yet parents, teachers, and other adults, in planning socialization experiences for children and adolescents, are probably making less than full use of these processes. In many learning situations where adults rely upon the methods of reward and punishment or upon didactic teaching, learning might well be left to the child's tendency to imitate and identify with admired people around him. In the classroom situation, for example, the processes of unconscious imitation and identification occur as frequently as elsewhere, yet they might occur even more frequently if teachers focused their attention upon them. The teacher who is first admired as a person will be more effective as a teacher.

Utilizing the processes of social learning just described, every individual becomes socialized by learning a set of social roles. A social role may be defined as a coherent pattern of behavior common to all persons who fill the same position or place in society and a pattern of behavior *expected* by the other members of society. The pattern may be described without reference to the particular individuals who fill the role. Thus, for example, all women behave in certain patterned ways when they fill the role of mother, and we speak of the social role of mother. All teachers are expected to behave in certain ways within the school room, regardless of how they may behave when school is over and when they are filling other roles such as father or mother, husband or wife, friend, or church member.

The growing child takes on a series of social roles and incorporates the expected behavior into his personality. A very young child learns first

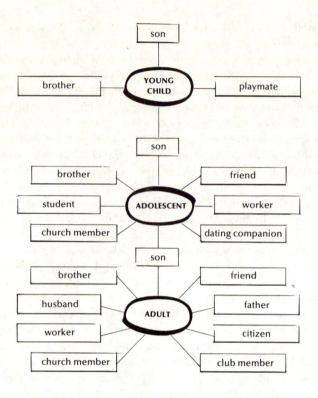

SOCIAL ROLES INCREASE WITH AGE

how to behave in the role of child; he learns that his parents take care of him and make decisions for him; that he may behave in certain ways, but not in other ways. Soon he learns to differentiate other social roles beyond the general one of child in relation to parent. He learns the role of brother or sister; then the role of playmate.

The child of school age has a wider range of social roles to fill. He is a son, a brother, a pupil, a friend, a playmate. For each of these roles he learns a number of expected and rewarded kinds of behavior; and he learns when to take each role. While in the school room, for example, he learns to behave foremost as a pupil and to subordinate his role of friend or playmate until he gets out on the playground. Later, as an adolescent and as an adult, he will fill a more complex set of social roles. As an adult he will be a spouse, a parent, a homemaker, a friend, a worker, a citizen, a church member, a club member.

Within these broadly defined social roles, there are narrower ones. As a brother, one may be an older or a younger brother; as a playmate, one may be a leader or a follower; as a pupil, one may be "teacher's pet" or the object of the teacher's disapproval.

70   *early experiences and early education*

The individual, as he grows older and as his circle of social interactions widens in scope, takes on an ever-increasing number of social roles, and incorporates the role behaviors into his personality and into "himself." In this sense, the social self consists, in large part, of the behavior the individual expresses in his various social roles. In this sense, too, the well-socialized individual is one who fills his various social roles successfully. While every person has his idiosyncratic pattern of role behaviors (thus no two women fill the role of mother in exactly the same ways), still the well-socialized person is one whose role behaviors are appropriate to the expectations set by the social groups with which he interacts.

THE FAMILY SETTING AS A LEARNING SITUATION

There are at least three factors that highlight the family setting as a crucial one for socialization and that differentiate family from nonfamily learning situations.

The first of these factors is the immaturity of the young child. As an infant and pre-schooler, the child is totally dependent upon the people around him for food, for physical care, for the very maintenance of life. His helplessness makes him extraordinarily dependent upon family members for approval and affection. A two-year-old cannot risk the mother's disapproval in the same way that a sixteen-year-old can risk the teacher's disapproval.

The child's immaturity makes him easily influenced and easily molded. As he lacks physical independence, so does he lack intellectual and social independence. He has no experience of his own and no standards of his own. He is accordingly at the most impressionable and most "teachable" period of his life.

A second factor has to do with the nature of the learning tasks set by the family. A great part of the learning that goes on within the first years of life has to do with biological functions: eating, sleeping, toilet-training, sexuality. To the immature individual who has yet very little in the way of intellectual and social development, and whose life is primarily circumscribed by his body and its functions, social learnings that have to do with the body are crucial. Dealing with the most basic of life processes, they reach to the very core of the personality. In this sense it is a momentous task for an infant to learn to drink from a cup rather than a bottle; and the methods used by the mother in weaning the child are likely to be of much greater significance in the child's social development than, say, the methods used by the teacher when an eight-year-old is learning to add and subtract numbers.

The third factor that distinguishes family from nonfamily learning situations is the highly charged emotional setting within the family. Generally speaking, there is more emotion, both positive and negative, within a family group than within a play group or a school room. Emotional ties are stronger and more complex, and both child and parent have a great deal of feeling invested in the learning and teaching situation. In this sense, a mother cares more than does a playmate or a teacher if little Johnny misbehaves or if he accomplishes an unusual feat.

Furthermore, American families today are smaller units than before. The typical household now consists of mother, father, and children; and not, as in earlier periods, of the more extended family when grandparents, aunts, and uncles were likely to live in the same household. This creates for our modern child a "tight" emotional atmosphere within the family, one in which the important persons in his life are few in number, with a proportionally greater influence of each one upon him. Within the setting, then, of the small unit of the immediate family, learning takes place in an atmosphere that is rarely neutral in tone but instead has strong emotional components.

These factors—the child's immaturity and impressibility, the crucial nature of the learning tasks, and the highly charged emotional atmosphere —add up to the fact that the learning situation within the family is a particularly sensitive one, with a quality very different from other learning situations the child will encounter. The social lessons the child learns at the hands of his family tend to go deep and last long; while they may be much modified by later experiences, they will tend to influence the individual all through his life.

THE FAMILY TEACHES THE CULTURE
AND SUBCULTURE

It is within a setting such as we have described that the family acts to teach the child the culture and subculture to which he belongs. In the gross sense, a child born into an American family learns the American culture. He learns to speak English rather than Spanish; to eat with a fork rather than with chopsticks; to dress in a suit rather than a bearskin; to cry when he is sad rather than to smile. He learns how to talk, walk, and think in ways that are distinctively American. He learns not only the overt behaviors; he learns also the social, moral, and economic values of the culture: how children relate to adults, and how men relate to women; how to curb his aggressiveness and yet to cultivate his competitiveness; how to develop loyalties and how to seek for self-achievement. The over-all expectancies and way of life of the culture are transmitted to the child through the family; any child raised in an American family emerges as an American.

The family also teaches the child its own variation of the culture, that which we have referred to earlier as the subculture. Thus a child born into a farm family learns to behave in somewhat different ways from the child born into a city family; the child born into a Catholic family learns a somewhat different set of values from the child born into a Protestant family; the child born into a Japanese-American family learns something different from the child born into a Mexican-American family; and the child born into an upper-class family learns a different way of life from the child born into a lower-class family. Ethnic, religious, racial, and social groups maintain their differences through time to the extent to which they provide their offspring with different and distinctive patterns of thought and action.

THE SPLIT-LEVEL AMERICAN FAMILY 7 URIE BRONFENBRENNER

Children used to be brought up by their parents.

It may seem presumptuous to put that statement in the past tense. Yet it belongs to the past. Why? Because *de facto* responsibility for upbringing has shifted away from the family to other settings in the society, where the task is not always recognized or accepted. While the family still has the primary moral and legal responsibility for developing character in children, the power or opportunity to do the job is often lacking in the home, primarily because parents and children no longer spend enough time together in those situations in which such training is possible. This is not because parents don't want to spend time with their children. It is simply that conditions of life have changed.

To begin with, families used to be bigger—not in terms of more children so much as more adults—grandparents, uncles, aunts, cousins. Those relatives who didn't live with you lived nearby. You often went to their houses. They came as often to yours, and stayed for dinner. You knew them all—the old folks, the middle-aged, the older cousins. And they knew you. This had its good side and its bad side.

On the good side, some of these relatives were interesting people, or so you thought at the time. Uncle Charlie had been to China. Aunt Sue made the best penuche fudge on the block. Cousin Bill could read people's minds (according to him). And all these relatives gave you Christmas presents.

But there was the other side. You had to give Christmas presents to all your relatives. And they all minded your business throughout the years.

They wanted to know where you had been, where you were going, and why. If they didn't like your answers, they said so (particularly if you had told them the truth).

Not just your relatives minded your business. Everybody in the neighborhood did. Again this had its two sides.

If you walked on the railroad trestle, the phone would ring at your house. Your parents would know what you had done before you got back home. People on the street would tell you to button your jacket, and ask why you weren't in church last Sunday.

But you also had the run of the neighborhood. You were allowed to play in the park. You could go into any store, whether you bought anything or not. They would let you go back of the store to watch them unpack the cartons and to hope that a carton would break. At the lumber yard, they let you pick up good scraps of wood. At the newspaper office, you could punch the linotype and burn your hand on the slugs of hot lead. And at the railroad station (they had railroad stations then), you could press the telegraph key and know that the telegraphers heard your dit-dah-dah all the way to Chicago.

These memories of a gone boyhood have been documented systematically in the research of Professor Herbert Wright and his associates at the University of Kansas. The Midwestern investigators have compared the daily life of children growing up in a small town with the lives of children living in a modern city or suburb. The contrast is sobering. Children in a small town get to know well a substantially greater number of adults in different walks of life and, in contrast to their urban and suburban agemates, are more likely to be active participants in the adult settings that they enter.

As the stable world of the small town has become absorbed into an ever-shifting suburbia, children are growing up in a different kind of environment. Urbanization has reduced the extended family to a nuclear one with only two adults, and the functioning neighborhood—where it has not decayed into an urban or rural slum—has withered to a small circle of friends, most of them accessible only by motor car or telephone. Whereas the world in which the child lived before consisted of a diversity of people in a diversity of settings, now for millions of American children the neighborhood is nothing but row upon row of buildings inhabited by strangers. One house, or apartment, is much like another, and so are the people. They all have about the same income, and the same way of life. And the child doesn't even see much of that, for all the adults in the neighborhood do is come home, have a drink, eat dinner, mow the lawn, watch TV, and sleep. Increasingly often, today's housing projects have no stores, no shops, no services, no adults at work or play. This is the sterile world in which many of our children grow, the "urban renewal" we offer to the families we would rescue from the slums.

Neighborhood experiences available to children are extremely limited nowadays. To do anything at all—go to a movie, get an ice cream cone, go swimming, or play ball—they have to travel by bus or private car. Rarely can a child watch adults working at their trades. Mechanics, tailors, or shopkeepers are either out of sight or unapproachable. A child cannot listen to gossip at the post office as he once did. And there are no abandoned houses, barns, or attics to break into. From a young point of view, it's a dull world.

Hardly any of this really matters, for children aren't home much, anyway. A child leaves the house early in the day, on a schoolbound bus, and it's almost suppertime when he gets back. There may not be anybody home when he gets there. If his mother isn't working, at least part-time (more than a third of all mothers are), she's out a lot—because of social obligations, not just friends—doing things for the community. The child's father leaves home in the morning before the child does. It takes the father an hour and a half to get to work. He's often away weekends, not to mention absences during the week.

If a child is not with his parents or other adults, with whom does he spend his time? With other kids, of course—in school, after school, over weekends, on holidays. In these relationships, he is further restricted to children of his own age and the same socioeconomic background. The pattern was set when the old neighborhood school was abandoned as inefficient. Consolidated schools brought homogeneous grouping by age, and the homogenizing process more recently has been extended to segregate children by levels of ability; consequently, from the preschool years onward the child is dealing principally with replicas of the stamp of his own environment. Whereas social invitations used to be extended to entire families on a neighborhood basis, the cocktail party of nowadays has its segregated equivalent for every age group down to the toddlers.

It doesn't take the children very long to learn the lesson adults teach: Latch onto your peers. But to latch he must contend with a practical problem. He must hitch a ride. Anyone going in the right direction can take him. But if no one is going in that direction just then, the child can't get there.

The child who can't go somewhere else stays home, and does what everybody else does at home. He watches TV. Studies indicate that American youngsters see more TV than children in any other country do. By the late 1950s, the TV-watching figure had risen to two hours a day for the average five-year-old, three hours a day during the watching peak age period of twelve to fourteen years.

In short, whereas American children used to spend much of their time with parents and other grownups, more and more waking hours are now lived in the world of peers and of the television screen.

What do we know about the influence of the peer group, or of television, on the lives of young children? Not much.

The prevailing view in American society (indeed in the West generally) holds that the child's psychological development, to the extent that it is susceptible to environmental influence, is determined almost entirely by the parents and within the first six years of life. Scientific investigators—who are, of course, products of their own culture, imbued with its tacit assumptions about human nature—have acted accordingly. Western studies of influences on personality development in childhood overwhelmingly take the form of research on parent-child relations, with the peer group, or other extraparental influences, scarcely being considered.

In other cultures, this is not always so. A year ago, at the International Congress of Psychology in Moscow, it was my privilege to chair a symposium on "Social Factors in Personality Development." Of a score of papers presented, about half were from the West (mostly American) and half from the Socialist countries (mostly Russian). Virtually without exception, the Western reports dealt with parent-child relationships; those from the Soviet Union and other East European countries focused equally exclusively on the influence of the peer group, or, as they call it, the children's collective.

Some relevant studies have been carried out in our own society. For example, I, with others, have done research on a sample of American adolescents from middle-class families. We have found that children who reported their parents away from home for long periods of time rated significantly lower on such characteristics as responsibility and leadership. Perhaps because it was more pronounced, absence of the father was more critical than that of the mother, particularly in its effect on boys. Similar results have been reported in studies of the effects of father absence among soldiers' families during World War II, in homes of Norwegian sailors and whalers, and in Negro households with missing fathers, both in the West Indies and the United States. In general, father absence contributes to low motivation for achievement, inability to defer immediate for later gratification, low self-esteem, susceptibility to group influence, and juvenile delinquency. All of these effects are much more marked for boys than for girls.

The fact that father-absence increases susceptibility to group influence leads us directly to the question of the impact of the peer group on the child's attitudes and behavior. The first—and as yet the only—comprehensive research on this question was carried out by two University of

North Carolina sociologists, Charles Bowerman and John Kinch, in 1959. Working with a sample of several hundred students from the fourth to the tenth grades in the Seattle school system, these investigators studied age trends in the tendency of children to turn to parents versus peers for opinion, advice, or company in various activities. In general, there was a turning point at about the seventh grade. Before that, the majority looked mainly to their parents as models, companions, and guides to behavior; thereafter, the children's peers had equal or greater influence.

Though I can cite no documentation from similar investigations since then, I suspect the shift comes earlier now, and is more pronounced.

In the early 1960s, the power of the peer group was documented even more dramatically by James Coleman in his book *The Adolescent Society*. Coleman investigated the values and behaviors of teen-agers in eight large American high schools. He reported that the aspirations and actions of American adolescents were primarily determined by the "leading crowd" in the school society. For boys in this leading crowd, the hallmark of success was glory in athletics; for girls, it was the popular date.

Intellectual achievement was, at best, a secondary value. The most intellectually able students were not those getting the best grades. The classroom wasn't where the action was. The students who did well were "not really those of highest intelligence, but only the ones who were willing to work hard at a relatively unrewarded activity."

The most comprehensive study relevant to the subject of our concern here was completed only a year ago by the same James Coleman. The data were obtained from more than 600,000 children in grades one to twelve in 4,000 schools carefully selected as representative of public education in the United States. An attempt was made to assess the relative contribution to the child's intellectual development (as measured by standardized intelligence and achievement tests) of the following factors:

1 Family background (e.g., parents' education, family size, presence in the home of reading materials, records, etc.)
2 School characteristics (e.g., per pupil expenditure, classroom size, laboratory and library facilities, etc.)
3 Teacher characteristics (e.g., background, training, years of experience, verbal skills, etc.)
4 Characteristics of other children in the same school (e.g., their background, academic achievement, career plans, etc.).

Of the many findings of the study, two were particularly impressive; the first was entirely expected, the second somewhat surprising. The expected finding was that home background was the most important element in determining how well the child did at school, more important than any of all aspects of the school which the child attended. This generalization, while especially true for Northern whites, applied to a lesser degree to Southern whites and Northern Negroes, and was actually reversed for Southern Negroes, for whom the characteristics of the school were more important than those of the home. The child apparently drew sustenance from wherever sustenance was most available. Where the home had most to offer, the home was the most determining; but where the school could provide more stimulation than the home, the school was the more influential factor.

The second major conclusion concerned the aspects of the school environment which contributed most to the child's intellectual achievement. Surprisingly enough, such items as per pupil expenditure, number of children per class, laboratory space, number of volumes in the school library, and the presence or absence of ability grouping were of negligible significance. Teacher qualifications accounted for some of the child's achievement. But by far the most important factor was the pattern of characteristics of the other children attending the same school. Specifically, if a lower-class child had schoolmates who came from advantaged homes, he did reasonably well; but if all the other children also came from deprived backgrounds, he did poorly.

What about the other side of the story? What happens to a middle-class child in a predominantly lower-class school? Is he pulled down by his classmates? According to Coleman's data, the answer is no; the performance of the advantaged children remains unaffected. It is as though good home background had immunized them against the possibility of contagion.

This is the picture so far as academic achievement is concerned. How about other aspects of psychological development? Specifically, how about social behavior—such qualities as responsibility, consideration for others, or, at the opposite pole, aggressiveness or delinquent behavior? How are these affected by the child's peer group?

The Coleman study obtained no data on this score. Some light has been shed on the problem, however, by an experiment which my Cornell colleagues and I recently carried out with school children in the United States and in the Soviet Union. Working with a sample of more than 150 sixth-graders (from six classrooms) in each country, we placed the children in situations in which we could test their readiness to engage in morally disapproved behavior such as cheating on a test, denying responsibility for property damage, etc. The results indicated that American children were far more ready to take part in such actions.

The effect of the peer group (friends in school) was quite different in the two societies. When told that their friends would know of their actions, American children were even more willing to engage in misconduct. Soviet youngsters showed just the opposite tendency. In their case, the peer group operated to support the values of the adult society, at least at their age level.

We believe these contrasting results are explained in part by the differing role of the peer group in the two societies. In the Soviet Union, *vospitanie*, or character development, is regarded as an integral part of the process of education, and its principal agent—even more important than the family—is the child's collective in school and out. A major goal of the Soviet educational process, beginning in the nursery, is "to forge a healthy, self-sufficient collective" which, in turn, has the task of developing the child into a responsible, altruistic, and loyal member of a socialist society. In contrast, in the United States, the peer group is often an autonomous agent relatively free from adult control and uncommitted—if not out-rightly opposed—to the values and codes of conduct approved by society at large. Witness the new phenomenon of American middle-class vandal-ism and juvenile delinquency, with crime rates increasing rapidly not only for teen-agers but for younger children as well.

How early in life are children susceptible to the effects of contagion? Professor Albert Bandura and his colleagues at Stanford University have conducted some experiments which suggest that the process is well developed at the preschool level. The basic experimental design involves the following elements. The child finds himself in a familiar playroom. As if by chance, in another corner of the room a person is playing with toys. Sometimes this person is an adult (teacher), sometimes another child. This other person behaves very aggressively. He strikes a large Bobo doll (a bouncing inflated figure), throws objects, and mutilates dolls and animal toys, with appropriate language to match. Later on, the experimental subject (*i.e.*, the child who "accidentally" observed the aggressive behavior) is tested by being allowed to play in a room containing a variety of toys, including some similar to those employed by the aggressive model. With no provocation, perfectly normal, well-adjusted preschoolers engage in aggressive acts, not only repeating what they had observed but elaborating on it. Moreover, the words and gestures accompanying the actions leave no doubt that the child is living through an emotional experience of aggressive expression.

It is inconvenient to use a live model every time. Thus it occurred to Bandura to make a film. In fact, he made two, one with a live model and a second film of a cartoon cat that said and did everything the live model had said and done. The films were presented on a TV set left on in a corner of the room, as if by accident. When the children were tested, the TV film turned out to be just as effective as real people. The cat aroused as much aggression as the human model.

As soon as Bandura's work was published, the television industry issued a statement calling his conclusions into question on the interesting ground that the children had been studied "in a highly artificial situation," since no parents were present either when the TV was on or when the aggressive behavior was observed. "What a child will do under normal conditions cannot be projected from his behavior when he is carefully isolated from normal conditions and the influences of society," the statement declared. Bandura was also criticized for using a Bobo doll (which, the TV people said, is "made to be struck") and for failing to follow up his subjects after they left the laboratory. Since then, Bandura has shown that only a ten-minute exposure to an aggressive model still differentiates children in the experimental group from their controls (children not subjected to the experiment) six months later.

Evidence for the relevance of Bandura's laboratory findings to "real life" comes from a subsequent field study by Dr. Leonard Eron, now at the University of Iowa. In a sample of more than 600 third-graders, Dr. Eron found that the children who were rated most aggressive by their classmates were those who watched TV programs involving a high degree of violence.

At what age do people become immune from contagion to violence on the screen? Professor Richard Walters of Waterloo University in Canada, and his associate, Dr. Llewellyn Thomas, showed two movie films to a group of thirty-four-year-old hospital attendants. Half of these adults were shown a knife fight between two teen-agers from the picture, *Rebel Without a Cause*; the other half saw a film depicting adolescents engaged in art work. Subsequently, all the attendants were asked to assist in carrying out an experiment on the effects of punishment in learning.

In the experiment, the attendants gave an unseen subject an electric shock every time the subject made an error. The lever for giving shocks had settings from zero to ten. To be sure the assistant understood what the shocks were like, he was given several, not exceeding the level of four, before the experiment. Since nothing was said about the level of shocks to be administered, each assistant was left to make his own choice. The hospital attendants who had seen the knife-fight film gave significantly more severe shocks than those who had seen the art-work film. The same experiment was repeated with a group of twenty-year-old females. This time the sound track was turned off so that only visual cues were present. But neither the silence nor the difference in sex weakened the effect. The young women who had seen the aggressive film administered more painful shocks.

These results led designers of the experiment to wonder what would happen if no film were shown and no other deliberate incitement were introduced in the immediate setting of the experiment. Would the continuing emotional pressures of the everyday environment of adolescents—who see more movies and more TV and are called on to display virility through aggressive acts in teen-age gangs—provoke latent brutality comparable to that exhibited by the older people under direct stimulation of the movie of the knife fight?

Fifteen-year-old high school boys were used to test the answer to this question. Without the suggestive power of the aggressive film to step up their feelings, they pulled the shock lever to its highest intensities (levels eight to ten). A few of the boys made such remarks as "I bet I made that fellow jump."

Finally, utilizing a similar technique in a variant of what has come to be known as the "Eichmann experiment," Professor Stanley Milgram, then at Yale University, set up a situation in which the level of shock to be administered was determined by the lowest level proposed by any one of three "assistants," two of whom were confederates of Milgram and were instructed to call for increasingly higher shocks. Even though the true subjects (all adult males) could have kept the intensity to a minimum simply by stipulating mild shocks, they responded to the confederates' needling and increased the degree of pain they administered.

All of these experiments point to one conclusion. At all age levels, pressure from peers to engage in aggressive behavior is extremely difficult to resist, at least in American society.

Now if the peer group can propel its members into antisocial acts, what about the opposite possibility? Can peers also be a force for inducing constructive behavior?

Evidence on this point is not so plentiful, but some relevant data exist. To begin with, experiments on conformity to group pressure have shown that the presence of a single dissenter—for example, one "assistant" who refuses to give a severe shock—can be enough to break the spell so that the subject no longer follows the majority. But the only research explicitly directed at producing moral conduct as a function of group experience is a study conducted by Muzafer Sherif and his colleagues at the University of Oklahoma and known as the "Robber's Cave Experiment." In the words of Elton B. McNeil:

> War was declared at Robber's Cave, Oklahoma, in the summer of 1954 (Sherif et al., 1961). Of course, if you have seen one war you have seen them all, but this was an interesting war, as wars go, because only the observers knew what the fighting was about. How, then, did this war differ from any other war? This one was caused, conducted, and concluded by behavioral scientists. After years of religious, political, and economic wars, this was, perhaps, the first scientific war. It wasn't the kind of war that an adventurer could join just for the thrill of it. To be eligible, ideally, you had to be an eleven-year-old, middle-class, American, Protestant, well-adjusted boy who was willing to go to an experimental camp.

Sherif and his associates wanted to demonstrate that within the space of a few weeks they could produce two contrasting patterns of behavior in this group of normal children. First, they could bring the group to a state of intense hostility, and then completely reverse the process by inducing a spirit of warm friendship and active cooperation. The success of their efforts can be gauged by the following two excerpts describing the behavior of the boys after each stage had been reached. After the first experimental treatment of the situation was introduced,

> . . . good feeling soon evaporated. The members of each group began to call their rivals, "stinkers," "sneaks," and "cheaters." They refused to have anything more to do with individuals in the opposing group. The boys . . . turned against buddies whom they had chosen as "best friends" when they first arrived at the camp. A large proportion of the boys in each group gave negative ratings to all the boys in the other. The rival groups made threatening posters and planned raids, collecting secret hoards of green apples for ammunition. To the Robber's Cave came the Eagles, after a defeat in a tournament game, and burned a banner left behind by the Rattlers; the next morning the Rattlers seized the Eagles' flag when they arrived on the athletic field. From that time on name-calling, scuffles, and raids were the rule of the day. . . .
>
> In the dining-hall line they shoved each other aside, and the group that lost the contest for the head of the line shouted "Ladies first!" at the winner. They threw paper, food, and vile names at each other at the tables. An Eagle bumped by a Rattler was admonished by his fellow Eagles to brush "the dirt" off his clothes.

But after the second experimental treatment,

> The members of the two groups began to feel more friendly to each other. For example, a Rattler whom the Eagles disliked for his sharp tongue and skill in defeating them became a "good egg." The boys stopped shoving in the meal line. They no longer called each other names, and sat together at the table. New friendships developed between individuals in the two groups.
>
> In the end the groups were actively seeking opportunities to mingle, to entertain and "treat" each other. They decided to hold a joint campfire. They took turns presenting skits and songs. Members of both groups requested that they go home together on the same bus, rather than on the separate buses in which they had come. On the way the bus stopped for refreshments. One group still had $5 which they had won as a prize in a contest. They decided to spend this sum on refreshments. On their own initiative they had invited their former rivals to be their guests for malted milks.

How were each of these effects achieved? Treatment One has a familiar ring:

> To produce friction between the groups of boys we arranged a tournament of games: baseball, touch football, a tug-of-war, a treasure hunt, and so on. The tournament started in a spirit of good sportsmanship. But as the play progressed good feeling soon evaporated.

How does one turn hatred into harmony? Before undertaking this task, Sherif wanted to demonstrate that, contrary to the views of some students of human conflict, mere interaction—pleasant social contact between antagonists—would not reduce hostility.

> . . . we brought the hostile Rattlers and Eagles together for social events: going to the movies, eating in the same dining room, and so on. But far from reducing conflict, these situations only served as opportunities for the rival groups to berate and attack each other.

How was the conflict finally dispelled? By a series of strategems, of which the following is an example:

> Water came to our camp in pipes from a tank about a mile away. We arranged to interrupt it and then called the boys together to inform them of the crisis. Both groups promptly volunteered to search the water line for trouble. They worked together harmoniously, and before the end of the afternoon they had located and corrected the difficulty.

On another occasion, just when everyone was hungry and the camp truck was about to go to town for food, it developed that the engine wouldn't start, and the boys had to pull together to get the vehicle going.

To move from practice to principle, the critical element for achieving harmony in human relations, according to Sherif, is joint activity in behalf of a *superordinate goal*. "Hostility gives way when groups pull together to achieve overriding goals which are real and compelling for all concerned."

Here, then, is the solution for the problems posed by autonomous peer groups and rising rates of juvenile delinquency: Confront the youngsters with some superordinate goals, and everything will turn out fine.

What superordinate goals can we suggest? Washing dishes and emptying wastebaskets? Isn't it true that meaningful opportunities for children no longer exist?

This writer disagrees. Challenging activities for children can still be found; but their discovery requires breaking down the prevailing patterns of segregation identified earlier in this essay—segregation not merely by race (although this is part of the story) but to an almost equal degree by age, class, and ability. I am arguing for greater involvement of adults in the lives of children and, conversely, for greater involvement of children in the problems and tasks of the larger society.

We must begin by desegregating age groups, ability groups, social classes, and once again engaging children and adults in common activities. Here, as in Negro-white relations, integration is not enough. In line with Sherif's findings, contact between children and adults, or between advantaged and disadvantaged, will not of itself reduce hostility and evoke mutual affection and respect. What is needed in addition is involvement in a superordinate goal, common participation in a challenging job to be done.

Where is a job to be found that can involve children and adults across the dividing lines of race, ability, and social class?

Here is one possibility. Urbanization and industrialization have not done away with the need to care for the very young. To be sure, "progress" has brought us to the point where we seem to believe that only a person with a master's degree is truly qualified to care for young children. An exception is made for parents, and for babysitters, but these are concessions to practicality; we all know that professionals could do it better.

It is a strange doctrine. For if present-day knowledge of child development tells us anything at all, it tells us that the child develops psychologically as a function of reciprocal interaction with those who love him. This reciprocal interaction need be only of the most ordinary kind—caresses, looks, sounds, talking, singing, playing, reading stories— the things that parents, and everybody else, have done with children for generation after generation.

Contrary to the impression of many, our task in helping disadvantaged children through such programs as Head Start is not to have a "specialist" working with each child but to enable the child's parents, brothers, sisters, and all those around him to provide the kinds of stimulation which families ordinarily give children but which can fail to develop in the chaotic conditions of life in poverty. It is for this reason that Project Head Start places such heavy emphasis on the involvement of parents, not only in decision-making but in direct interaction with the children themselves, both at the center and (especially) at home. Not only parents but teen-agers and older children are viewed as especially significant in work with the very young, for, in certain respects, older siblings can function more effectively than adults. The latter, no matter how warm and helpful they may be, are in an important sense in a world apart; their abilities, skills, and standards are so clearly superior to those of the child as to appear beyond childish grasp.

Here, then, is a context in which adults and children can pursue together a superordinate goal, for there is nothing so "real and compelling to all concerned" as the need of a young child for the care and attention of his elders. The difficulty is that we have not yet provided the opportunities—the institutional settings—which would make possible the recognition and pursuit of this superordinate goal.

The beginnings of such an opportunity structure, however, already exist in our society. As I have indicated, they are to be found in the poverty program, particularly those aspects of it dealing with children: Head Start, which involves parents, older children, and the whole community in the care of the very young; Follow Through, which extends Head Start into the elementary grades, thus breaking down the destructive wall between the school on the one hand and parents in the local community on the other; Parent and Child Centers, which provide a neighborhood center where all generations can meet to engage in common activities in behalf of children, etc.

The need for such programs is not restricted to the nation's poor. So far as alienation of children is concerned, the world of the disadvantaged simply reflects in more severe form a social disease that has infected the entire society. The cure for the society as a whole is the same as that for its sickest segment. Head Start, Follow Through, Parent and Child Centers are all needed by the middle class as much as by the economically less favored. Again, contrary to popular impression, the principal purpose of these programs is not remedial education but the giving to both children and their families of a sense of dignity, purpose, and meaningful activity without which children cannot develop capacities in any sphere of activity, including the intellectual.

Service to the very young is not the only superordinate goal potentially available to children in our society. The very old also need to be saved. In segregating them in their own housing projects and, indeed, in whole communities, we have deprived both them and the younger generations of an essential human experience. We need to find ways in which children once again can assist and comfort old people, and, in return, gain insight to character development that occurs through such experiences.

Participation in constructive activities on behalf of others will also reduce the growing tendency to aggressive and antisocial behavior in the young, if only by diversion from such actions and from the stimuli that instigate them. But so long as these stimuli continue to dominate the TV screen, those exposed to TV can be expected to react to the influence. Nor, as we have seen, is it likely that the TV industry will be responsive to the findings of research or the arguments of concerned parents and professionals. The only measure that is likely to be effective is pressure where it hurts most. The sponsor must be informed that his product will be boycotted until programing is changed.

My proposals for child rearing in the future may appear to some as a pipedream, but they need not be a dream. For just as autonomy and aggression have their roots in the American tradition, so have neighborliness, civic concern, and devotion to the young. By re-exploring these last, we can rediscover our moral identity as a society and as a nation.

8

BETTYE M. CALDWELL

CAN YOUNG CHILDREN HAVE A QUALITY LIFE IN DAY CARE?

A few years ago it would have been impossible to try to approximate an answer or series of answers to the question, "Does day care mean a quality life for young children?" for the simple reason that for many years nobody bothered to try to find the answers. Another reason is that we do not really know what we mean by a "quality life" for children. Day care in America has grown in spite of social planning rather than because of it. It is as though we tacitly assumed for many years that if we didn't pay any attention to it, it would simply go away. Strong forces of public opinion actively resisted the growth of day care, asserting that more available day care would mean that more mothers would go out of the home to seek additional employment, thereby neglecting their children and increasing juvenile delinquency and all sorts of other social ills. Finally social planners began to realize that failure to provide good day care did not keep mothers at home. Furthermore, day care was a mandatory, not an optional, service for the large number of mothers left with full responsibility for child rearing, whose children might not have subsisted without the income that the mother could provide. Rather, the alternative to not providing *good* day care was to force mothers to settle for *substandard* day care. And the assumption was made that if the child was kept at home, he automatically experienced a quality life.

But suddenly day care, as a means of trying to offer a quality life, is very much in our consciousness. Where did it come from? With many people, the experience is like learning a new word. Before you learned that word, you never heard it before; now suddenly you hear it three times a day and wonder why people are suddenly using it so often! Day care, or simply child care, as most of us prefer to call it, has suddenly emerged as a force in American life, and it will not disappear again. It is with us to stay. There are a number of reasons for that emergence, at least one of which is that we have reached a new level of community orientation in our personal lives. One by one, the major areas of life that have throughout history been taken care of predominantly within the family (except for a few people within each social group)—child bearing, routine health care, basic education, food preparation—have begun to be shared with others in the social group. Such sharing comes about in any field whenever specialization of function takes place and some members of the community are recognized as more skilled than others at a particular task. As techniques of child rearing have become a subject of scientific study, and as growth-inducing and growth-retarding practices have been identified, it has become inevitable that child care be gradually ever more professionalized. Whenever either self-proclaimed or consensually acclaimed "experts" appear who supposedly can do a better job at a given task, someone is sure to speak up quickly and say, "Then do it for me, or at least help me do it." It is useful to view day care in this context of social evolution as a manifestation of the professionalization of child care and not simply as an ad hoc procedure created to perform desired social services.

Day care in America took a quantum step during and after World War II. This increase in service did not include machinery that would provide objective feedback data on the effects of the service, for early day care programs grew up almost outside the boundary of planned scientific inquiry. Simultaneously with the increase in day care in America, there occurred a build-up in the area generally called nursery education or preschool education. But certainly the leaders in that field did not talk to the people in day care, and vice versa! Indeed not. For, after all, was not day care a service designed to provide *care and protection* for unfortunate children whose mothers were forced to work? And did not use of day care automatically identify a family as one in which there was *social pathology*? After all, if there were not such pathology, the family theoretically would not have sought day care. Nursery education, on the other hand, was for children from story book America, for the Dicks and Janes who would later appear in our readers, all blond and blue-eyed and fair-skinned, happily chasing their dog Spot in the grassy yard of their Cape Cod house surrounded by its picket fence. All of these children had two parents who went to PTA meetings. The father had a steady job (preferably as a physician or lawyer or a university professor), and the mother stayed home and baked cookies and lovingly applied band-aids when someone fell down. These children were exhaustively researched to the extent that we knew how they grew, what their conceptions of causality and deity were, how many words they knew at each age level, whether they played parallel or as isolates (heaven forbid), what their average IQs were, whether they responded better to autocratic or democratic leadership—and on and on and on!

But there were other children out there. It was just, as Michael Harrington (1962) charged, that they were invisible to us. And many of them were in day care—often of an improvised type, not in beautiful lab schools furnished with elegant equipment and futuristic jungle gyms. No, many of those of nursery school age were left with six- or seven-year-olds at 5:30 in the morning when mother had to leave the housing project to catch a train across town to arrive by 7:00 a.m. at the hospital where she worked. At 7:30 they went to an aunt's apartment three floors down, and she gave them breakfast and then took them, along with her two, to a decrepit day care center, following which she left for work. At 4:00 their mother picked them up, along with the two that belonged to the aunt, and took them home with her, where all the children stayed until the aunt came home—and so on. Certainly few people were interested in the child development of "those children." For how could we possibly generalize to the population as a whole if we used such a group for our research sample? That those children were probably far more representative than the small group being exhaustively studied never seemed to make an impression on anyone's consciousness until the early 1960s.

[This description obviously reeks of hyperbole and minimizes the contributions of pioneer workers in nursery school education and day care. However, as a description of the attitudes held by leaders in the broader field of early childhood, it appears accurate—as accurate, at least, as one can ever be when characterizing one time period from the vantage point of a different time period.]

But then things changed abruptly, and day care was given the impetus it needed to come into its own—into its own with full trappings of social respectability and that fraternity handshake of the intellectual crowd—data, facts, information. For it was in the early 1960s that early childhood as an important developmental period was discovered. Furthermore, with early childhood's discovery came the notion that it was not only *there* but that it might be *critical* for setting developmental limits for the child for the rest of his life. Intervention during the early years became the battle cry, and, for the first time, the primary target group was "those children" who previously had been totally neglected. Scientific ideas can never flourish, of course, unless they are compatible with the *Zeitgeist*. More and better nursery education of the two to three hour a day variety would not have filled a major social need. But more and better day care would indeed fill such a need. And so day care came out of the kitchen and, for the first time, began to eat in the dining room. It was no longer a pariah; it was really the prodigal son who had been misunderstood all along. And so, for the last six or seven years, we have been seriously trying to observe day care programs, to try to evaluate the extent to which they formulate objectives for the children and families and then meet those objectives, to conduct research on samples of children in day care and thus to understand them better and to broaden our understanding of all children. And, on the basis of the pool of knowledge now emerging, we can begin to determine whether day care can provide a quality life for children.

1: *A full range of experiences will be encountered by children in day care; one can no more speak of day care in the singular than one can of "school."* This has been documented more completely by Prescott, Jones and Kritchevsky (1967) than by anyone else. They observed for four 20-minute periods, daily for 10 days in 50 randomly selected day care centers in the Los Angeles area and noted such things as teaching style (use of restriction or encouragement), amount of training, program formats, spatial arrangements and staff attitudes. As would be expected if one paused to reflect on it, they found a wide variety on all their variables in the different centers they observed. Among their findings were such things as, in general, amount of training was a predictor of whether the program would be adult-centered or child-centered. More training was associated with a child-centered approach, although there were some very well-trained directors who were adult-centered and vice versa. Size of the facility and arrangement of equipment within the available space was an important determinant of teacher performance. They found that day care was most effective (as determined by the extent of the children's interest and involvement in the program) in those centers in which the staff was flexible and where children's needs were met. Positive behavior tended to be forthcoming in response to encouragement, to lessons in consideration, creativity, pleasure, awe and wonder, and to emphasis on verbal skills. Negative behaviors tended to be associated with restriction and to lessons in control and restraint and rules of social living. In short, in this important observational study, it was possible to place the programs of different centers along a variety of continua, both in terms of program input and child response. Neither in California nor in any other location can one refer to "day care" en masse and be doing anything other than obscuring important information.

2: *Children in day care develop motivationally and in terms of skills considered adaptive in today's world.*
A few years ago, when a number of people began to do serious research on the effects of day care, critics of the field took the position that the task for the researchers was to prove that the experience did not harm the children. This was especially true if the day care population included

children younger than three. This somewhat phobic reaction was generated by the fallacious assumption that group day care was the equivalent of institutional care, in which children experienced extremely depriving sensory circumstances and in which the problem of self-identity was difficult if not impossible to solve. Now we fortunately have an accumulation of data which demonstrates that quite the reverse can be true in well-planned and well-run programs. That is, children enrolled in day care on the average show significant gains on standard intelligence and achievement tests. One program from which data in support of this position can be cited is the Children's Center in Syracuse, N.Y. (Caldwell & Richmond, 1964, 1968). The underlying hypothesis guiding the Syracuse program was that the optimal time to begin enriching the experiential environment of a child was during early infancy—that is, after such time as he would have formed an attachment to his primary caregiver (his mother) and before such time as restrictive modes of communication and thinking had been established that would limit his future adaptivity. From 1966 to 1969, this program had a yearly enrollment of approximately 75 children, ranging in age from six months to five years and divided into five approximately equal subgroups. Age separations in the groups were not rigid, and during part of each day the children were in planned contacts with older and younger groups. Most of the children attended for a full six-to-nine hour day, with a teacher-pupil ratio being approximately 1:4 for all groups. The classroom activities offered a balance between teacher-initiated and child-initiated activities. That is, in each day's schedule there were some activities that were carefully planned by the teaching staff and others that involved completely free selection of activity and expression of interest by the children. All groups were racially balanced, and an attempt was made to have approximately equal numbers of boys and girls in each group.

At this time data are available from some 86 children who had entered day care prior to age three, 22 who had entered after age three and 49 controls from comparable socioeconomic backgrounds (Caldwell, 1971). Each child used in the analysis had remained in the program for at least six months; many had remained for two to three years. Each child was assessed shortly after enrollment on a standardized test of early development and again immediately prior to this data analysis. The difference between the initial score and the subsequent score was statistically significant for both subgroups of children, with neither group gaining more than the other. For both the early and the late entries, the difference between the amount of change shown by the day care and the control children was substantial and statistically reliable.

It has been suggested that such gains are spurious and merely reflect greater familiarity with the test situation and greater ease and relaxation during the assessment period. This may well be the case. However, it is significant to note that in the Syracuse study, controls were themselves tested in circumstances which corresponded very closely to those under which the day care children were tested. That is, a one-week "nursery school" was established and no child was tested until he had achieved familiarity with the situation and the examiners. But even if the gains in the day care children are motivational rather than intrinsic cognitive gains, this in itself is important. Whether such gains hold up with time is quite another matter, and one to which a great deal more research attention needs to be directed in the future.

Findings from other carefully evaluated day care programs have shown either similar gains (Robinson & Robinson, 1971), or else no difference between day care and control children (Keister, 1970). Probably the most accurate generalization that can be drawn is that the greater the proportion of children in a program from environments which differ from the middle-class norm, the greater the likelihood that results will indicate an increase in cognitive functioning associated with day care; the greater the proportion of children from backgrounds already geared to the acquisition of skills represented in the developmental tests, the less the likelihood that there will be a statistically significant difference between day care and control children. But above both of these conclusions can be placed the superordinate generalization that intellectual development need not be adversely affected by participation in day care, as many people seemed to fear might be the case if children were separated from their families for large segments of the time during their early years.

3: *Children in day care can be kept healthy.*
Certainly one aspect of a quality life is good health, and the question of the effects of day care on the health of children is a major one. Because of the potential health hazards, it would have been folly until just a few years ago to advocate bringing large numbers of young children, especially infants, together in groups—epidemics of measles or polio would have had disastrous consequences. Now, however, such illnesses can be controlled by immunization and, provided a family receives good medical care, they no longer need to pose a serious threat to the presence of young children in groups.

But what about the array of less serious, but still troublesome, illnesses that beset young children in groups? Specifically, what effect will day care have on the incidence and severity of colds and other respiratory illnesses? Will children in groups have perpetual runny noses and will one infant in a group so spread his illness that no one will be safe? These questions are especially relevant for infant day care.

Several infant centers are currently collecting data on this subject, but to date only the Chapel Hill, N.C., group has published results. Over a five-year period, this group studied respiratory illnesses in approximately 100 children who had participated for some length of time in the Frank Porter Graham Child Development Center. Most of the children entered day care before one year of age. The average incidence of respiratory illness by the group was 8.9 illnesses per child per year. The highest incidence rate of 10 per year was in the children under one year, with the figure dropping below eight per year in the three-year-olds. The Chapel Hill data were compared to data from a large metropolitan community which recorded an average of 8.3 illnesses per year for one-year-old children and 7.4 per year thereafter through age five. Glezen et al. (1971) concluded that infant day care might be associated with a slight excess of respiratory illnesses in children under one year of age, but that after that time the incidence figures were very similar to those reported for home reared children.

Data from this study should be very reassuring to those who are interested in operating infant day care programs. In the Chapel Hill Center, no attempt was made to isolate the ill children unless this appeared necessary for the ill child's own well being. Of course, high standards of cleanliness were maintained by the staff. Also, all children received excellent medical care through the program and, by 1967, a fulltime nurse and parttime pediatrician were part of the staff. Thus, one should not, from the results of this one study, rush to the conclusion that infant day care will never be associated with increased incidence of illness. Obviously the data at hand are from a high quality program which strove for optimal conditions for the maintenance of health. But these data are important in identifying a standard of excellence in the area of health to which all day care programs can strive.

4: *Children in day care do not lose their attachment to their mothers.*
The Syracuse group (Caldwell, Wright, Honig, & Tannenbaum, 1970) investigated another extremely important aspect of social and emotional development of children in day care—the attachment of children to their own mothers, and the reciprocal attachment of the mothers to their children. Primary maternal attachment is considered an essential foundation to all other social attachments that a child forms in later life (Ainsworth, 1969). In order to obtain some information on how early day care affects this basic attachment, the Syracuse staff compared two groups of mother-child pairs. Children in one group of 18 mother-child pairs had been involved in the day care program from the time they were approximately one year old. Children in the other group of 23 mother-child pairs had remained in the exclusive care of their mothers during that

same period. All assessments were made when the children were approximately 30 months of age. Based on observations of interaction between the mothers and the children in a three-hour session, interviews about the child's behavior at home and discussions of the mother's own child-rearing patterns, a cluster of ratings pertaining to attachment behavior was made for each mother and child.

In terms of the attachment of the children for their own mothers, there were no significant differences between the day care and the home-reared infants. That is, the children who had been enrolled in day care and had been exposed to several adults daily since before their first birthday were just as attached to their own mothers as were the children who had remained at home during this same period.

The children were also rated on *breadth* of attachment, i.e., in terms of their attachment to people other than their mothers. Their day care infants enjoyed interaction with other people more than the home-reared infants. This finding is compatible with data from a study by Schaffer and Emerson in Scotland (1964), which showed that infants who had had extensive contacts with other people tended to develop attachment to more people than infants who had been isolated.

In regard to strength of attachment of their *mothers* for their *children*, there were again no major differences between the groups. One important factor in this study was that all infants were at least six months old when they were enrolled in day care. This policy was adopted to permit the primary child-mother attachment to develop *before* the child was placed in a situation that might conceivably weaken it.

Other findings in this Syracuse study which, while not directly answering our question about the effects of day care upon attachment behavior, demonstrate the informational by-products that can generally be expected from broadbased research. For example, when the day care and home-reared samples were combined, we found that strength of attachment of a child for his mother was correlated with developmental level. That is, children whose development was *most advanced* usually were rated as the most attached to their mothers. Similarly, there was some evidence that the most advanced babies tended to have the most attached mothers. Both of these findings corroborate the generalization that one cannot effectively separate early manifestations of behavioral competence from other aspects of development.

Several other projects are continually monitoring the social and emotional development of infants whose early experience has included day care. Within the next five years a great deal of information on this topic should be available to us to help ascertain more definitively if this aspect of a quality life can be guaranteed children in day care.

5: *Young children in day care do not necessarily become emotionally disturbed.*

This conclusion is also stated negatively, as there were valid theoretical reasons to remain alert lest this occur. Again data from the Syracuse project can be offered to substantiate the point. In 1968, Dr. Samuel Braun, a child psychiatrist, was asked to do what is generally called a "blind" study on all the children in the group of three-four-year-olds (Braun & Caldwell, 1972). For many people, the only acceptable cutting point for enrolling children in day care was age three—any children put in such a situation at an earlier age were expected to become emotionally disturbed. Those who operated the Syracuse program were eager for reassurance that the procedure developed there to offer cognitive and social enrichment was not producing emotional damage. Accordingly, Dr. Braun spent a week with the children in the two oldest groups—helping in the classrooms, eating with them, going to the bathroom with them, riding to and from school with them, talking with their teachers, just observing them, etc. At the end of that time he rated each child on a scale of 1 to 5, with 1 indicating good adjustment and 5 indicating poor adjustment. Of the total group, only one child received a rating of 5 and only four received a rating of 4, indicating that, in general, the 30 children were relatively well adjusted. Then the data were examined to see whether the distribution of ratings differed for the children who had enrolled at or after age three. The distributions of ratings for the two groups were virtually identical, indicating that early enrollment (prior to age three) need not be associated with a high incidence of emotional disturbance.

6: *Children in day care develop a feeling of community.*

For some time we have thought that our early day care children "cared for" one another more than one usually finds in groups of children of similar age. They are often deeply concerned about another child's rights, about whether Mary has had her turn or whether the teacher dealt adequately with Eric when he pushed Gerald off the tricycle. A hint that this might be the situation can be found in published reports (see Freud & Dann, 1951) of the social behavior of parentless children who were released from concentration camps in eastern Europe after World War II. These children seemed to find their strength in each other and to resist for some time the establishment of close ties with new adults and with other children. Currently, Lay and Meyer are collecting some observational data on 20 kindergarten children who are "graduates" of the Syracuse Children's Center, most of whom have been together in day care from early infancy. These children are now enrolled in a school with 20 additional children who were not part of the original day care sample. Using a time sample observational technique, Lay and Meyer (1971) found that although the "new" children distributed their social encounters rather equally over the entire group of 40 children, the social interactions of the former day care children were largely among themselves. That is, they tended to stick with the children who had "graduated" to the new environment together, although over the course of the year (as new friendship patterns developed) this tendency weakened somewhat. This suggests that these little children from diverse family backgrounds moved to a new social setting as a small community—sticking together, helping one another, offering a familiar base until the new environment could be more readily apprehended. Several of the children were from unstable and disturbed families, and most were from families burdened in economic difficulties; yet their "togetherness" had helped them adjust to a new situation and had strengthened in them the feeling of community that we need to encourage in all children.

7: *Children in day care have a better chance of being Americanized.*
This now almost archaic-sounding term—Americanize—is used for this point to highlight the absurdity of some of the charges leveled against the Comprehensive Child Care bill at the time of the presidential veto in December of 1971. In his message accompanying the veto, the President condemned the child care provision of the act for its "fiscal irresponsibility, administrative unworkability, and family-weakening implications of the system it envisions." The President was justifiably concerned about this veto, as, shortly after taking office, he had by Executive Order created the Office of Child Development and had committed his office to do everything possible to strengthen programs for children during the first five years of life. Although participation in the programs was to be voluntary, and although local parent councils would guide all programs that became operational, the President claimed to fear that the child development programs would eventually become mandatory and thus serve to destroy the family. He said: "For the Federal government to plunge headlong financially into supporting child development would commit the vast moral authority of the National Government to the side of communal approaches to child rearing over against the family-centered approach."

An illustration of this position can be found in the following quote from the Congressional Record, the remarks made by a California legislator who shall remain nameless:

> *Of course, Mr. Speaker, they do not yet ask for power to take children by force. That never comes first. But, Mr. Speaker, as surely as twilight follows sunset and darkness follows twilight, it comes last. It is the end to which all such programs logically tend. The family is the backbone of any healthy society. Destroy the family and we destroy America. This "child development" legislation aims at providing a*

> substitute for the family in the form of committees of psychiatrists, psychologists, sociologists and social workers. But there is no substitute for the family. A Nation of orphanages cannot endure, and should not. It is an offense to God and Man.

This bit of impassioned rhetoric was followed by the *pièce de résistance:*

> Walk into the halls of the Department of Health, Education and Welfare and think of having it in place of a mother.

This charge has come to be labeled the "Sovietization" issue—such programs mean that we are changing our basic socialization pattern to conform to that used in collective societies. This is, of course, a spurious issue, deliberately employed to confuse and mislead. A few careful substitutions in part of the above quotation will perhaps help to strengthen my point:

> This "education" legislation aims at providing a substitute for the family in the form of committees of superintendents, principals, and teachers.

For is that not what we do in our public schools? Do we not now let teachers help our children learn how to read and cipher instead of their parents as used to be the pattern? And has not vocational education broken up the pattern of family apprenticeship? To assert that an experience which can help children achieve the goals for which this country stands will "Sovietize" them indicates just how far we have strayed from those original goals. Did we not develop a system of public education in this country precisely because our forefathers recognized that no set of parents could hope to do all that was needed to educate (i.e., socialize) their children?

Thus, to counter some of the irresponsible charges as to possible consequences of progressive child development legislation, this author would suggest that early child development programs can help to provide a quality life by helping to Americanize American children. The following poignant anecdote will illustrate the point.

This occurred in the kindergarten of our extended day school, a comprehensive educational day care facility for children ranging in age from under one year up through sixth grade. One of the most popular children was a little White child whose two best friends, one a boy and one a girl, happened to be Black. In the middle of the school year, the girl's parents indicated their intention to withdraw her from the school, as the racial composition had shifted from about 50:50 to 75:25 Black-White. "It seems that she never talks about anybody but the Black children," complained the parents. One of our social workers talked to the parents about the matter, trying to accept their feelings without remonstrance while reiterating our policy of admitting children without regard to race and urging that the child be permitted to remain in what was obviously a highly rewarding and enjoyable environment for her. The parents thought the matter over and kept the child in school. The morning after the conference, the little girl bounced into the room and, in her customary didactic style, pointed individually to each child in turn and announced, "I can play with you, and you, and you, and I can't play with you, or you, or you. . . ." It took no great categorizing skill to perceive that skin color was the basis of the classification. With the honesty of a child she freely verbalized the agreement that had allowed her to remain in school: "If I do, my momma's going to whip me and my brother's going to beat me up." The earlier favorite friends of the child were crushed and the child herself had obvious difficulty remembering the new rules as she fell into her school routine. Fortunately, with the help of a sensitive teacher who gently interpreted that homes had rules and school had rules and that they were not always identical, the admonition was quickly forgotten and old friendships were restored.

To whom did the teachers in our day care school have an obligation? To those parents, whose love and devotion to their child expressed itself in a very un-American concept and type of behavior? Or to the child who deserved a better chance to learn how to adapt in a pluralistic society in which representatives of all ethnic and cultural groups have equal rights and privileges? Was the child, who was being encouraged to behave in the context of a set of values that obviously contradicted those of the home, being Sovietized? Communized? Not at all, but she was being Americanized. One of the nicer things that can happen to children in day care is that it gives them an opportunity to acquire the breadth of vision necessary to realize the full meaning of that now seemingly anachronistic phrase, the American dream.

SUMMARY

In this paper an attempt has been made to marshal evidence that day care can help provide a quality life for young children. In the few programs in which systematic evaluations have been conducted, quality day care has been found to be associated with intellectual gains, with the acquisition of adaptive social skills, and with healthy physical and emotional development. A response to such data might be a rejoinder that such experiences can obviously be good for children, but that they are seldom found in day care. What is the proportion of such programs among the array of centers and day care homes scattered all over the country? In how many do you find happy children, and in how many do you find children eating lunch off the lid of the garbage pail (to cite one recently published horror story). And in what proportion is there a sensitive program, geared to children's developmental needs in contrast to a steady diet of TV throughout the day? Unfortunately, we do not know the answers to those questions, but one of the more encouraging trends of the past five years is that we are beginning to bring all categories of day care under public scrutiny. All states now have some kind of licensing procedure for day care, albeit the standards vary widely from state to state. And, although licensing can in some respects be seen as encouraging premature crystallization of operational patterns without ample opportunity to explore and try different forms of service, in general, it offers one of the best protective mechanisms that we have. If consumers are to get good day care, they must realize their obligation to find out about the situation, visit centers and keep in contact with state and national legislation programs.

A commendable step in this direction has been taken by Mary Dublin Keyserling who chose *Windows on Day Care* as the apt title for her study of the variety of available operating programs and of the need for additional facilities.

We definitely need to open all possible windows on day care in order to know and to influence what is happening in the field. As citizens—not just as professionals or as day care consumers—we must all demand systematic monitoring of day care programs to ensure experiences for our children that are conducive to wholesale development. Today one hears cries from potential consumers for more and better day care, and sometimes these demands appear to show little concern for the welfare of the children involved. "We need more day care centers so their mothers can go to work and get off the welfare rolls." And, "We want more child care centers so that women can realize their potential." These are legitimate concerns of our society, for we do want our citizens to be able to function independently, and we do want our women to have an opportunity to realize their own destiny. But sometimes it is hard to shake the fear that those who make these demands are minimally concerned about what happens to the children. If day care does weaken family life, we need to know this, for as of this time we do not know of a successful way to rear children (in terms of how our society has traditionally defined success) apart from families. We must, in short, keep constantly attuned to generate continuing answers to the question asked in this paper. We can have cheaper day care by not bothering to monitor, by not bothering to care. But in the long run it will cost us more.

9

A teacher cannot directly provide a child with learning. He can, however, provide materials that will engage the child's innate curiosity and make learning more likely. Through experience with such materials—animate and inanimate—children reorganize and extend what they know about themselves and their world.

The teacher's role in setting a rich environment for learning is therefore a serious responsibility. Rather than offer specific suggestions of appropriate choices, a task well accomplished elsewhere (Churchill & Leitman, 1966; Yeomans, 1967; Association for Childhood Education International, 1967; Technology for Children Project; Education Development Center Follow Through Program, 1969), I would like to suggest principles that can guide further selections, toward the end of reaching an optimal match between child and materials.

PRINCIPLE I: *Whenever possible, permit and encourage children to supply their own materials.*
One way a teacher can be sure the classroom contains materials capable of eliciting children's interest is to encourage them to bring items of their own to school to explore as a *legitimate* part of their academic day.

By contrast, the usual Show and Tell practice either serves primarily as an excuse to require children to stand up and talk before the class or as a means to convey to the teacher and class outside-of-school interests as though the latter belonged to some other world. What the child brings in is something he seldom is allowed to investigate during school time. Further, teachers usually limit the range of acceptable "sharing" materials so as to screen out such items as animals, tools, comic books, bicycles or other sports equipment and the like.

Given broader latitude to bring materials of their own special interests, children can offer the teacher important clues for subsequent selection of additional materials. For example, a packet of seeds brought in by a child having difficulties with arithmetic may lead to a planting, measuring, graphing project. A museum model-dinosaur brought in by a child with reading problems might suggest choices for an easy-to-read science book collection. And children can be encouraged to construct their own new materials or equipment in the classroom—such as devices to measure length, time or weight.

PRINCIPLE II: *Whenever possible, permit and encourage children to explore the real world outside of the classroom and outside of the school.*
Once we dismiss the notion of the teacher as the child's only source of

knowledge, the classroom is no longer sacrosanct. A child's proper place of learning is the entire world to which he has access. The countryside offers creatures of every kind, plants, streams; suburban and city environments abound with their own distinctive learning opportunities—everywhere are movement, change, pattern and excitement.

People are resources as valuable for children's learning as are objects or natural phenomena. Everyone is a potential "teacher." Many British schools, for instance, so view their entire staff (Hull, 1964):

> . . . in these schools, and others at both the infant and junior levels, the kitchen staff is not isolated. Often the women will be sought out by children for help with spelling words and other academic problems [p. 3].

Administrative rigidities notwithstanding, it is often possible and profitable for the teacher to release children from rigid adherence to a five-hour-a-day schedule in the classroom to allow for explorings of the learning awaiting outside. When everyone in a school and its neighborhood is regarded as a possible resource helper, when adults explore with children, all move together toward a much-sought-after and seldom-achieved goal, a *sense of community*, which implies a group of people working cooperatively toward common ends.

PRINCIPLE III: *Seek out common, inexpensive, familiar, easily available materials.*

Expensive materials often better serve teachers' and parents' needs than children's. Too many educational "innovations" involve little more than moving from old books, desks and buildings to new books, desks and buildings. Unasked and therefore unanswered go such questions as whether a new $12 textbook actually results in more learning than the old $4 copy.

With the availability of so many manufactured materials, American teachers sometimes are hesitant to scrounge, unsure that what they might select will be seen as valuable and acceptable to administrators and even to the children themselves. So viewed, selection becomes an act dependent upon budget restrictions and the offerings of the latest ed-biz catalogs.

This caution is doubly unfortunate. For one thing, many manufac-tured items used in school—microscopes, filmstrip viewers, reference encyclopedias for example—are to be used by children *only* in school, usually under strict terms laid down by the teacher who is made to fear their loss or damage. Again the effect is one of localizing and separating the child's in-school learning activities from his out-of-school living. If his work with multi-base blocks is felt to be restricted to the classroom, it becomes unlikely that he will carry either the materials or the learning activity associated with them home.

Common, less expensive materials, on the other hand, provide many advantages. Seeking them out, children and adults both learn to master the raw materials of the world around them. Teachers in many areas of the world *must* be resourceful, with no choice but to make the most of what they have. Again the British primary schools afford exemplary models. There, teachers and children alike are creative scroungers for all manner of things: old tires for swings, roots of trees from nearby woods for sculpture, popsicle sticks for "maths."

An interest in animals, clay, sand, water, once initiated at school, can easily be pursued by the child with similar materials at his own time, in his own place. If a child uses beans to count, approximate and play games while in school or to use common kitchen equipment for his science experiments, he will have no difficulty continuing these activities at home. Materials can help him integrate his two important worlds.

And children tend to respect and care for inexpensive, common materials with uncharacteristic zeal while they often abuse more expensive school equipment. The empty cereal box, pail of sand, or pieces of wood, rope or wire are seen by children, in some important sense, as their own, to be used as they please—to play store, add to, mix, cut, measure, drop, without constant concern and intervention from the teacher. In contrast to the constraint, dependence and resentment often associated with more "valuable" materials, children tend to surround ordinary things with independence and freedom. This freedom makes learning more possible.

PRINCIPLE IV: *Give preference to ambiguous, multiprogramed materials that suggest a variety of possible paths of use.*
Another important reason for preferring common, inexpensive materials over more expensive manufactured ones is that common materials tend to be more ambiguous and less directive, offering the child a greater role in determining their use.

Materials designed to exclude all but one or two possible paths for a child's exploration and thinking are not only limited but limiting. They teach dependence upon the structure inherent in the materials (and upon the adult who constructs them) and leave insufficient room for children to invent, improvise, modify and adapt. Revealing are such phrases as "the child will be led to" and "orderly stages," elaborate directions concerning "proper use," and suggested ways to get children back on the "right" path should their imaginations cause them to depart from it. The child can assemble a plastic model in only one way; he can use the filmstrip viewer only with those filmstrips available to him. The fact that such materials may be seen as exciting by the child and legitimate by the adult makes them no less limiting. A child should be instrumental in posing for himself both the problem and the path he will take in pursuing that problem. Materials are to assist him in these choices, not direct or restrict him.

Structure is not necessarily incompatible with good materials for children—many common materials that have not been designed for any one set purpose do have definite structure and the capacity to influence and organize children's thought. Magnets, sand, wooden blocks are examples. What is crucial is that they are ambiguous and multiprogramed; rather than confine a child, they offer him a major part in determining their use, depending upon the questions they suggest to him. They encourage inventiveness. With a magnet he can pick up dropped pins or thumbtacks; he can study polarity; he can build a motor. With blocks he can make balance boards, houses, forts, highways for his cars, or stands for his checker games. With sand he can also model, construct, cast, measure, weigh, pour, draw, paint—or even smooth wood.

As with other principles of selection, that of giving preference to multiprogramed materials must be employed with regard to the degree of independence of each child. For Andy, who is still dependent upon direct adult control or a source outside of himself to initiate and sustain his own learning, narrowly structured activities such as playing a board game or viewing a filmstrip are probably most appropriate, at least initially. This child might be at a loss before a sand table. For Steve, a more self-reliant child, ambiguous materials such as clay, water, blocks—which offer a variety of entry points and exploration paths—may be most helpful. He is free to determine their use just as is the potter, the biologist, the carpenter.

People, as well as materials, can be more or less directive, rigid, prescribing. What a teacher permits children to do with materials influences thinking and behavior as much as do the inherent properties of the materials themselves. The teacher faces therefore a dual task: to select materials that will provide multiple-structures and then to encourage each child to use the full range of possibilities in the materials and in himself. Hopefully, in time all will thereby develop competence, resourcefulness and confidence when confronted with unstructured and ambiguous situations—i.e., with the real world.

PRINCIPLE V: *Select materials that are likely to insure active exploration.*
Implicit in much of the preceding discussion is the belief that learning is a consequence of *active* exploration in a rich, manipulative environment. It cannot be assumed that all children will wish to explore a random collection of materials; selection can help make active exploration both likely and fruitful.

Children coming to school in September have little idea where they "left off" the year before. Their new teacher who does not know them may have little idea of their interests and capabilities, but he can provide materials that will invite questions, investigation, excitement. Last year's permanent record card may reveal a Sally who was fascinated by fish, an important clue for providing books or materials for her. Children's interests are often ephemeral, however; and most likely the teacher must select materials on the basis of what he suspects children of a given age, sex and background will find challenging. He shouldn't be surprised if children use materials in unanticipated ways.

Fortunately, the need to select materials without benefit of observation of the children who will use them is short-lived. Yesterday, three children made robots out of cardboard boxes, though the teacher may have guessed they'd make a train. Today he can provide paint, tin cans and buttons for these same children, should they want to embellish their robot. Robot books, robot models, robot pictures can also mysteriously appear. After the first few days the teacher is busy selecting materials to sustain and extend interests his pupils have revealed, but he may well continue to introduce new materials for which they may find use. His job becomes less speculative, then, and more based on careful observation of what children are saying and doing.

In sum, the teacher selects materials that appear appropriate for a particular child with a particular interest at a particular time. Lesson plans, curriculum guides and literature on child development are of little relevance in making these fine discriminations; only keen, firsthand observation can guide. Timing the introduction of materials can be as important as the nature of the materials. Thus, the role of the teacher in selection cannot be separated from the role of the teacher in observing and diagnosing children's behavior. To select and provide materials for the release of children's potentials tomorrow, we must take advantage of what they are telling us today.

DAILY ROUTINES AND GROUP EXPERIENCES 10 EVELYN BEYER

Although play is the core of the curriculum of good nursery schools, and teacher's energies and attention must be focussed on providing the best possible conditions for play, there are also routine facts of nursery school life that must be considered and planned for.

The way in which these routines are managed reflects the relative importance they hold in the total planning scheme. Cleaning up, putting away toys, toileting, washing, juice procedures are all part of everyday living in the nursery school. Obviously they offer little creative potential, but they deserve the kind of organization that will result in casual and effective functioning.

There have been varying degrees of emphasis on these routines over the years. There have been times when they, rather than play, seemed to be the core of curriculum planning. Most of the child's day was filled with energy-consuming attention to their correct fulfillment. I have observed nursery schools where children were greeted with cups of water (liquid intake), then steered to the toilet (liquid output), then put on cots for preplay rest. Play seemed grudgingly wedged into the more important activities of eating, washing, toileting and resting.

Today's emphasis on these routines is generally more casual. In relation to toileting, the teacher remains alert to signs and signals of individual children and reminds them to go to the toilet. She is fortunate if the bathroom is adjacent to the playroom, so that she can give help if it is needed. In less convenient situations, she may need to plan organized group toileting times for those who need it. It is usually a good idea to remind the children to go to the bathroom before getting into heavy outdoor clothing, when children are preparing to go outside. Some children may need frequent reminders, some children may be completely independent, some may not need to go to the bathroom during the morning, some may be actively resistant to using a toilet away from home.

It is usually helpful to the teacher to get information from the mother of each child about her child's characteristic toileting pattern, and to follow it as carefully as she can. Casualness is the key attitude to seek and foster. This is not always easy with children for whom toileting has been a battleground fraught with tension between mother and child.

"Accidents" also deserve to be treated with casual acceptance. As the teacher cleans up the child (standard equipment should include extra panties and socks for every child) she will remind him that he needs to tell her when he has to go to the toilet, and that she will always help him.

Washing hands is another routine that teachers need to provide for. The teacher with an exaggerated sense of cleanliness may insist on a formal ritual of soaping and rinsing after toileting and before juice as well as after using some of the messier materials such as paint, dough, paste, or clay.

In the not so olden days, half-day nursery school bathrooms were ringed with individual washcloths and towels hanging from hooks. In a university nursery school, in which I observed, the washing up period was conducted by the nurse (symbol of antisepsis) who stood in the doorway and chanted a washing-up ritual. The children responded in a seeming hypnotic daze. They undoubtedly emerged clean, but I question the value of spending twenty minutes to a half hour on something that might have been adequately accomplished in a few minutes.

The opposite extreme is the "dirt can't hurt" attitude of some teachers who don't even seem to see it, and except for major emersions in paint or mud or plastics, tolerate it.

There should be a middle ground characterized neither by toleration of grime, nor glorification of cleanliness. This middle-ground teacher will encourage casual wash-ups or "splash-ups" at low child-height sinks, under running water which rinses as it cleans. Liquid soap from a dispenser and paper towels constitute adequate equipment. A casual suggestion, "It might be a good idea to wash your hands now," is just as effective as the elaborate ritual which needs a conductor, and consumes most of the morning hours.

Putting away toys and play materials is another routine part of nursery school life which the teacher needs to consider.

Again, there are extremes of attitude and practice among nursery school teachers. There are those who insist that the termination of each activity be followed by immediate and proper putting away of materials before another activity is started. Each child is held accountable for his materials and their return to the proper place. This attitude results in a tidy classroom, but it has some limitations. I have seen children who have refused to build with blocks because they didn't want to pay the price of having to put them away. If this attitude of tit-for-tatness is carried to an extreme, as it tends to be, it puts a damper on creativity or even zestful exploration and discovery. "Neatness is all" as a classroom motto stultifies rather than releases.

The opposite attitude of "anything goes" or "leave it be" results in a hodgepodge of disorder that prevents creative use and enjoyment of materials. When blocks are scattered all over the floor, no one can build; when tables are cluttered with scattered puzzle pieces, mixed with pasting materials and dough or clay, no satisfying activity can take place there. Books should not be tossed carelessly around the room. Such treatment is not only damaging to books, but builds into children a kind of disrespect for books that should not be permitted to develop. Doll corners should be lived in with the kind of disorder that comes from active dramatic use, but should not be allowed to become a muddled mess of scattered toys and props.

Frequently teachers who promote this kind of chaotic scene do so with the best intentions. They feel that by insisting that children share in the cleaning up and putting away of materials, they are interfering with the child's constructive impulses.

Again I feel that there is a reasonable middle ground that permits and encourages creative use of materials and also teaches respect for them. Children can be helped by casual reminders to return one book or puzzle to the shelf before taking another. Or they can be reminded that they should use the blocks they have taken from the shelf before getting another pile.

In most nursery schools there is a general cleaning up or putting away time at the end of the work-play period. Children can be helped to participate in this. Sometimes it helps to assign specific areas to children, not necessarily because they have been engaged in that area. Picking up the block area is usually the most difficult, but this can be organized in a variety of ways. If the teacher piles the blocks of similar sizes, children can stack them on the shelves. Or children may be assigned a certain size or shape which will be their job. "Bob will be the cylinder loader." "Jill will be the animal and people loader." Sometimes singing the "piling song"—"Pile the blocks in even rows, Stephen knows where each one goes," inserting each child's name as it is repeated—is a pleasing accompaniment to clearing the block area.

When the job is completed, there should be a happy satisfied sense of accomplishment for everyone who has shared in it. "We really worked hard!"

To rest or not to rest in an official lying-on-mats-or-cots in the middle of the morning has been a somewhat controversial part of nursery school programs. The trend seems to be toward providing a quiet time of looking at books or listening to music rather than a formal lying on mats or rugs. Those of us who struggled with enforcement of the official lie-down rest period remember how unrestful it could be for those children who actively resisted it. Often it seemed to consume more energy than it restored. The mechanics of getting out individual mats (which usually occupied valuable storage space), putting them down, separating children of combustible potential, maintaining (policing) quiet atmosphere, and then, after a suitable interval reversing the process, often seemed to produce more tension than peace.

A more casual quiet time, a shift from active to passive activities, looking at books or pictures or a special exhibit of leaves or shells or something brought from home, a shift in pace seems more relaxing than an official lie-down period. We have found that the child who really needs to rest will quietly curl up or stretch out for a few minutes of relaxation without needing to have an official rest period in which to do it.

Following the busy work and play period and the clean-up time, it is a good idea to give a toileting and hand-washing reminder, before gathering for the snack and juice time that follows.

As in other routines, the juice time may have a wide range of "flavors." In some nursery schools it is a very formal affair. Juice is served by the teacher; crackers may be passed by her or a selected child, or placed on the napkin near the juice. In some schools a simple grace may be said. After finishing the snack, children are reminded to wipe their mouths, tuck the napkin in the cup, place the cup on the tray, and then go to the story group or whatever activity follows juice.

In one school that I observed, there seemed to be no structure to the juice time. A snack table apart from the work tables was set up with a pitcher of juice or milk and a basket of crackers. Children were informed of its presence. They came to it, received a cup of juice poured by the teacher, helped themselves to crackers, wandered off, eating and drinking wherever they happened to be. This method seemed too casual and shapeless. There was considerable spilling of juice en route, and crumbled crackers paved the floor.

Enthusiasm for children pouring their own juice seems to have subsided somewhat. However, if pitchers small enough to be successfully handled by three- and four-year-old hands are available, and children are helped to master the skill of pouring, it can be an enjoyable experience.

Since most eating situations involve sitting down, it seems reasonable to expect that juice time will be a sitting down rather than a wandering around occasion. It can also be a pleasant social occasion, a time for talking about things of interest to the group; something that happened on the way to school, something interesting that is going to happen, a trip, a current event of interest, plans for cooking. The teacher often needs to start the conversational ball, but she will be quick to take her cue from the children. Her goal is that the whole procedure will be a pleasant, enjoyable occasion. She will not fuss about manners, but she will demonstrate good manners herself. She will be gracious in thanking the child who passes the crackers, or she will politely ask for more if she wants more. She will comment favorably on children who do the same, not merely because it pleases her, but because it sounds pleasant and makes people feel good.

She will discourage disruptive behavior, deliberate juice spilling and cracker crumbling, as inappropriate and disturbing. She knows how contagious this can be, and how destructive to a happy snack time.

Some teachers are ingenious in varying the standard cracker and juice menu by introducing an assortment of raw fruits and vegetables, carrot and pepper sticks, apple quarters, tangerines and oranges, raisins, cereal. It is also fun for children to prepare special snack treats such as Jello, cut-up fruit, cookies, salads, puddings, even soups. Many of these can be prepared without an elaborately equipped kitchen. They provide interesting experiences in learning about the nature and variety of food products, as well as good nutritional experiences.

To the uninitiated observer of a nursery school classroom, the lack of organized group times is often puzzling. It may be difficult for observers to understand that important learning is going on in a room where each child is engaged in his own individual project. Their idea of a schoolroom is one where children are sitting down quietly and listening to the teacher, or following her directions.

Skilled nursery school teachers would be uneasy in such a classroom. They respect the needs of three- and four-year-olds to move about freely, and do not belittle the learning that takes place in a classroom of "movers." However, they also recognize that young children can be helped to enjoy brief "group times."

The juice or snack time is one of these. The story time and music time are other periods when the group assembles to share an experience.

In planning her day, the teacher will decide on the best time for these group experiences, usually a period immediately preceding or following the juice and snack time.

The mechanics of managing the group time are important. Shall the children sit in chairs or on the floor? Shall the children scramble for places, or be assigned special places? Where shall the teacher sit, on the children's level, or above them? What does the teacher do about potential disrupters of the peace? What about children who choose not to join the group? Should they be ignored or made to join? How does the teacher catch the attention of sixteen wiggling four-year-olds, and even more wiggling three-year-olds?

There is no standard set of rules that will guarantee success in managing a group story or music time. Each teacher has to discover her own characteristic way. Some teachers feel at home on the floor; others feel more comfortable sitting on a chair with children clustered at their feet. Some teachers like to have children seated in chairs; others feel that chairs complicate the situation or make it too formal.

The teacher with insight is not likely to insist that every child join the group the first time. She will respect the individual child who seems reluctant to join. However, she will not permit him to engage in activities that are disturbing and distracting to the group. She also has confidence that eventually he will be attracted to the group activity, and that his watching will not be wasted. She will quickly spot the combinations of children that stimulate disruption rather than participation, and she will separate them or arrange to have them near an adult who can help them.

She may begin (as Miss Bates did) by singing a simple song like, "Here we are together, together, together, Here we are together, all sitting on the floor. There's Billy and Buffy, and Timmy and Mary . . . (naming each child). Here we are together, all sitting on the floor." A song about shoes and sneakers, and who is wearing what color, is a sure way of catching the attention of shoe-conscious three-year-olds. Each child needs to hear his shoe or shirt described, and needs to hear his name. At first, this kind of singing tends to be a teacher solo, but as children catch on to it, they will join in and add to it.

Some teachers use finger plays as devices for capturing and holding group attention. Children seem to enjoy these action games as well as simple circle games like *Punchinello* and *Here We Go, Sandy Maloney*. They enjoy initiating the action in answer to the question, "What can you do, Punchinello, little fellow, what can you do, Punchinello, little dear?" Imitating Punchinello's choice of "doing" is equally delightful.

Many nursery school teachers who lack musical skills are reluctant to include music in their programs. The teacher who can play the piano certainly has an advantage over those who cannot. But there are simple instruments such as the autoharp and the recorder which can be mastered without an extensive musical background. The autoharp in particular provides a pleasant chord accompaniment to singing. Drum beats can substitute for piano accompaniment to rhythms—fast beats, slow beats, running beats, skipping beats. Singing-action games like *The Little Gray Pony* need no accompaniment except the singing voice or a drum beat.

Sometimes parents with musical skills can be recruited to share them with the group. A guitar-playing mommy or daddy is a welcome addition to any group.

The group music time, like the story time, should be an optional affair. There are often some children who seem reluctant to join the group, but who may watch and listen from a distance. The teacher accepts this watching-listening as a preliminary to participation. She knows that a happy group experience is usually irresistible, and that eventually each child will join it when he is ready.

The preschool group or "together" time needs to be an experience which children can enjoy, and from which they can learn some of the simple rules of being members of a group: the responsibilities of not disturbing the group activity, of contributing to the group enjoyment, of listening and responding appropriately. Early group times should be brief, and timed to end before they disintegrate. The teacher is the stage manager, the mood setter, and the terminator. If she enjoys it, the children are likely to enjoy it, too.

Nursery schools which have space enough to have a separate sleep room are fortunate. Most schools have to convert the play space into sleeping space, by hauling in cots and screens, and fitting them into the space. This is harder to manage, but it can be done, and done well.

The teacher soon learns which children are ready to nap and need little or no help in relaxing and getting to sleep. She also learns the ones who resist nap, who are potential disturbers of the peace, and she tries to place these in strategically "safe" zones. Some teachers begin the nap period by playing some quiet music, or they may tell or read a story or sing some gentle tunes. Some teachers may have a "signal" that announces the official beginning of nap time, the flicking off of the light or drawing the shades. Some teachers tiptoe around the room, patting or tucking in each child. A particularly restless child may need a teacher to sit beside him. One teacher that I know took a nap herself, after the last child had been tucked in!

Getting up from nap is another routine that presents the teacher with a management problem. However, not all children will be ready to get up at the same moment. The short nappers can be helped first, shoes tied, blanket folded and stowed away, cot removed to storage. Gradually the room is restored to its play space appearance and usage, as sleepers awake and resume their afternoon activities.

The important thing about all routines of nursery school life is that they be conducted in a casual way. The teacher's attitude will determine their nature and quality. If she is tense and rigid about them, her attitude will be reflected by tension and resistance in the children. If her attitude is loose and shapeless, routines will be equally loose and shapeless, and so will the children's behavior. If she sustains a spirit of sprightly clarity, this too will be reflected in the children's acceptance of them as a part of their nursery school day. Routines can be genial learning situations, or hectic periods of resistance and confusion. The teacher sets the tone by her attitude toward them. She neither glorifies them nor denies their importance. By accepting them herself, she helps her children to accept them matter-of-factly.

MARIO D. FANTINI
GERALD WEINSTEIN **11** TOWARD A CONTACT CURRICULUM

FROM: *Emphasis solely on cognitive, extrinsic content*
TO: *An equal emphasis on affective, inner content*

Since the importance of the affective or intrinsic domain cannot be minimized or merely hinted at, it is necessary to discuss this area separately [from curriculum, which deals chiefly with the selection of content, the form in which it is taught, and the manner in which it is organized and developed].

Many current teacher prescriptions lack contact because they lack intrinsic relevance for many children and for the disadvantaged in particular. What is relevant? There seem to be at least four causes of irrelevance in education, and consequently, four levels on which relevance may be achieved:

HOW IT IS TAUGHT Irrelevance is caused if teaching procedures and learning styles are not matched. The current literature on disadvantaged children indicates that they learn best in more concrete, inductive, kinesthetic, and less verbal situations. In view of this, their teachers should search for methodology coordinated with this learning style. Thus, if all techniques, practices and methods used by teachers are geared specifically to the pupil's own style of learning, then, regardless of content there is a degree of relevance in whatever is being taught because of *how* it is being taught.

WHAT IS TAUGHT Irrelevance occurs if the material presented is not within or easily connected with the learner's knowledge of his physical realm of experience. If the learner is from an urban area, for instance, teaching about his neighborhood or his city may be more relevant to him and make greater contact because he is experientially familiar with the topic.

Content that is most closely connected to the learners' reality—to their experiences—will have the best possibility for engaging the learners, especially those who are disadvantaged. This "experiential content" is based on what the child learns from experiences provided by his life space, or the social contact in which he lives. It is mainly cognitive and may or may not be related to more affective or "feeling" content. For example, a child may learn how to take care of his younger brothers and sisters, or how to use the streets as a playground. He knows the latest popular songs, the "in" language, what's happening in his neighborhood, or how a leader in his group must act. The migrant child may learn the characteristics of a good worker, a good boss, or ways for picking the most strawberries with least effort.

Thus, in an effort to achieve relevance on this level, the teacher must begin by asking himself several questions: "What content does the child bring to school? What does he already know? What can he teach me? What does he talk about when no one is structuring his talk?" In other words, relevance is achieved by making *what* is being taught germane to the learner's *knowledge* of his experience.

LEARNERS' FEELINGS The third level of irrelevance occurs if *what* is being taught and *how* it is being taught ignore the learner's *feelings* about his experiences. To be an effective teacher on this level involves a more intrinsic operation, since it is these deeper feelings about his experiences that, if tapped, may lead to the learner's greater involvement. For instance, an urban reading series or a unit on the city policeman may be used because the learner "knows" them. But, if the learner has a fear of policemen by virtue of his particular experience with them, then, because of the content selected, learning actually may be inhibited. Until the learner's real *feelings* about his experiences are utilized, until there is an emotional connection made, the third level of relevance has not been tapped.

In order to achieve relevance on this level, one of the continuing questions a teacher must ask the learners is "How do you feel about this?" An example of the use of this type of question and of making the connection with children's feelings occurred in a situation in which a teacher told her class that a nurse was coming to the school the next day to talk to them about hospitals and how they are run. The children, who conceived of the hospital as mysterious, forbidding, and associated only with people who are injured or dying, could not get interested in such questions as how many doctors were on the staff, how many rooms it contained, how much money was needed to run it, etc. But the visiting nurse quickly excited the children in the lesson when she asked: "How do you feel when you think about a hospital?" One child put up his hand and shouted, "Scared!" Other children indicated that they, too, saw the hospital as an object of fright. The nurse, who apparently had been used to dealing with the fears of young patients, immediately started from that point—the children's feelings in regard to the subject matter (the hospital)—and developed it. By the time she finished the lesson, she managed to explain a good deal about the real world of the hospital for the children as patients or as relatives of patients. The key to it all was her having started from their ground—in this case, a feeling of fear.

LEARNERS' CONCERNS The fourth level of irrelevance occurs if the *concerns* of the learners are ignored. Concerns also involve feelings and emotions but at a much deeper level than those described in the third level. Concerns are the most persistent, pervasive threads of underlying uneasiness the learners have about themselves and their relation to the world. The distinction between this level and the third level may be stated this way: Concerns always engage feelings, but feelings do not always involve concerns. For example, a person may have an immediate, spontaneous feeling about listening to a symphony orchestra or about another person, without having a concern (as defined above) about either. Feeling anger at having one's toe stepped on would be an immediate feeling; whereas, becoming angry *every* time someone criticized a particular group to which one belonged would represent a more pervasive feeling which probably reflects a concern. Relevance is achieved on this fourth level if the teacher attempts to deal with the questions that people most consistently ask themselves, such as, "Who am I? What can I do about things? Who am I really connected to or how do I fit into the scheme of things?" The difference between this level and the previous one is a difference in kind as well as degree.

Some cues to children's concerns that may assist teachers in selecting relevant content that deals with these concerns may be found in the following statements made by children:

Cues indicating self-rejection that reflects a concern for self-identity:

Why do I live in the slums?
I may be brown, but I'm not black!
How can you like me when I don't like myself?
We're the dumb special class!

These last two statements could easily occur across socio-economic lines, while the first two contain the added variables of class and caste.

Cues indicating disconnectedness that reflect a concern for greater connectedness:

Whenever I leave Harlem I feel like a fish out of water.
Why should I listen to my parents? Look at the way they live!
In order for me to get educated I gotta be like you? What about
me?
You can't trust nobody, white or negro.

Cues indicating powerlessness that reflect a concern for greater control over what is happening to them:

It's no use trying. There's nothing you can do.
I'm Hercules—I can do anything.

. . . what the hell can I do? This is the attitude; we can do nothing, so leave it alone. People think you're always going to be under pressure from the white man and he owns and runs everything, and we are so dependent on him that there's nothing I can do. This is the general impression I've gotten from most of the adults in Harlem [Harlem Youth Opportunities Unlimited, 1964, p. 344].

These statements are significant to us, because they are questions with which children are grappling which are rooted in the core of their being. They are questions that all humans face, but which for the disadvantaged have been so compounded and powerful that they have become the essence of their disadvantage. Such concerns lie at the core of what we term relevance, for very little could be more relevant to groups of children than what they actually *feel* most about.

Effective teaching utilizes all four levels of relevance. Educators are beginning to use the first two levels. What they are not meeting adequately are the third or fourth levels which constitute two different levels of the "affective" or feeling domain. Educators are not answering the spoken and more often unspoken questions children ask themselves: "Why do I feel the way I do? What makes me do that? Do they think I'm any good?" Rather than try to supply insights to these questions, the school, instead, asks children, "What do we mean by the Common Market?" "How are animals and people different?" Ignored in the process is one of the child's most persistent questions: "What does it have to do with *me?*" Unless there is this connection with the child's experiential and emotional framework, the knowledge he gains will be of little significance and may not be manifested in the types of behaviors spelled out by the aims of education.

It is our general hypothesis that what makes the most contact is that which is the most "relevant" to them and which makes a connection between the affective or feeling aspects and the cognitive or conceptualizing aspects of the learner.

The so-called Montessori method has three main characteristics. First is the adaptation of schoolwork to the individuality of each child. This principle is not, of course, new in the history of education. No teacher, however, has put more stress upon it than Mme. Montessori, and she has been more successful than most in selling the idea to the rank and file of the teaching profession. Mme. Montessori believed firmly that the first duty of each human being was to be himself and that anything which checked this development did him a serious injury. She therefore encouraged pupils to work at their own rate, to concentrate upon what interested them, and to use school materials in whatever way would serve to develop their latent abilities and to solve their current problems. In her teaching she made every effort to adapt what she had to say to each child, often teaching pupils individually so as to get the greatest possible adaptation. Moreover, she studied and tested and observed each pupil until she felt she had an understanding of him as a growing, developing individual before she tried to teach him at all.

A second feature of her method was her insistence upon freedom, which she considered an essential requirement for any true education. Both the teacher and the pupil must be free; the former should not dominate the latter, nor should the latter depend more than absolutely necessary upon the former. As she said: "No one can be free unless he is independent; therefore the first active manifestations of the child's individual liberty must be so guided that through this activity he may arrive at independence." And in another place: "My method is established upon one fundamental base—the liberty of the pupils in their spontaneous manifestations." Or again: "We cannot know the consequences of stifling a spontaneous action when the child is just beginning to be active; perhaps we stifle life itself."

The meaning of the above statements is perhaps best revealed by presenting an incident related by Mme. Montessori:

> One day, the children had gathered themselves, laughing and talking, into a circle about a basin of water containing some floating toys. We had in the school a little boy barely two and a half years old. He had been left outside the circle, alone, and it was easy to see that he was filled with intense curiosity. I watched him from a distance with great interest; he first drew near to the other children and tried to force his way among them, but he was not strong enough to do this, and he then stood looking about him. The expression of thought on his little face was intensely interesting. I wish that I had had a camera so that

I might have photographed him. His eye lighted upon a little chair, and evidently he made up his mind to place it behind the group of children and then to climb up on it. He began to move toward the chair, his face illuminated with hope, but at that moment the teacher seized him brutally (or, perhaps, she would have said, gently) in her arms, and lifting him up above the heads of the other children showed him the basin of water, saying, "Come, poor little one, you shall see too!"

Undoubtedly the child, seeing the floating toys, did not experience the joy that he was about to feel through conquering the obstacle with his own force. The sight of those objects could be of no advantage to him, while his intelligent efforts would have developed his inner powers. The teacher hindered the child, in this case, from educating himself, without giving him any compensating good in return. The little fellow had been about to feel himself a conqueror, and he found himself held within two imprisoning arms, impotent. The expression of joy, anxiety, and hope, which had interested me so much, faded from his face and left on it the stupid expression of the child who knows that others will act for him.

From some of Mme. Montessori's statements one might assume that she meant to give children perfect freedom and let them grow up à la Émile. Such was, however, not the case. She knew very well that life in a schoolroom makes "complete freedom" impossible. Moreover, Mme. Montessori is a well-born, cultivated Italian lady who would be most unwilling to let children dash about a schoolroom whooping like Indians because at the moment that was what they felt like doing. She tells in her own words her reactions to scenes of unrestricted freedom in certain schools that had taken her principles too literally: "I saw children with their feet on the tables and with their fingers in their noses, and no intervention was made to correct them. I saw others push their companions and I saw dawn in the faces of these an expression of violence, and not the slightest attention on the part of the teacher. Then I had to intervene to show with what almost rigor it is necessary to hinder and little by little suppress all those things which one must not do." These are not the words of an apostle of freedom, but those of a sensible woman who shares the world's disapproval of hoodlums. Her theory and her practice do not agree.

In a true Montessori school the teachers give no commands to the pupils, nor are there either punishments or rewards. The burden of control is thus put upon the children themselves, and they respond by learning to direct their own activity. Mme. Montessori expressed her basic idea about the control of children as follows: "The liberty of children should have as its limit the collective interest [of the group]; as its form, whatever we universally consider good breeding. We must therefore check in the children whatever offends or annoys others, or whatever tends to rough or ill-bred acts." In short, when Mme. Montessori was confronted by actual children she did what was sensible, practical, and possible—and did it superlatively well.

There were small, light chairs and tables that the children could move around at will. Each pupil selected from the available materials in the room whatever he wanted to work on, took them to a place that suited him, and went to work in his own way. There was no group instruction, although the children sometimes played group games or spontaneously did their work together. There was always a teacher present, but her function was to observe and guide. She helped each child when and if he needed it, suggested a better procedure if she saw him getting into difficulty, and gave him encouragement, but otherwise left him alone. If a pupil failed to complete an exercise he received no penalty; his failure was taken merely as an indication that he was not yet ready for the work, and the teacher suggested something else for him to do. Whenever possible the materials with which the children worked were self-corrective, so that pupils could find their own mistakes and thus become even more independent of the teacher.

Naturally, such an arrangement called for a new concept of discipline. The child who moves about the room as he needs to, intent upon carrying out his own purposes and indifferent to what the teacher is doing, is a "good" child, even if he is sometimes noisy. Under a repressive discipline, immobility is often confused with goodness and spontaneity with mischievousness. For forced immobility Mme. Montessori would substitute the quietness that comes from concentration upon a fascinating problem; for pressure from the teacher she would substitute the pressure of the children upon each other; for forced learning she proposed spontaneous interest. The pupils would thus learn to control themselves because they would find out that only by so doing could they accomplish the things their interest was urging them to accomplish.

Since freedom implies independence from the services of other people, it is natural that small children in the Montessori schools should be given "practical exercises in daily life," as they are called. The pupils learn in school to dress themselves, keep themselves clean, to dust the room, to care for school equipment, to help serve lunch, to attend to their own toilet needs. The youngest children begin with exercises in buttoning, hooking, and lacing pieces of cloth together. Later they learn, as a regular part of their schoolwork, to walk about quietly, to move their chairs without noise, to handle more and more delicate objects. At first they are helped by the older children, but such great prestige is associated with independence that new pupils dispense with aid as soon as they can. This practical training is especially characteristic of Mme. Montessori's attitudes and interests.

Finally, the Montessori system gives an important role to the training of the senses. Indeed, this emphasis upon sensory education is perhaps the most distinguishing mark of the system. The training is used not only as a means of development but as an introduction to reading, writing, and arithmetic, as will presently be shown. Training in sensory discrimination was given so prominent a place because Mme. Montessori believed that there was a close relationship between the senses and the intellect and that if the senses were neglected during the early years, the intellect would not develop as it should. She was so emphatic about this point as to state that a man whose sense training was inadequate might in later life learn all there is to be known about his profession and yet remain inefficient by reason of his sensory obtuseness. Thus a doctor might be well informed about diseases of the heart but be unable to apply his knowledge because his ears could not discriminate sounds sufficiently well.

Mme. Montessori's own statement of the objective in sense education was as follows: "The education of the senses has as its aim the refinement of the differential perception of stimuli by means of repeated exercises." These exercises are necessarily self-educative, since no teacher can do a pupil's seeing, hearing, and touching for him. Most of Mme. Montessori's exercises are also self-corrective. For example, the first in the series consists of a block of wood with ten holes of different diameters bored into it and ten little wooden cylinders that just fit the holes; obviously, a child cannot put a cylinder into a hole too small for it, and if he puts one into too large a hole he will have at the end of the exercise a cylinder left that will not go into the only remaining hole. When he makes an error, the materials automatically inform him of it. The exercises are so designed as to train all the senses and thus offset the predominance of vision, the one sense ordinarily so highly trained that many people depend upon it almost exclusively. It may not be true that a child adds a cubit to his mental stature by means of sensory training, but he certainly does develop finer powers of discrimination in many fields and thus lays the basis for a greater variety of experience than he might otherwise have.

It was not originally Mme. Montessori's idea to teach reading and writing or arithmetic to small children, but gradually she modified this view because she found so many children voluntarily trying to teach themselves the rudiments of these skills. She therefore added some further exercises that should furnish a transfer from purely sensory training to the school subjects. Children who can already recognize and sort figures begin to count them, forward and backward, to group them by twos and threes, to dissect them into halves, thirds, and quarters, thus laying the immediate foundation for arithmetic.

The transition from sense training to writing is especially good. After the children have had a good deal of experience in tracing contours made from sandpaper they are given cards, each containing a letter of the alphabet in sandpaper against a smooth background. The children learn to recognize the letters, but they also practice running their forefingers over each letter, again and again, often with their eyes closed; the object of this game is to see if they can follow the sandpaper quickly, lightly, and surely, from memory. In this way they practice the alphabet. To get proper control over a pencil they merely color in the outlines of pictures. They are soon familiar with the muscular-tactical sensations of writing and have a visual perception of each letter. They then learn the sounds of the letters. The pupil is provided with a box of letters identical in size and form with the sandpaper models but cut in cardboard and unmounted; there are three or four copies of each letter, which are kept in a fixed compartment. The teacher pronounces a short word, enunciating each component sound carefully, while the pupil selects from his letters the ones that the teacher is sounding. When he has laid out several words he reads them back to the teacher. In this way he builds up a small vocabulary of words he can both spell and read. He is now all ready to begin writing, since he has all the necessary skills. However, no one does anything about teaching him further except to provide some large sheets of paper and some soft pencils. He continues to play with the sandpaper letters, to make words from dictation, and to color pictures, until some day, when he spontaneously gets a paper and pencil and begins to write.

There is no question in the mind of one who has watched a child's natural burgeoning into penmanship that the Montessori method is the best possible introduction to the subject. Moreover, the time needed is very short; even four-year-olds require only about six weeks from the initial preparatory exercise to the spontaneous writing of words in better script than the average child twice their age.

Usually the transfer from sensory training to reading comes later than in the case of writing. When the children can produce written words and can read their own writing, the teacher gives them little packages of cards on each of which is the name of some object in the room. The pupil then scampers around the room putting the cards on the appropriate objects. After a while he gets cards with phrases such as "stand up," "jump three times," or "open the door"; he looks at the cards and shows his comprehension by carrying out the command. Although there is no pressure whatever upon the children, most of them learn the elements of arithmetic, reading, and writing before they enter the regular schools, and all of them have acquired the sensory discriminations upon which such achievements are based.

The Montessori system is, then, a fusion of somewhat divergent elements, of which three are outstanding. Two of these basic principles—respect for the child's individuality and encouragement of his personal freedom—compose what might be called the Montessori point of view. They determine not only the atmosphere of the schoolroom but the relation of teacher and pupil, the arrangement of the schoolroom, and the nature of the instructional procedures. The sense education, together with its transfer to the elementary school subjects, is better referred to as the Montessori technique. The two fundamental educational tenets and the specific methodology together give the Montessori method its distinctive character.

Before one can fairly criticize the Montessori system one has to realize that there is often a marked divergence between what Mme. Montessori wrote and what she did, between her philosophy and her pedagogy, between her theory and her practice. In general she seems to have gotten her theory out of a book and her practice from a shrewd observation of human beings. As a result, her teaching procedures may either contradict her general principles or else have no discernible relation to them. And it is her reactions to children, her grasp of their needs, her handling of them, and her methods of teaching that are right. As a clinician and a teacher she is magnificent, but like many other great teachers she is an indifferent philosopher. As a result, Mme. Montessori sometimes seems to do the right things for the wrong reasons.

A second point to consider skeptically is the claim that the Montessori system is rigidly scientific. No one could be any surer of its firm foundation in science than Mme. Montessori herself, but to the observer it seems that the essence of her method is highly intuitive. It is probable that Mme. Montessori's long training in science was invaluable to her in her work, but the main elements in her method of teaching are intuition, shrewdness, hard common sense, knowledge of the world, keen observation, and the same controlled guesswork that characterizes the conclusions of any other expert diagnostician. Mme. Montessori's work needs neither theoretical nor scientific justification—and in the writer's opinion it would be better off without them.

It seems quite clear that Mme. Montessori was in error in certain of her concepts about personality. One's personality is a fusion of biologically and socially determined elements, but Mme. Montessori so greatly overstressed the former as to regard personality as an inheritance through the germ cells. By overemphasizing biological inheritance and understressing social forces Mme. Montessori has produced a concept of personality and individuality that is at present untenable—in case it ever were defensible. An especially striking feature of her system is the absence of training for the emotions. Everything is intellectual. To be sure, the child is never forced, but the schoolwork makes little demand upon his spontaneous desire to play. There are almost no games, and what do occur seem to be tacked on as a sop to immaturity; little constructive use is made of them, and they are not regarded as educational. The children do not act out plays, nor does the teacher tell them stories. While spontaneous flights of imagination are not repressed, they are certainly not stimulated. Little provision is made for aesthetic interests. The pupils rarely sing, or play singing games, or play Victrola records, or look at pictures, or model with clay, or draw pictures, or mess about with paints—all activities dear to the childish heart. It is typical that when a child does color pictures it is to learn how to control a pencil, not to create something he thinks is beautiful. Naturally, such activities are not forbidden—on her own principle of freedom Mme. Montessori cannot reject anything a child does, provided it is not actually harmful or indecent—but there is little in the training to give nourishment to aesthetic sensibilities.

The method is deficient also in social training because the work is almost all individual. The children indulge in more or less free play together, but they fail to get the social training that comes from joint undertakings and group instruction. While the pupils inevitably educate each other socially to some extent in Montessori schools as elsewhere, the system itself does not arrange for and encourage the social growth that is now regarded as a chief result of schooling at all levels.

Even within its relatively narrow intellectual limits, the method shows other defects. The sensory education rests directly upon the laboratory psychology of the late nineteenth century. In the psychology of that day, mental life was conceived of as being built up out of elements which combine in thousands of different ways, just as chemical elements combine to produce the varied forms of matter. The experimental work of the period was one-sided because it dealt primarily with sensory discrimination and other simple phenomena in a laboratory atmosphere of artificial detachment and purposely suspended animation. Naturally, sensations are important, but they do not constitute the whole of one's mental life. Moreover, on the assumption that sensations are an early and simple form of mental activity, Mme. Montessori defended sense education as peculiarly appropriate for early childhood. The more modern view is that proper training of the emotions should come first. What might be called the subject matter of the Montessori method is, therefore, distinctly one-sided and based upon a type of psychology that has been outgrown.

Some critics have raised the objection that enough training of the senses for any ordinary purpose is automatically given by the processes of growing up and achieving an ordinary education, and that additional training, if needed for a particular job, can be acquired at any period of life up to senescence. Whether or not the average person gets "enough" sensory education by ordinary means is still an open question because no one can say with exactness how much is enough or even how much children usually get. In any case, the whole matter of sensory training has to be considered in the light of a child's total needs and such time assigned to it as will not interfere with the development of other and equally important abilities.

Finally, there is one defective point in the general procedure for building a curriculum. Mme. Montessori wanted everything in her school to spring from the nature of small children. Like everyone else who has based school work upon what came spontaneously from children, she is confronted with the problem of what fails to come. Mme. Montessori herself was greatly concerned because her system included no training in religion. Since she is committed to a learning that is free and unforced, she has automatically excluded didactic instruction of any kind, and cannot introduce what the children do not voluntarily show a desire for. She is not alone in this dilemma of curriculum building. Since 1900 many people in many places have tried to make a course of study out of childish activities and have all found the same difficulty: that the work is one-sided and does not contribute enough in the way of preparation for later stages of development. It has by now been demonstrated that while children's interests and spontaneous activities can and should be used to motivate schoolwork, they cannot be used as the sole basis for determining its content.

The Montessori system has, then, its virtues and its faults. As in the case of other systems that have come from the thinking of a single individual, it has the same strong points and the same shortcomings as its author. Mme. Montessori's outstanding virtues are her sturdy independence, her insistence upon being herself, her willingness to let other people be themselves, her devotion to science, her deep love of learning, and her intuitive understanding of children. Her shortcomings are her overintellectualized interests, her dogmatized science, and her lack of provisions for the emotions.

To a considerable degree Madame's great skill in teaching offset the weaknesses of her system, whenever she was doing the actual teaching. In her hands an exercise in walking on a chalk line became an exercise in manners and morals; a test for visual acuity was transformed into training in systematic observation; a drill in putting buttons through buttonholes developed into an exercise in independence. It has been said that a child who was exposed to nothing but the Montessori method during his preschool and school years would emerge as an individual cast in the same mold as Mme. Montessori herself: scientific, precise, objective, accurate, unemotional, independent, vigorously individual. Education has often fared worse than this, but certain modifications could eliminate the defects of the Montessori system and make it approach more nearly to the educational ideal.

intelligence and early learning

At the core of most programs in early education is the belief that such programs can help children become more effective in dealing with themselves and their worlds. This belief is generally based on the view that experiences in the early years can have a significant impact on a child's ability to be successful in his later life, an ability traditionally referred to as intelligence. Currently the meaning and modifiability of intelligence is a topic of considerable debate and controversy, with particular interest centering on the aspect of intelligence labeled "cognitive capacities." The abilities to remember and recognize previously experienced events, to organize information into a meaningful pattern, and to manipulate ideas, symbols, and concepts in adapting to the environment are all considered cognitive capacities.

Instead of entering into the controversy about the genetic basis of intelligence and whether intelligence can be modified, most educators and psychologists have focused on children's cognitive processes and ways of facilitating their development. It is in this context that the work of Jean Piaget, the Swiss developmental psychologist, has received such wide attention. It is also in this context that behavior modification (espoused by B. F. Skinner) has been introduced into the classroom. Underlying Piaget's approach is the belief that children's cognitive capacities develop in a specific series of stages and that children organize their psychological world according to a logic that is often different from adult logic. The behavior-modification approach derives from the belief that carefully sequenced instructional materials that provide specific and direct rewards will be effective in teaching children skills. The emphasis in the behavior-modification approach is on specific behavioral skills; in the Piagetian approach, on the other hand, the emphasis is on understanding the underlying structure and process by which knowledge is gained. Both positions have been the basis of early-childhood programs, but, quite obviously, the programs are markedly different from each other.

The six articles in this section deal with some of the basic issues regarding the cognitive capacities of young children. In "Preschool Enrichment and Learning," Article 13, Jerome Kagan points out that there are many ways to raise a child, and that what we regard as "enriching" or "ideal" will depend on the environment in which the child is reared. What is regarded as constructive, healthy, and growth-promoting is not so regarded for all children even in this country, much less the world. Kagan proposes that the word "intelligence" be discarded since it is often used loosely and judgmentally and has only limited scientific validity.

Article 14, "Children Have Ways of Understanding Their World," by Kenneth Wann, Miriam Dorn, and Elizabeth Liddle, is a presentation of research data on how children use their cognitive capacities in their daily lives. These researchers, basing their findings on extended observation, note that children derive inherent satisfactions from gaining and possessing information and that they use, organize and manipulate the information they gain. Most children are not passive; instead, they classify, generalize, infer, and conclude on the basis of what their world provides.

Article 15 by Celia Stendler-Lavatelli and Article 16 by Richard Copeland describe Jean Piaget's formal theory concerning how children actively process information and utilize experience in developing intelligence. The Stendler-Lavatelli selection, "Aspects of Piaget's Theory That Have Implications for Teacher Education," considers in some detail three aspects of Piaget's theory that are particularly important for teachers: his definition of intelligence; his analysis of logical thought in children; and his description of the stages in the development of logical intelligence. The Copeland selection, "Cognitive Development and Learning Mathematics," focuses specifically on implications of Piaget's theory for mathematics instruction. The author believes that it is necessary "for the child of four to eleven to begin learning about abstract mathematics inductively by using objects in the physical world." He also feels that deep and lasting cognitive growth results from the child's *equilibrating* (balancing and adapting) his current conceptual framework with new and discordant input from the environment. Finally, he recommends that teachers attune their teaching goals to the child's current developmental level in terms of Piaget's stages, a recommendation that is somewhat controversial. (The controversy stems from the fact that Piaget charts in laboratory and field settings the child's *previously developed* capacities rather than comparing in the classroom the differences between what a child of a given age can learn when instructed via non-Piagetian as opposed to Piagetian teaching strategies.)

In "Manipulatives in the Classroom," Article 17, Elizabeth Fennema discusses the appropriate use of physical, "touchable" teaching materials to assist children in developing, applying, and enjoying mathematics skills. Fennema indicates how the use of such materials in teaching dovetails on a theoretical level with Piaget's views on how children develop intelligence and learn to understand the physical universe. The author also describes a variety of further probable benefits that accrue when abstract mathematical principles are taught in a concrete and tangible context.

The last two articles in this section deal with theoretical issues related to the teaching of concepts in science and mathematics. Lee Shulman's analysis of the "Psychological Controversies in the Teaching of Science and Mathematics," Article 18, revolves around the central issue of how much and what kind of guidance is to be provided in the learning situation. Comparing the Piaget-derived views of Jerome Bruner with the Skinner-derived views of Robert Gagné, Shulman discusses the differences between discovery learning and guided programmed instruction. These theoretical differences imply drastically different practices for the classroom teacher.

Some features of the discovery learning process are described by Helen Heffernan in "Concept Development in Science," Article 19— among them the central part the child plays in gaining scientific concepts. The teacher must be aware that she cannot "give" the child concepts; rather, the child develops his own concepts out of his own experiences. The teacher can, however, make available a wide variety of sensory experiences that the child can then use in his own way to organize and understand his own world.

behavioral objectives *To be able to discuss the following points*

13 PRESCHOOL ENRICHMENT AND LEARNING
The concept of interaction between the organism and its surrounding environment
The belief that there is a single fixed definition of success
The differences between behavior, cognition, and motivation and the relationship of each to individual values
The concept of developmental goals
The basic units of cognition described by Kagan
The cognitive processes that involve manipulation of the units of thought
Four different meanings of intelligence

14 CHILDREN HAVE WAYS OF UNDERSTANDING THEIR WORLD
Three types of evidence that children gain satisfaction from their knowledge of the world
The idea that children attempt to organize their psychological world to deal with the constant bombardment of information
The terms "association," "classification," and "generalization" as they apply to children's thinking

15 ASPECTS OF PIAGET'S THEORY THAT HAVE IMPLICATIONS FOR TEACHER EDUCATION
The major focus of Piaget's work and several topics on which he has conducted studies
Piaget's concept of intelligence and the properties of logical thought
The stages in the development of logical intelligence

The role of maturation, experience, social transmission, and equilibrium in the development of logical intelligence

16 COGNITIVE DEVELOPMENT AND LEARNING MATHEMATICS

The sequence and basic features of Piaget's four stages of cognitive development

The results of studies on acceleration of learning

Equilibration and its implications for classroom teaching

The significance of reversibility of thought

The differences between IQ tests and Piaget-based tests of intelligence

17 MANIPULATIVES IN THE CLASSROOM

The value of using manipulatives in the classroom

The relationship between the use of manipulatives to teach mathematical skills and Piaget's theory of cognitive development

The relationship of cognitive skills to specific uses of manipulatives

The benefits that probably result from using manipulatives to teach mathematics skills

The relationship of manipulatives to the development of the child's self-concept

18 PSYCHOLOGICAL CONTROVERSIES IN THE TEACHING OF SCIENCE AND MATHEMATICS

The general process of learning as it is viewed by Bruner

The general process of learning as it is viewed by Gagné

The respective positions of Bruner and Gagné on the objectives of education, instructional style, and readiness

The views of Gagné and Bruner on curriculum sequence and transfer of training

The concept of guided discovery and the differences in its application by Bruner and by Gagné

19 CONCEPT DEVELOPMENT IN SCIENCE

The advances in science education in the last ten years

The meanings of the terms "concept," "symbol," "percept," and "generalization"

Four features of the classroom environment in which teachers can best facilitate concept development

The relative importance of what is taught and how it is taught versus how much is taught

Americans have become preoccupied with early intellectual development because of a fundamental assumption that our racial and ethnic problems will not be solved as long as there are enormous differences in the style of cognitive functioning among our school-age children. But since it is not clear how we should describe or conceptualize early cognitive development there is little agreement among educators and psychologists on strategies for change or intervention. The present paper addresses itself to these fundamental issues in the hope that it will inform practical, social-action plans.

The popular interpretation of the unfortunate fact that poor children find school difficult is that early experiences in the family, rather than demons, floating wombs, or excessive secretion of body humors, are the villainous cause of unsatisfactory academic achievement. It is possible that we, like the Greek and medieval physicians, have an exaggerated faith in the validity of our diagnosis. For it is unlikely that interactions with parents are the sole determinant of the complete sweep of psychological development. However it is probably safe to assume some truth to the idea that the child's experiences with adults during his first five or six years have a nontrivial influence on his future abilities and motivation. Since an increasing number of educated women want careers outside the home, and many poor women work in order to contribute to the economic stability of their families, our society has been nudged to create sources of supplementary care outside the home, and pushed to the lip of a major structural alteration in the form of child care. It is likely that we will soon have several million children under age six cared for outside the home by adults who, in most instances, are complete strangers to the parents. Since there is no firm body of data or theory that allows us to predict the consequences of this arrangement we should worry a little about its possible sequelae. Hence, the question of what to do with young children is relevant whether the location of child care be the home, a neighbor's apartment, a trailer, or a freshly built day-care center on a busy city street. How do we arrange the environment so that the child's growth is optimal?

Let me state a prejudice in the clearest form possible:

One cannot prescribe the correct experiences for a child unless one specifies the environment to which he must adapt.

The skills, strategies, beliefs, and motives that are useful in one environment may be irrelevant or, in some instances, debilitating in another. We allow our children to express their anger because we believe that suppression of this emotion will produce an overly inhibited and tense child, and that an excessively inhibited adolescent will not fare well in our competitive society. The Eskimo, by contrast, try to prevent expression of anger in older children because they believe it will destroy the close feelings of cooperation that must be maintained if one lives continually with six others in an area of 1000 square feet. Unfortunately most citizens prefer to assume a more absolute posture, believing in a fixed and special set of psychological attributes that permits an adult to be happy and successful, and a parallel set of environmental experiences that allows that psychological house to be built. This is much too simple a view. There are too many different profiles of successful psychological adjustment to ensure the truth of the first proposition, and too many local theories of child-rearing to bolster the second. The rural, poor mother in West Virginia believes that a slap on the bottom will teach her child to inhibit childish crying or teasing of a younger sibling. The middle-class Princeton mother is sure that deprivation of a privilege will accomplish the same goals. The Utku mother living northwest of Hudson Bay knows that there is nothing she can do until the child is old enough to understand that whining and teasing are wrong, until the child acquires what the Utku call *ihuma,* which is best translated as *reason.* And we should not be surprised that most seven-year-olds in all three cultural settings have stopped both of these undesirable behaviors. There are many ways to socialize a child, and a relativistic attitude toward psychological growth is the only rational attitude to promote. There is no recipe of caretaking practices that accomplishes some ideal set of goals independent of the cultural context in which the socialization proceeds. There is no wrinkled guru who possesses the universal "how-to-do-it" secrets of human development. Despite the intellectual attractiveness of this conclusion, our hearts boldly resist it and persuade us that some experiences must be more beneficial to growth than others, and we continue to search for a statement that summarizes them. Although there is no neat recipe for growth, it is true, nevertheless, that there are some basic assumptions about psychological development and this paper considers some of these ideas. Although this essay is primarily on cognition it is useful to distinguish among the three great psychological systems of *behavior, cognition,* and *motivation.*

The domain of overt public behavior is most easily specified. The child's repertoire of public actions is best described by its functions. Some responses are used to gratify biological needs. Others are used for defense—physical as well as psychological. Still others are employed to gratify learned desires and further psychological growth. Some behavioral systems, like the motor coordination necessary for walking or playing tennis, are acquired through the processes of conditioning. Other response systems—like language—are potentiated through mere exposure to the proper set of environmental events. The child's speech emerges naturally, though mysteriously, as a result of listening to a talking environment. Apparently structures in the temporal lobe have been specially prepared by nature for the reception and organization of language. Given the raw material provided by hearing people talk, these brain structures manufacture language products in their host. Still other behavioral systems are acquired through observation of others, followed by imitated practice. Learning how to open a window is perhaps the straightest example of this last category. Thus our first assumption is that if one prefers to use the word *learning* to cover all these types of *change*, it is appropriate to speak of different modes of learning.

Cognition—or more simply thought—is our second system, where cognition is assumed to refer to a set of mental units and a coordinated set of processes that manipulates these units in the intricate ballet of thought. The primary functions of cognition are (1) to allow the child to recognize the past, (2) to understand new experience, and (3) to manipulate his symbols, concepts, and rules in order to solve a problem. The basic units of cognition include schemata, images, symbols, concepts, and rules. The basic processes include perception, memory, inference, evaluation, and deduction, organized by special executive processes that are responsible for the permanent registration of experience, as well as its transformation and activation when problems have to be solved. Although we return to a discussion of the five units and five processes later, it is useful to explain now this last idea of the executive, since it has only recently attracted the attention of psychologists.

All children learn a language to label discrete aspects of their experience. These linguistic structures are placed in long-term memory and retrieved, as if by a special mental rake, by an executive process that organizes knowledge as it retrieves it, much as a construction foreman directs the depositing of bricks, boards, and pipes around the building site and, at the proper time, retrieves them from the correct location and organizes them into the proper architectural form. There are important differences among children in the efficiency with which this executive operates.

Consider the following empirical finding. Four-year-old and eight-year-old children are shown a row of six familiar objects—a pin, button, cup, fork, doll, and scissors. The examiner assures himself that each child can name each of the six objects correctly. Now the examiner touches four of the six objects once in a random order, perhaps button, fork, doll, and scissors, and then asks the child to touch the objects in the same order. The four-year-old performs poorly, the eight-year-old does very well. We know that the younger child's failure does not result from absence of a language label for each of these simple objects. We also know that a four-year-old is capable of remembering much more information than is required in this problem. For if he is asked to examine 60 pictures from magazines, for about two seconds each, and is then shown 120 pictures, 60 of which are new and 60 of which he looked at earlier, and asked simply to say which ones he saw, he is correct 90% to 100% of the time. Some children make no mistakes when tested two days later. The four-year-old can remember 48 hours later that he saw 60 pictures, if all he has to say is "yes" or "no," "old" or "new." But he cannot reconstruct a temporal pattern of only four events. Our explanation of this apparent paradox is that the young child did not activate the language label that he had in his repertoire while the adult was touching the objects. He did not use his knowledge to help him remember the temporal pattern he watched. Proof of this conclusion comes from a study in which five-year-olds, eight-year-olds, and adults looked through the 60 pictures under two different conditions. One group was given no special instruction, as in the experiment cited above. The second group was told to label the picture in some way. Then all the subjects were shown 120 pictures—60 old and 60 new—and asked to say which ones they saw earlier. For adults, who naturally activate a conceptual set of labels for experience, it did not make much difference which group they were in. They performed well under both instructions. However, for the children, especially the five-year-olds, those who were instructed to label benefited enormously and their performance was much better than those five-year-olds who examined the pictures under no special instruction, and who apparently did not activate any label for the pictures.

A second example comes from the Kpelle of Liberia, who do not have a written language. A list of words was read to the Kpelle adult, some of which belonged to one conceptual category, like weapons, and some to another conceptual category, say edible foods. The subject was asked to remember these words and to recall them when the complete list had been read. The subject remembered about as many words as an American adult on the very first reading. But with succeeding readings of the list, Americans improved dramatically, while Kpelle did not. It appears that the Kpelle did not have the mental set or disposition to organize the "weapon" words into one conceptual category and the food words into another, even though they had the individual words for the category. However, the more education a Kpelle had, the more his performance resembled that of an American. Education teaches the use of categories. The executive strategy of organizing experience into conceptual categories is one of the functions strengthened by formal education. We must make a sharp differentiation, therefore, between possessed knowledge and the active use and organized retrieval of that knowledge to solve a problem.

130 *intelligence and early learning*

Consider a final example of the executive process from the infant. Ten-month-old infants were allowed to play with a simple toy—say a toy animal—for a few minutes. Then six minutes later they were given a pair of toys, a new one and the one they had played with earlier. Some children went directly to the new toy. Others first visually scanned each of the two toys two or three times, and only then crawled to the new one. We do not believe that it is a coincidence that the infants who stopped to scan both toys had mothers who were more interactive and playful with them. This one-to-one interactive activity between caretaker and infant may facilitate the development of this executive process that compares the past and present and retrieves relevant knowledge in time of conceptual conflict. The closely tuned interaction, we believe, sets the baby to look for variations on an habituated theme. The child comes to expect "surprises" and becomes increasingly skilled at assimilating them. In short, we believe that one-to-one interactive play that is closely monitored by the adult and is, therefore, assimilable by the child sculpts a process that disposes the infant to compare "what is happening" to "what just happened," and to attempt to understand it. To be concrete, we are suggesting that a child who is exposed to games like "peek-a-boo" between caretaker and infant gradually develops an expectation of moderate surprises, becomes vigilant to those variations in the external environment, derives pleasure from that understanding, and, as a result, becomes increasingly alert for information in the external world and more strongly motivated to interpret it.

The third major system—after behavior and cognition—refers to motives in the broadest sense, and includes the varied goals the child desires to attain, his expectancy of obtaining them, and the affect that occasionally accompanies motivation.

If these are the three systems that form the bedrock of psychological development, we can ask about their relation to the title of this paper. The phrase preschool enrichment usually means providing experiences that will make poor children from ethnic minority groups similar to middle-class white children in behavior, cognition, and motivation. A more relativistic definition of enrichment would be concerned with how one arranges the environment so that the largest number of children eventually come to possess the behaviors, cognitive structures, and motives that will be most adaptive for their particular cultural setting. To illustrate, black English frequently omits syntactic forms of the verb to be. Thus, "I goes home" means the same as "I am going home." The former sentence is different from standard middle-class English, but it is not necessarily a cognitively deficient sentence. Hence the primary issue surrounding "what should be enriched" is as much an ethical as it is a scientific issue. The members of any society must decide on the profile of psychological qualities to promote, and a pluralistic attitude toward the goals of growth should be considered. But whether one route or many is selected, the issue of deciding goals cannot be ignored. Families and educators must make a value choice. It is suggested that parents and teachers cooperate in the elucidation of educational goals and in their implementation. This arrangement not only guarantees a commitment on the part of the family to the goals of the school or the preschool center, it also facilitates mutual identification on the part of all parties. Such an affective involvement with the child's growth can be only beneficial.

Each social community has an implicit catechism of ideal traits for its children. I suggest that most, but not all, Americans would support the following statement of developmental goals—a sort of psychological platform for children. Each child should believe he is valued by the adults who care for him so that he will develop an autonomous identity, be self-reliant, and come to believe he can determine his own actions and values. We should note that these simple premises are not shared by all societies. The Japanese, for example, reject our stress on individual identity and self-reliance and are convinced that an adolescent should not be completely self-determining. He should be ready and willing to rely on others for help and affective support. Americans, by contrast, generally regard such behavior in a late adolescent as immature and excessively childish. Each of us is a unique bundle of talents and temperaments with a best fit in some particular context. My profile happens to be in harmony with the community in which I live, and thus there are occasional moments of serenity. But I can imagine a half-dozen environments in which I would be miserable.

Each parent, parent surrogate, and educator must toss a prophetic fishline forward in time and estimate the talents, motives, and beliefs that will be most useful for 1990. Fortunately the set of traits to celebrate cannot be totally unrelated to those we promote now for there are sociological constraints on the amount of social change that will occur, as well as biological limits on man's psychological elasticity and imaginative capacity to invent a totally novel set of goals. It is reasonable to expect, therefore, that as far as cognitive processes are concerned, we shall continue to value the child who has a rich store of concepts and rules, and effective strategies for registration of experience and retrieval of knowledge. The more specific talents that fill out that abstract formula will probably include reading competence (despite McLuhan, since reading is so much more efficient than listening), quantitative skills, the ability to write coherently, and the capacity to discriminate effective from ineffective arguments. The required motivational processes will include, at a minimum, the wish to be intellectually competent, an expectancy of obtaining that goal, and a firm personal identity.

COGNITIVE UNITS AND PROCESSES

As promised earlier, we now consider in more detail the cognitive and motivational processes that make development appear progressive. First, we consider the cognitive structures that should be enhanced at home and in preschool educational centers.

The basic units in cognition consist of schemata, images, symbols, concepts, and rules.

SCHEMATA The schema, which is the infant's first acquired cognitive unit, is a representation of the salient aspects of an event. Although the schema is neither an image nor a photographic copy of the event, it does preserve the arrangement of the significant elements that define the event. Your schema of Atlantic City is likely to contain water as a critical element. The critical elements of a schema give it distinctiveness and, like the cartoonist's caricature, exaggerate the most salient attributes of the event.

During infancy the salient elements can include the sensory feedback from the infant's actions toward an object. Thus, a baby can represent, or come to know, his favorite rattle in terms of its visual appearance as well as through his actions toward it. Piaget believes that sensorimotor action with objects during the first year of life is necessary for cognitive growth, and he talks of the acquisition of sensorimotor schemes.

Most enrichment programs for infants—as well as toy departments— emphasize play with attractive toys. The single most common element in all day-care programs for infants in the United States is the presence of toys that permit the infant to shake, rattle, push, and pull them and receive feedback from this manipulation. It is assumed that these experiences help to teach the child about the object and, as a dividend, persuade him that he can have an instrumental effect on the world. Although this notion seems intuitively reasonable, it is not so obvious to all parents and professionals. Some Dutch physicians in the eastern part of Holland instruct the mother to minimize the amount of stimulation and play that the infant experiences during the first 10 months of life, and they lie alone in cribs, with no toys, for the first 40 weeks. And these children are intellectually adequate at age five, although they are a little retarded on American tests of intelligence at one year. Moreover, limbless infants born to mothers who had taken thalidomide have no opportunity to manipulate toys, yet their cognitive development seems perfectly adequate. Thus, despite the intuitive reasonableness of the idea that play with toys should be necessary for mental development, the empirical data force us to at least question the strong form of that proposition.

Perhaps the most compelling argument for this idea is that the child acquires knowledge of language merely by listening to other people speak.

The child does not have to speak, even though normal children do, in order to learn some of the complex knowledge represented by the meaning of language signs and the rules of syntax. This is also true for the learning of song among birds, for the young chaffinch can learn to sing the song of its species merely by listening to that song on tape. It does not have to make any sounds while it is exposed to those important auditory inputs. Although motor action probably facilitates cognitive development because it keeps arousal high and provides important feedback information, it can still be true that overt behavior may not be necessary for the acquisition of some cognitive structures.

IMAGES A schema is not synonymous with a visual image, for the child can have schemata for voices, odors, and textures. The image is a mental picture and is a special and more elaborate structure that is related to the schema and more easily manipulated. However, like the schema, it preserves the unique pattern of physical qualities in the event. Perhaps the best way to regard the relation between schema and image is to view the former as the basic skeleton from which the more detailed holistic image is built. A schema is used in the construction of the image when cognitive processes perform work on it.

SYMBOLS Symbols are qualitatively different from both schemata and images, for unlike the latter two, a symbol is an *arbitrary representation* of an event. The best example is the name for a letter, a number, or an animal. A child who can name the arbitrary collection of lines we designate as the letter M and can point to an M when asked possesses the symbol for that alphabetic letter. In most children, symbolic function begins around 15–18 months, but can begin as early as one year. Most enrichment programs encourage the development of symbols, especially linguistic symbols, by encouraging the caretaker to begin to name objects in the child's environment as soon as the teacher feels the child can understand them.

CONCEPTS All concepts are symbols but they are much more than that. A concept stands for a set of common characteristics among a group of schemata, images, or symbols, and is not a specific object. A concept is a representation of a feature or features common to a variety of experiences. Consider the drawing of a cross. The eight-month-old infant possibly represents the cross as a schema. The three-year-old, who may call it a cross, represents it as a symbol. The adolescent who regards it as the cross of Christianity and imposes on it a relation to religion and church possesses the concept.

One of the serious difficulties preschool children have is that they regard many concepts as absolute, rather than relative. When the four-year-old first learns the concept dark, he regards it as descriptive of an absolute class of color—black and related dark hues. The phrase "dark yellow" makes no sense to him, for dark signifies dark colors, not relative darkness.

It is important that the child appreciate both the absolute and relative qualities of many concepts, and to persuade him that the same concept can have several different meanings in different contexts. The set to appreciate the relativity of conceptual dimensions can be promoted by a number of game-like problems in which the child has to name the multiple attributes of objects. A banana is yellow and brown and long and soft and smooth and sweet and sticky. A rock is good for breaking glass but bad for bouncing. A glass is good for drinking, fair for making musical melodies, and absolutely useless for drawing. The child himself is many things: he is a boy, the son of his father, the smallest child in the family, but the largest child in his classroom. It is possible to help the young child appreciate the multidimensional quality of concepts, and this victory seems to facilitate other intellectual conquests.

RULES There are two kinds of rules. One states a relation between two concepts. The rule "water is wet" states that the concepts water and wet are related, for one of the dimensions of water is the quality wetness. A second type of rule is a mental operation or routine imposed on two or more concepts to produce a new one. Multiplication is a rule imposed on two numbers to produce a third. We call these rules transformations. Piaget claims that there are discrete stages in the acquisition of rules. The appearance of stages in the child's thought sometimes results from the fact that rules that are learned initially stubbornly resist retirement, for they have been so effective in the past. A child's rule, like a scientific theory, is never replaced by criticism alone, only by a better rule.

Having considered the basic units of schema, image, symbol, concept, and rule, we turn now to the cognitive processes that manipulate these units in thought. Cognitive processes include two general types, undirected and directed. Undirected thinking refers to the free flow of thoughts that occurs continually as the child walks home or stares out the window. Directed thinking, by sharp contrast, refers to the processes that occur when the child tries to solve a problem. He knows there is a solution and he knows when he has arrived at it. This problem-solving process typically involves the following sequence: comprehension of the problem, memory, generation of possible solutions, evaluation, and implementation.

COMPREHENSION OF THE PROBLEM Understanding the problem, which must be the first event in problem-solving, requires selective attention to the salient aspects of an event and organized interpretation of information. Most problems are presented in the verbal mode and, therefore, the richer the child's vocabulary—that is, his language concepts—the more successful his understanding. This is one reason why the majority of preschool programs emphasize the teaching of words. However, all concepts are not linguistic, and if the child becomes overly accustomed to using only language to understand a problem, he may fail to develop other strategies. Hence, problems and information must be presented in nonverbal modes, including pictures, sounds, and action.

The preschool child has difficulty focusing attention on more than one event at a time. If he tries to listen or watch many things at once he often becomes confused. Hence the teacher should guarantee that she has the child's attention when talking to him. The best way to accomplish this goal is to have an adult working 1:1 or with only a small group of children. Since it is impossible to have a half-dozen licensed teachers in every preschool center, paraprofessionals must be used. Mothers, older children, and college and high school students are an excellent reservoir of needed talent and help.

MEMORY Memory refers to the storage of experience. There are two major kinds of memory, short term and long term. This differentiation is based, in part, on special structures in the central nervous system that seem necessary for long-term memory. Information in short-term memory is typically available for 15 to 30 seconds. The easy forgetting of a new telephone number after it has been dialed is the best example. Unless one makes a special effort to transfer the perceived information to long-term memory, some or all of it will be lost. Young children display poor memory because (1) they have a less adequate set of cognitive units to encode information for placement in long-term memory, (2) they have not learned the trick of rehearsal and do not spontaneously repeat events to themselves in order to aid transfer to long-term memory, and (3) they are not efficient at retrieving what they know. Enrichment programs should include exercises in which the child is taught memory tricks, ways of grouping words, numbers, or pictures and strategies of free associating that will aid later recall. Moreover, anxiety is memory's major enemy; it interferes with focused attention and with the ability to recall the past. Curricula should help the child develop strategies for placing new knowledge in memory and for efficient retrieval, while keeping distraction and anxiety tamed.

GENERATION OF IDEAS The comprehension of a problem and remembering it are typically the first two processes in any problem-solving sequence. The third process is the generation of possible solutions, the thinking up of alternative ways to solve the problem. The child is motivated to seek solutions whenever he comes across a problem he does not understand, one for which he does not have an immediate answer. The child sees his mother weeping or watches a bird unable to fly. These events create a state of uncertainty because he cannot explain the event. He wants to resolve this uncertainty, to understand the experience, and so he dips into his reservoir of knowledge and searches for ideas that will allow him to explain what he has seen. One of the major obstacles to the generation of good ideas is the possession of beliefs that conflict with good solutions. A set of firmly held ideas that are inconsistent with the required solution is one cause of rejection of the correct idea, should it occur. Anxiety over possible criticism for suggesting unusual ideas also can be inhibiting, for fear typically blocks creative solutions. The easiest and most common reaction to fear of error is to withdraw from the task or, if the fear is mild, to inhibit offering answers. Every preschool teacher recognizes this syndrome, for each group has a few children who are intelligent, but overly inhibited. They know more than they are saying, and censor good ideas because they would rather avoid making a mistake than risk the joy of success. The teacher must reduce these fears by encouraging guessing and convincing the child that honest approximations are better than no response, any attempt better than none.

EVALUATION Evaluation refers to the degree to which the child pauses to evaluate the quality of his thinking and the accuracy of his conclusions. This process influences the entire spectrum of thought, including the accuracy of perception, memory, and reasoning. Some children accept and report the first hypothesis they produce and act upon it with only the barest consideration for its quality. If correct, they are called ebullient; if not, unruly. These children are best called impulsive. Others devote a long period of time to considering their ideas and censor many hypotheses. These children are reflective. If correct, they are called wise; if incorrect, dull. This difference among children can be seen as early as two years of age and seems to be moderately stable over time. Fortunately, the child's disposition to be reflective or impulsive can be modified by training.

The impulsive child can be made more reflective by direct instruction (Kagan, Pearson, & Welch, 1966), by reinforcement for a reflective posture (Briggs, 1966; Nelson, 1968), or by modeling procedures (Debus, 1968). It is even possible to move an impulsive first grade child toward a reflective attitude by placing him in a classroom with a reflective teacher (Yando & Kagan, 1968). Educators should consider this information in working with young children.

IMPLEMENTATION OF IDEAS: THE DEDUCTIVE PHASE Deduction or implementation is the application of a transformational rule to solve a problem, once the solution hypothesis has been generated. There are basic changes in the child's understanding and use of rules during his first 12 to 15 years. Some psychologists assume the child merely learns more good rules each day, storing them for future use, and there is no rule that is necessarily too difficult for a child to comprehend and apply. The alternative view, which I find a little more friendly, is that some rules are inherently too complex for young children to understand. Hence there must be maturational stages in the development of thought.

Let us summarize this section on cognition by noting the general changes that occur during the period from one through six years of age. The richness of the child's supply of symbols, concepts, and rules increases each year and these units undergo continual reorganization as a function of experience, especially experience that causes him to question what he knows.

The original function of thought is to help the child make sense of his experiences. If he witnesses an unusual event he does not instantly understand, he reaches back into his mind to pull out an explanation that will put him at ease again. The child becomes increasingly concerned with the amount of agreement between his concepts and those of others, and he becomes more apprehensive about making mistakes. Hence his conception of problems and the rules he activates to solve them begin to approach that of the adult community. The second function of cognition is to communicate thoughts and wishes to others. Finally, thought permits the pleasure that comes from having a good idea, which is one of the basic sources of joy nature has permitted us. You will note that I have refrained from using the word *intelligence* or *IQ*. This was a purposeful act for I believe we should think of mental phenomena as a set of coordinated, but separate processes—not as a global capacity. Let me defend this prejudice.

THE CONCEPT OF INTELLIGENCE

Human beings like to rank order people and things into categories of good, better, best. We are satisfied with noting that the rose is a deep red but feel pressed to add that it is the loveliest flower in the garden. Man automatically gives a goodness-badness score to most of his experiences. He also performs this evaluation on himself, for homeliness is bad and attractiveness good, weakness bad and strength good. Of the many attributes of man, three typically receive special attention in all cultures. We usually evalute physical qualities, inner feelings, and skills. There are very few cultures known to man that do not have special words to describe how a person looks, how he feels, and how competent he is—and these words imply that certain appearances, feelings, and skills are good, while others are bad.

But each culture's decision is somewhat arbitrary and may not be valid for another group or for its own membership at another time in history. In 17th century Europe, women whom we in America today would regard as hopelessly overweight and unattractive were viewed as beautiful and a comparison of a Rubens' nude with that of a Gauguin reveals the changing standard of attractiveness.

The skills that are tagged good or bad also vary with time and social group, although every society sets up certain talents as most desirable. Bushmen must be skilled at hunting and tracking and those who possess these talents are given a designation that has a connotation similar to our word intelligent. Intelligent is the word society uses to apply to those people who possess the mental talents the society regards as important. But those talents change with time. In the late 19th century Francis Galton suggested that those with extremely sensitive vision and hearing were intelligent because the dominant brain theory of the day emphasized the importance of transmission of outside sensory information to the central nervous system. Today we emphasize the salience of language and reasoning because our theories of the brain have changed. But, like Galton, we still use the word intelligent to designate those who have more of those skills we happen to believe are "better."

From a scientific point of view we should exorcise words like intelligent because they are primarily evaluative and explain very little. But this exorcism will not happen because most members of our society—scientists as well as nonscientists—believe that this word has an explanatory power that derives from differences in our brains. So let us consider possible meanings of this word.

There are at least four different meanings of the concept of intelligence that deserve mention. The first is not very psychological; the remaining three are, but are different in conception.

INTELLIGENCE AS ADAPTATION TO THE ENVIRONMENT The ability to adapt to the specific environmental niche in which an organism lives and grows is, for the biologist, the most important attribute of an animal species. Successful adaptation requires resisting predators, maintaining a capacity to reproduce the next generation, and having the capacity to cope with new environmental pressures by learning new habits and changing one's anatomy and physiology. Evolutionary history tells us that some species, like the opossum, have survived for many thousands of generations, whereas others, like the graceful heron, are about to become extinct. If intelligence is defined as the ability to adapt to an ecological niche, then the opossum must be more intelligent than the heron. Since this conclusion contradicts our intuitions, this view of intelligence has never become popular. But that attitude is a matter of taste, not logic.

PIAGET'S VIEW OF INTELLIGENCE Piaget believes that intelligence is the coordination of mental operations that facilitate adaptation to the environment.

Hence, in one sense, Piaget promotes the biological prejudice described above. The growth of intelligence is the resolution of the tension between using old ideas for new problems and changing old ideas to solve new problems. Intellectual growth is adaptation to the new through alteration of old strategies, and the intelligent child is the one who has the operations that allow him to solve new problems.

THE EASE OF LEARNING NEW STRUCTURES AND SKILLS The most popular layman's view of the concept of intelligence assumes that the more intelligent the child the faster he will be able to learn a new idea or skill. This belief rests on the notion that there is a generalized receptivity to acquiring new competences, regardless of their specific nature. This faith is opposed by the belief that there are important differences depending on what specific skill is being learned. The man who learns a foreign language quickly may not have such an easy time learning to sail. This tension between a generalized intelligence and a set of specific intelligences is the subject of much controversy among psychologists and is reflected in our ambivalent attitude toward experts. We announce preference for the doctrine of specific intelligences by surrounding the President of the United States with counselors of different expertise—economists, social scientists, physicists—assuming that insight into inflation is most likely to come from the person who has gained knowledge in economics. As citizens we tend to seek advice from varied people according to the problem. We ask for help with our fears from a psychiatrist, help with our investments from a broker, and advice on building a house from an architect. However, there are still lingering beliefs in a generalized intelligence, for the society is still willing to listen to the advice of a Nobel laureate in physics on how to solve the racial crisis in our schools, as if brilliance of insight into atomic structure indicated profound understanding of social psychological problems.

It is this issue that captures the intense controversy surrounding the current use of intelligence and the value of the IQ score. Parents and teachers who believe that intelligence reflects the capacity to learn new skills with ease are often impressed with the intelligence test because the IQ score of a 10-year-old does predict, to some degree, his grades in high school and college. Is this possible because there is a general ability to learn that is stable over time and domain? Or is it possible because the skills that are taught in most high schools and college are intimately related to the skills measured on the intelligence test? The ability of the IQ obtained at age 10 to predict high school English grades may merely reflect a specific intelligence. In this case, it is the capacity to master English concepts and vocabulary. One reason why this last conclusion is attractive is that there is no question on the standard IQ test that requires the child to learn any new concept, idea, or skill.

THE IQ TEST The notion that the IQ score defines intelligence is much different from the three conceptions considered above. Unfortunately, it has gained wide acceptance by Americans. The typical American parent is anxious about his child's IQ and attributes more value and mystique to it than to most characteristics his child possesses. Many believe that a person's IQ score is inherited, does not change very much over the course of a life, and can be measured in early infancy. These beliefs are gross exaggerations of the truth. Although most people regard intelligence as the ability to learn a new skill as a result of experience, the majority of questions on intelligence tests do not require any new learning, but ask the child whether he knows a particular segment of knowledge. Hence the IQ test does not measure the central attribute that most people believe defines intelligence.

However, the intelligence test is an excellent measure of how much the child has learned about the dominant concepts in his culture. That is why the IQ score is a good predictor of school grades.

Since middle-class children are more consistently encouraged than are lower-class children to learn to read, spell, add, and write, rather than to keep away from police or defend oneself from peers, the child's IQ, social class, and school grades are all positively related. The IQ is an efficient way to summarize the degree to which a child has learned the vocabulary, beliefs, and rules of middle-class American society. The IQ is extremely useful because it can predict how easily a child of 8 years will master the elements of calculus or history when he enters college. However, the specific questions asked on intelligence tests have been chosen deliberately to make this prediction possible. The child is asked to define the word "shilling" rather than the word "rap"; he is asked to state the similarity between a "fly" and a "tree," rather than the similarity between "fuzz" and "Uncle Tom"; he is asked what he should do if he lost one of his friend's toys, rather than what he should do if he were attacked by three bullies. IQ tests are not to be discarded merely because they are biased toward measuring knowledge that middle-class white Americans value and promote. But both parents and teacher should appreciate the arbitrary content of the test. It is not unreasonable that if the printed word becomes subordinate to tape recorders and television as ways to present knowledge, 100 years from now our culture—in the same way as the early Greek orators—might place higher value on the ability to imagine a visual scene than on richness of vocabulary. We may have a different test of intelligence a century hence because the skills necessary to adapt successfully will have changed. Perhaps the groups we call intelligent at that time will be different from those who have that label today.

We can only hope that public preschool centers will acknowledge that quality of intellect is relative to the demands of the culture and that these centers will promote pluralism in curricular content and educational goals. As indicated earlier, one way to protect against uniformity of philosophy is to have parents actively involved in the educational planning.

It will always be true that some people will be better adapted to the society in which they live than others, and man is likely to attribute their more successful adaptation to the possession of a set of superior talents. The society will then make a test to measure these talents and label the score as an index of "intelligence." This process is bound to continue as long as man continues to evaluate himself and others. What will change is the list of talents he selects to celebrate.

MOTIVATION

Let us, in the final pages, examine briefly the two problems surrounding the relation between motivation and the issue of enrichment. The pivotal assumption can be stated plainly:

> *Too many poor children in our country enter school with minimal motivation to master school tasks and no expectancy of succeeding.*

Since the school directs its tutoring procedures toward the average child, the second grader who has not learned to read or write is hopelessly behind four years later. Perhaps 5% to 7% of these children, but probably no more, have subtle nervous-system pathology that is undiagnosed, and normal curricular procedures may have less startling success with these children than with normal ones. But the vast majority of children who fail to show satisfactory progress in school do so because they enter that embattled house with frail motivation for mastering the arbitrary requirements of the primary grades, and a high expectancy of failure. But these children are motivated for some goals, and the teacher must graft a desire to read to the wishes that happen to be dominant. Motives, in the most general sense, are desired goals the child is uncertain of attaining. Many of the desirable things we seek are experiences we are not sure we can attain. During each successive stage in development, the profile of these uncertain delights changes, and so do the salient motives. The typical five-year-old is uncertain about his sex-role identity and whether he will be accepted and respected by extrafamilial adults. Hence he is motivated to acquire traits and skills that help define his masculinity (or femininity) and help him gain signs of acceptance from others. The teacher, and I use this term in its most general sense, should capitalize on these motives. The best structure for a young child in a learning situation is a one-to-one relationship with an adult. Such an arrangement is most likely to convince the child that the adult is aware of his existence and cares about his victories, joys, doubts, and fears. A one-to-one arrangement is most likely to persuade the five-year-old that intellectual skills are appropriate to his burgeoning identity and most likely to guarantee that his smallest victory will be praised. These experiences can thwart the temptation to withdraw, which continually shadows potential failure.

Since we do not have enough certified teachers to meet the one-to-one requirement for every child we must use high school and college students, parents, and interested adults in the neighborhood as part of a nation-wide plan. This suggestion is practical, economical, and a reasonable derivative from theory. It is difficult to understand why we did not think of it earlier. The goal of the tutor, be he student, parent, or neither, is to persuade the child to involve himself in a cognitive activity so that he can produce evidence of the competence hidden within him.

If there is anything new to these ideas, it is the simple plea that we stop thinking of the disadvantaged child as having a deficit in words or numbers that has to be "made up," a mental cavity that has to be filled, as we feed a child deprived of protein or carbohydrate. A more appropriate image is the tempting of a shy deer out from behind a tree in order to try our menu, in the hope that it will come to prefer it to its usual diet. Persuasion, not enrichment, should be the essence of educational procedures. We must convince a great many young children that the attainment of the intellectual talents that our society happens to promote holds a potential for joy, since mastery of the competences valued by a culture can be one route to the self-actualization that everyone requires.

If we are successful, we will be able to use de Gourmont's (1953) criteria for documenting our victory, for he suggests that, "to judge how high a child's talent will reach do not attend so much to his greater and smaller facility for assimilating technical notions, but watch to see whether his eyes are occasionally clouded with tears of enthusiasm for the work."

CHILDREN HAVE WAYS
OF UNDERSTANDING THEIR WORLD

KENNETH D. WANN
MIRIAM S. DORN
ELIZABETH A. LIDDLE

The lack of emphasis on the intellectual in educational programs for young children results from some very basic ideas of what young children can know and understand about the world. These have come from a number of sources and they tend to limit the interest and concern for mental development in this early period. Foremost among these ideas is the contention that children are not capable of critical thinking before seven or eight years of age. Those following this line of thinking hold that children below this age are not capable of critically interpreting the world they observe around them. They do not seek to understand cause and effect relationships. They rely on magic to answer questions about their world or to explain phenomena they observe. Animism is considered a characteristic of young children's interpretations of things about them.

Another idea of young children's abililty to understand their world holds that they can know only about their "here and now world." The here-and-now idea in early childhood education served a useful purpose when it was first introduced. It was emphasized to call attention to the great importance of helping children to become alert and sensitive to the world in which they lived. It was a reaction against content for children that had become highly abstract and removed from their daily experiences. Enabling children to utilize the immediate environment was seen as a means of understanding those things more remote in time and space. Unfortunately, however, this has become a limiting notion. To many people it suggests that young children can know only about their touch-and-see environment. It suggests that they are not capable of learning from vicarious experiences. They can learn only as they can see, touch, or otherwise experience at firsthand. They must be in contact in order to know. This idea can easily cause the educator of young children to overemphasize manipulative experiences for young children. From this emphasis it is all too easy to settle for a nursery school or kindergarten program based on sheer manipulation of certain materials.

A third idea of children's ability to understand their world and which limits concern for young children's intellectual development holds that their intellectual abilities extend no further than enumeration and identification. Adults frequently operate as if children can know only facts about "what is." An examination of science or social studies materials written for five- and six-year olds will verify this contention. These materials identify and elaborate the obvious. One book written for six-year olds uses five pages to "teach" children that they have four grandparents. Another uses several pages to identify the different colors of hair to be seen on the heads of people or the bodies of animals. The goal in this latter case is to "teach" children that people and animals differ in appearance, a fact children observe daily. We develop units of study in which we devote considerable time to identifying and enumerating the community helpers and landmarks in the community. On the other hand, when we listen to young children we find that most of their questions are "how" and "why" questions indicating a desire for a more penetrating understanding than simply being content with identification of "what is." These are the questions adults find very hard to answer for children because they believe the children cannot understand sufficiently the explanations required.

There are many reasons for questioning the validity of these ideas about the intellectual abilities of young children. Today's children live in a world that is vastly different from the world of a generation or two ago when these ideas about children's thinking were developing. Many factors make it possible for children to know more today at an earlier age. Young children have experiences now that were unheard of in the past. Their curiosities, their abilities to reason and think and make sense of their world are challenged today as they have never been before.

Today's children are bombarded by information. The advancement of science and technology, the compactness of living, the ease of communication, the closeness of the entire world because of speed of travel, and other new developments cry out to the children to look, test, and learn. What a stimulating world it is for those who want to know the why, what, and how of things. This is also a rapidly changing world. Every day new discoveries are being made and announced. Children in nursery schools and kindergartens today are space-age children.

HOW WE STUDIED CHILDREN'S
UNDERSTANDING OF THEIR WORLD

Our concern that we might be underestimating young children's ability to understand and interpret their world and as a consequence unnecessarily limiting their experiences sent us off to study how young children respond to their physical and social environment. We wanted to study their ways of thinking and the means by which they deal with their world of people and things. We were also interested in what they know about their world and how they use their information.

Three-, four-, and five-year-old children enrolled in five schools were studied. The schools were in communities of widely varying socio-economic levels. Three of the schools were day care centers. One was located in a community where the economic level was extremely low. The five schools had a total enrollment of 319 children. Anecdotal recordings were made on 233 children, or roughly 73 per cent of the entire enrollment. The test situations were administered to the total population.

Action research was the essential method employed. The evolving plan of research and action relied heavily on the participation of classroom teachers from the five schools involved in the study. Participation of a school was contingent on the interest and willingness of the teachers to study the children in their classrooms. In each school the director and teachers worked closely with the research team in defining each phase of the study and in developing research procedures. Many hours were spent in meetings devoted to improving observational techniques and developing means whereby teachers might effectively record their observations and at the same time carry on their classroom responsibilities.

This study was launched to test the growing belief that children could know more at this early period than many educators believed possible. The belief grew from observations which pointed to the great range of interest and knowledge of young children and to the apparent satisfactions they derived from gaining and possessing information. The relative lack of concern in nursery schools and kindergartens for extending and clarifying their understandings and information was a source of concern for the researchers.

Certainly, the research team did not believe nursery schools and kindergartens were completely lacking in interest and concern for the mental development of children. All schools for young children provide equipment and experiences for furthering this aspect of their development. For example, blocks are excellent for learning to recognize spatial relationships. Models of automobiles and trains and a variety of wheel toys give children play experiences with concrete materials which provide first steps for later development of abstract ideas. The arts have their beginnings in the early childhood years with impressionistic tempora paintings, clay animals, and collages full of fluffy cotton and gilt paper. The sciences are recognized, and a well-equipped room is invariably stocked with magnets, batteries, pots of plants, and a cage with an animal of some sort. There are also experiences in the social studies. Children are helped to categorize and formalize information about their mothers and fathers and sisters and brothers and they learn that the supermarket man, the shoemaker, the policeman are called "community helpers."

While equipment such as easels, blocks, potted plants, clay and puzzles can suggest content for mental stimulation, the emphasis often has not really been in this direction. Using clay or fingerpaint is considered to have a therapeutic value, to be a good release on "rainy days." Blocks are valued for helping children to play in groups and share in dramatic play. Stringing beads is a pastime to promote small-muscle coordination. In many cases science and social studies receive only minor emphasis.

KNOWLEDGE IS SATISFYING

Having information and being able to use it in appropriate ways was a source of great satisfaction to the children. Evidence for this conclusion comes from numerous recordings of occasions when children expressed pleasure at having gained information or at the prospect of learning. The five-year old's remark, "Oh, boy, dinosaurs," after the teacher had been persuaded to read another book about their favorite topic is a case in point. The great frequency with which children made a game out of testing their own or another's information is further evidence of satisfaction derived from having certain knowledge. The conversation of young children which begins with "You know what," or "Guess what," and ends with the disclosure of precious information was a frequent occurrence among the children. Emmy's greeting on a rainy winter morning illustrates this type of conversation.

EMMY: *You know what I heard over the radio this morning?*
TEACHER: *What?*
EMMY: *It's going to get cold and slippery.*
TEACHER: *Why is it going to get slippery?*
EMMY: *It's going to freeze.*
TEACHER: *What is going to freeze?*
EMMY: *Oh, the rain, because it's raining this morning and it will be slippery.*

CHILDREN USE THEIR INFORMATION IN DRAMATIC PLAY

Further evidence of the satisfaction which children derived from the possession and use of knowledge resides in the spontaneous way in which they used and tested their information. Dramatic play was an important means for testing and expressing what they know. Such play has long been considered an excellent way to help children gain insights into the behavior of themselves and others, to learn how to get along with one another as they dramatize experiences involving conflict and cooperation. It has been seen as a security-building device when children are helped to work through by means of play a life situation which might involve elements of threat. Dramatic play is recognized as a means of emotional release and children who need release are helped to let go their pent-up feeling of aggression or resentment toward their dolls or other inanimate accompaniments of play.

The children frequently used dramatic play in still another way. They found it a satisfying means to further their own intellectual development. It became a way to test and clarify and to extend their information.

Jim's conversation with his four-year-old friends during a block-building experience is an illustration:

Let's build a blimp and I'll be the driver. The driver sits in the back. We'll fill it with hydrogen. You know a zeppelin is filled with hydrogen.

And there is the incident where four-year-old Minnie, having seen "Around the World in 80 Days," is teaching her friend, Wesley, about bull fighting as they play with a piece of red cloth. "Now, you hold it this way. You see, bulls don't like red."

As we listened to such conversations as these we came to appreciate more and more the great capacity of young children for retaining and putting together information. Such inaccuracies as placing the Dutch "fifty total" miles away and the "driver" in the rear of his blimp or mixed concepts such as placing Florida and New York in the category of countries confirmed the need of young children for help in clarifying and interpreting what they are seeing and hearing on every hand.

CHILDREN USE THE ESSENTIAL PROCESSES OF CONCEPTUALIZATION

Just as it is important to make it possible for children to extend their knowledge and understanding so it is important to provide help and guidance in the interpretation and use of the information. Evidence from our study points to young children's struggles with the processes of thinking and reasoning. The complexities of their environment demand that they understand cause and effect relationships and that they seek reasonable explanations for what they see. The great amount of information with which they are bombarded must be put together into some kind of understandable whole. Three-, four- and five-year-old children were doing associative thinking and struggling to reach reasonable and logical conclusions in their attempt to explain satisfactorily observations of their surroundings. We have evidence that children were associating ideas; they were trying to see likenesses and differences in things and events; they were working on cause and effect relationships; and they were drawing conclusions and generalizing about their activities.

CHILDREN ASSOCIATE IDEAS

The process of seeing relationships was an active one. The examples given here are typical of a large number recorded for this study.

> *Dan, three years of age, was playing with dough. He picked up a star-shaped cookie cutter and observed, "Stars sometimes come out at night." He proceeded with his play and rolled out a round, flat piece of dough whereupon he observed further, "Looks like a moon in the sky."*

It is obvious that Dan is in the process of putting together these phenomena which he has observed at night.

CHILDREN CLASSIFY

Accompanying the process of relating ideas in concept development must be the process of discriminating between what is related and what is not related. Viewed in this light concept development is partially a process of classifying ideas. This is by no means a simple process especially when, as in the case of young children, experiences and vocabulary are limited. But young children work at this process. Our observations revealed attempts by young children to see likenesses and differences, to set up classes of things, and to rule out those things which to them did not make sense. The following illustration reflects children's attempts to see likenesses and differences and to make classifications.

> Susan, John, and Paul, also four years of age, were sitting "reading" Curious George Takes a Job.
> JOHN: *Is that an alligator or a crocodile?*
> PAUL: *It's a crocodile.*
> SUSAN: *Alligators have feet and hands and crocodiles don't.*

Susan's attempt to help her friends distinguish between alligators and crocodiles although not based on accurate information suggests to us the kind of clues and points of differentiation young children seek in their attempts to classify.

CHILDREN GENERALIZE

Numerous anecdotes were recorded in which children were generalizing. In many cases the generalizations were accurate and well based. In others the generalizations were premature and inaccurate. It was noteworthy, however, how frequently young children attempted to use this process since it is an essential element in concept formation. The inaccuracies and the too hasty generalizing simply indicated a need for help which adults can supply. Children, three, four, and five years of age were actively attempting to make generalizations.

> The children were in the hall waiting for an elevator. Miss Smith yawned, Billy yawned, Susan said, "I am tired too.

> On Friday the teacher in this day care center remained late in the day so she always arrived later on other days.
> ALICE: *Today we are going to eat fish.*
> MARIA: *Why?*
> ALICE: *Because when the teacher comes late we always eat fish.*

> The children were being served dessert. Phillip, looking at a dish of red Jello, said, "Oh, boy! Red! Right, teacher, this is red?"
> "Yes," replied the teacher.
> "Jello is red! Jello is red!" exclaimed Phillip.

CHILDREN ATTEMPT TO REACH LOGICAL CONCLUSIONS

Essential to the development of understanding and the successful interpretation of environmental data is the ability to see cause and effect relationships, to make inferences and to reach logical conclusions. We found children attempting to utilize these processes in dealing with their environment.

> *The children were talking about what they had for breakfast.*
> KAREN: *I had toast, eggs, milk, and fruit for breakfast.*
> LAURA: *I guess you were late for school trying to eat all that food.*

There were situations in which children were able to reason through several steps and arrive at sound conclusions.

> *Three-year-old Victor liked desserts very much. The policy in his school was to allow second helpings of all food except dessert. One day during lunch time he engaged the teacher in the following conversation. She was not quite prepared for the last question.*
> VICTOR: *My mother told me that spinach is good for me. Is that true?*
> TEACHER: *Yes, it is good for you.*
> VICTOR: *Are those potatoes good for me too?*
> TEACHER: *Yes, they are.*
> VICTOR: *Is this meat good too?*
> TEACHER: *Yes, it is.*
> VICTOR: *Is dessert good for me?*
> TEACHER: *Of course it is.*
> VICTOR: *Why can't we ask for more dessert from the kitchen?*

Many of the conclusions children reach are not logical and many of their concepts are inaccurate and inadequate according to adult standards. This is a natural consequence, since children are slowly building concepts about a complex world. They have nothing to start with and must add each new learning bit by bit. Their young age and more or less limited experience give them very little understanding against which to test the accuracy of their conclusions. From their own standpoint the conclusion seems logical and accurate. Each new experience extends understanding in some area, thus broadening the base and helping to modify and extend concepts. This process continues through adulthood for it is continually necessary to extend and modify existing concepts. Viewed in this light it is easier to recognize the fundamental nature of the process we have observed in children. It becomes easier to be serious with children about their struggles to understand and to resist considering their "boners" as simply delightful stories about young children. These stories are cues for adults to help with this important process.

15   CELIA B. STENDLER-LAVATELLI

The past ten years have seen a tremendous upsurge of interest in the work of Piaget, due in large part to America's increasing concern, following Sputnik, with the intellective development of children. The interest has centered not so much on Piaget's early work on language, judgment, and reasoning and moral development of the child (1926, 1928, 1932), as on his research into the psychology of intelligence (1950) and, with Inhelder and others, the development of logical thinking (1958, 1964). This is not to leave the reader with the impression that there was a gap in Piaget's productivity or that his interests took a turn in the last two decades. A glance over his very impressive bibliography (Flavell, 1963) shows steady production and persistent interest in problems of epistemology. His main concern is and always has been with questions of how does the child acquire knowledge and what happens to mental processes during the acquisition. Unfortunately, translations of his works have been limited to a few books, and publication involves an inevitable time lag. Gradual evolution of his theory has led him to his present investigations into the relations between perception and intelligence (1961) and the role of mental image in the development of cognitive structures, but reports on these investigations are not yet available in English.

Increased interest in Piaget has met with mixed reception. On the one hand, there are those who would dismiss his work as unworthy of the attention of either psychologists or professional educators because he has not tested an adequate sample and has not done carefully controlled research. But Piaget's theory is not founded on seemingly casual observations of children; research on large numbers of children has been conducted in Geneva, although only one report has been translated into English. Nor does his clinical method permit as much freedom to the experimenter as critics would make it appear. In the clinical method, a child is presented with a task to which he makes some kind of response; what the experimenter does next depends upon that response. But over the years, Piaget has discovered the type of response that is likely to be given, and directions for administering the task take into account the possibility of alternative responses.

On the other hand, there are critics who now attribute to Piaget every innovation in American education, from the emphasis upon teaching children the structure of subject matter to team teaching. The truth of the matter is that Piaget himself stoutly maintains in his lectures that he is not a pedagogue and that he does not concern himself with applications of his theory to problems of education. He acknowledges that there are, of course, implications for the education of children in what he has written, and he hopes that those in pedagogy will concern themselves with the task of searching out these implications. This paper considers those aspects of his theory that hold the most promise for application in the classroom.

From the wealth of ideas Piaget has given us, there are three in particular that are most relevant to problems of teacher education: his concept of intelligence, his concept of the properties of logical thought, and his concept of stages in the development of logical thinking.

PIAGET'S CONCEPT OF INTELLIGENCE

For Piaget, intelligence is a form of adaptation, a particular instance of biological adaptation (1952) involving a striving for equilibrium and mental organization.

As an individual acts upon his environment, certain elements from the experience are stored in mental structures. Construction of mental structures begins at birth, with new elements from fresh experiences being incorporated into those structures. These new elements upset equilibrium, but as old structures are altered according to the reality conditions being experienced at the time, equilibrium is restored. Piaget postulates twin processes—assimilation and accommodation—as being at work here, with assimilation the process by which information is taken into mental structures, and accommodation the modification of the thought patterns to adapt to reality. The reader of this paper may have brought to his reading a mental structure of what constitutes intelligence that is quite different from the concept being presented here. If he acts upon Piaget's notion and mentally digests its elements, equilibrium in mental organization will be upset. With a modification of the old concept to accommodate the new, a changed concept of what is intelligence emerges.

Self-activity is crucial in the adaptive process; for Piaget, "Penser, c'est opérer." If equilibrium is to be achieved at a higher level, then the child must be mentally active; *he* must transform the data. The elements to be incorporated may be present in an experience or the child may be *told* of the error in his thinking, but unless his mind is actively engaged in wrestling with data, no accommodation occurs. Children, like adults, are not convinced by being told they are wrong, nor by merely seeing evidence that contradicts their thinking. They have to act upon the data and transform them, and in so doing, make their own discoveries. As Piaget puts it, knowledge is not a copy of reality; to know something is to modify external reality (Ripple & Rockcastle, 1964). Knowledge always involves a mental operation which permits one to transform what one sees in the light of what one already knows. These operations are not the same at all ages; the thought of the young child and that of the adult are, hopefully, very different. Piaget describes the changes that occur with age in terms of stages; before turning to a description of the stages, it is necessary first to examine the properties of logical thought.

THE PROPERTIES OF LOGICAL THOUGHT

Piaget's model of logical thought is a logico-mathematical one. He sees the same properties in thought structures that have been identified in alegbraic structures. What do we do when we think logically? We perform some mental action upon data; we shift data about in our minds, performing displacements upon them. We put two and two together, figuratively speaking, to arrive at a conclusion. Or, we arrange things in some kind of order—perhaps a temporal one—thinking of which event happened first, which next, and so on, so that we may think about a problem in a more systematic way. Or, someone makes a sweeping analogy in the course of conversation, comparing race relations in the South and in the North. The mind then does a one-to-one correspondence between elements in each racial situation in an attempt to see whether or not they are identical. Or, the problem comes up of what is responsible for an increase in language problems among children entering kindergarten. Not only must we check out certain obvious variables to see if each is a contributing factor, but we must also check to make sure that the less obvious is not a factor. We must ask ourselves how we know it isn't such-and-such a thing. All of these are examples of operations performed upon data to arrive at consistent, noncontradictory—that is to say, logical—conclusions.

Piaget has systematically analyzed logical operations and described for us a grouplike structure that mirrors the thought of the child. The structure is not the same for children of all ages. During some of the elementary school years (7 to 12), certain mental operations are apparent in the child's thinking, operations which together form an ensemble or group.

One of the operations, reversibility, is for Piaget one of the most critical to develop. Every change, every displacement that we carry on mentally is reversible. We can combine robins and all-birds-not-robins to make up a class of birds, and we can also separate the class into the original subclasses.

Several of the tasks developed by Piaget to discover how the child thinks about a problem involve the conservation principle. An illustration of the conservation principle is the fact that such properties of matter as amount of substance, weight, and volume are conserved even with a transformation in appearance. Thus a ball of clay rolled into a hot-dog shape will contain the same amount of substance and weigh the same as it did to begin with. How do we know? Logically, it has to be the same, for the rolling-out process can be reversed and the hot dog restored to the ball.

This is exactly how the child solves the problem; he uses a reversible mental operation.

Logical operations, however, form a grouplike structure, and reversibility is not an isolated phenomenon. Present the conservation of weight problem to a nine-year-old, and his answer may go something like this: "They've got to weigh the same. The hot dog is longer, but it's skinnier, and that makes up for its being longer. Just put it back into a ball, and you'll see that it's the same." In other words, in shuffling the data about, not only is a reversible operation performed, but the child also sees that the hot dog is made of bits and pieces of clay (additive composition) that can be put together in various ways without a change in weight. The first is the operation of additive composition, and the second is the associative operation: the mind can reach the same goal by different paths. A change in one dimension can be compensated for by change in another.

Or, one can think about the clay-ball problem in still a different way. A child may say, "It's got to be the same. You didn't add anything, and you didn't take anything away, so there can't be a weight difference." Here the operation is one of identity.

What the child is doing here as he works on the problem is actually to perform one or more operations in his mind. He may reverse a process, or combine elements to make a whole, or put elements together in different ways, or perform an identity operation where two sets *must* be the same if there is a one-to-one correspondence between parts and all the parts are accounted for. To these four properties of logical thought—reversibility, additive composition, associativity, and identity—there is added a fifth, a case of special identities or tautology, which affirms the equivalence of members of a class. A class of red objects is still a class of red objects when more red objects are added. To call a spade a spade, figuratively speaking, means that we haven't changed the class with additions we make, provided the additions are identical in quality.

When a child is presented with one of the Piaget tasks, an analysis of his responses is made for evidence that his thinking is distinguished by these properties of logical thinking. Thus in the volumes by Piaget (1952, 1957) and those written with Inhelder (1958, 1964) we can find the gradual emergence of logical operations as the child matures. The most thorough and best analysis of the logic involved in the practical operations characteristic of seven-to-twelve-year-olds is to be found in Flavell's *The developmental Psychology of Jean Piaget* (1963), Chapter 5.

The operations described above characterize the child's thinking during most of the elementary school years, but during adolescence, changes occur in modes of thinking. Piaget describes the thought processes that emerge at this time as *propositional thinking*. The adolescent states propositions in terms of the variables he has identified and then proceeds systematically to combine the propositions so as to test all possible combinations.

There are four ways in which propositions can be combined. We can combine by conjunction, as when we say, "It's got to be this and this"; by disjunction, "It's got to be this or this"; by negation, "It's neither this nor this"; and by implication, "If it's this, then this will be true." In addition to combining propositions in these four different ways, we can also transform each of the combinations in four different ways, yielding a possibility of sixteen different products.

STAGES IN DEVELOPMENT OF LOGICAL INTELLIGENCE

From the foregoing analysis of logical thinking, it should be obvious that human beings are not capable of such thought processes at birth. For Piaget they develop in stages; he regards logical thinking as the greatest attribute of man, and his account of stages in the development of mental operations is geared toward the individual's growth in ability to think in this fashion. There are four main stages: the sensorimotor, the preoperational, the stage of concrete operations, and the stage of formal operations.

Piaget finds the origins of logical intelligence in the sensorimotor period. The infant comes into the world with two kinds of reflexes: those like the knee jerk that are not altered by experience, and others like grasping and sucking that are modified as the infant exercises them. The modification occurs through assimilation and accommodation. The infant, for example, accommodates the grasping reflex to the shape of the object to be grasped, curving the fingers in one way for a long, narrow object, and in a different way for a plastic play ring. Later, looking and grasping become coordinated; the infant can put out his hand and grasp that which he sees. Each newly discovered experience brings with it a need to repeat the experience; activity begets activity. And as the infant operates upon the physical world with his sensorimotor system, he acquires notions of objects, space, time, and causality. Ask a ten-month-old baby, "Where's Mommy?" and he looks toward the door through which Mommy has just disappeared; he "thinks" about the concepts of time and objects with his motor system, i.e., Mommy was here but is not now. However, she still exists. Objects have a permanence and do not cease to exist when out of sight.

During the sensorimotor period, the infant lays the foundation for later representational thought. Structures are built which are essential for the mental operations carried on at a later stage of development. The sensorimotor foundation of one structure that adults recognize most easily is that involved in orienting ourselves in space. A person giving directions to a motorist will often turn his body and put out his hands as he "thinks" with his motor system which way to direct the questioner. With a mental map, the need for a motor accompaniment to thinking disappears; thought has become representational. But the structures which enable the school child to deal with space are laid in the sensorimotor period. The concept of a grid system, of an object being displaced in both horizontal and vertical direction, has its primitive beginnings in infant actions.

Gradually actions become internalized; the child can represent in thought processes that which was first developed on the sensorimotor system. This second stage begins at eighteen months and extends to seven years of age (roughly). It is in this stage that we find most kindergarten and first-grade children; some second-grade; and of course, some children even older that seven years. This stage is called preoperational because the child does not use logical operations in his thinking. Piaget characterizes mental processes at the preoperational stage as follows:

1   The child is perceptually oriented; he makes judgments in terms of how things look to him. Piaget has shown that perceptual judgment enters into the child's thinking about space, time, number, and causality. It is only as the child goes beyond his perceptions to perform displacements upon the data in his mind that conservation appears.
2   The child centers on one variable only, and usually the variable that stands out visually; he lacks the ability to coordinate variables.
3   The child has difficulty in realizing that an object can possess more than one property, and that multiplicative classifications are possible. The operation of combining elements to form a whole and then seeing a part in relation to the whole has not yet developed, and so hierarchial relationships cannot be mastered.

So far this consideration of preoperational thinking has been largely negative. We have seen that the child lacks the ability to combine parts into a whole, to put parts together in different ways, and to reverse processes. What, then, can the child do. The development of logical processes is not at a standstill during this period and there are some positive accomplishments. We see, for example, the rudiments of classification; the child can make collections of things on the basis of some criterion. He can also shift that criterion. Thus, if we present a kindergarten child with a collection of pink and blue squares and circles, some large and some small, and ask him to sort them into two piles with those in each pile being alike in some way, he can usually make two different collections on the basis of color and shape (a few children discover the third criterion of size). Such an ability, of course, is essential to the formation of classes and eventually to the notion of hierarchy of classes.

The child is also beginning to arrange things in a series. He can compare two members of a set within a series when they are in consecutive order; he knows that Tuesday comes after Monday. But since Friday comes after Tuesday, which is after Monday, does Friday also come after Monday? This operation, involving seeing logical relations between things or events that are arranged in a series, is not yet possible to the preoperational child, but experiences with seriation are preparatory to the development of such operations.

By seven years of age, the logical operations of reversibility, associativity, etc., that I have already described, begin to appear. Piaget calls this the stage of concrete operations, because while the child uses logical operations, the content of his thinking is concrete rather than abstract. Fifth-grade pupils, if given a billiard-game problem when they are studying light, can do serial ordering, and establish a one-to-one correspondence between the two slopes of directions. "The more I put it like that (inclined to the right), the more the ball will go like that," a ten-year-old will explain. That the total angle can be divided into two equal angles does not occur to them, for they lack the formal operations necessary to such a discovery. They solve problems and give explanations in terms of the concrete data available to them; they do not try to state generalizations.

This stage of concrete operations lasts until twelve years, which is roughly the age for the onset of the stage of formal operations or propositional thinking. According to Piaget, most children at the high school level tend to do the if-this-happens-then-that-is-likely-to-happen (or not happen) kind of thinking. They are also more likely to think in terms of abstractions and can state, as in the case of the billiard game, the general principle involved.

Critics of Piaget have made this notion of development as occurring in stages one of their targets. Some mistakenly think that he uses the concept, as did Gesell, to refer to similarities among children of the same chronological age, with age being the critical antecedent of the similarities. As Kessen and Kuhlman (1962) point out, when the language of stages is used merely as a paraphrase for age variation, it is not useful. For Piaget, however, stages are convenient for helping us to think coherently about the course of development. His descriptions of stages are based upon changes in the child's comprehension of logic and emphasize sequence. They are not tied in any hard-and-fast way to age. In fact, as the students in Geneva discovered when they tried the Piaget tests on husbands, wives, or other adults, including themselves, adults are spotty in their logical development. Most adults have reached the stage of formal thought in solving many of the problems demanding logical solutions, but they may be a bit chagrined to discover that they are not even at the stage of concrete operations with respect to others. And with respect to operations at each of the stages, Piaget describes these in terms of probability; he would say that at a particular stage there is a probability which can be set at a certain figure that the child will select a particular strategy (not necessarily consciously) for solving a problem. Piaget explains the stage-age relationship in this fashion:

> *The age of seven is a relative one in a double sense. In our research we say that a problem is solved by children of a certain age when three-quarters of the children of this age respond correctly. As a result, to say that a question is solved at seven years old means that already one-half of the six-year-olds can solve it, and a third of the five-year-olds, etc. So, it's essentially relative to a statistical convention. Secondly, it's relative to the society in which one is working. We did our work in Geneva and the ages that I quote are the ages we found there. I know that in certain societies, for instance in Martinique, where our experiments have been done by Monique Laurendeau and Father Pinard, we have found a systematic delay of three or four years. Consequently the age at which those problems are solved is also relative to the society in question. What is important about these stages is the order of the succession. The mean chronological age is variable.*

The question arises, once we assume that age changes in logical thinking are not fixed, as to whether we can then speed up the development of logical thinking. This is a question that never fails to amuse students and faculty in Geneva, for they regard it as typically American. Tell an American that a child develops certain ways of thinking at seven, and he immediately sets about to try to develop those same ways of thinking at six or even five years of age. Actually investigators in other countries as well as in America have tried to accelerate the development of logical thinking, and we have available today a considerable body of research on what works and what doesn't work. Most of the research has not worked. Paper after paper reports the stubborn refusal of children to accept the conservation principle, despite a variety of training techniques. Efforts have not been successful because experimenters have not paid attention to the processes of assimilation and accommodation in equilibrium theory. The researchers have tried to teach a response rather than to develop operations. They have tried, for example, to teach the child that of course the hot dog will weigh as much as the clay ball; the subject can put both on a two-pan balance and get immediate feedback. But the child is completely unconvinced unless he acts upon the data in his mind, transforming them by means of one or more of the operations already described. In fact, an ingenious technique devised by Smedslund showed that external reinforcement leads only to a pseudo-concept. After children had been trained on the balance to give conservation responses, the experimenter tested each child by surreptitiously removing a piece of clay from the hot dog before it was put on the scale. The subjects who had learned the proper response immediately abandoned conservation in favor of perceptual judgment. Learning a fact by reinforcement does not in and of itself result in mental adaptation. Learning involves active assimilation resulting in momentary conflicts and compatibilities which the learner must himself resolve to reach a higher level of equilibrium.

What does work? Research by some investigators offers some promising leads. These might be summarized as follows:

1   It has been possible to accelerate the development of logical intelligence by inducing cognitive conflict in subjects. Smedslund (1961) devised a training procedure with the balls of clay where he both elongated the clay and also took away a piece of it, thus forcing the child to choose between two conflicting explanations. Can the hot dog weigh more when a piece has been taken away? Given this kind of choice, the child veers toward consistency. The number of successful cases was small, but they offered tentative support for the cognitive-conflict hypothesis.

2   Training children to recognize that an object can belong to several different classes at once aids in the development of logical classification. Morf (1959) and Sigel (1965) have had some success with this procedure. Sigel has worked with bright preschool children on conservation tasks, training them on certain logical operations considered to be prerequisite to conservation. Children were trained on multiple labeling, multiple classification, and multiplicative relations. For example, the teacher would first have a child label a piece of fruit, then another and another; then search for a class label; then define criteria of the class; and finally take the class apart and put it together according to various criteria. Only five children were trained, but four out of the five showed an increase in ability to deal with conservation tasks.

3   There is a tendency for conservation of number to be accelerated in children trained to see that addition and subtraction of elements change numerical value, and so, if nothing is added and nothing is taken away, number is conserved regardless of how the elements are arranged in space.

4   To help children move from the preoperational stage to the stage of concrete operations, it is helpful to make gradual transformations in the visual stimulus and to call the child's attention to the effects of a change in one dimension to a change in another.

Piaget himself has provided guidelines for acceleration of logical development in his identification of four factors that influence development from one stage to another. These factors help to explain individual differences in children's performance on the Piaget tasks.

MATURATION Maturation, defined as a ripening of neural structures with age, undoubtedly plays a part in the transformations in mental structures, and undoubtedly genes influence the ripening process. But maturation alone cannot account for changing mental structures. The Martinique studies (Laurendeau and Pinard, 1962), showing a four-year delay in development over the Geneva norms, reveal that maturation alone does not guarantee that children of a certain age will have reached a certain stage in logical development. And evidence from the Dennis (1960) studies in Teheran shows that maturation itself is dependent upon experience. Babies in an orphanage confined to cribs and terribly limited in motor experiences were shockingly retarded in age of onset of walking. Ripening of the nervous system is not something that is completely under control of the genes. A recent critical review by Moltz (1965) had this to say:

> An epigenetic approach holds that all response systems are synthe-sized during ontogeny and that this synthesis involves the integrative influence of both intraorganic processes and extrinsic stimulative conditions. It considers gene effects to be contingent on environmen-tal conditions and regards the genotype as capable of entering into different classes of relationships depending on the prevailing environ-mental context. In the epigeneticist's view, the environment is not benignly supportive, but actually implicated in determining the very structure and organization of each response system.

EXPERIENCE Piaget finds that experience alone is not enough to accelerate logical development, if experience is defined as exposure to objects or events only. There must be a logico-mathematical experience if logical structure is to develop. There must be a "total coordination of actions, actions of joining things together or ordering things, etc."

SOCIAL TRANSMISSION Social transmission is linguistic or educational trans-mission. Like the two preceding factors, this, too, plays a part in logical development, but it is not enough. As Piaget points out, young children hear everyday expressions involving whole-part relationship ("Champaign, Illinois"; "Some Indians lived in tepees"), but they do not understand the logic involved. Some Indians are no different for them from all Indians, and Champaign is not physically contained in Illinois. Linguistic transmis-sion is possible only when logical structures are present in children's thinking.

EQUILIBRIUM For Piaget, this is the critical factor. The three previously mentioned factors are necessary, but it is the mental activity of the subject when confronted with cognitive conflict and operating to compensate that determines the development of logical structures. Compensation is achieved through the operations of reversibility, etc., already described.

No attempt will be made here to spell out the implications of Piaget's theory for educators. Certainly his account of stages should be useful to curriculum makers interested not only in attending to subject matter to be mastered but also in providing for development of logical structures. And Piaget's equilibration theory should shake the faith in external reinforcements of all but the most orthodox of learning theorists. For the doubting Thomas, some experience in using external reinforcements to try to teach a child the conservation principle will prove to be shattering but rewarding.

COGNITIVE DEVELOPMENT AND LEARNING MATHEMATICS — 16 — RICHARD W. COPELAND

How does a youngster "learn" mathematics? Are his mental processes the same as those of an adult? Can we by a process of segmenting knowledge into simpler and simpler form come to a point where any child can understand it? This last question poses a premise that has sometimes been used as a basis for determining the level at which mathematics can be introduced to children. Mathematical content has been moved further and further down in the elementary grades.

Educators now recognize that a child is a developing organism and does not learn as a miniature adult. There are a number of limitations to his ability to solve problems. He may be unable to reverse a thought process, he has an egocentric outlook, he is unable to generalize, he needs concrete materials.

The man probably most responsible for our understanding of children's thinking as it relates to mathematics is Jean Piaget, a Swiss psychologist, biologist, and mathematician, now in his seventies (Copeland, 1970). He postulates that our mental processes work on the basis of a model similar to that of an electronic computer. This is in sharp contrast to Thorndyke's stimulus-response theory of learning.

In the stimulus-response theory the mind becomes a network of responses to myriad stimuli. Piaget maintains that cognitive development is more complex than this. The mind is not just a response mechanism. It is a logical structure, as is a computer, with feed forward, feed back, and branching networks. It can operate on its own in considering abstract problems without the necessity of prompting by stimuli from our external environment.

The logical structure of the child's mind is not the same as that of the adult, and it does not reach the adult stage of operation until 11 or 12 years of age. If this is true, instructional procedures for the child of less than 11 or 12 years must be planned on the basis of the level of development of the child.

STAGES OF DEVELOPMENT

Piaget finds several stages of development in children. The first is a *sensorimotor stage* lasting until approximately two years of age. The second is a *pre-operational stage* lasting from two until approximately seven years of age. The third is a *concrete operational stage* lasting on an average from seven to eleven years of age. Finally there is a *formal operational stage*, which is an adult level of thinking.

It is necessary that the teacher understand these stages and base the plan of her instructional program on the stage of development of each child in her class. Different children at different stages cannot learn the same content. They cannot learn about number, for example, until they reach the concrete operational stage.

The concrete operational stage marks a beginning of logical thought in children. Thinking logically is necessary to understand number. The transition from pre-logical to logical thought can be tested easily. The most pervasive concept, used by Piaget, as a basis for this test is the idea of *conservation* or *invariance*. It is a logical concept. Applying it as a test of conservation of number, the child is shown two sets of objects and asked if there are more objects in one set than in the other, or if the sets are the same:

X   X   X   X   X
X   X   X   X   X

The configuration of one set is then changed—for example, one set may be spread out—and the question repeated:

X   X   X   X   X
X   X   X   X   X

The child at the pre-operational level thinks there is more in the spread-out set. Sensory impressions are the basis for his answer. It looks like more since the objects cover a larger space. At the concrete operational level the child can use the "logic" that if there was the same number there is still the same number. Number is conserved, or invariant, as the shape or arrangement of the set of objects is changed.

Usually between six and seven years of age the child will reach the concrete operational level of thought as far as number is concerned. It is then that he can begin to learn about number in other than a rote fashion. At the pre-operational level the child may "count" the number of objects in each set, five, for example, and still tell you there are "more" in the spread-out set. It is obvious that the number 5 means little at this point of development. Many children in the first grade are still at this level, so that what passes as instruction in arithmetic may be wasted.

The child at the concrete operational level should have concrete objects as a basis for abstracting mathematical ideas; hence the name concrete operational level of thought. As the child manipulates objects he is at some point able to disengage the mathematical idea or structure involved. It is necessary for the child of four to eleven to begin learning about abstract mathematics inductively by using objects in the physical world. It is not sufficient to "tell" or "explain" or "show." The child should disengage the mathematics from the objects himself. This idea cannot be overemphasized because most of us are used to being "told" or having something "explained." According to Piaget, "Words are probably not a short cut to understanding; the level of understanding seems to modify the words that are used rather than vice-versa" [Duckworth, 1967, p. 319].

At approximately 11 or 12 years of age the child reaches the operational level of thought, at which time he can reason or consider at the abstract level without having to resort to the physical world. It is a hypothetical-deductive thought level. At this time it is possible to begin formal mathematics with some premise arbitrarily chosen and then to reason in deductive, logical steps. Such a level of thought, however, is not characteristic of the elementary school child.

TYPES OF KNOWLEDGE

In attempting to teach, it is necessary to differentiate between types of knowledge. Again, stages of development are crucial.

Knowledge of a sensorimotor type may be inherited or a part of the genetic structure, as exhibited by an infant's ability to suck, cry, and blink, for example. Just touching a baby's lips causes him to suck. Such responses are necessary for food and life.

A higher form of knowledge is physical knowledge—noting facts about objects based on their properties. Children learn colors at a relatively early age. Sensory impressions are sufficient to give them the correct answer. Going a step further, however, a child may observe that a piece of wood floats because "it is light" but may be unable to generalize and predicts that another piece of wood will sink because "it is heavy."

Logico-mathematical knowledge requires a higher level of thought because it may be independent of the physical properties of objects. In numbering sets of objects or considering the commutative property of addition, any objects can be used—blocks, beads, candy, and so forth. The physical properties are not important. It is the abstract property of number that is being considered. The child less than eight years old has great difficulty with the commutative property, unable to generalize that $a + b$ is equal to $b + a$ even when a and b are related to sets of objects. For example, "I give my doll four apples and two oranges. Now to be fair, give your doll just as much fruit, but since she likes oranges better, give her more oranges."

Similarly, concerning the transitive property, if *a* has a certain relation to *b* and *b* has that relation to *c*, then *a* has the same relation to *c* regardless of what *a*, *b*, and *c* are. To use such concepts the child must first reach the concrete operational level of thought. The teacher must differentiate between physical knowledge and logico-mathematical knowledge as she plans her lessons.

ACCELERATION OF LEARNING

Can the development of the child be "accelerated" so that he reaches the concrete operational level of thought earlier? Can conservation of number be "taught" earlier? A number of studies have been conducted on this subject, since America is a "hurry-up" country. Most of the studies find that little acceleration is possible (Almy, 1967; Elkind, 1968). Piaget does not even think it is desirable. There is, to him, an optimum time in each child's development for learning each concept.

Many teachers find it very difficult to accept this idea, thinking on the basis of the premise of the first paragraph above that if the idea is simplified enough the child can understand it. The writer observed a parent (also a teacher) attempting to teach conservation of number to her own four year old child until the child became very upset.

While seven has been given as an average age of the development of *conservation of number,* it is an average age and may occur at five and one half years for one child and at eight years for another. *Conservation of* other concepts such as *length, area,* and *distance* are also important. This variation in development suggests an individualized instructional program for maximum effectiveness.

As this was being written, an associate entered the author's office, much elated because his daughter had just been given the Stanford Binet Test and her score had jumped 40 percentile points. While there could be a number of reasons for this increase, such as test administration, the incident may point up a basic weakness of the test. If the child has moved from one basic stage of development to the next since the last testing, there may be quite a different performance. Tests which are more consistent with Piaget's theories are now being developed (Philips, 1969).

In a study of the cognitive development of Sioux Indian children, Voyat (1970) reported the following:

> The intellectual development of 70 children, ages 4 to 10, living on the Pine Ridge Indian Reservation, was studied using standard Piagetian tasks. Five conservation tasks (matter, liquid, weight, length, and one-to-one correspondence), two tests of special relations (geometrical drawings and perspective), and two tests of elementary logic (seriation and class inclusion) were administered.
>
> Contrary to the numerous studies which have shown Indian

children to have low IQ's, the Sioux children showed themselves to mature intellectually at about the same rate as Piaget's Geneva subjects. Also the succession of stages was shown to be clearly respected. Piaget's theory and many of his specific tasks were shown to be culturally fair. The test results will be discussed and contrasted to the poor school performance of many of the subjects [p. 124].

FACTORS AFFECTING LEARNING

While children are passing through the four basic stages of development just described, there are, according to Piaget, four factors important to what a child learns. These factors, such as experience or environment, may not speed up development, but they are necessary conditions for development to take place when it should. For example, some children at age 10 have not reached the stage of conservation of number. A proper environment in the form of a questioning teacher using physical objects such as counters should be available if the child is to reach this developmental stage at the normal age of six or seven.

The four basic factors involved in learning are *maturation, experience* with the physical world, *communication* with others such as the teacher, and *equilibration*. It is the last factor that is uniquely Piagetian. Consider again the child shown two sets of five counters that are equally spread out, and then two sets of five counters with one set spread out more than the other. Sensory perception tells him there is "more" in the spread-out set, but he has counted and found five counters in each set. There is an inconsistency. Finally he reasons that if there were five before and if there are still five, then logically the number of counters is the same. What it looks like must be deceiving. This reasoning process is an internal one. It accommodates or adjusts to the data at hand; logic, not sensory perception, produces the correct answer.

REVERSIBILITY OF THOUGHT

Many children do not have reversibility of thought at the nonconservation level. At the conservation level the child reasons that while the counters have been spread out they can be returned to their original position. Hence, the number of objects in the set has not changed. This conclusion results from a logical process. Similarly, if a child of seven or less is shown two sticks of the same length side by side, he agrees that they are the same length. But if one is moved further away, he usually "thinks" that it is now longer. He uses sensory perception as a basis for his answer, rather than the logic of reversibility or conservation of length, which would tell him that the stick could be moved back to where it was when it was the same length as the other stick.

Difficulty with reversibility is also readily apparent as the child attempts to learn addition. He can solve $3 + 2 = \square$ but is unable to solve $5 = 2 + \square$ or $2 + \square = 5$. Such addition and subtraction facts probably should not be taught until the child has achieved the necessary reversibility of thought, and this is often not in first grade. According to Piaget (1964):

> Addition is a reversible operation. There is therefore no more than a suggestion of it when, at the first stage, the child does not understand that a whole B divided into two parts A and A' is still the same whole $(B = A' + A; 5 = 3 + 2)$. The operation of addition comes into being when, on the one hand, the addenda are united in a whole $(3 + 2 = 5)$, and on the other, this whole is regarded as invariant irrespective of the distribution of its parts $(5 = 3 + 2 = 1 + 4 = 2 + 3 = 4 + 1)$ [p. 189].

The teacher can provide experiences for the child in joining and separating sets of objects and noting the number relationships involved. While this will probably not accelerate his cognitive development, it does provide the necessary physical or concrete experiences that precede understanding.

17

ELIZABETH FENNEMA   MANIPULATIVES IN THE CLASSROOM

Statements concerning the efficacy of manipulative materials in facilitating the learning of mathematical ideas abound in current mathematics education literature. Partly in response to such statements, mathematics laboratories, or activity-based curricula that include a heavy reliance on the use of such materials, are becoming more and more prevalent. This belief that manipulative materials do indeed enhance the learning of mathematics has gained much validity from learning theories such as those suggested by Bruner, Dienes, and Piaget. These theories strongly support the idea that children need physical involvement, such as might be provided by hands-on experiences with manipulative materials, in order to add new ideas to their cognitive structure. However, attempts to translate such theories into classroom practice and to empirically measure the results have not provided evidence that the use of such materials by teachers does indeed result in better learning than the use of symbols alone (Suydam & Weaver 1970; Kieren 1971; Fennema 1972). This difference between theory and research findings indicates that manipulative materials are no panacea; the use of materials does not automatically ensure that mathematics learning will follow. However, even without strong empirical support, a strong case can be built for the inclusion of manipulative materials in an elementary school mathematics program.

The most important reason for using manipulative materials in teaching is to make the abstract world of mathematics meaningful. This is done when such materials are used to enhance the relationship between symbols and reality. However, children should at some point learn to operate efficiently and effectively with symbols that represent the abstract nature of mathematics. For example, children should learn to understand what the numeral 9 means. In itself it has no meaning; it is merely a squiggle. However, it can represent nine discrete, real objects; a quantity greater than eight; or a quantity less than ten. It can be used in performing various mathematical operations and in interpreting a variety of real world situations—for example, what clothes to wear to school when it is 9°F outside. It should not be necessary to get out nine counters, a certain Cuisenaire rod, or any other material each time the number idea of 9 would be useful. In other words, symbols must become an integral part of the usable knowledge of each child. However, unless knowledge of these abstract mathematical symbols is based on meaningful, concrete experiences, children will be unable to use the symbols except in a cursory way. Manipulative materials can help to provide the real situations that enable a child to understand and effectively use symbols.

The mathematical ideas taught in the elementary school are not (or should not be) taught just as isolated ideas. A learned idea should facilitate learning of more advanced ideas and enable one to solve problems that lie outside the personal realm of experience; that is, learners should be able to transfer their learning. Although the process of transfer of learning is complex, it is of vital importance in the achievement of long-range goals such as the understanding of the wide applicability of mathematical ideas. One of the beauties of mathematics is that an abstraction such as $4 + 3 = 7$ can represent an infinite number of physical situations. For example, $4 + 3$ can represent 4 children and 3 children coming together, the length of a line when two lines of 3 and 4 feet are put together, or a total of 7 hours achieved by combining periods of 3 and 4 hours. Dienes (1971) believes that if mathematical ideas are learned as "a result of gathering together the common properties of a large variety of situations it is more likely that the final abstract concept will be applicable to a large variety of applications and situations" [pp. 30–31]. The use of manipulative materials in the classroom helps to provide the variety of situations that helps to ensure that the transfer of knowledge from learned to unlearned situations will occur.

The wide diversity of individual differences that exists in a classroom is well documented. There are differences in ability to learn, rate of learning, background of knowledge, and style of learning. To best provide for learning by children with so many differences, a variety of experiences must be available. Some individuals may learn certain ideas when they are represented by symbols, while other individuals may require a broader experience. The use of manipulative materials provides a diversity of learning environments, which permits a broader range of individuals to learn more readily than does the use of symbols alone. Acceptance of the idea that diversity of experiences is important leads to the conclusion that a variety of manipulative materials must be provided. No one set of manipulative materials is sufficient.

Improved motivation is another reason for using manipulative materials. Without the proper motivation, it is almost impossible to teach children to learn much mathematics. It is true that the learning of simple skills such as number facts or basic computational algorithms can be encouraged by extrinsic rewards. However, the broader goals of mathematics instruction, such as acquiring an understanding of the abstract interrelationships of mathematics or developing widely applicable skills in problem solving, can be reached only with great difficulty, if at all, unless children are intrinsically motivated to learn. Manipulative materials help to provide such motivation. One has only to take a set of Cuisenaire rods into a classroom of children to be aware of the motivating effects of materials. Manipulative materials attract attention and stimulate curiosity, both of which are important factors in arousing intrinsic motivation.

Attitude towards learning is closely related to motivation in learning. Children enter kindergarten or first grade with a positive feeling towards mathematics as a tool for handling their environment. However, this does not last. Neale (1969) hypothesizes, on the basis of several studies, that "current school programs result in a substantial decline in the favorableness of attitude toward learning mathematics as children progress in school" [p. 634]. Perhaps this decline in favorable attitude can be partly explained by the concurrent decline in the use of manipulative materials as children move through the grades.

Motivation and attitude are not unrelated to making mathematics meaningful. Certainly one has a more positive attitude and is more motivated to learn those ideas that are understandable and real. Nonsense information (which much mathematics often is to children) is difficult and boring to learn.

Another factor related to motivation and attitude is the child's self-concept. The role of self-concept, particularly in relation to the ability to solve problems, has become increasingly evident. Manipulative materials provide tools for problem solving. When a child has an aid to solve problems that is always available, his self-confidence is increased because he does not need to depend on the fallibility of his memory. The assurance of a child who is using his fingers (the most omnipresent manipulative materials), or any other manipulative material that he knows well, results in the belief that mathematics has meaning; mathematics is not just an abstract game played according to strange, unknowable rules that originated in the mysterious world of adults.

Having children demonstrate mathematical ideas with manipulative materials helps teachers gain insight into children's thinking. For example, consider a fifth-grade child who cannot remember the basic multiplication facts and, as a result, cannot progress towards mastery of the principle of multiplication of whole numbers. The teacher needs to know whether this blockage is caused by an incomplete knowledge of what multiplication is, or whether it is just an inability to commit the combinations to memory. With manipulative materials, such as counters of any type, the child can be asked to demonstrate how to find the answer to a simple multiplication problem. From the child's demonstration, it is often clearly evident whether he understands the principle of multiplication. If he does not understand the principle of multiplication, one type of remedial help is indicated. If he understands the principle, but does not know the necessary facts, a different kind of help is needed.

Despite the valid reasons for using manipulative materials, they should not be used in an elementary school mathematics program in a random, unorganized way that fails to attain important goals of mathematics instruction. Children should not learn merely to manipulate objects. Children should use this manipulation of objects as a means to learning important mathematical processes, principles, and skills. The use of manipulative materials is not an end in itself, and care must be taken that they do not become "seductive shibboleths" [Weaver, 1971, p. 263]. Hartung (1971) states that "mathematics is a conceptual subject and the physical activity that is used to promote learning is mainly a means to this end" [p. 280]. As Weaver (1971) says, "mathematics is essentially cognitive in nature; and the principal, distinguishing goals or objectives of mathematics instruction are (and should be) cognitive ones" [p. 263]. Only when manipulative materials help children understand the abstract nature of mathematics and assist them in becoming more efficient problem solvers is the use of manipulative materials justified.

PSYCHOLOGICAL CONTROVERSIES IN THE TEACHING OF SCIENCE AND MATHEMATICS 18 LEE S. SHULMAN

The popular press has discovered the discovery method of teaching. It is by now, for example, an annual ritual for the Education section of *Time* magazine to sound a peal of praise for learning by discovery (see, e.g., Pain and Progress in Discovery, 1967). *Time*'s hosannas for discovery are by no means unique, reflecting as they do the educational establishment's general tendency to make good things seem better than they are. Since even the soundest of methods can be brought to premature mortality through an overdose of unremitting praise, it becomes periodically necessary even for advocates of discovery, such as I, to temper enthusiasm with considered judgment.

The learning by discovery controversy is a complex issue which can easily be oversimplified. A recent volume has dealt with many aspects of the issue in great detail (Shulman & Keislar, 1966). The controversy seems to center essentially about the question of how much and what kind of guidance ought to be provided to students in the learning situation. Those favoring learning by discovery advocate the teaching of broad principles and problem-solving through minimal teacher guidance and maximal opportunity for exploration and trial-and-error on the part of the student. Those preferring guided learning emphasize the importance of carefully sequencing instructional experiences through maximum guidance and stress the importance of basic associations or facts in the service of the eventual mastering of principles and problem-solving.

Needless to say, there is considerable ambiguity over the use of the term *discovery*. One man's discovery approach can easily be confused with another's guided learning curriculum if the unwary observer is not alerted to the preferred labels ahead of time. For this reason I have decided to contrast the two positions by carefully examining the work of two men, each of whom is considered a leader of one of these general schools of thought.

Professor Jerome S. Bruner of Harvard University is undoubtedly the single person most closely identified with the learning-by-discovery position. His book, *The Process of Education* (1960), captured the spirit of discovery in the new mathematics and science curricula and communicated it effectively to professionals and laymen. His thinking will be examined as representative of the advocates of discovery learning.

Professor Robert M. Gagné of the University of California is a major force in the guided learning approach. His analysis of *The Conditions of Learning* (1965) is one of the finest contemporary statements of the principles of guided learning and instruction.

I recognize the potential danger inherent in any explicit attempt to polarize the positions of two eminent scholars. My purpose is to clarify the dimensions of a complex problem, not to consign Bruner and Gagné to irrevocable extremes. Their published writings are employed merely to characterize two possible positions on the role of discovery in learning, which each has expressed eloquently at some time in the recent past.

In this paper I will first discuss the manner in which Bruner and Gagné, respectively, describe the teaching of some particular topic. Using these two examples as starting points, we will then compare their positions with respect to instructional objectives, instructional styles, readiness for learning, and transfer of training. We will then examine the implications of this controversy for the process of instruction in science and mathematics and the conduct of research relevant to that process.

INSTRUCTIONAL EXAMPLE: DISCOVERY LEARNING

In a number of his papers, Jerome Bruner uses an instructional example from mathematics that derives from his collaboration with the mathematics educator, Z. P. Dienes (Bruner, 1966).

A class is composed of eight-year-old children who are there to learn some mathematics. In one of the instructional units, children are first introduced to three kinds of flat pieces of wood, or "flats." The first one, they are told, is to be called either the "unknown square" or "X square." The second flat, which is rectangular, is called "1 X" or just X, since it is X long on one side and 1 long on the other. The third flat is a small square which is 1 by 1, and is called 1.

After allowing the children many opportunities simply to play with these materials and to get a feel for them, Bruner gives the children a problem. He asks them, "Can you make larger squares than this X square by using as many of these flats as you want?" This is not a difficult task for most children, and they readily make another square, such as the one on the right.

Bruner then asks them if they can describe what they have done. They might reply, "We have one square X, with two X's and a 1." He then asks them to keep a record of what they have done. He may even suggest a notational system to use. The symbol $X^{\square}$ could represent the square X, and a + for "and." Thus, the pieces used could be described as $X^{\square} + 2X + 1$.

Another way to describe their new square, he points out, is simply to describe each side. With an X and a 1 on each side, the side can be described as $X + 1$ and the square as $(X + 1)(X + 1)$ after some work with parentheses. Since these are two basic ways of describing the same square, they can be written in this way:

$$X^{\square} + 2X + 1 = (X + 1)(X + 1)$$

This description, of course, far oversimplifies the procedures used.

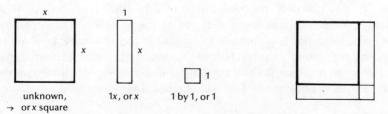

unknown,
→ or x square   1x, or x   1 by 1, or 1

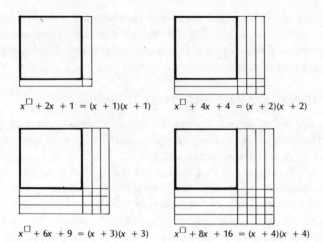

$x^{\square} + 2x + 1 = (x + 1)(x + 1)$ $x^{\square} + 4x + 4 = (x + 2)(x + 2)$

$x^{\square} + 6x + 9 = (x + 3)(x + 3)$ $x^{\square} + 8x + 16 = (x + 4)(x + 4)$

The children continue making squares and generating the notation for them, as shown above. At some point Bruner hypothesizes that they will begin to discern a pattern. While the X's are progressing at the rate of 2, 4, 6, 8, the ones are going 1, 4, 9, 16, and on the right side of the equation the pattern is 1, 2, 3, 4. Provocative or leading questions are often used Socratically to elicit this discovery. Bruner maintains that, even if the children are initially unable to break the code, they will sense that there is a pattern and try to discover it. Bruner then illustrates how the pupils transfer what they have learned to working with a balance beam. The youngsters are ostensibly learning not only something about quadratic equations, but more important, something about the discovery of mathematical regularities.

The general learning process described by Bruner occurs in the following manner: First, the child finds regularities in his manipulation of the materials that correspond with intuitive regularities he has already come to understand. Notice that what the child does for Bruner is to find some sort of match between what he is doing in the outside world and some models or templates that he already has in his mind. For Bruner, it is rarely something *outside* the learner that is discovered. Instead the discovery involves an internal reorganization of previously known ideas in order to establish a better fit between those ideas and the regularities of an encounter to which the learner has had to accommodate.

This is precisely the philosophy of education we associate with Socrates. Remember the lovely dialogue of the *Meno* by Plato, in which the young slave boy is brought to an understanding of what is involved in doubling the area of a square. Socrates maintains throughout this dialogue that he is not teaching the boy anything new; he is simply helping the boy reorganize and bring to the fore what he has always known.

Bruner almost always begins with a focus on the production and manipulation of materials. He describes the child as moving through three levels of representation. The first level is the *enactive level,* where the child manipulates materials directly. He then progresses to the *ikonic level,* where he deals with mental images of objects but does not manipulate them directly. Finally he moves to the *symbolic level,* where he is strictly manipulating symbols and no longer mental images of objects. This sequence is an outgrowth of the developmental work of Jean Piaget. The synthesis of these concepts of manipulation of actual materials as part of a developmental model and the Socratic notion of learning as internal reorganization into a learning-by-discovery approach is the unique contribution of Jerome Bruner.

The Process of Education was written in 1959, after most mathematics innovations that use discovery as a core had already begun. It is an error to say that Bruner initiated the learning-by-discovery approach. It is far more accurate to say that, more than any one man, he managed to capture its spirit, provide it with a theoretical foundation, and disseminate it. Bruner is not the discoverer of discovery; he is its prophet.

INSTRUCTIONAL EXAMPLE: GUIDED LEARNING

Robert Gagné takes a very different approach to instruction. He begins with a task analysis of the instructional objectives. He always asks the question, "What is it you want the learner to be able to do?" This *capability* he insists, must be stated *specifically* and *behaviorally.*

By capability, he means the ability to perform certain specific functions under specified conditions. A capability could be the ability to solve a number series. It might be the ability to solve some problems in non-metric geometry.

This capability can be conceived of as a terminal behavior and placed at the top of what will eventually be a complex pyramid. After analyzing the task, Gagné asks, "What would you need to know in order to do that?" Let us say that one could not complete the task unless he could first perform prerequisite tasks *a* and *b.* So a pyramid begins.

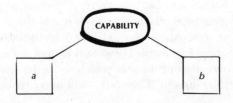

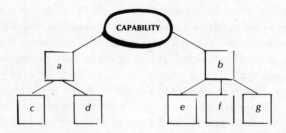

But in order to perform task *a*, one must be able to perform tasks *c* and *d* and for task *b*, one must know *e*, *f*, and *g*. So one builds a very complex pyramid of prerequisites to prerequisites to the objective which is the desired capability.

Gagne has developed a model for discussing the different levels of such a hierarchy. If the final capability desired is a *problem-solving* capability, the learner first must know certain *principles*. But to understand those principles, he must know specific *concepts*, and prerequisite to these are particular *simple associations* or *facts* discriminated from each other in a distinctive manner. He continues the analysis until he ends up with the fundamental building blocks of learning—classically or operantly conditioned responses.

Gagné, upon completing the whole map of prerequisites, would administer pretests to determine which have already been mastered. Upon completing the diagnostic testing, the resulting pattern identifies precisely what must be taught. This model is particularly conducive to subsequent programing of materials and programed instruction. When prerequisites are established, a very tight teaching program or package develops.

Earlier, we discussed the influences on Bruner. What influenced Gagné? This approach to teaching comes essentially from a combination of the neo-behaviorist psychological tradition and the task analysis model that dominates the fields of military and industrial training. It was precisely this kind of task analysis that contributed to successful programs of pilot training in World War II. Gagné was trained in the neo-behaviorist tradition and spent the major portion of his early career as an Air Force psychologist.

NATURE OF OBJECTIVES

The positions of Bruner and Gagné take very different points of view with respect to the objectives of education. This is one of the major reasons why most attempts at evaluating the relative effectiveness of these two approaches have come to naught. They really cannot agree on the same set of objectives. Any attempt to ask which is better—Michigan State's football team or the Chicago White Sox—will never succeed. The criteria for success are different, and it would be absurd to have them both on the same field competing against each other.

For Gagné, or the programed-instruction position which can be derived from him, the objectives of instruction are capabilities. They are behavioral products that can be specified in operational terms. Subsequently they can be task-analyzed; then they can be taught. Gagné would subscribe to the position that psychology has been successful in suggesting ways of teaching only when objectives have been made operationally clear. When objectives are not clearly stated, the psychologist can be of little assistance. He insists on objectives clearly stated in behavioral terms. They are the cornerstones of his position.

For Bruner, the emphasis is quite different. The emphasis is not on the *products* of learning but on the *processes*. One paragraph from *Toward a Theory of Instruction* (1966) captures the spirit of educational objectives for Bruner. After discussing the mathematics example previously mentioned, he concludes:

> *Finally, a theory of instruction seeks to take account of the fact that a curriculum reflects not only the nature of knowledge itself—the specific capabilities—but also the nature of the knower and of the knowledge-getting process. It is the enterprise par excellence where the line between the subject matter and the method grows necessarily indistinct. A body of knowledge, enshrined in a university faculty, and embodied in a series of authoritative volumes is the result of much prior intellectual activity. To instruct someone in these disciplines is not a matter of getting him to commit the results to mind; rather, it is to teach him to participate in the process that makes possible the establishment of knowledge. We teach a subject, not to produce little living libraries from that subject, but rather to get a student to think mathematically for himself, to consider matters as a historian does, to take part in the process of knowledge-getting. Knowing is a process, not a product [p. 72, emphasis added].*

Speaking to the same issue, Gagné's position (1965) is clearly different.

> *Obviously, strategies are important for problem solving, regardless of the content of the problem. The suggestion from some writings is that they are of overriding importance as a goal of education. After all, should not formal instruction in the schools have the aim of teaching the student "how to think"? If strategies were deliberately taught, would not this produce people who could then bring to bear superior problem-solving capabilities to any new situation? Although no one would disagree with the aims expressed, it is exceedingly doubtful that they can be brought about by teaching students "strategies" or*

"styles" of thinking. Even if these could be taught (and it is possible that they could), they would not provide the individual with the basic firmament of thought, which is subject-matter knowledge. Knowing a set of strategies is not all that is required for thinking; it is not even a substantial part of what is needed. To be an effective problem solver, the individual must somehow have acquired masses of structurally organized knowledge. Such knowledge is made up of content principles, not heuristic ones *[p. 170, emphasis added]*.

While for Bruner "knowing is a process, not a product," for Gagné, "knowledge is made up of content principles, not heuristic ones." Thus, though both espouse the acquisition of knowledge as the major objective of education, their definitions of *knowledge* and *knowing* are so disparate that the educational objectives sought by each scarcely overlap. The philosophical and psychological sources of these differences will be discussed later in this paper. For the moment, let it be noted that when two conflicting approaches seek such contrasting objectives, the conduct of comparative educational studies becomes extremely difficult.

INSTRUCTIONAL STYLES

Implicit in this contrast is a difference in what is meant by the very words *learning by discovery*. For Gagné, *learning* is the goal. How a behavior or capability is learned is a function of the task. It may be by discovery, by guided teaching, by practice, by drill, or by review. The focus is on *learning* and discovery is but one way to learn something. For Bruner, it is learning *by discovery*. The method of learning is the significant aspect.

For Gagné, in an instructional program the child is carefully guided. He may work with programed materials or a programed teacher (one who follows quite explicitly a step-by-step guide). The child may be quite active. He is not necessarily passive; he is doing things, he is working exercises, he is solving problems. But the sequence is determined entirely by the program. (Here the term "program" is used in a broad sense, not necessarily simply a series of frames.)

For Bruner much less system or order is necessary for the package, although such order is not precluded. In general Bruner insists on the child manipulating materials and dealing with incongruities or contrasts. He will always try to build potential or emergent incongruities into the materials. Robert Davis calls this operation "torpedoing" when it is initiated by the teacher. He teaches a child something until he is certain the child knows it. Then he provides him with a whopper of a counterexample. This is what Bruner does constantly—providing contrasts and incongruities in order to get the child, because of his discomfort, to try to resolve this disequilibrium by making some discovery (cognitive restructuring). This discovery can take the form of a new synthesis or a new distinction. Piaget, too, maintains that cognitive development is a process of successive disequilibria and equilibria. The child, confronted by a new situation, gets out of balance and must accommodate to achieve a new balance by modifying the previous cognitive structure.

Thus, for Gagné, instruction is a smoothly guided tour up a carefully constructed hierarchy of objectives; for Bruner, instruction is a roller-coaster ride of successive disequilibria and equilibria until the desired cognitive state is reached or discovered.

READINESS

The guided learning point of view, represented by Gagné, maintains that readiness is essentially a function of the presence or absence of prerequisite learning. When the child is capable of *d* and *e* below, he is by definition ready to learn *b*. Until then he is not ready. Gagné is not concerned with genetically developmental considerations. If the child at age five does not have the concept of the conservation of liquid volume, it is not because of an unfolding in his mind; he just has not had the necessary prior experiences. Ensure that he has acquired the prerequisite behaviors, and he will be able to conserve (1966).

For Piaget (and Bruner) the child is a developing organism, passing through congnitive stages that are biologically determined. These stages are more or less age-related, although in different cultures certain stages may come earlier than others. To identify whether the child is ready to learn a particular concept or principle, one analyzes the structure of that to be taught and compares it with what is already known about the cognitive structure of the child at that age. If they are consonant, it can be taught; if they are dissonant, it cannot.

Given this characterization of the two positions on readiness, to which one would you attribute the following statement? ". . . any subject can be taught effectively in some intellectually honest form to any child at

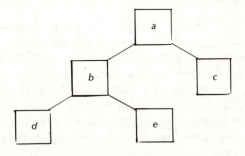

any stage of development." While it sounds like Gagné, you recognize that it isn't—it's Bruner [1966, p. 33]. And in this same chapter he includes an extensive discussion of Piaget's position. Essentially he is attempting to translate Piaget's theories into a psychology of instruction.

Many are puzzled by this stand, including Piaget. In a recent paper delivered in the United States, he admitted that he did not understand how Bruner could make such a statement in the light of Piaget's experiments. If Bruner meant the statement literally; i.e., *any* child can learn *anything*, then it just is not true! There are always things a child cannot learn, especially not in an intellectually honest way. If he means it homiletically, i.e., we can take almost anything and somehow resay it, reconstruct it, restructure it so it now has a parallel at the child's level of cognitive functioning, then it may be a truism.

I believe that what Bruner is saying, and it is neither trivial nor absurd, is that our older conceptions of readiness have tended to apply Piagetian theory in the same way as some have for generations applied Rousseau's. The old thesis was, "There is the child—he is a developing organism, with invariant order, invariant schedule. Here, too, is the subject matter, equally hallowed by time and unchanging. We take the subject matter as our starting point, watch the child develop, and feed it in at appropriate times as he reaches readiness." Let's face it; that has been our general conception of readiness. We gave reading readiness tests and hesitated to teach the pupil reading until he was "ready." The notion is quite new that the reading readiness tests tell not when to begin teaching the child, but rather what has to be done to get him more ready. We used to just wait until he got ready. What Bruner is suggesting is that we must modify our conception of readiness so that it includes not only the child but the subject matter. Subject matter, too, goes through stages of readiness. The same subject matter can be represented at a manipulative or enactive level, at an ikonic level, and finally at a symbolic or formal level. The resulting model is Bruner's concept of a spiral curriculum.

Piaget himself seems quite dubious over the attempts to acclerate cognitive development that are reflected in many modern math and science curricula. On a recent trip to the United States, Piaget commented:

> . . . *we know that it takes nine to twelve months before babies develop the notion that an object is still there even when a screen is placed in front of it. Now kittens go through the same stages as children, all the same sub-stages, but they do it in three months—so they're six months ahead of babies. Is this an advantage or isn't it? We can certainly see our answer in one sense. The kitten is not going to go much further. The child has taken longer, but he is capable of going further, so it seems to me that the nine months probably were not for nothing.*

It's probably possible to accelerate, but maximal acceleration is not desirable. There seems to be an optimal time. What this optimal time is will surely depend upon each individual and on the subject matter. We still need a great deal of research to know what the optimal time would be [Jennings, 1967, p. 82].

The question that has not been answered, and which Piaget whimsically calls the "American question," is the empirical experimental question: To what extent is it possible through a Gagnéan approach to accelerate what Piaget maintains is the invariant clockwork of the order? Studies being conducted in Scandinavia by Smedslund and in this country by Irving Sigel, Egon Mermelstein, and others are attempting to identify the degree to which such processes as the principle of conservation of volume can be accelerated. If I had to make a broad generalization, I would have to conclude that at this point, in general, the score for those who say you cannot accelerate is somewhat higher than the score for those who say that you can. But the question is far from resolved; we need many more inventive attempts to accelerate cognitive development than we have had thus far. There remains the question of whether such attempts at experimental acceleration are strictly of interest for psychological theory, or have important pedagogical implications as well—a question we do not have space to examine here.

SEQUENCE OF THE CURRICULUM

The implications for the sequence of the curriculum growing from these two positions are quite different. For Gagné, the highest level of learning is problem solving; lower levels involve facts, concepts, principles, etc. Clearly, for Gagné, the appropriate sequence in learning is, in terms of the diagram below, from the bottom up. One begins with simple prerequisites and works up, pyramid fashion, to the complex capability sought.

For Bruner, the same diagram may be appropriate, but the direction of the arrow would be changed. He has a pupil begin with *problem solving.* This process is analogous to teaching someone to swim by throwing him

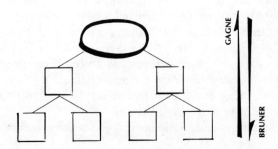

into deep water. The theory is that he will learn the fundamentals because he needs them. The analogy is not totally misbegotten. In some of the extreme discovery approaches we lose a lot of pupils by mathematical or scientific drowning. As one goes to the extreme of this position, he runs the risk of some drownings. For Gagné, the sequence is from the simple to the complex; for Bruner one starts with the complex and plans to learn the simple components in the context of working with the complex.

It is unclear whether Bruner subscribes to his position because of his concept of the nature of learning or for strictly motivational reasons. Children may be motivated more quickly when given a problem they cannot solve, than they are when given some little things to learn on the promise that if they learn these well, three weeks from now they will be able to solve an exciting problem. Yet, Bruner clearly maintains that learning things in this fashion also improves the transferability of what is learned. It is to a consideration of the issue of transfer of training that we now turn.

TRANSFER OF TRAINING

To examine the psychologies of learning of these two positions in any kind of comprehensive form would require greater attention than can be devoted here, but we shall consider one concept—that of transfer of training. This is probably the central concept, or should be, in any educationally relevant psychology of learning.

Gagné (1966) considers himself a conservative on matters of transfer. He states that "transfer occurs because of the occurrence of specific identical (or highly similar) elements within developmental sequences" [p. 20]. To the extent that an element which has been learned, be it association, concept, or principle, can be directly employed in a new situation, transfer will occur. If the new context requires a behavior substantially different from the specific capability mastered earlier, there will be no transfer.

Bruner, on the other hand, subscribes to the broadest theories of transfer of training. Bruner believes that we can have massive transfer from one learning situation to another. Broad transfer of training occurs when one can identify in the structures of subject matters basic, fundamentally simple concepts or principles which, if learned well, can be transferred both to other subject matters within that discipline and to other disciplines as well. He gives examples such as the concept of conservation or balance. Is it not possible to teach balance of trade in economics in such a way that when ecological balance is considered, pupils see the parallel? This could then be extended to balance of power in political science, or to balancing equations.

Even more important, for Bruner, is the broad transferability of the knowledge-getting processes—strategies, heuristics, and the like—a transfer whose viability leaves Gagné with deep feelings of doubt. This is the question of whether learning by discovery leads to the ability *to* discover, that is, the development of broad inquiry competencies in students.

What does the evidence from empirical studies of this issue seem to demonstrate? The findings are not all that consistent. I would generalize them by saying that most often guided learning or expository sequences seem to be superior methods for achieving immediate learning. With regard to long-term retention, the results seem equivocal, with neither approach consistently better. Discovery learning approaches appear to be superior when the criterion of transfer of principles to new situations is employed (Worthen, 1968). Notably absent are studies which deal with the question of whether general techniques, strategies, and heuristics of discovery can be learned—by discovery or in any other manner—which will transfer across grossly different kinds of tasks.

Why is transfer of training superior in the discovery situation when the learning of principles is involved? There are two kinds of transfer—positive transfer and negative transfer. We call something positive transfer when mastery of task X facilitates mastery of task Y. Negative transfer occurs when mastery of task X inhibits mastery of task Y. Positive transfer is a familiar notion for us. Negative transfer can be exemplified by a piece of advice baseball coaches often give their players. They tell them not to play golf during the baseball season because the baseball swing and the golf swing involve totally different muscles and body movements. Becoming a better golf swinger interferes with the baseball swing. In psychological terms there is negative transfer between golf and baseball.

What is needed for positive transfer is to minimize all possible interference. In transfer of training, there are some ways in which the tasks transferred to are like the ones learned first, but in other ways they are different. So transfer always involves striking a balance between these conflicting potentials for both positive and negative transfer. In discovery methods, learners may transfer more easily because they learn *the immediate things less well*. They may thus learn the broad strokes of a principle, which is the aspect most critical for remote transfer, while not learning well the detailed application of that specific principle, which could interfere somewhat with successful remote transfer.

If this formulation is correct, we are never going to find a method that will both allow for tremendous specific learning of products and broad transfer, because we are dealing in a closed system in which one must make a choice. To the extent that initial learning is well done, transfer is restricted. The instructor may have to decide which is more important—an immediate specific product or broad transfer—and choose his subsequent teaching method on the basis of that decision. This is a pessimistic view, and I hope that future studies might find it flawed.

SYNTHESIS OR SELECTION

Need we eternally code these as two alternatives—discovery versus expository teaching—or can we, without being heretical, manage to keep both of these in our methodological repertories as mathematics and science educators?

John Dewey was always very suspicious whenever he approached a controversy between two strongly stated positions, each of which insisted that the other was totally in error. The classic example of this is in his monograph *Experience and Education,* in which he examines the controversy of traditional versus progressive education. Dewey teaches us that whenever we confront this kind of controversy, we must look for the possibility that each position is massively buttressed by a brilliant half-truth from which is extrapolated the whole cloth of an educational philosophy. That is, too often a good idea wears thin as its advocates insist that it be applied outside its appropriate domain.

As educators, we find it extremely important to identify the conditions under which each of these theories can be applied most fruitfully. First, one must examine the nature of the objectives. More than half of this controversy can be resolved not at the level of which is the better psychology, but at the level of evaluative philosophical judgments. Given one set of goals, clearly the position Gagné advocates presently has more evidence in its favor; given another set of goals, there is no question but that Bruner's position is preferable to Gagné's.

But there are other questions. The age and personality of the learner must be taken into account. All things being equal, there are some kinds of children who cannot tolerate the ambiguity of a discovery experience. We all know this; some of us prefer to hear lectures that are well organized so that we can take notes in a systematic manner. Others of us like nothing better than a free-flowing bull session; and each of us is convinced that we learn more in our preferred mode than the others learn in theirs. Individual differences in learning styles are major determinants of the kinds of approaches that work best with different children.

Yet this is something we have in general not taken into consideration at all in planning curricula—and for very good reasons. As yet, we do not have any really valid ways of measuring these styles. Once we do, we will have a powerful diagnostic tool. Subject matter, objectives, characteristics of children, and characteristics of the teacher are all involved in this educational decision. Some teachers are no more likely to conduct a discovery learning sequence than they are to go frugging at a local nightclub.

There appear to be middle routes as well. In many of the experimental studies of discovery learning, an experimental treatment labeled *guided discovery* is used. In guided discovery, the subjects are carefully directed down a particular path along which they are called upon to discover regularities and solutions on their own. They are provided with cues in a carefully programed manner, but the actual statement of the principle or problem solution is left up to them. Many of the well-planned Socratic dialogues of our fine teachers are forms of guided discovery. The teacher carefully leads the pupils into a series of traps from which they must now rescue themselves.

In the published studies, guided discovery treatments generally have done quite well both at the level of immediate learning and later transfer. Perhaps this approach allows us to put the Bruner roller-coaster of discovery on the well-laid track of a Gagné hierarchy.

Thus, the earlier question of which is better, learning by discovery or guided learning, now can be restated in more functional and pragmatic terms. Under what conditions are each of these instructional approaches, some sequence or combination of the two, of some synthesis of them, most likely to be appropriate? The answers to such questions ought to grow out of quite comprehensive principles of human learning. Where are we to find such principles?

THEORIES OF LEARNING AND THE SCIENCE AND MATHEMATICS CURRICULUM

There is a growing psychology of learning that is finally becoming meaningful to curriculum construction and educational practice. Children are being studied as often as rats, and classrooms as often as mazes. Research with lower animals has been extremely useful in identifying some principles of learning that are so basic, so fundamental, so universal that they apply to any fairly well-organized blob of protoplasm. But there is a diminishing return in this approach insofar as transfer to educational practice is concerned. Today, a developing, empirically based psychology of learning for *homo sapiens* offers tremendous promise. But it can never be immediately translatable into a psychology of the teaching of mathematics or science. Mathematics and science educators must not make the mistake that the reading people have made and continue to make. The reason that the psychology of the teaching of reading has made such meager progress in the last 25 years is that the reading people have insisted on being borrowers. Something new happens in linguistics and within three years a linguistic reading series is off the press. It is an attempt to bootleg an idea from one field and put it directly into another without the necessary intervening steps of empirical testing and research.

Mathematics and science education are in grave danger of making that same error, especially with the work of Piaget and Bruner. What is needed now are well-developed empirically based psychologies of mathematics and science learning. Surely they will grow out of what is already known about the psychology of learning in general, but they must necessarily depend upon people like yourselves, your students, and your colleagues who are interested in mathematics and science conducting empirical studies of how certain specific concepts are learned under certain specific conditions with certain specific kinds of pupils. If anything is true about the field of mathematics and science education today, it is that rarely have any disciplines been so rich in theory and brilliant ideas. But we must seriously consider the admonition of Ivan Pavlov, the great Russian psychologist, who is said to have told his students the following:

> *Ideas and theories are like the wings of birds; they allow man to soar and to climb to the heavens. But facts are like the atmosphere against which those wings must beat, and without which the soaring bird will surely plummet back to earth.*

19

HELEN HEFFERNAN   CONCEPT DEVELOPMENT IN SCIENCE

To anyone who has had a lifelong interest in the place of science in the education of young children, the developments of recent years have been a source of much gratification. We are much farther ahead than we were ten years ago.

"Farther ahead" means a number of things. Children are more involved in the processes of science. Children are having more firsthand experiences, greater opportunity to conduct explorations of scientific phenomena, and more opportunity to do critical thinking.

Also, teachers are participating in in-service education programs specifically directed toward the maturity level of the children they teach. Teachers and children have access to more ample material. Much effort is being directed to curriculum planning. School districts are developing laboratory centers for teachers.

As science education moves forward on so many fronts, critical needs command renewed attention. Much must be done to lessen the lag between what is now known about science teaching and classroom practice. As cases in point, how rapidly can we provide the focus, freedom, and responsive environment essential to J. Richard Suchman's inquiry program? Dr. Suchman has made a significant contribution to learning in his demonstration that a child must confront a discrepancy in events which cannot be explained by the theories with which he is operating.

Another significant forward thrust has been given by Ben Strasser (1966) of the staff of the Los Angeles County School Superintendent who has focused his interest on the teacher's self examination of his own teaching behavior. Mr. Strasser is concerned about what it is that learners do when they inquire and what are the behaviors a teacher exhibits which stimulate learners to perceive, to inquire, to discover, and to experiment. Mr. Strasser views teaching as a truly dynamic process. To achieve education of the quality he envisions requires conditions of reasonable class size and opportunity for in-service education. Observation of learners, their actions and interactions, interpreting such data, making diagnoses in terms of the learner, the situation and the goals and resultant change in teacher behavior in terms of the diagnoses made will not happen in overcrowded classrooms with harassed teachers and inadequate facilities.

A third most promising line of thinking and research is being carried on at the University of Arizona, by Alphoretta Fish (1965). She indicates another level to which inquiry can be taken. In her model, inquiry shifts from the level on which alternative methods of science inquiry are focal, to the level on which decisions about which methods to select are focal. Her purpose is to guide pupils to make the decisions about the method to use in their science inquiry, experience the consequences of their decisions, and assess the consequences by inquiring into the science inquiry methods which produced the consequence. Dr. Fish is aiming at five goals in her research:

1 Expanding meanings by expanding relations instituted
2 Analyzing the questions children ask and the methods they use for inquiring in science
3 Evaluating their questions and methods-building criteria
4 Reconstructing the questions and the methods of their science inquiry, and finally
5 Evaluating and reconstructing their criteria

These three sophisticated studies point toward the development of the rational powers of the learner. All aim toward learners becoming more independent; learners dealing with problems of significance to them; learners able to perceive discrepancies and invent theories which satisfy their explanations; learners able to draw and test their inferences; and finally learners with wide experience with a variety of phenomena. The studies focus on scientific method but we need also to consider how children secure their wide experience with a variety of phenomena.

CONCEPT DEVELOPMENT

The psychologist tells us that "a concept is a generalization about related data." The philosophers say that "a concept is a mental image of a thing formed by generalization from particulars." We know that a concept is arrived at through various kinds of *perceptions*.

To illustrate: Looking out into your garden, you *perceive* some colorful, fluttering, strutting, chirping, flying objects. Some time in your past experience, someone has helped you to attach *verbal symbols* to these objects and you proceed to recall: robin, blue jay, woodpecker, dove, finch, English sparrow. Each of these is a *percept,* an impression gained solely by the use of the senses. When you *generalize* from these percepts and say "birds" you have arrived at a concept.

But for few, if any, is the concept of "bird" ever complete. The exception might be an ornithologist with a global range of study in the field of his specialization. He would come nearest to perceiving all facets of the concept.

Your concept of "bird" will change over the years with the addition of new percepts. You may travel to Africa and for the first time make contact with a bird that cannot fly—the ostrich. This may mean you will correct your previous concept if your experience had led you to generalize "that all birds fly."

This illustration, beginning with what seemed a relatively simple concept, could take us far—to South America for a glimpse of the scarlet ibis, to New Guinea to see the bird of paradise, to Europe to see the great white stork, to Australia to see the amazing plumage which gave the lyrebird its name. Your expanding concept of "bird" might lead you to learn about the pattern and variety of bird structures, their nesting habits, birds' eggs, feeding habits, migrations, their evolution probably from reptilian ancestors, extinct birds and much, much more.

By elaborating on the concept "bird" we have a good illustration of the vast number of related experiences that contribute to expanding knowledge and an increasingly more accurate concept about one familiar object in our global environment. Sensations, recalled percepts or memories, mental images of things not actually present to the senses at the moment all enter into the complex process called concept building.

We discuss this process because it is essentially the process of education. Concepts develop out of related perceptual experiences and as a result of the child's reorganization of his experiences to solve a problem or to express himself creatively.

The teacher who is aware of the way concepts are developed will seek continuously to provide children with a wide variety of sensory experiences. Children learn first through perceptions; their sensory equipment provides the means through which they observe their world. Not solely through vision, on which education has relied far too much, but on all the senses—through hearing, smelling, tasting, and through handling and manipulating objects.

The teacher at any level of the elementary school enters the life of a child at a point in a continuum in the process of concept development. All children at every stage of development have been acquiring concepts. They have been perceiving the world around them, and attempting to relate to it. They have modified, corrected, or enlarged their concepts through each relevant experience.

Sometimes we forget that when a child is born he knows nothing about the world, people, his relation to that world, what to do, and how to make it yield what he must have to satisfy his basic human needs. All he will ever know he must learn. What he learns will depend upon his experiences, because experience is the basis of all learning. A child can learn to know and do *only what he has access to through experience.*

Every human being has a life-space, an area of the world with which he comes into contact. What this life-space contains, the people in it, what they do, how they act, how they feel, how they speak is the culture the child internalizes. Only as his life-space is expanded by family trips; by experiences his home, school, and community provide for him; the motion pictures or television programs he sees; his opportunity for personal exploration of his community; or by talking and reading can he acquire knowledge beyond his immediate life-space. And he will interpret whatever he hears or reads about beyond his life-space in terms of the word meanings, concepts and attitudes learned in it.

Nothing is more important to the teacher than to understand the essential relationship between the child's life-space and what the child himself knows, does, says, thinks, feels, and understands. Let us not expect all children of the same age to know more or less the same things, have the same interests, think and feel in the same way, and associate the same meaning with words. Children's life-spaces and the ways in which people within their life-spaces act, think, feel, and believe are dramatically varied, with the result that children vary widely in their concepts, attitudes, ways of acting, language patterns, and skills.

We see concepts as providing the material for children's thinking. They develop slowly from percepts, mental images, and need verbal symbols attached to them to make them manageable by a child. We see children arriving at, expanding, and correcting concepts by an inductive process.

The nursery school is not too early to begin to develop concepts leading to basic understandings of the structure of science (California State Department of Education, 1964). To understand about

1 Variety and pattern in living and nonliving things
2 Continuity and change and that continual change occurs with living and nonliving things
3 Interaction and interdependence that occurs among living organisms and nonliving things
4 Evolutionary development where changes have occurred over a long period of time and continue to occur among living and nonliving things

Gerald Craig has said:

The question of how much of the content of science is taught is not of nearly so great importance as is the question of what *is taught,* how *it is taught, and the* purpose *for which it is taught.*

The Head Start program, begun in the summer of 1965, has offered young preschool children an enriched program of educational experiences. Fortunately, for their science education, these babes cannot read. Their educative experiences, therefore, do not need to be restricted by the limitations imposed by their mastery of printed symbols. They learn directly from the realities of their environment and follow the discovery-exploration-experimental approach to learning which educators generally extol.

Neither children nor teachers in the Head Start program are expected to know about science, but science learning goes on as children observe and talk about the behavior of frogs, or ducks, or chickens, or guinea pigs, or tortoises, or guppies, or any of the animals encountered on study trips.

As Dr. Craig points out, our success in helping young children to understand their scientific environment does not depend primarily upon the specific *content* selected. The content is limitless and can be explored to any depth the interest of children take them. No teacher could possibly know all the facts of science but she can know the sources of data and the process by which needed information can be secured.

With young children the real success comes as a result of the skills of the teacher in arranging an environment that

1 Opens up new experiences about weather, seasons, temperature, variety in plants and animals
2 Impels children to observe carefully and to formulate significant questions
3 Encourages them to discover for themselves
4 Leads them to gain new *ideas* and *feelings*
5 Excites them to express their ideas and feelings in words, in construction, in painting, in modeling, in dramatic play, in rhythmic expression

Where there is zest, meaning, and depth in the science experiences the skills of the language arts and mathematics fall into their proper relations. Education has in the past focused inordinately on the *skills* of learning. We need an about-face and a focus on all the wonderful *content* which makes this a world of wonders.

WELL-DESIGNED MATERIALS

Well-designed curriculum materials are needed for use by teachers who are not and can not become specialists in science. Such curriculum should be organized in terms of a sequence of science experiences appropriate for three- and four- and five-year-olds. Each experience should be clearly presented as a separate unit showing the materials needed to carry on appropriate activities in which children may engage, types of questions designed to result in concept formation and thinking and variations in the opportunities for learning related to the major purpose of the experience.

For example, suppose the activity proposed were gardening, the materials suggested would include short shovels, hand rakes, hoes, watering pot, and seeds such as carrot, radish, sweet pea. The suggestion to the teacher might include use with the children of *Carrot Seed* by Ruth Kraus and *Up Above and Down Below* by Irma Webber. The teacher's questions during the activity would concern preparation of soil, depth to plant seeds, putting in seeds, watering. Later the children would return to the garden for weeding, watering, and talk about the growth of their plants. The unit might suggest other experiences such as: growing plants indoors and exposing them to various amounts of sunshine, giving plants varying amounts of water. Each child might have a piece of sponge in which grass seeds are grown; they might grow plants from bulbs and cuttings according to the season.

In addition to the preparation of explicit curriculum material for use by teachers, well-qualified science educators are needed to work in programs set up for training assistants to work with young children in nursery school and in child-care or child-development programs.

In this new expansion of educational experience to the very young, are to be found unparalleled opportunities for research in selection of curriculum content and use of scientific processes in teaching. My hypothesis here is that if we based a preschool program on significant firsthand science experiences so children had faith in their own observations and conclusions based on experience we would then have a far more meaningful and much less bookish science program through the elementary school. In an effort to answer the demand for a standard or pattern of effective science courses in the elementary school, over twenty or more groups of scientists and educators are experimenting with new elementary science curriculum programs.

Presently, many of the individual units produced by these groups are excellent, but they represent unorganized fragments of the broad scope upon which a program having continuity depends. Therefore, for the future, professional organizations are challenged to set up task forces to coordinate current promising efforts and expand science education experimentation to the end that science education throughout the nation achieve horizontal coherence and vertical continuity. The challenges at this moment lie chiefly in an intensive study of science education and in providing present teachers with the time and leadership essential to measure up to the changing, emerging, dynamic, creative world of which they are a part.

language and the language arts

Traditionally the schools—usually beginning with grade 1—have emphasized the development of reading and writing skills. (The emphasis is well
warranted because written language has enabled the human race to
develop complex ethical-technological cultures and refined powers of
describing, organizing, and understanding the world.) As a prelude to the
teaching of reading and writing, many kindergarten and preschool
programs include the teaching of letter recognition and other more
directly obvious reading-readiness skills.

Recent research indicates that the preschool children who are
superior in the use of oral speech are also superior in thinking skills. This
research also indicates that the children more highly skilled in the use of
oral speech in grade 1 are also more skilled in reading in grades 3 to 6.
Consequently, educators have begun to see the promotion of effective oral
speech in preschool and kindergarten-aged children as being of major
importance.

Numerous programs for teaching oral speech have been designed,
some considerably more successful than others. Generally, the more
successful programs incorporate a theory of learning (any one of several
are equally effective) and involve specific goals and structured plans for
achieving them. Until recently educators have attempted to teach all
young children to speak in the manner popular in the white middle-class
culture (standard English). Now some leading educators are advocating

teaching speech in the child's native language or dialect and teaching standard English as a second language.

Five articles are included in this section. Oral speech is the subject of the first three: how children learn to speak and use speech and how teachers promote speaking skills in preschool and day-care settings. The next article is a discussion of reading readiness and teaching rudimentary reading skills. (Article 40 in Section Seven deals with teaching reading to "disadvantaged" children.) Nonverbal communication, the messages teachers and children convey to each other without words, is the final topic in this section.

Most of "Values and Issues in Young Children's Literature," Article 21, concerns a research analysis of the stories nursery-school children tell when they are asked to tell a story. Evelyn Goodenough Pitcher's analysis focuses on the ways children use language and on the underlying concerns and interests that the children reveal in their stories. Pitcher also discusses children's literature and on the basis of her research makes some recommendations about appropriate children's literature.

Wanat's article (22), "Language Acquisition: Basic Issues," is a clear discussion of three competing theories regarding how children acquire oral speaking skills. It serves as a good introduction to Article 20, "Language Development in Day-Care Programs" (by Courtney Cazden and others). This selection, although published in a manual on day care, is equally applicable to preschool and kindergarten settings. Courtney Cazden and the other authors of Article 20 discuss the extensive research literature on competing theories of language acquisition. They also dispel some myths about the various dialects English-speaking American children use and offer background information and guidelines useful to the teacher who wishes to promote oral speaking skills.

In Article 23, "Confusions and Misconceptions in the Controversy About Kindergarten Reading," Dolores Durkin describes the current and continuing controversy over what is the best age for children to begin receiving formal reading instruction. She offers considerable evidence in support of beginning such teaching in preschool or kindergarten. Durkin also discusses what "reading readiness" means.

Although verbal language is man's most sophisticated vehicle for communication, much meaning is also conveyed (less deliberately, but equally emphatically) by various nonverbal actions. Galloway's article on "Nonverbal Communication " (24), lists the most frequent and significant ways by which teachers and students communicate nonverbally in the classroom setting. In addition to describing the "body language" of gestures, eye movements, facial expressions, and clothing style, Galloway discusses "classroom cues." By such cues as the arrangement of desks teachers convey attitudes and information about themselves to their students. Galloway suggests several assignments that should prove interesting and revealing to the student interested in communicating effectively.

behavioral objectives   *To be able to discuss the following points*

20 LANGUAGE DEVELOPMENT IN DAY-CARE PROGRAMS
The processes by which children learn the grammatical construction of language
The extent to which children learn language by imitation
The relationship between a child's early verbal behavior and the teacher's attitude toward him
The basic grammatical structure of nonstandard English and sources of some of the linguistic characteristics of black English
The relationship between developmental forms and dialectal differences in the language usage of young children
Some implications of the social attitudes relating to the use of standard English
Differences in the verbal styles of young children and some possible ways of dealing with them

The three functions of talk among young children and ways in which this talk can be utilized to facilitate language development
The factors involved in constructive adult-child talk with a child who speaks some dialect other than standard English

21 VALUES AND ISSUES IN YOUNG CHILDREN'S LITERATURE
The differences between children's literature and adult literature in terms of form, plot, language, and characterization
The themes that are most appealing to preschoolers and the basis of their appeal
The effect on children of exposure to violence and death in literature
Two positive emotions reflected in the stories children tell
The thinking of children as revealed by their stories, specifically with reference to sex differences, concepts of morality, and their understanding and use of language

22 LANGUAGE ACQUISITION: BASIC ISSUES
Some of the skills producing competence in spoken language and the relationship of these skills to reading
The basic precepts of the behavioristic, nativistic, and cognitive theories of language development
Wanat's recommendations for teaching dialect speakers how to read
The general implications of the three theories of language development for the teaching of verbal skills

23 CONFUSION AND MISCONCEPTIONS IN THE CONTROVERSY
ABOUT KINDERGARTEN READING
The meaning of reading readiness
The relationship of reading readiness to chronological or mental age
The relationship between reading ability and the age when reading began
The nature of reading instruction, as distinguished from formal instruction, and its application to kindergarten teaching
The factors that constitute pushing a child to read and ways of teaching kindergarten children to read without pushing them

24 NONVERBAL COMMUNICATION
The forms of nonverbal communication
The kinds of information acquired through nonverbal communication and the relative value placed on nonverbal messages
Some types of nonverbal phenomena in student behavior and their implications for the teacher
Some aspects of the classroom situation that have nonverbal

significance for students and four specific behavioral cues that contribute to effective teaching

Factors that affect the student's response to a teacher's behavioral cues

COURTNEY B. CAZDEN
JOAN C. BARATZ
WILLIAM LABOV
FRANCIS H. PALMER

20

LANGUAGE DEVELOPMENT IN DAY-CARE PROGRAMS

One of the responsibilities of any day-care center is to extend each child's verbal abilities. This means continuing his learning of the structure of his native language or dialect, and probably helping him learn standard English (SE) as well. It means extending his repertoire of words and meanings for talking about the objects, events, and ideas in his expanding world. And it means giving him rich opportunities to use language for private thought and for social communication in ways satisfying to him and important for school success.

Certain conditions should be met if this responsibility is to be fulfilled. Our concern here is not with specific curriculum options, but with the more general conditions which apply in any program for the traditional preschool years of three to five.

LANGUAGE DEVELOPMENT

By and large, children do not learn language from their teachers. Most children come to school, even to preschool, with a basic knowledge of the grammar of their native language.

When we say that a child learns his native language, we mean he is learning a limited set of rules which linguists call a grammar. On the basis of this knowledge, the child can speak and understand an infinite set of sentences. He doesn't know the rules in any conscious sense; for that matter, neither do most adults. Few adults can actually state the rules for adding -s or -z or -iz sounds to form plural nouns; yet if they are asked to supply the plurals for nonsense syllables, such as *bik* or *wug* or *gutch*, all native speakers of English can do so with ease. If you say these words to yourself, you will quickly see how easy it is to decide which plural sound to add. Most six-year-old children can also add these plural sounds correctly. We infer knowledge of the rules from what adults or children are able to say and understand.

Children learn the grammar of their native language gradually. One might assume, therefore, that the stages they pass through on their way to adult knowledge are partial versions of it. However, this is not the case.

194 *language and the language arts*

One of the most dramatic findings in studies of children's acquisition of language is that these stages have striking similarities in all groups of children, but equally striking deviations from adult grammar.

For example, during a certain period when children are learning to form noun and verb endings, they will say *foots* instead of *feet*, *goed* instead of *went*. Children do not hear anyone around them say *foots* or *goed*. Instead, these words are overgeneralizations of rules that each child is somehow extracting from the language he does hear.

Sometimes we hear dramatic evidence of how resistant to external correction the child's rule system can be. Jean Berko Gleason (1967) had the following conversation with a four-year-old:

C: *My teacher holded the baby rabbits and we patted them.*
JBG: *Did you say your teacher held the baby rabbits?*
C: *Yes.*
JBG: *What did you say she did?*
C: *She holded the baby rabbits and we patted them.*
JBG: *Did you say she held them tightly?*
C: *No, she holded them loosely.*

With rare exceptions, all children learn to speak the language of their parents and home community. They do so with speed and ease, at pre-school ages when other seemingly more simple learnings such as color identification are absent. One naturally wonders how they do it and how the environment helps. Here we can contrast research knowledge with common folk beliefs.

FOLK BELIEFS
MYTH: *Children learn language by imitation.*
The common view of how children learn to speak is that they imitate the language they hear around them. In a general way, this must be true. A child in an English-speaking home grows up to speak English, not French or some language of his own. But in fine details of the language-learning process imitation cannot be the whole answer. As *foots* and *goed* and *holded* show, children use the language they hear as examples of language to learn from, not samples of language to learn.

Although imitation is not as important as commonly believed, identification with particular models is very important. How any person speaks depends not only on who he is, but also on how he sees himself in relation to others, on who he wants to be. From the beginning of the language-learning process, children pick their models. They do not do this consciously, but we have already noted how powerful nonconscious knowledge can be. If children didn't pick their models, there would be no way to explain why black children, for example, speak like their parents or peers despite considerable exposure to standard English on television. The power of attitudes to influence language learning is of critical importance for education, since they influence teachers' responses to children as well as childrens' responses to teachers. We shall return to this point later.

MYTH: *Children learn language by being corrected.*
Along with the common belief that the child's language-learning process is basically imitation, there is a belief that the adult's contribution is to shape the child's speech by correcting him when he is "wrong" and reinforcing him when he is "correct." Nevertheless, all analyses of conversations between parents and children whose language is developing well show that neither correction of immature forms nor reinforcement of mature forms occurs with sufficient frequency to be a potent force. This has been demonstrated by studies of white children in Cambridge, Massachusetts (Brown et al.), and Madison, Wisconsin (Friedlander) and of black lower-class children in Rochester, New York (Horner), and Oakland, California (Kernan).

During conversations with their children parents do correct misstatements of fact (such as the time a particular television program comes on), they clarify word meanings (such as the difference between *beside* and *under*), and they correct socially inappropriate language. Ursula Bellugi-Klima's picture (1968) of one family's conversations applies to all:

> *The mother and child are concerned with daily activities, not grammatical instruction. Adam breaks something, looks for a nail to repair it with, finally throws pencils and nails around the room. He pulls his favorite animals in a toy wagon, fiddles with the television set, and tries to put together a puzzle. His mother is concerned primarily with modifying his behavior. She gives him information about the world around him and corrects facts. Neither of the two seems overtly concerned with the problems that we shall pursue so avidly: the acquisition of syntax.*

The language that mothers speak to young children has been studied by students of Dan Slobin in California (black mothers in Oakland) and by Judith Phillips in Baltimore (hospital staff workers). Mothers do use simpler language with young children than with other adults, and as the child's utterances become longer and more complex, so do the mother's. Other than this simplification, there is no sequencing of what the child has to learn. He is offered a cafeteria, not a carefully prescribed diet. And seemingly impelled from within, he participates in the give-and-take of conversation with adults and other children as best he can from the very beginning, and in the process takes what he needs to construct his own language system.

Although the course of language development is similar for all children, individual differences in the rate of development will be striking in any day-care center. These differences appear in both speaking and under-standing, and they pose special problems for teachers.

For example, at age two and a half many children talk a great deal, while others do not utter a word. The child who talks well at age two is not necessarily brighter nor will he necessarily be more verbally capable at age three. A little later in life, roughly from three-and-a-half on, there is a relationship between how verbal a child is and how verbal he will be in the future. But in the earliest months of talking this is not the case.

Individual differences in the amount of talking in very young children pose a special problem for teachers, because adults tend to talk more to children who talk back. (Adults like reinforcement too.) Thus a day-care center may unwittingly magnify initial differences. Talkers who are reinforced for talking by someone they like and trust will talk even more; nontalkers may be even less inclined to talk if they are ignored. Teachers must be exceedingly careful about how they distribute their attention during the day.

Variability among children in understanding language is probably as great as their variability in talking. Consider, for example, Palmer's (1970) research on New York City children's comprehension of words for basic concepts like *on top of, fast, wet, same as,* or *many.* Children were asked to demonstrate their understanding by manipulating objects. For instance, they were given a tow truck and a car and asked to "make the car go *up*" and "make the car go *down*." Out of 50 such concepts, some children at age two understood only six or seven, while other children understood as many as 40.

Some concepts, and the words associated with them are easier to learn than others and are learned earlier by most children. For example, of 240 children from three ethnic groups in Palmer's study, the following percentages of all children responded correctly to particular words:

On top of	93%	*Slow*	29%
Into	82%	*Biggest*	26%
Open	74%	*Under*	18%
Wet	68%	*Around*	10%

The comprehension vocabulary of a child is seldom as well rec-ognized by those around him as his productive vocabulary. Yet good teaching presumably requires that the teacher talk with each child in words he can understand while helping him always to learn more. Teachers need to listen sensitively to children in a variety of situations. (Cazden, in press, offers some specific suggestions.)

A child's background appears to influence his knowledge about certain concepts even as early as age two. For reasons we don't understand, the Puerto Rican children in Palmer's study were considerably better in responding to concepts of movement, such as *fast* and *slow*, even though the three groups were matched for socioeconomic status. Thus, although some concepts are, in general, more difficult for children, the immediate home environment contributes to their understanding of specific concepts. As a result, the knowledge that children bring to a day-care program depends to some extent on the population it serves.

In a center where age groups are mixed, the extent of individual differences will, of course, be greater. By age three most children have learned to comprehend many of the simple concepts. For example, Palmer found that, in the same sample of 240 children at age three, 70 percent of the children comprehended the concept *under*, whereas only 18 percent had done so at age two. Concepts which were still very difficult for the three-year-old were *bottom, backward*, and *side*. Still other concepts, such as *same* and *different*, are still difficult for children at the age of four.

Words representing such concepts as *into* are learned first in specific situations. Even when a child shows that he understands the message *Put the toy into the box*, we cannot assume that he has a general understanding of the spatial relationship *into*. He may simply know what one normally does with toys and boxes. One characteristic of language learning is growth from meanings that are situation-bound to meanings that are situation-free, and a child will vary in this respect with different words. Teachers should try to use even those words that children "know" in a limited sense in a rich variety of contexts.

Since language development in the growing child is partly a function of the education and occupation of his parents, there are also differences that correlate with socioeconomic level. This is particularly true with knowledge of word meanings, which is what most language tests (and also some intelligence tests) evaluate. This fact has led some teachers and researchers to infer that differences in all forms of language development begin very early in life, shortly after the child begins to talk. This is not true.

Palmer (1970) compared the language comprehension of black boys from widely varying socioeconomic backgrounds at age 2.0, 2.8, 3.0, and 3.8. Care was taken to ensure that each child was comfortable in the testing situation; hence 4 to 15 hours was required to finish the test battery, depending on the child's age and individual characteristics. There were no significant differences relating to socioeconomic level except in a select group whose parents had exceptional educations; a small group at the highest end of the socioeconomic scale may perform better as early as three. However, no differences between the child of average parents and the child of ghetto parents emerges until about four-and-a-half.

This fact has significant implications for preschool education. Since two to four and a half is the age at which children frequently are first placed in day-care centers and nursery schools, day-care programs offer an opportunity to reduce the differences that would otherwise emerge.

LANGUAGE DIFFERENCES

Most children differ from their teachers in the language system, or grammar, that they use. They also differ among themselves in verbal styles. It is not possible to plan effective educational programs without taking these differences into account.

DIFFERENCES IN GRAMMATICAL SYSTEMS

One important source of language differences is, of course, a foreign-language background. Some children of immigrant families come to school without knowing English, although in most cases they are already using English before the age of five. In the United States the pattern has been for foreign-born parents to promote the use of English by their children; hence even first-generation children usually have only a passive knowledge of their parents' native language. The Italian or Yiddish backgrounds of many first-generation children, for example, has surprisingly little influence on their English.

This pattern of the decline of the immigrant language is also evident in Puerto Rican communities. Although the continual transmigration in those communities makes Spanish seem a more stable language than its predecessors in Eastern cities, researchers report no strong influence of Spanish grammar on the English of first-generation Puerto Rican adolescents. Younger children, still under the influence of their parents at four or five, may show a much heavier Spanish overlay in their English.

In those regions of the United States that border directly on a foreign-language area the situation is different. There are two such regions: the portion of Maine adjacent to French-speaking Quebec and the Mexican border areas in the Southwestern states. Spanish continues as the native language of children in the Southwest and shows no signs of disappearing. In this region there are also large numbers of Indian children—Navaho, Apache, Papago, and others—for whom English is a second language.

Many more children have different grammatical systems from their teachers because they speak some nonstandard dialect of English. There is a general consensus among educated speakers on the grammar of standard English, and controversies are confined to a few issues such as *It's me* vs *It's I* and other fine points which rarely arise in natural speech. But most children use a number of familiar nonstandard forms which actually constitute a general subordinate social dialect. Although many teachers may also have used these forms in their native vernaculars, they have adopted standard English as a consequence of their own education. In most regions of the United States the number of differences involved is surprisingly small—a dozen or so rules concerning the objective case in pronouns, agreement between third-singular subject and verb, irregular forms of the perfect, the comparative and adverbial -ly, a few conjunctions, and such well-known markers as *ain't*. The persistence of these forms is a tribute to the strength and utility of the nonstandard dialects, rather than to any inherent difficulty in converting to the standard rules.

REGIONAL DIALECTS Some regional dialects differ much more from the standard English (SE) of the classroom than the usual urban nonstandard speech. In rural New England, Appalachia, and many regions of the South the nonstandard grammars have striking points of contrast with SE. Southern dialects freely employ negative inversion for emphasis. *Didn't anybody see it* can only be a question in the North, but in the South it may be a statement. There are also deeper social differences in the South than elsewhere. Thus the most common nonstandard equivalent of this regional form is *Ain't nobody see it*.

In most cases the teachers in these areas are native to the same region; hence they have an intuitive grasp of these grammatical forms even though they may lack a full enough understanding to teach the contrasting sets of rules to children.

However, when a regional dialect is transplanted to another region, usually from a rural to an urban region, it typically becomes a subordinate, stigmatized social dialect. As a result, the linguistic distance between child and teacher is greatly increased, since there is now both a regional *and* a social barrier. This is the case with the speech of blacks from the rural South who move to the Northern cities. The same is true of Appalachian dialects transplanted to Midwestern cities such as Columbus or Cleveland.

CREOLE LANGUAGES There is another form of English spoken within the United States which differs from SE more than any of the dialects, but not as much as a foreign language. This is Creole, a distinct language which has a largely English vocabulary but is not readily intelligible to speakers of SE. The Creoles are native languages descended from contact vernaculars or pidgins—reduced forms of language developed as a means of communication by speakers of radically different languages. One such English Creole is Gullah, spoken in coastal South Carolina and Georgia by blacks, especially on the Sea Islands; Gullah directly or indirectly influences all the English spoken in that region. Another is Hawaiian Creole, generally known as "pidgin" in Hawaii, which is the native language of most of the noncaucasian population on the islands. Adults and older youth use a modified form of these Creoles in conversation with outsiders, so that many outsiders believe that the Creoles no longer exist as distinct languages. But children coming to school maintain the Creole tradition, and most of them preserve it as their basic vernacular at least until their early twenties. The term "Creole" originally referred to the French-based vernacular spoken in Louisiana, which still has an influence on the speech of children in some areas.

BLACK ENGLISH   Black English, or "nonstandard Negro English," is a remarkably uniform dialect used by black children in all the inner-city ghetto areas and throughout most of the South. Current studies by William Labov, Roger Shuy, William Stewart, Walter Wolfram, and others show that the grammar of black English (BE) is essentially the same in Boston, New York, Philadelphia, Washington, Cleveland, Detroit, Chicago, St. Louis, New Orleans, San Francisco, and Los Angeles. There is evidence that BE has a Creole origin—that it has inherited certain grammatical features from an earlier Creole spoken throughout the South, similar to those spoken in the Caribbean, and is itself the product of language contact between European and African languages. BE is therefore a combination of all the differentiating factors mentioned above. It is a nonstandard regional dialect, transported to other regions in a subordinate position, it has a Creole pattern originating in contact between English and another language, and it shares with general nonstandard English such features as negative concord (double negatives) and irregular perfects (e.g., *I had came*).

The overall results of Labov's research on black English show that the most apparent differences from SE are superficial from a linguistic standpoint. Although it differs from SE more than any other nonstandard dialect, it is not a foreign language in any sense of the word; the underlying set of meaningful categories are the same, with one or two notable exceptions. The striking differences in surface structures are largely due to (1) the rules for contraction of grammatical particles, (2) phonetic realization of a few sounds, (3) different intonational patterns, and (4) different distribution of a few redundant elements.

The situation with the regular past tense illustrates the general point. Black children often say *He pick me up yesterday*; the word *pick* seems to have no ending. But careful examination of a number of dialects shows that the rule which results in *pick* is used by all speakers of English to a greater or lesser extent: optional deletion of a phonetic *-t* or *-d* after another consonant. BE carries this rule further and includes the past tense *-ed* in its scope much more often, but there are no speakers of BE who never use the full *-ed* form. The plural *-s* also occurs in BE, although there are some differences in irregular forms, such as *deers* in place of *deer*. In contrast, the Creoles based on English have a very different grammatical apparatus. Jamaican Creole has no *-ed* and no plural *-s*. The past tense is usually not marked at all, and the habitual present is marked by prefixing *a-* to the verb. The plural is marked by the suffix *dem*: *di buk dem* corresponds to SE and BE *the books*. Hawaiian Creole also has no *-ed*, but uses the auxiliary *went* instead: *He went pick em up* for SE *He picked it up*.

The use of forms of the verb *to be*—called the "copula"—is even more central to the child's logic as evidenced by his language (Labov, 1970). Some psychologists working with preschool children have construed the omission of the copula in such expressions as *They mine* and *He my brother* as an inability to make logical statements. The present-tense copula *is*, of course, not logically necessary; most languages dispense with it in such sentences. However, in this case, BE is merely extending the contraction rule to omission of the copula when it is not emphasized, under the same conditions that govern the SE contractions *They're mine* and *He's my brother*. (BE has, in addition, an undeletable copula *be* which marks the habitual present.) In any case, we find that all BE speakers have an abstract copula which appears with emphasis or whenever contraction is not permitted, as in *He is too my brother* and *That's what he is*. Children of four to eight use the full form *is* even more than older children who have mastered the BE vernacular.

DEVELOPMENTAL VERSUS DIALECTAL DIFFERENCES

The view of dialectal language differences is further complicated by the fact that in a day-care program many children still have an incomplete grasp of the grammar and phonetics of their basic dialect, standard or nonstandard. Moreover, at this age they often have problems with the articulation of *l* and *r*, so that contracted forms of *will* and *are* in *He'll* and *They're* are particularly elusive. They have difficulty with the sound of *th*, as in *them* or *thin*, and produce instead *t* and *d* or *f* and *v*. They have problems with such consonant clusters as *-st* and *str-* in *passed*, *test*, and *strong*, as well as *thr-* in *throw*. Labov has found that in black or Puerto Rican children these developmental patterns sometimes coincide with and reinforce a pattern of their nonstandard dialect. For example, many children use *skr-* for *str-* in *street*; this happens to coincide with a regional South Carolina pattern which is often heard in black English in the North.

There is also a certain amount of similarity between nonstandard grammatical patterns and early childhood developmental forms. Very young children often fail to reverse the subject and auxiliary with *wh-*questions: *Can he go?* but *Where he went?* BE speakers seem to follow this pattern longer than speakers of other dialects, although the standard *Where'd he go?* is more common in fully formed BE. Hawaiian Creole has no such reversal even in yes-no questions; there is only *He can go*, with a special high falling intonation to denote the question form.

Many four-year-olds show negative concord in their speech: *He don't like nobody*, which coincides with the general nonstandard form. The distinction between subjective and objective pronouns, especially *he-him* and *she-her*, is occasionally missing in the speech of black children until it is acquired in adolescence. It is possible that both of these irregular patterns survive longer in BE as an inheritance from Creole patterns, which do not differentiate subjective and objective or masculine, feminine, and neuter. This does not mean that the young child is confused about sex distinctions.

The fact that many nonstandard speech forms coincide with early developmental forms in standard English has led to a common assumption that nonstandard English is simply retarded language development—a viewpoint which has been reinforced by the low verbal output and scholastic performance of speakers of nonstandard English in the traditional school environment. However, there is an equally large body of evidence that nonstandard dialects are more advanced developments, and more remote from childhood patterns, than standard English. Negative inversion and the deletion of the copula are actually additional steps in language development. It is incorrect, therefore, to equate nonstandard language with underdeveloped language. Rather, the teacher or tutor in a day-care program must realize that the differences between his speech and the children's speech represent a mixture of developmental and dialectal differences.

FOLK BELIEFS

Any program for teaching day-care center personnel about language differences will have to come to grips with a set of powerful folk beliefs (see Baratz & Baratz, 1970, for more extended discussion).

MYTH: *Some languages are better than others.*
Although some people believe that the Indian languages are little more than a series of grunts and groans, or that standard English is better than black dialect for abstract thinking, there is no evidence to support such assertions. All languages are inherently equal in the complexity of their basic grammatical and logical structure. All languages have highly structured rules of sound and syntax, and all languages are used for interpersonal and intrapersonal communication. Cultures differ in the topics considered worthy of discussion; for example, people in nontechnological societies spend less time discussing scientific matters than those in technological societies. But any language has the potential to deal with any topic if the speakers want to introduce or develop the appropriate vocabulary.

MYTH: *Some dialects represent bad language usage.*
A dialect, as linguists use the term, is one of the many varieties of a language which, when taken together, make up that language. English, for

example, includes all the dialects used throughout North America and the United Kingdom, and what we refer to as standard English in the United States is merely one of these dialects. The fact that it is the official form for conducting the affairs of state, business, and education does not mean that in terms of linguistic properties it is any better than white Appalachian dialect, black nonstandard dialect, or Hawaiian pidgin English. All dialects of a language (including the standard) are systematic, highly structured language codes.

MYTH: *People who speak a nonstandard dialect have low intelligence.*
On the false premise that a dialect is bad English, people who speak nonstandard dialects are often considered lacking in intelligence. Such an assumption presupposes that any utterance that is not in standard English is the result of poor learning of standard English, rather than the result of good learning of a dialect other than the standard. The language variety one learns reflects those with whom one lives, not the intelligence with which one is endowed.

In many instances those who deprecate nonstandard dialects fail to separate the linguistic reality from the social one. The fact that standard English is the employed dialect for negotiations by the larger mainstream society, and the fact that the larger mainstream society devalues and rejects other dialects, does not make these dialects any less valid in terms of linguistic features. Such social devaluing based on the ethnocentrism of the mainstream society is an indication of how language myths have inadvertently generated prejudice.

MYTH: *Learning a nonstandard dialect is not learning a language.*
This myth has led to the common assumption that children from economically deprived backgrounds are verbally destitute. Educators and psychologists unversed in language learning and language usage have contributed greatly to such an assumption because they have erroneously equated verbal ability with proficiency in standard English. Thus they have construed nonstandard utterances as "underdeveloped" language.

Moreover, many of the experiments designed to elicit language have used stimuli which were not only linguistically biased in favor of standard English, but which also violated the social conventions of the children being tested. Language learning involves not only acquiring the rules of the structure of the dialect, but also learning the social conventions of its usage—what topics are talked about, with whom one talks, and so on. In certain cultures it is inappropriate behavior for a child to make a "display" of his knowledge to an adult even if the adult happens to be kind, like the proverbial friendly white examiner. The black child's *I 'on' know* may more often reflect his perception of the alien social situation than his ignorance.

The prevalence of these myths among teachers may be related to their own social background. According to one estimate 80 percent of all teachers come from the middle class, and a good proportion of this group comes from the lower middle class, which Labov has found to be frequently the most linguistically insecure. No comparable estimate is available for day-care personnel, but the large numbers of paraprofessionals involved suggests that the problem of adult insecurity about language may be even greater. People who are themselves insecure are often rigid and hostile toward children who display speech patterns which they hate in themselves.

Unfortunately these folk beliefs about language differences are more damaging to a good day-care program than folk beliefs about language development. The expectations that the teacher has for a child will influence how he teaches and how much the child learns, and there is mounting evidence that one of the principal cues to which the teacher responds in developing these expectations is the child's speech. Frederick Williams in Chicago and Wayne Shamo in Memphis found that teachers evaluate children more negatively when their speech has nonstandard pronunciation and syntax. Judith Guskin in Ann Arbor found that teachers-in-training rated black speakers as less likely to succeed academically than white speakers. Seligman, Tucker, and Lambert in Montreal found that a recorded speech pattern or a child's photograph carried more weight than the quality of a child's composition or drawing in third-grade teachers' ratings. There is no reason to believe that preschool teachers, inservice or preservice, would be less susceptible to these prejudiced reactions. Monica and Douglas Holmes compared the evaluations of a Head Start teacher in Coney Island with observations and IQ tests of the children in her class. The teacher's ratings of her children's intelligence were not correlated with actual intelligence-test scores, and they were biased by such actual behaviors as the child's willingness to respond to directions and his general verbal skills.

We do not know how a training program for teachers should be designed to deal with such ethnocentric biases. Since these reactions are deeply founded in the teachers' own past experiences, they probably will not be changed merely by learning the facts about language differences.

DIFFERENCES IN VERBAL STYLES

Children differ markedly in their strategies for learning. (1) Some make every bit of new knowledge explicit and insist on repeating aloud everything they know. (2) Others store up knowledge like blotters, rarely producing it even on demand. (3) Others avoid new learning and insulate themselves from it as much as possible. The difference in these strategies or individual styles is crucial in planning a successful program.

It has been considered the task of teachers to diagnose such individual differences in behavior. No test now in use seems to differentiate children who are following path (2) from those who follow path (3). However, certain general sociolinguistic principles operate beyond the influence of individual personalities. There is a striking difference between the way children talk to each other and the way they talk in the presence of adults. Oldest children or only children show the fastest verbal development and more of it, in the sense of strategy (1). Since practice in communicating with adults leads to more explicit verbalization, better performance on reading-readiness tests, and better initial performance in school, most teachers conclude that the less vocal children lack the necessary requirement for verbal development—contact with adult speakers of standard English—and need more individual attention from the teacher, or even one-to-one tutoring.

Some children do indeed talk more fluently with adults. But empirical studies show that many children talk less with adults than with their peers; their responses to adults may also be less complex than the kind of speech they produce among themselves. Children who are tagged as "nonverbal" in test situations with an adult often show remarkable verbal skills when adults are absent. This is particularly true among black and Puerto Rican children, who have a highly developed verbal culture of their own which is not easily accepted or appreciated by parents and teachers. Teachers need to be imaginative in trying a variety of methods for adapting to individual differences in verbal style.

Teachers often want samples of a child's language, either for evaluation or for instruction, and in such cases they may use the same technique as testers: they ask the child to tell a story about a picture. The following examples are taken from such a teacher-tester situation, in which the most elaborate language elicited consists of such simple, unconnected sentences as *The girl got a bike. . . . The boy's playin' football.* In the typical exchange the adult does most of the talking:

TEACHER: *Where are they playing, James?*
JAMES: *On the street.*
TEACHER: *Do you think the street's a good place to play in?*
JAMES: *Yes.*
TEACHER: *You do? Alright, go ahead. Tell me some more. Why do you think it is a good place to play in?*
JAMES: *'Cause they like to play.*

The main sociolinguistic control in this situation is the unequal power relation between adult and child. No matter what demands are made on the child, no matter how obscure and pointless the questions may seem, he is obliged to answer. The typical reaction of many preschool children is to give minimal responses, sometimes the exact reverse of the answer the adult is demanding. This happens most often when the adult combines moral instruction with his inquiry and thus confuses the roles of preacher and teacher:

TEACHER: *Mays, do you see all that paper in the street?*
MAYS: *Yeah.*
TEACHER: *How do you think it got there?*
MAYS: *It blew there.*
TEACHER: *Do you think that children could do anything to help keep the street clean?*
MAYS: *Nah.*

The temptation to act as an agent of social improvement is difficult to resist, even in the midst of an exploration of the child's verbal skills. Day-care programs are particularly prone to this line of adult-child relationship, since many adults think their primary responsibility is to keep the child out of trouble and improve his social behavior. As a result, they often provoke the monosyllabic defensive behavior illustrated above, which they then take as evidence of the child's restricted verbal skills. On the basis of such false evidence, many educational programs are devoted to the task of providing children with a "new language" instead of creating a school setting that stimulates each child to use all the language he has.

LANGUAGE IN THE DAY-CARE CENTER

In the day-care center children can talk to other children and to adults. It is important to make maximum use of all these human resources.

TALK AMONG CHILDREN
Most children in day-care populations will use their fullest grammatical skills when talking to other children. This means, as a minimum, that teachers should encourage as much talk among children as would normally occur in unsupervised situations. Ideally, more can be done to provide the maximum benefits of child talk for each participant. Three functions of speech seem particularly important as incentives for complex language.

SPEECH FOR SELF-AGGRANDIZEMENT The primary factor here is power relations. The most language is produced when there is no one present of superior status—in other words, when nothing the child says can be held against him. It is even helpful to have someone of clearly inferior status present, an argument for mixed-age grouping. One of the major uses of language is self-aggrandizement with respect to others: raising one's own status and lowering theirs. Children use the system of adult norms as an instrument for this purpose and become involved in complex propositions on the future consequences of present or future acts. To illustrate this point, we can use extracts from the free conversation of the same six-year-olds quoted above. Those present are James, his close friend Mays, a smaller and younger boy named Harold, and a rabbit:

MAYS: *James, I told you not to move with him no more! If he fall out your lap and hurt hisself, that's your fault an' you gonna pay for it! . . .*

JAMES: *You better sit back down, boy, before he get ma-ad and beat you up for some carrots.*

LANGUAGE FOR EXPLICATION A second major incentive for complex language is the need for explication, as would be the case in puzzling out the complex workings of machinery:

MAYS: *Look at it, look at—that's why it's turnin' around. You know why it's turnin' around? 'Cause makin' that thing. . . .*

The first two functions are combined in:

MAYS: *How can a bunny rabbit talk to you! He only don't even know how to speak!*

LANGUAGE FOR ESTHETIC PLEASURE The third motivating factor for complex speech is *esthetic*. Children play with syntax as well as sound and can demonstrate skills that go far beyond any current program of instruction. The following example combines the esthetic and the normative functions of language:

JAMES: *The more he get nervous . . .*

MAYS: *. . . the more he gonna jump off!*

JAMES: *Uh-uh. The more he get nervous, the more he die, the more Harold gonna hafta pay the doctor bills!*

MAYS: *Right. 'N' the more he get nervous . . .*

JAMES: *Tsk! The more he die, the more Harold gonna hafta pay the doctor bills.*

The linguistic skills of these children are beyond the school program that is being offered them. The task of the day-care program, if it is to be successful, is to draw on the energy and versatility displayed here for constructive ends. This can be done by creating social situations in which these abilities naturally come into play. Children should be helped to organize themselves into groups with considerable age range, where it is the natural task of the older to explain things to the younger (and where the younger is not necessarily degraded for not knowing something). Also, they should have available objects of considerable mechanical complexity, where their desire for explication can be given full scope.

208 *language and the language arts*

Many day-care programs use puppet plays and other role-playing situations to stimulate language. This can be a successful device if three basic relationships are incorporated. Adults should provide roles and situations, but not model behavior or the plot. Characters can be constructed who are in an inferior role in relation to the children, for example, puppets, animals, or robots who know less than the children themselves. Objects and settings for such roles can be complicated up to the point where it is possible for any small child to get lost in them.

These suggestions for maximizing the value of talk among children come from sociolinguistic analyses of children's spontaneous speech. They are important because so often in discussions of programs for young children the impression is given that planning for one-to-one talk between adult and child is all that matters. We may learn more about how to create conditions for complex talk among children by analyzing what happens when these ideas are tried out. Whatever situations are most likely to elicit a child's most complex language are also useful contexts for diagnosing his growth in verbal abilities over time.

ADULT-CHILD TALK

Adults can talk to children in ways that are uniquely beneficial to their language and cognitive development, and day-care programs should make maximum use of such opportunities. What counts, however, is the quality of adult-child talk, not just the quantity, and the organizational conditions in which constructive talk is most likely to occur.

QUALITY OF TALK The first major step is to shift the role and behavior of the adult away from that of interviewer to that of a resource for the child to draw on. Unfortunately many language curricula depend largely on question-answer sequences. Questions put by the adult should be true requests for information, rather than known-answer questions or requests for a display of knowledge. To the extent that an adult takes on the role of disciplinarian, he can hardly serve as the center of a free exchange of ideas.

Barbara and Jack Tizard (1970) studied the conditions in residential nurseries in Great Britain that promote language development. They found that " 'informative' remarks by the staff tended to evoke a response in the children, while commands and 'time passing' remarks did not. The more frequent the prohibition in an adult's talk, the less often was she answered by the children."

Surprising as it may seem, many adults need help in learning how to talk to children in productive ways. Polly Greenberg (1969) reports on a workshop session from the Child Development Group of Mississippi:

> Talking *about talking with children didn't work. If people don't habitually talk lengthily with children, they don't know* how *to talk lengthily with children. So we actually practised it:*

TEACHER: *Oh, you tease Tom, what are you telling Winston?*
TOM: *I tellin' him my brother Gary a bad bad boy.*
TEACHER: *Oh, now that ain't nice.*

The group analyses and discusses this. Then the same teacher goes to find Tom, who is waiting for out staff meeting to be over so one of the teachers will drive him home. The same teacher runs through the same conversation. I tape this conversation too, and afterward we discuss it to see if and how the teacher prolonged and enriched the verbal exchange:

TEACHER: *Tom, what was you tellin' Winston this mornin' when you was playin' with the ball?*
TOM: *I tole him Gary my brother.*
TEACHER: *You like Gary?*
TOM: *Yeah, I lahk him, but he bad.*

. . . *[three teacher-Tom interchanges]*

TEACHER: *Why's dat?*
TOM: *'Cause he walked up and set with his friend when they was singin' 'bout Jesus and the preacher was preachin'.*
TEACHER: *Who whipped him?*
TOM: *Daddy—he tuk him outside and whupped him with a red belt.*
TEACHER: *Did Gary cry?*
TOM: *Oh, yeah, he got tears in his eyes. Mama wiped his eyes with a rag when he come back in. Then he popped his fingers. That boy can't* never *be quiet.*

. . . *[and so on for at least five more teacher-Tom interchanges; pp. 165–66].*

In the above conversation adult and child are talking about a past event. Sometimes it may be easier to engage a child in extended conversation about some object actually present. David Hawkins, a philosopher of science, relates how he learned from his wife Frances, a nursery school teacher, how to talk with small children (1967):

I learned . . . that one of the very important factors in this kind of situation is that there be some third thing which is of interest to the child and to the adult, in which they can join in outward projection. Only this creates a possible stable bond of communication, of shared concern. . . . So the first act in teaching, it seems to me, the first goal necessary to all others, is to encourage this kind of engrossment. Then the child comes alive for the teacher as well as the teacher for the child. They have a common engrossment for discussion, they are involved together in the world [p. 7].

In these conversations teachers should try, even at the risk of initial self-consciousness, to use elaborated and precise language themselves (within the limits of the child's comprehension). There is evidence that the elaboration of teacher talk is reflected in the talk of the children (Smothergill, 1969) and that it is the quality of talk, not the quantity, that counts (Tizard, 1970). Oralie McAfee (1967) gives suggestions for vocabulary, and Celia Lavatelli (1970) gives suggestions for syntax.

Finally, the reinforcing nature of the affective relationship between child and adult can be used to facilitate learning in the child. When a warm and trusting relationship between the two has developed, games and other forms of play may serve as a context for learning. But for maximum effect, the child must learn that from the games the teacher will expect some response. Just as there is a difference for an adult between reading a detective story for his own satisfaction and reading a drivers' license manual to pass an examination, so there is a difference between play for play's sake and play designed to provoke responses from the child in a context of learning. If the child learns that the blocks or toys with which he is playing are related to a response the teacher will expect of him, he seems to learn to process the experiences in a more systematic manner. This ability to organize information with the purpose of an eventual response to an adult or peer is probably most efficiently learned in a one-to-one situation between adult and child, where the adult can, with smiles, nods, and words of encouragement, reinforce the responses that order the materials the child is playing with. Organizing information for response to others is an essential characteristic of most human intellective abilities, no matter how one wishes to define intelligence.

ORGANIZATIONAL CONDITIONS The Tizards' research points to organizational conditions in day-care centers which probably affect the frequency of quality conversations between adult and child. The adult-child ratio is not the only factor, although it is important. They found that nurseries in which the children's language development was highest were also characterized by a smaller proportion of children under three, greater staff stability, and greater staff autonomy. Where the proportion of very young children was high, the staff was preoccupied with the burdens of physical care. Where staff turnover was high, the adults were less likely to understand the early speech of the young child. Where staff autonomy was low, the adult saw her job more as " 'minding' the children under the eye of her supervisor." Finally, within any given adult-child ratio, conversation may depend on how staff responsibilities are allocated. The Tizards found that "when two staff were on duty with a group of six children, the junior of the two tended to talk less and interact less with the children than when she was alone in charge of the group." Adults as well as children are influenced by the power relations inherent in speech situations. We need more studies like the Tizards' of how features of complex organizations influence behavior and thereby affect the child's development.

WHICH LANGUAGE TO USE

Day-care programs must take into account the fact that most of the children will have limited command of standard English. The basic approach in the past has been the "Sink-or-swim" method, where speakers of a foreign language or of BE were confronted with an SE-speaking classroom. Children have a surprising ability to cope with such an abrupt switch. Experiments in Quebec show that English-speaking middle-class children can accept a totally French-speaking school without any obvious problems. However, this is under the most favorable circumstances. The obvious fact remains that BE- , Creole- , French- , Spanish- , or Indian-speaking children do not take full advantage of the English-speaking schools, and their overall educational achievement is very low. From all indications, the low performance of black, Chicano, or Indian children is the result of general cultural factors. Although the absence of their native language in the classroom may not present insuperable cognitive obstacles, it may be decisive in defining the school or preschool as an alien and hostile environment.

It follows that ideally both the children's native language or dialect and standard English should be used in the classroom. How much English and how much of the other language is an open question. A further and more difficult question concerns the selection of day-care personnel, either as staff for a center or as mothers for home day care. Which is more important: fluency in the child's native language or some degree of fluency in standard English? As certification requirements for educational personnel change from academic degrees to performance criteria, the question of criteria in language becomes important.

Obviously, the best-qualified adult would be fluent in all languages and dialects represented, but the supply of such multilingual experts is extremely limited. Answers to these questions will depend on the attitudes and goals of the parents, on the availability of bilingual personnel, and on more knowledge than we now have of how best to teach children a second dialect or language in a school setting while at the same time promoting their fluency in their first language as well. (See John & Horner, in press, for discussions of bilingual programs for young children.)

TEACHING CULTURAL PLURALISM

We assume a goal of cultural pluralism: many different ethnic groups living together, sharing and borrowing while retaining their ethnic distinctiveness. The early childhood day-care center offers a unique opportunity for children to learn about their own cultural identities while learning at the same time to respect others. A curriculum for young children can be designed to provide learning about the language, culture, and mores not only of their own group or of mainstream America, but also of the many other ethnic groups that are a part of American society.

For example, food is a topic dear to all children, and exploration of the food tastes of various ethnic groups can serve as an excellent beginning for learning about cultural differences. It should not be difficult, especially in urban areas, for teachers to obtain samples of the foods of Jews, Italians, blacks, Poles, Chinese, or Mexican-Americans from neighborhood stores. Information on songs, dances, games, and the social customs of children from different cultures are available from such sources as Folkways Records, UNESCO, and organizations such as B'nai B'rith, the Knights of Columbus, and the NAACP.

It is important that all such experiences be related to what the children already know. It will not help for a white child in Los Angeles to learn wonderful things about Pedro in Seville while he remains contemptuous of Jose in the inner city of Los Angeles, or to admire Aki the Nigerian boy while he considers Leroy ignorant because he says "*ain't.*" By the same token, it seems at best devious, and perhaps futile as well, to teach a lower-class American black child to respect himself by learning to respect tribal Africans on the one hand or middle-class American Negroes on the other. The kind of identity that he must learn to respect is his own, including his own variety of walking style, dress, and language.

Undoubtedly the most important resource is the variety of backgrounds within the day-care center itself. Language differences among children and staff—and cultural differences of all kinds—should be welcomed, openly discussed, and utilized in the curriculum. It is to be hoped that adults as well as children will gain greater confidence in themselves and more realistic attitudes toward others through these experiences.

21

VALUES AND ISSUES
IN YOUNG CHILDREN'S LITERATURE   EVELYN GOODENOUGH PITCHER

It is rewarding to consider in some general ways how and why children's literature is different from adult literature. A difference perhaps too obvious to mention is the relatively more simple form, plot and language. There is usually quick action, an uncomplicated, episodic plot; endings are sudden, descriptions are sparse. Repetitive oral formulae are popular, particularly for quite young children.

Such adaptations in levels of organization show that, contrary to several centuries ago, we realize that children are not just small adults, but that they have different developmental levels of understanding, interest, and ability. We are also aware now that children perceive the environment in quite different ways from the ways adults view it. At the pre-school and early school level, children tend to a certain animism, seeing nature in anthropomorphic or personal terms. Children's literature, therefore, rarely has a theme reflecting impersonal, or causal, forces. We need to know what children's personal concerns are likely to be and how they may differ from those of adults.

The literature is different also in that it does not deal with large social issues or a complicated society. Although there is a laudable trend to introduce Negro children and urban life into literature, such characters and environments are home-oriented. The books present social roles that are easily understood, such as those of garbage man, fireman, cowboy, nurse, king, princess, mother, or father. The social group most attractive and comprehensible to children is the family. Indeed, even when books may be allegedly or superficially dealing with a wider society, they probably do not move far from the home front in their communications to young children.

Another difference arises with regard to complexity of characterization. Although certain characters, such as Mr. Badger in *Wind in the Willows* briefly and symbolically represent recognizable psychological types, it is not likely that children fully appreciate Badger's satirical prototype of a gentleman of coarse manners, high position, and kind heart. In general, characters (from adult standards) are "flat" because children themselves are not sufficiently aware of inner differentiation of psychological traits to appreciate complexity of psyche.

THEMES

The matter of themes is more difficult to interpret, and often misunderstood. Although stories for children sometimes present themes seemingly suitable and popular in adult literature, such as war and death and various aspects of ethics or morality, it is unlikely that the themes have the same impact on children as on their elders. Death and warfare are forms of aggression, and as such are also favorite themes. Children are fascinated by what is good and what is bad, and seek constant interpretations of these values. Yet they really come to grips with morality in simple black or white terms. (I shall return to this idea in more detail later). But the impact of such themes is highly personal, understood in a childlike way. Children take from their reading only as much as they can receive. Matters beyond their own experience or receptivity are not likely to affect them deeply.

First I would like to consider what I will label generally as themes of "catastrophe." War and death, hurt and misfortune, various kinds of injury are alluring in that they present themes emotionally meaningful to children to which they seem to respond with more enthusiasm than to a fact-setting story. We can understand this more when we realize how insecure young children are, how mysterious and threatening the outside non-family world can be, and how important their own physical intactness is. Children have an avid interest in stories where characters fall and get hurt and Band-Aids have to be applied or doctors summoned. The story of Johnny's visit to the doctor, with the exciting shot in the arm, brings rapt attention.

NEBRASKA CURRICULUM

"A Curriculum for English," presented by the University of Nebraska (1966) suggests four structural motifs of children's literature which are related to the child's sense of insecurity and his sense of family and other than family:

> (1) a small person's journey from home to isolation away from home; (2) a small person's or a hero's journey from home to confrontation with a monster; (3) a helpless figure's rescue from a harsh home and the miraculous creation of a secure home; and (4) a conflict between a wise beast and a foolish beast. The family unit and the home are described as ultimately good, even if, as in (3) above, it may not be so originally for a small hero. That terrors lurk outside the home in many stories—wolves, tigers, the "dread of the forest"—may reflect the mystery of the technologically-oriented outside world for the child [p. 18].

Three books that are currently popular with pre-schoolers deal in various ways with the motifs described above: Curious George, Harry the Dirty Dog, The Story of Ping. All such motifs seem to me to reflect stage-crucial problems in a young child's life dealing with his initial and basic sense of insecurity, both physical and emotional, and his battle with issues of independence and dependence. Erik Erikson (1950) has demonstrated the importance of these issues in the psycho-social development of children. Another motif, getting knowledge, building skills, relates to the issue of industry versus inferiority. This theme is particularly appealing to children 5–8, as is the next theme, that of identity—a finding one's role or place in society. Needless to say, older children do not give up their interest in themes of security and independence, and many younger children begin reaching out in interest toward themes more absorbing to older children.

CHILDREN TELL STORIES: ANALYSIS OF FANTASY

A project at Bank Street College (1966), reported as "The Story Reader as Teacher," revealed the greater interest of a group of young children in stories that involved themes in what was termed "stage crucial" emotional problems, personally meaningful and understandable. A detailed and documented study of the relevance of some crucial issues in development that seem to appear in stories young children make up themselves is presented in my book, *Children Tell Stories: An Analysis of Fantasy* (1963).

I was prompted to make such a study, inspired by an awareness of some conscientious educators toward certain kinds of literature and fantasy. Fairy-tales, Bible stories, even Mother Goose were considered unfit and psychologically damaging. Was it right to give children notions of boys drowning kittens in wells, birds plucking off noses, dogs suffering pangs of unrequited hunger, boys made of sticks and stones and puppy-dog bones? What is the value of reading of wicked stepmothers who are often witches; is it not dangerous to offer children themes based on deceit, betrayal, hypocrisy, and threats of devouring or dire death in wolves, bears, dragons, and malevolent fairies? Would a child project personal abandonment into the story of Moses in the bulrushes? Tales of battles such as those of David and Goliath, the seige of Jericho, Gideon's defeat of the Midianites seemed but to foster savage aggressiveness in the young child.

So I tried to get some answers from children themselves, children between the ages of two through five in a nursery school where I was teaching. I asked them to tell me a story and I recorded and analyzed the stories thus told, assuming that the kind of story they remembered, the sort of theme most dominant would suggest important interest and concerns. Many of the stories initially offered were a complete or partial telling of a fairy tale, a story of cowboys or Indians remembered from television, or a recital of some *Mother Goose*. Favorite tales were *Hansel and Gretel, Red Riding Hood, Three Little Pigs, Three Bears, Three Billie Goats Gruff.* Almost every child of four and five knows these tales and would rank them on his best seller list. Basic concerns I have already mentioned—those of security and independence, are incorporated into these tales of strong drama, action, vitality, daring, aggressiveness, suffering. Forces of evil (threats from outside) are usually overcome by forces of good (the home, the individual of physical and emotional integrity).

The children also told some original stories, and I collected and analyzed 360 of these. They represented many categories: realistic and fantastic, humorous and dull, dramatic and humdrum. Most surprising, however, was to see the predominance of themes of aggression, involving violence and death and catastrophe, involving hurt and misfortune. Sometimes the aggressions ended in the healing touch or Band-Aids of the mother; sometimes simply, like Hamlet, in all the characters being killed. Sometimes there were episodic recitals of calamities, with no particular resolution. Here are some examples of such stories from children of two, three, and four:

ULF S. 2:10: *I hurt my leg and I tell my mommy. I got a scratch and she put band-aid on it. And I put band-aid on my hand. And I went on a good truck ride. I fall down in the truck, and the car run over me. And I hurt myself in the street, and it was a bone. I got in the truck and the man shut the door so I won't fall out the truck. And then I bumped my head in the truck. Then I ride in the airplane and go to my grandpa.*

COLIN M. 4:11: *Once upon a time there was a man and a typewriter [pronounced typawriter]. And then you know something? The man always wanted to type it. One day this lady came and wanted to type it. And then the man said, "Mrs. Lady, don't type this typewriter." And then the lady just pushed the man down and typed the typewriter. And then the man pushed the lady off the chair she was typing on. And then the man typed what he wanted. And then you know something? The lady got up and when the man started to put his finger on the button she pushed one of the buttons that the man didn't want on there. And then the man got angry at the lady and the lady got a stick and whipped the man and then the man got a sword and then the lady got a sword and they both got two baskets to put over their faces and they both had a sword fight. And then the lady killed the man with her sword. And that's all of that story.*

HOW DO STORIES AFFECT CHILDREN?

Except in unusual instances, it is not likely that children will be made aggressive or overly anxious because they hear of such matters in stories they are told. The mainsprings of aggression and insecurity are fundamental, and methods of dealing with them represent varied and life-long problems. To be sure in some instances sensitive children who are already anxious may hear a story which aggravates their fears. But even here it is not likely that the fear is created by the story, and in most instances an expression of fear or aggressive impulse in the presence of other children, or in the presence of a loving adult offers a means of working toward its solution. Children, like adults, enjoy being a little frightened, especially if matters turn out all right, and if the fright is presented in an art form which could be classified as good literature. Such presentations are subtle and somewhat fantastic; they do not dwell excessively on the gruesome and lurid and sensational. Contrast, for example, the horrid and horrible witch in Walt Disney's *Snow White* with the much vaguer, less frightening original in Grimm. Consider also the sadistic and frightening book *Struwelpeter*, such a source of anxiety to many children in the last century. The first poem in the book which tells with excruciating realism in picture and text how the thumb-sucking Peter will have his thumb cut off leaves nothing to the imagination; in its too vivid description it brings a stage-crucial concern too prominently into focus. *Mother Goose* handles the same concern with far greater finesse in "Along came a blackbird and plucked off her nose." Here the hurt and misfortune fascinate the children, but do not trouble them with overly concrete, personally threatening details.

HUMOR AND NONSENSE

I have particularly dwelt on the darker emotions, but it would be misleading to suggest that children do not respond to exciting events in ordinary living and to lighter and positive emotions, to humor and nonsense. Perhaps we can call these happy emotions our human heritage, and our aggression our human predicament. There are many examples of light and happy stories from children, some perfectly delightful nonsense which sometimes made the children laugh so much they could scarcely speak:

> TITUS B. 5:10: *Silliest civil war you ever heard of—worms are fighting us, the alligators. You know who always wins—the worms. The giant alligators have fourteen and the worms have 125. The alligators haven't sent up their satellite yet, but the worms have. The worms have sent up 255 satellites. And already fourteen worms are in space—even the babies have little suits the worm size. They have alligator's dead teeth (because they shot a lot of alligators in the war). They don't like to do it because they used to like alligators. But now it's their duty. They are just really strong worms. The snake family is with the worm family—that's why they always win. They are not allowed to go around because there is always a guard that spears them—they have fourteen spears and the worms have none. They have fourteen pieces of metal. Alligators have fourteen metals too. They both have fourteen space suits.*
>
> *Fish in these days never ate worms but they ate big fish. There were dinosaurs too. Dinosaurs were terrible lizards. They helped the worms and snakes and fish. The meat-eaters eat dead fish—and they were all allergic to plant eaters. All the plant eaters were too old to be eaten—155 years old. The meat eaters didn't like to eat anything that old. Then the dinosaurs said, "We can beat up the alligators." Then the meat-eaters won. And they didn't like to have those meat-eaters; they speared them.*
>
> PENNY O. 4:10: *A little giraffe lived in a zoo, and he had a little giraffe but the thing was every time he went to sleep a clown woke him up. And then he said, "It's Valentine's Day. You can't go to sleep. You have to work." So he woke up and he got holly, and leaves with berries and then the dog said, "Arf! Arf! Don't believe the clown. Tear up all your work for it's not Valentine's Day. It's Easter!" So then one*

clown said, "Don't believe your dog for it's not Easter, it's Christmas!" And the dog came, and said, "Don't believe the clown. It's not Christmas, it's summer! Then the clown said, "Don't believe your dog, and it's not summer. It's spring!" And the dog said, "Don't believe the clown. It's winter." And then the elf said, "You darn silly things. What is summer and Christmas, and winter and spring, and fall and Easter?

TRACY H. 5:8: *There was a boy named Johnny Hong Kong and finally he grew up and went to school and after that all he ever did was sit all day and think. He hardly even went to the bathroom. And he thought every day and every thought he thought up his head got bigger and bigger. One day it got so big he had to go live up in the attic with trunks and winter clothes. So his mother bought some gold fish and let them live in his head—he swallowed them—and every time he thought, a fish would eat it up until he was even so he never thought again, and he felt much better.*

A SENSE OF WONDER

Then there are a number of stories which seem to belong to a group reflecting—in Rachel Carson's words a "sense of wonder." Such stories seem particularly alert to the joy and excitement and mystery of the world, to communion with and appreciation of the beauties of nature. Their language is the idiom of the child, but the themes have overt tones of wonder.

One such story comes from a four year old which seems to express the association of feminine sexuality and the sea which appears so often in myths:

LILA P. 4:8: *Once there was a fish named Flower. She went down in the water and said, "Oh, my gosh, where's my lover?" She went down in the cellar where my house is. She saw a big father fish which had a sword in his nose. She ran away from the house and hid in another house. She ran up the water and flapped out. She ran away. She went to another house in a deep, deep river. She saw her own home which had her lover in it. They kissed each other. That's the end.*

Another of the passing of the seasons and birth and reproduction:

HARRIET S. 5:1: *Once there was a big, big, Christmas tree. There was a kitty that owned the Christmas tree. And every year the kitty chipped off a bit of the tree for her Christmas. And when Christmas Eve came, Santa planted another big tree for the little kitty. Then years and years and years more trees came and more Christmases came. But then the years grew shorter and the days longer: the trees began to go* *away. Every year the kitty chopped down a tree and every year she got a new big tree.*

And the little kitty had a dog she thought was a kitty. And she didn't know this, 'cause it was in an egg—and she knew kitties didn't come out of eggs. But all of a sudden she went to go away and went and had a squirrel come. And she said, "Will you please, please sit on these eggs. I laid another one just today. But maybe you will lay one for me."

Then she took a ride. She was only gone for a day, but then it snowed. And this little squirrel got so tired. But then she came back. "Where are my eggs?" "Right here." One popped out, two popped out, three popped out. And then they were all squirrels 'cause the little kitty did not sit on them long enough. She only sat on them half a day. They turned out to be squirrels with wings. She said, "Will you please take these little squirrels away. I do not like them. You always lay them the way you are and not the way I am."

But years and years passed and she lay more and more eggs—they were all kitties—and the kitties all grew up and they all were the beginning again.

Here there is influence of Jonah in the whale, with fresh interpretations:

BONNIE C. 4:9: *It's about first in the beginning there was a big ship. It was round and then there were five people living in it. And then they went to bed leaving the grease on the stove and the boat burned down. They all fell in the water and they got swallowed by one whale. And then they had a stick before they jumped in the water so they hit the whale's throat with a stick. And then you know what happened? Then they were free and they jumped out of the whale's mouth. Then they ran up on top of the water and they found a new boat and they found a piece of money on the sky and they caught it when it fell down and they paid for the houseboat and they never left the grease on the stove again and the stove on.*

A three year old manages to get a certain beauty into his description of a nightmarish chaos:

UPTON S. 3:9: *A goat man. The goat man said, "Gone over to the movie." And then the house came over to the movie, and then crash again! And no one cried again, and the world was all over. Then another world came, and they fighted to another war. Then the war came into the house. And they had a big fight in the house. They knocked down the chairs and tables and candles. And then police came and put them in jail and they had to stay forever and ever. Then the war was all gone and then there was coming for night.*

CHILDREN AND THEIR THINKING

There are several other areas I should like briefly to consider without offering further examples from the stories, since those already quoted support what I have to say. I should like to make a few comments about sex differences, morality, and children's understanding and use of language.

First, sex differences: even at an early age there seems to be a sex-difference in the type of story children tell. Girls are more likely to talk about people or themselves; they introduce romantic themes, mentioning love, marriage and children. Boys tend to like themes of action, and talk more about objects than persons.

There are studies of reading interests of older children which show a preference along the same lines (Children's reading interests, 1932). Whether we go along with such sex-typed interest, or try to widen horizons, it is worth considering a child's sex in connection with providing his books.

Next, children's understanding and use of language: since study of children's own stories makes one ponder about what they are understanding from the words they hear. Particularly at younger ages, language is so chaotic, episodes are so unrelated, that there is a real question in my mind as to whether a plot as such registers in sequence with children under five years of age. I recall that when *David Copperfield* was read to me, I had no realization it was a single story; it seemed a new tale on each reading occasion. A study I mentioned earlier, carried on at Bank Street College, found it rewarding to question childrens' understandings, and then attempt to clarify them. Even the word *deck* in *Curious George*, as well as the word *curious* had to be explained. The pre-schooler's verbal world is like the infant's total world—"a booming, buzzing confusion"; even the child who handles language well is probably coping with fuzzy understandings.

I would not, for this reason advocate simplifying the language in books, nor would I have vocabulary reviews in connection with each book, but it does seem wise for adults to realize the limitations of children's verbal understandings, in contrast for instance, to their extraordinary capacity for emotional experiences. Relating unfamiliar words to familiar ones, providing repeated usages of words, explaining words in numerous ways can help the development of a child's language, and his appreciation of books.

Despite their limitations in using language, there is considerable educational significance in children making up their own stories. They experience pleasure, and grow in self-confidence with an adult's attention to what they have to say, and profit from practice in expressing thoughts and feelings. Stories from pre-school children that are written down and then typed and then read back to them flatter their ego and promote a realization of the origin, usefulness and delight of the written word. Older children can write their own stories and books. Such productions should be appreciated for what they express; it is wrong to discourage such efforts by excessive or ill-timed correcting of grammatical, spelling, or other technical inadequacies.

Finally, I should like to return to the matter of morality in children's literature: as you recall I have already referred to children's interest in themes about good and evil. Children's original stories suggest that ideas of right and wrong may be determined by what they have been told is right or wrong, or by their sensitivity to the parents' approval or disapproval of behavior. Their ideas represent the "morality of constraint" as Piaget (1932) describes it. That which is wrong seems most of the time to be that which is destructive or aggressive as defined by parents or parent substitutes. There is, of course, a development in the complexity of children's understanding of wrong-doing. By the age of three there is an awareness in some children that goodness and badness can exist in the same persons or species. Some four year olds cope with the idea that good qualities may exist in seemingly bad characters. The five year old increasingly mentions more subtle forms of ethical misbehavior involving social responsibility: lying, stealing, sending in false fire alarms, letting sick children go to school. Despite this progression, however, ideas of good and bad are not very sophisticated or complicated. It is interesting that young children (and perhaps adults, too) spend more time describing what is bad than setting forth what is good. They often have difficulty, indeed, in defining just what "good" is. In one story, for example, there is an alligator described as good "because his tongue lasts all the way down to his stomach."

We already mentioned that books dealing with questions of good and bad, either subtly or overtly expressed, are very popular, since this is an early concern, laden with emotion. If we consider the young child's point of view, it is impressive to review all the variables that may go into parental judgment of a bad action. A child who has squeezed toothpaste from a tube may be punished in quite different ways depending upon whether the toothpaste goes into the bowl or on the wall paper, whether the wall paper is plastic or not, whether he squirts out just a little or a lot, and, if the latter, whether it is the last tube of paste in the house! What *is* good and what is bad? It seems to me that young children need help with clear-cut answers. Certain kinds of learning and other problems can come to children who do not develop the ability to analyze good and bad, and to be self-critical about the behaviors which may get them into trouble. Clearly it takes a long time to learn about right and wrong. Books that set forth how such and such consequences come from certain actions are both appealing and educationally significant, since anxieties are aroused when a child gets into emotional predicaments he does not understand. Because children's concepts of morality are so primitive, it seems to me that books with moral messages for young children should not be fuzzy, but should be clearly and explicitly expressed. I am *not* in favor of the moral message in the book *Nubber Bear* (Lipkind, 1966), for example, which conveys a curious and confusing message of a bear who is naughty, told what he should not do, is spanked, but manages to get what he wants. For the same reason I oppose the "morality" in *Where the Wild Things Are* (Sendak, 1963), where a child is sent to bed without his supper, has a hallucination and then, for no clear reason, finds his hot meal suddenly awaiting him. It seems to me ill-advised to present a child with a problem, and offer no solution except dreaming. *Nubber Bear* and *Where the Wild Things Are* are appealing books in many ways, yet, in my opinion, their moral lessons would probably confuse rather than help a young child's emerging sense of right and wrong.

Thus there are many insights about children and their thinking, their problems and their joys that may be learned from the stories they tell and write and the tales they like to read.

LANGUAGE ACQUISITION: BASIC ISSUES 22 STANLEY F. WANAT

The way a child acquires his language is a "natural process" in the sense that we don't have to teach it to him in the same way we have to teach him mathematics. When he enters school, the child can already understand and use a wide range of grammatical structures. How is the child able to do this? And how is his language development related to reading?

Answers to these questions were sought by a team of scholars who were part of the U.S. Office of Education's Literature Search in Reading. Twenty-five researchers drawn from fourteen universities worked the past year examining 1) studies of the reading process; 2) studies of learning to read; and 3) studies of language development related to reading. Martin Kling of Rutgers held overall responsibility for the project, along with John J. Geyer (also of Rutgers), and Frederick B. Davis (University of Pennsylvania). . . .

LANGUAGE DEVELOPMENT

What is language development and why bother about it? The study of language development (also referred to as "developmental psycholinguistics" or "developmental linguistics" or "the study of language acquisition") tries to account for how the "meaningless" cooing, gurgling, and babbling sounds made by the infant turn into the meaningful language spoken by the adult. This field is important to reading specialists because some theorists (notably Eleanor J. Gibson) maintain that competence in the spoken language is an essential first step in learning how to read. The steps in Gibson's theory are: learning to use spoken language, learning to discriminate between graphic symbols, learning spelling-sound correspondences, and learning to handle larger units of structure.

Noam Chomsky of M.I.T. claims that language acquisition is a process in which the child formulates a theory ("description") of the structure of his language. It is as if the child were a linguist writing a new grammar, but Chomsky qualifies his claim by saying that the child's grammar-formulation is intuitive, and that the child is probably not even conscious of the rules he formulates. Some of the skills which underlie language development are: the mental ability to deal with the world, the ability to remember things, the ability to break down the language one hears into units of sound and units of meaning and recombine these units, and the ability to generalize.

How do the child's linguistic skills develop? Some theorists stress the child's own active role in the acquisition of language. Other researchers emphasize the innate aspects of language development while a third group concentrates on the rewarding or reinforcement of certain kinds of behavior as the determining factor in language acquisition. These three viewpoints can be labelled Cognitive, Nativistic, and Behavioristic, respectively.

BEHAVIORISTIC THEORY

Following B. F. Skinner's views, the acquisition of language is based on rewarding the child when he imitates or tries to imitate models of adult language. There has been much discussion about the nature of the reward or reinforcement and about the stimulus—the thing which brings about a response from the learner. Techniques based on behavioristic theory have been successful in the classroom: Rewards such as food, use of play equipment, and teacher approval brought about changes in the speech of children in experiments. Two questions posed to behaviorists are: "Is reinforcement the most important factor?" and, "If imitation is so central, why is it that a response learned in one way is also used in many other ways by the speaker?"

The imitation of models that the child hears and the frequency with which he hears these models are key concepts in behavioristic theory. Studies of language acquisition have indicated that although children do imitate what they hear, they also produce many variations of the model. Research has also shown that the child may ignore the model, as in the case where the adult speaker repeatedly presents a correct model, but the child continues to make the same error. Yet, imitation clearly is an important factor in language development, for children raised in an English-speaking environmer learn English, and not some other language. The role of frequency of hearing the model is also at issue, since "telegraphic" speech leaves out high-frequency words, and researchers note that language acquisition includes a period of telegraphic speech. Concern with the frequency of items is reflected in basal readers, but such strict vocabulary control may be stifling the curiosity of young readers.

Given the research findings that techniques involving imitation frequency, and reinforcement do affect the child's acquisition of language, how do we best help the development along? The next theory of language development stresses the innate aspects of language.

NATIVISTIC THEORY

Very briefly, the nativistic position holds that language development is related to the growth of the human brain, and that maturation in language parallels maturation in motor and thinking skills. While the behaviorists emphasize outside events, nativistic theory concentrates on what is "inside" the child. Chomsky has been particularly critical of Skinner for ignoring what the child himself brings to the task of language learning. Eric Lenneberg's nativistic theory is based upon the notion that language development is biologically determined, and that no other creature besides man has language.

Lenneberg's theory is based upon evidence from the study of language development in normal children, and of children with abnormal language development resulting from congenital and environmental factors. As evidence of the innate biological basis of language, Lenneberg cites the universal properties of language—the characteristics which all languages share. Major issues concerning nativistic models include whether or not language is unique to Man, and the nature of language universals. Chomsky's transformational-generative grammar is based on the existence of universals in the mind. Some people have argued that universals across different languages occur because there are universals in the subjects people think about and want to talk about. A problem with nativistic theory is that it does not explain how we get from the child's innate knowledge to his actual language performance.

One aspect of nativistic theory has potentially important implications for the teaching of reading. Lenneberg maintains that there is a "critical" period for language acquisition which is biologically determined. Since, as has already been mentioned, some reading theorists hold that reading is dependent upon language development, there may be some optimal relationship between stages in language development and stages in learning to read. Current language intervention programs are not directed at children during the time they experience maximum growth in language development, which is before they are four years old.

The nativistic position stresses the internal mechanism—the innate language learning capacity—which the child brings to the task of language acquisition. But trying to account for *all* aspects of language learning in terms of its biological basis is no more informative than trying to account for all aspects of learning how to drive a car in terms of its biological basis. The nativists also fail to take into account the possibility that there may be differences in the innate cognitive and language structure of different children.

Chomsky claims that the child's acquisition of language is relatively independent of intelligence or the particular experiences that the child has had. On the other hand, Basil Bernstein, a British sociologist, holds that social settings bring about particular forms of communication which determine the intellectual orientation of the child. Chomsky maintains that his theory of language holds for the "ideal" speaker in an environment where all the other people speak pretty much alike. Some critics strongly argue that the linguists' assumption of an "ideal" speaker is a basic error, and that all children do not possess the same skills in thinking. As linguists start to analyze actual language behavior, rather than dealing with fictionalized "ideal" speakers, they will move closer to the concerns of psychologists, and linguistic and psychological theories may begin to merge. One of the problems with describing language development is that the goal towards which the child is progressing—the fluency of the mature speaker—has not been adequately described by linguists.

COGNITIVE THEORY

A third theory of language development, cognitive theory, holds that the child takes an active role in learning. The child's cognitive, or thinking, activity is a kind of information processing. Major theories of the ways in which thinking develops in the child take the form of language for granted. Jean Piaget, the Swiss psychologist, states that transformational grammar is close to some of his views. Piaget's concept of "stages" in cognitive growth has implications for reading. If, for example, a child is still at the stage where his perception is "centered," then he can only attend to one part of a situation. He will thus have problems discriminating between a figure and its background. This has obvious implications for the perception of letters. Also, the child whose perception is at this stage will have trouble dealing with the sound of a letter while he is dealing with its visual form, since "centration" is characterized by the inability to deal with more than one thing at a time.

THE DIALECT SPEAKER

The language of the dialect speaker—a relatively recent concern in language development—also has implications for the teaching of reading.

226 *language and the language arts*

The child who does not have a good grasp of the language to be read must either be taught that language before reading instruction begins, or else the reading materials must be put into the language or dialect that he speaks. The middle class child has an advantage because the language he hears and speaks at home is very close to the language he must read in school. Consequently, he has a better chance of success in using context cues to the form and meaning of the sentence.

In teaching dialect speakers how to read, one must try to minimize differences between how they speak most naturally and their reading materials. The establishment of a program to teach reading in the home dialects of American children would necessitate preparing materials in at least seven dialects. Since programs for teaching reading through the use of materials in dialect have not been evaluated, success with this approach is not assured. If, for example, a child does not pronounce the plural marker on words when reading aloud, this does not mean that he cannot read. It may be that his home language is French and that he is transferring language habits from French to English. The same may be true of dialect speakers who "can't read" past tense forms. Black Americans who talk so-called "nonstandard" Negro English may not pronounce the past-tense marker of verbs when they converse. Therefore, it is not necessarily the case that they "can't read" because they transfer language habits from their home dialect when they read the variety of English we expect to hear in the classroom.

The following implications for teaching are associated with dialect differences: First, the student's task of having to learn a second dialect should be explicitly taken into account. Second, the decoding process should take place within one dialect, and not between dialects. Third, a great deal of attention must be paid to the social context in which learning to read takes place, since there are strong pressures from peer groups against reading in some ghetto settings. For many children, the home situation is so chaotic that instead of developing strategies for attending to information, the children are forced into strategies of "tuning out" information.

NEEDED RESEARCH

Research has generally ignored differences between and within groups. Consider the relation between sex differences and reading problems: 90% of the referrals to reading clinics in the U.S. are boys, whereas in some countries there may be a higher rate of referrals for girls than for boys.

In summary, group differences have generally been ignored in research on language development. Thus, dialect differences, possible ethnic differences in capacities and strategies for processing information, differences in thinking-style, and emotionally-related factors are not adequately taken under consideration. None of the theories reviewed gives an adequate explanation of the way a child acquires his language. Each of the theories is wrong in that each unjustifiably claims to provide a complete explanation. Yet, each of these theories is valuable in that each provides part of the information we need to understand language development.

23 CONFUSION AND MISCONCEPTIONS IN THE CONTROVERSY ABOUT KINDERGARTEN READING

DOLORES DURKIN

It is not wise to introduce reading formally in the kindergarten because most five-year-olds have neither proper eye-hand coordination nor the patience to sit still for too long in an imposed program of sequential learning. It is certainly not wise as a matter of policy because too many of the children who enter our elementary schools are simply not ready. The few who are will not be harmed by waiting; the many can be soured on reading for life by being pushed too soon . . . [Rudolph & Cohen, 1964, p. 9].

The material just quoted portrays some characteristics of typical opposition to kindergarten reading. That this type of opposition *is* so typical is a reason for discussing the issues that are central to the ever-present controversy about the optimum time to start teaching reading. The more important of these issues—as the quoted material demonstrates—concern the very nature of readiness to become a reader, as well as the question of the value of an earlier start. Of considerable relevance, too, is the meaning that is assigned to terms such as *reading instruction, formal instruction,* and *pushing* children.

NATURE OF READING READINESS

In any discussion of reading readiness, two points must be emphasized and reemphasized. The first is that reading readiness *is not one thing.* That is, it is not a single package of certain kinds and amounts of abilities. Consequently when we talk about readiness for reading, we are referring to different things in different children. We are really talking about readiness*es*—a rather awkward word—not *a* readiness.

The idea that readiness refers to *various* combinations of abilities and understandings becomes clearer when a second basic point is emphasized; namely, that the concept of readiness denotes a *relationship*—in this case, a relationship between the abilities and understandings of a child and the type and quality of reading instruction that will be offered. One implication of this relational dimension is that a given child might be "ready" if one type of instruction is available, but "unready" if other types are offered. Gates, as early as 1936, made the same point when he wrote, "The optimum time of beginning reading is not entirely dependent upon the nature of the child himself, but it is in a large measure determined by the nature of the reading program [p. 684]."

The varying nature of readiness, as well as its relational dimension, has still other implications that need to be highlighted in this discussion. One obvious implication is that readiness can never be determined by some single-factor criterion such as chronological age or even mental age. It is important to remember that the practice of starting children to read in first grade and at the age of six is a product of convention, not of any evidence that there is something special about six-year-old children which makes age six a particularly productive time to start teaching reading.

But now, you might be asking, what about mental age? And, especially, what about the frequently reported idea—even in current texts—that a mental age of 6.5 years is necessary for success with reading? This particular notion . . . is closely associated with a study of first grade reading described by Morphett and Washburne in a 1931 article, "When Should Children Begin to Read?" Central to their research was a particular kind of first grade reading instruction given in a particular kind of setting; and for success the combination appeared to require a mental age of about 6.5. As Chall (1964) has noted:

> The Morphett-Washburne findings make sense when we realize that the children in their sample were a superior group intellectually–the median mental age at the beginning of Grade I was about seven. Their criterion of success was high, and instruction was based mainly on independent silent reading. Isn't it possible, then, that a child with a mental age below six in such a situation would find himself a failure, both by the stringent definition of reading success used by the investigators and by his own perception of his ability as compared with the other children? [p. 20]

The close association that developed in earlier decades between success with beginning reading and the mental age of 6.5 resulted in postponing school instruction in reading; but it also fostered the related belief that any child who was able to learn to read even before he entered school must surely be a genius. That such is not the case was learned by this writer in carrying on studies directly focussing on preschool reading ability (1966). To relate some of the findings of one of these studies to the present discussion of mental age and reading readiness, Table 1 is presented below.

TABLE 1: *Reading progress of forty-nine preschool readers over five school years as related to chronological age, mental age, and intelligence quotient when home help with reading began*

READING GRADE-LEVEL MEDIAN		CHRONOLOGICAL AGE, IN YEARS	MENTAL AGE, IN YEARS		INTELLIGENCE QUOTIENT	
Start of grade I	*End of grade V*		*Median*	*Range*	*Median*	*Range*
2.6	9.2	3.5 (N = 13)	4.5	3.2–5.6	128.0	91–160
1.8	6.6	4.5 (N = 22)	5.0	4.5–7.2	111.5	99–161
1.7	7.6	5.5 (N = 14)	7.0	5.1–8.3	127.0	93–151

° *In a slightly different form, this table appears in* Children Who Read Early *(Durkin, 1966), (8), a description of findings from two longitudinal studies of preschool readers.*

Examination of the table shows, first of all, that among the early readers in one of the studies, Stanford-Binet IQ's ranged from 91 to 161. (More detailed examination of the data would also show that one-third of the total group of 49 children had IQ's of 110 or less.) The table points out, too, that the children began reading at home at ages ranging from three to five years, when their mental ages varied from 3.2 years to 8.3 years.

Your attention should also be called to one other set of data in Table 1. These are the findings that indicate that the best readers, after five years in school, were the children who began to read at the earliest age. It seems tempting to ask whether such data begin to suggest a generalization like: the earlier the start, the better the reader. The answer, of course, is "No." Like the Morphett-Washburne research referred to earlier, this study is a description of just one small group of children. In this case they are children who began to learn to read in a highly specialized setting—the home. Consequently all that the findings can do is to point out—as all of this discussion has tried to do—that it makes no sense whatsoever to think about readiness for reading as being defined by some specified chronological or mental age.

VALUE OF EARLIER READING

In the past, opposition to kindergarten reading was often expressed via the claim that five-year-olds are unable to learn to read. Now, though, with the existence of children who are reading even earlier than age five, such a claim is not very meaningful. One result is that opposition to reading in the kindergarten concentrates on a newer question: Even though children younger than six can be taught to read, *should* they?

According to some who disapprove of kindergarten instruction in reading, five-year-olds should *not* be taking the time to learn to read because, they say, the achievement advantages of earlier reading are only temporary. Other children, without the earlier start, soon "catch up" (Ilg & Ames, 1964; Olson, 1949).

Because claims about the temporary value of early reading are part of the current discussion of "when to begin?" and because this characteristic of "here today, gone tomorrow" has traditionally been cited as one of the reasons why parents should not try to teach their preschoolers to read, it is important to examine the correctness of the indictment. *Is* an earlier start in reading only of temporary advantage? *Do* children without an early start ultimately read as well as those who begin sooner?

If nothing else, this question of the future value of earlier reading does one thing very successfully. It exemplifies the unfortunate tendency—even among those who ought to know better—to reach "conclusions" before the facts are in. For, actually, we know very few facts about the results of earlier reading, including the effect it has on a child's later achievement in reading. The few researchers who have studied pre-first grade reading generally omitted attention to its future effects (Brown, 1924; Davidson, 1931; Wilson, 1938). In fact, it was because of such a serious and unfortunate omission that this writer, in 1958, undertook the two longitudinal studies of preschool readers which, in one case, followed 49 children for all of their elementary school years, and, in the other, followed 156 children for the first three years of elementary school (Durkin, 1966). While there is no pretense that two studies of small groups of children could arrive at definitive conclusions about all early readers, the findings of the research are still significant—if only because of the dearth of information about an important issue. What the research findings indicate is that the average achievement of preschool readers, over as many as six school years, remains significantly higher than the average achievement of equally bright schoolmates who did not begin to read until after they started first grade.

Two additional points about this research must also be made here in order to make sure that its findings are put into the right perspective. First, the early reading that was the focus of both studies resulted from help given at home, not in a school setting such as the kindergarten. For this reason the research only provides information about the effect of early reading that is *not* of school origin. It can say nothing directly, for instance, about the future value of reading instruction given in the kindergarten (Sutton, 1964). With its positive findings, however, the research can at least claim the right to raise questions about the notion that the achievement advantages of reading which starts in the kindergarten are only temporary.

A second, equally important point that must be stressed is that the preschool readers in the research did not always receive what could be called appropriate instruction in reading once they started school. Although they entered first grade reading at second, third, and, in a few instances, even fourth grade levels, some of the early readers received typical first grade instruction, beginning with the preprimers of the various basal reader series. Such a practice must be mentioned here because it indicates that, even when preschool readers do not receive appropriately challenging instruction when they get to school, their average achievement in reading still remains significantly higher than the average achievement of equally bright non-early readers. (What favored the early readers, of course, were the various characteristics of their home life that got them reading in the first place.) Future research must consider what their achievement would have been with more individualized school instruction.

The important message for now is that if there are to be changes in the timing of reading instruction so that it begins for some children during their kindergarten year, then, quite obviously, there must be corresponding changes in the level of instruction offered in subsequent years. Considering kindergarten reading as being isolated from the rest of the school program is narrow and meaningless.

DEFINITION OF TERMS

Whether the point being discussed is as basic as the nature of readiness, or as complicated as the question of the future value of earlier starts in reading, the meaning assigned to a term like *reading instruction* is of paramount importance. But the meanings of other terms and descriptions also take on significance, especially as they become key points in the controversy about when to begin teaching reading. For example, because *formal instruction* is so often criticized as being inappropriate for kindergarten children (see the sample quotation that opens this article) some attention needs to be given to the meaning of *formal* instruction as opposed to any other kind. And because opponents of kindergarten reading frequently warn about the dangers of *pushing* children, it is also meaningful and even necessary to ask what *pushing* means in this context.

While it is true that a discussion of these few terms will not resolve the controversy about the optimum time for starting instruction in reading, it should, nonetheless, foster better communication among the participants and, especially, among the readers of this text.

WHAT IS "READING INSTRUCTION"?

Definitions of this term can be so narrow that it comes to be equated with only one type of teaching or so broad that nothing very specific is communicated. For instance, it is all too common to confine reading instruction to the use of basal readers and workbooks. In fact, the close association between teaching reading and using basal reader materials is so dominant in the thinking of many professional educators—and probably parents too—that when they consider the possibility of having reading in the kindergarten they automatically envision a program of instruction which is defined by the content and sequence of basal readers and by the teaching suggestions in their manuals. One current, concrete result of such a narrow outlook is the existence of kindergartens with reading programs that can be described as a good imitation of unimaginative first-grade instruction. Consequently, one further result has been a sweeping condemnation of kindergarten reading that fails to make a distinction between a type of instruction that might be inappropriate, but a timing that is just right—at least for some kindergartners.

On the other hand, the tendency to define reading instruction in broad, general terms encourages teachers of young children to believe that just about anything they do is somehow contributing to a child's later ability to read. Within such a framework, of course, it is easy to be a "good" teacher. And it is also easy to have a school program that amounts to little more than first-class baby sitting.

What this text [*Teaching Them To Read*] has already proposed as a definition of reading instruction lies somewhere between the two viewpoints just described:

1   A child's ability to read is related to, and even dependent upon, his earlier abilities in listening and speaking. In fact, reading ought to be seen as an extension of these skills. Within such a framework of relationships, whatever a teacher does to extend a child's ability in using and comprehending oral language is considered to be a part of reading instruction.

2   Because the ability to spell and write a word results in the ability to read it, any help a teacher gives a child in spelling and writing is considered to be another aspect of reading instruction.

3   The form reading instruction takes varies. From a teacher, for example, instruction might be an explanation, a reminder, a description, a question, or a response to a request for assistance. Depending on what is available in a classroom, instruction in reading can also come from materials; for instance, in a picture dictionary an illustration can identify for a child the written word that is its label.

4   Many sources of written language are useful in teaching a child to read. This means that the use of street signs, television commercials, calendars, magazines, labels on food packages, and all other materials which display written language is appropriate and even desirable in teaching reading. Consequently, in this book "instructional materials" comprise much more than just books.

To summarize, then, *reading instruction* refers to the many and varied ways in which teachers and materials can help a child to recognize—that is, to "read"—the written form of his language. Because comprehension of meaning eventually becomes the very essence of reading, whatever a teacher does to help a child increase his ability to use and understand oral language is also a type of reading instruction.

WHAT IS "FORMAL INSTRUCTION?"

The word *formal* is frequently used in descriptions of teaching. Writers who use the word in their condemnations of kindergarten reading communicate the idea that *formal* instruction with five-year-olds is "bad." But they do not explain clearly the precise kind of teaching to which they are so strongly opposed. Because of this omission, all that can be done here is to suggest what appears to be the inferred meaning of *formal instruction.*

Formal instruction in reading seems to be a teaching that is directed to a whole class of children, rather than to small groups or individuals. It would appear that the content or focus of this instruction is fixed and highly prescribed, probably by published materials rather than factors like children's interests, special abilities, or particular learning problems. It is also likely that formal instruction would be accompanied by fixed expectations of what is to be achieved by all of the children.

If these few details are an accurate description of formal instruction, then it appears to be a type of teaching in which everybody gets the same thing at the same time at the same rate and out of the same book. If this is so, it merits nothing but criticism. However, if this *is* an accurate description, then formal instruction is merely one type of classroom teaching and should not be portrayed as the only possible way of teaching kindergarten children to read.

WHAT DOES IT MEAN TO "PUSH" A CHILD?

As an everyday expression, *pushing* often describes efforts to get a child to achieve a certain goal, even though it is too difficult or, perhaps, of no interest to him. If the goal is one that could be achieved and might even be of interest, then *pushing* could denote efforts to get the child to reach the desired goal at a pace that is too fast. It could also refer to efforts to keep a child working toward a goal, even when he needs or wants to stop.

Does the prospect of kindergarten instruction in reading mean that children will be pushed? The answer, quite obviously, depends upon many factors, most of all on the kind of instruction that becomes available. For instance, if a kindergarten teacher were to establish achievement goals which all members of her class were expected to reach at the same time and in the same way, then it is very likely that at least some of the children would be pushed or bored. But if, to the contrary, the teacher carries on a type of reading instruction that (a) is not always, and maybe even seldom, directed to the whole class; (b) takes into account the interests of the children; and (c) allows for varying rates and amounts of learning, then it is not too likely that a child will be "pushed"—or, for that matter, bored.

24 NONVERBAL COMMUNICATION CHARLES GALLOWAY

When second-grade teacher Ruth Harris was getting dressed for school one dull Monday, she hesitated between a black suit and a bright print dress. Choosing the print, she thought, "It will brighten the day for me and the children." Things did seem to go well all day. . . .

As Paul Trask entered the school building, he saw the principal at the end of the hall. Expecting a smile and a wave, he was surprised to get a curt nod and the sight of a disappearing back. Paul wondered what could be wrong. . . .

Annette Webster looked at her fourth-year arithmetic group as they bent over the problem she had presented to them. She noticed Chris scowling at his paper and biting his lip and moved to help him. . . .

What happened with these teachers? Each one either sent or received a message without saying or hearing a word. What happened was *nonverbal communication*. Nonverbal communication is behavior that conveys meaning without words. It can be symbolic or nonsymbolic, spontaneous or managed. It can be expressive, transmitting emotion; or it can be informative, transmitting facts. It can be as specific as a gesture or as general as the atmosphere of a room. It can be either dynamic or static. Nonverbal communication takes a certain amount of time and occurs at a certain tempo. It can be quick or slow. It can be negative or positive—something that doesn't happen as well as something that does. Or it can be a combination of any of these—and there's even a nonverbal component in verbalisms.

All human beings are compelled to send and receive messages. They try constantly to discover information which lessens confusion or increases understanding. When messages are carried by words, the participators are consciously aware of hearing or seeing the words. But nonverbal communication is given much less conscious thought. The operations of giving information through nonverbal action and reading the meaning of another person's nonverbal behavior usually occur without deliberate reflection.

The clothing you wear, your posture, or how you walk transmits a message to others. You may be saying, "I am a teacher; I am meeting your expectations (and mine) of how a teacher should look." Depending on your emotional needs, you may also be trying to say, "I am an alert modern teacher," or even, "I may be a teacher, but at heart I'm a swinger!"

So we can say that nonverbal clues are evident in any situation where people are with other people. In fact, the most subtle and covert kinds of information can be discovered in this way. Here are three examples:

NONVERBAL PHENOMENA ESTABLISH THE STATUS OF INTERACTION At a party you are talking to someone, but his eyes are following someone else around the room. His posture and manner indicate his desire to be off. What conclusion do you come to?

NONVERBAL BEHAVIOR INDICATES WHAT THE OTHER PERSON THINKS OF US You are discussing a controversial topic with a small group. Everyone is reacting politely, but you are aware of those who approve of your ideas and those who disagree. How do you know?

NONVERBAL CLUES ARE USED TO CHECK THE RELIABILITY OF WHAT IS SAID You had mailed a coupon indicating interest in an expensive set of books. The man who shows up at your door is poorly groomed and shifty-eyed. Although his credentials seem in order, you hesitate even to let him in.

The significance of nonverbal behavior in the classroom is an idea about teaching that is growing in importance. Until now, it has seldom been recognized or understood, at least in a formal, specific way. Now persons interested in improving the teaching act are studying the implications of nonverbal communication—implications that are important for you to understand.

ASSIGNMENTS

1 Think of at least one classroom situation in which each of the three conditions described above occurred.
2 Review the last two days of school. Can you recall an incident in which a child's behavior belied his remarks?
3 When a nonverbal cue disagrees with or contradicts a verbal remark, we tend to accept the nonverbal message as representative of the real meaning. Discuss why this occurs.

NONVERBAL PHENOMENA

Nonverbal behavior consists of such events as facial expression, posture, gestures, movement, even the arrangement of space or objects around the behaver. It involves use of the body, use of space, and even the use of time. Although we are often unaware of the process, we are very conscious of the eloquence of nonverbal cues. We all agree that "actions speak louder than words," and realize that *how* we say something can be as important as *what* we say. We also know the feeling of being "in tune" with someone—immediately understanding him and having him understand us. Most of us believe that the most personal and valid kinds of information are discovered by what we call intuition. What really happens is that we subconsciously respond to nonverbal clues transmitted by other persons.

During the school day, many graphic portrayals of nonverbal phenomena occur. Here are some common ones, and as you read them, think about your class. Undoubtedly you will recall many examples like them, and will be able to add others.

SUBSTITUTE EXPRESSION A child shrugs his shoulder in an "I don't know" manner after being accosted in the hallway for running. Probably this means he feels guilty at being caught, yet he hesitates to engage the teacher in a verbal debate. This is especially true if his verbal defense is likely to be employed against him later in the conversation. One of the places events like this occur repeatedly is in inner-city schools, where children are already conditioned to express their frustrations and defiance in a nonverbal way.

QUALIFYING EXPRESSION Ann says, "I don't sing well," but what does she mean? Stated one way, it suggests that she *does* sing well; or it may mean that she *would like* to sing well; or, that she truly *does not* sing well. The intent of verbal remarks is usually qualified through intonation and inflection. Facial expressions and gestures also qualify verbal language.

NONVERBAL SYMBOLIC John observed the teacher watching him. Now he is painting with large dramatic strokes, one eye on the teacher, hoping she will look his way again. When we know we are being observed, our behavior is designed to have intent or purpose for the observer. It symbolizes our thoughts or intentions. Eyes alone may beckon or reject. Many gestures and facial expressions symbolize our deepest feelings.

NONVERBAL NONSYMBOLIC You are watching a child who is observing another child, totally unaware that you are watching him. His behavior is considered nonsymbolic since it is free of overt intent. When you observe the unobserved observer, it is a profound process—for his reactions are genuinely his own with no desire to create an impression. Observing a person who is unaware of our presence is both informative and fun.

ATTENTIVE OR INATTENTIVE Your students are pretending to listen while their minds wander in fields of fantasy, and when they respond it is in a bored fashion. Nonverbally they are being inattentive. As an experienced teacher, you are able to detect such reactions and use them to change the pace and direction of what is being taught. Observing when students are involved and interested and when they are not is a skill that teachers learn. But teachers vary widely in their ability or willingness to use these pupil reactions as directions for their own behavior.

There are other nonverbal occurrences, but these are good ones to start with. Undoubtedly you can add other specific types from your own experiences.

ASSIGNMENTS

1 Identify children in your class who typically react nonverbally to either reprimand or approval. Do you know what they are really trying to communicate?
2 Experiment with positive body and facial qualifying expressions, especially when you feel a need to support a request or judgment you are making.
3 Think of a nonsymbolic situation in which your observation was later confirmed; another one which later proved wrong.

CLASSROOM CUES

Nonverbal behavior is not limited to personal practices. Many classroom phenomena serve as nonverbal communicators. Their impact on the course and direction of an activity can strongly affect the contextual meaning that is derived from it. Methods of distributing materials can affect the activity that follows; the way a group is formed influences its practices; even the degree of neatness required suggests behavior to the pupil. Nonverbal cues either reinforce or minimize verbal messages. They become the focus of attention and *carry conviction that lingers long after the verbal event has passed.* Why this is so is difficult to answer, but the strong influence of nonverbal cues is unmistakable.

Classroom phenomena often play a more significant role in students' learning than the formal teaching which takes place. In any classroom, the extent and duration of teacher-pupil contacts are great. It is vital to have mutual understanding in the exchange of the messages that are nonverbal in character and import. Consider phenomena that are typical of any classroom:

USE OF SPACE Classrooms are divided into territories. Both teacher and students occupy space. Some arrangements of territorial rights are traditional, with the teacher's desk at the front of the room and students seated in rows. Other arrangements are more imaginative. Some uses of space are fluid, others are static. Space arrangement shows the teacher's priorities—what she thinks important; what she thinks about her children; how she envisions her own position. A change in a spatial arrangement influences the potential meaning of a learning context.

TEACHER TRAVEL Where and when a teacher chooses to travel in a classroom is significant. In the past, teachers usually moved around their own desks as if they were isles of security. They rarely ventured into territories of student residence, unless they wished to check up on or monitor seatwork. Today that picture has changed. Some teachers have done away with desks; others have put them in less focal places. To move toward or away from students signifies relationships. Teachers may avoid some students or frequent the work areas of others. All of those movements have meaning that students recognize.

USE OF TIME How teachers use their time indicates the value and importance they place on types of work, on subject areas, and on acceptable activities. Spending little or no time on a topic indicates a lack of interest in or knowledge about it so that even little children are aware of teachers' preferences. Teachers often fail to recognize the implications of their use of time. One teacher spends two hours marking papers. A teacher in the next room spends the same amount of time in helping children mark their own papers. Certainly these teachers have different concepts of evaluation, and it is revealed by their uses of time.

CONTROL MANEUVERS Teachers engage in various nonverbal tactics to control the behavior of students. These silent expressions serve as events reminding students of teacher expectations. Some typical examples of nonverbal maneuvers: the teacher indicates inability to hear due to classroom noise; places finger to lips; stands with hands on hips and stares in silence; scans room to see who is not working; records in grade book while student is making a report. Negative maneuvers tend to "put children in their place." Similarly, positive maneuvers can give encouragement, help a child overcome fear, put a nervous child at ease, or resolve a tense situation.

As the teacher works to establish better classroom phenomena, he must be careful to avoid *incongruity*. This is an event where there is a contradiction between what is said and what is done, and it may occur many times in a day. The thing to remember about an incongruity is that it is nonverbal behavior that makes the impression that is most lasting and most difficult to overcome.

Incongruous behaviors occur frequently during times of praise or encouragement. Teachers use words such as "good" or "nice job" but the praise can appear false or unbelievable. When we are not honest with children, it is the nonverbal clues that trip us up.

Nonverbal phenomena should not be thought of primarily in negative terms. Many classrooms are well arranged. The teacher's approach to an activity provides excellent motivation. Or, through meeting a child's eyes or with a small gesture, a teacher builds confidence. Such nonverbal events can be highly conducive to good classroom climate.

Nonverbal qualities that contribute to effective classroom interaction are suggested:

ATTENTION The event of listening to pupils when they talk. This is essential. When a teacher fails to listen, a pupil is likely to believe that what he says is unimportant.

RECEPTION Behavioral evidence that a teacher is listening, by maintaining eye contact while a pupil is talking. The event of attending to pupils when they talk assures pupils and encourages them to believe that their verbal communication is valued by the teacher.

REINFORCEMENT A look or gesture to reinforce approval of an act by a student. Not only the timid but also the seemingly forward child may need reinforcement if he is to go ahead on his own.

FACILITATION A movement toward a student for the purpose of helping or assisting. Teachers quite often detect needs or unexpressed feelings by students, and initiate a move toward the student to alleviate his concern. Teachers engage in such events because, either consciously, or subconsciously, they have become sensitive to the nonverbal cues given by their students.

We all recognize that expressive cues are fleeting and transitory. Nonetheless, they transmit emotion and feeling, and are detected as indications of meaning far more quickly than speech. *It is the appearance of such cues that especially suggests to others the attitudes we hold at a given time.* Therefore, they are particularly important in establishing the classroom environment and in working out good rapport with each child.

ASSIGNMENTS

1 Draw some alternate layouts for your classroom. List changes in nonverbal phenomena that each layout would imply.
2 Make a two-day study of how often you contact each child in any

of many ways. Keep a list of children's names and devise a simple code to indicate times of approving or disapproving, individual or group sharing, listening, or other interaction.

FEEDBACK

Improving classroom nonverbal behavior is not easy, especially in discovering incongruity. Yet we probably all agree that such improvement should be a conscious goal for any teacher.

One enlightening and sometimes disconcerting way to check your present behavior is by watching yourself on film or video-tape. Another way is to listen to the comments and suggestions of an observer whose judgment you trust. *A teacher's major source of feedback, however, is the responses of students.*

To become more knowledgeable about the nonverbal reactions of your youngsters to your behavior is a difficult quest. Even when you begin to recognize the reactions, it is naive to believe that change is imminently possible. Most of us have been observing and behaving in patterned ways for a long time. Ridding oneself of past habits and attitudes is a difficult undertaking and must be a continuing process. The best way to start is to develop an attitude of *openness*. Openness to one's experience and the realization that a rich and available source of data exists in the classroom is crucial. Openness is necessary if an improvement of perceptual skills and style of behaving is to be effected.

Assuming that a teacher has an open attitude toward self and others, the steps for becoming better informed involve *awareness, understanding,* and *acceptance*. To be aware is to observe more fully and to be open to the nonverbal reactions of others and oneself. To understand implies the need to analyze the meaning of your observations and to suspend judgment until you are reasonably certain of their real meaning. To accept is to acknowledge that your behavior means what it does to students, even though the meaning is not what you intended to imply. This last step is especially difficult because most of us do not like to admit even to ourselves that others perceive us differently. But once you can accept what your behavior represents to others, the door is open to behaving differently.

Does it seem odd to be talking about the *behavior* of teachers? That is a word usually reserved for children, yet the teacher's conduct in the classroom is of vital importance to every child. In being open to nonverbal cues, it is useful to recognize behavior as a cultural, social, and psychological phenomenon. The behavior of a teacher or of students arises from experiences that have been learned over a period of time. Here are some points to consider as you view students' reactions.

SIMILAR EXPERIENCES CAN MEAN DIFFERENT THINGS A pat on the back to one child may imply friendliness and support, whereas to another exactly the same behavior may be interpreted as an aggressive and threatening gesture. Similarly, an aggressive act by a child may be in defiance of controls, or in response to something in your classroom climate that has encouraged him to go ahead on his own.

REACTION TO PHYSICAL CONTACT VARIES To some children who are accustomed to adults' maintaining a physical distance from them, too close a proximity by the teacher might well stifle and embarrass. Conversely, other children prefer the close contact and warmth of teacher-pupil contacts. One broad cultural understanding among us that you may not have realized is that we do not stand too close to one another while talking in public. When the appropriate distance is broken, talking ceases.

NONVERBAL EXPRESSIONS AMONG RACIAL, ETHNIC, AND SOCIAL CLASSES CAN DIFFER MARKEDLY Similarly, the behaviors of suburban, rural, and inner-city children vary. The teacher must be sensitive to behavior differences and seek to learn what they imply rather than coming to premature conclusions.

MEETING EXPECTATIONS APPEARS TO BE A DEVELOPMENT ABILITY If meeting expectations is a learned process, it explains why the behavior of young children appears so unaffected and natural. Much of their behavior is spontaneous and unrehearsed. With older children, activities of pretending to listen in class, appearing busy during seatwork assignments, and putting on a front of seeming to be interested, may all be games that they have learned to play. There are perhaps many such games that children learn to play in school, and the longer they go to school the better their skills develop. This is a necessary step in preparing for adult roles; but on the other hand, children who do need help may be able to conceal their need.

RESPONSIVENESS MAY BE MISLEADING Parents who want their children to succeed often stress the importance of "pleasing the teacher." In actuality, the student less overt in his responsiveness may be more receptive to what is going on. Nonverbal clues are the best way to judge responsiveness.

DEPRIVED CHILDREN MAY BE INCAPABLE OF MEETING THE BEHAVIORAL EXPECTATIONS OF THE TEACHER They may neither understand the rules of the school game nor be able to control their behavior satisfactorily. Indeed, many teachers do not facilitate their fumbling efforts, but, rather, try to catch them in the act. Such students need practice in what it means to be a student.

Awareness of the behavior of yourself and your students and what it means does not come all at once. Interpretations change as realization increases. But the processes of awareness and realization are concomitant. You perceive to greater depths, you are more attuned to those around you, and you begin to employ nonverbal clues for positive purposes. Having opened the door, you realize you have the ability to change and improve.

ASSIGNMENTS

1   A company selling video-tape recorders may be willing to give a demonstration of its product in your school. Volunteer to be photographed. It may take courage! Or make a class movie, letting children take footage with a movie camera. (Don't try to be in the film. Chances are you will be automatically included.) Study it to see how your nonverbal behavior could improve.

2   Make a study of the feedback at times when you are an observer—for example, of children's reactions to the librarian, music teacher, or other classroom visitors.

3   Discuss feedback in a teachers' meeting. Let teachers anonymously mark profile sheets showing impressions they have of other teachers, including yourself. (The results may amaze you.)

EXPERIMENTING

Since nonverbal communication is so basic and certainly old as mankind, why the recent interest in its role in education? Are teachers now expected to search for hidden meanings behind everything that happens in their classrooms? Must they become overly sensitive to ordinary behavior? Not at all. Teachers need not set out to discover meanings that lurk in the subterranean caverns of the mind. Indeed, they shouldn't. Instead, the purpose is to become more aware of nonverbal cues because they operate as a silent language to influence teacher-student understandings and interactions. And it is through these understandings and interactions in the classroom that the business of teaching and learning goes forward.

Your final assignments in your nonverbal course are an invitation to experiment in every phase of classroom nonverbal communication. The possibilities are limitless.

ASSIGNMENTS

1   If you customarily work with small groups of children, experiment with the spread of the chairs. When the chairs are touching each other, do children react differently from when they are a foot apart? What about two feet? Does it make a difference whether you sit on a higher chair or one the same height?

2   Nonverbal acts are often preferable to words, and many studies

show that the teacher's voice is heard far too often. Without telling the children of your intentions, experiment with giving nonverbal instead of verbal directions. Use devices such as a tap of a bell to tell children you want their attention, or the flick of lights to show that a period is about to end.

3 Make a definite attempt to react more effectively to signals. A kindergarten teacher found that she could avoid calamity by observing more closely a boy with bathroom problems. The child chewing his pencil may be hoping you will come to his desk. Or, the one wanting to sharpen his pencil may be lacking an idea to write about.

4 Try to match your degree of nonverbal behavior to the child's and examine the results. For instance, sometimes teachers tend to be overarticulate with a nonarticulate child, subconsciously compensating for his lack. In contrast, a child who sits quietly beside the teacher may be getting warmth and comfort from the teacher's sitting quietly beside him. Matching the nonverbal behavior of a child is a kind of approval.

5 Experiment with light and heat—both important factors in classroom climate. Some teachers flick the switch as soon as they open the door, yet in most classrooms, any artificial light is not necessary on a normal day. Light affects mood, and so does heat. Deliberate changes in temperature can also be an effective device for changing classroom atmosphere.

6 Use nonverbal displays. The old adage that a picture is worth a thousand words applies in establishing classroom climate, especially if you employ humor and relaxation. One teacher experimented with two signs. The first said, "Pick up paper and put it in the wastebasket." The second was a silhouette of a child neatly dropping paper in the wastebasket. The second proved to be by far the better reminder.

7 Provide opportunities for children to express emotions by nonverbal means. Pantomimes are not only highly expressive for the actors but also give teachers insight into their feelings and emotions. Various forms of rhythm and creative dance are good nonverbal expressions, and so of course are all types of art work.

8 Talk about nonverbal patterns with your children, but do it astutely. Give them the opportunity to express themselves about nonverbal behavior on the part of adults that gives them pleasure or causes them frustrations.

9 Increase your practice of looking students in the eye. Experiment with glance exchanges for individual-to-individual contact.

10 Increase the frequency of your relevant gestures. They are an excellent way of underlining points you are trying to make.

11   Check your relevancy by checking your degree of effectiveness in transmitting ideas. This is not easy to do but it is especially important. Do you often feel misunderstood? Does a particular point you tried to make fail to get across? Your nonverbal behavior may have an incongruity that cancels out the effectiveness of your words.

12   Experiment with new movement patterns. Things you have been doing, do differently for a while. You may be making yourself too available or not available enough. Be sure, however, that your accessibility is not just a sneaky way to maintain close supervision.

13   Let children experiment with furniture arrangement that involves group interaction. One teacher tried putting desks in groups of four with the children facing each other. Two days later the desks were reversed so that this time the children faced away from each other.

14   Individualize your attention. You can't listen to all of the children all of the time, so experiment with listening very intently to a child for a brief period. As long as he is talking, look directly at him.

These suggested experiments aren't new. You've known about them all before. What's new is the emphasis on their nonverbal aspects. Considering them from this new point of view can help you understand their impact. Your goal is to use nonverbal communication more effectively in your quest for better ways of teaching.

personality development

Unlike elementary school curricula, which traditionally place the greatest emphasis on developing the three R's, preschool and kindergarten programs usually give equal attention to the fostering of affective (social-emotional) and cognitive (intellectual) skills. Section Five comprises selections that define the features of "healthy" personality development and present some classroom strategies for the enhancement of such development in basically normal children. (Articles 31, 32, and 35 in Section Six suggest strategies useful to teachers whose classrooms contain children manifesting some forms of personal maladjustment.)

What is healthy personality development in the young child can be viewed in the light of three themes prominent in the discussions in this section: values and moral choice, competence and general effectiveness, and a balance between traits of independence and dependence.

The first three articles focus on the related themes of values and moral choices. A "value" is a belief about the worth and importance of a given trait or enterprise; a "moral choice" is a decision in which a value (or values) plays a role. For example, a child who refrains from hitting another child because he believes that hurting others is "bad" is making a moral choice based on his values. In our present society, when children are exposed to a greater number of life-styles than ever before, many educators think it is particularly important that children be prepared to make personally valid choices from among the array of alternatives.

David Elkind's article, "Increasing and Releasing Human Potentials," is a consideration of some of the general factors in this society that make it difficult for children to maintain healthy personality development. These factors exert an impact in the classroom as well as in the society at large because the classroom is an extension and agent of the society. One particularly important factor inhibiting healthy personality development is the existence of stereotyped value hierarchies, which result in some skills' and enterprises' being considered more respectable than others. Elkind notes that these prejudices can, for example, cause a child whose skills are mechanical to feel less self-respect than a child whose talents are in language and mathematics.

In Article 26, "A Strategy for Developing Values," James Raths discusses methods for teaching values in the classroom. He contrasts the traditional methods with innovative teaching practices that attempt "to help each student to build his own value systems."

Lawrence Kohlberg considers "moral development" and differentiates six stages through which children progress in Article 27, "Moral Education in the Schools." Kohlberg's suggestions are useful to the teacher concerned with fostering movement from lower to higher stages of moral reasoning and action.

Stanley Coopersmith examines "The Antecedents of Self-Esteem" in Article 28, focusing on the theme of competence and general effectiveness.

In particular, Coopersmith considers the child-rearing practices that are associated with high self-esteem (self-respect) in children. His evidence indicates that high self-esteem is promoted by a combination of acceptance of the child, the setting of limits beyond which the child is not allowed to stray, and respect for the child as a decision-making individual.

The last two articles in this section take up those aspects of personality involving the traits of independence (being able to accomplish goals for and by oneself) and dependence (needing other people for affection or assistance).

In "Early Pressures in Child Development," Article 29, Willard Hartup discusses the development of independence, dependence, and achievement strivings (the desire to do well) in children. He concludes, as does Coopersmith, that a complex middle-ground approach between the excercise of authority and permissiveness promotes healthy personality development in children.

Article 30, "The Right to Feel," is an investigation into the role of emotions in the development of independence and dependence. Selma Fraiberg discusses how adult-child "love" involves a mutual giving and receiving by both child and adult. She also points out the importance of allowing children to feel anger while teaching them at the same time to control aggression. More generally, Fraiberg advocates allowing children to experience negative emotions such as anger and grief, stating that: "In our efforts to protect children from painful emotions we may deprive them of their own best means of mastering painful situations."

behavioral objectives   *To be able to discuss the following points*

25 INCREASING AND RELEASING HUMAN POTENTIALS
The effects of heredity and environment on individual development and the relationship of these effects to the realization of human potential
Four barriers to the realization of human potentials
Classroom practices whereby teachers can counteract the societal barriers to the realization of human potentials

26 A STRATEGY FOR DEVELOPING VALUES
The development of values as a function of education
The benefits and shortcomings of four common approaches to value development used in schools

The three processes involved in the establishment of psychological safety

The nature of clarifying strategies and their role in helping a child to develop his own values

The relationship of psychological safety to the effective use of clarifying strategies

27 MORAL EDUCATION IN THE SCHOOLS:
A DEVELOPMENTAL VIEW

The view that moral education is synonymous with mental health and social adjustment

The implications of Hartshorne and May's findings regarding the value of moral education

The theory that moral behavior is related to deep-seated emotional states and the effect of this theory on programs of moral education in the schools

The concepts of ego strength and level of moral judgment and their relationship to each other

The six stages of moral reasoning and the motivation for moral action at each stage

28 THE ANTECEDENTS OF SELF-ESTEEM

Three parental behavior patterns that have been found to be antecedents of self-esteem in children

The function of parental limits in the development of high self-esteem in children

The two combinations of patterns which are likely to be found in the parents of high self-esteem children

The relationship between high self-esteem and rigid, submissive, and insensitive behavior in children

Some teaching practices suggested by the parental behaviors associated with high self-esteem in children

29 EARLY PRESSURES IN CHILD DEVELOPMENT

The issues in the controversy over early pressures in child development

Hartup's recommendations concerning early pressures for independence, and demonstrate an understanding of the relationship between dependence and independence

Parental practices associated with high achievement motivation in children

The constructive use of conflict in changing the behavior of children and the limits necessary to prevent it from becoming a destructive learning tool

Some teaching practices suggested by the parent-child relationships associated with high achievement in children

The value of allowing children to experience painful emotions such as sorrow and anxiety

The factors involved in children's expression of anger against their parents

Ways of dealing with sibling rivalry

The nature of an optimal love relationship between parent and child

The implications for classroom practices of the child's right to express grief and anger

DAVID ELKIND **25** INCREASING AND RELEASING HUMAN POTENTIALS

One of the miracles of human genesis is the way it permits both freedom and constraint, both flexibility and direction in individual development. This miracle is the result of two different circumstances. On the one hand, the genetic endowment of any given individual is dependent upon the gene-complexes present in the chromosomes he receives from his parents. At the moment of conception, the number of possible chromosomal pairings is almost infinite; this well-nigh unlimited number of possible pairings constitutes the freedom component in individual genesis. On the other hand, once the chromosomal pairing has occurred and a viable organism has been formed, the growth of the individual takes a definite direction and follows a pattern characteristic of the species. This pattern of growth, followed by every individual within the species, is the constraint evolution places upon individual development.

I would like to take nature's example of freedom and constraint within individual development as a keynote theme. In the past, discussion of human potentials often went to extremes. *Environmentalists* like John Watson argued that given proper training any child could become a butcher, baker, beggarman, thief. At the other end of the spectrum *maturationists* like Arnold Gesell emphasized the extent to which the child's development was an "unfolding from within" that was relatively impervious to environmental influence. The contemporary view, which parallels the example set by individual genesis, falls between the two extremes and emphasizes both the limits set by genetic endowment and the opportunities provided by experience. Indeed the modern view of human potentials is that of elastic limits, of boundaries which are set by heredity but which can be stretched to an unknown extent by experience and by training.

The notion of freedom with constraint applies not only to the *how much* of development but also to the *what*. Modern genetic and ethnological research suggests not only the multitude of human abilities and talents but also that even complex behavior traits may have a genetic component. Here again, however, the "gene-complexes" operative to any given trait are so variable between individuals that genetic linkage in no way implies uniformity. Accordingly, even when we are concerned with the *what*, the range of possible human talents, as well as with *how much*, we encounter the same principle of freedom *with* restraint, of flexible limits and elastic boundaries.

As I see it, this conception of freedom with constraint underlies the human potentials movement—the aim of which is to find opportunities for every individual, whatever his background; to find his *vein*, the area of activity in which he can work creatively and productively. Having already considered the individual component of this process of realization, let us look for a moment at the social component. In particular I want to consider some of the social barriers that both limit the individual's freedom and impose undue constraints on his efforts to realize his potentials. The first step in any successful encounter is to know one's opponent.

Perhaps the most significant and difficult barrier the human potentialities movement confronts is the established value-hierarchy with respect to human abilities. Our society values the academic and scholarly abilities required to enter the professions and the managerial abilities required for success in business. Artistic abilities are also valued but to a somewhat lesser extent. Lowest in the value hierarchy are the manual trades and service occupations. As a consequence, the work of, say, many talented carpenters, plumbers and electricians, who every day solve difficult problems with imagination and creativity, is neglected and rarely made visible to young people. For children gifted in the manual domain, full realization of their abilities is marred by a value system that attributes little worth to what they can do best.

This value-hierarchy, present in both teachers and parents, is conveyed to children in a myriad of ways. Parental praise for high marks in math and reading far exceeds parental praise for the child's productions in arts and crafts, which are usually dismissed with "That's nice." Moreover if a child is not gifted in the arts but does well academically, parents are not a bit concerned. But, when the reverse is true, concern is obvious and the child who draws when he should be doing math is severely disciplined. The values implicit in such differential responsiveness are not lost upon children who then incorporate them into the scale upon which they rank the worth of activities and themselves.

A second, equally significant, barrier to programs for the realization of human abilities lies in our lack of knowledge in this domain. Most of our tests and assessment procedures are geared to the academic. Only in recent years have we begun to assess such areas as creativity and multiple talents, wherein our devices for assessing the range of talents among children are crude and insufficient at best. Clearly one of the directions in which we can move, and move rapidly, is toward better instruments for assessing the wide range of potentials children bring with them into the world.

Development of adequate assessment procedures is, however, only half of the problem. Once we have instruments that can point up a child's strengths across a wide range of talents, we need to discover means by which we can help the child realize those talents most efficiently and productively. If individualized instruction means finding ways to teach individuals so that they all come out alike at the end, the "individualization" is a farce. Truly individualized instruction should help the child to realize his talents, to find his *vein* in his own way and at his own pace.

A final barrier to the realization of human potentials must be mentioned. Even if parents and educators change their value hierarchies and even if we devise adequate assessment and self-realization procedures, the human potentials program will fail without the support of other social institutions. Media such as television must begin to reflect the valuation of multiple talents and abilities that parents and educators are encouraging. Always presenting the carpenter or handy man as an oaf in a TV series could undo much of what the human potentials movement is all about. Likewise, restrictions by labor unions of the entrance of young people into their ranks undermine the value of human potentials training. Business, too, could do more in the way of recognition for all types of employees. Likewise, the university might give at least as much recognition to teaching talent as it does to research and to grant-getting abilities. Additional examples could be given, but these should suffice to illustrate that if we really want to make it possible for individuals to realize their potentials, institutional as well as individual changes must be made in value-hierarchies.

These barriers to helping each individual realize the possibilities of his talents and abilities are formidable but not unsurmountable. Pressures to tear down the barriers come from such diverse directions as the Women's Liberation Movement and the rapid spread of sensitivity or encounter groups. Each of these movements is, in its own way, concerned with the value-hierarchies on the individual and institutional levels that block some individuals and groups from the opportunity to develop themselves to the full. Progress is being made. To be sure, dangers cannot be discounted, because one cannot predict the direction in which the realization of human potentials will go; and humans have the potential for evil as well as for good. But no freedom is possible without risk. Like all educational movements, the human potentialities movement also has political import and is perhaps our greatest defense against the anarchy that demands freedom without constraint and the dictatorship that demands restraint without freedom. Realization of human abilities involves freedom *with* constraint and is thus democratic in the truest and most positive sense.

A STRATEGY FOR DEVELOPING VALUES 26 JAMES RATHS

"A great and continuing purpose of education has been the development of moral and spiritual values." With this pronouncement, the Educational Policies Commission opened its 1957 report. As important as developing values seems to be to the DAR and the VFW; to the FBI and the HUAC, the area is even more important to us as educators, it seems to me, because of its implications for the learning process. Let me briefly spell out some of these implications.

First, Kubie (1959) suggests that learning is swift, spontaneous and automatic. At times, learning is blocked—many times by what Kubie calls preconscious motives and drives. He recommends that teachers concern themselves with developing self-knowledge on their students' part to remove blocks to learning—to free children so that they may learn in a spontaneous fashion. Second, Ginsburg (1950) suggests that good mental health, assumed to be a necessary condition for learning, is merely a process of living up to a set of values. Finally, several researchers, following the ideas of Louis Raths, have identified pupil behaviors associated with a lack of values (Jonas, 1960; Keevan, 1958; Raths, 1961, 1962). These classroom behaviors, including overconforming, indifference, flightiness and several others, it is argued, interfere with concentration, involvement, and openness in the learning process. Therefore, value development, it seems, should be one of the many central concerns of teachers.

While the area of value development has been a major concern of educators for many years, the public and many professional people, too, have had a feeling that our efforts in this area have not been too effective. The studies summarized by Jacob (1957) in his *Changing Values in College* tend to support this hunch. Teachers have been unable, it seems, to translate their genuine concerns about the value problem into effective patterns of action in their classrooms.

Essentially, there are four basic approaches to the development of values current in our schools. These methods include the teaching of values by the lecture method, by the use of peer-group pressure, by finding or setting examples for children to respect and emulate, and by a reward and punishment rationale. These methods are neither mutually exclusive nor exhaustive of all the approaches we use in schools, but they seem to me to be among the most prevalent in our classrooms.

METHODS IN USE

Perhaps the most common approach is the use of lecture methods. Teachers seem ever ready to tell students what they should believe or how they ought to act. It is easy to burlesque this method in harsh tones. Actually, it may be employed by the kindest, most sincere teachers as well as by the overly self-righteous, would-be reformers found on some school faculties. While it is possible to cite cases in which a lecture or even a "bawling out" did bring about changes in students' values, basically this method is not too successful. Attesting to this is the common cry of many teachers—"You can't *tell* those kids anything." In general, this remark has been found to be accurate.

Teachers' judgments and convictions seem, from a student's point of view, to be out of the framework of things. (Analogously, it may be akin to the feelings teachers in the field have of the "should's and should not's" of professors from schools and colleges of education.) Jones (1960) has suggested a basis for explaining the ineffectiveness of the lecture method. He states that a teacher must be emotionally accepted by his students before he can contribute much to their development of self. By their moralizing and preaching, teachers may set themselves apart emotionally from their students. To the extent that teachers are not accepted by their students, it can be presumed that they will have little effect upon students' values. Students may leave the lecture all full of enthusiasm about what the teacher said, but they may not internalize what they admire and all too often they do not.

A second approach to the value development problem has been in the main popularized by exponents of the core curriculum. During a special period of the school day, students address themselves to self-evaluations and group evaluations. They are encouraged to speak freely, frankly and openly to the entire class judging their own behavior, criticizing group performances and perhaps pledging themselves to future improvements. In general, such statements are accepted by the teacher with little or no comment while other pupils are free to make suggestions, recommendations and comments.

The pressure of group approval or disapproval is a powerful force in bringing about changes in values. This method seems successful in some cases but it has some disturbing by-products. The most distressing of these is the tacit approval of the teacher of the notion that group consensus is correct or at least worthy of very serious consideration. This method, in effect, helps develop "other-directed" persons. Another disadvantage inherent in this group technique is the passive role of the teacher. In a sense, the insight, experience and skills of the teacher are muted. In their place, naïve students play the dominant role in value development, and they do it quite unconsciously.

A third approach for developing students' values is one of acquainting students with examples of exemplary behavior. Instances of model behavior may be drawn from history, literature, and legend or, more directly, from examples set by teachers.

Literature for all levels of schooling has been selected for the past several hundred years on the basis of the ethical and moral lessons with which it dealt. As in other methods discussed previously, some students are truly inspired by these vicarious experiences but we have little evidence that attributes found in a student's reading are readily transferred to daily life.

Teaching values by a living example is a related tactic. Here it is assumed that "values are caught, not taught." It is argued that as teachers demonstrate values students will learn to prize these values. Surely people have been inspired by the goodness of a teacher with whom they have had the good fortune to be associated. However, teachers, especially in secondary schools, have little opportunity to demonstrate many key values. Problems that represent the real issues of life rarely present themselves in a 50-minute subject-matter period in such a way that students can observe their teacher's handling of them. It would truly be unfortunate if we had to rely on this approach as the only positive way teachers can help youngsters develop a set of values.

A fourth method deals with indoctrination and habit formation. Here it is assumed that when students are required to follow rules and regulations, when they are punished for infractions and praised for obedience, they will take on the values associated with the requirements. We are all familiar, however, with what students do when they are free *not* to obey the rules.

It is my contention that these four methods are rather ineffective.

Perhaps their relative ineffectiveness arises partially because they are based on the assumption that the knowledge of ethical and moral choices necessarily leads to ethical and moral conduct. As pointed out many years ago by John Dewey (1909), this assumption has little basis in fact.

Yet more important, these methods seem intent on utilizing external factors, such as lectures or peer-group pressures, to develop values. Friedenberg (1962) analyzes the current problems in developing values as follows:

> . . . it is the inner discipline that is lacking; the school fails to provide a basis for it. The undisciplined behavior which sometimes results is often a sign of the anguish which results from having no core of one's own [emphasis added].

The most promising approach would seem to be one that attempts to help each student build his own value system. This idea is supported by Allport (1955) who asserts that no teaching is more important than that which contributes to a student's self. Clearly, this statement echoes the ideas of Kubie mentioned in the opening paragraphs. Are teachers able to help children in this way? B. O. Smith has said that teachers use little psychological knowledge beyond that found in common sense. What knowledge can we, as teachers, use in this area? Louis Raths has developed a teaching method designed to provide some direction for teachers who are interested in helping students develop their own value systems (Raths, 1957, 1960, 1963).

USE OF CLARIFICATION PROCEDURES

The teacher's role in this method is neither that of a preacher nor that of passive listener. Instead the teacher strives to (a) establish a climate of psychological safety, (b) apply a clarification procedure. An elaboration of these procedures follows.

ESTABLISHMENT OF PSYCHOLOGICAL SAFETY

NONJUDGMENTAL ATTITUDES It has been said that teachers have difficulty responding to an idea without saying, "That's good," "That's bad," or "What good is it?" To provide an atmosphere in which children will feel free to express themselves without threat of ridicule and derision, teachers must refrain from making harsh unnecessary judgments. Of course at times some judgments become necessary in situations in which the health and/or safety of students are threatened in any real sense.

MANIFESTATIONS OF CONCERN While the teacher may be nonjudgmental, it is important for him to be concerned with the ideas expressed by his students. If the concern is apparently lacking, then often the number of student ideas shared with a teacher tends to diminish. Perhaps students are reluctant to share their ideas with someone who is not interested in them. One of the most effective ways to show concern for a student's ideas is to *listen* to them. Busy teachers sometimes overlook this basic and effective technique for communicating interest to their students. Another method for a teacher's communicating his concern for a student's ideas is to *remember* them. As a teacher is able to cite a student's idea in a later conversation, the student cannot help but feel genuinely flattered and impressed.

OPPORTUNITIES FOR THE SHARING OF IDEAS Teachers must organize their courses in such ways that children have the opportunity to express their opinions, purposes, feelings, beliefs, hunches, goals and interests, about moral issues. These attitudinal-type statements may then be examined by the child who expressed them with the teacher acting somewhat as a catalytic agent in the process. Some methods used by teachers in various researches by classroom teachers include: (a) question-answer discussion periods involving moot questions for the class to consider; (b) special written assignments; (c) role-playing techniques; (d) behavior manifestations of individuals or groups that may indicate attitudes, e.g., cheating or being tardy.

The task of finding issues that children may react to is no small problem. While our lives are filled with many, many moral and ethical questions to consider, even within our formal disciplines, it is difficult to find these issues in our textbooks, or *Weekly Readers*. Alexander (1960), a textbook consultant for the New York City schools, has found that "few or no serious problems" are present in our current textbooks.

CLARIFYING STRATEGIES
ASKING QUESTIONS The teacher may attempt to clarify the ideas elicited from his students by asking probing questions. The key criterion for selecting these questions is that they must be questions for which only the student knows the answer. Of course, to be effective they must be asked in a nonjudgmental manner. If a student seems seriously challenged by one of the questions, the teacher should make efforts to "save face" by accepting his bewilderment. For example, the teacher may pass on by saying, "That's a hard question for anyone to answer, isn't it?" "Let's think about it for a while and maybe an answer will come to us later." A list of questions that a teacher may ask is included below. Of course, this list is not exhaustive,

and teachers may add to it as they become more fluent in the use of this procedure.

Reflect back what the student has said and add, "Is that what you mean?"
Reflect back what the student has said with distortions and add, "Is that what you mean?"
"How long have you felt (acted) that way?"
"Are you glad you think (act) that way?"
"In what way is that a good idea?"
"What is the source of your idea?"
"Should everyone believe that?"
"Have you thought of some alternatives?"
"What are some things you have done that reflect this idea of yours?"
"Why do you think so?"
"Is this what you really think?"
"Did you do this on purpose?"
Ask for definitions of key words.
Ask for examples.
Ask if this position is consistent with a previous one he has taken.

It is important that teachers ask these questions of students who express ideas with which they agree as well as with those students who express ideas with which they disagree.

CODING WRITTEN WORK Researchers have found the coding of written work very effective in value clarifying. Whenever students seem to express an attitude, belief, goal, purpose, interest, or aspiration, teachers may mark a V+ or V− in the margin to reflect this idea back to the student. This code works much like other more familiar codes we already use in our schools, e.g., WW for wrong word, or SP for misspelled word. There is one crucial difference. When a teacher marks WW in the margin, there usually *is* a wrong word. When a teacher marks V+ in the margin, it is understood that she is really asking, "Do you believe this?" or "Do you want to change it?"

ACCEPTANCE WITHOUT JUDGMENT It has been found that teachers feel awkward trying to draw the clarification exchange to a close. The verbal interaction between teacher and student is not to win an argument or to gain a debating point. The purpose of the exchange is to clarify students' ideas. It is important that teachers find a way to accept the students' ideas without communicating agreement or praise of them. In a sense, the exchange does not have an ending. Neither the teacher nor the student arrives at a conclusion. Neither is there a need for summarizing. Questions left unanswered are thought about and dwelt on by the student (and perhaps the teacher) at night before going to sleep, or during moments of quiet during the day. Some ways that have been found successful in closing an exchange are as follows:

Silence with a nod.
"Uh-huh."
"I see."
"I understand you better now."
"I can see how you would feel that way."
"I understand."
"I can see that it was difficult for you to decide that way."

In summary, the clarification procedure developed by Louis Raths attempts to elicit from students statements of an attitudinal nature and to clarify these statements for the student. By developing an emotional acceptance of himself on the part of his students, and asking students questions which will serve to clarify their own purposes, goals, attitudes, beliefs, etc., teachers can play an effective role in developing values in their classrooms.

This procedure can be time consuming or it may also take just a few seconds. For example, consider the following hypothetical exchange:

STUDENT: *I hate math.*
TEACHER: *You have never liked math?*
STUDENT: *Well, I did like it at one time.*
TEACHER: *What changed your mind?*
STUDENT: *I don't know.*
TEACHER: *Oh.*

Without trying to lecture the student about what he "ought" to like, without preaching about the dangers inherent in not liking math, the teacher is attempting to help the student understand his own preferences and values.

In passing, it may be appropriate to add that several researchers (Jonas, 1960; Keevan, 1958; Raths, 1961, 1962) have successfully attempted to test these ideas in classrooms in New York State and Wisconsin. Other studies are needed, of course, to test further the efficacy of this procedure. The experiences of a number of researchers in this field suggest also that learning to use the process of clarifying is not easy. It is clearly a difficult matter to enter into a significant interaction with a student. The problem is much less that of identifying with a student, but one of identifying with the student's concerns, of listening, and of taking seriously what he has said and reacting thoughtfully to it.

It must be clear that teachers who apply the clarification procedure must have a tremendous respect for their students. As teachers agree or disagree with students' expressed ideas they must be able to consider them as tenable ones to hold. If teachers believe it is their role to "convert" students to a "right way" of thinking, then it seems they must basically disrespect the views their students hold now. The distinction I am trying to make is one between accepting and respecting. It would seem possible for me to respect the views of a colleague, let us say, without accepting those views. This is the spirit that I believe must dominate a teacher's conversations with his students. Of course, this statement must be modified to the extent that a student's views may threaten the health or safety of himself or society. It is my contention that such cases are rare in our classrooms. Yet there is still plenty of room for many safe differences of opinion and behavior between students and teachers.

Most of us have become accustomed to the association of teaching with changes in student behavior. Too frequently, quite without being aware of it, we look for "instant" changes. We hope for miracles on the "values front." We do not pay enough attention to the fact that it took many years for our students to learn their present almost valueless behavior, and that it may take a long sustained effort to help students to develop serious purposes and aspirations through the clarifying processes. For a free society, opportunities to clarify and to choose must be created again and again.

Norman Cousins (1963) has written about his concern for the predatory quality of life in human form. He suggests that what makes our society so much like a jungle is the misfits who exert power over honest men.

> There are those . . . who insist on projecting their warped ideas to the people around them. They are the agents of chaos. . . . Maybe this is what makes a jungle a jungle.

Cousins continues to say that the way out of the jungle is not just emptying it of these misfits. "There must be some notion about what is to take the place of the jungle. That is why ideals and goals are the most practical things in the world. They conquer the jungle, make men mobile, and convert humans from fawning and frightened animals into thinkers and builders." As teachers learn to develop the ideals, goals and values of students by applying the clarification procedures outlined in this paper, they may perhaps become truly "influential Americans."

MORAL EDUCATION IN THE SCHOOLS:
A DEVELOPMENTAL VIEW

27

LAWRENCE KOHLBERG

For many contemporary educators and social scientists, the term "moral education" has an archaic ring, the ring of the last vestiges of the Puritan tradition in the modern school. This archaic ring, however, does not arise from any intrinsic opposition between the statement of educational aims and methods in moral terms and their statement in psychological terms. In fact, it was just this opposition which the great pioneers of the social psychology of education denied in such works as John Dewey's *Moral Principles in Education* (1911) and Emile Durkheim's *Moral Education* (1925). Both of these works attempted to define moral education in terms of a broader consideration of social development and social functions than was implied by conventional opinion on the topic, but both recognized that an ultimate statement of the social aims and processes of education must be a statement couched in moral terms.

Unfortunately, the educational psychologists and philosophers who followed Dewey's trail retained his concern about a broad phrasing of the goals of education in terms of the child's social traits and values (e.g., co-operation, social adjustment, "democraticness," mental health) without retaining Dewey's awareness that intelligent thought about these traits and values required the concepts dealt with by moral philosophers and psychologists. More recently, however, thoughtful educators and psychologists have become acutely aware of the inadequacies of dealing with moral issues under cover of mental-health or group-adjustment labels. We have become aware, on the one hand, that these mental-health labels are not really scientific and value-neutral terms; they are ways of making value judgments about children in terms of social norms and acting accordingly. On the other hand, we have come to recognize that mental-health and social-adjustment terms do not really allow us to define the norms and values that are most basic as ideals for our children. The barbarities of the socially conforming members of the Nazi system and the other-directed hollow men growing up in our own affluent society have made us acutely aware of the fact that adjustment to the group is no substitute for moral maturity.

It is apparent, then, that the problems of moral education cannot be successfully considered in the "value-neutral" terms of personality development and adjustment. In this paper, I shall attempt to deal with some of the value issues involved in moral education but will approach these issues from the standpoint of research findings. I believe that a number of recent research facts offer some guide through the problems of moral education when these facts are considered from Dewey's general perspective as to the relationship between fact and value in education.

One of the major reasons why the social functions of the school have not been phrased in moral-education terms has been the fact that conventional didactic ethical instruction in the school has little influence upon moral character as usually conceived. This conclusion seemed clearly indicated by Hartshorne and May's findings (1928–1930) that character-education classes and religious-instruction programs had no influence on moral conduct, as the latter was objectively measured by experimental tests of "honesty" (cheating, lying, stealing) and "service" (giving up objects for others' welfare). The small amount of recent research on conventional didactic moral education provides us with no reason to question these earlier findings. Almost every year a professional religious educator or community-service educator takes a course with me and attempts to evaluate the effect of his program upon moral character. While each starts by thinking his program is different from those evaluated by Hartshorne and May, none comes away with any more positive evidence than did these earlier workers.

While recent research does not lead us to question Hartshorne and May's findings as to the ineffectiveness of conventional, formal moral education, it does lead us to a more positive view as to the possibility of effective school moral education of some new sort. In particular, recent research leads us to question the two most common interpretations of the Hartshorne and May findings: the interpretation that moral behavior is purely a matter of immediate situational forces and rewards and the interpretation that moral character is a matter of deep emotions fixed in earliest childhood in the home. Instead, recent research suggests that the major consistencies of moral character represent the slowly developing formation of more or less cognitive principles of moral judgment and decision and of related ego abilities.

The first interpretation of the Hartshorne and May findings mentioned was essentially that of these authors themselves. Their conclusions were much more nihilistic than the mere conclusion that conventional moral-education classes were ineffective and essentially implied that there was no such thing as "moral character" or "conscience" to be educated anyway. Hartshorne and May found that the most influential factors determining resistance to temptation to cheat or disobey were situational factors rather than a fixed, individual moral-character trait of honesty. The first finding leading to this conclusion was that of the low predictability of cheating in one situation for cheating in another. A second finding was that children were not divisible into two groups, "cheaters" and "honest children." Children's cheating scores were distributed in bell-curve fashion around an average score of moderate cheating. A third finding was the importance of the expediency aspect of the decision to cheat, that is, the tendency to cheat depends upon the degree of risk of detection and the effort required to cheat. Children who cheated in more risky situations also cheated in less risky situations. Thus, non-cheaters appeared to be primarily more cautious rather than more honest than cheaters. A fourth finding was that even when honest behavior was not dictated by concern about punishment or detection, it was largely determined by immediate situational factors of group approval and example (as opposed to being determined by internal moral values). Some classrooms showed a high tendency to cheat, while other seemingly identically composed classrooms in the same school showed little tendency to cheat. A fifth finding was that moral knowledge had little apparent influence on moral conduct, since the correlations between verbal tests of moral knowledge and experimental tests of moral conduct were low ($r = 34$). A sixth apparent finding was that where moral values did seem to be related to conduct, these values were somewhat specific to the child's social class or group. Rather than being a universal ideal, honesty was more characteristic of the middle class and seemed less relevant to the lower-class child.

Taken at their face value, these findings suggested that moral education inside or outside the school could have no lasting effect. The moral educator, whether in the home or in the school, could create a situation in which the child would not cheat, but this would not lead to the formation of a general tendency not to cheat when the child entered a new situation. Carried to its logical conclusion, this interpretation of the findings suggested that "honesty" was just an external value judgment of the child's act which leads to no understanding or prediction of his character. It suggested that concepts of good or bad conduct were psychologically irrelevant and that moral conduct must be understood, like other conduct, in terms of the child's needs, his group's values, and the demands of the situation. "While from the standpoint of society, behavior is either 'good' or 'bad,' from the standpoint of the individual it always has some positive value. It represents the best solution for his conflicting drives that he has been able to formulate (Josselyn, 1948)." This line of thought was extended to the view that moral terms are sociologically as well as psychologically irrelevant. From the standpoint of society, behavior is not clearly good or bad either, since there are a multiplicity of standards that can be used in judging the morality of an action. As sociologists have pointed out, delinquent actions may be motivated by the need to "do right" or conform to standards, to both the standards of the delinquent gang and the great American standard of success.

A second interpretation of the Hartshorne and May findings was somewhat less nihilistic. This interpretation was that suggested by psychoanalytic and neopsychoanalytic theories of personality (Freud, 1930; Fromm, 1949; Horney, 1937). In this interpretation, moral instruction in the school was ineffective because moral character is formed in the home by early parental influences. Moral character, so conceived, is not a matter of fixed moral virtues, like honesty, but of deep emotional tendencies and defenses—of love as opposed to hate for others, of guilt as opposed to fear, of self-esteem and trust as opposed to feelings of inadequacy and distrust. Because these tendencies are basically affective, they are not consistently displayed in verbal or behavioral test situations, but they do define personality types. These types, and their characteristic affective responses, can be defined at the deeper levels tapped by personality projective tests, but they are also related to other people's judgments of the child's moral character. This point of view toward moral character was mostly clearly developed and empirically supported in the writing and research of Robert Havighurst and his colleagues (Havighurst & Taba, 1949; Peck & Havighurst, 1960).

While both the "situational" and the "psychoanalytic" interpretations of moral-character research have some validity, recent research findings support a different and more developmental conception of moral character with more positive implications for moral education (Kohlberg, 1963a, 1963b, 1964). While a specific act of "misconduct," such as cheating, is largely determined by situational factors, acts of misconduct are also clearly related to two general aspects of the child's personality development. The first general aspect of the child's development is often termed "ego strength" and represents a set of interrelated ego abilities, including the intelligent prediction of consequences, the tendency to choose the greater remote reward over the lesser immediate reward, the ability to maintain stable focused attention, and a number of other traits. All these abilities are found to predict (or correlate with) the child's behavior on experimental tests of honesty, teacher's ratings of moral character, and children's resistance to delinquent behavior (Kohlberg, 1964).

The second general aspect of personality that determines moral conduct is the level of development of the child's moral judgments or moral concepts. Level of moral judgment is quite a different matter from the knowledge of, and assent to, conventional moral clichés studied by Hartshorne and May. If one asks a child, "Is it very bad to cheat?" or "Would you ever cheat?" a child who cheats a lot in reality is somewhat more likely to give the conforming answer than is the child who does not cheat in reality (Kohlberg, 1966). This is because the same desire to "look good" on a spelling test by cheating impels him to "look good" on the moral-attitude test by lying. If, instead, one probes the reasons for the moral choices of the child, as Piaget and I have done (Piaget, 1932;

Kohlberg, 1963b), one finds something quite different. As an example, we present the child with a series of moral dilemmas, such as whether a boy should tell his father a confidence about a brother's misdeed. In reply, Danny, age ten, said: "In one way, it would be right to tell on his brother or his father might get mad at him and spank him. In another way, it would be right to keep quiet or his brother might beat him up." Obviously, whether Danny decides it is right to maintain authority or right to maintain peer "loyalty" is of little interest compared to the fact that his decision will be based on his anticipation of who can hit harder. It seems likely that Danny will not cheat if he anticipates punishment but that he has no particular moral reasons for not cheating if he can get away with it. When asked, the only reason he gave for not cheating was that "you might get caught," and his teacher rated him high on a dishonesty rating form.

Danny's response, however, is not a unique aspect of a unique personality. It represents a major aspect of a consistent stage of development of moral judgment, a stage in which moral judgments are based on considerations of punishment and obedience. It is the first of the following six stages found in the development of moral judgment (Kohlberg, 1963b):

LEVEL I: PREMORAL

Stage 1 Obedience and punishment orientation. Egocentric deference to superior power or prestige, or a trouble-avoiding set. Objective responsibility.

Stage 2 Naïvely egoistic orientation. Right action is that instrumentally satisfying the self's needs and occasionally other's. Awareness of relativism of value to each actor's needs and perspective. Naïve egalitarianism and orientation to exchange and reciprocity.

LEVEL II: CONVENTIONAL ROLE CONFORMITY

Stage 3 Good-boy orientation. Orientation to approval and to pleasing and helping others. Conformity to stereotypical images of majority or natural role behavior, and judgment of intentions.

Stage 4 Authority and social-order-maintaining orientation. Orientation to "doing duty" and to showing respect for authority and maintaining the given social order for its own sake. Regard for earned expectations of others.

LEVEL III: SELF-ACCEPTED MORAL PRINCIPLES

Stage 5 Contractual legalistic orientation. Recognition of an arbitrary element or starting point in rules or expectations for the sake of agreement. Duty defined in terms of contract, general avoidance of violation of the will or rights of others, and majority will and welfare.

Stage 6 Conscience or principle orientation. Orientation not only to actually ordained social rules but to principles of choice involving appeal to logical universality and consistency. Orientation to conscience as a directing agent and to mutual respect and trust.

Each of these stages is defined by twenty-five basic aspects of moral values. Danny's responses primarily illustrated the motivation aspect of stage 1, the fact that moral motives are defined in terms of punishment. The motivation for moral action at each stage, and examples illustrating them, are as follows:

Stage 1 Obey rules to avoid punishment. Danny, age ten: (Should Joe tell on his older brother to his father?) "In one way it would be right to tell on his brother or his father might get mad at him and spank him. In another way it would be right to keep quiet or his brother might beat him up."

Stage 2 Conform to obtain rewards, have favors returned, and so on. Jimmy, age thirteen: (Should Joe tell on his older brother to his father?) "I think he should keep quiet. He might want to go someplace like that, and if he squeals on Alex, Alex might squeal on him."

Stage 3 Conform to avoid disapproval, dislike by others. Andy, age sixteen: (Should Joe keep quiet about what his brother did?) "If my father finds out later, he won't trust me. My brother wouldn't either, but I wouldn't have a *conscience* that he (my brother) didn't." "I try to do things for my parents; they've always done things for me. I try to do everything my mother says; I try to please her. Like she wants me to be a doctor, and I want to, too, and she's helping me to get up there."

Stage 4 Conform to avoid censure by legitimate authorities and resultant guilt. Previous example also indicative of this.

Stage 5 Conform to maintain the respect of the impartial spectator judging in terms of community welfare or to maintain a relation of mutual respect. Bob, age sixteen: "His brother thought he could trust him. His brother wouldn't think much of him if he told like that."

Stage 6 Conform to avoid self-condemnation. Bill, age sixteen: (Should the husband steal the expensive black-market drug needed to save his wife's life?) "Lawfully no, but morally speaking I think I would have done it. It would be awfully hard to live with myself afterward, knowing that I could have done something which would have saved her life and yet didn't for fear of punishment to myself."

Corresponding to these stages of moral judgment and stages in motivation for moral action are stages in the more general beliefs to which moral judgment is related. While these stages are age-related, they also generally appear in the same step-by-step sequence in different cultures. Ages but not the sequence generally vary cross-culturally.

The information from the Hartshorne and May work, from the psychoanalytic literature, and from the research on ego development and stages of moral judgment combine to present a third alternative to a state moral-indoctrination system and to the current American system of moralizing by individual teachers and principals when children deviate from minor administrative regulations or engage in behavior personally annoying to the teacher. This alternative is to take the stimulation of the development of the individual child's moral judgment and character as a goal of moral education, rather than taking as its goal either administrative convenience or state-defined values.

THE ANTECEDENTS OF SELF-ESTEEM **28** STANLEY COOPERSMITH

What summary statements and conclusions can we make about the conditions associated with the development of high self-esteem? Or, more exactly, what differentiates the antecedent conditions and personal characteristics associated with the occurrence of high self-esteem from those associated with less favorable self-appraisals? The most general statement about the antecedents of self-esteem can be given in terms of three conditions: total or nearly total *acceptance* of the children by their parents, clearly defined and enforced *limits,* and the *respect* and latitude for individual action that exist within the defined limits. In effect, we can conclude that the parents of children with high self-esteem are concerned and attentive toward their children, that they structure the worlds of their children along lines they believe to be proper and appropriate, and that they permit relatively great freedom within the structures they have established. Examination of this combination of conditions reveals some general relationships between childrearing practices and the formation of self-esteem. The most notable of these deal with parental behavior and the consequences of the rules and regulations that parents establish for their children. These relationships indicate that definite and enforced limits are associated with high rather than low self-esteem; that families which establish and maintain clearly defined limits permit *greater* rather than less deviation from conventional behavior, and freer individual expression, than do families without such limits; that families which maintain clear limits utilize *less* drastic forms of punishment; and that the families of children with high self-esteem exert greater demands for academic performance and excellence. Taken together, these relationships indicate that, other things being equal, limits and rules are likely to have enhancing and facilitating effects and that parental performance within such limits is likely to be moderate, tolerant, and generally civilized. They suggest that parents who have definite values, who have a clear idea of what they regard as appropriate behavior, and who are able and willing to present and enforce their beliefs are more likely to rear children who value themselves highly. Parents who can act this way apparently have less need to treat their children harshly, and, from all indications, are viewed with greater affection and respect by their offspring.

There is, of course, an underlying question about the nature and enforcement of the limits and rules espoused by the parents of children with high self-esteem. Two sources of evidence lead us to believe that the limits established are reasonable, rational, and appropriate to the age of the child, and are not arbitrary and inflexible. The first basis for this belief is the consistent and marked acceptance of their offspring that these parents express. They are concerned for their welfare, are willing to exert themselves on their behalf, and are loyal sources of affection and support. They express their acceptance in a variety of ways, with expressions of interest and concern being perhaps the major underlying feature of their attitudes and behaviors. The second reason for believing that the limits are moderate and reasonable comes from our evidence concerning the parents. Our study indicates that the parents of children with high self-esteem are themselves active, poised, and relatively self-assured individuals who recognize the significance of childrearing and believe they can cope with the increased duties and responsibilities it entails. The parents generally appear to be on relatively good terms with one another and to have established clear lines of authority and responsibility. Both father and mother lead active lives outside the family and apparently do not rely upon their families as the sole or necessarily major sources of gratification and esteem. The concern that these parents show for their children, the attention they give them, and their calm, realistic, and assured demeanor lead us to believe that they would be unlikely to impose harsh or extreme restrictions, or to behave in a capricious manner; firm, clear, but extensive limits appear to be much more consistent with their personalities. There are no indications—and several contraindications—that these (high self-esteem) parents are harsh, vindictive, emotional, or power seeking. They apparently believe strongly in the validity of their perceptions and values and guide the lives of their children accordingly, yet at the same time accept and tolerate dissent within the limits that they have established.

Why well-defined limits are associated with high self-esteem can be explained in several ways. First and foremost we should note that well-defined limits provide the child with a basis for evaluating his present performance as well as facilitating comparisons with prior behavior and attitudes. The limits serve to define the social geography by delineating areas of safety and hazards, by indicating means of attaining goals, and by pointing out the landmarks that others use to judge success and failure. When the map drawn by the parents is a realistic and accurate depiction of the goals accepted by the larger social community and the means used to reach them, it serves as a guide to the expectations, demands, and taboos of that community. As such, the map clarifies the ambiguities and inconsistencies of social behavior and also endows such behavior with a sense of meaning and purpose. If provided early, and accurately enough, and if it is upheld by behavioral as well as verbal reinforcement, limit definition gives the child the conviction that there is indeed a social reality that makes demands, provides rewards, and punishes violations. Imposition of limits is likely to give the child, on a rudimentary nonverbal and unconscious level, the implicit belief that a definition of the social world is possible and that the "real" world does indeed impose restrictions and demand compliance with its norms. On this level limits result in differentiation between one's self and the environment and thus serve to increase self-definition. In sum, imposition of limits serves to define the expectations of others, the norms of the group, and the point at which deviation from them is likely to evoke positive action; enforcement of limits gives the child a sense that norms are real and significant, contributes to self-definition, and increases the likelihood that the child will believe that a sense of reality is attainable.

That persons with high self-esteem come from homes notable for their definition of limits raises the question whether persons with positive self-attitudes are likely to be more rigid, submissive, and insensitive. In more neutral and descriptive terms the question is whether persons reared under clear, enforced limits are likely to comply automatically with the desires of others, lose their initiative, and assume a pedestrian and simple way of perceiving and thinking. The issue, in effect, is whether the gains of self-esteem that flow from definite standards may be offset by inflexible opinions, sanctimonious convictions of personal correctness, and a close-minded insensitivity to possibilities and alternatives. From the evidence available to us, the response to this question would appear to be generally negative. We find that individuals with high self-esteem who are reared under strongly structured conditions tend to be more, rather than less, independent and more creative than persons reared under more open and permissive conditions. From other indications it appears that children reared within definite limits are also more likely to be socially accepted as peers and leaders by their associates and also more capable of expressing opinions and accepting criticism. Thus many of the presumably negative effects of limit definition are not supported by empirically derived evidence. Once the loaded terms and value judgments are cast aside and specific behavioral indices are employed, it appears that parents who are less certain and attentive of their standards are likely to have children who are more compliant to the will of their peers and less likely to perceive alternatives—as well as lower in self-esteem.

Psychologically, the distinctive feature of the home in which limits are clearly defined is that the standards, information, and cues it provides are cognitively clear. This clarity enables a child to judge for himself whether he has attained a desired goal, made progress, or deviated. In a home where standards are ambiguous, a child requires the assistance of others to decipher its cues, recognize its boundaries, and understand its relationships. In the cognitively clear world he learns to rely upon his own judgments and interpretations of events and consequences; the locus is internal and personal rather than external and social. Detailed definition of standards, and their consistent presentation and enforcement, presents the child with a wealth of information that he himself can employ to appraise and anticipate the consequences of his actions. A psychological world that provides sparse, ambiguous, or inconsistent information makes it difficult for the child to make rational decisions—that is, decisions with predictable outcomes—and increases the likelihood that he will either continually seek aid in interpreting his environment or will gradually withdraw from it: in neither case will he come to believe that he can, by himself, interpret his environment and guide himself through the thickets of its ambiguities.

Despite the benefits that they confer, would cognitively clear limits have beneficial effects upon children without the warmth and respect expressed by their parents? In more specific terms we may ask whether our results indicate that a *pattern* of conditions is necessary to produce high self-esteem, whether any single condition or set of conditions plays a greater role than others, and whether the self-esteem of the parents is invariably related to the child's self-esteem and to parental patterns of behavior. Although our results do not permit a definitive empirical answer to all of these questions they do provide the basis for a tentative response. First, and foremost, we should note that there are virtually no parental patterns of behavior or parental attitudes that are common to all parents of children with high self-esteem. Examination of the major indices and scales of acceptance, limit definition, respect, and parental self-esteem provides explicit support for the view that not all of these conditions are essential for the formation of high self-esteem. Thus, we find that 21.2 percent of mothers of children with high self-esteem rate low on acceptance, 12.1 percent of them do not enforce limits carefully. 19.4 percent do not believe that children should be permitted to dissent from their parents' views, and 24.3 percent are themselves rated as below average in self-esteem. The other side of this analysis—that is, examination of the attitudes and actions of parents whose children have low self-esteem—is equally revealing: 56.7 percent of them rate high on acceptance, 60.0 percent enforce definite limits, 50.0 percent tolerate dissent and expression, and 56.7 percent have high self-esteem. These findings apparently indicate that although we have established the general conditions associated with producing high self-esteem, not all of these conditions (or others) are essential to its development in any given individual nor is any single one of them sufficient to produce marked enhancement. Even though errors of measurement, scaling, and so on may contribute to the distribution of responses in any single analysis and the distributions differ for different analyses, it nonetheless appears that the apparent basic conditions of parental treatment and personal characteristics are not individually necessary nor sufficient to produce high self-esteem. This would suggest that combinations of conditions are required—more than one but less than the four established by this study (acceptance, limit definition, respect, and parental self-esteem). In addition it is likely that a minimum of devaluating conditions—that is, rejection, ambiguity, and disrespect—is required if high self-esteem is to be attained.

At least in theory, two combinations are likely to occur with considerable frequency: high parental self-esteem is likely to be associated with acceptance; firm limit definition is likely to be found in concert with respect for individual expression. The rationale for the relationship between high parental self-esteem, acceptance, and the child's high self-esteem stems from the findings of other investigators of the process of identification (Bateson, 1944; Sears, 1957; Whiting, 1954). Their general conclusion appears to be that the child's identification with his parents is markedly increased and to a great extent derives from parental acceptance. A close affective tie apparently establishes the desire to emulate, and also the likelihood that parentally approved behaviors will be expressed. In effect, the child is more likely to follow in the footsteps of his parents and accede to their desires if they indicate their approval of him than if they disapprove of him and treat him in a punitive, rejecting manner. Doll play, used as an index of underlying attitudes, reveals that parental nurturance is positively associated with preference for adult dolls (Levin, 1952): a child is less likely to adopt an adult role when he is physically punished or rejected. Studies of institutionally reared children (Goldfarb, 1945; Bowlby, 1951) suggest that persons who have not had a history of nurturant experience with a parental figure tend to be socially immature and shallow in their emotional responses. Our own results indicate that children with high self-esteem are more likely than others to be close to their parents, to confide in them, to respond to the punishments they administer, to be socially skilled and emotionally responsive. This leads us to the initial conclusion that, to the extent that identification plays a role in the formation of self-esteem, children with high self-esteem are more likely to identify, as well as more likely to have a favorable model with which to identify.

The second suggestion—that clear, enforced limits are related to respect for individual expression—stems from the observation that openly expressed rules and restraints provide a framework for discussion and hence require less supervision and restriction. From a purely structural viewpoint, rules that are fixed and accepted make it possible, although not certain, that persons exercising authority will be less concerned and threatened by differences of opinion. If such rules of conduct do not exist, persons in authority are more likely to consider that differences of opinion threaten their position. An external code of specified practices and rights that is enforced provides those governed by it with at least some degree of assurance against arbitrary actions and also permits those who exercise authority to be more casual in their treatment of dissent; it engenders a more relaxed attitude for those who must administer social organizations as well as for those who must live within them.

The relation between parental self-esteem and the child's self-esteem indicates that unconscious identification and conscious modeling may well underlie the self-evaluations of many individuals. These processes need not contribute equally to the history of each person but there does appear to be a general relationship between the parent's self-esteem and the manner in which he treats his children. Parents with high self-esteem are generally more accepting of others, decisive, inclined to lead active personal lives, and convinced of their powers. They presumably have less need to gain vicarious successes from the accomplishments of their children and are able to provide their children with a definite idea of what they expect and desire. The parent with low self-esteem who is accepting of his child may provide a negative model for esteem building but at the same time the pattern of his actions may well lead the child to a higher level of self-appraisal than he has himself attained. The combination of a high self-esteem model and an enhancing pattern of treatment should provide the highest and most stable levels of positive self-evaluation. Some recent attempts (Bandura & Walters, 1963) to modify the antisocial actions of adolescents suggest that an effective, rewarding model establishes the motivation for change and provides the specific cues for desirable action patterns.

29

What to demand of a child? How much to demand of him? When to demand it? The problem of early pressures is a core concern within the field of practical child psychology. Also, much of the scientific work currently being conducted in the areas of learning, motivation, cognitive processes, and personality development in children has implications for this problem. More and more frequently, responsible educators are endorsing the concept of early pressures in child development. Francis Keppel, the U.S. Commissioner of Education, has recently added his support by suggesting that we have been wasting enormous creative powers by beginning education too late, by assuming that there is some magical, fixed age at which learning takes place, and by adhering slavishly to the notion of predetermined developmental levels.

As a consequence of changing educational views, present-day parents and teachers are caught in a bind. "Should I help my four-year-old pick out words in 'Cat in the Hat?' I hear the first-grade teacher doesn't like parents to do this." "Should reading, or prereading experiences, be part of every nursery school and kindergarten curriculum?" "How far should I go in urging my three-year-old to fight back when the neighbor kids have pre-empted his toys?"

Descending to us, on the one hand, is a tradition which suggests that those responsible for the socialization of children exercise their responsibility best by helping children do what they are free or ready to do without trying to force them into particular channels of expression. The idea that children develop optimally in a benign, hot-house type of environment is identified, albeit mistakenly, with the tradition in pedagogy known as "progressive education" and with the psychological theories of the psychodynamic schools. Such terms as *permissiveness* and *liberalism* are closely associated with these child-rearing approaches, and few words in the lexicon of social psychology have been so overworked or badly misused.

Running counter to educational doctrine based on concepts of readiness and free expression is the doctrine of early pressures. Those who hold this view argue that there should be early and persistent demands for conformity to accepted standards of moral and social conduct, as well as early demands for excellence in cognitive performance and self-motivated achievement. Further, these demands should be buttressed by "old-fashioned" discipline stemming from strong, watchful, authoritative parents, teachers, preachers, and law-enforcement officials. Advocacy of early pressures in the educational development of the child has a long-standing tradition, but it has been particularly strong since the advent of the space age. Emphasis on early pressures for characterological development has been particularly intense since the advent of the "new conservatism" in American politics.

The philosophical conflict experienced by those who live and work with children is intense. I regard this conflict with the utmost seriousness. Occasionally, the conflict between opposing child-rearing ideologies can be resolved by rational methods. A teacher can say to himself, coolly and objectively, "Let's look at the evidence concerning the results of structured language experiences for children of preschool age. To be sure, the evidence is not very good and more research should be done, but the choice can be a rational one."

Unfortunately, the problem is complicated by feelings or, as Leon Festinger (1957) has termed it, *cognitive dissonance*. Acceptance of a permissive philosophy of child-rearing is, after all, to act in opposition to an old and strong cultural tradition that endorses the necessity for pressure. A certain amount of discomfort or dissonance inevitably follows for the individual who deliberately chooses the permissive view. Further, because rearing children is extremely serious business, the amount of dissonance evoked by the necessity for choosing an educational philosophy is likely to be great rather than minimal. It is the rare parent who, when his child has successfully gotten away with something, can dismiss this without a feeling of "maybe I should have been tougher on him." For example, in our house, we have a 22-month-old named Barry who misbehaves by opening the oven door on the kitchen stove, climbing up, and nonchalantly lighting the burners. (One Playskool toy and at least two pans have been permanently scorched as a consequence of Barry's actions.) Our reaction to Barry's behavior has been a kind of disorganized attempt to evoke verbal mediational processes in our son. I experienced enormous dissonance one day when a very child-centered, liberal-minded colleague informed me that she had instantly stopped similar behavior in her child. She simply said, "Hot, hot, Benjy," and then deliberately burned him! The dissonance experienced by people responsible for the rearing of children ranges from that evoked by simple, specific instances such as the one just described to conflict evoked by whole philosophies. For example, the most dedicated, psychodynamically-oriented preschool teacher seldom has personal defenses of sufficient strength, or the "tunnel vision" needed, to escape dissonance evoked by the rising popularity of the Montessori schools—and, vice versa.

The antecedents of the child-rearing traditions being discussed here are pertinent. After some historical remarks, selected research evidence supporting an eclectic philosophy of child-rearing will be presented. The point of view to be expressed is based on social learning principles. It will be argued that pressures of certain kinds should, indeed, be brought to bear on the young child. It will be argued, however, that these pressures should be exerted within a context of nurturance and permissiveness. No admixture of liberal and conservative philosophies of child rearing stressing that the adult should keep an iron hand concealed in a velvet glove will be proposed here. Rather, it will be argued that, when the child's early years include encouragement of dependence and trust in adults, early pressures for independence and achievement, for appropriate identifications, for motivation to learn, and for competence in certain areas of intellective functioning are not only appropriate but desirable. It should be emphasized that this is not a simple middle-of-the-road philosophy.

The doctrine that children accomplish best what they are ready to do in the absence of pressure for accomplishment is the culmination of two ideologies concerning the nature of the child. First, this doctrine is based on a belief in the innate capacity for goodness in children. The name of Jean Jacques Rousseau is usually identified with the point of view that, if the child is permitted to express his natural impulses and to develop without restriction the abilities given him by nature, he will show little of the depravity characteristic of adults and his capacity for constructive social good will be maximized.

A second influence on present-day liberal education has been the hypothesis of "critical periods." The notion of critical periods is comprised of two interrelated hypotheses. First, it is assumed that both the physical and behavioral development of children proceed according to more or less orderly sequences. For most children, turning over, creeping, walking, running, and jumping proceed in an orderly sequence. We have thoroughly adequate norms concerning both the average ages at which these events occur and the amount of variability across groups of children in the timing of each of these events. Probably the most famous critical periods postulated in all child psychology are Freud's psychosexual stages; others who have recognized critical periods in behavioral development are Erik Erikson, who has described regularities in psychosocial development, and Piaget, who has argued that intellectual development takes place according to a patterned sequence.

Implicit also in the critical-periods principle is the notion that "there is a time to plant and a time to pluck up that which is planted." That is, it appears that interference with certain developmental phenomena seems to be of greater significance for the later development of the child when the interference occurs at some points in the life history rather than at others. This component of the critical-periods hypothesis is supported by developmental observations at many different levels. Students of human embryology report that there are clear-cut periods in the morphogenesis of the embryo during which neural tissue, visceral tissue, and other parts of the physical structure of the organism are sensitive to extrinsic stimulation, but beyond these periods the embryo is fairly resistant to such influences. Similarly, McGraw (1935) found that attempts to speed learning of certain motor skills were ineffectual when introduced at an inappropriate time. Students of personality development have argued that attachment to a love object during the first months of a child's life is prerequisite to successful subsequent socialization. Piaget and other students of cognitive development have suggested similar critical periods in intellectual functioning.

Virtually all students of developmental processes have acknowledged that the timing of developmental events is, to some extent, unique for each individual child. The time schedule or stages formulated for various aspects of behavioral development are not rigid but apply within fairly broad limits. Nevertheless, the critical-periods notion is the reason why eight out of ten textbooks in child psychology are organized in terms of chronological age and why children are not taught to read until they are six.

Descriptive norms relating to the behavioral development of children are, and will continue to be, very useful in constructing educational programs for masses of children. "Best guesses" about the capacities of children at various ages, when based on adequate normative research, facilitate many a sound educational decision. But norms are seductive. For example, they do not by themselves furnish a parent or teacher with an adequate basis for a philosophy of child rearing. "Slavish attention to developmental levels" (to use Mr. Keppel's phrase) draws attention away from a more basic issue in child development—the processes which bring behavioral changes about. The question that educators, as well as research psychologists, should persistently seek to answer is *why* development occurs rather than *when* development occurs.

Educational emphasis on the concept of early pressures does not stem from a clearly identifiable group of principles within developmental psychology. The notion of early pressures is reminiscent, in some ways, of the prescientific view that children are smaller, weaker, more stupid versions of adults, or the Calvinist view of childhood as the crucial period for containing and eliminating the evil in man's nature. But the doctrine of early pressures has picked up support from more modern quarters. Espousal of the belief that man is "infinitely perfectible," or general endorsement of the belief that nurture has much power over maturation, supports the concept of early pressures. Such sharply differing theorists as John B. Watson and Maria Montessori have enunciated views consonant with the early-pressures notion. Further, those applied psychologists who have argued for cultural enrichment, or that good nursery school experience increases the child's competence in intellectual functioning and social adjustment, imply an endorsement of the early pressures concept.

To be sure, some of these viewpoints emphasize appropriate *experiences* for the young child, rather than appropriate early *pressures*. The distinction between experiences and pressures, however, is not clear-cut. The simple act of sending a child to nursery school is a form of pressure; the simplest limits for social conformity are pressureful; the simplest curriculum activity involves pressure, too. Only the condition of *laissez faire* does not imply pressure. But *laissez faire* is an abstraction and is not a philosophy of education; it is, rather, the absence of education and need not concern us further here.

Educators of young children have accepted many of the ramifications of the critical-periods hypothesis, but they have also recognized the child's early capacity for relatively complex forms of learning. The "right pressures at the right times" has been the educational touchstone of many nursery school teachers. But child psychology is a young and tentative science. Continuing questions have been formulated concerning the developmental stages. Would intellectual competence be enhanced by introducing achievement demands earlier than we do now? Are the developmental stages we have abstracted from our studies of children immutable? Even if these stages accurately represent the facts of development for most children, are there necessarily harmful consequences for the individual child when social-learning demands are introduced earlier than usual (or, for that matter, later than usual)? These are the problems, traced in historical perspective, that we now face. The dissonant position in which teachers and parents now find themselves stems from the convergence of long-standing beliefs concerning the nature of child development.

Selected research that bears on these problems is now relevant. But first, a word about independence and achievement and some of the determinants of these aspects of child behavior.

To begin with, I am familiar with no evidence that suggests an optimal age for beginning either training for independence or attempts to motivate the child toward achievement. The evidence we have, however, suggests that the preschool years, as a whole, are crucial in developing both of these qualities.

Independence, for the young child, involves taking initiative, overcoming obstacles, persistence in activity, just wanting to do things, and wanting to do things by oneself. Research by Beller (1955) has shown that independence and dependence are only *partially* separable components of social behavior. Preschool children are neither independent nor dependent, at one end or the other of a single continuum. Instead, young children are a mixture of two quite distinct clusters of traits—self-reliant striving for mastery, on the one hand, and dependency, on the other. The preschool child is learning simultaneously to depend on others and to be independent of others, paradoxical as this sounds. The child is learning new ways for *being helped* at the same time that he is learning to *help himself.*

Virtually all theories of socialization consider early learning to rely on other people as a necessary vehicle for later social learning. Therefore it would not seem sensible to set about teaching a preschool child to *inhibit* his dependent behavior in order to establish self-reliance. On the contrary, support and reinforcement for dependence need to be forthcoming during the early preschool years, rather than systematic inhibitory influences. Some evidence suggests that early, strong, inhibitory socialization in the area of dependence has undesirable consequences. Cross-cultural studies, for example, Whiting & Child (1953), suggest that severe handling of dependence in early childhood is associated with adult anxiety about social relationships and personal insecurity. Also, the folklore of cultures that inhibit dependence in children at early ages frequently contains aggressive and hostile themes. Finally, the work of other investigators (e.g., Sears, Whiting, Nowlis, & Sears, 1953; Gewirtz, 1954) suggests that early deprivation of dependency gratifications serves in many instances to motivate the child to redouble his efforts to gain attention and approval from adults. I conclude that independence training should not begin by abrupt, premature attempts to decrease dependency behavior.

At the same time, early direct training and encouragement of self-reliance and assertiveness seems to increase such efforts by the child. This statement does not contradict the foregoing thesis that reinforcements for dependency should not be pervasively withdrawn from young children. Studies with preschool children indicate that independence is increased both by reinforcement of independent effort and by providing the child with experiences that increase his proficiency in the task at hand. For example, Fales (1944) trained nursery school children to take off their wraps; she also praised some of the children for their endeavors. Later observations showed that the trained *and* reinforced group refused assistance far more frequently than did the untrained and unreinforced groups. In another, quite different investigation, Winterbottom (1958) studied the child-rearing antecedents of independent and achievement-oriented behavior in elementary school boys. This study will be mentioned again further on in this paper. Suffice it to say here that information was obtained concerning the demands made by the mothers of the subjects for independent accomplishment, the rewards given for fulfillment of these accomplishments, and the restrictions placed on autonomous performance. The nine-year-old subjects in this investigation showed more signs of independent accomplishment when their mothers reported themselves as placing fewer early restrictions on independent activity and furnishing more early rewards for autonomous behavior.

Thus far, I have postulated that two conditions are requisite for optimal development of independence in the child: (1) dependence should not be broadly inhibited; and (2) independent activity should be rewarded frequently and early. In addition to these child-training components I would add a third. As independent, self-reliant behavior emerges and becomes a stable part of the child's hierarchy of social responses, *inappropriate* forms of dependent behavior can be weakened. But weakening of inappropriate dependency should stem from withdrawal of reinforcement, rather than the application of criticism or punishment. Recent work in the area of behavior modification conducted in the Laboratory of Developmental Psychology at the University of Washington suggests that careful withdrawal of reinforcement for inappropriate behavior is a necessary component in the execution of early pressures for more desirable activity (Harris, Wolf, & Baer, 1964).

It should be made clear that effective early pressures for independence do not involve withdrawal of reinforcement for all, or even most, manifestations of dependency. As mentioned earlier, socialization cannot proceed (conscience development is impeded, for example) in the absence of motivations for reliance on people. Dependency is a kind of social glue; culture, social institutions, the family, existence as we know it, could not be maintained in the absence of emotional interdependence among people. Dependency, however, is a form of social behavior that is "changeworthy." Rather than being pressured to give up social attachments, young children need to be pushed in the direction of altering the *objects* from whom they seek gratification. Children of two and three years of age certainly require ready access to the affection and attention of teachers, parents, and other adults. On the other hand, Heathers (1955) has shown, in his very interesting observational studies, that a shift to peers as objects for dependency occurs during the later preschool years. Active encouragement of this shift would seem desirable; the teacher of four-year-olds should gradually withdraw some of her reinforcement for dependence on adults, at the same time stepping up rewards for seeking attention from, and seeking contact with, peers.

Pressure can also be brought to bear on young children concerning the *methods* used for obtaining dependency gratifications. Whereas regular reinforcement for clinging and affection-seeking may be appropriate for three-year-olds, reinforcements for these components of dependence should be given under more selective circumstances in the case of the four- and five-year-olds. Older children may be appropriately pressured to seek approval for completing tasks well and to seek praise for accomplishing things. In our society, seeking approval is a "mature" form of dependence. By instituting early pressures for approval-seeking, teachers not only facilitate maturity in the ways children seek social gratification; such early pressures also set in motion strivings for excellence and achievement.

Achievement behavior refers to attempts to perform well—to perform efficiently or quickly, or to produce something of quality. McClelland, Atkinson, Clark, & Lowell (1953) have emphasized two major factors leading to the development of achievement motivation. First, the child must have opportunity to associate feelings of satisfaction produced by simple changes in the environment with his own striving or effort. That is, children need the opportunity to exert themselves in an independent and effortful way and to observe satisfying environmental changes as a consequence of their actions.

Second, early achievement efforts are enhanced by attempts of parents and teachers to structure performance standards and by adult demands for striving and excellence. This means that children must know or be informed as to what worthwhile effort is. Put in another way, the child must be helped to discriminate between a good try and a poor try. He must learn to differentiate between a good product and a poor product. Further, he must understand that the important people in his environment hope and desire that he will produce effective tries rather than lackadaisical efforts and good products rather than poor ones. This point of view implies that parents and teachers should not praise indiscriminately every intellectual, creative, or athletic effort made by young children. It is easy (and probably comforting to children) to respond to every painting or every high jump with, "Oh, that's nice," or with the noncommittal "Umhum." To be sure, at certain stages major interest may lie in simply getting the child involved in activities—in getting *any* response at the easel or *any* move on the climbing apparatus. At such times, wholesale reinforcement of the child's efforts may be defensible. But excellence in subsequent endeavor is, by definition, not possible unless the child has some idea as to what excellence is. Both parents and teachers frequently underestimate the capacity of young children for making such discriminations. It is my belief that at least rudimentary concepts of excellence can be conveyed to most children of preschool age with respect to such diverse activities as singing, physical movement, the graphic arts, and verbal communication.

It follows from the preceding discussion that the teacher's own esthetic values—her own evaluations of grace and elegance in movement and dance and her own judgments concerning excellence in verbal functioning—are key contributors to the acquisition of behavioral standards by the child. Children cannot be pressured to acquire definitions of excellence if those doing the pressuring do not have valid conceptions of excellence. But the process of structuring standards for young children is not simply a matter of transmitting the teacher's own values to the children. The idiosyncratic potentialities of the individual child and his family are pertinent to this problem. Further, the value structure of the

280 *personality development*

cultural milieu in which the teacher finds herself with the child should supplement, and not work at cross purposes, with the school's efforts to teach the young child what excellence means.

The late Vaughn Crandall (1963) and his associates (including his wife, Virginia, who has written an excellent review of research on achievement behavior in young children for a recent issue of *Young Children* (1964), have also studied the early childhood determinants of achievement. This group has argued that the emergence of autonomous achievement-striving depends on direct approval and reinforcement of the child's early efforts at mastery. Of particular significance is reinforcement of early achievement efforts by means of attention, approval, and affection from adults. Earlier in this presentation I endorsed the hypothesis that the first meaningful step toward independent striving for excellence consists of learning to use performance as an avenue through which one can acquire dependency gratifications. Perhaps the point should be made once again. It is important that the young child learn to seek approval for things he does. This is important not only because seeking approval happens to be a mature, socially acceptable way for expressing dependency needs, but because this kind of social learning is a prerequisite for later stages in development wherein autonomous, self-sustaining, prideful, self-approving efforts to achieve will be required of the child.

Early reinforcement for achievement is probably only one determinant of motivation for learning in children. For example, I doubt if social approval for achievement-striving could ever produce the autonomous determination necessary for the consistent "A" report card, the contributions of a great scientist, or the world's record in the 10,000 meter run. Intrinsic rewards stemming from within acts of learning or mastery are themselves obviously important. The efforts of the infant to roll over, to reach for objects, and to orient toward complex stimuli are primitive demonstrations that intrinsic motivation contributes significantly to strivings for excellence. It is for this reason that I have always been gratified by those nursery school teachers who feel pressured themselves to provide young children with a broad array of rich, intrinsically rewarding experiences. A simple occurrence, such as watching what happens when blue and yellow paint are mixed together, is probably rewarding to the young child for intrinsic perceptual reasons. Early social reinforcement for skillful paint-mixing probably contributes far less than these intrinsic perceptual gratifications to the child's motivation for excellence in the large, molar process of painting. But the point is made, I am sure. Early reinforcement for achievement-striving appears to be related to the strength of the child's later achievement efforts. Other factors, such as early opportunities to experience intrinsic motivation, also contribute to the strength of achievement efforts. Social reinforcement for achievement cannot, in all likelihood, do the job alone; at the same time, it is doubtful that strong achievement efforts seldom emerge when this kind of early reinforcement is absent.

Research evidence supporting the assertions contained in the preceding paragraphs stems from several different sources. For example, data are beginning to emerge from projects studying the effects of nursery-school experience on the achievement behavior of culturally deprived children. The experimental nursery schools involved in these projects usually provide frequent positive reinforcement for the child's autonomous efforts at mastery. Consequently, findings showing increases in IQ or elementary school achievement among children who have attended experimental nursery schools suggest that reinforcement facilitates the development of an achievement orientation. But the experimental effort to offset the effects of cultural deprivation also involves frequent opportunity for the child to experience intrinsic gratifications from cognitive and social experiences. At best, then, the evidence emerging from these projects is only suggestive concerning the role of early reinforcement for achievement behavior in increasing autonomous achievement-striving in the child.

Other evidence is to be found in studies of child-rearing practices. In a study mentioned previously Winterbottom (1958) reported that nine-year-old boys evincing strong motivation for achievement had mothers who expected self-reliant behavior relatively early, who provided more frequent and larger rewards when their sons succeeded in performing independently and well, and who placed fewer restrictions on their sons' spontaneous independent behavior. Another investigator (Feld, 1959) studied these same boys after they had reached adolescence. The mother's behavior with respect to her son's early autonomous efforts continued to be related to the strength of achievement motivation in adolescence. This is a particularly interesting finding since the mother's tendency to reinforce independence *after* her son reached adolescence was actually negatively related to strength of achievement motivation. Tentative as these data are, they suggest that early pressures for achievement are more effective than late ones.

A quasi-experimental study by Rosen & D'Andrade (1959) involved elementary school boys, their fathers, and their mothers. It was found that parents of boys with strong motivation for achievement had higher aspirations, set higher standards, and expected better performance than parents of boys with lower levels of achievement motivation. Mothers, in particular, gave more approval for successful achievement efforts and were quicker to criticize unsuccessful efforts in the case of high achievement-oriented boys than the mothers of low achievement-oriented boys. Crandall, Preston, & Ralson (1960) also report a positive relation between maternal reinforcement of achievement behaviors and the frequency of achievement efforts on the part of nursery school children. And finally, longitudinal data from the Fels Institute (Moss & Kagan, 1958) indicate that children of pushing, achievement-oriented mothers scored higher on IQ tests early in the preschool years and increased their scores on IQ tests during the elementary school years more than children of nonaccelerating mothers. Taken together, the few studies mentioned here point clearly to early reinforcement of achievement behavior as a major determinant of efforts at mastery in later childhood.

In her forthcoming review, Mrs. Crandall concludes that "our education for excellence is accompanied by certain psychological costs." While achievement-oriented preschoolers seem to enjoy relatively good social and personal adjustment, some evidence suggests that older children and adolescents with high achievement motivation suffer disruptions in their social relationships, manifest higher levels of anxiety, and the like. More information is needed than is currently available concerning the correlates of achievement motivation in children. It is possible, however, that the extant results do not tell the whole story. For example, research on level of aspiration in children suggests that striving and aspiring to excellence have at least two motivational roots. Some children, boys in particular, seem to be intrinsically motivated toward competence and task-mastery; one might say these children wish to do well for the sake of doing well. Others, girls somewhat more often than boys, seem to strive because of strong fears of failure. Relatively little is known concerning the child-rearing antecedents of these two forms of motivation for high aspiration and achievement.

To recapitulate: there is reason to believe that early positive pressures for achievement are beneficial to the young child. Early, successful achievement efforts need to be vigorously supported. Next, the young child needs to be helped to discriminate between successful and unsuccessful effort. Finally, the consequences of early failure probably should not include withdrawal of adult esteem, strong criticism and punishment, since these pressures may enhance achievement striving at the cost of strong fears of failure.

Finally, I should like to touch on conflict, frustration, and anxiety as these motivational forces act on the child. Most of the literature (both scientific and popular) concerning conflict in child development emphasizes the dangerous and debilitating consequences of the so-called negative emotions. Thousands of pages in hundreds of volumes, as well as parent meetings too numerous to estimate, have focused on the relation of conflict to hostility, to disrupted social relationships, to defensive processes, and to learning inhibitions. There is little question that frustration and conflict are key determinants of many disturbances in the personality and intellectual development of young children. Until recent years, however, very little has been said concerning the constructive role in human development played by the negative emotions. One recent plea for recognition of the positive consequences of conflict was heard at the Philadelphia meeting of NANE. The paper, "conflict and Controversy in Child Development," by Meyer Sonis (1963), included the following statement: ". . . the potential for good or bad, constructive or destructive, resides in conflict *but conflict itself is not good or bad.*" I urge you to reread Dr. Sonis's address.

Constructive consequences of conflict, frustration, and anxiety can be found in many aspects of behavioral development in children. Consider, for example, the development of identificatory behavior. Conflict is a key construct in virtually every modern theory of identification. The Oedipal conflict was emphasized by Freud. To be sure, Freud regarded the Oedipus complex as an antecedent of neurosis, but he also argued that "the superego is the heir to the Oedipus complex." That is, Freud recognized conflict as an important antecedent of appropriate sex-typing, self-control, and resistance to temptation—conscience, in a word. Consider also the theory which suggests that identification stems from the conflict over loss of love. Consider, too, the sociological theories which suggest that children identify with powerful figures or with people perceived as prestigeful, or privileged, or in possession of important gratifications.

Conflict motivates much cognitive learning. Would children learn to read if no conflict were present? I do not mean that conflict produced by telling a child, "You'd better learn to read, or else!" Rather, being aware of what it means to be able to read and realizing that one *cannot* read is a form of conflict which probably helps greatly in motivating the child to acquire reading skills.

Conflict also contributes significantly to social behavior. The cohesiveness of children's groups and the frequency of constructive social activity are, in many instances, enhanced by frustration and conflict. Wright (1940) for example, found that preschoolers who were best friends actually became more socially outgoing and cooperative under frustrating circumstances than under satiation conditions. Further, the frustration used in the Wright experiment (the Lewin barrier, which prevented the children from reaching attractive toys) reduced the interchild hostility characteristic of ordinary play. Instead, the frustrated children pointed their aggression in a highly appropriate direction—toward the experimenter! And in still another area, my own recent studies of peer reinforcement (Hartup, 1964) have demonstrated that preschool children worked more vigorously and sustained higher levels of performance on simple tasks when they received praise and approval from another child who was *not* liked than when reinforcement was forthcoming from a child whom the subject regarded as a good friend. Even elementary school children, we find, work harder at simple tasks when reinforced by unpopular children than when praised by children regarded as popular.

All the foregoing illustrations of constructive responses to conflict have one element in common, namely, that conflict was attached to an *appropriate, socially-desirable response.* Thus, conflict and frustration are powerful, effective forces for socialization, but only when conflict-reduction reinforces appropriate behavior. Those instances in which conflict-reduction is associated with undesirable responses are, of course, to be eschewed; still, this does not mean that children need to be protected from all contact with conflict and frustration.

There are certain heretical elements in this philosophy concerning the role of conflict and frustration in child behavior. In one sense, these comments furnish a modern rationale for the old "spare the rod" approach to child rearing. These comments also suggest that the ends justify the means in the process of bringing up children. Most certainly, these implications *are* present in the position here put forward. Unquestionably, however, limits must be placed on the deliberate use of conflict and frustration in child rearing. Even though the behaviors to be acquired on the basis of conflict may be socially appropriate, high and sustained levels of pressure are probably harmful. For one thing, in many instances, the arousal of particularly strong emotions interferes with learning instead of facilitating it. Also, some sort of balance between frustration and more positive inducements for learning is surely needed. Other motivational bases are available for learning; several have been mentioned (e.g., desire for mastery and intrinsic motivation). But my major thesis must not be obscured nor made to sound like the arguments of the devil's advocate. Everyone engaged in child rearing needs to recognize the fact that conflict carries constructive possibilities; to deny this is probably to deny that children can be educated.

To conclude: This has been a social-learning approach to the problem of early pressures in child development. The emphasis has been on reinforcement, withdrawal of reinforcement, and conflict-reduction. All these factors are known to produce desirable modifications in behavior and they can all be brought to bear on the young child. Social-learning theory remains, in 1964, a set of principles derived mostly from studies of simple behavioral phenomena. Thus, in using this theoretical framework to explain and predict complex patterns of behavior (such as those dealt with in this paper) simplifications are bound to occur. That is, the principles on which this discussion is based may not be entirely adequate, by themselves, to account for all of the variability involved in complex patterns of behavior such as independence and achievement-striving. I am confident, however, that these principles have wide applicability in child rearing and in education. If the theory fails at certain points to account for all the complexities contained in child development, please understand that this does not mean that the theory is wrong. It simply needs improvement. In the meantime, I submit that a social-learning approach has many immediate, applicable, constructive implications for every one of us who lives and works with children and for every one of us who is concerned about early pressures in child development.

30

SELMA H. FRAIBERG   THE RIGHT TO FEEL

Early one morning I received a telephone call from a friend—the mother of a five-year-old boy. "I'm calling from upstairs," she said in a low voice: "so Greg won't hear this." There was a pause. "Ernest died this morning! What shall I tell Greg?" "How terrible!" I said. "But who is Ernest?" "Ernest is Greg's hamster!" she said. "This will break his heart. I don't know how to tell him. Bill is going to stop off at the pet shop on his way home from work tonight and pick up a new hamster, but I just dread breaking the news to Greg. Please tell me what to say to him." "Why don't you tell him that his hamster died?" I said. "Died!" said my friend, shrinking at my crudity. "What I want to know is how I can break the news gently to him and spare him the pain of this whole experience! I thought I would tell him that Ernest went to heaven. Would it be all right to tell him that?" "Only if you're sure that Ernest went to heaven," I said in my best consulting-room voice. "Oh, stop!" my friend begged. "This is very serious. I don't mean the hamster. I mean this is Greg's first experience with death. I don't want him to be hurt."

"All right," I said. "Then what right do we have to deprive Greg of his feelings? Why isn't he entitled to his grief over the death of his pet? Why can't he cry and why can't he feel the full measure of pain that comes with the discovery that death is an end and that Ernest is no more?" "But he's only a child!" said my friend. "How can he possibly know what death means?" "But isn't that how he will know what death means? Do we ever know more about death than this—the reaction to the loss of someone loved?"

And so we argued, my friend wanting to prevent her son from feeling a loss and I defending Greg's human rights in feeling a loss. I think I finally convinced Greg's mother when I told her that Greg would be better able to endure the loss of his pet if we allowed him to realize the experience fully, to feel all he needed to feel.

In our efforts to protect children from painful emotions we may

286 *personality development*

deprive them of their own best means of mastering painful experiences. Mourning, even if it is mourning for a dead hamster, is a necessary measure for overcoming the effects of loss. A child who is not allowed feelings of grief over a pet or a more significant loss is obliged to fall back on more primitive measures of defense, to deny the pain of loss, for example, and to feel nothing. If a child were consistently reared on this basis, deprived of the possibility of experiencing grief, he would become an impoverished person, without quality or depth in his emotional life. We need to respect a child's right to experience a loss fully and deeply. This means, too, that we do not bury the dead pet and rush to the pet store for a replacement. This is a devaluation of a child's love. It is like saying to him, "Don't feel badly; your love is not important; all hamsters, all dogs, all cats are replaceable, and you can love one as well as another." But if all loved things are readily replaceable what does a child learn about love or loss? The time for replacing the lost pet is when mourning has done its work and the child himself is ready to attach himself to a new animal.

Other stories come to mind which illustrate the problems of parents in dealing with the painful emotions of children. I once knew a little boy who was unable to cry and reacted to loss and to separations from loved persons with an inscrutable indifference, although he regularly produced allergic symptoms at such times. Often he spoke to me about his grandfather whom he had loved dearly and who died when my patient was five. He had many memories of his grandfather and spoke of him with much affection, but he had no memory of the grandfather's death or the year that followed his death. Neither was there any emotion attached to the idea of grandfather's death. But the death of the grandfather had been a great calamity in this child's family and the circumstances of the death were tragic in the extreme. Why was nothing of this remembered? And why was there no emotion attached to the loss of the grandfather or to death or separation from loved persons? All of this was exceedingly complex, but one very significant factor was the reaction of the child's mother at the time of the grandfather's death. Her own grief had been nearly unsupportable, but she was determined not to break down in the presence of the children: "It would make things harder for them." With heroic self-discipline she contained her feelings and presented a façade of her accustomed self to the children. With this I could understand my patient's strange reaction to death and loss. It was not "indifference" as it appeared on the surface, but an identification with his mother's outward behavior at the time of his grandfather's death. Since mother had not permitted her own grief to be revealed, the child behaved as if grief were an impermissible emotion. His suppressed longing to cry could only be satisfied by the symptomatic weeping that accompanied his allergy. It would have been much better for this child if his mother had not concealed her grief from him, for if he could have shared her grief in some way he would have received permission, as it were, to have his own feelings, and mourning for the loved grandfather would have helped him to overcome the shock of his death.

Many times, quite unconsciously, we cut off a child's feelings because they are so painful to us. I think now of Doug, a six year old, who had terrible anxiety dreams and wet his bed each night but presented a day-time picture of a cheerful, buoyant carefree little boy. He insisted that in the day-time he wasn't afraid of anything and never thought of scary things. He was actually being quite truthful, it turns out. Other children hate having their teeth drilled at the dentist's. Not Doug. He liked it. How come? "I always get a chocolate sundae afterward." "But even so, drilling hurts and don't you worry about that, Doug?" "Oh, no. I never think about how it's gonna hurt. I just think about the chocolate sundae." Other kids might worry about an appendectomy. But Doug didn't. "All I think about is all the presents I'll get when I'm in the hospital." Whenever unpleasant subjects appeared in our talks together he automatically switched to his Index of Pleasant Topics and began to talk about the baseball game he was going to tomorrow, the birthday party next Saturday or the new electric train he had just received. When I saw him once on the morning after a particularly terrifying dream that had kept him awake half the night, he could not bring himself to talk about the dream but spent the better part of an hour talking about his new bike.

Now, of course, if Doug were able to worry about the dentist and the appendectomy and other unpleasant events *before* they occurred, he would not be the sort of fellow who has recurrent anxiety dreams as his chief symptom. For some reason, we had to assume, he did not build up the anticipatory anxiety that would help him to meet crises. It was in the anxiety dreams that he experienced the anticipatory anxiety that was omitted in waking life. We learned that one of the important determinants in his unusual way of handling anxiety was his parents' way of helping him meet danger from the earliest days on.

They were good parents and devoted parents and Doug was their first child. Even when he was a baby they found themselves very upset by any of the usual manifestations of distress or pain or anxiety. Their impulse at such times was to step in quickly and offer a distraction or an amusement or something that would provide immediate solace. "Don't cry, dear. Look, look. See the pretty bird! Here are Daddy's keys to play with. Here's a cookie." Later the same principle was employed in the handling of many of Doug's fears or his encounters with unpleasant circumstances. He was educated not to cry or react to the shot in the doctor's office by the promise of surprises, something very pleasant, immediately afterwards. The educational principle was "Let's not think about the nasty shot. Let's just think about the nice surprise afterwards." Or a variation: "Let's not think how lonesome it will be when Mother and Daddy are on their trip. Let's just think about the presents and the surprises they will bring back."

Now it's probably true that nearly every parent has sometimes employed such tactics in helping a child meet an unpleasant experience, but in the case of Doug's parents this was truly an educational principle applied broadly and fairly consistently to the handling of every circumstance where anxiety might develop. His parents moved in so swiftly to prevent anxiety from developing that the child scarcely had a chance to become aware of it himself. He could not prepare for danger by developing anticipatory anxiety because this was not "allowable"; it was so painful to the parents. Gradually, as we see, he acquired the parents' method of handling his anxiety and made it his own. Every time anticipatory anxiety might have emerged into consciousness he substituted a pleasant thought for the dreaded event or the danger. In this way both Doug and his parents were spared unpleasant feelings, but Doug was also deprived of an important means for preparing for danger, anticipatory anxiety. I do not want to oversimplify the problem of night terrors in a child, but *one* of the contributing factors in Doug's disturbance was the inability to prepare for danger, something which his parents had innocently and unknowingly deprived him of.

A half century ago the right of a child to feel anger toward parents and siblings would have been disputed. Curiously enough, as I write now about children's rights to have feelings, I cannot easily find an example of a child known to me now who has been denied the right to feel anger. It is strange that in the whole gamut of emotions, hostility has been singled out in recent years as the prerogative of the young and there is hardly a parent today who does not regard it as such. But the "right" to have a feeling is not the same as a license to inflict it on others, and in the matter of license we appear to have erred gravely in the education of today's child.

A child may have the right to feel angry and to give expression to his feelings—within certain limits. But should a child be permitted to strike his parents? When Jimmy of an earlier chapter [in *The magic years*] struck his father in a fit of temper, his father felt that he had had quite enough and sent Jimmy off to his room. Many modern parents would have felt more indulgent. After all, they would say, the child was very upset, he lost control, and maybe he got rid of a lot of pent-up feelings and felt much better afterwards. But I do not think that Jimmy felt relieved afterwards; on the contrary, we find that the child who strikes a parent is made more anxious afterwards. I think that Jimmy's father acted wisely. He did not retaliate with an act of aggression toward the child, but he firmly called a halt to this and said in effect, "I can't allow you to do this!" I do not know if Jimmy's father knew why he felt he had to put a stop to this behavior, but his instincts were right. For when a child loses control of himself to the extent of striking his parent, he is really very frightened to find that he cannot control his own aggression and he is relieved to have the parent step in and put the brakes on when he can't stop himself. We can see this in Jimmy's anxiety dream, too; he called to his father to save him from the enraged tiger, that is, Jimmy himself.

The child's fear of loss of control is something that needs more widespread understanding among parents. It can even be an important motive in creating a neurosis. I recall a little seven year old who had a severe neurosis. Along with the neurotic symptoms he had rages of such intensity that often he wantonly destroyed any objects within reach. He had a recurrent anxiety dream which he told me about. He was riding downhill on his bike at tremendous speed and when he tried to apply the brakes to stop himself nothing happened and he and his bike went sailing downhill toward destruction. This child was tremendously relieved when I helped him understand his dream and told him that I would be able to help him so that whenever he needed his brakes to work they would work for him, in other words, that I would help him achieve self-control.

Let's consider other limits of aggression within the home. If we can see good reasons for placing striking of parents out of bounds how about some of the verbal forms of aggression that we are so indulgent of today? Should we allow name-calling of parents and abusive language? I cannot imagine how it can serve the mental health of any child to be permitted such displays of uncontrolled verbal aggression. This is very close to physical assault and the child who is permitted such license in verbal attack is just as likely to suffer bad effects as the child who is permitted to hit his parents. Of course, we do not need to make the child feel that he is a black sinner and will be struck by a bolt of lightning for his name-calling. It should be enough for a parent to call a halt to this display, "That's enough. I don't care to hear any more of this. You're completely out of control and I don't like this one bit. When you've calmed down we'll discuss this business like two human beings." A child can be permitted to express his anger without resorting to savage name-calling. If he does so, if he loses control, he needs to know from his parents that he has overstepped the line. This doesn't go.

Let's consider, too, the limits of aggression in sibling situations. "Sibling rivalry" is regarded as another prerogative of today's child and the licensed hostility in this area sometimes reaches the point of barbarity. We find that physical attacks by siblings on each other are regarded by many parents as one of the natural accompaniments of family life. "Just as long as they don't murder each other," parents may say indulgently. Yet I can think of no good reason why children beyond the nursery age should settle their differences through jungle tactics, and even in the nursery years we should begin the education away from physical attack. I have known households where nine- and ten-year-old boys and girls were continuing a war that began the day a baby came home. The quarrels of these older children were like the quarrels of toddlers. "That's my chair! She's sitting in my chair!" Or, "He got a bigger piece of pie than I did!" Tears. Stamping of feet. A slap. Shrieks. A deadly battle is on.

But why should the nursery rivalries persist in unmodified form for eight years—or longer? Is it because the jealousies were more severe or because these children were never required to find solutions to their rivalries beyond those of the early years? I suspect that in most cases it was because these children were not required to give up the infantile forms of their rivalry. The right to have sibling rivalry is so firmly entrenched in the modern family that parents show a tendency in their own behavior to protect those rights. In the case of two big children engaged in battle over the rights to a chair it would not be unusual to find their parents solemnly presiding over the dispute, seriously listening to the claims on both sides and issuing a sober judgment giving property rights to one of the contestants. It then happens that the contestant whose case was thrown out of court accuses the judge of favoritism, reproaches his parents for not loving him and preferring his sister, and there follows a lengthy protestation of love from the parents and the quarrel and reproaches are renewed. It might have been more to the point if the parents had treated the whole matter as it deserved to be treated, as a piece of nonsense.

On the other hand, we find that many times parents do not step in to prevent their children from destroying each other through words or the subtler forms of sadism. In the name of sibling rivalry, children today are permitted extraordinary license in cruel name-calling and refined torments designed to undermine each other's personalities. Parents who would never themselves do anything to depreciate the masculinity of a young son may find that the older sister is making a career of it, devoting herself to the work of undermining his self-confidence through taunts, disparaging remarks, and cruel jokes. If we close our ears to all this ("After all, brothers and sisters will fight, you know!") we do nothing to help the older sister overcome her aggressive feelings toward boys, and we are allowing her to damage the personality development of her younger brother.

It seems to me that we have to draw the line in sibling rivalry whenever rivalry goes out of bounds into destructive behavior of a physical or verbal kind. The principle needs to be this: *Whatever* the reasons for your feelings you will have to find civilized solutions.

What are the good and the healthy solutions to sibling rivalry? Not all sisters and brothers continue their rivalries for all the years of their lives. A good many of them develop strong and enduring ties of love, and the rivalries and petty jealousies are overcome by the stronger forces of love. Somewhere along the line of development the rivals must accept the impossibility of any of them obtaining the exclusive love of a parent. In coming to terms with this fact the hostilities die down and the rivals, who all have in common their love of the same set of parents, find themselves bound together through a common love. This has obvious implications for parents in handling sibling rivalry. It means that we educate the child to an acceptance of the impossibility of achieving the exclusive love of a parent, that we do not behave in any ways that encourage the rivalries, that we are not amused or flattered by the signs of jealousy and that we very clearly show our expectations that children beyond the nursery age can find solutions to their rivalries without resorting to infantile displays.

All of this brings us finally to another group of "rights" in the emotional development of the child. These rights have to do with love and the valuation of love. We grant that every child has the right to claim the love of his parents. But if a child is to grow in his capacity to love and to emerge as an adult capable of mature love, parents must be able to claim the love of their children—and to make claims upon this love! The parent who loves his child dearly but asks for nothing in return might qualify as a saint, but he will not qualify as a parent. For a child who can claim love without meeting any of the obligations of love will be a self-centered child and many such children have grown up in our time to become petulant lovers and sullen marriage partners because the promise of unconditional love has not been fulfilled. "I know I am selfish and I have a vile temper and I'm moody and a spendthrift, but you should love me in spite of my faults!" these spoiled children say to each other in marriage. And because they believe in their right to be loved—in spite of everything—they do not alter themselves to make themselves worthy of love, but change partners and renew the quest for unconditional love. It is a mistake to look upon these capricious lovers as incurable romantics. They are really in love with themselves. Even their most unattractive qualities are absorbed and forgiven in this self-love, and what they seek in a partner is someone who can love them as well as they love themselves. In all such cases we can conclude that something went wrong in the education for love. These were the children who never relinquished the self-love of the earliest years.

There are obligations in love even for little children. Love is given, but it is also earned. At every step of the way in development a child is obliged to give up territories in his self-love in order to earn parental love and approval. In order to sacrifice many of his private and egocentric wishes he must put a high valuation on parental love, which means that parents themselves need to look upon their love not only as "a right" but as a powerful incentive to the child to alter himself.

social behavior

The years of early childhood mark the emergence of the child into the social world that exists outside the home. This world is a world of children, a world of strange adults, and a world of classrooms and playgrounds. The environment outside the home brings new experiences and satisfactions as well as new demands and frustrations. Children are asked to share, take turns, and play with one another; to dress themselves, accept responsibility, and begin learning skills and information. The reorientation required is perhaps greatest for the middle-class child, but all children experience it to some degree. This experience is even more acute when the child enters a school environment. Although young children may have been catered to at home or given great freedom of action, when they move out of the home they are faced by more impersonal, structured, and demanding environments. Even the most understanding teacher does not know the child as well as his parents do. In addition, teachers are not necessarily willing to cater to a child's whims, and other children may not be willing to grant him their toys, accede to his desires, or be sympathetic to his requests. To the young child who has little understanding of his own feelings, let alone the feelings of others, the social world he enters is likely to be a source of confusion as well as challenge. The five articles in this section examine several key issues in the social world of the young child and how they can be understood and handled.

In "Aggression and Timidity in Young Children," Article 31, Ronald Feldman describes normal expressions of anger and timidity in children of two and one-half to six, who have not yet developed social-interaction skills and learned more mature methods of resolving their conflicts. He differentiates this behavior from aggression and discusses some of the factors in the child's world that can be indirect causes of aggressive behavior.

Article 32, "Disagreements Between Children," is an examination by Elsa Barnow and Arthur Swan of the sources and significance of youthful combat. Cautioning against the view that all combat necessarily stems from hostility, these authors indicate that physical encounters also signify play, exploration, and tests of strength. Barnow and Swan believe that since disagreements are an inevitable and normal part of life, it is important that children learn to solve their own problems and gain skills in dealing with conflicts.

Article 33 on "Sex Roles in Early Reading Textbooks," by Ramona Frasher and Annabelle Walker, concerns the part the school plays in teaching sex-role behavior. As the authors point out, school is a social experience in which children learn social attitudes and values as well as academic skills and facts. These attitudes are conveyed not only through the child's direct interaction with others, but also through the content of the materials used to teach skills. Hence the roles and behaviors depicted in early reading materials contribute to the formation of the child's own sense of identity and to the selection of goals considered "appropriate." Walker and Frasher present an analysis of the sex-role stereotypes presented to children in early reading textbooks and discuss some implications of these stereotypes for the development of both male and female children.

Going beyond textbooks to "The Student's World," Philip Jackson describes in Article 34 some of the basic aspects of school life that influence student attitudes and motivation. Among such aspects he considers the teacher's roles as supply sergeant, traffic director, and timekeeper and the occurrence of delay, interruption, and denial as an inevitable part of classroom procedure. Jackson also considers the two curriculums—one involving academic skills and the other dealing with rules and regulations. He proposes that these most obvious features of classroom organization have a profound effect on the ways in which children relate to the school and concludes that the student's world is marked by contradictory demands for active involvement on one hand and docility on the other.

The behavior-modification approach to social learning is exemplified by Article 35, "A Social Reinforcement Technique for the Classroom Management of Behavior Disorders." R. E. Vallett, applying the procedures developed by B. F. Skinner to children who are inattentive and lacking in self-control, describes how the occurrence of such "behavior disorders" can be reduced. The goal is to change the frequency of certain specified behaviors, reducing inappropriate ones by inattention and increasing appropriate ones by rewarding their occurrence. As Vallett points out, rewards are only part of the broader context of acceptance, which is made up of materials and a program designed to fit the child's level and needs. The behavior-modification approach is only one approach to treating behavior problems, but it has been widely used in the past five years. It is notable that the children in Vallett's study were labeled "exceptional children," a term applied to children who require specialized attention in their school programs.

behavioral objectives *To be able to discuss the following points*

31 AGGRESSION AND TIMIDITY IN YOUNG CHILDREN
Age-related characteristics of aggression in children
Four causes of aggression in young children
Some ways in which teachers can deal with timidity in children
The relationship of verbal skills to aggression and timidity

32 DISAGREEMENTS BETWEEN CHILDREN
Some causes and functions of physical encounters among children
The point at which a teacher should intervene in a conflict between young children
The ways teachers can deal constructively with such encounters

33 SEX ROLES IN EARLY READING TEXTBOOKS
The ways in which early reading textbooks may influence a child's development
Three areas in which early reading textbooks differentiate between male and female roles
Areas in which sex-role stereotypes differ from reality

34 THE STUDENT'S WORLD
Three aspects of the teacher's role which conflict with the education of the individual student
Some institutional factors that lead to an attitude of resignation and their effect on academic performance
The conflict between the goals of school as a social institution and as an educational institution

35 A SOCIAL REINFORCEMENT TECHNIQUE FOR THE CLASSROOM
MANAGEMENT OF BEHAVIOR DISORDERS
The characteristics of behavior disorders in children which tend to interfere with learning
Six social-learning principles that may be used in modifying problem behavior
Three forms of social reinforcers that may be used in the classroom
The model training program outlined by Vallett

3]

AGGRESSION AND ANGER

Teachers of young children justifiably are concerned with aggression and anger in their students, for during the period from two and one-half to six children are learning and consolidating basic patterns of social interaction. In earlier times many teachers viewed all forms of aggression and anger as undesirable. In those days, a teacher's objective often, but not always, was to teach the young child to *control* his more violent impulses as much as possible and as soon as possible. With today's dual emphasis on control and on expression of feelings, anger and aggression are being seen in a more differentiated fashion. Teachers are interested in understanding what forms of aggression and anger are normal and less normal for young children, in how the expression of these impulses changes with age, in determining whether or not the aggression takes a potentially dangerous form, and in understanding the causes of or reasons behind a child's expression of anger or aggression.

The categories described are intended to convey the author's general interpretation of "adequate" self-control without at the same time drawing a hard-and-fast line as to the meaning of "adequate." Human behavior is too varied and complex for such simple categories, and judgments are most suitably made with appreciation of the child's life circumstances, cultural background, individual personality, and life expectations. For our purposes "aggression and anger" include all actions, physical or nonphysical, with which force, threat, or anger-related emotions are associated. Thus a child can display anger by hitting or pinching a playmate, by grabbing a toy that belongs to another child, by chasing a child who has taken a toy from him, or by yelling in anger at a playmate, "You give it to me."

Some general information concerning aggression and anger in young children may be of interest to teachers. Aggressive encounters between young children rarely last longer than one minute, and more often than not the actual quarreling ceases within thirty seconds after the episode has begun (Dawe, 1934; Jersild & Markey, 1935). During these episodes pushing, hitting, pulling, foot stamping, pinching, and the throwing of relatively harmless objects are all common and normal behaviors (Dawe, 1934). Not normal, however, are such actions as hitting a playmate time and time again after he has fallen to the ground, frequent loss of temper, physically dangerous actions, or prolonged feuds that last tens of minutes or even days (Jersild & Markey, 1935).

298 *social behavior*

Young boys, on the average, are more aggressive than young girls. Aggression, indeed, seems to follow boys around. Boys quarrel more frequently with boys than girls do with girls. In addition, young girls quarrel more often when interacting with boys than they do when playing with other girls. Boys tend to use physical means of aggression. Girls tend toward more frequent use of verbal tactics (Green, 1933; Muste & Sharpe, 1947).

Aggressive episodes tend to last slightly longer as children become older because the problems that children ages four or five encounter are more complex than those encountered by children two and one-half or three (Dawe, 1934). On the other hand, aggressive behavior becomes less physical and more verbal and is exhibited less and less frequently as children mature in years during this early period of life. This gradual replacement of aggressive behaviors by other equally effective but less violent conflict-resolving processes is one of the most important changes taking place between years two and one-half and six. Teachers can play an important role by helping to guide children through the involved set of associated learning experiences.

SPONTANEOUS VERSUS DELIBERATE AGGRESSION Child-child conflicts often arise suddenly, and the children involved frequently do not fully understand how the situation even came about. Aggression in such circumstances may be the involuntary result of a "flooding of feeling." On other occasions a child will employ aggressive behavior for a very practical reason: aggression helps him to get his way. Quite frequently aggression in child-child conflict situations is in part spontaneous and in part deliberate.

Deliberate aggression itself is a complex and varied phenomenon that may not always deserve the concern and excitement generated in teachers and parents. Very young children (ages two and one-half to three and one-half) have difficulty understanding the desires and rights of other children and have only limited verbal capacity to express their feelings. Even though most children employ aggression from time to time, they usually do so infrequently, and few express it in dangerous forms. Aggression can take harmless as well as dangerous forms, and can vary in purpose from legitimate self-defense to gaining the property and privileges of other children.

INDIRECT CAUSES OF AGGRESSION Most episodes of aggression probably stem directly from conflicts of desires—one child's desire to own a toy, to play in a given area, or to conduct play in a certain fashion conflicts with the desires of other children. On other occasions aggression results from less obvious, more indirect causes or motives. Four such indirect causes are notable.

1 Curiosity and the desire to tease. Children are curious about how others will respond to their actions; they also sometimes enjoy upsetting other children.

2 Social ineptness and feelings of being socially rejected. Nursery school is often the child's first social encounter outside the family. Quite often, the young child does not know how to approach other children successfully, and, as a result, he or she is repeatedly rejected. Feeling rejected, these children often become angry and vent their hostilities on other children. At the same time they are being aggressive, they desire peer acceptance and hope they will be able to join in social play with classmates.

3 Desire to gain attention. Children are sometimes aggressive as a means of gaining attention from their playmates and teachers. They may act this way because they receive too much or too little attention at home or because they are accustomed to being the center of interest. Causing trouble is an almost certain way of getting adult attention.

4 Boredom and the need for diversion (Green, 1933). Children who have been inactive or engaged in uninteresting activities sometimes engage in vigorous play either during or immediately after these periods. In these instances aggression may be either displaced from its original target or merely a release of pent-up energy.

TIMIDITY AND INHIBITION

Aggressive actions by a child disrupt the play of other children, produce considerable noise and disturbance, and frequently involve the teacher and occupy her time. Equally important, but not likely to receive as much attention, are episodes in which children fail to express or to act upon legitimate and acceptable desires. Future adult life can be as unsatisfying for a person who fails to defend his rights or to communicate his feelings or opinions as it can be for a person whose self-centered, aggressive manner causes others to avoid social contact with him. Between ages two and one-half and six some children may begin to develop problems of either type. As with aggression, we shall avoid hard and fast guidelines and dwell upon general considerations.

COMMUNICATION OF DESIRES OR OPINIONS Timid children often fail to communicate what they want and need even when they have a right to do so. They may fail to ask for a turn or be reluctant to ask for toys and materials that are common classroom property. As a result of their timidity, they are often ignored and fail to receive the attention, approval, and treatment they ardently desire.

PROTECTION OF RIGHTS Children who do not express their wants often allow themselves to be dominated. Other children may take their toys, ignore their turns at games, and attempt to intimidate them. For such children, learning to ignore or deal with threats is as important as asserting their rightful place in the group.

SEEKING TEACHER ASSISTANCE If a young child depends too much on teachers for assistance, he may not learn how to express his desires to other children. Seeking teacher assistance is not bad in itself, but it may detract from the child's developing his own capacities for dealing with problems. Teachers should be wary of becoming so helpful that they inhibit the child from acting in his own behalf. Encouragement of personal initiative as well as assistance by the teacher help the child to become more expressive.

RESPONSE TO FAILURE OR DISAPPOINTMENT In childhood, as in adulthood, things do not always turn out as one might wish, even after one has expressed his desires and communicated his opinions. In some circumstances, the failure or disappointment may be undeserved or unjust. In other circumstances, the frustrating outcome is a just one. Learning that disappointments are inevitable and that they must be coped with is an important element in learning to persist and explore the world of people, tasks, and play.

32

DISAGREEMENTS BETWEEN CHILDREN

ELSA BARNOW
ARTHUR SWAN

It should not be assumed that all physical encounters between children stem from feelings of hostility. On the contrary, children revel in playful combat. They very much resemble puppies in their desire to wrestle, roll about, and test their strength against one another. It is one of their means of getting acquainted. Children learn best through their muscles and it is often through physical contact rather than by the medium of language that they establish friendships.

Two-year-olds may appear to be unfriendly when they are merely exploring their classmates as they do the other objects in the room. Their techniques may include poking, pushing, biting, hugging, or hair pulling.

The fact that a big hug elicits tears often astonishes a young cave man. It takes a long time to learn that other children have feelings and desires much like his own.

To gain entry into a desired circle, a child may often find it necessary to prove his strength. When William entered one four-year-old group in the fall, his great wish was to be Eddy's friend. The previous year Eddy had managed to establish himself as the acknowledged leader. William had none of the physical competence which Eddy displayed. He was tense, somewhat awkward, and unable to defend himself. But he was fortunately endowed with courage and determination, and before a month had gone by he was willing to accept Eddy's challenge to a boxing match. William suffered hard blows without wincing, and though defeated he won admiration for his good sportsmanship. As the weeks progressed the two boys became firm friends. William had plenty of other skills and abilities to offer, but he knew how best to win the friend he craved.

A little girl, Cynthia, was so flattered one day at being invited to box with Charlie, whom she deeply admired, that she was willing to don the gloves and take her chance. She was warned that Charlie might give her some hard blows, but she said she didn't mind and faced the test with courage. Girls can often box as well as boys. Some have an advantage in that they are taller and more developed. A very subdued Chinese girl, who was blocked in speech, won fame because of her astonishing wallops. None of the boys dared take her on after one experience. "I'm not going to fight that whacking lady," announced one of the cautious young males. The confidence which she acquired through this one skill helped in overcoming her speech difficulties.

Children rarely harbor grudges against one another, unless their elders keep harping on past injuries. Peter came home several times with battle scars on his face. His nurse called for him one day and was distressed to see a new lump on his forehead. As they reached home she said to Peter's mother, "That bad boy, Johnny, has hit him again." Peter blazed up angrily, "Don't talk that way about Johnny. He's not a bad boy. He's my friend."

It is also wise for parents not to take their children's complaints about each other too seriously. "Who is Leslie?" asks an anxious mother. "Alice says he's so rough that she's afraid to come to school. Would you be sure to protect her from him?" Her teacher replies that she had noticed that Leslie likes to tease Alice. In fact, he is very much aware of her. As Alice also appears to be talking about Leslie, it may be that his interest is reciprocated.

"Perhaps Alice needs to learn how to cope with Leslie's teasing," adds the teacher. "Yesterday he called her 'scribble-scrabble Alice' and she burst into tears. I suggest you invite him over for a visit some day so that they can get better acquainted."

Alice's mother agrees to try this suggestion and leaves with a somewhat lighter heart. A few days later, Leslie saves the seat beside him at the snack table for Alice. Though he never goes so far as to try to include her among his rowdy cronies, he stops pestering her and Alice no longer regards him with fear.

The aggressive child is usually singled out as a cause for concern, but there may be a far more deep-seated problem in the child who never gets involved in any sort of fracas or faces any issue squarely with his peers. His behavior may be a sign of unhealthy withdrawal which may be very hard to cure, whereas the aggressive child's problems are constantly in the open and can therefore be more easily recognized.

A persistent urge to pick fights may stem from various causes, though a frequent one is lack of confidence and a longing to be accepted in the group. A good example is Philip, who joined a four-year-old group without previous school experience. A small, indecisive child, he was at first completely unable to cope with the other children. Soon he began to center his attentions on Lucy, the tiniest, most delicate-looking child. Her timid, frail appearance gave him courage. He teased her by hugging her about the waist so tightly that she was actually hurt. He pushed her slyly so that she fell from the seesaw, bit her to make her give up a tricycle, and so completely demoralized her that she wept and quailed at his approach. His teachers never accused Philip of having bad intentions. They suggested to both children that what Philip was trying to convey to Lucy was that he wanted her for a friend, that he would like her to play with him. They made it clear to Philip, however, that Lucy did not like it when he hurt her. And to Lucy they pointed out that one reason he teased her so much was that she cried so easily. Philip nodded agreement with these sentiments, and even made use of his teachers' arguments when he felt a bit guilty about what he had done. "I only wanted to love her," he explained with cheerful duplicity as he had just made her cry. During the year the staff gave Lucy some pointers on self-defense. After a time she was brave enough to don the boxing gloves in gentle bouts with trustworthy girl friends. On one momentous morning she resisted Philip's advances with such surprising vigor that he retreated in amazement. This was a turning point in their relationship. They had developed a healthy respect for one another and were on the road to becoming friends.

Lyman was a boy of exceptionally small stature. His classmates referred to him as "the baby." In order to prove he was not, he got involved in numberless frays and frequently had to be rescued from beneath a formidable opponent. He always fought back his tears and valiantly announced, "I'm glad I hit him." The intense urge to prove his worth by means of physical combat declined when Lyman was able to accept himself with his own particular limitations. He soon found more satisfying ways of winning respect, for he was an intelligent and gifted boy. Eventually he could say quite calmly when questioned about his age, "Im four and a half, but small for my age."

Wherever people live together, disagreements are certain to occur. Small children are no exception. As their paths cross and their interests conflict they are bound to have some clashes. There are innumerable ways in which children meet or fail to meet their social problems. Some make a hasty exit, leaving a clear field for the aggressor. Others rush for aid from grownups or more sturdy classmates. Others simply weep. Some shriek so dramatically that the opponent beats a hasty retreat. Others hang on for dear life to the object under dispute. A few resort to hitting, biting, or hair pulling as an effective mode of attack or defense. Among older preschool children bargaining, offers of substitute toys, threats, and promises begin to replace the more primitive physical tactics. Though the staff may be keeping hands off, they never relax their vigilance. They are on the alert for any signs of physical danger and also stand by to prevent unfair dealings. Obviously one cannot allow such behavior as kicking, biting, and scratching to continue unchecked, but there are ways of helping both the attacker and the attacked to find better means of coping with their differences.

It is a good idea to encourage children to take an active part in solving their own problems rather than always relying on the adults to smooth things out. Otherwise they will find themselves unprepared to meet life's simplest threats. If Martha comes to her teachers weeping and complaing that Barbara took her dolls away, their attitude is to encourage Martha to do something about it instead of expecting them to settle the situation for her.

"Go and get it back," they may urge her. They stay by, however, to see what happens. It is of paramount importance that justice prevails in the classroom. Children sense whether teachers are fair in their dealings, and can only feel at ease if they are certain that there is no favoritisim or disregard of serious injustice.

Should Nicholas come in tears saying, "Danny hit me," the staff does not say, "Well, hit him back." They do suggest, however, that Nicholas find some way to cope with it himself. Nicholas may be quite satisfied to inform Danny, "That hurt me. I don't like you when you hit me." He may decide, on the other hand, to repay Danny in kind. If he does hit back, the idea was his own and not one recommended by the teacher. This is an important point, for it leaves room for him to cast off his primitive solution as he discovers better social techniques. If the adult has urged him to use the "eye-for-an-eye" method, however, this may seem to him the noblest solution and one which must be carried out at all costs. There is an added danger in telling a child to strike back at an aggressor. If he hasn't the courage to do so, he may feel he has failed in the eyes of the adult. By encouraging him to work out his own solution, he can go as far as he feels able at the moment.

Many children are at first leery of applying physical force because of the disapproval they have sensed at home or in the community. Once they feel confident that both teachers and parents do not disapprove, they can use their fists without misgivings or burden of guilt.

With the older children, especially, a point is made of coaching them in the use of fair methods of fighting. "Use your fists," "Don't kick," "No scratching or pinching allowed," "Two against one is not fair." The children soon learn these rules and remind each other of them.

The stable adult can watch two children fight without growing panicky about it. It is not a major crisis. In fact, it is astonishing how often an apparent death struggle comes to a sudden conclusion and the two combatants continue their play together as if nothing had come between them. Adults should keep hands off unless one child is no match for the other. However, the weaker child needs to be taught better methods of self-defense.

If tension between two children reaches a venomous pitch and they fly at each other in a blind rage, one must hurry to step in before damage is done. If it is necessary to break up a fight, the teacher may suggest that the two children put on boxing gloves and have an organized match. This suggestion may be rejected, but tensions are cooled off because of the interruption. As long as emotions are under control and the fight is fair, teachers do not interject themselves except as referees.

If organized fights between children are properly refereed and kept within fair limits, there is little danger of hostile feelings developing between the combatants. In fact, the opposite usually occurs. When children select an opponent for a boxing match, they invariably decide on a friend. And it is impressive to note how often the choice is a fair one. The teachers could hardly show better judgment than do the children in pairing themselves off. Great hilarity often accompanies these sparring events. Now and then a child will get a bloody nose or a painful whack, but if these matches are properly supervised, serious damage is not likely to result.

Occasionally injuries inflicted accidentally or intentionally by a classmate do occur at school. Sometimes teachers need to be as concerned about the child who has caused the mishap as the one who is hurt. His feelings of guilt may be a heavy burden. It may help the aggressor if he is allowed to assist in applying medication. If Peter has bitten Margaret, for example, the teacher may take them both to the bathroom and ask Peter to help to treat the wound. Peter will see the result of his action but is also given a chance to do something constructive about it. Although Peter is made to understand that biting hurts and is not acceptable behavior, his teacher will not belabor the point. It is well not to let such an incident be overdramatized, lest it should seem interesting enough to warrant repetition.

Conflict is sometimes necessary in shaping character. Judy, who had always played second fiddle to her friend, Jane, suddenly turned the tables on her and began to challenge her assumed leadership. As they were playing in the doll corner an angry argument could be heard.

"I don't want to be the baby today! I'm the Mommy," announced Judy.

"No, I'm the Mommy. You have to be the baby," retorted Jane, stamping her foot.

"I don't want to," parried Judy, whacking her friend angrily. "I won't play with you any more." And to Jane's obvious amazement, Judy stalked away.

This was the beginning of a revolution in the longstanding friendship between these two girls. The teacher who overheard the argument was secretly delighted, for she had been troubled about their relationship in the past. Though free of conflict, the attachment had never been a wholesome one, for Judy had always submitted unquestioningly to Jane's suggestions and commands. For several weeks life between them became stormy and quite disagreeable from the onlooker's point of view. But the turn of events meant growth for both girls. Jane gradually learned to accept suggestions from others while Judy discovered that it was not always necessary to do what she was told. Eventually, a fine relationship was established between them, based on mutual respect.

Eloise and Marjorie, both on bikes, met face to face beneath a bridge made by high ladders. Neither wanted to back out. They bumped their bikes in the middle. Eloise appealed to Mr. De Mott: "Make Marjorie get out."

Mr. De Mott did not seem to hear. Both looked more determined, knocking each other's bikes harder. Suddenly Eloise found a face-saver.

"Marjorie! Push me out with your bike," she suggested.

This solution came as a happy relief to both girls.

Children often welcome a face-saver when in conflict. They hate to give in when they have reached an impasse. They are no different from grownups or nations in this respect. This is a valuable thought for teachers and parents to keep in mind, for tense situations often can be cleared up by suggesting an honorable way out.

None of the incidents recounted above is at all unusual or abnormal. They are fairly typical of the sort of behavior that can be expected at the nursery school age level. Now and then, however, a wave of aggression and hostility may sweep through a particular group and cause a lot of unhappiness. If there seems to be an undue amount of friction, bad language, negativism, and other signs of resentment and fear, it is well for the staff to make a thorough analysis. It is not at all impossible that the teachers themselves are at fault. If they are critical of one another and fundamentally at odds, the children will sense this and respond unconsciously to the emotional tone set by them. Sometimes physical conditions of the play area may cause increased tension. Children need plenty of room in which to move about. Some of them become high-strung if they feel hemmed in too long, and a series of rainy days may coincide with stormy weather in the classroom.

An individual child may come to school in an angry mood and transfer his feelings to his associates. Certain children have especial need to let off tensions accumulated in a difficult home situation. Close contact with their families usually enables teachers to gain some insight into the underlying causes. If they realize that John's father is fretting because he is unemployed or saddled with an uncongenial job, that there is conflict over discipline between Barbara's parents, or that overly high standards of conduct and achievement are demanded of Arthur, they can better understand why these children need to let off steam in the school situation. Just as the business man who has had a hard day at the office may take out his annoyance on his wife, so do children carry their troubles from home into school or from school into the home.

There are, of course, methods of sublimating one's antisocial drives. Pounding with a hammer, bashing one's fist into a heap of clay, tackling a dummy, or delving into a colorful mass of fingerpaints may serve as a useful surrogate and provide the hoped-for release. Yet such tactics do not always satisfy the deep underlying need of a child. He may want to come face to face with the problem that haunts him rather than having it diverted into side channels.

Adults need to have an abiding faith that all children, no matter what their present behavior may be, have a deep-seated desire to grow toward maturity. Without this trust, no one can do a truly satisfactory job. The confidence and genuine friendship of both parents and teachers are the child's strongest allies in his struggle to grow up and find better ways of behaving.

33

SEX ROLES IN EARLY READING TEXTBOOKS

This study was undertaken on the assumption that sex role behavior is culturally determined and is produced by social learning. This learning takes place through many channels and includes both sex role expectations and examples for identification. Children thus come to have a sense of self-identity which is pervaded by the behavior, appearance, activities, personality characteristics, and achievement goals considered socially appropriate to their own sex.

It is further assumed that school is a social experience and a vehicle for the transmission of social values and attitudes, textbooks being one agent of this transmission. Other reading research has been based on this rationale. Blom and others (1968), in "Content of First Grade Reading Books," say that "cultural attitudes and values are conveyed through the content of stories."

The authors of reading series, too, recognize the influence of story content on social learning. In the introduction to one basal reading series (Robinson et al., 1962) are the statements: "At the most formative period of children's lives, it would be unfortunate if the power of books to mold character were overlooked or ignored in the reading lesson" and ". . . built into each story is some aspect of social relationship that children can make their own and apply to their behavior," indicating that a conscious effort is made to manipulate this learning.

It therefore seems reasonable to investigate what is being presented to children through reading textbooks in the area of sex role differences, in view of its possible effect on the molding of their identities, attitudes, and values.

PURPOSE AND PROCEDURES

The purpose of this study was to compare the roles, relationships, activities, and relative importance assigned to male and female characters in stories in readiness and first and second grade reading textbooks.

The method of content analysis was selected for the study. Two recent articles pertaining to a similar analysis of children's literature (A feminist look, 1971; Meade, 1971) and a study of nursery Sunday school materials (Doely, 1970) were helpful in determining specific categories of activities and role related characteristics to be recorded. Selected textbooks at various levels from the series under study were analyzed concurrently by both writers, following a predetermined outline. The following dimensions were selected for evaluation of the stories:

I. Main characters
    A. Male
    B. Female
    C. None or shared
II. Adult occupations
III. Adult role in the family
    A. Breadwinner-provider
    B. Homemaker-shopper
IV. Child activities and play
    A. Quiet
    B. Active

The unit for analysis was the story, and all results were based on stories rather than individual incidents. Thus an appropriate category was checked once if relevant evidence appeared in the story, even though multiple instances may have occurred.

Readiness books and first and second grade readers from four major basal reading series were selected for analysis: Harris (1970), Ousley and Russell (1966), Robinson and others (1962), and Sheldon and others (1968). A total of 734 stories was read and analyzed. Since the purpose of the study was the examination of sex roles, consideration was limited to stories dealing with human beings except in instances where animals were the main characters in stories with humans. Animal fantasies and folk and fairy tales were excluded.

ANALYSIS OF DATA

MAIN CHARACTERS Table 1 clearly indicates that a majority of stories analyzed had male main characters. Males were main characters in more than three times as many stories as females. Total stories with male main characters not only appeared in a strong majority over those with females, but even outnumbered stories in which the main roles were shared.

ADULT ROLES: OCCUPATIONS Stefflre (1969) found that elementary school reading textbooks present a distorted picture of American working women.

TABLE 1: *Distribution of main characters by story*

SERIES	MACMiLLAN	SCOTT, FORESMAN	ALLYN & BACON	GINN	TOTAL	TOTAL PERCENT
Male	118	98	82	43	341	46
Female	19	49	25	15	108	15
None or shared	36	86	103	60	285	39
Total stories	173	233	210	118	734	100

He found that readers he analyzed depicted women as comprising only 7 percent of the labor force, when actually they comprise 37 percent; that readers depicted women working in occupations that did not accurately reflect those occupations in which most women actually work; that few women are seen working in "masculine" jobs such as engineering; and that only a tiny fraction of married women work.

Our findings corroborate those indicated by Steffire. Adult males were observed in occupations outside the home in 196 stories. Adult females were observed in occupations outside the home in fifty-two stories, about one-fourth as many as males. The list of occupations in which males were observed is long and varied, containing fifty-eight different occupations, from street workers to doctors and scientists. The list for women is short and limited, containing only eleven different occupations, all of which are traditional female jobs, such as teacher, nurse, librarian, stewardess. Moreover, teachers accounted for over half of the women workers shown in these fifty-two stories. Working women were titled "Mrs.," indicating their married state, in only five stories.

ADULT ROLE IN THE FAMILY The setting in most family stories was the home or a family outing. Therefore, the adults were not frequently observed in the role of "Breadwinner-provider." However, forty-six stories clearly indicated that an adult fulfilled this role by showing parents on their way to work, coming home from work, by indicating ownership of a house or farm, or actually by showing a specific parent at work. Forty-five of these stories showed fathers in this role. One story, in the Scott, Foresman series, indicated that a mother was obviously the breadwinner for her one-child family.

One hundred sixty-five stories showed mothers as "Homemaker-shopper," that is, doing housework, cooking, buying groceries, clothing or household items, or wearing the ubiquitous apron. Fathers were seen in this role in fourteen stories.

Fathers assumed almost entirely the role of family leadership. They were often pictured taking the children on outings, giving factual information, and solving problems. Almost all of the fathers' activities, including the cooking they did, seemed to take place outdoors. They did the traditional male-related tasks of mowing the lawn, painting and repairing the house, and maintaining the car. They also drove the car and carried packages for the family.

Mothers, on the other hand, stayed indoors most of the time. In addition to their housekeeping activities, they performed their traditional nurturing role—comforting their children when sick or distressed, checking children's personal hygiene habits, and reminding them to play carefully and to pick up their toys. Fathers were observed in a nurturing role in only a few instances. Mothers rarely played with their children, rarely helped them to solve problems, and rarely gave any factual answers to questions.

CHILD ACTIVITIES AND PLAY Quiet activities included playing dolls, house, and "dress-up," painting, reading, cooking, sewing, picking flowers, watching TV, and observing. "Observing" meant that a child was simply watching while others engaged themselves actively in a game or activity. Activities included running, jumping, climbing, riding bikes, building, playing ball, and swimming. This category was checked only when a child was shown as fully participating in such activities. Table 2 shows the results obtained in this area.

The overall ratio of percentages of stories picturing girls in quiet games, to those showing boys, was 70/30. This ratio was even higher in favor of girls in two series which presented girls in quiet games 76 percent of the time, or over three times as often as boys. The other two series showed girls about twice as often as boys in quiet games. The overall ratio of percentages of stories showing girls in active games, to those showing boys, was 30/70.

Another treatment of sex role differences can be shown in the proportion of quiet to active games picturing girls, and of quiet to active games picturing boys. This ratio was 60/40 for girls and 20/80 for boys. The proportion of quiet to active games for girls was higher in only one series—70/30 (Robinson et al., 1962). This ratio seemed to occur in spite of the presence of Sally, the preschooler in this series. Sally was usually pictured in active games and activities, as one would expect of a preschool child. Therefore, although no separate tally was kept for her activities, the ratio obtained was felt to reflect an unusually large proportion of quiet activities assigned to Jane, the schoolage girl in the series.

The overall quiet/active ratio for boys (20/80) was so extremely disparate as to require special comment. By comparison to the quiet/active ratio for girls (60/40) it indicates that boys were shown in a narrower range of activities than girls. It was noted by the writers that the quiet activities which were shown for boys were such things as reading or

TABLE 2: *Distribution of girls and boys in quiet and active games by story*

SERIES		MACMILLAN	SCOTT, FORESMAN	ALLYN & BACON	GINN	TOTAL
Quiet:	Girls	29	68	42	24	163
	Boys	9	21	24	9	63
Active:	Girls	23	28	34	18	103
	Boys	66	79	65	32	242

watching TV. Never did a boy of any age play with a doll or dollhouse, nor sew or pick flowers. In a few stories, a boy did participate in cooking, though not nearly as often as girls did, and never with his mother, as girls often did.

ACTIVITIES AND PLAY: FURTHER OBSERVATIONS

Some further observations were made in the area of Activities and Play which deserve comment. It was noted that clearly differentiated, sex related roles were often assigned. In one story, for instance, both boys and girls participated in setting up a store. However, the girls were shown baking the food to sell while the boys built the store (Sheldon et al., 1968). In another story, the children visited a farm. A boy said, "We boys can look at the animals in the barn. You girls can go to see the baby in the house" (Robinson et al., 1962).

One whole group of stories centered around a boy's embarrassment at having to carry home a doll from a shop (he bought it, not for himself, but to give to a girl in exchange for an old printing press she had). These stories described the great lengths to which this boy went to avoid being seen with the doll. In the final story, the girl accepted the doll happily, exclaiming over how pretty it was, in exchange for the printing press, which the boy told her he intended to use to put out his own newspaper (Harris, 1970).

The strangest aspect of this group of stories was that the girl had originally asked for and received the press from a store giving it away. One wondered what she intended to do with it, if anything. At no time did she use it in the stories, nor even show that she knew how it worked. Instead, she was shown sitting and watching while the boy operated it.

The behavioral characteristics of boys and girls as displayed in the course of their activities, while difficult to measure precisely on a quantitative scale, were found, in the writers' opinion, to differ obviously and strongly by sex. These differences appeared to relate to the kinds of activities in which each sex was portrayed.

Girls were shown much more frequently as needing help and protection, giving up easily, and lacking competence in many tasks. Timidity, docility, and dependence seemed characteristic in general of girls throughout the series. Their personalities came across to the reader as containing a high degree of passivity.

Boys, however, appeared to show a much higher degree of positive-striving qualities: leadership, independence, initiative, curiosity, assertiveness, perseverance, bravery, and logical thinking or problem-solving ability. Their personalities conveyed, in general, to the reader a high degree of aggressiveness.

It seemed significant that even the teacher's manuals were found in some cases to openly support such a view of sex differences in behavioral characteristics. In one series, for example, a boy and a girl were pictured bathing a dog, in an apparently shared activity. Yet the teacher's manual interpreted this picture by saying, "Boy-like, Dick occupies the center of the stage in a situation where, as Spot's master, he obviously feels he is in charge" (Robinson et al., 1962). The term "boy-like" seems clearly prejudicial and designates leadership as a characteristic not only of Dick's behavior, but of boys in general and not, of course, of girls.

Although no formal count was kept of the ages of the children shown, it was impossible not to notice that a boy was shown as the oldest child in almost every family throughout all of the series.

DISREGARDING REALITY

Males predominated as main characters in readiness books and first and second grade readers in all of the series analyzed. Therefore, it seems logical to conclude that the publishers of these four reading series regard males and their activities as far more important and interesting to children than females and their activities.

Women's occupational roles in the textbooks analyzed were limited, distorted, and stereotyped. The following picture of women workers was presented:

1 Female workers are uncommon, compared with male workers.
2 Females work in very few occupations.
3 Females who do work are rarely married.

This representation does not portray the actual roles and characteristics of working women, but presents a severely limited range of occupational opportunity. Tradition has already imposed upon women a narrow field of occupations. The textbook publishers have taken it upon themselves to restrict even further the female child's choice of occupational identification and possible aspiration.

Reality was also disregarded as far as family relationships and activities were concerned. Parents were depicted as filling only traditional, stereotyped roles. Fathers were presented as the sole providers and decision makers for families. They were shown almost exclusively in traditional stereotyped "male" activities. Mothers were depicted virtually unanimously as homemakers and nurturers. They were found in traditional, stereotyped "female" activities.

One series (Robinson et al., 1962) suggested that Mother be introduced to students as follows:

Dick, Jane, and Sally's mother is like your mother. She takes care of the house and the children.

The results above indicate that in the readers analyzed for all four series, the mothers did, indeed, "take care of the house and the children." If they did anything else, the authors took great pains to conceal it.

MOTHER ROLES

The role of "Mother" in these primary reading materials deserves a special discussion in this report, although her role was not originally singled out for special attention. Early in the study the writers observed that mothers were the least effective, albeit the most visible, adults in the stories. Time and time again, mothers were represented as dull, ineffectual, almost totally preoccupied with housework and shopping, incapable of solving problems, and even stupid.

In story after story, when Father reads, Mother knits. When Mother does read, it is usually a magazine. She is seldom seen without her apron and almost never seen in slacks or shorts. Once in a while, she drives the car, but not if Father is around. She turns to Father or her oldest son when confronted with the overwhelming task of carrying a picnic basket or the problem of recovering a lost pet. She speaks occasionally, observes a great deal, and almost never gives factual information. She appears timid and avoids getting involved in the action of the stories. She cooks, and cooks, and cooks. Although she rarely scolds, she utters numerous "Be carefuls."

After reading the many family and home-oriented stories, one has difficulty identifying "Mother" as anything but a supreme bore. Considering the influence which real mothers have on the lives of young children and the time and energy which most real mothers spend on their children, it seems remarkable that they must be represented in their children's textbooks as such insipid creatures.

CHILD ROLES

The child roles in these series were also strongly stereotyped by sex. When children were shown in quiet activities or merely watching others, those children were much more often girls than boys. Boys, on the other hand, were physically active in many more stories than girls, and, in fact, were rarely seen doing anything else. Also, the quiet activities they did engage in appeared to be fewer in variety than those of girls.

In addition, instances were noted where boys actively avoided being associated with a "girl-type" activity, as well as cases where boys objected to the "intrusion" of a female in a "boy-type" activity. The writers felt that the strongly stereotyped activity picture of boys presented in these series was one which might well contribute to, rather than relieve, the greater

314 *social behavior*

number of reading problems boys have. By giving the impression that boys should nearly always be playing ball, riding bikes, or climbing trees, little reinforcement is given to the idea that reading and other language-related activities are also appropriate and fun for boys.

Behavioral characteristics observed appeared also to differ strongly by sex and to parallel the sex differences in activities and play described above. Girls displayed many more passive characteristics than boys, while boys showed strongly aggressive characteristics. This sex difference was even assigned directly, in some cases, by the language of the teacher's manuals.

The writers also noted that an overwhelmingly large majority of families depicted in these textbooks had a son as the oldest child. The authors of these series would appear to believe that

1 Most American parents have a son.
2 Most American parents have a son first.
3 This is the ideal way to distribute the sexes in the production of progeny.

CONCLUSIONS AND IMPLICATIONS

The present study indicates that a considerable degree of sex role stereotyping is present in the content of readiness books and first and second grade readers. The writers consider the images thus presented to children poor ones by reason of casting models for possible identification into a limited mold which is unrealistic and does not allow for individual differences. This model is particularly limited and inadequate for female children, and includes fewer of the activities, possible occupational goals, and characteristics which are accorded greater prestige and held higher in esteem in our society.

The results of this study, which are shocking when viewed in the light of the public school's avowed purpose of educating all children to strive for the achievement of their greatest potential, imply that further research in the area of sex role treatment is imperative. Reading textbooks in the intermediate and upper grades move away from the family-oriented setting toward a heavier emphasis on boy-girl relationships, biographies of famous people, and school subject oriented stories. Would their analysis yield similar results?

Our final suggestion is that further research be done in all aspects of possible school influence on the social learning process as it relates to sex role expectations and models. This would include all textbook and other reading material, school games and activities, educational philosophy, and the relationships of teachers and administrators to students.

34

And I have seen dust from the walls of institutions,
Finer than flour, alive, more dangerous than silica,
Sift, almost invisible, through long afternoons of tedium,
Dropping a fine film on nails and delicate eyebrows,
Glazing the pale hair, the duplicate gray standard faces.

THEODORE ROETHKE, "DOLOR"

Prehensile sophomores in the tree of learning
Stare at the exiled blossoming trees, vaguely puzzled.

JOHN MALCOLM BRINNIN, "VIEWS OF THE FAVORITE COLLEGES"

When you were a child, how many times did you find yourself cornered by an adult, usually a strange aunt or uncle, who opened the conversation with that oldest of all gambits: "Well, how do you like school?" As an adult how often have you been left alone with someone else's child and, not knowing what else to say, found yourself falling back on some variant of the standard query: "How's school?" If you have not had both of these experiences, and each of them several times, you must be something of a recluse, for talk about school, when the dialogue is between an adult and a child, is almost as popular a social maneuver as talk about one's health or the weather.

Yet such talk, despite its popularity, rarely yields much information about what life in school is really like or how that life is experienced by the student to whom we are speaking. There seem to be two major reasons why this is so. First, in most instances neither the child nor the adult takes the query seriously. Both know that questions about school, like questions about personal health, are polite social gestures and usually are not intended to be answered fully or honestly. Thus, when asked about his classroom experiences, the fourth-grader who is having a miserable time with long division and who hates his teacher with a deep and abiding passion knows that he is expected to respond in much the same way as the victim of a migraine headache whose health is inquired into. Custom requires both sufferers to grin and say, "Fine, thank you."

A second limit to what we can learn about school life by talking to students arises from the fact that students may themselves not be acutely aware of what is happening to them in the classroom. Or, more precisely, they may never have tried to express the vague feelings and intuitive knowledge engendered by that experience. School life, like life in the military service, is not easy to describe to outsiders. You have to have been there.

But even being there is not enough, for when fellow students, or army veterans, discuss their common experience they often overlook or fail to mention some of the obvious and pervasive aspects of that experience. And often it is these familiar and seemingly trivial features of life that are the most revealing when it comes to capturing the flavor or unique quality of membership in a social institution. Accordingly, the remainder of this essay will focus on some aspects of school life that students rarely talk about in the presence of adults or even, in all probability, in the presence of other students.

The subjects to be discussed are not dramatic, or even intrinsically interesting, though I shall do my best to keep them from becoming deathly dull. What is more important, they concern things we all know, even though we do not think about them too much. My only justification for asking you to attend to such mundane matters is my hope that a consideration of these trivial but neglected events will deepen our insight into the character of the student's world and, hence, might lead us to ask new questions about our responsibility for establishing and maintaining that world.

Two warnings are necessary. First, I do not bring words of uplift and inspiration. In fact, some of the things I am going to say about schools and schooling will not be pleasant. They may even sound harsh. But I am convinced that educators are ready for such talk, provided it stems from good intentions, and that they prefer frankness, even though it may hurt, to the sticky sentiment and clichés that have come to characterize educational discussions from college courses to inservice workshops. Second, I am not going to present a plan of action for your consideration. Indeed, I am going to raise many more questions than I shall answer. Here again, I believe that more and more teachers are becoming tired of hearing experts, whether from the university or the central office, hand out the latest panacea for eliminating our educational woes. For a change, therefore, I will ask you to do nothing but think. If there are practical implications that follow from what I have to say, it is up to you to find them.

THE SOCIAL TRAFFIC OF THE CLASSROOM

Anyone who has ever taught knows that the classroom is a busy place, even though it may not always appear so to the casual visitor. Indeed, recent attempts to describe that busyness have yielded data that have proved surprising even to experienced teachers. For example, we have found in our studies of elementary-school classrooms that the teacher engages in as many as a thousand interpersonal interchanges each day. No comparable data are available for high-school teachers, but there is reason to believe that the interpersonal demands are equally severe at that level. A look at these and other demands is instructive as we try to understand what life in the classroom is really like.

First, consider the rapidity of the teacher's actions. What keeps her hopping from Jane to Billy to Sam, and back again, in the space of a few seconds? Clearly much of this activity is done in the interest of instruction. In most classrooms the teacher acts as a gatekeeper who manages the flow of interaction. When more than one person wishes to say something (a common condition in educational gatherings), it is the teacher who decides who will speak and when. Or we might turn our observation around and say that it is the teacher who determines who will not speak, for usually the number of students who want to say something exceeds the number who are granted the privilege.

SUPPLY SERGEANT

Another time-consuming task for the teacher, at least in the elementary school, is that of serving as a supply sergeant. Classroom space and material resources are limited, and the teacher must allocate these resources judiciously. Not every student can use the big scissors at once; only one child at a time can look through the microscope or drink from the drinking fountain or use the pencil sharpener. Again, it is important to recognize that the number of students who want to use these resources at any given moment is often greater than the number that can use them.

Closely related to the job of doling out material resources is that of granting special privileges to deserving students. The teacher frequently must decide whether a student is to be allowed to hand in his homework paper late or make up a quiz that he missed or have an extra day to finish his laboratory assignment. In elementary-school classrooms it is usually the teacher who assigns coveted duties, such as serving on the safety patrol, running the movie projector, or clapping the erasers. Students soon learn that in school, as in life in general, many are called, but few are chosen.

OFFICIAL TIMEKEEPER

A fourth responsibility of the teacher, and one that calls our attention to another important aspect of classroom life, is that of serving as an official timekeeper. The teacher sees to it that things begin and end on time, more or less. He determines the proper moment for switching from discussion to workbooks, or from spelling to arithmetic. He decides whether a student has spent too long in the washroom or whether those who take the bus may be dismissed. In many schools the teacher is assisted in this job by elaborate systems of bells and buzzers, but even when the school day is mechanically punctuated by clangs and hums, the teacher is not relieved of his responsibility for watching the clock. School is a place where things often take place not because people want them to, but because it is time for them to happen.

Our concern here is with the student and the quality of his life in the classroom. Therefore, the frenetic activity of the teacher, as she goes about calling on people, handing out supplies, granting privileges, and turning activities on and off, is of interest to us only insofar as the student experiences that behavior. We are interested, in other words, in what it is like to be on the receiving end of the teacher's action.

To begin, it is safe to say that for most students, some of the time, and for some students, most of the time, the classroom is a great place to be. When new insights are formed and mastery is achieved, when the teacher's queries can be answered with confidence, when privileges are granted and praise bestowed, when natural interests and desires coincide with institutional expectations—at such moments (and such moments do occur more or less regularly for many students) life at school must be extremely satisfying. A sufficient number of such experiences might well create the desire for further education and could set the stage for a lifetime of scholarship and academic pursuits.

But it is probably also true that for most students, some of the time, and for some students, most of the time, the classroom comes close to resembling a cage from which there is no escape. When activities are dull and repetitious, when the student is not called on even though he has signalled the desire to be heard, when privileges are not granted and blame, rather than praise, is bestowed, when natural interests and desires are antithetical to the demands of the institution—at such moments (and such moments probably occur more or less regularly for many students) life in school must be extremely irksome.

The important point is that these unpleasant aspects of school life are experienced not only by those who are failing in their schoolwork (although students with low achievement might receive more than their share of these discomforts). Nor are they simply a function of the cantankerousness or maladroitness of particular classroom teachers (although poor professional preparation and psychological disorders of teachers may well add to the student's burden). It would seem, in other words, that much of the pain of school life is a natural outgrowth of the problems of institutional living and the management of social traffic. Given the arrangement in which one person is chiefly responsible for serving the educational needs of thirty or thirty-five others and for articulating the demands of this group with those of several other groups in the same building, three of the most salient features of school life—delay, denial, and interruption—are almost inevitable.

Consider for a moment the frequency of delay. When we examine the details of classroom life carefully, it is surprising to see how much of the student's time is spent in waiting. In the elementary school, the students often line up for recess, for lunch, and for dismissal, and they frequently have to wait for the lines to be straight before they move. During individual seatwork they wait for the teacher to come around to their desk to inspect their work. When the whole class is working together, there is the waiting for the slower pupil to finish the work that the faster ones have completed. During discussion there is the waiting for fellow students to answer the teacher's query. When motion pictures or slides are shown, there is usually a delay as the room and the equipment are made ready. As time for the bell approaches, students are waiting for it to ring, even though they may still have their eyes on the teacher.

No one knows for sure how much of the student's time is spent in neutral, as it were, but it is certainly a memorable portion. How many of us who have lived thousands of days in schools can remember waiting anxiously for the minutes to tick away until the dismissal bell freed us? How many of us whose lungs are lined with chalk dust can recall the hours spent looking out the classroom window as we waited for the group in which we were imbedded to move sluggishly along? How many of us respond sympathetically to the following image of school life presented by George Santayana (1947), as he describes his student days at Boston's Boys Latin School: "No blackboard was black; all were indelibly clouded with ingrained layers of old chalk; the more you rubbed it out, the more you rubbed it in. Every desk was stained with generations of ink-spots cut deeply with initials and scratched drawings. What idle thoughts had been wandering for years through all those empty heads in all those tedious school hours! In the best schools almost all schooltime is wasted [p. 487]."

Idleness, unfortunately, is only part of the picture, and perhaps not even the most important part. Waiting is not so bad and may even be beneficial when the things we are anticipating ultimately happen. Indeed, Longfellow was probably speaking with the voice of wisdom when, in his *Psalm of Life*, he advises us to "Learn to labour and to wait." But he was just a shade too optimistic when, in another poem (the title of which ironically is *The Student's Tale*), he promises his reader that "All things come round to him who will but wait." At least it is doubtful that Longfellow was referring to things that go on in classrooms, for there the waiting is sometimes in vain.

DENIAL

The denial of desire is a commonplace in school, and likely it has to be. Not everyone who wants to speak can be heard, not all the students' queries can be answered to their satisfaction, not all their requests can be granted. It is true that, considered individually, most of these denials are psychologically trivial; but considered cumulatively, their significance increases. Part of learning how to live in school involves learning how to give up desire as well as waiting for its fulfilment.

Typically, things happen on time in school, and, as a result, activities are often begun before interest is aroused and terminated before interest wanes. Once again, there is probably no alternative to this unnatural state of affairs. If we were to wait until students requested a history class on their own, as an instance, we would have a long wait. Similarly, if we allowed students to remain in their physical education classes until they grew tired of the game, there likely would not be time for other things. There seems to be no alternative, therefore, but to stop and start things on time, even though it means constantly interrupting the natural flow of interest and desire for at least some students.

INTERRUPTIONS

But interruptions in the classroom are not confined to the beginning and ending of subject-matter periods. There are also more subtle ways in which activities are broken into. The irrelevant comment during class discussion, as an instance, often breaks the spell created by the relevant remarks that have preceded it. When the teacher is working individually with a student while others are present—a common arrangement in elementary-school classrooms—petty interruptions, in the form of minor misbehavior or students coming to the teacher for advice, are the rule rather than the exception. In countless small ways the bubble of reality created during the teaching session is punctured, and much of the teacher's energy is spent in patching up the holes, just as much of the student's energy is spent in attempting to ignore them. Students are constantly "turning back" to their studies after their attention has been momentarily drawn elsewhere.

Here, then, are three of the unpublicized features of school life: delay, denial, and interruption. As educators what do we make of them? Or better, what should we make of them? Let's dispense with extreme reactions first.

On the one hand, there is the temptation to ignore these aspects of classroom experience. After all, delay, denial, and interruption are features of life in several other settings. Why pay particular attention to these petty annoyances when they occur in school? Students themselves do not seem to be too upset by these occurrences, the argument continues; therefore, it is probably safe to ignore them, with perhaps a passing cluck of disapproval, and move to more pressing educational problems.

On the other hand, there is the temptation to magnify these

undesirable events until they become all that can be seen of school life. This alternative, which might be called the school-is-hell approach, seems to be dominant on many of our college campuses these days. It is the credo of the new undergraduate religion: anti-establishmentarianism.

The trouble with these extreme positions, as with most, is that they can be maintained only by choosing to ignore certain salient features of our educational scene. Defenders of the optimistic leave-well-enough-alone point of view preserve their calm by remaining blind to the fact of widespread discontent in our schools. Defenders of the school-is-hell point of view must keep the edge on their fury by failing to acknowledge that there is massive satisfaction as well as massive dissatisfaction in our classrooms.

A more dispassionate point of view, although one that is unlikely to capture newspaper headlines, might lead us to examine the strategies that students develop to adapt to these mundane features of school life. What must be done, in other words, if the student is to live a large portion of his life in an environment in which delay, denial, and interruption are inevitable? Further, how do the strategies for adapting to these demands combine with, complement, or contradict the strategies for acquiring knowledge and developing intellectual mastery?

PATIENCE AND RESIGNATION

The quintessence of virtue in an institutional setting is contained in the single word: *patience.* Without that quality life can be miserable for those who must spend time in our prisons, our hospitals, our corporation offices, and our schools. But virtue can become soured if tested too severely. And the conditions that lead to the development of patience can also, if carried too far, set the stage for the development of resignation—a much less virtuous condition. Indeed, the distinction between the patient person and the resigned person is not always easy to make on the basis of surface appearances, even though there is a world of difference in the psychological strength of the two.

While the patient person maintains a firm grasp on his own plans for the future and, hence, retains a sense of integrity, the resigned person does not. Resignation involves an act of psychological surrender in which one's own desires, plans, and interests are abandoned and action is taken on the basis of the desires, plans, and interests of others. The resigned person has not only given up hope, he has given up many other linkages between his motives and his actions. Resignation involves, in other words, a loss of feeling and a sense of no longer caring about what happens.

Returning to the situation in our schools, we can see that if students are to face the demands of classroom life with equanimity—rather than with disappointment, anger, and rebellion—they must learn to be patient.

This means that they must be able to disengage, at least temporarily, their feelings from their actions. The hope is that the disengagement will not become permanent, that patience will not fade imperceptively into resignation. Yet in expressing this hope we acknowledge a real danger, for the one condition lies just beyond the other, along the same path. The problem, for the teacher, is to help students become uninvolved when conditions demand it, but not too uninvolved. We want students to be calm in the face of some of the frustrations caused by collective life in an institution, but we do not want them, in the jargon of adolescence, to "cool it."

MASQUERADE

The second-grader who groans with disappointment when an enjoyable classroom activity is terminated, and the fourth-grader who zestfully waves his hand while his classmate is struggling to answer the teacher's question, both will likely be transformed by the time they reach high school or college into the jaded "professionals" of the classroom—those living inkblots whose enigmatic silence and languid slouch effectively mask both the presence and the absence of enthusiasm for educational affairs. Which ones are merely being patient, and which resigned? It is sometimes hard to tell.

Students also know that teachers like to see evidence of enthusiasm and involvement, and this knowledge causes alertness and other signs of interest to be worn as masks in much the same way as signs of indifference. Classroom courtesy demands that you keep your eye on the teachers and frown intensely at appropriate times even though your mind may be miles away. Again the teacher is faced with the problem of deciding which students are really with her as she goes about her work and which ones just appear to be with her.

The business of faking involvement and of masking withdrawal is not limited to the simple procedure of showing signs of attention when class is in session. These are not the only strategies by which students adapt to classroom demands. Nor are delay, denial, and interruption the only unpleasant aspects of school life with which the student must cope. The classroom, it must be remembered, is an evaluative setting in which the student must learn not just to comply with commands, but to comply in a way that yields a positive evaluation.

Thus arises the common practice of giving the teacher what she wants on written assignments and test questions, even though the assignments seem meaningless and the questions inane. Along with this practice goes the technique of disguising ignorance, of responding to the teacher's queries with sufficient ambiguity or with only thinly veiled flattery so that she will not discover and no longer care whether the student knows anything or not. (When I was a high-school student, this ploy was known as giving the teacher a "snow job." I do not know what name it goes under these days, but I am fairly confident that it is still being practiced.)

These forms of student behavior may be laughed off as harmless pranks, and sometimes they are nothing more than that. But all these acts of detachment and deception, each of which might be considered harmless, or even "cute," when used in moderation, grow out of attempts to deal with institutional constraints. When used excessively and in combination, they are the marks of the educational con-man, the student who has learned to size up teachers and give them what they want with all the shrewdness and feigned sincerity of a dishonest second-hand car dealer.

THE TWO CURRICULUMS

Much that has been said up to this point can be summarized by suggesting that every school and every classroom really has two curriculums that the students are expected to master. The one that educators traditionally have paid the most attention to might be called the official curriculum. Its core is the three R's, and it contains all of the school subjects for which we produce study guides and workbooks and teaching materials. It is the curriculum that all the curriculum reform groups are shouting about these days.

The other curriculum might be described as unofficial or perhaps even hidden, because to date it has received scant attention from educators. This hidden curriculum can also be represented by three R's, but not the familiar one of reading, 'riting, and 'rithmetic. It is, instead, the curriculum of rules, regulations, and routines, of things teachers and students must learn if they are to make their way with minimum pain in the social institution called *the school.*

THE REWARD SYSTEM

Two or three important observations might be made about the relationship between these two curriculums. One is that the reward system of the school is tied to both. Indeed, many of the rewards and punishments that sound as if they are being dispensed on the basis of academic success and failure are really more closely related to the mastery of the hidden curriculum. Consider, as an instance, the common teaching practice of giving a student credit for trying. What do teachers mean when they say a student tries to do his work? They mean, in essence, that he complies with the procedural expectations of the institution. He does his homework (though incorrectly), he raises his hand during class discussion (though he usually comes up with the wrong answer), he keeps his nose in his book during free study period (though he does not turn the page very often). He is, in other words, a "model" student, though not necessarily a good one.

It is hard to imagine any of today's elementary-school teachers failing a student who tries, even though his mastery of course content is slight. And elementary-school teachers are not alone in this respect. At higher levels of education as well rewards go to the solid citizen as well as to the budding scholar. Surely many of our valedictorians and presidents of our honor societies owe their success as much to institutional conformity as to intellectual prowess. No doubt that bright-eyed little girl who stands trembling before the principal on graduation day arrived there at least partly because she typed her weekly themes neatly and handed her homework in on time.

This manner of talking about educational affairs may sound cynical and may be taken as a criticism of teachers or as an attempt to subvert the virtues of neatness, punctuality, and courteous conduct in general. But nothing of that kind is intended. The point is simply that in schools, as in prisons, good behavior pays off.

Just as conformity to institutional expectations can lead to praise, so can the lack of it lead to trouble. As a matter of fact, the relationship of the hidden curriculum to student difficulties is even more striking than is its relationship to student success. Consider, as an instance, the conditions that lead to disciplinary action in the classroom. Why do teachers scold students? Because the student has given the wrong answer? Or because, try as he may, he fails to grasp the intricacies of long division? Not usually. A student is more likely to be scolded for coming into the room late or for making too much noise or for not listening to the teacher's directions or for pushing while in line. The teacher's wrath, in other words, is commonly triggered by violations of institutional regulations and routines rather than by the student's intellectual deficiencies.

Even with the more serious difficulties that clearly entail academic failure, the demands of the hidden curriculum lurk in the shadows. When Johnny's parents are summoned to school because their son is not doing too well in arithmetic, what explanation will be given for their son's poor performance? More than likely blame will be placed on motivational deficiencies in Johnny rather than on his intellectual shortcomings. The teacher may even go so far as to say that Johnny is *un*-motivated during arithmetic period. But what does this mean? It means, in essence, that Johnny does not even try. And not trying, as we have seen, often boils down to a failure to comply with institutional expectations, a failure to master the hidden curriculum.

There is a further question that must be asked about the relationship between the official and the unofficial curriculums in our schools: To what extent does the mastery of one interfere with the mastery of the other? In other words, how do the demands of intellectual achievement relate to the demands of institutional conformity? Are they complementary or contradictory?

We have already seen that many features of classroom life call for patience, at best, and resignation, at worst. As the student learns to live in school, he learns to subjugate his own desires to the will of the teacher and to subdue his own actions in the interest of the common good. He learns to be passive and to acquiesce to the network of rules, regulations, and routines in which he is imbedded. He learns to tolerate petty frustrations and to accept the plans and the policies of higher authorities, even when their rationale is unexplained and their meaning unclear. Like the inhabitants of other institutional settings he learns that he must frequently shrug and say, "That's the way the ball bounces."

But the personal qualities that play a role in intellectual mastery are of a very different order from those that characterize the Company Man. Curiosity, as an instance, that most fundamental of all scholarly traits, calls forth the kind of probing, poking, and exploring that is almost antithetical to the attitude of passivity that has just been described. The productive scholar must develop the habit of challenging authority and of questioning the value of tradition. He must insist on explanations for things that are unclear. The scholar must certainly be a disciplined man, but his discipline is developed in the service of his scholarship, rather than in the service of other people's wishes and desires. In short, intellectual mastery calls for sublimated forms of aggression rather than submission to constraints.

DOCILE SCHOLARS

These brief descriptions exaggerate the real differences between the demands of institutional conformity and the demands of scholarship, but they do serve to call our attention to points of possible conflict between the two sets of demands. Can both sets be mastered by the same person? Apparently so. Certainly not all our student council presidents and valedictorians are academic Uriah Heeps. Some have clearly managed to retain their intellectual aggressiveness while at the same time acquiescing to the laws that govern the social traffic of our schools. Apparently it is possible, under certain conditions at least, to breed docile scholars, even though the expression might appear at first glance to be a contradiction in terms. But how are these successes achieved? At what cost? And how many fail to achieve the synthesis of the so-called well-rounded student?

The cost of scholastic success must be measured not only in terms of the intellectual energy expended or the non-academic gratifications denied. For many students there is also a social cost. The students who accede willingly and sincerely to both the intellectual and the institutional demands of the school run the risk of being perceived as defectors by their peers. At the lower levels of education these students are likely to be called *goody-goodies, tattletales,* and *teacher's pets;* at the upper levels they are called *greasy grinds, eager beavers,* and *squares.* In the eyes of many of their classmates the students who receive the highest praise from the authorities of the school are the ones who have sold out to the system. For many students this kind of name-calling, which is often correctly perceived as reflecting envy, is not difficult to endure and is a small price to pay for the admiration of adults whom they respect. For other students it is more important to appear to be a "regular guy." Many would rather be seen as a "buddy" than as a "brain."

The number of failures in our schools is much larger than the number of students who do not come up to snuff on our achievement tests or final exams. The failures include an untold number who seemingly succeed but who turn off their intellectual motors when the dismissal bell rings. These children have learned how to give the teacher what she wants all right, but in the process they have forgotten how to use their mental powers to give themselves what they want when the teacher is not around. This group includes the students who make the honor rolls and the dean's lists during the school year but who do not know what to do with themselves during the summer vacation. It includes the thousands who, after their formal schooling is finished and diploma hung on their wall, will never again be stirred by the quest for knowledge. It includes the millions for whom a childhood of teacher-watching is followed by an adulthood of television-viewing, with hardly a change of posture or facial expression to mark the transition. One almost expects them to raise their hands and ask Johnny Carson if they can go to the bathroom. Adequate as students? Yes. Adequate as adults? No.

TWO WORLDS

And who is to blame for these failures? The schools? The society? The individual? All three share the responsibility, I suppose, but it is the school's role with which we are particularly concerned at present. The school, it would seem, asks the student for a commitment to two worlds—the world of the institution and the world of scholarship. Unfortunately, it often succeeds in obtaining only a feigned commitment to either one.

What about our own commitment to these two worlds? How have we partialled out our own loyalty? How much have we ourselves become Company Men, more interested in an up-to-date register than an up-to-date idea, more concerned with straight lines than with straight thinking? After all, we too, like our students, are rewarded for doing things neatly, and on time, with a minimum of fuss and bother. How often have we received compliments from our principals for the surface show of scholarship, for the attractiveness of our bulletin boards rather than for the vigor and imaginativeness of the ideas we present to our pupils? Nor are our administrators the villains of the piece, for they, in their turn, are caught in the same bind. The public wants its institutions to be run quietly, efficiently, and economically. The best-attended school-board meeting is almost always the one at which the budget is discussed. And who is this elusive public but the very people we educators had yesterday in our classrooms. So the circle is complete. No one is responsible, yet everyone is.

What, then, is life like in school? It would seem to be a life of contradictory demands and competing tendencies, a life in which discovery and disappointment go hand in hand, where the unpredictable and the routine are combined daily. These monotonous settings of desks and blackboards and books provide a stage for the cyclic enactment of a dull drama, a play that is at once boring and exciting. No wonder our young friend only says, "Fine!" when we ask him how things are going in the classroom. School is a puzzling place, and the puzzles are not all intellectual ones.

35

R. E. VALLETT

A SOCIAL REINFORCEMENT TECHNIQUE FOR THE CLASSROOM MANAGEMENT OF BEHAVIOR DISORDERS

The child with a behavior disorder characterized by inattentiveness, distractibility, hyperactivity, and lack of self-control usually has great difficulty in learning. Children with neurological perceptual problems, mental retardation, emotional disturbance, and specific learning dysfunctions often present such behavior problems; however, these behaviors are occasionally manifested in regular classrooms and have been encountered by most experienced teachers. Where such behavior is allowed to continue, the child experiences increasing failure in learning which, together with growing frustration and social maladjustment, may seriously interfere with the educational program of the entire class. In such situations, it is obvious that some system of positive intervention must be instituted if the entire learning situation is not to be jeopardized.

Every teacher has some system of classroom and pupil control which supposedly enhances effective learning. In most cases, an interested teacher with a flexible curriculum, well organized lesson plans, and realistic marking system is sufficient to provide the structure, motivation, and reward essential to learning. Children with chronic behavior disorders, however, need more than these basic essentials. First and foremost, they require a teacher capable of love and understanding, who is concerned about doing more to help the child learn. Of equal importance is the ability to define the pupil's educational needs; develop specific learning programs with realistic goals; set consistent limits; provide direction, training, and guidance; and encourage gradual and continued success through reinforcement systems of praise and rewards.

BASIC PRINCIPLES

In order for learning to occur, the pupil must be motivated to attend, concentrate, and respond to appropriate stimuli; continued interest and motivation are dependent upon some measure of success and reward for effort expended. For many children with behavior problems, the fundamental difficulty has been the lack of motivation resulting from repeated failure and uninteresting lessons. For example, the pupil who is continually given work beyond his basic skills or ability seldom experiences success sufficient to motivate him to keep working. Obviously, a strong and well organized system of rewards is essential if we wish to keep children interested in learning.

Most children who have been reared in a home and community environment where their primary needs of physical care, love, and attention have been adequately provided for have been taught to respond to such secondary reinforcers as encouragement and recognition. These pupils are more capable of self-control and deferring immediate gratification of their inclinations. Other pupils, however, must be taught to attend, respond, cooperate, and gradually acquire self-control and responsible behavior.

It is now well accepted that children can be taught appropriate responses through conditioning procedures which are sure to reinforce or reward the specific behavior that is desired. What is necessary is the development of a reinforcement system around the appropriate responses that have been clearly identified. Furthermore, to be educationally effective, the technique must provide for immediate and primary rewards to the single pupil when necessary and must also encourage total classroom or peer group support of the individual and the group learning situation.

Azrin and Lindsley (1956) were among the first to demonstrate experimentally that a system for the reinforcement of cooperation between children was feasible. Since then, Lindsley (1963) has analyzed the terms and conditions necessary for a social reinforcement system and Hewett

(1964) has defined the levels of educational tasks which can be programed in a reinforcement system. Hewett (1966) has also demonstrated the effectiveness of a reward system in shaping the behavior of educationally handicapped pupils. More recently, *Newsweek* magazine (Golden grades, 1966) has focused public attention on the value of reward systems for keeping dropouts in school and in transforming low achieving pupils into honor students.

On the basis of available studies, several simple principles have emerged which can and should be used in any practical educational system interested in modifying pupil behavior and improving learning. These might be briefly summarized as follows:

1 Pupils must be educationally programed according to their level of development and achievement.

2 Material to be learned must be systematically organized and able to elicit response and success from the pupil.

3 Success in learning (e.g., desirable behavior) should be immediately rewarded. If necessary, primary reinforcement (food, praise, etc.) should be used.

4 Immediate primary reinforcements should be part of a broader system involving varying rewards and social reinforcement.

5 Rewards should be attainable after a reasonable period of effort (lessons should not be too long and may have to be broken down into smaller units with subsequent reinforcement as necessary).

6 The pupil must be able to understand the desired behavior change, the rewards involved, and the operation of the total system. The system should be available (e.g., written out) and as concrete as possible.

SOCIAL REINFORCERS

Within the educational setting, social tolerance is basic to the operation of any reinforcement system. That is, the pupil must be capable of being physically present in order to become part of the system. Not all children with behavior disorders can be tolerated in the public school setting. If a student's behavior is inimical to the welfare of the class or school, it may be essential to limit him to a shorter school day or, in extreme cases, to exempt him from attendance.

Most children with behavior disorders can learn to control themselves for given periods of time by reduction of attendance to a half day, a period or two, or even for only the amount of time that self-control can be maintained. Sometimes such children are further aided by a mild tranquilizing medication which, together with a limited day, may make some school attendance possible. Over a period of time, most children come to prefer the stimulation of their peer group and, therefore, school attendance itself becomes a strong social reinforcer.

As long as the child is part of the class, he is a member of a social system that can be managed to control his behavior. Primary reinforcers such as candies, raisins, fruit loops, and peanuts have been found to be effective in eliciting responses and stimulating basic motivation; these rewards, however, should always be accompanied by verbal praise (i.e., "very good," "good boy," etc.) and occasional physical reinforcers such as pats on the head and back and hugging.

Tokens, such as poker chips, may also be used as immediate reinforcers if they are exchangeable later for food, simple toys, or social privileges. Check marks for correct responses ("C") can also be strong reinforcers if they, too, lead to extrinsic rewards. Tokens and check marks can also be used by the pupil to gain access to classroom activity corners, such as listening centers for records and tapes, science puzzle centers, library reading centers, or arts and crafts centers. Some reinforcement systems provide for the further encouragement of good marks through awarding stars, which are exchangeable for tangible goals.

Perhaps one of the more effective social reinforcers is earned eligibility to student citizens councils, where recognition pins, special privileges, and honors are available. Of course, formal grades or report card marks can also serve as reinforcers if they are awarded relative to the pupil's ability and achievement; however, for most children with behavior disorders, report card marks are usually too removed and abstract and seldom prove effective by themselves in motivating pupil behavior.

MODEL SOCIAL REINFORCEMENT TECHNIQUE

One model social reinforcement technique applicable to elementary classes and programs for the mentally retarded or educationally handicapped is presented here. It can be modified according to the age of the pupils and the nature of their learning and behavior problems. This approach integrates both primary and secondary reinforcers and is based on the careful programing and constant evaluation of pupil behavior. A Weekly Work and Reward Record is retained by the pupil and serves to constantly remind him of his progress and attainment at any given time.

As pupils arrive at their desks, they find their individual work packets with basic assignments for the day. Specific lessons, work sheets, page references, etc. for arithmetic, reading, writing, and special training (such as visual motor exercises) are there. The children take their first assignment and, upon demonstrating that they are ready to work, they are rewarded by the teacher, who hands them a poker chip. Following completion of the assignment, the child's work is immediately evaluated, and he is rewarded with a chip for each assignment completed and with another chip if the assignment was accurately done with the overwhelming majority of the items correct. The teacher also marks the child's Work and Reward Record with a "C" following presentation of the chip.

The teacher marks each individual assignment item "C" if correctly done; wrong answers are not checked in any way and should become the basis for individual work with the child in order that he may understand and correct his errors and then obtain a "C" mark. Upon satisfactory completion and correction of an assignment or two (depending upon the pupil), the child is further rewarded by the teacher by being allowed to go to an activity corner of his choice for a period of time. The pupil follows a regular daily schedule of individual and class activities in order that he may come to anticipate the general behavioral requirements to be made of him.

Under this particular system, it is possible for the child to earn 15 chips during a normal school day. One chip is awarded for completion of the assignment in writing, reading, arithmetic, music, special training, and physical education and games; another chip is awarded for accuracy of work in each of these areas. One chip is awarded after the lunch period to students displaying readiness to work, self-control, and good behavior during the morning class; another chip is awarded near the end of the day to students exhibiting self-control and good behavior during the afternoon. Another chip is awarded for helping others as the occasion demands.

At the end of the school day, the teacher schedules a council meeting, where the day's work records are reviewed, problems discussed, and chips exchanged for candy, peanuts, or other food items. The number of chips earned is then totalled by each pupil in the daily column. When 15 chips have been earned, a Blue Star Award is gummed on the record sheet. Where some children may easily earn a blue star each day, it may take two or more days for other children to earn this award. When five blue stars have been earned, the pupil is presented with the Gold Star Award, which is affixed to his record and the date indicated.

On Friday afternoons the council meeting is extended to include an award party. First, each pupil counts the total number of chips he has earned during the week, and an equal number of food items is placed in the class party dish. These food rewards are then shared equally by the class as a whole. During this party, pupils who have earned the Gold Star Award are allowed to select a special award from the Gold Star Surprise Box; the surprise box usually contains small trinkets, such as plastic cars, whistles, balloons, and other simple inexpensive toys.

Children who have earned two gold stars are eligible for the Citizens Council Award. Nomination and election are done by the council members, who meet near the end of each school day. Following one week on the Citizens Council, the pupil is presented with a "C" pin, which he is encouraged to wear during class. If a pupil fails to continue to earn at least four blue stars weekly or breaks any special conduct code established by the council, he may then be voted off the council and must earn his way back. Occasional privileges, such as messenger, game leader, etc., are awarded to council members.

Following four continuous weeks on the Citizens Council, pupils are automatically given the Citizens Honor Award. This may consist of special privileges, such as bowling, an unusual field trip, luncheon out, or related social activities.

SUMMARY AND IMPLICATIONS

Social reinforcement systems, such as the model presented, can be devised to aid in the classroom management of children with behavior disorders. For exceptional children, the reinforcement system must be based on learning programs derived from the pupil's pattern of psychoeducational abilities, interests, and past accomplishments.

The system is most effective when clearly understood by the pupil and his parents. Teachers can obtain further reinforcement of desirable behavior by involving parents through conferences which help them to become aware of the program and to lend support to the social reinforcement system used.

Through such a reinforcement system, children begin to experience success and derive pleasure from learning and self-control. Formal report card marks must be used relative to the total reinforcement system and should not be based on arbitrary standards. Experimental programs of social reinforcement systems should be teacher devised and applied in public school classes for exceptional children with behavior disorders.

disadvantaged and minority children

Much of the emphasis on early childhood education during the past decade stems from efforts to improve the achievement of disadvantaged children. At the beginning of the decade the definition of "disadvantaged" was considered relatively clear-cut; it referred to those who were poor (and in many cases belonged to minority groups). It was believed that early childhood programs that applied the then available findings of psychology would stimulate and enrich the intellectual development of the disadvantaged child and thereby increase the likelihood that he would be academically successful and financially independent in later life. A decade of experimentation and implementation not only has raised questions about these beliefs, but also has revealed that our knowledge of such children is limited and our ability to change their behavior even more limited. As the following articles show, there are many kinds of deprivation, and the middle-class child is deprived in some ways in which the lower-class child may be enriched. As these articles also indicate, it is not very productive to institute early childhood programs that do not stem from an awareness and appreciation of the actual conditions that exist in the life of these children or an acknowledgement of the ways in which they are capable and gifted. This section deals with several concerns that are central to programs for facilitating the educational progress of disadvantaged youth.

In Article 36, Robert Coles describes "Like It Is in the Alley" of America's urban ghettos. The slums that have become the dwelling places of poor blacks are marked by distrust, sickness, hunger, fear, and the fatalistic view that life will always remain the same. Coles presents a graphic picture of the physical and psychological conditions of life that entrap the young child in poverty. School is an alien world for ghetto youth, and they feel neither accepted nor trusting within its doors.

In Article 37 Miriam Goldberg takes us from this description of ghetto life to an examination of the "Issues in the Education of the Disadvantaged." After defining "disadvantaged," Goldberg examines several explanations that have been advanced to account for the learning difficulties of disadvantaged children. These explanations are relevant to the questions of what the teachers and schools can do to overcome such difficulties and why various efforts at intervention are effective or not. In a sober appraisal, the author concludes that slow progress can be made and that programs with a broader range than those that are contained in present-day classrooms will be required.

"Prejudice and Your Child," Article 38, is an examination of the significance of racial identification and racial preferences of white and black children. Studies indicate that children as young as three mirror the racial attitudes of their parents and that the broader community of peers, school, and mass media contribute to the formation of these attitudes. As Kenneth Clark points out, the racial attitudes of children are more easily changed than those of adults. The potential significance of early educational experiences is obvious.

Children from minority groups are likely to suffer economically based disadvantages; the middle-class white child suffers other kinds of deprivations. In "The Shortchanged Children of Suburbia," Article 39, Alice Miel and Edwin Kiesler, Jr., spell out some limitations of life in America's suburbs. Like the ghetto child, the suburban child has little direct experience with persons outside his own group. Both in school and at home there is a heavy emphasis on materialism and status and a generally patronizing attitude toward the poor. The schools of suburbia are highly competitive and are marked by strong pressures for achievement, with relatively little concern for other social or moral values. As a result, the suburban child is often disadvantaged in these basic areas of personal development.

In Article 40 Esther Levin, a first-grade teacher, concludes that "Beginning Reading Is a Personal Affair." After appraising the educationally and economically deprived backgrounds of her students, she found that the key to the problem was individual motivation. To overcome her students' shyness, distractibility, and short attention spans, she focused on each child's unique background and developed procedures to enhance his sense of pride and confidence.

behavioral objectives *To be able to discuss the following points*

36 LIKE IT IS IN THE ALLEY
The experiences of the ghetto family with public institutions
Peter's relationship with school
The adult-child authority relationship evidenced in Peter's family
Peter's beliefs concerning his ability to control his destiny
Some of the special skills and strengths of the ghetto child

37 ISSUES IN THE EDUCATION OF THE DISADVANTAGED
The characteristics of the population referred to as disadvantaged
The relationship between social-class status and school achievement
Five theories concerning the learning difficulties of disadvantaged children
The philosophy behind school intervention programs and the effectiveness of such programs

The issues involved in proposals for helping the disadvantaged student

LIKE IT IS IN THE ALLEY **36** ROBERT COLES

"In the alley it's mostly dark, even if the sun is out. But if you look around, you can find things. I know how to get into every building, except that it's like night once you're inside them, because they don't have lights. So, I stay here. You're better off. It's no good on the street. You can get hurt all the time, one way or the other. And in buildings, like I told you, it's bad in them, too. But here it's o.k. You can find your own corner, and if someone tries to move in you fight him off. We meet here all the time, and figure out what we'll do next. It might be a game, or over for some pool, or a coke or something. You need to have a place to start out from, and that's like it is in the alley; you can always know your buddy will be there, provided it's the right time. So you go there, and you're on your way, man."

Like all children of nine, Peter is always on his way—to a person, a place, a "thing" he wants to do. *"There's this here thing we thought we'd try tomorrow,"* he'll say; and eventually I'll find out that he means there's to be a race. He and his friends will compete with another gang to see who can wash a car faster and better. The cars belong to four youths who make their money taking bets, and selling liquor that I don't believe was ever purchased, and pushing a few of those pills that *"go classy with beer."* I am not completely sure, but I think they also have something to do with other drugs; and again, I can't quite be sure what their connection is with a "residence" I've seen not too far from the alley Peter describes so possessively. The women come and go—from that residence and along the street Peter's alley leaves.

Peter lives in the heart of what we in contemporary America have chosen (ironically, so far as history goes) to call an "urban ghetto." The area was a slum before it became a ghetto, and there still are some very poor white people on its edges and increasing numbers of Puerto Ricans in several of its blocks. Peter was not born in the ghetto, nor was his family told to go there. They are Americans and have been here *"since way back before anyone can remember."* That is the way Peter's mother talks about Alabama, about the length of time she and her ancestors have lived there. She and Peter's father came north *"for freedom."* They did not seek out a ghetto, an old quarter of Boston where they were expected to live and where they would be confined, yet at least some of the time solidly at rest, with kin, and reasonably safe.

No, they sought freedom. Americans, they moved on when the going got *"real bad,"* and Americans, they expected something better someplace, some other place. They left Alabama on impulse. They found Peter's alley by accident. And they do not fear pogroms. They are Americans, and in Peter's words: *"There's likely to be another riot here soon. That's what I heard today. You hear it a lot, but one day you know it'll happen."*

Peter's mother fears riots too—among other things. The Jews of Eastern Europe huddled together in their ghettos, afraid of the barbarians, afraid of the *Goyim,* but always sure of one thing, their God-given destiny. Peter's mother has no such faith. She believes that *"something will work out one of these days."* She believes that *"you have to keep on going, and things can get better, but don't ask me how."* She believes that *"God wants us to have a bad spell here, and so maybe it'll get better the next time—you know in Heaven, and I hope that's where we'll be going."* Peter's mother, in other words, is a pragmatist, an optimist, and a Christian. Above all she is American: *"Yes, I hear them talk about Africa, but it don't mean anything to us. All I know is Alabama and now it's in Massachusetts that we are. It was a long trip coming up here, and sometimes I wish we were back there, and sometimes I'd just as soon be here, for all that's no good about it. But I'm not going to take any more trips, no sir. And like Peter* said, this is the only country we've got. If you come from a country, you come from it, and we're from it, I'd say, and there isn't much we can do but try to live as best we can. I mean, live here."

What is "life" like for her over there, where she lives, in the neighborhood she refers to as "here"? A question like that cannot be answered by the likes of me, and even her answer provides only the beginning of a reply: "Well, we does o.k., I guess. Peter here, he has it better than I did, or his daddy. I can say that. I tell myself that a lot. He can turn on the faucet over there, and a lot of the time, he just gets the water, right away. And when I tell him what it was like for us, to go fetch that water—we'd walk three miles, yes sir, and we'd be lucky it wasn't ten—well, Peter, it doesn't register on him. He thinks I'm trying to fool him, and the more serious I get, the more he laughs, so I've stopped.

"Of course it's not all so good, I have to admit. We're still where we were, so far as knowing where your next meal is coming from. When I go to bed at night I tell myself I've done good, to stay alive and keep the kids alive, and if they'll just wake up in the morning, and me too, well then, we can worry about that, all the rest, come tomorrow. So there you go. We do our best, and that's all you can do."

She may sound fatalistic, but she appears to be a nervous, hardworking, even hard-driven woman—thin, short, constantly on the move. I may not know what she "really" thinks and believes, because like the rest of us she has her contradictions and her mixed feelings. I think it is fair to say that there are some things that she can't say to me—or to herself. She is a Negro, and I am white. She is poor, and I am fairly well off. She is very near to illiterate, and I put in a lot of time worrying about how to say things. But she and I are both human beings, and we both have trouble—to use that word—"communicating," not only with each other, but with ourselves. Sometimes she doesn't tell me something she really wants me to know. She has forgotten, pure and simple. More is on her mind than information I might want. And sometimes I forget too: "Remember you asked the other day about Peter, if he was ever real sick. And I told you he was a weak child, and I feared for his life, and I've lost five children, three that was born and two that wasn't. Well, I forgot to tell you that he got real sick up here, just after we came. He was three, and I didn't know what to do. You see, I didn't have my mother to help out. She always knew what to do. She could hold a child and get him to stop crying, no matter how sick he was, and no matter how much he wanted food, and we didn't have it. But she was gone—and that's when we left to come up here, and I never would have left her, not for anything in the world. But suddenly she took a seizure of something and went in a half hour, I'd say. And Peter, he was so hot and sick, I thought he had the same thing his *grandmother did and he was going to die. I thought maybe she's calling him. She always liked Peter. She helped him be born, she and my cousin, they did."*

Actually, Peter's mother remembers quite a lot of things. She remembers the "old days" back South, sometimes with a shudder, but sometimes with the same nostalgia that the region is famous for generating in its white exiles. She also notices a lot of things. She notices, and from time to time will remark upon, the various changes in her life. She has moved from the country to the city. Her father was a sharecropper and her son wants to be a pilot (sometimes), a policeman (sometimes), a racing-car driver (sometimes), and a baseball player (most of the time). Her husband is not alive. He died one year after they all came to Boston. He woke up vomiting in the middle of the night—vomiting blood. He bled and bled and vomited and vomited and then he died. The doctor does not have to press very hard for "the facts." Whatever is known gets spoken vividly and (still) emotionally: *"I didn't know what to do. I was beside myself. I prayed and I prayed, and in between I held his head and wiped his forehead. It was the middle of the night. I woke up my oldest girl and I told her to go knocking on the doors. But no one would answer. They must have been scared, or have suspected something bad. I thought if only he'd be able to last into the morning, then we could get some help. I was caught between things. I couldn't leave him to go get a policeman. And my girl, she was afraid to go out. And besides, there was no one outside, and I thought we'd just stay at his side, and somehow he'd be o.k., because he was a strong man, you know. His muscles, they were big all his life. Even with the blood coming up, he looked too big and strong to die, I thought. But I knew he was sick. He was real bad sick. There wasn't anything else, no sir, to do. We didn't have no phone and even if there was a car, I never could have used it. Nor my daughter. And then he took a big breath and that was his last one."*

When I first met Peter and his mother, I wanted to know how they lived, what they did with their time, what they liked to do or disliked doing, what they believed. In the back of my mind were large subjects like "the connection between a person's moods and the environment in which he lives." Once I was told I was studying "the psychology of the ghetto," and another time the subject of "urban poverty and mental health." It is hoped that at some point large issues like those submit themselves to lives; and when that is done, when particular but not unrepresentative or unusual human beings are called in witness, their concrete medical history becomes extremely revealing. I cannot think of a better way to begin knowing what life is like for Peter and his mother than to hear the following and hear it again and think about its implications: *"No sir, Peter* has never been to a doctor, not unless you count the one at school, and she's a nurse I believe. He was his sickest back home before we came here, and you know there was no doctor for us in the county. In Alabama you have to pay a white doctor first, before he'll go near you. And we don't have but a few colored ones. (I've never seen a one.) There was this woman we'd go to, and she had gotten some nursing education in Mobile. (No, I don't know if she was a nurse or not, or a helper to the nurses, maybe.) Well, she would come to help us. With the convulsions, she'd show you how to hold the child, and make sure he doesn't hurt himself. They can bite their tongues real, real bad.

"Here, I don't know what to do. There's the city hospital, but it's no good for us. I went there with my husband, no sooner than a month or so after we came up here. We waited and waited, and finally the day was almost over. We left the kids with a neighbor, and we barely knew her. I said it would take the morning, but I never thought we'd get home near suppertime. And they wanted us to come back and come back, because it was something they couldn't do all at once—though for most of the time we just sat there and did nothing. And my husband, he said his stomach was the worse for going there, and he'd take care of himself from now on, rather than go there.

"Maybe they could have saved him. But they're far away, and I didn't have money to get a cab, even if there was one around here, and I thought to myself it'll make him worse, to take him there.

"My kids, they get sick. The welfare worker, she sends a nurse here, and she tells me we should be on vitamins and the kids need all kinds of check-ups. Once she took my daughter and told her she had to have her teeth looked at, and the same with Peter. So, I went with my daughter, and they didn't see me that day, but said they could in a couple of weeks. And I had to pay the woman next door to mind the little ones, and there was the carfare, and we sat and sat, like before. So, I figured, it would take more than we've got to see that dentist. And when the nurse told us we'd have to come back a few times—that's how many, a few—I thought that no one ever looked at my teeth, and they're not good, I'll admit, but you can't have everything, that's what I say, and that's what my kids have to know, I guess."

What *does* she have? And what belongs to Peter? For one thing, there is the apartment, three rooms for six people, a mother and five children. Peter is a middle child with two older girls on one side and a younger sister and still younger brother on the other side. The smallest child was born in Boston: "It's the only time I ever spent time in a hospital. He's the only one to be born there. My neighbor got the police. I was in the hall, crying I guess. We almost didn't make it. They told me I had bad blood pressure, and I should have been on pills, and I should come back, but I didn't. It was the worst time I've ever had, because I was alone. My husband had to stay with the kids, and no one was there to visit me."

Peter sleeps with his brother in one bedroom. The three girls sleep in the living room, which is a bedroom. And, of course, there is a small kitchen. There is not very much furniture about. The kitchen has a table with four chairs, only two of which are sturdy. The girls sleep in one big bed. Peter shares his bed with his brother. The mother sleeps on a couch. There is one more chair and a table in the living room. Jesus looks down from the living room wall, and an undertaker's calendar hangs on the kitchen wall. The apartment has no books, no records. There is a television set in the living room, and I have never seen it off.

Peter in many respects is his father's successor. His mother talks things over with him. She even defers to him at times. She will say something; he will disagree; she will nod and let him have the last word. He knows the city. She still feels a stranger to the city. *"If you want to know about anything around here, just ask Peter,"* she once said to me. That was three years ago, when Peter was six. Peter continues to do very poorly at school, but I find him a very good teacher. He notices a lot, makes a lot of sense when he talks, and has a shrewd eye for the ironic detail. He is very intelligent, for all the trouble he gives his teachers. He recently summed up a lot of American history for me: *"I wasn't made for that school, and that school wasn't made for me."* It is an old school, filled with memories. The name of the school evokes Boston's Puritan past. Pictures and statues adorn the corridors—reminders of the soldiers and statesmen and writers who made New England so influential in the nineteenth century. And naturally one finds slogans on the walls, about freedom and democracy and the rights of the people. Peter can be surly and cynical when he points all that out to the visitor. If he is asked what kind of school he would *like*, he laughs incredulously. *"Are you kidding? No school would be my first choice. They should leave us alone, and let us help out at home, and maybe let some of our own people teach us. The other day the teacher admitted she was no good. She said maybe a Negro should come in and give us the discipline, because she was scared. She said all she wanted from us was that we keep quiet and stop wearing her nerves down, and she'd be grateful, because she would retire soon. She said we were becoming too much for her, and she didn't understand why. But when one kid wanted to say something, tell her why, she told us to keep still, and write something. You know what? She whipped out a book and told us to copy a whole page from it, so we'd learn it. A stupid waste of time. I didn't even try; and she didn't care. She just wanted an excuse not to talk with us. They're all alike."*

Actually, they're all *not* alike, and Peter knows it. He has met up with two fine teachers, and in mellow moments he can say so: *"They're trying hard, but me and my friends, I don't think we're cut out for school. To tell the truth, that's what I think. My mother says we should try, anyway, but it doesn't seem to help, trying. The teacher can't understand a lot of us, but he does all these new things, and you can see he's excited. Some kids are really with him, and I am, too. But I can't take all his stuff very serious. He's a nice man, and he says he wants to come and visit every one of our homes; but my mother says no, she wouldn't know what to do with him, when he came here. We'd just stand and have nothing to talk about. So she said tell him not to come; and I don't think he will, anyway. I think he's getting to know."*

What is that teacher getting to know? What *is* there to know about Peter and all the others like him in our American cities? Of course Peter and his friends who play in the alley need better schools, schools they can feel to be theirs, and better teachers, like the ones they *have* in fact met on occasion. But I do not feel that a reasonably good teacher in the finest school building in America would reach and affect Peter in quite the way, I suppose, people like me would expect and desire. At nine Peter is both young and quite old. At nine he is much wiser about many things than my sons will be at nine, and maybe nineteen. Peter has in fact taught me a lot about his neighborhood, about life on the streets, about survival: *"I get up when I get up; no special time. My mother has Alabama in her. She gets up with the sun, and she wants to go to bed when it gets dark. I try to tell her that up here things just get started in the night. But she gets mad. She wakes me up. If it weren't for her shaking me, I might sleep until noon. Sometimes we have a good breakfast, when the check comes. Later on, though, before it comes, it might just be some coffee and a slice of bread. She worries about food. She says we should eat what she gives us, but sometimes I'd rather go hungry. I was sick a long time ago, my stomach or something—maybe like my father, she says. So I don't like all the potatoes she pushes on us and cereal, all the time cereal. We're supposed to be lucky, because we get some food every day. Down South they can't be sure. That's what she says, and I guess she's right.*

"Then I go to school. I eat what I can, and leave. I have two changes of clothes, one for everyday and one for Sunday. I wait on my friend Billy, and we're off by 8:15. He's from around here, and he's a year older. He knows everything. He can tell you if a woman is high on some stuff, or if she's been drinking, or she's off her mind about something. He knows. His brother has a convertible, a Buick. He pays off the police, but Billy won't say no more than that.

"In school we waste time until it's over. I do what I have to. I don't like the place. I feel like falling off all day, just putting my head down and saying good-bye to everyone until three. We're out then, and we sure wake

up. *I don't have to stop home first, not now. I go with Billy. We'll be in the alley, or we'll go to see them play pool. Then you know when it's time to go home. You hear someone say six o'clock, and you go in. I eat and I watch television. It must be around ten or eleven I'm in bed."*

Peter sees rats all the time. He has been bitten by them. He has a big stick by his bed to use against them. They also claim the alley, even in the daytime. They are not large enough to be compared with cats, as some observers have insisted; they are simply large, confident, well-fed, unafraid rats. The garbage is theirs; the land is theirs; the tenement is theirs; human flesh is theirs. When I first started visiting Peter's family, I wondered why they didn't do something to rid themselves of those rats, and the cockroaches, and the mosquitoes, and the flies, and the maggots, and the ants, and especially the garbage in the alley which attracts so much of all that "lower life." Eventually I began to see some of the reasons why. A large aparemtnt building with many families has exactly two barrels in its basement. The halls of the building go unlighted. Many windows have no screens, and some windows are broken and boarded up. The stairs are dangerous; some of them have missing timber. (*"We just jump over them,"* says Peter cheerfully.) And the landowner is no one in particular. Rent is collected by an agent, in the name of a "realty trust." Somewhere in City Hall there is a bureaucrat who unquestionably might be persuaded to prod someone in the "trust"; and one day I went with three of the tenants, including Peter's mother, to try that "approach." We waited and waited at City Hall. (I drove us there, clear across town, naturally.) Finally we met up with a man, a not very encouraging or inspiring or generous or friendly man. He told us we would have to try yet another department and swear out a complaint; and that the "case" would have to be "studied," and that we would then be "notified of a decision." We went to the department down the hall, and waited some more, another hour and ten minutes. By then it was three o'clock, and the mothers wanted to go home. They weren't thinking of rats anymore, or poorly heated apartments, or garbage that had nowhere to go and often went uncollected for two weeks, not one. They were thinking of their children, who would be home from school and, in the case of two women, their husbands who would also soon be home. *"Maybe we should come back some other day."* Peter's mother said, I noted she didn't say *tomorrow*, and I realized that I had read someplace that people like her aren't precisely "future-oriented."

Actually, both Peter and his mother have a very clear idea of what is ahead. For the mother it is *"more of the same."* One evening she was tired but unusually talkative, perhaps because a daughter of hers was sick: *"I'm glad to be speaking about all these things tonight. My little girl has a bad fever. I've been trying to cool her off all day. Maybe if there was a place* near here, that we could go to, maybe I would have gone. But like it is, I have to do the best I can and pray she'll be o.k."

I asked whether she thought her children would find things different, and that's when she said it would be *"more of the same"* for them. Then she added a long afterthought: *"Maybe it'll be a little better for them. A mother has to have hope for her children, I guess. But I'm not too sure, I'll admit. Up here you know there's a lot more jobs around than in Alabama. We don't get them, but you know they're someplace near, and they tell you that if you go train for them, then you'll be eligible. So maybe Peter might someday have some real good steady work, and that would be something, yes sir it would. I keep telling him he should pay more attention to school, and put more of himself into the lessons they give there. But he says no, it's no good; it's a waste of time; they don't care what happens there, only if the kids don't keep quiet and mind themselves. Well, Peter has got to learn to mind himself, and not be fresh. He speaks back to me, these days. There'll be a time he won't even speak to me at all, I suppose. I used to blame it all on the city up here, city living. Back home we were always together, and there wasn't no place you could go, unless to Birmingham, and you couldn't do much for yourself there, we all knew. Of course, my momma, she knew how to make us behave. But I was thinking the other night, it wasn't so good back there either. Colored people, they'd beat on one another, and we had lot of people that liquor was eating away at them; they'd use wine by the gallon. All they'd do was work on the land, and then go back and kill themselves with wine. And then there'd be the next day—until they'd one evening go to sleep and never wake up. And we'd get the Bossman and he'd see to it they got buried.*

"Up here I think it's better, but don't ask me to tell you why. There's the welfare, that's for sure. And we get our water and if there isn't good heat, at least there's some. Yes, it's cold up here, but we had cold down there, too, only then we didn't have any heat, and we'd just die, some of us would, every winter with one of those freezing spells.

"And I do believe things are changing. On the television they talk to you, the colored man and all the others who aren't doing so good. My boy Peter, he says they're putting you on. That's all he sees, people 'putting on' other people. But I think they all mean it, the white people. I never see them, except on television, when they say the white man wants good for the colored people. I think Peter could go and do better for himself later on, when he gets older, except for the fact that he just doesn't believe. He don't believe what they say, the teacher, or the man who says it's getting better for us—on television. I guess it's my fault, I never taught my children, any of them, to believe that kind of thing; because I never thought we'd ever have it any different, not in this life. So maybe I've failed Peter. I told him

the other day, he should work hard, because of all the 'opportunity' they say is coming for us, and he said I was talking good, but where was my proof. So I went next door with him, to my neighbor's, and we asked her husband, and you know he sided with Peter. He said they were taking in a few here and a few there, and putting them in the front windows of all the big companies, but that all you have to do is look around at our block and you'd see all the young men, and they just haven't got a thing to do. Nothing."

Her son also looks to the future. Sometimes he talks—in his own words—"big." He'll one day be a bombadier or "something like that." At other times he is less sure of things: "I don't know what I'll be. Maybe nothing. I see the men sitting around, hiding from the welfare lady. They fool her. Maybe I'll fool her, too. I don't know what you can do. The teacher the other day said that if just one of us turned out o.k. she'd congratulate herself and call herself lucky."

A while back a riot excited Peter and his mother, excited them and frightened them. The spectacle of the police being fought, of white-owned property being assaulted, stirred the boy a great deal: "I figured the whole world might get changed around. I figured people would treat us better from now on. Only I don't think they will." As for his mother, she was less hopeful, but even more apocalyptic: "I told Peter we were going to pay for this good. I told him they wouldn't let us get away with it, not later on." And in the midst of the trouble she was frightened as she had never before been: "I saw them running around on the streets, the men and women, and they were talking about burning things down, and how there'd be nothing left when they got through. I sat there with my children and I thought we might die the way things are going, die right here. I didn't know what to do: if I should leave, in case they burn down the building, or if I should stay, so that the police don't arrest us, or we get mixed up with the crowd of people. I've never seen so many people, going in so many different directions. They were running and shouting and they didn't know what to do. They were so excited. My neighbor, she said they'd burn us all up, and then the white man would have himself one less of a headache. The colored man is a worse enemy to himself than the white. I mean, it's hard to know which is the worst."

I find it as hard as she does to sort things out. When I think of her and the mothers like her I have worked with for years, when I think of Peter and his friends, I find myself caught between the contradictory observations I have made. Peter already seems a grim and unhappy child. He trusts no one white, not his white teacher, not the white policeman he sees, not the white welfare worker, not the white storekeeper, and not, I might add, me. There we are, the five of us from the 180,000,000 Americans who surround him and of course 20,000,000 others. Yet, Peter doesn't really trust his friends and neighbors, either. At nine he has learned to be careful, wary, guarded, doubtful, and calculating. His teacher may not know it, but Peter is a good sociologist, and a good political scientist, a good student of urban affairs. With devastating accuracy he can reveal how much of the "score" he knows; yes, and how fearful and sad and angry he is: *"This here city isn't for us. It's for the people downtown. We're here because, like my mother said, we had to come. If they could lock us up or sweep us away, they would. That's why I figure the only way you can stay ahead is get some kind of deal for yourself. If I had a choice I'd live someplace else, but I don't know where. It would be a place where they treated you right, and they didn't think you were some nuisance. But the only thing you can do is be careful of yourself; if not, you'll get killed somehow, like it happened to my father."*

His father died prematurely, and most probably, unnecessarily. Among the poor of our cities the grim medical statistics we all know about become terrible daily experiences. Among the black and white families I work with—in nearby but separate slums—disease and the pain that goes with it are taken for granted. When my children complain of an earache or demonstrate a skin rash I rush them to the doctor. When I have a headache, I take an aspirin; and if the headache is persistent, I can always get a medical check-up. Not so with Peter's mother and Peter; they have learned to live with sores and infections and poorly mended fractures and bad teeth and eyes that need but don't have the help of glasses. Yes, they can go to a city hospital and get free care; but again and again they don't. They come to the city without any previous experience as patients. They have never had the money to purchase a doctor's time. They have never had free medical care available. (I am speaking now of Appalachian whites as well as southern blacks.) It may comfort me to know that every American city provides some free medical services for its "indigent," but Peter's mother and thousands like her have quite a different view of things: *"I said to you the other time, I've tried there. It's like at City Hall, you wait and wait, and they pushes you and shove you and call your name, only to tell you to wait some more, and if you tell them you can't stay there all day, they'll say 'lady, go home, then.' You get sick just trying to get there. You have to give your children over to people or take them all with you; and the carfare is expensive. Why if we had a doctor around here, I could almost pay him with the carfare it takes to get there and back for all of us. And you know, they keep on having you come back and back, and they don't know what each other says. Each time they starts from scratch."*

It so happens that recently I took Peter to a children's hospital and arranged for a series of evaluations which led to the following: a pair of glasses; a prolonged bout of dental work; antibiotic treatment for skin lesions; a thorough cardiac work-up, with the subsequent diagnosis of rheumatic heart disease; a conference between Peter's mother and a nutritionist, because the boy has been on a high-starch, low-protein, and low-vitamin diet all his life. He suffers from one attack of sinus trouble after another, from a succession of sore throats and earaches, from cold upon cold, even in the summer. A running nose is unsurprising to him—and so is chest pain and shortness of breath, due to a heart ailment, we now know.

At the same time Peter is tough. I have to emphasize again *how* tough and, yes, how "politic, cautious and meticulous," not in Prufrock's way, but in another way and for other reasons. Peter has learned to be wary as well as angry; tentative as well as extravagant; at times controlled and only under certain circumstances defiant: *"Most of the time, I think you have to watch your step. That's what I think. That's the difference between up here and down in the South. That's what my mother says, and she's right. I don't remember it down there, but I know she must be right. Here, you measure the next guy first and then make your move when you think it's a good time to."*

He was talking about *"how you get along"* when you leave school and go *"mix with the guys"* and start *"getting your deal."* He was telling me what an outrageous and unsafe world he has inherited and how very carefully he has made his appraisal of the future. Were I afflicted with some of his physical complaints, I would be fretful, annoyed, petulant, angry—and moved to do something, see someone, get a remedy, a pill, a promise of help. He has made his "adjustment" to the body's pain, and he has also learned to contend with the alley and the neighborhood and *us,* the world beyond: *"The cops come by here all the time. They drive up and down the street. They want to make sure everything is o.k. to look at. They don't bother you, so long as you don't get in their way."*

So, it is live and let live—except that families like Peter's have a tough time living, and of late have been troubling those cops, among others. Our cities have become not only battlegrounds, but places where all sorts of American problems and historical ironies have converged. Ailing, poorly fed, and proud Appalachian families have reluctantly left the hollows of eastern Kentucky and West Virginia for Chicago and Dayton and Cincinnati and Cleveland and Detroit, and even, I have found, Boston. They stick close together in all-white neighborhoods—or enclaves or sections or slums or ghettos or whatever. They wish to go home but can't, unless they are willing to be idle and hungry all the time. They confuse social workers and public officials of all kinds because they both want and reject the city. Black families also have sought out cities and learned to feel frightened and disappointed.

I am a physician, and over the past ten years I have been asking myself how people like Peter and his mother survive in mind and body and spirit. And I have wanted to know what a twentieth-century American city "means" to them or "does" to them. People cannot be handed questionnaires and asked to answer such questions. They cannot be "interviewed" a few times and told to come across with a statement, a reply. But inside Peter and his brother and his sisters and his mother, and inside a number of Appalachian mothers and fathers and children I know, are feelings and thoughts and ideas—which, in my experience, come out casually or suddenly, by accident almost. After a year or two of talking, after experiences such as I have briefly described in a city hall, in a children's hospital, a lifetime of pent-up tensions and observation comes to blunt expression: *"Down in Alabama we had to be careful about ourselves with the white man, but we had plenty of things we could do by ourselves. There was our side of town, and you could walk and run all over, and we had a garden you know. Up here they have you in a cage. There's no place to go, and all I do is stay in the building all day long and the night, too. I don't use my legs no more, hardly at all. I never see those trees, and my oldest girl, she misses planting time. It was bad down there. We had to leave. But it's no good here, too, I'll tell you. Once I woke up and I thought all the buildings on the block were falling down on me. And I was trying to climb out, but I couldn't. And then the next thing I knew, we were all back South, and I was standing near some sunflowers—you know, the tall ones that can shade you if you sit down.*

"No, I don't dream much. I fall into a heavy sleep as soon as I touch the bed. The next thing I know I'm stirring myself to start in all over in the morning. It used to be the sun would wake me up, but now it's up in my head, I guess. I know I've got to get the house going and off to school."

Her wistful, conscientious, law-abiding, devoutly Christian spirit hasn't completely escaped the notice of Peter, for all his hardheaded, cynical protestations: *"If I had a chance, I'd like to get enough money to bring us all back to Alabama for a visit. Then I could prove it that it may be good down there, a little bit, even if it's no good, either. Like she says, we had to get out of there or we'd be dead by now. I hear say we all may get killed soon, it's so bad here; but I think we did right to get up here, and if we make them listen to us, the white man, maybe he will."*

To which Peter's mother adds: *"We've carried a lot of trouble in us, from way back in the beginning. I have these pains, and so does everyone around here. But you can't just die until you're ready to. And I do believe something is happening. I do believe I see that."*

To which Peter adds: *"Maybe it won't be that we'll win, but if we get killed, everyone will hear about it. Like the minister said, before we used to die real quiet, and no one stopped to pay notice."*

Two years before Peter spoke those words he drew a picture for me, one of many he has done. When he was younger, and when I didn't know him so well as I think I do now, it was easier for us to have something tangible to do and then talk about. I used to visit the alley with him, as I still do, and one day I asked him to draw the alley. That was a good idea, he thought. (Not all of my suggestions were, however.) He started in, then stopped, and finally worked rather longer and harder than usual at the job. I busied myself with my own sketches, which from the start he insisted I do. Suddenly from across the table I heard him say he was through. Ordinarily he would slowly turn the drawing around for me to see; and I would get up and walk over to his side of the table, to see even better. But he didn't move his paper, and I didn't move myself. I saw what he had drawn, and he saw me looking. I was surprised and a bit stunned and more than a bit upset, and surely he saw my face and heard my utter silence. Often I would break the awkward moments when neither of us seemed to have anything to say, but this time it was his turn to do so: *"You know what it is?"* He knew that I liked us to talk about our work. I said no, I didn't—though in fact the vivid power of his black crayon had come right across to me. *"It's that hole we dug in the alley. I made it bigger here. If you fall into it, you can't get out. You die."*

He had drawn circles within circles, all of them black, and then a center, also black. He had imposed an X on the center. Nearby, strewn across the circles, were fragments of the human body—two faces, an arm, five legs. And after I had taken the scene in, I could only think to myself that I had been shown *"like it is in the alley"*—by an intelligent boy who knew what he saw around him, could give it expression, and, I am convinced, would respond to a different city, a city that is alive and breathing, one that is not for many of its citizens a virtual morgue.

37

MIRIAM L. GOLDBERG

ISSUES IN THE EDUCATION OF THE DISADVANTAGED

The population currently referred to as the "disadvantaged" is not a homogeneous population. Although characteristically its members live under substandard economic conditions, they come from a variety of cultural backgrounds and exhibit varying behavior patterns. Many come from groups that have suffered and continue to suffer discrimination (Indians, Negroes, Mexican-Americans, Puerto Ricans); many have migrated to industrial centers from isolated rural backgrounds (Appalachians). The majority of these individuals (but by no means all of them) perform poorly in school, fail to develop adequate symbolic skills for later economic independence, and show excessive rates of crime, dope addiction, and mental disorder.

The relationship between social-class status and school achievement is well known. It is clearly seen in scores on tests of intelligence and reading. The retardation appears to be cumulative; pupils fall further and further behind national norms with each additional year of schooling. For example, Negro pupils who had migrated to New York City sometime before third grade were, at the end of third grade, 7 months retarded in reading comprehension; comparable Negro pupils at the end of grade six were almost 2 years retarded. In junior high school, the lowest quarter of the population moved from 3.6 years of reading retardation in grade seven to over 5 years at the end of grade nine (New York City, 1957). Taking all the schools in central Harlem (Haryou, 1964), 30 percent of third graders were reading considerably below grade level; at the end of sixth grade, 81 percent fell below the norm. On a nationwide survey (U.S. Department of Labor, 1967), white-Negro achievement differences increased from 2.4 years in grade six to 3.5 years in grade 12. Similar data are found for lower-class Puerto Rican and Mexican-American children.

Social-class differences were also reported in studies of achievement motivation. In one study (Rosen, 1956) 83 percent of boys from the upper two socioeconomic levels (on a five-level scale) demonstrated high need achievement compared with 23 percent of boys from the lowest-level group.

In many of the groups, learning problems are compounded by language difficulties. Both in the Puerto Rican and Mexican-American populations, large numbers of children are Spanish speaking and have little knowledge of English when they enter school. Similarly, Southern Negro immigrant children, and even some second-generation residents in Northern urban centers, speak a dialect that differs in pronunciation, syntax, and even vocabulary from the language of the school.

Learning difficulties are often accompanied by social-behavior problems that manifest themselves in infractions of classroom and school discipline and in the pupils' failure to accede to the social norms set by the school. Drop-out rates are high (in some high schools over 50 percent). Many drop out at reading levels below grade five, the level of "functional literacy." Large numbers remain unemployable, even after special training, unable to function adequately on the job. However, at least for the Negro population, high school drop-out rates have decreased significantly since 1960. Even so, as noted earlier, there has been no comparable decrease in the gap between their achievement status and national norms (U.S. Department of Labor, 1967).

SOME CONFLICTING OR OVERLAPPING THEORIES

Various theories have been drawn upon to account for the learning difficulties of disadvantaged children.

GENETIC SELECTION Perhaps less prevalent than in the past but still fairly common, is the belief that the learning difficulties of disadvantaged children are due to genetic selection. The argument goes as follows: there is considerable evidence of intellectual variability (IQ scores) not only within social classes (about 70 percent), but also between social classes (about 30 percent) (Terman & Merrill, 1937), since the variance between groups is greater than can be accounted for by the variance which differentiates identical twins reared apart (about 11 percent), it is due, at least in part, to genetic factors. This theory is further bolstered by the assumption that in a relative mobile society, the more able move up, while the least able remain at the lowest rungs of the ladder. Examination of scores on "culture-free" tests shows that middle-class children are still performing at higher levels than lower-class children. It is therefore argued that the poor achievement of lower-class children is in some measure a function of lower innate ability.

SCHOOL AND TEACHER EXPECTATIONS AND PREJUDICES A diametrically opposed position is taken by those who explain the learning problems of disadvantaged children in terms of school and teacher prejudice and the "self-fulfilling prophecy." Most often expressed among civil-rights groups is the belief that slum and ghetto children are no different from all other children. They are just as bright or just as dull. They come to school no less ready for learning than others, but the school personnel, because of its own white middle-class orientation, rejects them, expects little from them (this view is reinforced by their low IQ scores), and fails to teach them. Thus, little learning takes place, and the situation is often described by the statement, "Children don't learn because teachers don't teach." Or, as stated in the Haryou report (1964), ". . . underachievement is the result of an accumulation of deficiencies while in school rather than the result of deficiencies prior to school." The theory of the self-fulfilling prophecy has been supported by evidence (Rosenthal, 1968) that indicates a positive relationship between level of teacher expectation and level of pupil performance. In addition, it is argued that slum children are shortchanged in available facilities: studies have shown that slum school buildings are the oldest and have the fewest amenities, and because of excessive teacher turnover, less-experienced teachers work in these schools. Thus less money is spent per pupil in slum-area schools (Sexton, 1961).

MOTIVATION AND CLASH OF VALUES Another set of explanations is put forth by those who view the problems as resulting from motivational and value conflicts. Because of slum or ghetto children's distance from the cultural mainstream, they see little relevance in the demands of the school to what they perceive as the needs of real life. The pupils see themselves, just as they see their parents, barred from economic opportunities beyond those at the lowest level. Although they may verbalize positive attitudes toward school, they have not internalized the belief that good work in school is the road to economic success. Many of the children have no adequate achievement models with which to identify, so achievement drive is not internalized. Various surveys of disadvantaged adolescents show that they do not consider reading ability or success in school to be particularly important in their life scheme.

Basic values also differ, which produces different approaches to school achievement. The ethnic and behavior patterns that have traditionally characterized the dominant middle-class culture—hard work, shame associated with dependent status, acceptance of delayed gratification, and verbal-conceptual styles of problem solving—all contrast with the lower-class motoric and physical style, poor time orientation, and need for immediate gratification. The boys, who see their physical (and later, sexual) prowess as representative of manhood, and who may be frightened by their own lack of masculinity (particularly if they are reared in fatherless homes) often may view the school's rewards for intellectual achievement as especially "sissyfied" and threatening (Bronfenbrenner, 1967). Thus, they reject the school and its demands, and their negative attitudes are reinforced by their failures.

COGNITION AND LANGUAGE Without denying the importance of motivational factors or completely exonerating the school from responsibility for pupil failure, another current theory has stressed the inadequate preparation of disadvantaged children for school learning. Their cognitive deficiencies, which are already apparent at the preschool level, impede academic learning in the early school years and put the children at a disadvantage for their entire school career. Assuming that intelligent behavior results from the interaction of genetic structures and environmental exposures, learning difficulties common to the majority of disadvantaged children are seen largely as the result of limited opportunities for the cognitive stimulation and interpretation that would enable their abilities to develop. Poor academic performance is thus viewed as a consequence of deficiencies in perceptual discrimination (especially where more than one sensory modality is involved at the same time), inadequate grasp of relational concepts, and limited listening skills (related to a common tendency to "tune out"). It is also affected by their language, which, though expressive and communicative within the peer group, lacks the transactional terms that enable mediation between the concrete and the abstract. Consequently the child's movement from a perception-bound to a conceptually ordered world is slowed (Ausubel, 1965).

As a result of these deficits, the child is prone to failure as he enters school and is confronted by the need to master reading, which is a highly complex and abstract symbol system. Early failure slows even further the already slow learning pace of the concretely orientated child and leads both cognitively and motivationally to cumulative difficulty in handling the increasingly abstract conceptual tasks of the school.

EFFECTIVE POWER AND MASTERY A further explanation of the shortcomings of the early experiences of most disadvantaged children stresses the lack of opportunities for the child to develop a sense of power over his environment, a recognition that his behavior has a direct and predictable effect on the behavior of others. The middle-class child soon learns which of his acts (and later words) will bring about the desired results. He internalizes a set of probabilities that help him to decide the relative merit of several behaviors. He "practices" those that most consistently have a high probability of success, simultaneously gaining mastery over his own skills and over his environment. He comes to school with many developed strategies for problem solving. Although he may have to give up some of these or modify them in the light of new demands made by the school, most of them serve him well.

One of the most important coping procedures that he brings with him to school is effective language. As Strodtbeck (1964) suggests, power through language is the "hidden curriculum" of the middle-class home. The child has learned that both the attainment and maintenance of power is best achieved through words, so he extends and elaborates his use of words into a powerful instrument, one that is as effective at school as it is at home.

For the disadvantaged child, raised in a large, struggling, and often disorganized family, the outcomes of his own behavior are far less predictable. The problems that confront him even at early stages are too difficult and too complex for his available resources. Because his own early behaviors do not have consistent outcomes, he does not develop a sense of power or evolve effective problem-solving strategies except as these are required for sheer survival. He does not learn to appreciate the power of language either. Language is not the means by which his environment is controlled, so he has no drive to master linguistic complexities. The strategies he does develop often take the form of physical aggression, a kind of random striking out both as a response to frustration and as a means of control. Such behavior impedes rather than aids problem solving in school.

SCHOOL INTERVENTION PROGRAMS AS OUTGROWTHS OF THEORIES

Each theoretical formulation underlies particular views about what educational programs should be. Some have actually provided the impetus for special programs.

Clearly, the theories that support genetic inferiority are at the base of efforts to retain school segregation, no matter what other reasons may be offered. These theories persist despite evidence on the interactive nature of genetic structures and environmental experiences. They fail, for example, to take account of the fact that retardation is far more common among Negro boys than girls, a fact that questions direct genetic explanations. They ignore the excessive physiological impairment found in youngsters who live in poverty, an impairment that so often leads to intellectual or academic malfunction (Bronfenbrenner, 1967). Furthermore, they ignore the social realities that have barred upward mobility, especially for the Negro population.

Many special programs have grown out of the conviction that, schools as presently constituted are not teaching effectively. An example of one such approach is the More Effective Schools in New York City, which look toward improving the climate of instruction through such methods as smaller classes, more remedial and guidance services, and more materials. Another approach accepts teacher inadequacy as a cause of poor pupil learning, but attributes the teacher's failures to poor preparation in the teaching procedures appropriate for dealing with the slum learner. Special teacher-preparation programs that stress internship experience in slum schools; materials-development projects that are preparing methodologically structured lessons and activities for teacher use, and publication of multiethnic, urban-orientated reading series are examples of attempts to improve teacher preparation. Most vociferous among the school blamers, however, are those who insist that the schools will not become responsive to the pupils until they are under the control of the local community, and staffed by administrators and teachers selected for their acceptance of and empathy with the children (generally, this means of similar ethnic background). They view the present curriculum as a "foreign body" imposed upon the learners, who because of it do not become engaged in the learning process. This movement is most pronounced in the Negro ghettos and underlies the development of new curricula that stress Afro-American history, culture, and so forth, as well as various proposed and existing large-city decentralization plans.

Many programs have been derived from the motivational theories. Best known of these was Higher Horizons, a program that attempted through trips and other forms of direct exposure (as well as personal-guidance services and remedial help) to bring slum children into contact with the "cultural mainstream." The Banneker Project in St. Louis is another example of a motivational approach, although attempts were also made to raise teachers' expectations of their pupils. The project achieved organized parent and community support for school achievement through parent pledges, radio programs, and other motivational devices. Support for the importance of school integration also has a motivational base. From the evidence, it would appear that lower-class children tend to perform at least somewhat better and have higher academic aspirations when they are in predominantly (proportion unspecified) middle-class schools (Coleman et al., 1966; Wilson, 1959). Both the desire to achieve and actual achievement in school are thus seen more as a function of the peer group than of factors related to patterns of school organization, teacher characteristics, or variations in methods or materials.

The cognitive-deficit theories have probably had the greatest impact on educational innovations giving rise to a variety of "compensatory" programs, of which Head Start is the most widespread. On the assumption that the pupils come to school poorly prepared to learn and thus face almost certain failure, preschool opportunities to acquire necessary preparation for learning seemed most appropriate. However, compensatory programs are not limited to the nursery-school years. Some current efforts extend downward to work with infants (usually through training parents) while others, like the Upward Bound programs, attempt to ready disadvantaged students for college attendance. Similarly, much work is being done under various auspices to upgrade the academic and vocational competencies of high-school dropouts. Special programs at the elementary and secondary level have tended more often to represent organizational changes: for example, addition or extension of remedial or guidance services, ungraded units, involvement of social services, and lowered pupil-teacher ratios. But even at these levels, there are efforts to introduce special training in the cognitive processes.

EFFECTS OF INTERVENTION PROGRAMS

To date, the accumulated evidence on all types of special programs, although not completely negative, is not highly encouraging. Higher Horizons programs, widely viewed as a panacea, have now almost disappeared. Even their strongest proponents could not wish away evaluation findings that demonstrated no significant effects on academic achievement. Similarly, serious questions have been raised about programs such as those represented by the New York City More Effective Schools: (smaller classes, ancillary staff, and more materials) following an objective evaluation. In fact, none of the special elementary and junior high school programs (including those that focused on integration) has been able to demonstrate consistent gains.

The evidence on the effects of prekindergarten programs is not very encouraging, either. Those that have been carefully evaluated are shown to have produced significant improvement in IQ scores and languages scores at the end of the intervention period. But in almost all instances, assessments at the end of the following year have found fewer differences between treated and untreated groups. With further follow-ups, these differences almost completely disappeared. For example, in the Perry Preschool Project (Weikart, 1967), at the end of the nursery year the experimental group scored a significant number of IQ points higher on the Stanford-Binet than did the control group. By the end of second grade, however, the difference was less than two points, representing a smaller advantage than the experimental group had before entering the project. Even in those programs where some gains in IQ or language were sustained beyond the period of active intervention, they invariably decreased significantly from the level reached at the end of the special programs. However, in some instances results of primary-level achieve-ment tests did show some advantage for children who had had compensa-tory preschool programs. The Perry Project found significant differences in reading, arithmetic, language, and total achievement-test scores at the end of grade two. The experimental pupils scored on the average in the bottom 18 percent of the population; the controls scored in the bottom 5 percent. By the end of second grade, however, percentile ranks for the experi-mental groups were slightly lower than they had been at the end of first grade.

Even where slight gains were demonstrated by the experimental groups and retained beyond the intervention period, the gains became less and less marked with increased schooling, and at no time did either the mean IQ scores or the mean achievement scores reach the national average. Thus, the pupils remained at a disadvantage even after varied forms of intensive early training.

The assumption that a year or even two of some form of prekinder-garten experience can bring the poorly prepared learner to a level of academic readiness sufficient to enable him to function "normally" without further special help in his later schooling no longer appears tenable. Current efforts are moving both downward—beginning compensatory programs at ever-younger ages—and upward—extending compensatory procedures into the primary and intermediate grades.

As the absolute numbers (and in the large cities the proportion) of disadvantaged children increases, more and more teachers are confronted by pupils whom they do not know how to teach. Although there are certainly some in the teaching profession who are disinterested in, prejudiced against, or even hostile toward the pupils, the majority of teachers want to do an effective job and want their pupils to learn. What they find, however, is that their training has not prepared them for the task and their knowledge is inadequate to it. What they know and know how to do doesn't work. Their efforts too often meet with failure. They become frustrated and externalize the blame for their failure on the pupils' lack of ability, poor backgrounds, disinterested parents, and inadequate preparation. Those teachers who remain on the job respond by going more slowly, making lesser and fewer demands, and becoming more concerned with the pupils' behavior than with their accomplishment. Mandated grade-level curricula, which require all pupils to master a common set of learnings in a given year, add to the teacher's problems because the pupils' lack of basic learning skills slows their pace in coping with the required material.

The problems of the teacher are further exacerbated by the mobility of the pupils. In some schools, there may be almost 100 percent turnover during any one school year; a 40–50 percent turnover is fairly common in slum-area schools. Some evidence indicates that the pupils who remain within a single school from grade three through grade six achieve at higher levels than those who change schools. The greater the number of changes, the lower the achievement (Justman, 1965). To what extent these findings reflect the deleterious effects of school discontinuity and to what extent they reflect differential mobility rates among different population groups is not known.

The discontinuity between the world of the school and the child's own world is daily confronted by the teacher just as it is by the child. The teacher believes that his task is to enable the children to acquire a repertoire of skills and knowledges that will free them from the constraints of their slum or ghetto life. But neither his training nor his experience has provided him with the means to achieve his goals. Blaming the teacher for the pupils' failure is no more justified than blaming the pupils or their parents. If one is to lay the blame anywhere, perhaps it should be laid at the door of the professional educators, the curriculum builders and teacher trainers, not because they have failed to produce effective answers, but because for too long they have failed to recognize the problems and initiate experimental procedures to search for answers. Even today the literature is replete with pious words about positive attitudes and great expectations, but devoid of tested procedures that would give teachers concrete help.

FUTURE DIRECTIONS

It is too soon to determine the possible effects of early and extended intervention: too many programs have not been clearly specified; curricular procedures are still being developed; and convictions about what programs should be vary widely. From the limited data available, one is led to hypothesize that the academic achievement of disadvantaged learners can be raised more effectively through a combination of the various current approaches than through any one of them: home programs for very young children (ages zero–three) through training mothers to provide them with necessary early learnings; carefully planned and structured procedures at the nursery and kindergarten level that stress development in the areas essential to further academic learning (Bereiter & Engelmann, 1966); and continuing individually tailored programs through the early and intermediate grades. This combination may enable a larger proportion of children to proceed with relative success through the higher grades.

But to reach the majority of our disadvantaged population, a much wider range of experimental programs will have to be initiated, programs that go well beyond the present conception of schools and schooling. Rapid technological developments suggest more than new methods of teaching. They suggest the possibility for more individualized progress, greater opportunities for self-pacing and self-teaching, and the added advantage of learning under conditions of immediate feedback without confronting the negative reinforcement of the frustrated teacher. The new technology also opens up possibilities of approaching early learning through channels other than the printed page with procedures that engage the learner actively in learning by way of varied media. Extensions of what Moore (1965) calls the "responsive environment" may enable at least some children who are now failing to become successful at learning as they find that they can control what happens and be reinforced by their power as well as their success. But the school may have to go still further: it may have to open its walls into the community, using it as a learning laboratory. New and far more effective procedures than are now available will have to be found for working with parents and community agencies and for using existing services outside the formal school setting to bolster the development of learning abilities.

There are programs for training prospective teachers within slum schools to bring them to a closer understanding of the lives and learning styles of their pupils. Inservice programs, summer workshops, and various institutes are now available for similar purposes. But before teachers can become truly effective in the classroom, such efforts will have to be bolstered with concrete procedures and materials. Unfortunately, many more ways of working will have to be experimentally tested before teachers can be given the help they need.

PLURALISM AND
THE COMMON CURRICULUM

Children bring with them to school different traditions, different cultural mores, even different cognitive strengths and weaknesses. Recent evidence suggests not only that differences in cognitive functions are related to social-class level, but also that particular abilities are more or less highly developed in particular ethnic groups, regardless of social class (Lesser, Fifer, & Clark, 1968). When middle- and lower-class Jewish, Chinese, Negro, and Puerto Rican children were compared on verbal ability, reasoning, number, and space, the middle-class children within each group performed at a higher level on all tests, but the patterns of high-low performance were similar within ethnic groups. For example, in the Jewish group middle-class children excelled lower-class children on all four scales, but both groups scored highest on verbal, second on number, third on reasoning, and lowest on space. In the Chinese group, both SES levels scored highest on space, only slightly lower on reasoning and number, and lowest on verbal performance. What are the implications of these differences for the school? Despite protestations of a belief in pluralism, in a many-faceted culture allowing for great variation in ways of living, the schools have traditionally attempted to make the children as similar as possible by exposing them to a common body of knowledge and a common set of skills. Children are evaluated in terms of their status vis-a-vis national norms. The only concession that is made to individual differences is to vary the pace, or "water down" the required content, making it less abstract and less conceptual, more concrete and applied. How then does or can the school support the notion of pluralism? What allowances can it or, for that matter, should it make to accommodate subgroup as well as individual differences? For example, treating English as a second language in the initial learning stages for foreign-language- and dialect-speaking children is now being tried in several schools. Similarly, one may be able to develop approaches that capitalize on the strengths of a particular ethnic group.

But even if compensatory programs successfully prepare the slum or ghetto child to meet both the academic and social demands of the school and to enter the middle-class world, is this a desired outcome? Loud voices are currently raised in strong opposition to such a goal. They decry the middle-class curriculum as inappropriate for lower-class children and do not want them to be reconditioned into ways of life that require them to replace their own values and mores with those of the dominant culture. Compensatory programs are viewed as denigrating and as further attempts on the part of the dominant society to rob the child of his identity. In a recent publication (Spache, 1968) put out by the highly respected National Society for the Study of Education, one finds this paragraph:

> *Reading well and widely (particularly in good literature) may itself be a middle-class status symbol . . . are . . . standards of skill and appropriate materials not reflections of the teachers' middle-class values? Reading instruction may need to be perceived as training in a tool which is to be used to achieve the pupil's own goals and social and vocational aims rather than as training in a skill which should be possessed to a maximum degree by all pupils [p. 246].*

There is, of course, the possibility that the current "common curriculum" fails to provide the learnings that will be most universally useful in a technological society characterized by constant, rapid changes and a high rate of obsolescence, not only of material goods but also of the means of communication, knowledge, ideas, and, indeed, ways of life.

These questions are currently generating often acrimonious debate. It is certainly in keeping with a pluralistic philosophy to support the contention that black children should be exposed to learnings that reinforce their unique characteristics and values and that give them a sense of pride in their own identity and a sense of power and control over their environment. By the same token, however, such procedures could, if not carefully tempered, build even higher walls around the black ghetto, curtailing the individual's options in determining his own future and widening the rift between white and black.

Despite the importance of these issues, despite the ferment they have created, and even despite-the direct effects their resolution will have on school control, organization, staffing, and curriculum, the teacher in the classroom, be he black or white, of lower- or middle-class origins, will still have to teach the children to read and write and manipulate numbers (unless or until it is decided that even these skills are not essential in our age of computers and television screens). And he will still have to confront the problem of finding effective ways of teaching these skills to disadvantaged youngsters.

To find these ways will require imagination and a willingness to break with existing educational models. It will be necessary to test these ideas through a series of complex, interrelated, and carefully planned and controlled experimental programs. It is not enough to devise exciting ideas from theoretical concepts. These must be translated into materials and carefully specified procedures. They must take account of relevant factors in the learners, in the school, and in the community, and they must be carefully assessed. It may be a slow and costly process, but as an alternative to the cost of our present failures, it may be cheap indeed.

38

Studies of the development of racial awareness, racial identification, and racial preference in both Negro and white children present a consistent pattern. Learning about races and racial differences, learning one's own racial identity, learning which race is to be preferred and which rejected—all these are assimilated by the child as part of the total pattern of ideas he acquires about himself and the society in which he lives. These acquired patterns of social and racial ideas are interrelated both in development and in function. The child's first awareness of racial differences is found to be associated with some rudimentary evaluation of these differences. Furthermore, as the average child learns to evaluate these differences according to the standards of the society, he is at the same time required to identify himself with one or another group. This identification necessarily involves a knowledge of the status assigned to the group with which he identifies himself, in relation to the status of other groups. The child therefore cannot learn what racial group he belongs to without being involved in a larger pattern of emotions, conflicts, and desires which are part of his growing knowledge of what society thinks about his race.

Many independent studies enable us to begin to understand how children learn about race, how they identify themselves and others in terms of racial, religious, or nationality differences, and what meaning these differences have for the growing child. Racial and religious identification involves the ability of the child to identify himself with others of similar characteristics, and to distinguish himself from those who appear to be dissimilar.

The fact that young Negro children would prefer to be white reflects their knowledge that society prefers white people. White children are generally found to prefer their white skin—an indication that they too know that society likes whites better. It is clear, therefore, that the self-acceptance or self-rejection found so early in a child's developing complex of racial ideas reflects the awareness and acceptance of the prevailing racial attitudes in his community.

Some children as young as three years of age begin to express racial and religious attitudes similar to those held by adults in their society. The racial and religious attitudes of sixth-graders are more definite than the attitudes of pre-school children, and hardly distinguishable from the attitudes of high-school students. Thereafter there is an increase in the intensity and complexity of these attitudes, until they become similar (at least, as far as words go) to the prevailing attitudes held by the average adult American.

The racial ideas of children are less rigid, more easily changed, than the racial ideas of adults. It is probable, too, that racial attitudes and behavior are more directly related among adults. The racial and religious attitudes of a young child may become more positive or more negative as he matures. The direction these attitudes will take, their intensity and form of expression, will be determined by the type of experiences that the child is permitted to have.

Who teaches a child to hate and fear—or to respect as his equal—a member of another race? Does he learn from his mother and father? From his schoolteachers? From his playmates? Or does he learn from those impersonal but pervasive teachers, the television set, the moving picture, the comic book? Probably it is all of these that teach him to love or to hate. Studies indicate that such attitudes are determined not by a single factor but by all of the child's experiences.

When white children in urban and rural sections of Georgia and in urban areas of Tennessee were compared with children attending an all-white school in New York City, their basic attitudes toward the Negro were found to be the same (Horowitz, 1936). Students of the problem now generally accept the view that children's attitudes toward Negroes are determined chiefly "not by contact with Negroes but by contacts with the prevailing attitudes toward Negroes." It is not the Negro child, but the *idea* of the Negro child, that influences children.

Rarely do American parents deliberately teach their children to hate members of another racial, religious, or nationality group. Many parents, however, communicate the prevailing racial attitudes to their children in subtle and sometimes unconscious ways. Parents often forget their influence on the formation of their children's opinions and frequently deny that they have ever said anything to their children tht would encourage race prejudice. A group of southern white children told one investigator (Horowitz) that their parents punished them most often when they went to play with Negro children who lived in their neighborhood. He concluded that the development of attitudes of southern children toward Negroes has its source in community pressures brought to bear upon the parents, who then transmit them to their children. The particular way in which this happens is frequently forgotten by the parents, and eventually they develop a system of rationalizations to support their behavior and the behavior they impose upon their children.

It is possible that these community pressures are transmitted to children not only through their own parents, but also, as they grow older, through their friends and their friends' parents. Some investigations suggest that the attitudes of parents have a greater influence on younger children than on older ones. From about ten years of age, the child is being more directly influenced by the larger environment; if his racial attitudes and behavior are still consistent with those of his parents, it is probably because the larger environment agrees with his parents.

There is no consistent evidence that parents always play a crucial continuing role in the transmission of the prevailing racial attitudes in their children. Studies dealing with the attitudes of Negro children show that these children generally have negative attitudes toward other Negroes. It would seem unlikely that the negative attitudes of these children toward their own group are a result of the direct influence of their parents. Although some Negro parents have mixed feelings about their own racial status, the average parent would be careful in the way he expressed such feelings in the presence of his children. But some children of a minority group may be sensitive to the unexpressed racial feelings of their parents. An occasional offhand disparaging remark, an occasional overheard adult conversation, may contribute to the development of the child's racial feelings. On the whole, however, it seems that Negro children, like white children, get their negative attitudes toward other Negroes as much from the outside community as from the home.

At a parent-teacher meeting devoted to the development of racial attitudes in young children, a white mother arose to present a problem. She said that she and her husband, concerned with problems of racial justice, had sought to provide for their children the type of democratic home atmosphere that would foster a sensitivity for and appreciation of the equality and dignity of all human beings. She had friends of different racial and religious groups who visited her home and whom she visited with her children. Nevertheless, her oldest child had come home from the first grade of school with disparaging remarks about Negroes. Once he used a particularly offensive racial epithet. She and her husband were disturbed about this and wanted to know how such a thing could happen and in what ways they had failed as parents. The guest speaker at the meeting pointed out that, once her child left the sheltered environment of the home, he was naturally exposed to other social influences. This child was learning about the attitudes that existed among the majority of his playmates and a few dominant individuals in his class who had been influenced by their parents or other adults.

Certain evidence seems to indicate that parents who are primarily preoccupied with their personal status, and parents who impose upon their children harsh and rigid forms of discipline, are likely to foster in their children intense prejudices toward individuals of another race or religion. Some students claim that children who are personally secure and happy are not as likely to develop rigid prejudices. But other observers maintain that it is misleading to explain the development of prejudices in terms of the personal happiness or security of the child within his family. Many children, growing up in the normal American environment, do not have the opportunity to learn any attitude except one that stereotypes individuals of a different race.

In understanding the growth and elaboration of racial attitudes in children, one must emphasize that the many institutionalized forms of prejudice are of primary importance. The various types of racial segregation that children observe—must take part in—are crucial in the formation of their racial attitudes. A white child who attends a segregated school from his earliest grades up through high school, or a child who is told that he must not play with Negro children because they are dirty or delinquent, is being taught that there are people who are "inferior" and that he himself is "superior" by virtue of race or skin color alone.

A study of 173 New York City children between the ages of seven and thirteen showed that the judgments of children are more likely to be influenced by the attitudes of their classmates than by the authority of their teacher. The investigator asked these children to estimate the length of lines, to compare one line with a standard line, and to match lines with lines of different lengths. These tasks varied in difficulty. The experiment was designed so that small groups of children were pitted against other groups, an individual child against a number of other children, and a child against his teacher. Always the majority group was instructed, unknown to the individual subject, to give answers that were sometimes obviously incorrect. The investigator found that an individual child, confronted with the fact that the majority of his own classmates were unanimous in making an incorrect judgment, tended to modify his own judgments according to the opinion of the rest. The younger children were more dependent upon the group than were the older children. (Berenda, 1950) On the other hand, when a teacher tried to influence the child's judgment by a clearly false opinion, not one of the children followed the teacher's judgment completely. The role of the teacher in influencing the opinion of these children was therefore much weaker than the role of their classmates. Although this particular study was not concerned directly with the problem of racial attitudes, it suggests that children of this age group are more likely to be influenced by friends of their own age than by adults.

There have been no consistent conclusions about the effect of individual teachers and the role of the school in the fostering of good intergroup relations among children. While there might be some question concerning the effects of direct attempts at indoctrination by teachers—particularly when these attempts are clearly in contradiction to observable facts—the influence by subtle and indirect means of adults on children's attitudes cannot be discounted. A school may have an excellent over-all human-relations program, but individual teachers with negative racial attitudes may present such a program in a way that cancels out the positive aims of the larger program. Allport and Kramer, after studying the racial attitudes of college undergraduates, concluded that, although many of their subjects remembered learning something about racial attitudes in elementary and high school, they could not recall anything specific. About 8 percent reported that they had learned some "scientific facts about race." These were generally the less prejudiced individuals.

Although many people continue to believe that schools and teachers have a direct influence on the development of racial attitudes in children, this view is not supported by any substantial body of evidence. There have not been enough specific studies of the role of the schools in the development of racial attitudes of children; the real extent of their influence is therefore unknown. A cautious interpretation of the available evidence suggests that the influence of schools and teachers is more passive than active. For the most part, educators seem to approach this problem somewhat in the way in which they approach the problem of sex education. Rather than taking the leadership in educational programs designed to develop more positive racial attitudes, the schools tend to follow the existing community prejudices. The few experiments in dynamic race-relations programs as integral parts of the school curriculum reflect the general inadequacy of our educational institutions in this area. They also show what could be done if teachers and other school officials were sufficiently alerted to their social and educational responsibility.

Given this tendency to passivity on the part of our schools and educators, episodes demonstrating the prejudice of individual teachers may become important factors in the development of negative racial attitudes in children.

It has been observed that lower-class children are more likely to react with violence and anti-social behavior, since they are generally taught to defend themselves by striking first. Aggressive patterns of behavior are a part of the struggle for survival within the lower-class pattern of living. The self-destructive implications of overt aggression and violence in reaction to minority status are less threatening to lower-class Negro adolescents and adults, because they have less to lose than middle- or upper-class Negroes.

The middle-class Negro parent in preparing his child for life teaches him—at least in words—that in spite of racial restrictions and taboos he is in fact equal to whites. Children of this class are trained to control their impulses, to adhere strictly to the demands of respectability, to avoid negative contacts with whites—in short, to keep out of trouble. This parent-child relationship would not be consistent with direct expressions of aggression, overt violence, or anti-social behavior.

The major parental pressure upon the middle-class or upper-class Negro child is the demand that he be a living refutation of the stereotyped picture of the primitive and inferior Negro. Parents sometimes attempt to conceal from their children the lower status of the Negro people in American society. They believe that they thus protect their children from the deep psychological scars resulting from an awareness of belonging to a rejected minority group. However, this tendency is not without its high human costs. These parents often require that their children behave with unrealistic virtues; that they be compulsively clean; that they repress normal aggressive impulses or sexual curiosity; that they assert racial equality by over-compensatory academic, artistic, or athletic achievements. Sometimes this results in exceptional achievement. At other times, when the particular child is not endowed with the necessary intelligence or talent, it results in a psychological casualty.

THE SHORTCHANGED CHILDREN OF SUBURBIA **39** ALICE MIEL
EDWIN KIESLER, JR.

How well is suburbia—the home of vast numbers of Americans, and increasingly the trend-setter for the entire population—preparing the young people of today for life in the future? Lacking first-hand contact, how do suburban children learn about human difference, and what do they think about it? How can they acquire respect for persons whom their middle-class society brands less acceptable than themselves? And what can adults—parents, school administrators, classroom teachers, community organizations—do to groom the coming generation for a proper role in a multicultural society?

Some time ago, a group of us—teachers, sociologists and researchers from Teachers College, Columbia University—set out to shed some light on these questions. We focused on New Village as a reasonably typical American suburb.

Of course, we knew that New Village was not a precise counterpart of every suburb. No single community could be, for each has developed according to his own pattern. Some were built on open land, others grew up around an existing community. Some belong almost wholly to one social class, others have at least a small range of socio-economic difference. In some, one faith predominates; in others, religious groups are more evenly represented. Some have stopped growing while others are still increasing in size. Yet, all seem to have a number of characteristics in common. They consist almost wholly of young adults and children. Fathers commute, and mothers dominate the children's upbringing. Adults have at least a high-school education and own their homes. Parents are greatly concerned with how their youngsters are raised. In all these respects, we found, New Village strongly resembles suburbs around the country.

SOME GENERAL IMPRESSIONS

The study points up certain troubling aspects of growing up in New Village—and, by extension, in any suburban community. To begin with, it was found that extraordinary effort was required to bring about any encounter between a child of the suburbs and persons different from himself. In big cities today—as in the small towns of the past—youngsters are virtually certain to encounter ethnic, economic or racial diversity, in the course of their school or social life. But the suburban child's life and social contacts are far more circumscribed; in fact they are almost totally controlled by his parents, whether or not the parents recognize this. He depends on his mother to chauffeur him wherever he goes. As a result, he knows little beyond his own home, the very similar homes of friends, the school, and the inside of the family car; he is largely insulated from any chance introduction to a life different from his own.

Second, we observed that children learn to be hypocritical about differences at a very early age. At first, many said things like "I wouldn't care if a person were white or black, I'd play with him if I liked him." But on further probing, it became evident that this supposed tolerance was only skin-deep: when the same children were given any test which involved just such a choice, they almost invariably shied from choosing the Negro. The prejudices of their society were still very much with them, but they had had it drilled into them that it was "not nice" to express such feelings.

Third, group prejudices, of whatever nature, evidently take root early and go deep. Many stereotypes about race and religion cropped up even among the youngest children. Six- and seven-year-olds, for instance, pictured Negroes as poor, threatening or inferior. With such early beginnings, any fight against prejudice is bound to be a difficult uphill struggle.

Fourth, and more hopefully, the study found a good many parents united in desiring more emphasis on certain kinds of human difference. For example, they were greatly in favor of children's learning about nationality differences; many also hoped the schools would help youngsters achieve respect for other faiths and even teach what the beliefs of these faiths were.

Finally, it appears that one area of human difference is almost completely ignored in the American suburb. Many parents and teachers were found eager to bridge religious differences; many recognized, however uneasily, the need for discussion of racial differences. But with a few notable exceptions, neither parents nor schools were facing up to economic inequality. Occasionally, a social-studies class would take up the poor of other nations, or a fund drive would focus attention on the less fortunate in the United States; but the fact that there were impoverished families within a stone's throw of New Village was seldom noted, and how they got there or what kept them impoverished was seldom investigated.

The overall impression one carries away is that something is missing in New Village. People who have moved to the suburbs since the Second World War often say proudly that they did so "for the children." And, of course, the children of communities like New Village do have a host of advantages, by no means all of them material. But in one aspect of their education suburban children are underprivileged. Though other races, other nationalities, other generations have a great deal to teach them, there is little in their education, formal or otherwise, to familiarize them with the rich diversity of American life.

In this sense, despite the many enviable features of their environment, the children of suburbia are being shortchanged.

RICH AND POOR

"Goodness, they really don't know much about poor white children, do they? They don't see many, I guess."

A New Village teacher was talking about her fifth-grade students. She had just heard them comment on some pictures our Teachers College study group was using to sample their knowledge of persons with economic backgrounds different from their own. These pictures showed three poor children from one of the Southern states, leaning against a fence. The girls' hair was stringy and unkempt, their faces were dirty, their dresses ill-fitting and soiled. Almost all the New Village children quickly rejected the idea that the children were Americans. "You can tell by looking at them. . . . No white children in our country would look like these three."

These comments point up one of the most suprising—and appalling —gaps in suburban children's knowledge about differences among people. The children of New Village knew almost nothing about persons less well off than themselves. Moreover, their attitude toward the less fortunate was almost insufferably patronizing—a response that was not surprising in view of the great emphasis placed on material wealth in New Village, as in most suburbs. It is, of course, possible that the children's attitude is changing with the current "war on poverty." But such a shift would also presuppose a changed climate in the home or the school—neither of which, at the time of our study, was doing much to fill in the blanks in the children's knowledge.

For any New Village child to know a person from an underprivileged class would be highly unusual, for the simple reason that there are few such persons around. New Village has little range of income. According to our sociologist's profile of the community, 21 per cent of heads of families there were professional people, 27 per cent were proprietors or managers, 20 per cent clerical employees, 16 per cent skilled workers and 12 per cent semi-skilled workers. Only 3 per cent were unskilled, and only 1 per cent unemployed.

The same kind of pattern was found in housing. New Village can be loosely divided into four different types of neighborhoods, each more or less homogeneous economically, but none of the four is really poor. First there are the prestige areas, where the land is hilly and wooded, and zoning restrictions require lots of at least one or two acres; here live mostly professionals, in homes valued from $25,000 upward. Second best are various developments, each with roughly identical houses, some occupied by upper-middle-class families and valued at $20,000 to $25,000, others by lower-middle-class and in the $15,000 range. A third type of neighborhood is mixed, reflecting the invasion of a former small village by suburban development; here there are both old and new houses, the latter generally valued at about $15,000. The fourth type and the least desirable grouping consists of older houses and apartments located within business areas along highways. In such a neighborhood live New Village's handful of Negroes.

Although New Village children were not acquainted with poverty, they certainly knew all about the slightest gradations among the community's residents—and so did their parents. Interviews showed that adults paid close attention to neighbors' earnings and possessions and were extremely money-conscious. They not only were aware of the different neighborhoods, but rated them in economic terms. Outright economic snobbery was sometimes apparent. "Something must be done to prevent small homes from being built next to large, beautiful ones," was a frequent comment.

Some parents wished their children could come to know impoverished families—for the rather ironic reason that they thought it would make the youngsters more appreciative of what they had at home. Conversely, a few parents were displeased that their children rubbed elbows with those of more affluent families in the community: it made them envious of the others' status. Still others practiced social climbing through the children. In discussing dances sponsored by one school, a teacher commented, "Parents looked on these dances as social opportunities for their children—a chance to move up the social ladder." In the wooded, hilly areas, where homes are most expensive, parents "pushed" their children socially at an early age, another teacher noted.

Perhaps the most flagrant instance of parental money-mindedness in relation to children occurred in a class election. One father openly attempted to help his daughter "buy" a class office. He gave her money to buy a candy bar for each voter—and was indignant when the school forbade her to distribute them.

In some cases, teachers told us, children managed to rise above these influences. Referring to the most affluent wooded-hill area and a less prosperous neighborhood across the highway from there, one teacher commented, "The children from the two sections help each other and learn from each other." Another said, "If the highway weren't so difficult to cross, the two groups would draw together even more."

The consensus of teachers, however, was that the children, like the adults, rated their peers in terms of economics. "Quite a little break exists between the children in the developments and the others," said one. Differences were noted openly. "In 'Show and Tell' it comes out that 'He doesn't have as much money as we do,' or 'They don't have as many cars as we do,' " another teacher reported. Still another teacher recalled the time a student asked another, "Why don't you get dressed nicer for school?" "It didn't bother the other boy at all," the teacher added.

Some of the teachers were quite disheartened by their students' values. "They are greatly concerned with material gain—lots of getting and little giving on their part," one wrote. Others told of students who constantly boasted of what they had at home—"cars, maids, toys, etc." A discouraged third-grade teacher told of the time her husband brought in a horned grebe, a water bird, which he had found on the road and was taking to a sanctuary. "I had hoped our careful observation of the bird and my talk on our responsibility to our nation's wildlife would be felt a little," the teacher reported. "But they were principally interested in how much money a bird like that would bring and how one could shoot such a bird since they were so fast in protecting themselves in water."

MATERIALISM BEGINS AT HOME

Our talks with students, and with teachers about students, revealed an early and widespread concern with such material matters as zoning, preserving neighborhoods, keeping out "undesirables"—all of which, of course, preoccupied their parents. Older children, for all we know, might have been more critical of the adults' values, but the elementary-school youngsters seemed to accept them unhesitatingly. One child wrote on a questionnaire: "People should cooperate about doing something to stop crowding because all the people from the city are moving in and it is getting too crowded."

During one stage of the study, children were asked: "If you had to move to a new house or apartment, where would you like it to be?" A considerable percentage mentioned areas where children would be "clean and nice," and houses bigger. Some said they were dissatisfied with their present neighborhoods because of the kinds of people living there.

In another set of interviews, we asked children to list three wishes they would most like to see fulfilled. We then classified the answers according to whether the wishes concerned the children themselves or others, and whether they were for material objects—a go-cart, a football, money, etc.—or for nonmaterial ones such as happiness in the child's own family or eliminating illness in the world. In some schools, as many as 60 percent of the students named either two or three wishes involving themselves alone. Interestingly, however, exclusively material wishes were listed less often by children of the more affluent families.

One of the more startling disclosures of the study came with still another test, originally designed to explore children's attitudes toward racial difference. Second- and third-grade children were shown pictures of two well-dressed Negro girls and two rather sloppily dressed white girls, and were asked whose party they would rather go to. To our astonishment, economic considerations seemed to outweigh racial ones. The majority said they would prefer the Negro girls. "I would go to the party of the girls who are dressed in pretty clothes," is the way one child put it. Another said, "The Negroes look like they have more toys so most children would want to go to their party."

Later, fifth-grade children were asked to comment on the answers given by the younger ones. "It is true, most children don't usually choose Negroes for friends," one fifth-grader said, "but they are thinking of themselves when they choose a party—they want an enjoyable time, and that is the most important thing."

"Do you mean that most children would not care who is giving a party, so long as they have a good time?" the interviewer asked.

"Sure," was the reply. "If the party is going to be fun, and if they were invited to one given by children who had a lot of toys and could show them a good time, they wouldn't care if they like the ones giving the party or not."

Added another: "Yes, most would choose to go to the party given by the Negroes, because they look as if their party would be fancier and more fun because they look rich and well dressed."

And one boy said flatly: "Most kids would want to go where they could get the most."

SILENCE IN THE CLASSROOM

In the face of disquieting attitudes like these, what are the schools of suburbia doing to teach children about economic difference, its causes and consequences? On the basis of our study in New Village, the answer must be: very little. In none of the classrooms we visited and in none of the reports drawn up for us by teachers in the town's seven elementary schools did we find any real attention devoted to the subject. Although poverty was often touched upon in discussing other nations, the issue was carefully sidestepped in studying American society. Yet the teachers themselves agreed that this area ought to be explored. In the very first stage of the project, more than one-fourth of them suggested that the socio-economic structure of New Village was itself worth studying.

With the need so widely admitted, why was not more done? We cannot be sure; but it may well be that teachers excused themselves from this responsibility because the topic simply did not seem to fit anywhere into the established curriculum. Classroom study of the local community concentrated on so-called community helpers, such as police and firemen, and ignored how others earn their living; discussions of nationwide matters focused on "current events," military and governmental history, or patterns of manufacturing and trade. Textbooks skimmed over the subject of economic inequality, and teachers had no other prepared materials to draw upon. Even more important, perhaps, teachers themselves frequently felt insecure about the subject. Being in a lower economic group than many of their pupils, they did not always feel on solid ground in discussing wealthier persons—or poorer ones, either.

A few did attempt more than a superficial exploration of economic differences. One sixth-grade teacher, for instance, devoted several class discussions to Rudyard Kipling's *Captains Courageous*, a tale in which a millionaire's pampered son falls off a yacht and is saved from the sea by a Gloucester fisherman. The teacher tried to help the children understand both the economic gulf between the boy and the fisherman and the socio-economic gap that accompanied it. The major lesson, as the teacher explained it, was "what democracy means in interpersonal relations between those who have great wealth and those who do not."

Similar ground could have been broken by other teachers. Yet most shied from such discussions, apparently because they felt that attitudes could not be changed by classroom teaching.

PORTRAIT OF THE SUBURBAN CHILD

To understand the attitudes of suburban youngsters toward human difference, one needs to know something about their values and their family milieu. For it appears that this sort of influence has as much bearing on how they regard human diversity as do their more precisely measurable feelings about Negroes, Jews, poor people or foreigners.

To draw a general profile of the suburban child and his setting, we used not only our findings in New Village, but also comparative data from other suburbs and from cities and rural areas. These comparisons indicate that while many of our conclusions apply solely to the suburban child, some may well be true of many or most children throughout the country.

As we have already seen, the child of suburbia is likely to be a materialist and somewhat of a hypocrite. In addition, he tends to be a striver in school, a conformist, and above all a believer in being "nice," polite, clean and tidy. Besides dividing humanity into the black and the white, the Jew and the Christian, the rich and the poor, he also is apt to classify people as "smart" or "dumb," "clean" or "dirty," and "nice" or "not nice." What is more, he is often conspicuously self-centered.

In all these respects the suburban child patterns his attitudes and goals chiefly after those of his parents. But he can never be sure that he won't fall short of their hopes for him—that he is measuring up to the standards (especially of academic achievement, behavior and tidiness) that they have set for him. He is therefore likely to be an anxious child. Our study as well as other inquiries indicate clearly that to grow up in an American suburb today is not a wholly enviable lot.

There is a good deal of evidence to suggest that academic striving, conformism, self-centeredness, the urge for cleanliness and order, and related traits have a bearing on how children feel about persons different from themselves.

ACADEMIC STRIVING

One of the foremost yardsticks children use to measure differences is academic achievement. The suburban child is quite aware of who learns quickly and who does not, who gets good grades and who does not, who is articulate and who is not. And he judges the worth of his peers accordingly.

This observation should come as no surprise. Suburban parents, schools, and communities at large use the same yardstick; they fill the atmosphere with pressure for academic attainment. This came out clearly in interviews, though they were not intended to measure people's wishes for their children's education. When the sociologist on our team asked parents why they had moved to New Village, the largest single bloc said: "To have better schools"; and when he inquired what they liked best about the community, most mentioned the school system.

"Competition here is keen and strong; the push from the home is hard in some cases," one New Village teacher wrote. "We have kids here who are making 90 and 95, and still there is a terrific push and drive. If the child drops a few points, the mother is very much concerned and the child is made conscious of it."

Other teachers said that parents often became indignant when some child was put in a higher group on the grounds of ability and their own child was left out. The barest hint of partiality brought recrimination;

individual pupils couldn't even be allowed to take a book home unless there were enough books for all. And not infrequently, the teachers continued, parents paid their children for academic effort, offering rewards for high marks on report cards.

Not all the pressure came from home, however. Teachers themselves, we observed, constantly urged the children into academic striving. They, in turn, were being prodded from above. At a fall orientation meeting, school administrators told the teachers that while they must take an interest in children's moral, spiritual and social values, acquiring academic concepts was more important than any other accomplishment.

Teachers' responses to our project sometimes echoed this thinking. "How will this study influence children's values?" one teacher asked us. "We have to prepare children for passing examinations, you know." Our tests were not always welcomed. At one point, for example, we asked teachers to distribute cards with words like *parents, neighbors, friendly, lonesome, not popular*. Children were to choose one of the cards and illustrate the concept with a drawing or a few sentences, so as to give a clue to their feelings. Some teachers allowed the children to write responses, but not to draw. One refused to participate at all, because "it would encourage the children to waste time."

As for the children of New Village, they readily joined in the quest for grades. "One thing I've run into this year that really amazes me is the importance attached to marks," a new teacher commented to us. "If one child gets an 'E,' other children want to know why they didn't get one. . . . They're very, very pushy." Children also discriminated sharply against classmates who could not keep up the pace. As noted earlier, a Puerto Rican boy and a Norwegian girl were slighted because of poor reading skills. A few youngsters even refused to play with children who did not read or otherwise do as well as they themselves did.

WHAT CAN THE SCHOOLS DO?

We came away from New Village convinced that public schools in suburbia, and possibly elsewhere, could do more than any other institution to increase children's understanding of persons different from themselves, and to replace handed-down prejudices with attitudes more in keeping with the modern world. It would, of course, be naive to assume that the schools, acting alone, could completely sweep away the problems of inter-group understanding among suburban children. But teachers who approach the task with imagination, conviction, and willingness to invest time and effort can introduce alternate ways of thinking, feeling and acting from which children might choose. To this end, we recommend several important changes to schools, plus certain steps that PTAs, community groups, parents and others might also take in support of such improvements.

RACE IN THE CLASSROOM

Of the specific areas of human difference, the issue of race—both at home and abroad—is the one where improved teaching is most urgently needed today.

Any such improvement will require introducing new subject matter, since race prejudice is in part the fruit of ignorance. At the same time, it is necessary to aim directly at children's attitudes, for subject matter may eventually become obsolete, but attitudes usually stick for life. Here are some things that can be done:

1 The curriculum and the teacher can emphasize what is common to all humans—birth, marriage, death, the family, making a living, providing basic necessities. It should be noted that these things are handled differently by different people for physical, economic or other reasons, so that children will not feel differences are bad or unmentionable.

2 In social studies, broad perspectives can be offered on all races of mankind, to help students understand that some things—such as tradition, language and religion—often cut across racial lines.

3 At the same time, children must be taught to recognize that the predominantly white society surrounding them is very different from the rest of the globe, where the overwhelming majority of the population is non-white.

4 Customs of unfamiliar human groups should not be presented as quaint or fantastic. Instead, it should be shown that the ways of each group make sense within the context of its particular culture.

5 Facile generalizations about groups or regions can be exploded. For example, in studying Africa, emphasis can be placed on the continent's variety of countries and peoples, and on its many living styles, rural and urban, so that children will not stereotype Africans, or Negroes generally, as backward or uncivilized.

6 Slavery should not be presented as a phenomenon peculiar to Negroes in the United States, but as an institution with a long history involving many races, nationalities and civilizations. In any given class, a large number of children are likely to be ultimately descended from people in bondage: from serfs in medieval Europe or Czarist Russia, from Jews, who were slaves in Egypt, and so on.

7 Stereotypes can be combated through personal contact with Negroes (students or adult visitors), and through films or other information media. In this way, it can be shown that Negroes may be professionals as well as menials, that they may speak with a Brooklyn or Midwestern as well as a Southern accent, and so forth.

8   Students at every age level can be helped to understand, in their own terms, race issues in the news—riots, voting-rights suits, school desegregation drives, Negroes' demands for acceptance by labor unions, and so forth. Teachers should recognize that children already know something of these matters from television, but that they need to have them clarified.

9   Above all, the teaching at every level must reflect that Negro Americans are full and equal citizens, possessing the same rights and privileges as all other Americans.

Over and above curriculum improvements, spontaneously arising classroom incidents can also become a vehicle for learning about race. Both have their uses. An unplanned incident has an impact and immediacy which deliberately introduced abstract material can rarely match. On the other hand, to wait for such an incident may mean never tackling the subject at all.

To turn classroom incidents to full advantage, there must be a coherent policy for dealing with them. For example, teachers should be warned against disposing of bigoted talk by a simple reprimand, because this might cause children to cover up rather than change their attitudes. Teachers should also be instructed under what circumstances an incident might best be ignored, and should be helped to plan a course of action which will prevent a recurrence or even bring a positive gain.

LEARNING ABOUT ECONOMIC STATUS

One of the goals of every social-studies program should be to clarify that all persons do not share equally in material things, under the American system, but that all, nonetheless, are full and equal members of democracy, and that the work of some is no less worthy for being less highly rewarded than that of others.

In a classic example, long antedating our study, a teacher in a look-alike middle-class suburb used field trips to slums and mansions to make her second-graders understand that the amount of grass a child has at home has nothing to do with his human worth, but depends merely on what his daddy can pay for. We believe that, within the limit of children's understanding, teachers could get across many other points concerning economic difference just as eloquently—again both by deliberately introducing studies of other people or the human condition generally, and by making use of incidents as they occur. The following steps are suggested for all ages:

1 Develop basic concepts about economic wants and resources, and about the choices open to different families.

2 Instill some ideas of the work of the world: the usefulness of different occupations, how people are trained or educated for them, and what is pleasant, difficult and rewarding about each.

3 Show how our society values the individual, regardless of his occupation or income—including explanations, in terms appropriate to the particular age levels, of institutions like Social Security, Medicare, public welfare or housing aid. It is important to have children understand that democracy seeks to provide adequate schooling, housing, food and care for every child.

4 Help children realize that members of minority groups are to be found at various socio-economic levels, but that discrimination often deprives them of access to opportunities.

5 Explain the war on poverty and unemployment, using the best literature, films, photographs and magazine articles available. This important topic should be introduced in an early grade and taken up again each year, with more advanced concepts and broader insights each time. The lesson should focus initially on the fact that not all American children live as the suburban child does; but it should also touch on other nations, as well as the work of such agencies as the United Nations, UNESCO and the Peace Corps. In addition, historic aspects of poverty should be covered—the Depression, the sweat-shop and similar features of the American past.

6 Constantly seek to help children understand that Americans—partly through their own doing, partly through the good fortune of a land blessed with resources—are much better off than the rest of the world; and that most suburbs are even better off than much of America.

ESTHER LEVIN **40** BEGINNING READING: A PERSONAL AFFAIR

After several weeks of close observation, I found that thirteen children in my "heterogeneous" first-grade class of twenty-three were not ready to read. All thirteen came from educationally and economically deprived areas. Three of the thirteen were amost eight years old and were attending school for the first time. They had spent the first seven years of their lives in isolated farm or mining areas, where apparently there had been no pressure to enrol young children in school.

378 *disadvantaged and minority children*

All thirteen children had at least one of the following characteristics: fearfulness, excessive shyness, submissiveness, high distractibility, and short attention span. Most of the children were inarticulate. They spoke in monosyllables. Their speech patterns were poor: they constantly slurred and mispronounced words. Many of them could not use verbs and articles. The children were interested in learning to read, but they were so bewildered, so inarticulate, so fearful, and so unable to listen that the idea of reading may have seemed awesome to them.

If I concentrated on the readiness skills, this group would soon be ready for beginning reading. Or so I thought until I discovered that the children lacked not only skills that are ordinarily learned before school age but also skills essential to a readiness program.

The children were confused about the meaning of *top* and *bottom, up* and *down, above* and *below. Left* and *right* meant nothing to them. Numbers, letters, words, and sounds were all one big jumble. Directions brought no response. Listening to directions was, I suppose, like listening to commercials on TV: just bear with them, and they will soon go away.

The ability to distinguish likenesses and differences had to be developed from an almost primitive level. The children had no comprehension of the meaning of the words *shape, form, different, alike, same, first, last, row,* and *line.* Just remembering what to look for was a problem, and the problem of recall was compounded by ineptness with crayons, pencils, chalk, and paint.

SEARCH FOR A SOLUTION

Stories were read to the children and told and retold to encourage them to speak; however, their impoverished vocabularies blocked any but the most meager verbal response. Rhyming games were played, but from one second to the next the children forgot the rhyming words. Visual recall games were also unsuccessful. The children seemed to have no conception of what a word was. To them words seemed to be a conglomeration of sounds. At the children's hesitant dictation chart stories were written, but these group experiences were soon discarded because of the continuous struggle to muster words. Stories the teacher made up were also unsuccessful; they failed to hold the children's attention. A completely different approach was needed, but what was it to be?

I considered an extended readiness program, but decided against the idea. A more rapid approach seemed necessary to keep these children interested in learning to read. A structured program had to be found—one that emphasized the language arts and used the children's unique backgrounds. With such a program, perhaps, I could find a key to unlock the door to their dormant abilities.

Obviously each child needed individual attention. Yet it seemed desirable to teach these children in a group, since the rest of the class and the rest of the curriculum could not be neglected. Besides, in a group the children would learn from one another; each could act as a catalyst, and they would profit from one another's mistakes, achievements, and experiences. The children worked in a group of six or seven.

By stressing each child's name, I hoped to enhance his self-image and his self-confidence, and establish for him a beginning association between the spoken and the written word. Each child was given a name card with his name in large black manuscript writing. All the names were listed on a large chart, each name in a different color. Each child then matched the name on his card with his name on the chart. Almost immediately afterward, each child was able to find his name without his name card, using only the color cue. Soon the configuration of the name alone was sufficient, and the color cue was discarded.

As each child found his name on the chart, he was shown how to use his right hand in a left-to-right movement under his name. Special attention was called to names with the same beginning sounds. A great to-do was made about each name—the way it sounded, its configuration, the tall letters, the short letters, the tail letters, the hump letters, and the names that were on "one track." As might be expected, talking about names seemed to give the children a feeling of importance and satisfaction, and seemed to release vague and unexpressed thoughts about themselves and their families.

PICTURES AND STORIES

At the same time that the children were learning to read their names, they were being encouraged to speak in complete sentences. A collection of large colorful pictures of classic fairy tales was used to motivate the children to talk. One of these pictures was displayed as the teacher told the story. She deliberately made mistakes to test the children. They were quick to make corrections, and they began to speak more freely and in complete sentences. Another device used during story time was to ask some outlandish question about the story to stimulate the children to react and to respond.

In time, the children began to take an active part in the story-telling. Later, dramatization was used. The teacher or one of the more able children acted as narrator while other children acted out the various parts and supplied the necessary dialogue.

After the children had learned to recognize their names and had participated in story-telling, large colorful picture alphabet cards were adapted by the teacher for the children's use. Each letter of the alphabet was represented by a picture. The teacher wrote the name of the object pictured at the bottom of the card and always used her right hand in a left-to-right motion under the word as she said it or helped each child use this motion as he called the word. As the children identified and discussed each picture, they learned to look at words from left to right. They did not learn to read the words under these pictures until weeks later, but they did become aware of the fact that things—like children—have names and that these names can be written as words.

One day the children were talking about themselves and their families, and were expressing complete thoughts. It seemed a propitious time to let the children see their thoughts in print. Here is the conversation that took place that day:

> **TEACHER:** *Listen to what I say. I'm going to tell you something, and then I am going to write what I say on this paper (indicating large chart paper). The words that come out of my mouth are going to be written here. Listen and then watch me write, "I am a teacher." (Writes: "Mrs. Levin said, 'I am a teacher.'" Repeats sentence and uses left-to-right motion. Then looks at the first child.) Now, Susan, you tell me something, and I will write what you say on this paper. The words that come out of your mouth I will write here. They will be your words—only yours.*
>
> **SUSAN:** *(After a great deal of thought) I'se a girl.*
>
> **TEACHER:** *(Rightly or wrongly) I am a girl.*
>
> **SUSAN:** *I'se am a girl.*
>
> **TEACHER:** *(Writes and repeats) Susan said, "I am a girl." That's fine, Susan. These are your words. They came out of your mouth. (Susan is mute but beaming with pride.)*
>
> **TEACHER:** *(looks at Lisa) Now, you tell me something you want to say, and I will write it down here. They will be your words—only yours.*
>
> **LISA:** *Hello, Mrs. Levin.*
>
> **TEACHER:** *(Writes and reads) Lisa said, "Hello, Mrs. Levin." Very, very good, Lisa. (Now many hands were waving. The other children wanted to see their names in print and their thoughts on paper.)*
>
> **JANE:** *Hi, Mrs. Levin.*
>
> **HENRY:** *Howdy, Mrs. Levin.*
>
> **MAGGIE:** *Goodbye, Mrs. Levin.*
>
> **LARRY:** *Bye, bye, Mrs. Levin.*

As each child spoke, his name was written on the chart, and what he said was set off by quotation marks. It was then quite simple for each child to frame and read what he or she said. This was the children's first attempt to read a sentence. Success was theirs to cherish. The chart held a precious personalized though from each of them. Interest was maintained because they were eager to repeat what they had said. They were fascinated by the fact that what they had said was written in black and white on the chart.

Several thought-charts along these lines were made. Popeye and the Three Stooges were among the subjects the children chose. Always I emphasized the fact that each sentence belonged to a particular person. This personal involvement in the sentences plus the interest inspired by familiar subjects helped maintain the children's interest in learning to read. My fortuitous reading of the book *Spinster* (Ashton-Warner, 1958) gave further impetus to this personalized approach to reading.

On a later occasion, I introduced another technique through which the children learned to read their own personal words. Each child was told to think of a word he would like to learn to read. The word was to be written on a card five inches by eight inches and given to the child as his very own. Each child was asked to think carefully, to choose a word that was important to him. Here are the first seven words the children wanted to read: *lunch, telephone, lamp, television, bald-headed baby, monkey,* and *peaches.* Each child dictated his word and watched to see how it was written. Then each child was asked to tell why he wanted that word. Here are some of the reasons:

> *Ma telephone's not workin'.*
> *Ma mother's lamp's pretty.*
> *Telebision set's new.*
> *Duane's ma ball-head baby. He ma doll baby [Her brother].*
> *Monkeys they's funny.*
> *Ah hates peaches.*

The cards were kept in individual brown envelopes with the children's names on them and were given to the children only at reading time or on special occasions. Each day one additional word was written for each child. The same procedure was followed each time: the child thought of the word, he watched it being written, and he told why he wanted that word. After a child had three or four words in his envelope, any words that he repeatedly misread were discarded. Few words had to be eliminated.

MOUNTING PRIDE

As the words accumulated, so did the children's excitement. They pleaded to read their word cards to one another, to the school secretary, to the principal, to other teachers, and to their parents. Praise and encouragement were constant and came from all quarters: from the teacher, from children in the group, from other members of the class, and from the staff. Fear vanished as the children's feeling of security and power grew.

After each child had accumulated seven to ten words, another procedure was used for reinforcement. Words were taken from the cards at random and written on a chart. The children then identified and read their words and illustrated them whenever possible. Later, each child was given a notebook. The children dictated simple sentences to the teacher, who wrote them in the notebooks for the children to illustrate. This device, though successful, proved too cumbersome and too time-consuming, and was discarded.

Before long the children began to ask for the vocabulary from the basic textbooks used by the other children in the regular reading program. Soon all the first preprimer words were among their word cards. Words with the same beginnings were emphasized. When the children themselves began to find similarities in word beginnings, it became a great source of pride to them and a signal to the teacher that progress was truly being made.

MOUNTING CONFIDENCE

Now that the children had overcome their fear of the unknown and had gained confidence in themselves, they were eager to read books. Their enjoyment of their first book was full, and their success complete. As they progressed in a regular reading program, more phonics skills were introduced and there was less emphasis on sight recognition of words. The word cards continued to interest the children and were not entirely forgotten. The children's main interest, however, turned more and more to books.

By the end of the year, eight of the thirteen children had read three preprimers, one junior primer, one primer, and halfway through a first reader. One child left the school; the other four had read three preprimers, one junior primer, and halfway through a primer.

The experience was rewarding for the teacher and hopefully for the children as well. The personalized approach seemed to release unplumbed depths of interest, ability, and individuality. Having a set of word cards of his own gave each child the feeling of possession and a personal involvement that made reading something of unique importance. The teacher gained many insights into the children's backgrounds, problems, and personalities that would not have been possible otherwise.

Reading became an exciting adventure. Learning to read *monkey*, *peaches*, and *bald-headed baby* was far more exciting than reading *come*, *look*, or *see*. The phrase *bald-headed baby* had a zip to it that could never compare with "*look, Baby, look*," especially when the bald-headed baby was someone's own "doll baby" of a brother. The word *monkey* had far more personality than any little old stuffed bear. And the word *peaches*. How could you forget it when you "hates peaches!" To the children these words express love, laughter, and hate. These words have interest, color, and vitality. They are personal, positive, picturesque, and using them helped the children learn to read.

new directions in early childhood education

Two current trends in contemporary society are having a particularly marked impact on early childhood education. The first trend is an effort to apply educational technology to the problems of education, particularly the education of minority youth. It has resulted in refined procedures for teaching cognitive skills to young children and in programs for giving a cognitive head start to so-called disadvantaged children. The second trend involves the humanization of our culture—that is, the mounting emphasis on reducing the alienation individuals feel from the institutions designed to serve them. Part of this trend is an increasing concern with providing each member of our society with a life that is psychologically as well as materially rewarding. One result has been a redefinition of the relationship between school and society, shown in such efforts as individualized instruction and affectively toned materials and practices. Another has been the creation of programs that humanize the relationship between teacher and child and curricula that educate the total child, not just his cognitive capacities.

Change breeds controversy, and this current period of flux in early childhood education has produced a host of critics—critics of both the old and the new. The critics of the old make such points as the following: educational procedures are inefficient; children are bored and "turned off" to learning; children learn to conform rather than to pursue self-development in the schools. The critics of the new counter with such assertions as: the wisdom of the past is being discarded for mere fads; new educational procedures are not being carefully appraised; and schools that merely "turn on" children will not effectively prepare pupils for the realities of the outside world.

The first two articles in this section give a general perspective on what the critics are saying about current developments in early childhood education. Both essays are thoughtful and probing and maintain relative objectivity on a topic more noted for conviction than for objective appraisal. The remaining selections detail various proposals and procedures advocated by proponents of educational change. Each of them concerns an *aspect* of a total school program, rather than a total package for educational reform.

Article 41, Robert Havighurst's "Requirements for a Valid 'New Criticism'," criticizes the critics of traditional school practices. Havighurst notes that these critics have failed to credit schools for their many real contributions and pinpoints areas in which some proposals for school reform are shortsighted. He then offers some reform proposals of his own which, while attuned to the circumstances of economically disadvantaged children, are generally applicable to schools for middle-class children.

Joseph Featherstone, the author of Article 42, "Open schools II: Tempering a Fad," is an early advocate of bringing to American children the open-classroom procedures pioneered in the Infant Schools (preschools) of Great Britain. He discusses some of the dimensions characterizing open classrooms as well as the reasons why attempts to put into practice such ideals have often failed.

In Article 43, "Reach, Touch, and Teach," Terry Borton reviews some important new programs in affective education. "The new programs make what was covert the subject of overt discussion. . . . They legitimize feelings, clarify them for the student, and suggest a variety of behaviors which he can use to express them."

The selections by Robert Hess et al. (Article 44) and Peggy Lippitt (Article 45) concern the innovative use of personnel in a way that promotes the curriculum goals of the school and at the same time reduces the alienation of children from the adult world and from children in different age groups. Hess and his coauthors, who advocate "Parent Involvement in Early Education," make concrete suggestions regarding parent involvement, and review some of the research findings on the importance of the parent-child relationship as an influence on both the cognitive and affective development of their children. Both the Lippitt and the Hess articles discuss "cross-age tutoring," that is, programs in which older children participate in the teaching of younger children. In Article 45, "Children Can Teach Other Children," Lippitt takes a more enthusiastic view of the positive features and benefits of such tutoring schemes.

The selections by Dorris Lee (Article 46) and by Pat Anzalone and Dona Stahl (Article 47) present a set of interrelated concepts for humanizing the learning experiences of children. In Article 46, "What Is the Teacher's Role in Diagnostic Teaching?" Lee discusses specific procedures and roles that teachers can use to change their traditional classroom practices. Anzalone and Stahl supplement their discussion of "Creative Teaching" with a question-and-answer section on related teacher concerns and a self-test for teachers which serves as a useful practical evaluation.

behavioral objectives   *To be able to discuss the following points*

41   REQUIREMENTS FOR A VALID "NEW CRITICISM"
The validity of the views of educational critics regarding the problems of the schools and the basic orientation of these critics
Three school-reform proposals put forth by the critics and the two weaknesses in these proposals

The differences and similarities in the anarchist and activist approaches to educational change

The focus of the recent successful innovations teaching disadvantaged children

The relationship between motivation and learning and some examples of motivating situations

42 OPEN SCHOOLS II: TEMPERING A FAD

The effectiveness of content-oriented and open-classroom reforms

The differences between the superficial and profound educational use of the word "freedom"

The difference between legitimate and arbitrary authority and the reasons that legitimate authority can result in more actual guidance than exists in traditional schools

Arguments against the totally child-centered but passive approach to teaching

The relationship between liberalizing the repressive atmosphere of schools and the promotion of intellectual development

The relationship between teacher-training programs and school reform

The order of importance of educational problems in American society

43 REACH, TOUCH, AND TEACH

The influences that are causing educators to place greater emphasis on educating students' feelings

The differences between the curriculum reforms of the 1960s and present programs of educational reform

The nature and correlates of achievement motivation and the implication of such motivation in individuals for the society at large

The goals and procedures transferred from the psychotherapy setting to the classroom setting

Reasons for emphasizing nonverbal communication and games in education

The problems associated with feeling-oriented education, what the most fundamental problem is, and why this problem is considered to be fundamental

44 PARENT INVOLVEMENT IN EARLY EDUCATION

Parental influences associated with independence, achievement orientation, and assertiveness in children

Parental influences associated with a positive self-concept in children

The relationship between verbal ability and opportunities for verbal interaction at home

The relationship between maternal employment and the child's cognitive development

Five implications for day care of the research findings on parent-child attachment

Four explanations of how experiences of being disadvantaged affect the educational attainment and capabilities of young children

The five roles that parents can play in education programs for young children

The two major sets of findings resulting from the evaluation of programs where parents are involved in the education of their children

Procedures for engaging parents and sustaining their interest in involvement in early education and day-care programs

The value of cross-age helping relationships

45 CHILDREN CAN TEACH OTHER CHILDREN

Four educational goals promoted by having children help other children

Three studies of programs in which older students become helpers for children three years or more their juniors

The objectives of a program for training children to help other children or to receive help from other children

What teachers who are receiving or sending child assistants can do to facilitate a student-helping program

The benefits for teacher and student when the teacher's role is to support growth rather than maintain control

46 WHAT IS THE TEACHER'S ROLE IN DIAGNOSTIC TEACHING?

The importance of flexibility in diagnostic teaching and some ways in which a teacher in this tradition can show openness to change and variety

The four eventual goals to be achieved in reorganizing a classroom for diagnostic teaching, and the step that is most important

Four approaches to meeting individual learning needs, and the effectiveness of each

The teacher's role in stimulating learning, serving as a resource person, and asking questions

Confusing the means and the ends in teaching

The conditions determining whether or not evaluation is useful

41

REQUIREMENTS FOR A VALID "NEW CRITICISM"   ROBERT J. HAVIGHURST

On November 2, 1967, the New York City School Board reported the results of school achievement tests that had been given the preceding April to all pupils in the second and fifth grades. *The New York Times* reported the results in a page of tables and headlined the story on page one with "City Pupils Losing Ground in Reading and Arithmetic." Let us examine some of the test results.

The national average reading scores for these grades in April were 2.7 and 5.7 respectively. New York City school children averaged definitely below these levels, and there was some evidence that the New York City average was lower than it had been the year before.

The New York Times did not point out the fact that almost 300 of the 650 elementary schools had reading averages for their second grades of 3.0 or higher—that is, three-tenths of a year above the national average. Nor did *The Times* report that 44 elementary schools had reading scores for their fifth grades averaging 7.0 or more—1.3 of a year above the national average.

During that same month of November, the New York State Board of Regents called for "a concerted effort to reform urban education." The "Bundy Report" of the Mayor's Advisory Panel on Decentralization of the New York City Schools, which was published November 9, commences with the statement, "The New York City school system, which once ranked at the summit of American public education, is caught in a spiral of decline." *The Times* on that date referred in an editorial to what it called "the deterioration of New York's gigantic school system."

The Saturday Review for November 18 carried the following headlines on its front cover—*Requiem for the Urban School* and *Education in Washington: National Monument to Failure.*

The unwary middle-income parent, with several school-age children, is very likely to read these pieces in *responsible* newspapers and journals, and to decide to move to the suburbs, where he is assured by the same press that the schools are good. This person may live in Queens District 27, where 20 out of 27 schools are well above average in reading achievement, or in Queens District 26, where every one of the 24 elementary schools averaged at least .4 of a year above the national average at the second grade and at least one year above the national average at the fifth grade. But if he follows the *responsible* press, unless he explores the fine print, he is misled to suppose that he cannot find "good" public schools in the city.

Although these examples are taken from New York City, they can be duplicated in every large city. In some areas of the city, where the people of average and above-average income live, school achievement is above the national average, and about the same as it is in the "better" suburbs. In the low-income areas, school achievement is low.

HOW BAD IS URBAN EDUCATION?

How bad is education in our big cities? Does a dispassionate examination of the facts justify such widely publicized statements and slogans as "our children are dying," "requiem for urban education," "the end of the common school," "death at an early age," all applied to the work of the public schools in large cities?

We spend much more on education now than we did in 1955, much more per child, and a great deal more of our gross national product. Yet we are not making much headway with the education of disadvantaged children.

The children who are doing so poorly in our public schools constitute about 15 percent of the total group of children. They come predominantly from the homes of parents who are in the bottom quarter of the population in income, educational level, and occupational status. An equal number of children in such homes do fairly well in school—hence we cannot simply say that the children of the poor do poorly in school. Many of them do very well. But about 15 percent of children come from poor families *and* do poorly in school. We call these children "socially disadvantaged" because there is ample evidence that their home environments give them a very poor preparation for success in school.

Since World War II the families that produce these children have collected in large numbers in the slums of the big cities. Before World War II the majority of these children were living in rural and relatively isolated areas, and consequently their failure in school did not create an obvious social problem.

The other 85 percent of American children are doing quite well in school, according to the ordinary standards of judgment applied by most Americans to the schools.

I find the situation far from desperate. It is encouraging, but rough in spots, and the rough spots are most clearly seen in the big-city slums. We are learning to do the job for disadvantaged children, but making a good many mistakes in the process.

THE CRITICISMS OF URBAN EDUCATION

What are the criticisms? There are two major themes of criticism of urban education, and they are quite different. The first and most general is that the schools are failing to educate the children of the poor, and it is the fault of the schools rather than the fault of the slum culture and home environment to which the children of the poor are subjected.

The second criticism is that the educational system is doing a poor job for the middle-class child and youth. The argument is that the present middle-class establishment is failing to govern the country effectively and failing to solve the country's international and domestic problems, and at the same time attempting to train the next generation to carry on this pattern of civic failure. One of the leading critics (Goodman, 1968b), writing an article entitled "In Praise of Populism," says "Indeed, the essential idea of this resurgent populism, in my opinion, is that the powers-that-be in the world are incompetent, their authority is irrational, they cannot cope with modern conditions, and they are producing ultimate horrors."

WHO ARE THE CRITICS?

There is a group who appear at this time to have easy access to the responsible newspapers and journals. These include Paul Goodman, Edgar Friedenberg, Nat Hentoff, John Holt, Herbert Kohl, and Jonathan Kozol. These are not irresponsible people. On the contrary, they feel a tremendous moral responsibility to report their perceptions of the schools and their hypotheses for the betterment of the schools.

There are certain personal characteristics of these critics which are relevant to their criticisms. I do not propose to psychoanalyze them, and I have shared these qualities at one time or another in my own career. All of these characteristics do not apply equally to all of the critics. For one thing, they tend to be anarchists. That is, they do not like rules and institutions set up by society to regulate the conduct and development of its members. For another, they tend to be hostile to authority and therefore critical of the Establishment. A third characteristic is that some of them are young men agonizing in public over their discovery that the world is a difficult place.

To this group of critics should be added another group who are especially concerned with one or another disadvantaged minority group, and claim that the schools are failing to educate properly the children of these groups either by discriminating against them or by offering them inappropriate forms of schooling. The principal minority group on whose behalf these critics speak is the Negro group, though there are similar arguments on behalf of Puerto Ricans, Spanish-Americans of the Southwest, rural whites of the Appalachian-Ozark mountain area, and American Indians.

WHAT IS WRONG WITH THE SCHOOLS?

The critics tend to attribute the shortcomings of the schools to the fact that they are operated by "the Establishment." The Establishment consists of the bureaucrats who administer the schools and who in turn are supported by the political leadership of the big cities, backed by a middle class satisfied with the school system in its present form. Thus Jason Epstein, writing on the Bundy Report that recommends decentralization of the public schools of New York City, says (1968):

> . . . the urgent matter is to wrench the school system away from the bureaucrats who are now running it and whose failure now threatens the stability of the city itself. As a practical matter the children of the ghetto, who now comprise nearly half the total public school enrollment, are largely without a functioning educational system at all, and the present school administration has shown that it is incapable of supplying them with one [p. 26].

Related to this criticism is the contention that the size of big-city systems makes them bad. When a single school board and a single superintendent and his staff have to take responsibility for more than about 50 schools or 50,000 pupils, it is argued that the school system becomes rigid, unable to adapt to the various educational needs of various subgroups and sections of the city.

Third, there is the criticism of the common school, or the system of public education. Thus Peter Schrag, editorializing in The Saturday Review for April 20, 1968, on the subject "The End of the Common School," says:

> Although criticism of schools and teachers has always been a great national pastime, there is something fundamentally new in the declining faith in the possibilities of reform, and particularly in the kind of reform that can be accomplished within the existing school structure. The characteristic view, reflected in the pressures for decentralization and for the establishment of competing institutions, is that school systems tend to be self-serving, bureaucratic monsters that need replacement rather than reform. Although these demands

have arisen during a time when the schools can attract more resources and more sophisticated staffs than ever before, they also coincide with the moment when the schools have achieved a near-monopoly position as gatekeepers to social and economic advancement: Where the schools were once considered benign, happy institutions for the young, they are now increasingly regarded as instruments of power.

Schrag says that there will have to be a number of alternative forms of education that may replace the single public school.

A few such competing institutions have already been established. In the large cities there are a few community schools, storefront academies, and programs for dropouts. Most of these operations are considered in some measure remedial and temporary. Most of them are inadequately financed and do not begin to meet the problems of miseducation, even in the communities where they are located. Yet the problems that led to the establishment of such institutions are going to be with us for a long time, and unless the public schools begin to accommodate far more diversity and to offer far more choice than they now do, the desperate need for alternatives will continue.

WHAT DO THE CRITICS PROPOSE?
As one would expect from critics who tend to be anarchists and who are hostile to the forms of authority, the positive proposals for educational improvement tend to be few and weak. There are three broad approaches:

1 Abolish the present school system and allow new institutions to emerge. This kind of proposal tends to be supported by critics who believe that there is too much bureaucracy with consequent rigidity in the present school system. They are not much concerned with the nature of the new institutions, since they tend to distrust institutions. With John Holt in *How Children Learn*, they follow Rousseau in their belief that children will learn best if allowed to initiate their own education. Paul Goodman writes (1968a), "We can, I believe, educate the young entirely in terms of their free choice, with no processing whatsoever" [p. 73].
2 Experiment widely and freely with new procedures, looking for teachers with enthusiasm, creativity, and iconoclasm. New ways of working successfully with disadvantaged children and youth will emerge from such experiments.
3 Require the schools and their teachers to do a much better job of teaching disadvantaged children. This is the proposal especially of some Negro educators, who believe that the school system at present,

both North and South, tends to *reject* Negro children, to assume they cannot learn well, and to avoid the effort of teaching them effectively.

There are two principal weaknesses in the positions taken by the critics. First, many of them, and especially those who speak for minority groups, are ignoring the basic research on the importance of the pre-school years in the preparation of a child for success in school. They ignore the following basic proposition:

The child's cognitive and social development in the years before age five are extremely important in his readiness for school work and his achievement in school. This proposition has been established by the empirical work of Bernstein in London, Martin Deutsch in New York, Robert Hess and his coworkers at the University of Chicago, and Skeels and Skodak at the University of Iowa. This proposition is widely discussed and amplified in the writings of J. McVicker Hunt, Benjamin Bloom, and Jerome Bruner.

Second, they ignore the post-war work on methods and materials of teaching mathematics, science, social studies, and foreign languages which has effectively reformed the curriculum of the intermediate and high school grades, and vastly improved the education of the majority of children and youth who do average and superior work in school.

Nevertheless, the critics serve a valuable purpose in contemporary education. They are sensitive people, aware of the needs for improvement in our society and in our education. They are especially useful as our social conscience.

WAYS OUT OF THE EDUCATIONAL MESS

Granting the proposition that major changes must be made in big-city education, how shall we decide what changes to make, and how shall we make them? There are three groups of people with something to say on this topic—the establishment, the anarchists, and the activists. All are prepared to talk about changing, though all are not equally prepared to take actual responsibility for changes.

THE ESTABLISHMENT AS A CHANGE AGENT

It is customary to describe the Establishment as a bureaucratic organization wedded to things as they have been in the past. The national organization of school superintendents and the organization of school principals have been accused of standing athwart the path of progress.

Yet some city school systems have been remarkably ready to exercise leadership in the making of changes. For instance, the New York City system which has been pilloried in *The New York Times* as a deteriorating system has been one of the most flexible, most experimental, and most responsive of all big-city systems to the social situation and the social needs of the big city.

It is a curious thing for the critics to proclaim the proposition that New York City schools are failing, when these schools are leading the country in working at the problem of educating socially disadvantaged youth, defining the problem, and studying it scientifically and experimentally.

During this period of the last 30 years, the great majority of books on the problems of education in the big city have come from New York City. These have been written by a wide range of people with a wide range of motives and experience.

Still, many of the great cities have been slow to innovate, and there certainly is a problem in all big-city systems where a bureaucratic structure stretching from the office of school principal to that of superintendent tends to perpetuate practices to which the organization has already grown accustomed. An example is the use of federal funds under Title I of the Elementary and Secondary Education Act to supplement educational services in schools located in poverty areas. The tendency has been to use these funds to support "more of the same" rather than to innovate. That is, the money has been used to pay teachers for an extra hour of classes after school, for Saturday morning instruction, for summer instruction, and to reduce the size of classes. This has not worked very well, and has given rise to criticism of big city systems for failure to try bold new experiments.

THE ANARCHISTS AS CHANGE AGENTS

The anarchists have been strong on criticism and weak on constructive proposals for change. They are, of course, opposed to the creation of a new set of organized and institutional practices, since, as anarchists, they mistrust procedures which tend to become rigid and confining. They proclaim "the end of the common school" and tell us that we are killing off the minds and spirits of children, but they are wary of writing proposals that could be put into an organized educational system. They favor experimentation of many kinds, but do not argue for careful evaluation of such experiments.

But the ablest of the anarchists recognize the need for new institutionalized procedures. Thus Paul Goodman, who calls himself an anarchist, also says explicitly that new institutions are necessary. After speaking of the present educational establishment as a hoax on the public and calling for an end to it, he says, . . . "Of course our society would then have to re-open or devise other institutional arrangements for most of the young to grow into the world; and in my books I propose many of these, since this is the problem."

To see the anarchist position most ably stated, and stated in most positive terms, one should read more of Goodman's writing [see Goodman, 1968a]. He argues that the educational system which has developed into such a large and expensive set of operations since 1900 is a hoax on American society. It tends to force conformity on the younger generation, and conformity to a set of adult institutions which are bad for everybody. He calls for more free choice in learning and says, "Free choice is not random but responsive to real situations; both youth and adults live in a nature of things, a polity, an ongoing society, and it is these, in fact, that attract interest and channel need. If the young, as they mature, can follow their bent and choose their topics, times, and teachers, and if teachers teach what they themselves consider important—which is all they can skillfully teach anyway—the needs of society will be adequately met; there will be more lively, independent, and inventive people; and in the fairly short run there will be a more sensible and efficient society."

Up to age 12, Goodman says, there is no point to formal subjects or a prearranged curriculum. Teaching should be informal, and should follow the child's interest. If let alone, a normal child of 12 will, Goodman believes, learn most of what is useful in the eight-year elementary curriculum by himself.

However, Goodman recognizes that some families do not provide an adequate setting for their children to learn the elementary school curriculum, and he has a proposal for a kind of school to serve these disadvantaged children. He says:

> Since we have communities where people do not attend to the children as a matter of course, and since children must be rescued from their homes, for most of these children there should be some kind of school. In a proposal for mini-schools in New York City, I suggested an elementary group of 28 children with four grownups: a licensed teacher, a housewife who can cook, a college senior, and a teen-age school dropout. Such a group can meet in any storefront, church basement, settlement house, or housing project; more important, it can often go about the city, as is possible when the student-teacher ratio is 7 to 1. Experience at the First Street School in New York has shown that the cost for such a little school is less than for the public school with a student-teacher ratio of 30 to 1. . . . The school should be located near home so the children can escape from it to home, and from home to it. The school should be supported by

public money but administered entirely by its own children, teachers, and parents.

Looking at the positive suggestions of the more constructive anarchists, of whom Goodman is a good example, we see that they want education to be institutionalized to a minimal degree, with a wide variety of small school and college units in which pupils and teachers work as far as possible on their own initiative.

THE ACTIVISTS AS CHANGE AGENTS

A broad group of people are prepared to work within the present educational system but want major changes or additions to it. This group might be called "institutional meliorists," to distinguish them from the anarchists. This group accepts the notion that the educational system must have a complex institutional structure and therefore differs from the anarchists on this major point. The activists want broad and fundamental changes in the educational system.

There is much disagreement among the activists. Many of them have just one program which they emphasize, such as:

Pre-school programs for disadvantaged children starting as early as age 3

Decentralization of the public school system to place responsibility and decision making more in the hands of parents and local community leaders

Educational parks

Black teachers for black schools

Alternative educational systems to the public schools, supported with public funds

The U.S. Office of Education has been promoting activist programs through its very large funds under Title III of the Elementary and Secondary Education Act. Several of the educational foundations have been supporting activist projects.

To this writer, who is an activist, it appears that there are some serious weaknesses in the activist approach, but that these weaknesses are being corrected.

A major weakness is a general lack of systematic reporting and evaluation of the results of experimental work. Several major big-city programs of compensatory education for disadvantaged children have been given wide publicity as successful on the basis of preliminary and inadequate evaluation, only to withdraw their claims after more systematic study of their outcomes.

But there have been some outstanding examples of careful research evaluation of innovative programs. For instance, the Higher Horizons

Program in New York City elementary schools was evaluated by the Bureau of Research, and its successor program, the More Effective Schools, has been carefully studied by the Center for Urban Education. The fact that these evaluations did not support some of the hopes and expectations of the sponsors of the programs is an unfortunate fact which the big city systems must learn to use constructively.

WORKING ON MOTIVES RATHER THAN SKILLS

Recently some of the activists appear to have discovered a principle that may produce much more effective ways of teaching disadvantaged children than the conventional way. The conventional way is to work directly on the mental skills of the child—his vocabulary, reading, writing, arithmetic. *Teach, teach, teach* with all the energy, time, patience, and techniques available. This has not worked very well. Hence some experimental methods have been tried that work on *motives* rather than skills and drills. The aim is to help the pupil *want* to learn, to help him see himself as a learner in school, as he now may see himself as a basketball player, a fighter, an attractive person to the opposite sex, a helper in the home, etc.

The theory underlying this approach might be outlined as follows: When a person *wants* something, he *tries* to get it. For example; when a child wants to read, he tries to read, and will use whatever help he can get from teachers, parents, other pupils, television, street signs, books around the house. He will drill himself, or accept the teacher's drill methods.

The desire to learn may be conscious or unconscious. One may have an explicit desire to be a good basketball player, or a good dancer, or a good reader, or a good singer. In this case, one seeks opportunity to improve oneself. On the other hand, one may have only a generalized and vaguely felt desire to please somebody else, or to be like somebody. In this case one accepts opportunity to move in the desired direction, but does not actively seek it.

Programs aimed directly at improving mental skills have had remarkably little success with children beyond the age of 7 or 8. Only a few people, generally with highly personal methods, appear to have succeeded with classes in slum schools beyond the third grade. For example, Herbert Kohl taught a sixth-grade class in Harlem with a kind of freedom and spontaneity that seems to have motivated many of his pupils to care about their school work. Perhaps it is significant that he did relatively little drilling, and did not bother to correct spelling and grammar. In fact, he drew criticism from his supervisors because he did not emphasize the mental skills in the usual way. And Jonathan Kozol, in Boston, made friends with his pupils, took them on trips with him, visited their homes, but did not seem to stress the conventional training.

A rather common element of motivating situations is the presence of a model—a person who is accepted by the pupil as one he would like to be like. The habit of *modeling* one's behavior after that of others is learned very early in life, and becomes largely unconscious. A person forms the habit of imitating his parents and other persons in authority and persons who are visible to him and attractive to him. Teachers may or may not be effective models, depending on their behavior toward pupils and on the attitudes of pupils toward them.

EXAMPLES OF MOTIVATING SITUATIONS

There are a growing number of experiments with inner-city youth that seem to be successful and yet do not represent what we think of conventionally as good teaching. The methods are erratic; the teachers are not well-trained. *These experiments have in common a motivating element.*

STOREFRONT ACADEMIES AND MINI-SCHOOLS small, informal schools and classes springing up in the inner city appear to be accomplishing more than the conventional schools with disadvantaged youth. For example, the "street academies" of New York City appear to be working successfully with some dropouts and failing students from the high schools. These are described in an article by Chris Tree in *The Urban Review* for February, 1968, and are now a part of the Urban League's Education and Youth Incentives Program. The mini-school idea has already been presented.

Such projects must have methods, and the methods are being worked out pragmatically. It is too soon to say with any assurance what such a program would accomplish if it were expanded and made a part of the school system. Careful, empirical evaluation will have to be made to find out what kind of children and youth profit from this type of school and what kind do not.

Perhaps the essential factor in whatever success these schools have is that of acceptance by the teachers of the pupils as persons who want to learn, and the acceptance by the pupils of the teachers as people they want to be like.

TUTORING PROJECTS A few years ago there was a wave of tutoring projects which put college students and middle-class adults in the role of tutors to inner-city pupils of the intermediate and high school grades. These seem to have been largely discontinued, even though the tutors often reported that they got great personal satisfaction from their work and that it helped them to understand better the social structure of their society. Several careful evaluations of the effects of tutoring on mental skills of pupils throw some doubt on the value of the project from this point of view.

More recently there has been a development of tutoring by students only a little bit older and more skilled than the pupils being tutored. Some of these projects have shown surprising success. For example, Robert Cloward of Rhode Island University has evaluated a tutoring program in New York City in which teen-agers somewhat retarded in reading tutored middle-grade pupils in slum schools. Both tutees and tutors gained more in reading achievement tests than their controls did in a carefully designed experiment.

I have been told by several teachers of primary grades that they have occasionally asked an older or more advanced child to help a slow first-grader, with good results.

Whatever success these procedures have must be due more to motivation than to method. Getting *involved* with someone in a helping relationship apparently increases the desire to learn on the part of both the helper and the helped.

GAMES Games have an accepted place in schools, as activities for recess and sometimes physical education and even spelling lessons. Generally they have been used as a change from the serious business of the school. But now games are being used as part of the planned curriculum. The reason is that games are motivating to most players, and they try to learn in order to win the game. There are now a good many mathematical games available, as well as games in geography. James S. Coleman and his colleagues have been working out games for high school students. The Mecklenberg Academy in Charlotte, North Carolina, has a number of games available for high school students.

It is not clear to what extent games can be used in slum schools, though there seems to be no reason to suppose that inner-city children cannot be interested in games aimed at teaching geography and arithmetic.

SELF-CONCEPT BUILDING Middle-class white Americans have difficulty understanding the demand for courses in African culture and history, for African languages such as Swahili, and for units on the Negro in American history in the elementary school. It is a waste of time if one is only interested in understanding the present world and in learning "useful" foreign languages.

But the need of a disadvantaged minority group to learn about its own cultural history in a positive way is related to the need for a positive self-concept—a self-concept of a person as a member of a social group that has a dignified and competent past. This need is hardly recognized by the white middle-class American, partly because he does not feel the need consciously and partly because his own competence and success as a person give him a positive self-concept which he can pass on to his children. Yet many children of Negro and other disadvantaged groups are told by their parents that they come from inferior stock, that they have "bad blood," that they suffer from their social past of slavery or of defeat by the white man.

While the best basis for a positive self-concept as a person who can learn in school and can succeed in American social and economic life is achievement—in school, in play, and in work—it may be that Negro children, in particular, would gain something from a study in school of the contributions of the Negro group to American life and culture, and of African history and culture.

When we find the good and effective ways to teach disadvantaged children and youth, we will still have to solve the problem of social integration of ethnic and poverty-plagued minority groups into the economic and political life of our large metropolitan areas. The solutions will go hand in hand. Big city and suburban governments as well as big city and suburban school systems will be remade in this process of social urban renewal.

I see the educational establishment reorganized and revitalized, together with the socio-political establishment. The work will largely be done by activists who learn to innovate creatively and to evaluate their innovations scientifically.

OPEN SCHOOLS II: TEMPERING A FAD JOSEPH FEATHERSTONE

Word of English schools reaches us at a time of cultural and political ferment, and the American vogue for British reforms must be seen as one element in a complex and many-sided movement. Within our schools, there is nearly a pedagogical vacuum. Few reformers have come forward with practical alternatives; even fewer have deigned to address themselves to working teachers. The grass-roots nature of the English reforms, with their emphasis on the central importance of good teaching, has a great appeal for people who are victims of the general staff mentality of our school reformers and managers. Blacks and other minorities are interested in new approaches simply because they reject all the workings of the schools as they stand; some of the best of the community control ventures, such as the East Harlem Block Schools, have been promoting informal methods, as have some of the parent-controlled Headstart programs. And there are growing numbers of middle- and upper-middle-class parents in favor of "open" and "informal," not to mention "free," schooling, even though they are vague on the pedagogical implications of these terms.

The most cogent chapters in Charles Silberman's *Crisis in the Classroom* are a plea for American educators to consider the English example. Silberman's book is interesting as a cultural document, as well as a statement in its own right. For it registers an important shift in opinion. Silberman is arguing that too many American schools are grim and joyless for both children and teachers. What was once said by a handful of radical critics is now very close to being official wisdom. Silberman, it should be added, distinguishes himself from many critics of the schools in that he is deeply sympathetic to ordinary classroom teachers and has a clear sense of the crucial importance of the teacher's role in creating a decent setting for learning.

By now I've visited a fair number of American classrooms working along informal lines. The best are as good as anything I've seen in England; the worst are a shambles. In the efforts that look most promising, people are proceeding slowly, understanding that preparing the way for further improvements and long-term growth is more important than any single "innovation." (As I've noted, there are too few entire school environments run along informal lines.)

Understanding the need for slow growth and hard work with teachers and children, many of the informal American practitioners I've talked to are alarmed at the dimensions of the current fad for "open" schools. There are reasons for skepticism. From today's perspective, which is no doubt morbid and too disheartened, it seems that our successive waves of educational reform have been, at best, intellectual and ideological justifications for institutions whose actual workings never changed all that much. At the worst, the suspicion is that past reform movements, whatever their rhetoric, have only reinforced the role schools play in promoting social inequality. The realization that schools alone cannot save the social order—which should have been obvious all along—has prompted some to despair over ever getting decent education.

Added to these sobering reflections is a fresh sense of dismay over the outcomes of the past ten years of "innovation." For we have finished a decade of busy reform with little to show for it. Classrooms are the same. Teachers conduct monologues or more or less forced class discussions; too much learning is still rote; textbooks, timetables, clocks set the pace; discipline is an obsession. The curriculum reform efforts of the '60s brought forth excellent materials in some cases—materials still essential for good informal classrooms—but they took the existing environment of the schools for granted. Perhaps because so many were outsiders, the reformers failed to engage teachers in continuous thought and creation, with the result that the teachers ended up teaching the new materials in the old ways. Being for the most part university people, specialists, the reformers were ignorant of classrooms and children: of pedagogy. They concentrated on content— organized in the form of the standard graduate school disciplines—and ignored the nature of children and their ways of learning. Too often children were regarded as passive recipients of good materials, and teachers as passive conduits. The reformers lacked a coherent vision of the school environment as a whole. It was characteristic of the movement that it ignored the arts and children's expressiveness.

In the philosophical chaos of the curriculum projects, the proponents of precision had a debater's advantage. They were able to state their goals in precise, measurable, often behavioral terms. For a time this false precision encouraged a false sense of security. And for a while the behaviorists and the education technology businessmen were allies: they imagined that a new era of educational hardware was dawning, promising profits commensurate with those in the advanced defense and aerospace industries. Now that the bubble has burst, it seems evident to more and more people that this curious alliance had all along been talking about training, not education. Training means imparting skills. It is an aspect of education, but not all of it. I suggest a reading example: if I teach you phonic skills, that is a kind of training. Unless you go on to use them, to develop interests in books, you are not educated. This ought to be the common sense of the matter, but it isn't. Our technicians conceive of reading as a training problem on the order of training spotters to recognize airplane silhouettes. If a sixth grader in a ghetto school is reading two years below grade level, as so many are, the problem may not be reading skills at all. A fourth grade reading level often represents a grasp of the necessary skills: part of the problem is surely that the sixth grader isn't reading books and isn't interested.

Another reason why some practitioners are dubious about "open" education reflects a further skepticism about the evangelical American mode of reform, with its hunger for absolutes and its weakness for rhetoric. Our "progressive" education movement often neglected pedagogy and the realities of life in classrooms and instead concentrated on lofty abstractions. It will be essential in promoting good practice today to abandon many old ideological debates. Yet the English example is now part of a whole diverse American cultural mood, which means that it is already ranged on one side of an ideological debate. The American milieu is polarized culturally and politically; this polarization conditions American responses to accounts of informal teaching. The responses tend to fall into the stereotyped categories of a cultural cold war raging between the hip, emancipated upper middle class and the straight middle and working class.

It is a class and cultural conflict, and it takes the form of battles between those who see life as essentially a matter of scarcity—and defend the virtues of a scarce order, such as thrift, discipline, hard work—and those who see life as essentially abundant—and preach newer virtues, such as openness, feelings, spontaneity. Hip people like the idea of open classrooms, because they seem to give children freedom; straight people fear the supposed absence of order, discipline and adult authority.

If I portray this conflict in highly abstract terms, it is because it seems to me remote from the concerns of good American and British practitioners actually teaching in informal settings. Take the issue of freedom, for example. Letting children talk and move about is helpful in establishing a setting in which a teacher can find out about students; it helps children learn actively, to get the habit of framing purposes independently, using their own judgment. But this freedom is a means to an end, not a goal in itself. As a goal, freedom is empty and meaningless— "a breakfast food," as e. e. cummings once put it.

There are always those who argue that freedom is something negative—freedom from—and those who argue that freedom is positive. From authoritarians like Plato to libertarians like Kant and Dewey, the second line of argument has linked freedom with knowledge—the free use of reason or intelligence and, sometimes, action with knowledge. Whatever the merits of the positions in this fascinating, perpetual debate, it is surely more appropriate for educators of the young to conceive of freedom in the second sense, not a momentary thing at all, but the result of a process of discipline and learning. Informality is pointless unless it leads to intellectual stimulation. Many children in our "free" schools are not happy, and one suspects that part of the reason is that they are bored with their own lack of intellectual progress. As William Hull remarks in a trenchant critique of the current fad for "open" education: "Children are not going to be happy for very long in schools in which they realize they are not accomplishing very much."

Or take the issue of authority. That it *is* an issue is a mark of deep cultural confusion, as well as a reflection of the frequent misuse of legitimate authority in America. Whatever their politics, good practitioners assume as a matter of course that teachers have a responsibility to create an environment hospitable to learning, that there is what might be called a natural, legitimate basis for the authority of an adult working with children. In his superb little book, *The Lives of Children*, George Dennison outlines some aspects of this legitimate authority:

> *Its attributes are obvious: adults are larger, more experienced, possess more words, have entered into prior agreements with themselves.*

When all this takes on a positive instead of a merely negative character, the children see the adults as protectors and as sources of certitude, approval, novelty, skills. In the fact that adults have entered into prior agreements, children intuit a seriousness and a web of relations in the life that surrounds them. If it is a bit mysterious, it is also impressive and somewhat attractive; they see it quite correctly as the way of the world, and they are not indifferent to its benefits and demands. . . . [For a child] the adult is his ally, his model—and his obstacle [for there are natural conflicts, too, and they must be given their due].

Disciplinary matters and the rest of the structure of authority in American schools work against the exercise of legitimate authority. And thus, in reaction to the schools, the education opposition movement foolishly assumes that all adult guidance is an invasion of children's freedom. Actually, in a proper informal setting, as John Dewey pointed out, adults ought to become more important:

Basing education upon personal experience may mean more multiplied and more intimate contacts between the mature and the immature than ever existed in the traditional schools, and consequently more rather than less guidance.

If you remove adult authority from a given group of children, you are not necessarily freeing them. Instead, as David Riesman and his colleagues noted in *The Lonely Crowd*'s critique of "progressive" education, you are often sentencing them to the tyranny of their peers. And unacknowledged adult authority has a way of creeping back in subtle and manipulative ways that can be more arbitrary than its formal exercise.

Another fake issue in the debate on open education is the distinction between education as something developed from within and education as something formed from without, the old, boring question of whether to have, as they say, a child-centered or an adult-directed classroom. There are, to be sure, certain respects in which the best informal practice is child-centered. The basic conception of learning, after all, reflects the image of Piaget's child-inventor, fashioning an orderly model of the universe from his varied encounters with experience. The child's experience *is* the starting point of all good informal teaching. But passive teaching has no place in a good informal setting, any more than passive children do. Active teaching is essential, and one of the appeals of this approach to experienced teachers is that it transforms the teacher's role. From enacting somebody else's text or curriculum, the teacher moves toward working out his own responses to children's learning. The teacher is responsible for creating the learning environment.

Still another confusion on the American scene lies in the notion that liberalizing the repressive atmosphere of our schools—which is worth doing for its own sake—will automatically promote intellectual development. It won't. We need more humane schools, but we also need a steady concern for intellectual progress and workmanship. Without this, it is unlikely that we will get any sort of cumulative development, and we will never establish practical standards by which to judge good and bad work.

Some American practitioners question the utility of slogans such as the "open school," or "informal education." The terms are suspect because they become cliches, because they don't convey the necessary values underlying this kind of teaching, because they suggest a hucksterized package and because they divide teaching staffs into the "we" doing the open approach and the "they" who are not. Some imitate the philosopher Charles Saunders Pierce, who changed his "pragmatism" to the much uglier-sounding "pragmaticism"—in order, he said, to keep his ideas safe from kidnappers. They prefer an awkward and reasonably neutral term like "less formal." A brave few are modestly willing to march under a banner inscribed "decent schools."

This suspicion of slogans can be carried to ludicrous extremes. But at the heart of the evasiveness is an important point: educating children or working with teachers is an entire process. A good informal setting should not be thought of as a "model" or as an "experiment," but as an environment in which to support educational growth in directions that have already proved sound.

Some observers fear the manner in which our schools implement reforms in a way that destroys the possibility for further development of teachers. (There are already instances where principals have dictated "open education" to their staffs.) There is a deep—and I think altogether justified—mistrust of the conventional channels of reform from the top down: pronunciamentos by educational statesmen, the roll of ceremonial drums, the swishing sound of entrepreneurs shaking the money tree. Most of the serious American informal practitioners are self-consciously local in their orientation. They are interested in planting themselves in Vermont, Philadelphia, New York City, North Dakota or wherever, and working at the grass roots. They imagine that it will take a very long time to get good schools, and they do not believe that big-wig oratory or White House Conferences on Education are any substitute for direct engagement with teachers and children in classrooms.

The changes they are starting are small but they have large implications. All teachers, no matter how they teach, suffer from the climate of our schools, and every serious attempt at reform will soon find itself talking about lunchrooms, toilet passes, the whole internal control structure of the schools, relationships to parents, relationships to supervisory staff, the ways in which supplies are ordered, the links between an individual school and the central bureaucracies; ultimately issues of politics, power and money.

As schools move in informal directions, there will be an increasing criticism of our system of training and credentialing teachers and administrators. (Here, with the exception of outstanding institutions like London's Froebel Institute, the English do not have examples to emulate: their teachers colleges are improving, but they have trailed behind the work of the best schools.) The training of administrators will come under attack, and in some places separate training programs for administrators will be abolished. The inadequacy of teacher training will also become more evident, although it is far from clear how to improve it. What we do know is that theory has to be reunited with practice. Without a solid grounding in child development, much of our informal teaching will be gimmickry; and without a sound base in actual practice in classrooms, theory will remain useless.

The enormous variety of the American educational landscape makes it difficult to speak in general terms. In certain areas, education schools willing to restore an emphasis on classroom practice may unite with school systems ready to move in informal directions. In other areas, where the education schools are unable to change their mandarin ways, school systems will have to assume more and more of the responsibility for training and credentialing teachers. Whichever the pattern, a central feature of successful programs will be periods of work in good informal settings. Thus a prerequisite to any scheme of training will be the existence of good schools and classrooms to work in. The single most important task is the reform of schools and classrooms, for good informal classrooms provide the best teacher training sites.

Whether the current interest in informal teaching leads to cumulative change will depend on many things. Two are worth repeating: whether enough people can understand the essentially different outlook on children's intellectual development which good informal work must be based on, and whether our schools can be reorganized to give teachers sustained on-the-job support. I'm somewhat optimistic about the first: the ideas are in the air, and many teachers, on their own, are already questioning the assumptions behind the traditional classroom. The second question will be much harder to answer satisfactorily. In some places, the schools are ripe for change; in others change will come slowly and painfully, if at all; and in others the chances for growth are almost zero. Those promoting informal teaching ought to be wary of suggesting good practices to teachers working in institutional settings where real professional growth is out of the question. In such a setting, all obstacles mesh together to form what people rightly call the System. Right now it seems unlikely that the System in our worst school systems will ever permit teachers to teach and children to learn. But things may have looked that way to some British educational authorities in the '30s, too.

A final word on the faddishness of our educational concerns. The appearance of new ideas such as the clamor for open, informal schools does not cancel out old ideas. "Open education" will be a sham unless those supporting it also address themselves to recurring, fundamental problems, such as the basic inequality and racism of our society. The most pressing American educational dilemma is not the lack of informality in classrooms: it is whether we can build a more equal, multiracial society. Issues like school integration and community control have not disappeared, to be replaced by issues like open education. The agenda simply gets more crowded. It will be all the more essential, however, to keep alive in bad times a vision of the kind of education that all wise parents want for their children.

TERRY BORTON **43** REACH, TOUCH, AND TEACH

There are two sections to almost every school's statement of educational objectives—one for real, and one for show. The first, the real one, talks about academic excellence, subject mastery, and getting into college or a job. The other discusses the human purpose of school—values, feelings, personal growth, the full and happy life. It is included because everyone knows that it is important, and that it ought to be central to the life of every school. But it is only for show. Everyone knows how little schools have done about it.

In spite of this, the human objectives describe the things all of us cite when we try to remember what "made a difference" in our school careers: the teacher who touched us as persons, or the one who ground out our lives to polish our intellects; the class that moved with the strength and grace of an Olympic team, or the dozens of lessons when each of us slogged separately toward the freedom of 3 o'clock. What we learned, and what we became, depended to a significant degree on how we felt about ourselves, our classmates, and our teachers. The schools were right—the human purposes *were* important. But with the exception of those teachers who were so rare we never forgot them, the schools did little to put their philosophy into practice.

Recently, however, a variety of programs have begun to build curricula and teaching methodology that speak directly to the human objectives. These programs, stemming both from within the schools and from various branches of psychology, point the way to a school practice which not only recognizes the power of feelings, but also combines academic training with an education directly aimed at the student's most important concerns. Schools may soon be explicitly teaching students such things as how to sort out and guide their own psychological growth, or increase their desire to achieve, or handle their aggressive instincts in nonviolent forms.

The new impetus has a variety of names: "psychological education," "affective," "humanistic," "personological," "eupsychian," "synoetic." Some of these names are a bit bizarre, and none has yet gained wide acceptance. But taken together their presence indicates a growing recognition that in the world's present state of social and moral turmoil, the schools' traditional second objective can no longer be for show. Riots, poverty, war, student rebellion, swollen mental hospitals, and soaring crime rates have involved an enormous number of people. They have generated a broadening conviction that society is as responsible for the psychological well-being of each of its members as is each individual. And that conviction has created a receptive audience for new kinds of educational critics.

The new critics do not simply attack the schools for their academic incompetence, as did the Rickovers of a decade ago. They are equally concerned with the schools' basic lack of understanding that students are human beings with feelings as well as intellects. Jonathan Kozol has given a gripping sense of the "destruction of the hearts and minds of Negro children" in his *Death at an Early Age*. In *How Children Fail* John Holt has shown that even in the best "progressive" schools, children live in constant fear which inhibits their learning, and Paul Goodman's *Compulsory Mis-Education* has made a powerful case for his contention that "the present school system is leading straight to 1984." The intuitive warnings of these "romantic critics" have been backed up by statistical evidence from the largest survey of education ever conducted, James Coleman's *Equality of Educational Opportunity*. This survey correlates academic achievement with attitudes such as a student's self concept, sense of control over his fate, and interest in school. The study concludes that these attitudes and feelings are more highly correlated with how well a student achieves academically than a combination of many of the factors which educators have usually thought were crucial, such as class size, salary of teachers, facilities, curriculum.

The pressure to deal more directly with student feelings (increasingly a pressure from students as well as critics) has given rise to dozens of different projects. None of the three examples which I will discuss here has yet reached the size or influence of the giant curriculum centers (such as the Educational Development Corporation) which grew up as a result of the post-Sputnik criticism. But in the long run they may be much more important. For the post-Sputnik curriculum reforms were essentially attempts to find better ways to teach the traditional disciplines of math, science, or social studies—often with the effect of moving the college curriculum into elementary and secondary schools. The programs I am describing not only operate with different techniques, but also begin to define and develop new curriculum subjects and a new school orientation toward practical and applied psychology. If expanded, they will make a profound change in American education—hopefully a change toward a more humane educational process, and a more human student.

The project which I co-directed with Norman Newberg, the Philadelphia School Board's specialist in "affective education," is an example of such a curriculum. It is being developed from within the schools—in this case by a group of urban teachers trying to find a philosophy and method which would work with the students they were asked to teach. The program is based on the assumption that every person handles massive amounts of information, and needs to be taught both logical and psychological processes for handling it. Two semester-long courses, one in communications, and one in urban affairs, isolate such processes as symbolization, simulation, dreaming, and de-escalating pressure, and teach them in an explicit fashion. At the same time the classes are designed to tie these processes to the amorphous undercurrent of student concerns for self-identity, power, and relationship.

I dropped into a high school communications class one hot day during last summer's field testing, when the teacher was working on "taxonomy of process," or a way of looking at what, why, and how behavior occurs and changes. The purpose of the class was to show the students a simple technique for analyzing their own habitual forms of processing the world around them, and then to show them how they could develop new responses if they wanted to. The class was working in groups of twos, filling in "What Wheels" for each other. One boy in the back was without a partner, so I joined him, and we agreed that I would make a What Wheel for him, and he would make one for me. I drew a circle, filled in the spokes, and wrote down my first impressions of him: "strong, quick, Afro, shy, bright."

The teacher asked us to read each other our What Wheels, select one adjective which interested us most, and ask our partner to draw a "Why Wheel" to explain *why* that adjective was meaningful to him.

Charlie read me his What Wheel—he was perceptive, as students usually are about teachers. Then I read him mine.

"Why'd you write 'shy'? I ain't shy."

"Well, I just met you, so I can't fill out a whole Why Wheel about it. But when I first sat there, I noticed you looked down at your desk instead of up at me. So I just guessed you were shy with strangers—maybe just with strange teachers."

Charlie took his What Wheel from me and looked at it. "You know, that's the truth. I thought nobody, except maybe my mother, knew that about me, but well, it's the truth anyhow."

The murmur of the class's conversation quieted while the teacher told us how to make up "How Wheels" with our partners. We were supposed to write down the range of actions which would either increase or decrease the trait we had been discussing.

"Aw, man, it would be easy to increase being shy," laughed Charlie. "I just wouldn't look at nobody."

"And decreasing it?"

"I'd look at you like I'm looking at you right now," he said, looking me straight in the eye. "And more than that, I'd look at you like that when you first came in here. Teacher, or white man, I wasn't afraid of you; no reason why I should act like I was."

We talked for a while—about my wheels, about the effectiveness of the what, why, how process questions for looking at behavior, and about school. When the bell rang, we shook hands. "See ya around," he said.

"See ya around," I said.

While many teachers have been experimenting with techniques similar to ours, research psychologists usually have been rather disdainful of the messy problems in the schools. Increasingly, however, psychologists such as David McClelland of Harvard are beginning to work on problems of motivation and attitude in schools. The progression of McClelland's study is a good example of how basic research may be applied to problems in education. McClelland began working on problems of measuring the motivation of rats deprived of food, performed a series of experiments to measure hunger motivation in humans, and then devised a system for measuring "achievement motivation" in men by counting the frequency of its appearance in fantasy images. He defined the need for achievement (n-Ach; as a pattern of thought and fantasy about doing things well, and discovered that those people who had such a pattern were characterized by a preference for moderate risk goals, a desire for immediate feedback on their performance, and a liking for personal responsibility. McClelland reasoned that if a society had a great number of such individuals, the society itself should show outstanding achievement. Twenty years were spent in a mammoth research effort to substantiate his claim that achievement research provided a "factual basis for evaluating theories that explain the rise and fall of civilizations." The next step was to devise educational methods for increasing the achievement motive in people who did not have much of it, and to test out these methods in this country and abroad.

Dr. Alfred Alschuler, director of the Harvard Achievement Motivation Development Project, which is one result of McClelland's research, is in charge of a federally funded five-year research project to assess what factors lead to effective achievement training. The project has devised many classroom techniques for increasing achievement motivation in students, most of them involving experiential learning that takes place in a game situation. I visited one training program for teachers in a nearby city, and sat in on a session that used a contest in making paper airplanes to demonstrate to the teachers how achievement motivation affects their students.

There was a lot of joking around the table, as everyone was a little nervous.

"Now they're going to use the old carrot on us," cracked a little physics teacher sitting on my right.

The head of the math department, an enormous man, smiled broadly, first at the physics teacher, and then at me. "Feeling cut-throat?" he asked.

I didn't say so, but I was, and he knew it. My "n-Ach" was way up. We eyed each other while we set our own quotas for the number of planes we would make.

Dr. Alschuler gave us the start sign. I was making planes feverishly; out of the corner of my eye, I could see the math department head moving more slowly, but doing a better job—the quality control check at the end of the game might go in his favor. The physics teacher was using mass production techniques, making one fold at a time.

At the end of five minutes the game was up, and we were all laughing at the tension it had produced. The physics teacher had more planes than any of us, but his mass production assembly had failed—all the planes were missing one wing. I had the second largest number of planes, but several had sloppy folds and were disqualified.

"Nuts to this," said the physics teacher. "I'm not going to get another heart attack over a bunch of paper airplanes. Next time I'm dropping my quota in half. I'm only going to make six."

I was swearing at myself—I should have been more careful. Next time through the game I would set a slightly lower quota and do a better job.

The math teacher was smiling broadly. He had won.

Later we all talked about our experience in the game and how our own behavior did or did not reflect the characteristics of a high achiever. Did we set moderate risk goals? Did we utilize information on our success or failure? Then we began to dig into the more fundamental value issues that were involved. Suppose that we could use games like the paper plane construction to teach students the characteristics of a high achiever, and through a variety of such exercises could actually train him to think and act as one. Was that a good thing? Did we want to subject our students to the pressure that we had felt? Could we decide that achievement training was good for some students who were not achieving up to our standards, and bad for those who were too competitive? On what basis?

Just as researchers are becoming involved in the practical questions of education, so clinical psychotherapy is getting up off its couch and finding ways to add its skill to solving school problems. Dr. Carl Rogers, founder of client-centered therapy, is presently working with Western Behavorial Sciences Institute and a group of Catholic schools to devise ways to use "sensitivity groups" in the schools. (A "sensitivity group" or "T-group" is composed of about a dozen people who meet for the purpose of giving feedback on how each person's behavior affects the other people in the group.) The National Training Laboratory, an associate of the National Education Association, is now running a year-round series of T-groups and related experiences for teachers and administrators. And in San Diego, child psychiatrist Dr. Harold Bissell and educator Dr. Uvaldo Palomares have set up the Human Development Training Institute which has written a two-year sequence of lesson plans to improve a primary school child's self-confidence and awareness, and has trained 1,000 teachers to use it.

One of the most eclectic approaches in the clinical tradition is the project run by Dr. George Brown of the University of California at Santa Barbara. Brown's project, sponsored by the Ford Foundation through the ebullient Esalen Institute, utilizes many different approaches, but particularly the theories of Gestalt therapy which attempt to get youth in touch with how they are feeling in the "here and now." With such theoretical orientations in their background, the teachers in Brown's project are encouraged to devise their own techniques to integrate academic with affective or emotional learning in order to achieve a more "humanistic education."

I joined the teachers at one of the monthly meetings where they learn about new ideas, and share with each other the techniques they have developed. Gloria Siemons, a pretty first-grade teacher, was describing an exercise that she had first conducted with the entire class, and then used when one child became angry at another. She lined the class up in two rows on the playground, had them find a partner, put their hands up facing each other, and push.

Push they did, laughing all over the field, especially at their teacher, who was being pushed around in a circle by several of the bigger kids.

Later, when two kids got into an argument at recess, Mrs. Siemons simply asked them: "Are you angry now? Would you like to push?"

"Yes, I'm angry. I'm angry at him."

Both agreed to the contest, pushed for a minute as hard as they could, and then collapsed into each other's arms giggling. Their anger was worked out, but without hurting each other.

"What would happen," I asked Mrs. Siemons, "if one kid pushed another hard enough to hurt him?"

"We have a rule about that. 'It's OK to be angry with someone, and it's OK to push, but it's *not* OK to push him into the rosebush.' "

Good teachers, particularly good first-grade teachers such as Mrs. Siemons, have always responded to the emotional side of their students' lives, and it is precisely this intuitive gift which Dr. Brown is capitalizing on. By systematizing such techniques and relating them to a general theoretical framework, he and the teachers of his staff have begun to generate hundreds of ways to integrate the feelings of students with the regular curriculum taught from kindergarten to high school.

The techniques being developed, the dozens of programs, and the various theories differ in many respects, but they have several features in common. First, and most important, all of them deal in a very explicit and direct way with the student's feelings, interpersonal relations, or values. It is the fact that they are so explicit and direct which sets them apart from the vague protestations that schools have usually made about this area. While schools were concentrating on math, science, or English, they often ignored or actively suppressed feelings. The new programs make what was covert behavior the subject of overt discussion; they make the implicit explicit. They legitimize feelings, clarify them for the student, and suggest a variety of behaviors which he can use to express them. They do so on the assumption that these feelings exert a powerful effect on a student's behavior, both in the present and in the future. If schools want to influence behavior, then it makes sense to deal directly with its major sources, not just with the binomial theorem, the gerund, or the Seventeenth Amendment.

A factor in the new field which often causes misunderstanding is that most of the programs use non-verbal experiences, either through physical expression and involvement, or through art, sculpture, or music. For the most part, this involvement with the *non*-verbal is not *anti*-verbal or *anti*-intellectual. Non-verbal educational techniques are based on the obvious but little-utilized fact that a child learns most of his emotional response patterns at a very young age—before he can talk. His knowledge of love, rejection, anger, and need does not come through words, but through his physical senses—touch, a flushed face, a gnawing in his stomach. Even later, when he begins to talk, the words he learns are "Mama," "doggie," "see"—words for things and actions, not feelings. Indeed, many children seem entirely unable to give a name to their current feelings—they have been taught how to say "I am bad," but not "I feel bad." Education that deals with feelings is often facilitated by skipping over the verbal labels which have been learned relatively late in life, regaining the other senses, and then reintegrating them with verbal thought and new behaviors.

Another common technique which causes confusion is the reliance of many of the programs on games, dramatic improvisations, and role-playing. Again, though those utilizing the techniques believe in fun and use games, few of them are simply advocating "fun and games." Their interest stems from an insight into the learning process of small children. By playing games—house, fireman, office, war—little children learn what it will be like to be an adult, and begin to develop their own style in that role. But our culture provides few such opportunities for older children or adolescents, even though the society is changing so fast that many of the response patterns they learned as a three-year-old may be no longer relevant, or even dangerous. Games and improvisation allow a simulation of the self. While they are real and produce real emotions, their tightly defined limits provide a way to try out new behavior without taking the full consequences which might occur if the same action were performed in ordinary relationships.

There are answers for questions about non-verbal and gaming emphasis, but there are many other questions which the programs raise for which there are no answers. At best, solutions will come slowly, and that is bound to produce tremendous strain in a time when events wait for no one. Many of these problems are already developing. Though Dr. Alschuler at Harvard and Dr. Willis Harmon at the Stanford Research Institute are both engaged in large surveys to find out what techniques and philosophies are presently being employed in the field, there is still no common theoretical base for the programs, and very little research on their effectiveness. The Achievement Motivation Development Project has by far the most extensive research program, and Dr. Alschuler's experience with it has made him feel strongly about the need for additional evidence before program expansion:

> *We have very little hard evidence that programs in this new field accomplish much more than natural maturation. We have claims,*

promises, and fascinating anecdotes. But we should not insti-
tute these programs without first using the most sophisticated
research techniques we have to improve them and explore their con-
sequences.

In addition to unanswered questions about effectiveness, there are practical limitations to all of the programs. Few have done an adequate job of integrating their material with the usual skills and knowledge that everyone recognizes the schools must continue to teach. No attempt has yet been made to work together with the free-flowing academic programs (such as the Leicestershire movement) which seem natural complements. Though all of the projects I have discussed here stress their responsiveness to student concerns, it is not yet clear how they can do that and yet not be heavily dependent on the skills and personalities of a few teachers like Mrs. Siemons who can both legitimize anger and make the rosebush out of bounds.

Politically, programs with both the potential and the liabilities of these are obvious hot potatoes. It is unclear as yet how projects designed by psychologists will fit in with current efforts toward more community control and what seems to be the resulting concentration on "teaching the basics." Even a mode of politics that is in consonance with the ideals and methods of the new programs is unknown, for the vision they present is often as utopian as that in George Leonard's exciting new book, *Education and Ecstasy.* How to get from here to there without waiting until 2001 is a complex political problem. Suppose, for instance, that a school district decided to adopt an entirely new curriculum and school organization based on the concepts I have been discussing. Would the teachers be able to change? Great care would have to be taken with their feelings and concerns, for not only are they as human as the children, but—as recent events in New York have indicated—they will strike if they feel they are being treated unfairly.

The most fundamental problem, and the one which is likely to get people the most upset, is the ethical question caused by changing the expectations of what schools are for. At present, students go to school to "learn stuff," and though they may expect schools to provide information, they do not expect schools to change them in any fundamental way, or even to offer that opportunity. As long as schools continue to have relatively little explicitly acknowledged impact on the students' values, attitudes, and behaviors, no one is likely to worry much about ethical issues. If schools consciously begin to make important changes in students' lives, people will suddenly become very concerned about what is happening to immature minds that are forced to accept this kind of education for twelve years. They will begin to ask whether there should be compulsory education, or whether students should be free to accept or reject schooling. And they will begin to ask hard questions about what should be taught, and how it should be presented.

If, for instance, all children should be motivated, should they also be "achievement motivated"? At what age? Who decides? And who teaches? What is to stop teachers from working out of their own needs rather than for those of their pupils? Should teachers who share an important confidence have the same legal privilege which a lawyer or a minister has? How can parents and children be assured of the privacy which is their right?

The ethical problems are likely to be compounded by the reporting of the mass media. The new field is peculiarly open to parody ("HARVARD PROF TEACHES PAPER AIRPLANE CONSTRUCTION") and to easy association with the exotic and erotic. (*Life* recently stuck a single misleading paragraph on Brown's project into a long article on Esalen Institute. By far the most arresting thing in the article was a two-page picture spread on a nude sensitivity group that had nothing to do with either Brown's project or Esalen.) Sensational publicity is not what the new field needs. It does need the time, the careful research and planning, and the critical reporting which will allow it to grow or decline on its merits. The alternative is a series of fads, created by ignorance and publicity, and death—after a short and enthusiastic life—in disillusionment.

The new programs are too important to allow that to happen. They are delicate, and they are moving into an area which is fundamentally new, so they can be expected to suffer from the attention they attract, to make mistakes, and to run into blind alleys. If it takes the big curriculum development corporations a million dollars and three years to build a single course in science or social studies, it will be even more difficult to build a fully developed curriculum in a new field. But the effort should be encouraged. For while it may not be novel to assert that a man's feelings are a crucial determinant of his public behavior and private well-being, there is no question about the novelty and significance of school programs that explicitly educate both the feelings and the intellect. Such programs raise many of society's basic questions about purpose and meaning—tough questions which will not be easy to answer. But they also offer a possibility for building a saner world—a world where people are more open about their feelings, careful in their thinking, and responsible in their actions.

ROBERT D. HESS
MARIANNE BLOCK
JOAN COSTELLO
RUBY T. KNOWLES
DOROTHY LARGAY

44

PARENT INVOLVEMENT IN EARLY EDUCATION

One of the most significant features in the expansion of early education in the United States over the last decade has been the increase in parent participation and involvement in various cooperative educational and policy-making roles. The pressures and influences that stimulated the rise in parental involvement in their children's education came from two broad sources: (1) the persuasion of empirical data and theoretical argument from education and socialization research; and (2) direct political pressure for community involvement.

The arguments that led to the establishment of Head Start and other large programs of early education at the preschool level were almost inevitably applied to justify parent participation in educational programs. Perhaps the two most significant influences were the growing number of publications that discussed the importance of early experience upon subsequent cognitive growth and education achievement (Bloom, 1964) and general psychosocial development (Kagan & Moss, 1962); and a body of research and writings on the specific influence of home and maternal factors in the socialization of cognitive behavior in young children (Bernstein, 1961; Coleman, 1966; Hess & Shipman, 1967; Gordon, 1969). This research has emerged, in turn, from earlier studies of parent-child interaction and the apparent effects that parents have upon the development of aggression, compliance, and other patterns of behavior in children (Sears, Maccoby, & Levin, 1957; Rosen & D'Andrade, 1959; Freeberg & Payne, 1967; Grotberg, 1969).

The argument of the importance of early experience carries with it the assumption that the mother and early home influences are likely to be particularly significant in shaping the experience to which the child responds. These conceptions of the family's role and of early experience, although by no means new, gained in intellectual and empirical vigor and in visibility during the early 1960s. In a number of writings they were combined to form a concept that during early stages of the education campaigns of the war against poverty was fundamental to the planning and establishing of programs of compensatory education. A compelling line of argument was developed for parent participation in early education programs. It contended that early experience affects subsequent intellectual and educational growth and achievement and that children who grow up in homes disadvantaged by racial discrimination and poverty have a deficit of the experiences presumably essential for academic achievement in the public schools. Further, this deficit, which initially is the responsibility of the community and family, becomes cumulative during the preschool and elementary school years. Therefore, compensatory programs should involve parents and assist them in providing a more adequate educational environment for their young children. In light of our present knowledge about early experience in ghetto and low-income homes, this view obviously is simplistic and in some respects false. Even so, it provides a significant part of the motivation and justification for involving parents in their children's education.

Parallel to this line of argument, but not entirely consistent with it, was an influence that came primarily from social and political origins. One feature of the civil-rights movement was a bitter and articulate criticism of the public schools, especially in urban areas. Criticisms concentrated upon the lack of relationship between the educational experiences offered by the school and the local community's cultural experiences and needs. The rise in ethnic nationalism—as represented by Black Power, for example—combined with criticisms of the school to create demands for community control over educational policy and decision making in the schools and other institutions that serve the local community.

The recognition of the family's role in early cognitive development and the pressures for community control were reflected in guidelines of major federal programs such as Head Start and Follow Through, in which parent and community participation was mandatory.

The growth in parent-involvement programs has been dramatic and seems likely to lead to consequences that were not altogether anticipated, either by the researchers who argued for parent involvement as an educational resource or by those oriented toward communication who saw involvement and control as one way of expressing the needs for self-determination in ghetto neighborhoods. It was not widely recognized at the time that the rationale and points of view that underlay these two influences—educational and political—soon would come into conflict. There may be an inherent contradiction between the arguments that have to do with cumulative deficit and those that support ethnic pride and self-determination for ghetto communities.

Our discussion of parental involvement in day-care programs will be from the perspective of these two points of view. Within this context, we shall consider parental influences upon the development of young children, parent involvement in early education, cross-age helping relationships, and the implications of both research and programmatic efforts for day-care planning and practice.

THEORY AND RESEARCH ON PARENTAL INFLUENCES ON EARLY DEVELOPMENT

Although it has been obvious for some time that parents influence their children's development, it is not clear what aspects of interaction between parent and child are relevant for understanding parental influence on cognitive and emotional development of young children. A knowledge of parental influences on early development, especially those that are relevant to specific day-care populations, could provide a basis for planning and practice both for day-care facilities and other early educational settings.

Parent-child research is subject to many methodological criticisms. Individual studies use slightly different variables and instruments, define their concepts, such as maternal warmth and independence training, in vague or noncomparable ways, and often fail to differentiate the effects of parental behavior upon boys and girls. Much of the earlier research that we shall discuss has used white, urban, middle-class samples exclusively. Thus, generalizations to other ethnic and socioeconomic groups, especially those expected to be represented in day-care populations, are limited.

The following are common categories of results that suggest that several global clusters of parental (largely maternal) behavior affect not only educationally relevant capabilities but also affective and social development of children.

AFFECTIVE INFLUENCES ON COGNITIVE AND EMOTIONAL DEVELOPMENT

DEMANDS FOR INDEPENDENCE-DEPENDENCE Several studies have suggested that parents who train their children from an early age to be independent in thinking and action while supporting early needs for emotional dependence, help their children toward the independence necessary for school success. Their children are usually high achievers (Rosen & D'Andrade, 1959; Crandall, Preston, & Robson, 1960; Chance, 1961).

WARMTH AND A HIGH-INVOLVED RELATIONSHIP BETWEEN PARENT AND CHILD Evidence from observations and parent reports shows that maternal warmth, high emotional involvement and interaction, and general parental interest are positively associated with children's achievement (Milner, 1951; Rosen & D'Andrade, 1959; Bing, 1963; Baumrind & Black, 1967; Slaughter, 1968; Solomon, Parelius, & Busse, 1969). One of these studies, however, shows that low-income black mothers, compared with middle-class black mothers, may accompany their warmth and support for the child with negative attitudes toward both teacher and school (Slaughter, 1968).

On the other hand, overindulgence, overprotection, and actual intrusiveness by parents results in lowered reading and IQ scores after four years of age (Stewart, 1950; Bayleyley & Schaffer, 1964).

RESTRICTION AND REJECTION IN THE CHILD'S HOME ENVIRONMENT It has been frequently claimed that middle-class mothers are more accepting and permissive about certain aspects of their children's behavior than low-income mothers (Bronfenbrenner, 1958), but this assertion is disputed, especially in regard to its interpretation (Hess, 1970). Research shows that although early independence training helps the child succeed in school, parents who establish well-defined limits for their children during later years facilitate their children's continuation of high school achievement (Drews & Teahan, 1957; Rosen & D'Andrade, 1959; Bing, 1963). Firmness or restriction during the early years would, on the other hand, encourage dependence and passivity (Baumrind & Black, 1967). One study of Mexican-American high school students, however, indicated that boys whose mothers were quite dominant were usually low achievers; girls, however, were high achievers in the same situation.

Implicit or explicit rejection by parents encourages independencelike behaviors in the child; often these children become high achievers (Stewart, 1950; Brody, 1969). Independent behaviors of the child resulting from maternal rejection are accompanied by increased signals for approval, praise, and attention toward the mother (Brody, 1969).

Consistency of discipline techniques used by parents over time, and between parents, is important for independence and assertiveness in boys and affiliation in girls (Baumrind & Black, 1967).

PARENTAL STYLES OF CONTROL Studies concerned with the kind rather than the severity of control of child behavior show that control accompanied by explanation, requests, consulting, and giving reasons for discipline, is associated with increased responsiveness to children's needs and achievements (Kagan & Freeman, 1963; Kamii & Radin, 1967).

Bronfenbrenner (1958) suggested that middle-class mothers are more responsive to inner states and have a more "democratic" accepting relationship with their children than do working-class mothers, who are more concerned with external standards of conduct and adherence to community norms. Several studies have identified the kinds of control that mothers use. *Imperative-normative* control (commands based on norms of groups or position within a family system) is typical among working-class families. Middle-class families tend more often to include control strategies based on either inner feelings of the child or approaches that emphasize the future consequences of given acts or patterns of behavior (*personal-subjective* or *cognitive-rational*) (Hess et al., 1968). Observations in both home and laboratory indicate that mothers in low-income families less often include explanations with their commands and more often give punishment for improper behavior than offer reinforcement for good behavior (Kamii & Radin, 1967; Bradshaw, 1968).

THE INTELLECTUAL RELATIONSHIP BETWEEN PARENTS AND CHILDREN

PARENTAL INFLUENCE IN THE SOCIALIZATION OF MENTAL ABILITIES Studies in cognitive socialization among different ethnic groups in New York and Boston found that both social class and ethnicity have strong and varied effects on performance on tests that covered four different mental abilities (verbal, reasoning, number, and spatial conceptualization) (Lesser, Fifer, & Clark, 1965; Lesser & Stodolsky, 1967). Ethnicity seems to affect the pattern among mental abilities. The results showed a very different pattern of scores for each ethnic group studied. Furthermore, the social-class variations within the ethnic groups did not alter the basic pattern. In verbal ability, Jewish children scored high, blacks average, and Puerto Ricans lowest. In spatial conceptualization, Chinese children exceeded all others; black children were relatively low on this and numerical tasks. These results tentatively suggest that there are subtle variations in the patterns of parent-child interaction across ethnic groups that are associated with differences in the pattern of mental abilities. However, no direct evidence supports this supposition.

Recent research in infant development suggests that parents begin to influence the cognitive development of their children from birth. The mother's touching, looking, smiling, holding, and manner of talking influence the infant's behavior in ways that are important for cognitive development (Lewis, 1965; Rubenstein, 1967; Lewis & Goldberg, 1968; Moss & Robson, 1968; Goldberg & Lewis, 1969).

PARENTAL EXPECTATIONS AND ATTITUDES TOWARD SUCCESS AND COMPETENCE Just as patterns of interaction in the home can shape children's mental abilities, so can parents' expectations, attitudes, and values influence their children's behaviors and the formation of the children's own expectations, attitudes, and values. A mother's high aspirations for her child and pressure on him for school achievement influence the child's motivation to achieve as well as his actual achievement (Rosen & D'Andrade, 1959; Bing, 1963; Wolf, 1964). Expressed satisfaction with the child's level of achievement reinforces the child's further achievement efforts (Rosen & D'Andrade, 1959; Crandall et al., 1964). If a parent has high expectations for his child, it is evidenced by greater participation in his child's work at home (Kagan & Moss, 1962; Katkovsky, Preston, & Crandall, 1964).

Several studies show that low-income mothers value achievement highly (Mannino, 1962; Coleman, 1966; Hess et al., 1968). However, there are indications that many black mothers, and probably those of other ethnic minority groups, feel a sense of powerlessness regarding their ability to help their children achieve in school (Kamii & Radin, 1967; Hess et al., 1968; Slaughter, 1970).

Feelings of "futility" in the role mothers play in the education of their children appear to be a necessary but not sufficient explanation of many black children's poor achievement (Slaughter, 1968). Although maternal membership in community organizations and feelings of control or power in the schools increases children's achievement (Hess et al., 1969), it is necessary to examine other experiences of children that might account for differential abilities for school achievements.

PARENTAL INFLUENCES ON CHILDREN'S SELF-CONCEPT AND SENSE OF EFFICACY A child's self-concept and sense of control over his environment accounts for more variation in achievement in grades 9 and 12 than other family background or school characteristics (Coleman, 1966). There has been very little study of parental influences on self-concept and sense of control. It appears, however, that parental acceptance of the child, firm and clear regulation in the home, parental respect for individuality, and high parental self-regard all foster positive self-esteem in children (Coopersmith, 1967; Sears, 1970). Belonging to a large family or being born in later ordinal positions increases the possibility that the child will have a poor self-concept (Sears, 1970).

With respect to locus of control, an individual is described as "internal" or "external" according to the "degree to which he perceives that the reward follows from or is contingent upon his own behavior or attributes versus the degree to which he feels the reward is controlled by forces outside himself and may occur independently of his own actions (Rotter, 1966)."

Maternal babying, protectiveness, affection, and approval increase the young child's internal sense of control over his environment. A father's positive and negative reactions to his child's behaviors encourage or discourage, respectively, the child's sense of internal control; mother's praise and criticism have little effect (Katkovsky, Crandall, & Good, 1967; Davis & Phares, 1969). There are conflicting results about whether there is a relationship between parents' own sense of control over rewards and their child's feelings of control (Davis & Phares, 1969; Hess, 1969). Davis and Phares (1969) found that fathers of children with greater internal control believed that parents should be indulgent while allowing the child to be self-reliant and independent; their wives, however, did not share these beliefs. Opposite views were held by parents of children who felt less control over the environment.

VERBAL ABILITY AND OPPORTUNITIES FOR VERBAL INTERACTION IN THE HOME A significant relationship exists between a child's verbal ability and opportunities for verbal interaction in the home. Opportunities for conversations at mealtime or other times, parental efforts to enlarge the child's vocabulary, and less use of punishment for poor speech relate to high verbal ability (Milner, 1951; Bing, 1963; Wolf, 1964). Other important factors are provision of resources for children such as toys, books, play space, and opportunities for self-initiated play (Milner, 1951; Bing, 1963; Wolf, 1964; Honzik, 1967; Kamii & Radin, 1967; Hess et al., 1968; Moore, 1968).

It is assumed that there are differences in quantity and quality of verbal stimulation of children from different social classes and ethnic groups that influence cognitive development. Recent research has shown that low-income black and bilingual families may be highly verbal and use complex speech patterns (Labov et al., 1968). Some difference in patterns and modes of linguistic exchange between members of different social classes do appear, however (Cazden, 1970).

MATERNAL TEACHING BEHAVIORS Several recent studies have looked at the strategies by which a mother helps her child learn or perform a task. In one instance, for example, a mother may help her child focus his behavior at the beginning of a task. She can also enhance learning by specific feedback, giving more positive than negative reinforcement, and modeling correct behavior by accompanying it with explanations (Hess & Shipman, 1967; Bee et al., 1969; Busse, 1969; Brophy, 1970). These studies have shown that lower- and middle-class black mothers give less positive feedback, fewer suggestions in the form of subtle questions, and spend less time in interaction with their children during problem-solving sessions than lower- and middle-class white mothers. Low-income white mothers give more negative feedback than low-income black mothers or middle-class mothers of either race (Bee et al., 1969; Hess et al., 1968). Middle-class black mothers seem to spend more time in task orientation and explanation and in focusing their children's actions than black mothers from low-income homes (Brophy, 1970). In a replication of Hess's Block Sort Task, lower-income Spanish surname mothers in San Francisco responded to their children with more negative feedback and had a stronger emphasis on physical response than their middle-class counterparts (Hubner, 1970).

INFLUENCE OF MATERNAL EMPLOYMENT AND FATHER-ABSENCE
ON COGNITIVE AND EMOTIONAL DEVELOPMENT
Children in day care are separated from either the father, mother, or both during most of the day. As with other separations, employment creates its own patterns of influence.

Although there is much evidence on the deleterious effects of long-term maternal separation or deprivation in the case of institutionalized children (Bowlby, 1958), there is little indication that maternal employment has harmful effects on either the cognitive or emotional development of children. Moore (1968) found that English middle-class children who had had daily substitute care from age two and one-half until five years showed little difference in IQ or achievement at age eight years.

The effect of maternal employment on children varies with the mother's attitude about working and her desire to work (Hoffman, 1959). Working mothers who dislike their work have reported less power over their children and more independent actions on the part of their children toward them than mothers who like their work. In peer-group interaction, their children show less impulse control, use physical force more often, and respond to frustration in nonadaptive ways. However, mothers who like their work are relatively higher on affect toward their children, use milder discipline, and impose fewer household tasks on their children. Their children are less assertive and less effective in social relations.

Little research is available on the effects of father-absence because of employment, other than studies dealing with prolonged times away from home. Father-absence is often ambiguously defined; hence, the results are difficult to interpret. One study sheds some light on the effects of variations in the father's employment patterns on girls. Girls whose fathers never worked on night shifts or whose fathers worked on night shifts after their daughters' ninth birthday had higher college-entrance scores than girls who either had no father or whose father worked on night shifts before age nine (the latter two groups did not differ) (Landy, Rosenberg, & Sutton-Smith, 1969). In their review of the effects of father-absence on boys, Herzog & Sudia (1970) note that father-absent boys usually show a ration reversal of the usual verbal-quantitative ratio in aptitude-test performance and do better on the verbal section than they do on the quantitative section. Typically, boys score higher on the quantitative section.

In a national sample, Coleman (1966) found that father-absence accounted for little of the variance in achievement among black children. However, for other minority groups—Oriental-Americans, Mexican-Americans, Puerto Ricans, Indian-Americans—father-absence was an important source of variance in school achievement relative to other home background variables studied. In another study, Hess and his associates (1969) presented evidence that father-absence may have a cumulative effect on school performance of black children that appears during the primary grades, but not during the preschool years.

From our discussion, it is evident that the effects of decreased interaction with either parent because of employment is an area of research that has been neither well defined nor explored. From available research, it is impossible to determine what specific variables are present or absent when parents work and hence to establish relationships between these variables and behavioral outcomes in the children.

THE FAMILY AS A UNIQUE INFLUENCE IN EARLY DEVELOPMENT

The advent of day care on a national scale has implications for the family's existence as the major agent of socialization during the child's early years. There is little research on the question of whether the extensive use of day care in the caretaking and education of young children will diminish the individuality of personality and culture now transmitted to children through their families. If we are to continue to value the "uniqueness" of each child, it seems even more important to have day-care staff work closely with the parents so that extrafamilial care can incorporate some of the individuality of each parent-child pair.

A related area of concern for day-care personnel is the development and maintenance of attachment between parents and child when the child is in day care many hours of the week. Recent writing (Ainsworth, 1969; Bowlby, 1969; Maccoby & Masters, 1970) stresses the importance of attachment for the child's total cognitive and emotional development. Attachment is formed primarily through the amount of emotional interaction between the attachment figure and the child. It depends on more than simple caretaking and is usually formed by the end of the child's first year, although it may occur at a later time. Infants may be "attached to" several people; however, usually there is one person to whom attachment is strongest. This is typically the mother because of the amount of time she spends in interaction with the infant during the first year. Infants who have a strong principal attachment are later attached to a greater number of other adults than infants who have weaker principal attachments. Children who are not attached to a primary figure usually have difficulty with socioemotional development in later years (Bowlby, 1969).

Several studies point to the importance of attachment between caretaker and child for cognitive and emotional development. Proximity to the mother encourages exploration of the environment. If children are alone or with strangers, they are usually inhibited in their exploration (Arsenian, 1943; Cox & Campbell, 1968; Rheingold & Eckerman, 1969; Ainsworth & Bell, 1970; Bell, 1970). Learning through modeling and social reinforcement is increased as a function of the child's emotional attachment to the model or reinforcer. Also, the effect of the model or reinforcer increases if the child perceives him to have a high degree of competence, status, and control over resources (Bronfenbrenner, 1970). Since parents usually develop this combination of emotional bond and status in the eyes of their young child, they seem to be in a unique position to foster his development. However, the extent to which other caretakers develop this combination of love and status would determine how effectively they provide a secure learning environment for the child.

Other research highlights the desirability of one-to-one relationships for cognitive development during infancy (Piaget, 1952; McCarthy, 1954; Gewirtz, 1969). These findings give tentative support to the conclusion that early development is fostered by a high frequency of contact involving a small number of adults.

Bettye Caldwell and her associates (1970) designed a research-oriented day-care center in which each infant would have high frequency of contact with as few caretakers as possible. The plan was not entirely feasible because of high staff turnover, but an analysis shows that children who have been in day care from ages one to two and one-half exhibit no difference in attachment behavior toward their mothers compared with a comparable sample of children reared entirely at home.

Research from the Israeli kibbutzim is also relevant. As Hava Gewritz has noted, the collective rearing of children does not preclude strong attachments between children and parents. However, attachments are also formed with the nurse. This becomes important when the nurse is replaced; the resulting discontinuity in caretakers during the child's daily life exposes the child to different personalities, attitudes, and in some cases, conflicting socialization techniques. The readjustment period usually is more difficult for very young children (Spiro, 1965). Thus, many kibbutzim recently have begun to keep the same nurse with children from the time they leave their mothers (six months) until they are four years old.

From our brief discussion of the attachment literature, there are several implications for day care:

1 The formation and maintenance of primary attachment is necessary for optimal emotional and cognitive development. It is important, then, that if at all possible nothing interfere with the child's ability to form a primary attachment.

2 Ideally, caretaking responsibilities should not be shared by many adults. Children up to ages five to six, but especially those under 12 months of age, need consistent figures with whom attachment can be formed and maintained and a stable pattern of socializing and educational techniques.

3 Infants who have not yet developed a stabilized primary attachment should be provided with experiences that would facilitate this, either in the home or day-care setting. If a primary attachment has been formed and stabilized, this attachment will not be diminished by the amount of time spent in the day-care center.

4 For children who have weak or insufficient parental inputs and attachment, the caretakers can supplement the parent and optimize the total development of the child.

5 Attachment to peers and adults other than the principal attachment figure can enrich a child's cognitive development by providing him with multiple models, which will increase his reactions to and attitudes about complex situations. This is relevant only if a child can differentiate among the values, attitudes, and behaviors of different models.

PARENT INVOLVEMENT IN EARLY EDUCATION PROGRAMS

ASSUMPTIONS AND RATIONALE OF PARENT PROGRAMS

Like other programs designed by middle-class professionals to meet the needs of minority and low-income groups, programs of parental involvement are based on conceptions of the social, cultural, and educational world in which families live and with which they interact. In one sense, these conceptions represent an implicit hypothesis about the nature of the educational problem and the point of the system that most needs to be changed; thus, they contain implications for the type of program that would provide a remedy. Many of the programs of the past decade have been based on the assumption that the educational system essentially is sound and that the greatest energy should be expended in helping families and children orient themselves successfully toward the school. Many of the program policies, procedures, and curriculum are built upon this cluster of assumptions.

Several implicit or explicit models of how experiences of being disadvantaged affect the educational attainment and capabilities of young children can be found in various forms in the literature of the last decade. (For a more detailed description of the models presented here and their assumptions, see Hess, 1969, and Gordon, 1969.)

THE DEFICIT MODEL One conception of the educational problems of the low-income child is that he has not had many of the experiences that confront a middle-class child during his preschool years and that help to prepare him for successful entry into the public schools. This leads to the belief that the poor child is deprived, that his home denies him the cognitive input needed for adequate growth, and that he is behind his middle-class peer in accumulating the information and skills needed for successful classroom work. The child is unable to deal successfully with early school tasks and finds himself getting farther and farther behind in a cumulative-deficit pattern. It is obvious that a conception of this kind would lead to remediation programs for the child and to educational programs for the mothers.

THE SCHOOLS-AS-FAILURE MODEL In contradiction to the deficit model is the view that the locus of difficulty is in the school and the school curriculum and the staff. From this standpoint, the problem is not so much within the child as in the schools' inability to deal adequately with the child's resources. The school is challenged as irrelevant, the teachers as unsympathetic and uninformed. The description of the problem changes from the "culturally deprived child" to the "educationally rejected child." The locus of blame is clearly in the institution that has failed in its responsibility to meet the community's educational needs. The emphasis on innovative programs is toward teacher training and retraining, toward increasing the sensitivity of the teachers and their knowledge about the child's culture and his resources, on curriculum changes, and mutual communication between the community and school. There is also a focus on the role of community persons as teaching personnel in the hope that greater participation will produce reform.

A CULTURAL-DIFFERENCE MODEL Another view of the educational problems of the minority child is that he has a learning experience that, although not deficient, differs from that of his middle-class peers and the assumptions upon which schools are based. He has grown up in a culture that has its own language, traditions, and strengths. The essential educational problem is one involving the difference between this culture and the one offered by the school. Proponents of this view believe that education should accommodate to cultural pluralism and that the curriculum should be adapted to include the need to transmit the community's culture to the young child.

A SOCIAL-STRUCTURAL MODEL The fourth point of view defines the problem in terms of general social processes. From this perspective, the behavior of individuals in a social system is related to their status, to the prestige and position they occupy, and to societal demands and expectations of them. The mother's interaction with her young child is a reflection of the societal demands and expectations. It is also a reflection of the society's treatment of her and her family. These modes of interaction eventually may have educational consequences. Because the social structure in which the family lives establishes cultural and community values, there is little to be gained from attempting to change individual children through remedial efforts unless there are also programs intended to change the social structure.

Programs that emerge from this approach are much broader in scope and deal with policies affecting communities rather than individuals.

ROLES PARENTS PLAY IN EARLY EDUCATION PROGRAMS

Parents play many different roles in early-education programs, and it is conceivable that they may assume one or more of these roles at different times depending on the program structure as well as on personal and situational demands. As we see it, there are five different, identifiable roles that parents play in early-education programs. They can be described along a continuum of involvement in educationally relevant activities.

PARENTS AS SUPPORTERS, SERVICE GIVERS, AND FACILITATORS

First, parents may plan a supportive and facilitative role in relation to the teachers and the school. Typically, parents contribute services in the forms of clerical, and custodial-maintenance work to support the nonacademic functioning of the school. They may engage in fund-raising activities, form baby-sitting services for visiting parents, and assist in the preparation of food served at the school. So that parents can learn about the staff and program, the staff may sponsor annual family nights, tours, or group discussions to inform parents about their responsibilities and roles as parents.

In all these activities, parents are typically in the roles of observers and bystanders and are not involved in activities that have a *direct* effect on or relationship to their children's education.

PARENTS AS LEARNERS

Second, parents may be involved as learners. Usually, the purpose is to improve the parents' skills and abilities so they can enhance the quality of family life for the child. Parents may attend formal education classes in child development, general education, or home management as is required in California cooperative schools. They may attend meetings to discuss problems of child-rearing.

Parents also may be involved in observing their children in the classroom, followed by a discussion of their observations with teachers who explain and interpret the child's behavior. During these parent-teacher conferences, the teacher may explain principles of child development, techniques for responding to the child in the home, and materials to use in the home to stimulate cognitive development.

Parents play the role of learner in all these activities, and the school (in the form of a teacher, psychologist, teacher aides, social worker) is the expert, or teacher. It is assumed that as parents learn to be better parents, they will enhance the development of their children.

PARENTS AS TEACHERS OF THEIR OWN CHILDREN

Third, parents may be involved as primary teachers of their own children, usually in the home. Mothers are trained to stimulate, reinforce, and support their child's cognitive development. The home visitor or teacher comes to the home with materials and toys and attempts to provide a model that the mother can imitate in her interaction with the child. The teacher may explain the purpose of the activities and how they relate to the child's development and how materials can be used in various ways with the child. In many programs, parents are taught to praise their children, stimulate their exploratory activities, and use various control and language strategies (e.g., Weikart & Lambie, 1969).

In this role, the parent is both a learner and a teacher who is involved in a one-to-one relationship with the child. Although some outside agency (e.g., the program or teacher) is still assumed to be the expert, parents are actively and directly involved in changing their behavior to affect positively their children's development.

PARENTS AS TEACHER AIDES AND VOLUNTEERS IN THE CLASSROOM   Parents may serve as paid teacher aides or volunteers in the classroom setting. Usually, this is seen as a program component that offers opportunities to low-income families to upgrade their employment levels; sometimes it is seen as a step to new careers in education.

Parents may supervise small groups of children, help teachers with preparation of materials, read stories, and implement other goals of the educational program. In some programs, parent teacher aides may train other parents to work as future teacher aides.

PARENTS AS POLICY MAKERS AND PARTNERS   Fifth, parents may be involved as policy makers who in partnership with the school can affect educational policy and thereby their children's development. They may take part in the planning, operation, and overall evaluation and direction of the program. In the Head Start, Follow Through, and Parent Child Center programs, parent participation in policy making is mandatory. For example, in Head Start, parents establish the criteria for staff selection, hire nonprofessional staff, and plan activities for the children and parents in the center. In other programs, such as the Coperativa De Niños (Children's Cooperative) in Chicago, the center is totally parent-controlled and staffed. Professionals act purely as resource personnel.

The rationale for parent participation in decision making is the belief that people will not be committed to decisions in which they have no involvement. Further, it is believed that the processes of considering information, decision making, and implementation are in themselves educational and help in developing leadership skills. It also is argued that since parents know their own situation best, they must be involved in planning for their children's education.

In planning for parent involvement in day-care programs, the various roles parents can play will depend on a number of factors, including program goals, assumptions about parents and children, local and organizational settings, ethnic and cultural factors, the developmental needs of children, and so forth. For example, in parent cooperative schools, parents play many roles at different times. They are involved in the administration of the school, are required to participate regularly as aides in the classroom, and in many cases must attend adult education classes. In other programs such as the home-instruction program, parents function almost exclusively as teachers of their own children.

EVALUATION OF PARENT PROGRAMS

Efforts to evaluate most of the existing programs that implement the various parental roles we have discussed are concerned primarily with the child's cognitive development and fostering positive parent behaviors and attitudes toward education. Evaluation procedures vary from program to program. In general, children are administered the standard tests of intelligence (e.g., Bayley Infant Scales of Development, Peabody Picture Vocabulary Test, and Stanford-Binet) at specific time intervals, typically before and after participation in the program. Besides these tests, a variety of standardized and nonstandardized instruments are used to assess social and emotional behavior and language development.

The evaluation of the effects of programs on parents is highly descriptive and generally based on informal evidence such as anecdotal reports and testimonials. In addition, various measures of mother-child interaction are made using tests and procedures developed by individual researchers as well as written reports of home visits that describe the mother's use of program materials, the quality of participation, and mother-child interaction (e.g., Gordon, 1969). Attendance records sometimes are used to determine the stability of involvement in the program, along with ratings of participation levels during group discussions (Badger, 1969). More promising attempts are underway to develop instruments to measure the impact of intervention programs on adult attitude change and behavior (Stern et al., n.d.; Hanson, Stern, & Kitano, 1968).

The wide variety in program inputs and evaluation procedures makes it difficult to draw definitive conclusions about program impact. It is virtually impossible to speak clearly about curricula, settings, intensities, durations, or specific characteristics of program inputs that may be associated with long- or short-term effects. The following are tentative conclusions representing the state of our knowledge.

Programs that attempt to involve parents as primary teachers of their own children appear to have positive effects on the cognitive development and achievement of their children (Klaus & Gray, 1965; Weikart &

Lambie, 1967; Gordon, 1969; Levenstein, 1969; Karnes et al., 1969). These effects appear to spread to other siblings and to children in the neighborhood who are not involved in the program (Klaus & Gray, 1965; Miller, 1968; Gordon, 1969), although it is difficult to identify the factors that led to these effects. Little evaluation has been done of the impact of programs on aspects of children's noncognitive development, partly because of the underdeveloped state of instrumentation in this area.

Participation may have some impact on the development of competence and self-esteem in the parents involved (Miller, 1968; Scheinfeld, 1969; Badger, 1970). It can be noted that these programs actively engage and involve parents in teaching their own children while emphasizing respect for their potential worth as individuals and confidence in this potential for continuous development. None uses psychotherapy, counseling techniques, or formal lectures, but each has attempted in some way to provide models for imitation, to provide support for the parents' problems and concerns in all aspects of family life and to express a firm commitment to self-determination and the elevation of self-esteem.

Parents involved in Head Start programs express a strong positive attitude toward their child's experience in the project. They feel that Head Start had a positive impact on their own lives by providing opportunities to make new friends, engage in more activities outside the home, read more, and get assistance from a social agency (Westinghouse Learning Corporation, 1969).

ENGAGING PARENTS IN EARLY EDUCATION AND DAY-CARE PROGRAMS

Because communities differ in life-styles, each particular school-community setting needs to be evaluated before methods of parent involvement are determined. Factors such as ethnic-group values, family patterns, the number of mothers working, whether the community is migrant or resident, and the physical setting will prove to be important to the needs of such programs. The evaluation process should be conducted in collaboration with community representatives.

Most of the innovative projects appear to follow a number of general principles that are applicable to day-care programs in establishing and continuing cooperation with parents.

There are, however, several obstacles to successful parent involvement. One is that the parents and teacher often have images of one another that do not promote cooperation. Both, for example, may feel unwelcome, the mother at school and the teacher in the home. The teacher may be viewed as less helpful and interested in the family than she really is, and the school staff is likely to underestimate the mother's strong desire to be involved with her child's education. Another hazard is that the family and community may come to expect more from this contact than is realistic and may eventually be disappointed. Further, a relationship that is established by one teacher may not be continued by another if the first leaves. Teachers are usually not experienced or prepared for working with parents, and their successes are often a result of personal charisma, confidence, and openness. Parent participation in the schools is a form of social commitment on both sides and deserves care and attention. It is one thing for both sides to want involvement, but quite another for either to know how to develop a workable arrangement.

INITIAL CONTACT WITH PARENT

The importance of the step of initial contact is recognized in virtually all programs, many of which learned its importance from harsh experience. Very often the school takes the initiative in establishing the relationship, especially since there has been an emphasis on parent-involvement programs in communities where parents have not felt free to participate. The impressions that the school initially creates about the program and the motivations of the staff may influence the level of participation of both sides and the program's success. Many experienced personnel believe that the most effective means of contacting parents is a home visit, preceded by arrangements made by note or telephone. Other program directors prefer to invite parents to an open house and to follow this social event with a home visit. The courtesies appropriate for visiting a home as well as the exact procedures vary with the cultural values of the community. Fathers in Mexican-American families, for example, play a strong role in decisions affecting the wife and children, and they are likely to want to participate from the beginning. In other communities, the father's participation and interest may be difficult to obtain if the responsibility of child-rearing is exclusively with the mother.

The home visit not only gives the teacher a more personal contact with the family and home but also expresses to family members the school's interest in them. The personal interchange enables the teacher to meet the mother on social terms and interact with her on a more personal level. This is an important step for many low-income families whose contact with the school is typically over behavior problems and criticisms of their children. Perhaps the most important objective of the initial visit is to begin to change the attitudes of mistrust and caution to those of trust and openness. Skills in clear and sensitive communication are essential in order that both parties understand each other's intentions. It may be useful to emphasize that the school and parents are working collaboratively toward a mutual goal—the education of the child. Through these visits the mother realizes she is wanted and needed in the program, and she feels less ignored and uninformed. In some programs, home visits are made by community members. This strategy has been successful because community members can anticipate the parents' reactions and establish rapport more easily. Frequently several home visits are necessary to establish trust and cooperation. However, the patience and understanding required is well worth the effort because the home visit is the most effective method of contact (Scott, 1964; Lane, 1968).

INCENTIVES

All parent-education programs offer incentives to encourage participation. Perhaps the most effective psychological incentive is the mother's interest in her child and her concern about the enhancement of his cognitive growth. Another psychological incentive is the experience that increases the mother's understanding of her child and helps her develop effective ways to deal with him.

Few programs offer financial incentives in the form of pay for involvement. Those that do may provide little more than the mother's expenses for joining the program (baby-sitting and transportation) unless she is employed as a teacher's aide (Lane, 1968; Badger, 1970; Levenstein, 1970). Parent participation in teaching, of course, does provide opportunity for the mother to upgrade her employment because she could eventually be employed as an aide or teacher.

The incentives mentioned are applicable to the day-care center, but insufficient with working mothers. For instance, parent involvement is possible during the day in the classroom only for mothers with flexible working schedules. The majority of employed mothers, however, do not have this advantage and cannot participate unless there is some change in the present work schedules. It may be possible for a day-care center operated by a corporation to arrange time for employees to participate regularly in the program. Also, provision of baby-sitting facilities after hours and meals for the mother and child enables the mother to participate in some education programs or as a member of a policy-making committee. These are arrangements that would enable employed mothers to participate in their children's education.

SUSTAINING THE PARENT'S INTERESTS

Once parents are engaged in a program, the difficult task of sustaining their motivation remains. In a successful program, the mother's interest in her own contribution to her child's education and the positive experience she gains in enhancing it may be enough to maintain participation. Her motivation is strengthened by feedback from the school about her child's progress. For example, one day-care center invited mothers before or after school to have coffee while discussing their children; nearly all the mothers responded and continued to attend the informal meetings throughout the year. If parents are involved in policy making, they must see concrete results from their efforts; otherwise, they feel ineffective and lose interest.

Other sustaining incentives include new social relationships and a curriculum geared to enhance the mother's personal growth. The teacher's genuine and constant interest can create a new and influential relationship. Badger attributes her 80 percent attendance record (Badger, 1970) to the teacher's persistence and interest. For instance, the teacher may make a special home visit to inform the parent of the events of a meeting the parent missed and to encourage future attendance. Other participating mothers may form a cohesive group, which tends to promote mutual interdependency and support that sustains the group over time. Some programs provide cookouts and field trips for the parents, which broadens their circle of friends. Several provide a special curriculum, such as a career-development component, which expands the parents' personal interests. Other projects provide courses to improve the homemaking skills of the mother (e.g., cooking and sewing). Such social and personal growth components can be incorporated easily into day-care programs.

AN ALTERNATIVE TO PARENTAL INVOLVEMENT: CROSS-AGE HELPING RELATIONSHIPS

The application of experience and knowledge of parent involvement programs to day care will vary with the circumstances of families in the program. Presumably, when day care is offered at low cost to nonworking mothers, there might be some point in establishing programs in which parents are encouraged actively to prepare their children for primary school. However, in programs that serve working mothers, particularly those employed in jobs demanding significant physical labor, using mothers as teachers is much more difficult. The mother's employment leads to constraints on her time and energy. In such instances the involvement of other family members, especially older siblings, might be particularly useful. Cross-age tutoring models thus offer an alternative means to serve the child, benefit older children in after-school programs and free the mother's evening time for affective and social interaction with her child. Cross-age helping relationships deserve consideration as potential resources for the school and family in day-care programs.

In recent years, educators have experiemented with ways to bring younger and older children together under conditions that will offer them pleasurable and productive learning experiences. These programs have been described as helping relationships (Thelen), cross-age teaching (Lippitt), interage classrooms (Yerry), and tutoring programs of one kind or another. All these programs share a common concern with developing helpful interactions and with bringing older and younger children together to facilitate the learning of concrete skills. Many of the program's proponents are as concerned with broadening social and interpersonal learning experiences as they are with academic achievement.

Cross-age helping programs thus far have been concerned primarily with elementary and high school students who focus on academic skills with their tutees. While a tutoring focus may be adaptable to day-care centers serving school-age children, the notion of helping relationships has broader implications and can be extended in a number of ways to increase individual attention for all children in group care. For older children, helping relationships provide experiences in supervised childcare and offer both older and younger children the chance to learn from and enjoy one another's growth as persons.

CROSS-AGE RESEARCH

Even though the research findings reported ʰy various programs document the effectiveness of cross-age relationships in improving academic achievement, school attitudes, and self-concept, one is led to conclude that the research findings are pale when compared with the enthusiasm of older and younger participants, teachers, parents, and administrators. On the whole tutors, tutees, parents, and teachers have reported that tutoring programs are effective. Despite these testimonials, Rosenshine and Furst (1969), in reviewing tutoring research, found that only half of the projects studied reported a significant impact on achievement. Moreover, none of the projects that included affective measures reported affect changes; affective measurement is not well developed, however, and such results are difficult to interpret. None of the tutor characteristics studied had any impact on success, that is, level of achievement, intelligence, and so forth.

The research dilemma may be stated from at least two perspectives: (1) the discrepancy between testimonials and data may reflect the impact of tutoring experience on some variable or process that has not been clearly identified; or, (2) the effects of tutoring on the variables being measured may be delayed rather than immediate, and the testimonials may be a clue to the impact, which may later show up as sustained gains. At present, these are only speculations.

In our view, there are two major advantages in including cross-age helping programs in day-care centers. One is that all children can use more individual attention than caretakers can provide. Through cross-age relationships, both younger and older children can receive additional attention to satisfy their personal need for recognition and to enhance their feelings of self-esteem.

A second advantage is that as older children learn more about younger children, they learn more about themselves. They also have a better understanding of adult roles, especially those of helping and teaching, and are better prepared for later parenthood.

PRACTICAL CONSIDERATIONS

The use of helping relationships between older and younger children in day-care centers depends on a number of factors, such as the population served and the available physical facilities.

Although in the past day-care centers generally have served pre-school children, there is increasing recognition of the need for after-school and before-school care for children whose parents are unable to provide for their care during nonschool hours. In any community where day care is needed, the children who must be considered are a variety of ages. The age range depends in part on the availability of recreational programs or extended school day programs as well as on local customs and attitudes that determine the age at which children are considered "responsible" for their own supervision during daytime hours.

To facilitate the development of optimal cross-age helping experiences, it would be useful to locate new day-care centers within or adjacent to schools, recreation centers, churches or factories. This would allow maximum flexibility in the use of space and in the assignment of children and make it possible to draw from a larger population of both older children and siblings. In the case of schools, it would be advisable to introduce cross-age programs into the curriculum during the regular school hours and to maximize opportunities for learning about younger children and helping roles while simultaneously offering individual attention to day-care youngsters.

SUMMARY AND IMPLICATIONS

Our discussion has several implications for parent involvement in day-care programs. Parents are not likely to be involved in programs when their life conditions demand that time and energy be primarily focused on meeting noneducational needs such as adequate housing, clothing, and food. If fully employed parents are to participate, the programs must have incentives that will allow them to do so without excessive loss of time and energy.

The recruitment and continued involvement of parents is a difficult and arduous process. Staff persistence and commitment is crucial to success. It appears that when parents feel genuinely involved and have a self-determined part in ongoing activities, they are likely to continue to participate and to initiate activities.

There is a trend in parent-involvement programs to move from passive roles, where parents are recipients of aid and information, to more active roles in which parents act as teachers aides, decision makers, and teachers of their own children. This trend probably is a function of the increasing awareness and experience of workers in parent education that information-dissemination and attitude change-oriented programs have dubious impact on parents and children unless they are used in connection with active and direct involvement of parents in the education of their children.

The involvement of parents has definite implications for the teacher's role. Traditionally, teachers have been child-oriented and have attempted to attain autonomy in the classroom with little interference from and interaction with parents. Parents have been viewed as competing agents of authority and respect.

Based on their home-instruction program, Weikart and Lambie (1969) have reached a number of conclusions about the role of the teacher in the home: (1) the teacher should assume a position of low power; (2) should provide immediate evaluation of teaching; and (3) be able to adjust to economic and social differences. The power and functions of teachers working in the classroom with parents changes with: (1) the availability of other adults besides the teacher in the classroom; (2) the supervision exercised by the mother over the teacher; and (3) the differences between teacher and parents in style and orientation toward the children.

It is essential that teachers and parents be involved in training that will give them some basis of cooperation and coordination once they are together in the classroom. Teachers must learn to be responsive to parents' questions and concerns and to be genuinely interested in and committed to the growth and development of parents as well as their children.

We need to understand the effects of intervention into family life and its implications for programs that can successfully involve parents in their children's education. It may be that fathers will be involved differently than mothers and in ways that respect their feelings about what are appropriate masculine behaviors (e.g., Tuck, 1969). Futhermore, day-care planners should be alert to the changing needs and growth of parents and children as they participate in intervention programs. For example, how do we move parents from "supporters" to "teachers of their own children," when and if they so desire? Flexibility and sensitivity to emerging needs is required in any kind of programmatic planning.

Finally, the concern about the impact of early-education institutions upon the nature and structure of the family has implications that go well beyond socialization and educational issues. In the sense that the family and the school perform similar functions in child care for the very young, they can be seen as "competing" agents of socialization, each attempting, intentionally or not, to shape the child's behavior toward a desired cluster of value and activities. It seems possible that the teacher will begin to play the role of expert vis-a-vis the mother in a range of child-care activities that include more than the customary educational concerns. The image of the mother's role as the most effective, and therefore the best, teacher and socializing figure in the child's life may be weakened by new institutions that not only offer in many ways the care provided by the mother but also presumably supply it more efficiently and effectively. A teacher becomes, in effect, the expert and may be seen in many instances as representing a governmental agency with access to special information and expertise. Since this system assumes responsibility for the child, it will certainly have effects upon the mother as an individual and upon her role in the family. The impact of the system thus deserves careful study, both because of its long-term implications for society and because of the educational needs that may be created by these fundamental shifts in institutional structures.

PEGGY LIPPITT **45** CHILDREN CAN TEACH OTHER CHILDREN

The door of the principal's office opened. A red-headed fifth grader brushed past the visiting teacher, and disappeared down the corridor.

"What's Billy Schwartz up to now?"

The principal smiled. "You'd be surprised. He came to show me the spelling test of a second grader he's been helping. Every word spelled correctly. Billy is as thrilled as if it were his own."

"Will wonders never cease?" murmured the teacher, who had been called on more than once to try to resolve Billy's continual referrals to the office and his negative attitude toward school. "What caused this change?"

"I changed first," the principal explained. "I cast myself in a new role with these discontented bigger students. I approached ten of our most influential and bored underachieving boys and girls, not as the big boss laying down the law, but as an educational leader with problems. I laid it on the line—how could I make school more fun for second graders who were having a hard time learning? Since they knew what it was like not to be getting along so well, what solutions did they have for the problems of the smaller youngsters? Then I invited these fifth graders to team up with me and the second-grade teachers to help the younger ones become more successful in school.

"They bought the idea that they could help, and began to work on a one-to-one basis. Now they keep coming in to show me how well their young students are doing."

This episode illustrates the growing recognition among educators that children helping other children learn may be a partial answer to four educational challenges: providing individualized instruction; increasing motivation; scheduling enrichment opportunities; and helping build self-esteem.

Children in the same grade often help each other. Recent experimentation reveals even greater advantages when older students become helpers for children three years or more their juniors. These outstanding gains are apparent:

1 Children receiving help from olders do not compare their skills unfavorably with those of their tutor.

2 Slower older students profit from tutoring. For example, sixth graders prforming at fourth-grade level can readily help second graders performing at or below grade level.

3 The tutoring can provide enrichment for brighter students as well as remedial work for slower ones.

If you need a rationale for cross-age helping, certainly all children need more individual help than a teacher can possibly give by himself. Furthermore, older children, because they *are* children, offer resources adults cannot provide as well. They are closer in age and can often reach a child who is having difficulty when an adult cannot; they provide more realistic models of behavior; and they offer opporunity for friendship within the peer culture. Studies show a direct ratio between feelings of peer acceptance and ability to use one's learning potential.

But cross-age helpers need training to be successful. Without it, older children tend to boss youngsters because of their own frustrations at being bossed. Youngers are apt to distrust olders while at the same time copying their attitudes and behaviors.

Training of older helpers should include development of a sympathetic, caring attitude toward youngers and skill practice in how to make them feel useful, successful, and important. Youngers need reassurance that everyone needs help; that it is not dumb to ask for it, or stupid to receive it. With this training teachers notice changes such as increased academic skill, more class participation, better school attendance, improved grooming, and growth in self-confidence for both the helper and the helped.

At the University of Michigan, social scientists, administrators, and teachers have been testing a Cross-Age Helping Program for six years, trying it out in suburban and inner-city elementary and secondary schools.

Older helpers have an in-service training seminar once a week on how to relate successfully to younger children. Also once a week they have a briefing session with the teacher of the younger pupil to exchange ideas on how to meet remedial needs, enrich learning opportunities, and increase motivation to learn.

Helpers work directly with the younger children for 20–50 minutes (depending on age and interest) three or four days a week in reading, writing, spelling, math, physical education, shop, or other activities. Sometimes the olders work with small groups instead of a single individual. The helping sessions take place whenever and wherever convenient; at the younger's desk, at the back of the room, in the hall outside the door, or in the library or special activity room.

Teachers can make or break a cross-age helping program. If you are a teacher of younger children you must consider the help of older students as a chance for your children to have individualized learning opportunities otherwise difficult to arrange. The helpers should be appreciated partners, and you should do for them what they hope to do for the youngers—give clear directions and check to see if these are understood; voice appreciation and build self-esteem; and act as a model of how one person can relate constructively to another. As a receiving teacher you must create a classroom attitude that cross-age helping is a desirable opportunity for everyone.

If you are a sending teacher, you must regard the program as a valuable experience from which children can learn a great deal in academic and social skills they might not otherwise be motivated to attain. You must think of it as an opportunity for them to be appreciated by other teachers and younger children and to develop their resources by using them. The experience does not compete with the learning you provide, but makes the learning in their own classroom more meaningful.

In all cases, the role of the teacher is to support growth rather than maintain control. You become a promoter of collaboration, an establisher of the norms of helpfulness rather than competition. You delegate responsibility and share the limelight. In turn, you get a high level of cooperation and commitment to learning. The youngers enjoy school more because they are more successful. The olders grow in academic achievement, gain insights, and learn service-oriented techniques.

46

DORRIS M. LEE

WHAT IS THE TEACHER'S ROLE IN DIAGNOSTIC TEACHING?

Since the pattern of diagnostic teaching differs from that of traditional teaching, its organization must differ also. Flexibility will be the keynote. Furniture will be arranged in many different ways, according to the immediate purposes. Schedules will utilize large blocks of time and provide for further changes or modifications as the needs demand.

There will be times when the teacher and the total group will be working together. At other times, small groups may be working by themselves or individuals will be working alone. Perhaps most often there will be a combination of small group individual activities with the teacher working first with one and then another.

The room will be a busy, active learning laboratory with children moving purposefully about the room, carrying out their explorations of the resources, conversing, seeking the ideas of their peers, discussing what they find, and coming to increased understandings. They will often be reading or writing, as individuals or groups, to gather or synthesize information and understandings they need. It will not be a pin-drop quiet place or an all-in-straight-rows orderly one. But it will be alive with children on their way to becoming tomorrow's capable and concerned citizens.

The teacher's role will be far different in this classroom than in the traditional one. This will require change, and teachers can change. The eagerness with which many are seeking a new and better way; the number who tried diagnostic teaching, greatly modifying their way of working with children; and the consistent response that having once worked this way they never are able to go back to the old way: all bode well for wide and successful changes.

Several cautions should be mentioned. The teacher must understand the why, the point of view, the basic understanding on which this way of working with children is built. A change in purposes and the teacher's feelings about children—increasing confidence in them and respect for them—is necessary. A recognition of the different role the school needs to take today from that of 30, 40, or 50 years ago leads to the recognition of the difference in the role the teacher needs to play.

Another caution is that unless a teacher feels very confident, it is wise to make changes gradually rather than doing an overnight total reorganization, especially with older children. They have acquired some fairly well-formed expectancies about school. Freeing them to be self-confident and self-directing will take time and patience. They must learn changes as well as the teacher. Once having accomplished this, progress can be most satisfying.

REORGANIZING

Teachers will initiate procedures for reorganizing at different rates and in different order. For this reason, suggestions will be made in light of eventual goals rather than as steps to follow, the order being from the larger overall aspects to the more specific.

ESTABLISHING PURPOSE Most basic of all is the establishment of purpose, broad and specific, by the learners. When they do not know, understand, or accept a reason for doing what is expected of them, little useful learning can take place. Purpose may be established in a variety of ways and, as things progress, should be. One important way is through teacher-pupil planning. The teacher may or may not set the broad framework within which planning takes place. Essential is the sincerity with which teachers invite suggestions and decisions by the children; children's right to make decisions within the limits that have been set must be genuinely honored. Unless the teacher sincerely feels this, the "exercise" of offering a choice that is really not available to them does children far more harm than good. It is probably more accurate to say that such a practice harms the relationship of the teacher with the children since it exhibits to the child a lack of trust, and mutual trust is a basic ingredient of any good learning situation.

ACCEPTING INDIVIDUAL DIFFERENCES Another basic step in reorganizing is to truly accept a frequently verbalized fact that children's purposes will vary and that therefore their activities and learnings will vary. A roomful of youngsters may all want to explore important issues . . . , but their concerns with the issues will vary with the learner. All may really want to be able to read better, but what they read and what they do to increase their reading abilities will be somewhat different for each. This means an end to blanket assignments, to the use of any one book as a text, to expecting always that all learners do the same thing at the same time for the same reason.

In group singing or group games or group planning, all may be dealing with the same content and procedures; but we must recognize that even here purposes and procedures will be different—and should be. For instance, a child may either try to be caught or try to escape while playing a game. He may be figuring out his own way to accomplish whatever aspect of the game best serves him, giving little regard to other aspects. Or he may look for ways of avoiding active participation as far as possible. And maybe these purposes are legitimate and desirable, or perhaps they are cues to feelings of inadequacy which need to change. Teachers must remember, however, that they cannot change these feelings of inadequacy by requiring more active participation. Feelings of adequacy are built on successful fulfillment of purposes, not going through motions on command.

ACHIEVING COMMITMENT This leads to a further basic step in reorganizing our classrooms: Stop requiring! Instead, encourage commitment of learners; expect them to set their own goals and do their own planning of what they need to do, how much and when. This may seem most difficult of all to accept. If so, it is because faith in children has been lost. Believe that children want to learn, that with guidance they can and will move ahead significantly, more confidently, and, ultimately, more rapidly by taking the responsibility for their own learnings.

Instead of the usual practice of making assignments, teachers can raise the question of what the learners feel they most need to do or what they need to do next that would be most helpful. If children have never experienced this, they will need help as a group and as individuals in order to think in these terms. And, let's face it, some teachers will also need to learn to think in these terms. Too often, what children "do next" is the next page or the next story or the next chapter, regardless of what they have or have not learned from previous assignments or from their experiences of living. In situations where diagnostic teaching prevails, teacher and children can learn together in a healthy environment of cooperation, mutual help, and increasing respect for each other.

MEETING INDIVIDUAL LEARNING NEEDS

It cannot be assumed that children will respond perfectly during the learning stages, that the learning stage is of the same duration for all, or that all mistakes have identical causes.

LEARNING FROM MISTAKES Errors must be expected and accepted. They are not bad, yet they are almost always punished—by word or look, by red marks on the papers or a lower grade, by imposing drill or staying after school. After all, a mistake is just a cue to something not learned yet. Since learning is the business of the school, teachers should welcome each mistake as a cue to what a child needs to learn that he thus far has not accomplished. It may well provide the basis for a learning experience in the near future.

Punishing errors has led to all sorts of undesirable results, such as cheating, disregarding assignments, and not responding for fear the comment is unacceptable. So much anxiety results that little learning is able to take place and the child's confidence in himself is lowered. This, in and of itself, impairs learning and leads to many other harmful results. In addition, punishing errors brings no useful results. For some time, many teachers have been asked whether they had any evidence that marking children's errors brought learning which later was applied in similar situations. Thus far no one has been willing to subscribe to the belief that checking mistakes really leads to significant learning.

USING INDIVIDUAL RECORDS How then can we make use of the mistakes children make? An important part of diagnostic teaching is the keeping of records on each individual. This has nothing to do with grading but does supply information which is helpful in helping children learn. There are many ways to keep such a record. One common one is the use of a loose-leaf notebook or ring binder that accommodates full-sized sheets. Each child's name can be put on a tab so his pages can be found quickly. Or the teacher may keep a file box containing index cards, each with a child's name on it. Whatever the device, the record needs to be flexible, expandable, and easily and quickly available.

The purpose of the record is mainly to note learnings the child has achieved and those he needs but has not yet acquired. More will be said about it as various areas of the curriculum are discussed. In any area it can provide the basis for teaching to meet an immediate need, either in groups or with individuals. It helps to organize learners into useful and defensible teaching groups. As teachers identify specific, current needs in the individual conferences and record them, they can organize temporary groups who need the same specific learning at the same time; each includes those who need the same sort of skill or understanding right now. Lessons can be planned and the group can work together with the teacher for 15 or 20 minutes, for one or two days or perhaps a week. Children may leave the group as they acquire the learning for which the group was established, and perhaps others may join it, either at the suggestion of the teacher or by their own request. Various groups may work during any day for a variety of purposes and disband when the specific need for which they were established has been met. Continuing such groups, using them to present one learning after another, is self-defeating. It indicates an assumption that all children need all learnings in a prescribed sequence. *This concept must be abandoned as it simply is not true.* This will be further explained in the discussion of the various curriculum areas.

FOSTERING SELF-EVALUATION Increasing self-evaluation on the part of the child is one of the greatest contributing factors to success in working with children. It is the essential key that frees children to become aware of their own needs and able to move ahead to satisfy them. When a person is dependent on outside judgment as to his competencies and his needs, there is little use in making these determinations for himself. In fact, it soon ceases to be an available alternative. Instead of developing as self-confident, self-directed individuals who understand themselves and know where they are heading, children become drifting, rudderless people waiting for pushes and steering by others. They lose confidence in their own ability to manage themselves and set their directions. This has produced some of the greatest ills of our society and will produce more as the world's pace speeds up and individual commitment becomes increasingly important.

Adults cannot wait until a child is old enough and then expect self-evaluation. Helping the child to assess his own behavior starts, hopefully, at a very tender age but certainly as soon as he enters school. It is amazing how kindergartners can identify what they can do well and what they would like to do better. Teachers who work this way with children all through the grades consistently report that as the program gets under way, most children can identify their own needs with increasing confidence and frequently with greater accuracy than can the teacher.

Teacher judgments on children's learning, in either the curriculum content or the processes of learning or of living together effectively, cannot form the bases of action. Children undoubtedly will need help in making accurate evaluations. This help should come *after* the child has made his evaluation and then only if it seems inadequate. At such times, rather than stating a judgment, the teacher raises questions that may help the child analyze the situation, inquiring about aspects he seems not to have taken into account. When he has been made aware of the main areas of pertinent data, his evaluation must then be accepted, at least for the time. It may well be more accurate than ours. If it is not, he will find it out as the teaching-learning proceeds and his own discovered mistakes will provide a most favorable learning situation. Never—oh never—does the teacher say, "I told you so!"

DEVELOPING SELF-DIRECTION   Self-evaluation is the basis for self-direction. As one knows where he is and has established a purpose, he can easily and surely move toward fulfilling it. The path that a learner takes may not be one the teacher sees or would have suggested. However, a purpose that the child sees and has commitment for is far more important and will produce far more success. As the teacher listens and becomes aware of the child's intended procedures, he may, if he feels it important, raise a question such as, Have you thought about————? Having made him aware of another possibility, it becomes the child's prerogative to follow it or not, to the extent that he feels it may be useful. If the teacher persists, the child decides this is something he is going to be compelled to do, whether or not he feels he needs to, and the effectiveness of the teacher-pupil relationship suffers.

INSTRUCTING

To consider the teacher's role in instruction, there must be agreement on the meaning of terms. Here, the term *instructing* will be used to mean the relationships and interactions which the teacher establishes within the situation for the purpose of the growth and development of each child toward the goals and purposes of the school. It includes, then, all the aspects previously considered in this chapter, as well as others. The aspects more commonly thought of as *teaching* will be considered in this section.

STIMULATING LEARNING A large part of teaching for many has been telling. The teacher is "on stage" usually at the front of the room presenting facts, information, and procedures. It is now known that this is not effective and often prevents more learning than it produces. It creates the false impression that knowledge and understanding can be *given* to one person by another. This, of course, is not true: each person must do his own learning. The only contribution another person can make is to create a situation in which the learner is most likely to see personal meaning and be challenged by an idea which he sees is of value to him. This will help to ensure that the learner deals with it intellectually in such a way as to understand its meaning for him and in sufficient depth as to be able to have it affect his thought and actions.

Therefore, a teacher's job becomes one of arranging a stimulating situation (few will be equally stimulating to all) and raising pertinent questions about it for the consideration of the children involved. It also means moderating—not controlling—the discussion that follows. When a pertinent point is being missed, the teacher needs to raise the level of awareness of the group by posing a question which calls attention to this area. From the reaction he must judge if more discussion of this is needed now, if more background experience is needed so children can bring personal meaning to it, or if the point should be dropped for the time being. Having introduced the concept, it may continue growing in some children and make them more ready to deal with it later. This is another kind of diagnostic teaching: diagnosing the pertinence of certain concepts for group thinking at any particular time.

SERVING AS A RESOURCE PERSON Another teaching role is that of a resource person. Helping children learn how to learn is one of the teacher's responsibilities. One of the important skills in accomplishing this is to be able to locate readily accessible sources of information or discussion materials on the topics of concern. This means different things for children of different ages. It may bring defeat if useful materials are so difficult to locate that children give up trying to find them. In short, the teacher's task is one of providing resources so that children are able to use them successfully for their purposes and also gain competence and confidence in their ability to find what they need.

At times, with children of any age and capability, sources of information may be so difficult to find or use or of such a tangential nature that a child's learning is better served when the teacher becomes the resource and directly provides the information needed. When telling is in response to a request to know, it can be very useful in learning.

Another sort of telling that is also a valuable part of the teacher's role is an extending of children's understanding through vicarious experiences. The teacher, in seeking to raise the level of thinking, may ask the children if they have thought about a certain aspect of a topic under study or what the significance of a specific related incident might be. Thus the teacher in a learning situation supplies not only material resources but also supplementary ideas that only a teacher can bring at the pertinent time. This does not mean providing conclusions but rather bringing more data for the children's consideration that will raise new questions and result in further clarification.

ASKING QUESTIONS Perhaps one of the most important instructional roles of a teacher is that of questioner, raising issues for the purpose of stimulating thinking rather than developing memory. This is far different from asking questions in the recitation situation. Questions are basically of two kinds, open and closed. The closed question requires convergent thinking to arrive at the one right answer, while the open question asks for divergent thinking, recognizing that there may be many answers or perhaps none at all. Both kinds of questions have their place and usefulness but neither can serve the purpose of the other. In general, the closed question has to do with specifics or details, while the open deals with broader aspects of the subject.

The question, "Where does it tell what Jimmy did about it?" (closed) requires different thinking than, "What might others have done in the same situation?" (open). The closed question, "What is the answer to this problem?" is different from, "How else might you find the answer?" (open). "What is this word and what does it mean?" (closed) does not provide the stimulation of the open question, "How can you change this word by adding suffixes and prefixes, and what difference does this make in use and meaning?" Very different kinds of exploration and thinking are required by the closed question, "What were the causes of the Revolutionary War?" and the open question, "How are recent revolutions around the world like or different from our revolution?"

EVALUATING

Another role for the teacher is that of evaluating the learning and progress of each child. Of course, all evaluation must be in terms of goals and purposes. Also, it should mainly be in terms of the ends or goal rather than the *means* by which the child is moving toward the goal.

CONFUSING THE MEANS AND THE ENDS

There is a great deal of confusion on this point. We are too apt to say a child does not know his arithmetic when we mean he cannot give immediately on demand the answers to his number combinations. The reason for knowing his number combinations is so that he can solve quantitative problems—have the means for attaining the end. However, he may do this very well and with reasonable accuracy and speed by using aids of various sorts. If so, he *does* know his arithmetic! When the aids prove inadequate or get in his way, the teacher may through diagnostic teaching help him to become independent of them, thus improving the means rather than treating the skill as an end.

To cite another example, many children are evaluated on their knowledge of phonics. The use of phonics is one way some children may be helped to learn to read. They are solely a means to an end and have no value of their own. So the evaluation should be in terms of the goal, the ability to deal with ideas on a printed page, and not of phonetic rules or information. A teacher may find that a child's reading at some point might be improved by developing some aspect of phonics through diagnostic teaching. However, this should not enter into the teacher's evaluation of the child's reading competence. In many other situations the means to learning is considered a goal. The many roads to learning and the fact that no two learners ever trod an identical path are ignored, as is the knowledge that for some the variations are wide indeed.

SELF-EVALUATING

For various reasons, evaluation always needs to involve the self-evaluation of the child. One often-overlooked reason is that the child's interpretation of his own learning often brings insights possible only to him. It can help the teacher avoid making serious and embarrassing mistakes. Even more important, however, is the increase in learning or understanding on the part of the child.

Yet the teacher has a responsibility for making his own judgments of the learner's stage of development as accurately as is possible. The process of evaluation can be more or less useful and comfortable for all, according to how it is carried out. Conditions such as the following determine whether the evaluation is less useful or more useful:

LESS USEFUL	MORE USEFUL
External	Internal
Done by others	Done by self
To meet a standard	To note progress
Once a term a year	Daily
Determines major decisions in organization (pass or fail)	Determines next steps in learning

Goals uncertain	Goals self-determined with guidance
Unrelated to real purposes	In line with real purposes
To judge performance	To analyze needs
Same for all.	Tailored to each individual.

Evaluation needs to be clearly distinguished from testing. The purposes of evaluation are to determine the stage of learning and the amount of progress, to reaffirm or adjust purposes, and to plan next steps. Testing is a contrived, in-or-out-of-context situation in which the teacher gets a paper-and-pencil response to certain facts, information, skills, or understandings which, hopefully, the child or usually the group has learned. Since learning is of little or no value unless it functions in pertinent real situations, testing may be quite irrelevant. Evaluation is most useful when the learning is reflected in the real situation. A child may spell all his words correctly on a test but write them incorrectly in a creative story. Or, he may respond quite inadequately to a question about a social studies concept yet use it effectively in dealing with his particular project. Many such illustrations might be given to document the fact that test scores are of little value. The only valid proof of learning is the evidence that the learner sees the relationship and is able to use the learning in a real situation.

CREATIVE TEACHING **47** PAT ANZALONE
DONA STAHL

CREATIVE TEACHING IS BASED ON THESE
HYPOTHESES ABOUT CHILDREN AND LEARNING

There are many patterns of learning and no one teaching method meets the varying needs of all children. It is vitally important to provide alternatives in the educational program.

The teacher cannot tell a child how to think, but must provide him with the freedom, the encouragement, and the opportunity to do so.

Learning is an active, not a passive, process and must involve participation in a task rather than mere absorption of information.

Children are consistent in their need for success experiences, but vary greatly in their levels and rates of achievement.

Discovering and developing uniqueness in individuals is a major goal not to be thwarted by ignoring or minimizing differences.

Children bring to each new experience varying amounts of informa- tion and misinformation, which may clarify or distort concept formation.

Setting goals and evaluating progress are the privilege and the responsibility of the child, and are essential to long-term learning. Teachers must not let a marking system distort evaluation.

The unstructured and inductive experiences which occur outside school are often the most profound and influential activities of childhood.

Children learn from each other, through observation, imitation, and cooperative consideration of a mutually challenging task.

Learning is both positive and negative. When the activity does not fit the child's unique personal need, negative learning is certain to occur.

It is more important for children to appreciate and practice self-con- trol than to be controlled by an adult authority figure.

Intrinsic motivation makes children capable of meaningful self-selec- tion and self-correction of appropriate learning activities.

CREATIVE TEACHING MEANS CHANGE FOR YOU

Intellectually it is not too difficult to accept the hypotheses above. But the emotional impact that comes from experiencing their realization could be another matter. It is rewarding, but it may be somewhat of a shocker, too.

Let us assume that you are both accepting the hypotheses and acting upon them. What kinds of things are likely to happen?

Your classroom will become the setting for an experience in community living by the children. You will be the most important person there, but the room activity will not revolve around your personality. Instead, you will encourage your group to develop value systems by setting standards, making decisions, and conducting themselves to gain acceptance by their peers.

Your room environment will be created in terms of personal and group efficiency rather than the traditional standards of quietness. As a result, the noise level will be somewhat higher than in other classes. The schedule will be far more flexible, with larger blocks to allow for creative activities and more reading and experimentation. Pupils will help to make the schedule, and it will be evaluated and changed from time to time.

Your goal will be to individualize instruction as rapdily as possible, and fixed groups will be replaced with flexible ones. Children will be paired, or will meet in small groups to work on particular problems or activities.

You will employ a multisensory approach to learning with far more related materials. Because of this, your room, though neat to your children, may be disorderly by adult standards.

Discussions involving inquiry or discovery will promote the trying out of ideas or the setting up of hypotheses. Questions you ask will be for both diagnosis and teaching, and often they will have several acceptable or correct answers.

As you work for individually tailored programs, the textbook will no longer determine classroom procedure. You will want many, many books and other materials but few, if any, sets with a copy for every child.

You will spend less time marking papers or hearing children perform, and more in pupil conferences. You will spend more time gaining background in various subjects and preparing work materials tailored to children's individual needs.

You will be constantly alert to better means of evaluating, and you and the children will recognize that grading is only one phase of evaluation.

As you try to give less direction and to help children become more objective about their work, you may at times become frustrated. (You will soon see that a poor teacher who can keep the children quiet is less likely to encounter difficulty than a creative teacher who has not totally mastered techniques of the new process.)

These conditions present a real challenge. Change doesn't come overnight, and you are very likely facing such situations anyway. However, they are not without their rewards. Here are some pluses you can expect:

Inherent politeness based on respect for each individual will develop among the children.

Individual interests and special talents will become far more evident. Children will have a sense of possession about the classroom and library, and increasingly they will use equipment and materials on their own.

Differences in children will be more evident than similarities, making them more interesting and providing grounds for respect and admiration.

You will be less likely to have nonreaders, or non-anything for that matter. If individual children have learning problems, they will help each other work on them.

Children will be more sensitive to art, music, literature, and other artistic expressions as well as to the feelings of those around them.

Integrity in thought and act will develop, with children seeing the need for supporting their ideas.

Parents who tend to be hostile at first will change their minds, mostly because their own children have sold them on what is happening. You and the children will strike a truce with the janitor. Pupils will try harder for order, and the janitor will become less stringent in his demands.

Your moments of satisfaction will increase as you watch each child working at his own speed on a program tailored especially to his needs.

Q AND A ABOUT OUR CREATIVE TEACHING STRATEGIES

How can I get started with multilevel activities? Is my first move to individualize one curriculum area?

Before getting started, it is a good idea to give plenty of thought to where you want to go, and what you have to work with. Know your objectives, even write them if you work best this way. Give plenty of time to diagnosing the levels and needs of the members of your class. Commercially designed tests will help you, and for certain purposes, teacher-made tests and observation.

There is a great deal to do in advance of attempting any amount of individualization if you are going to avoid later confusion and frustration. To differentiate instruction you cannot be merely one jump ahead of the class, because some students will soon out-jump the materials you have ready, and you won't be able to maintain your lead. Work into individualization gradually and in one area at a time.

How do I select and arrange materials? Are there criteria to determine their value?

During your preparation period you established both your objectives and the levels you need to provide for. Now you are ready to gather and organize materials for each level. Select or make instructional materials which are largely self-directing and self-correcting. Look at old materials in a new way as well as selecting appropriate new items. Workbooks can be torn apart and the pages used in many ways. Commercially available self-directing and self-correcting materials can often be used in part or *in toto*. Textbooks from lower levels can be disassembled and useful pages packaged into booklets or pasted on cards. Old worksheets can be brought into use. Share duplicator copies with teachers from other grade levels so you can provide for various levels in a skill or content area. You will find yourself looking for potentials in materials that previously you would not have considered.

Could you give a few specific examples of materials I could try using at first?

Pages from an easy reading workbook can provide a simple map around which you can prepare questions for geography skills work to be used by a small group of children whose reading level would prohibit a class text or grade-level workbook. Pictures cut from an arithmetic readiness book can provide material for small-group activities in classification. Magazine illustrations might be used by an advanced group, together with guiding questions (on a card), for making inferences leading to concept formation and eventually to statements of generalizations.

So far you've discussed how the teacher gets ready. How about the children? Don't they need to be prepared?

They certainly do, and you should spend plenty of time in training them. Show them how to use the various self-directing, self-correcting materials. Let the children know exactly how to proceed through programs you have set up, and how to keep the necessary records. Be sure they know where and how to go from one step to another. They will also need to establish routines for obtaining materials, for storing materials in use, and for handling completed work. Agree upon a procedure for children who need help.

At last, I feel ready to start and I think the children are ready, too. What now?

It is wise to begin one group at a time, in a program of self-directing, self-correcting materials. Work with them step by step until they are thoroughly familiar with the program. Then let them begin to work at their own rates. Be alert to the child who may be misplaced or who may suddenly spurt ahead. Place individuals in programs at other levels as the need becomes apparent.

A few suggestions to help you retain your sense of equilibrium during this period: Expect more noise and moving about than you may be used to, but notice that it is probably working noise made by many children actively involved in a learning experience. Expect some days to be better than others, some programs to work more smoothly than others, and some children to operate more independently than others. Plan for a variety of other types of activities, such as whole-class discussion, independent supervised study, and short lectures, to provide a change of pace.

How can I keep track of everyone when so many different things are going on?

Keeping track of individual students working at different levels and with different materials need not be complicated. Determine what you must know about a pupil working in a program (it will vary) and how often you want to know. Then design various kinds of record sheets for pupils to keep.

In a program with a sequence of activities, pupils might have a checklist, merely checking off each activity as it is completed. When activities may be selected in random order, a control sheet can identify each activity by number or title. Then the child circles the number of the activity he is currently working on and puts an X through the circle when he completes it. Simple bar graphs of scores can be kept in many programs. The purpose of each record should determine its design.

Such records must be simple enough so the student can keep them without teacher assistance. They must be clear enough to show at a clance what a child is working on and how well he feels he is doing.

Exactly what is the purpose of these records? How do I translate them into marks?

These records are not meant to be used as a basis for marking. They are indications of mastery concept or levels of performance. Every meaningful learning sequence should present one or more basic concepts, allow for practice and application, and then have a formal teacher-administered and teacher-scored test of mastery. Student-kept checklists and graphs are designed to record the pupil's individual progress through the program of materials. Mastery tests are used at appropriate stages to determine what he has learned and at what place in the program he should resume further work.

What kind of physical organization is necessary for multigroup activities?

Your classroom may already have movable desks and chairs, an extra table or two, countertops, bookshelves, filing cabinets, and storage cupboards. These provide an ideal starting point for the physical arrangement needed for multilevel, multigroup activities, but a lack of them does not prevent a room from being used for such activities. However, you may have to show ingenuity in "making do" with what you have.

Clustering desks or tables provides for flexibility in grouping children for work, study, small-group instruction, and use of audiovisual materials. It is also the most economical use of classroom space, leaving large peripheral or central areas cleared for action. Even a classroom with stationary desks will yield corners where small groups of children can gather. Pupils need not remain in chairs—they like the floor!

How do you house materials? Is it important for each child to have a storage area?

It is very important. Also you must arrange for storage of a variety of self-directing, self-correcting programs. They should be all easily accessible to pupils, be clearly labeled, and be organized so that children can return completed items to the proper place with minimum effort. Boxes containing well marked file folders or manila envelopes of lessons or activities in a logical order provide a relatively simple, inexpensive storage system. Don't place too much material in each, for the children will be moving them from place to place as the need arises.

Is there portable equipment that would help me organize and store materials?

A wagon such as a kitchen utility cart or a set of shelves mounted on wheels, with a long extension cord, makes an easily moved, versatile "audiovisual center." Such a vehicle can house the tape recorder and earphones, overhead film loop or filmstrip projector, and boxes of materials for use with the audiovisual equipment. (Your room should have its own pieces of equipment mentioned.)

A shadow box with a white background can be made from a large cardboard carton to serve as a screen for use by small groups in viewing slides, filmstrips, or film loops. Any cluster of desks or section of rows of desks can become a listening corner by taking the tape recorder and earphones to it.

Even if I can adjust to more room noise, won't classroom control be a big problem?

Not if your real concern is to develop self-controlled, independent learners. We found that we first had to establish a classroom environment offering many worthwhile activities from which individuals could choose. Allowing them to use freely materials which interested and challenged them did much to eliminate the source of discipline problems.

Boredom, lack of interest, and frustration are the real causes of most classroom mismanagement. Such attitudes toward a teacher-proposed activity yield minimal performance by many students, and by others a complete refusal to perform. Work which is too difficult for a child frustrates him. He doesn't learn what the teacher intends him to learn, but instead, he learns the futility of trying. The boredom which the bright child experiences in an unchallenging task is expressed in undesirable pupil behavior.

Do the children still respect you as teachers, or do you get "lost in the shuffle"?

First, they respect us as fair, responsible individuals. Secondly, they respect us for respecting them as fair, responsible individuals (not children). They know we have responsibilities just as they do. As for the shuffle, a ringing bell means we want their attention, and we get it quickly!

Rate yourself first on each of the five topics, on the basis of 25 possible points. Enter your score beside each topic. Then rate yourself on each question on a 1 to 5 basis (1 as lowest, 5 as highest). Enter your scores as before, and add them by sections.

DEVELOPING A SPIRIT OF ADVENTURE WITH REGARD TO DIFFERENTIATION OF INSTRUCTION

Are my objectives different for various children? ____

Is my "class" time lessening and activity or work periods increasing? ____

Am I now more inclined to watch how individual children learn? ____

Do I talk to the whole class less and less frequently? ____

Am I likely to have several types of activities going on at one time in one curriculum area? ____

PROVIDING FOR DIFFERENT RATES AND LEVELS OF ACHIEVEMENT

Do I form reading groups for specific skill instruction as well as for reading level? ____

Do different children take different mastery tests at different times? ____

Is virtually no child consistently failing in the tasks provided for him? ____

Do I frequently regroup in arithmetic according to individual skills? ____

Do I rarely give whole-class homework assignments in social studies, science, or other nonskill areas? ____

ALLOWING PUPILS TO BECOME MORE SELF-DIRECTING

Have pupils planned some of our learning activities for this week? ____

Do some children work independently in pairs or small groups each day? ____

Are pupils correcting their own work more and more often? ____

Does each child keep systematic records of progress for some of his work? ____

Do I hear "I'm finished. What shall
I do now?" less and less frequently?   ____

PROVIDING OPPORTUNITIES FOR CHILDREN TO
DEVELOP THINKING SKILLS

Have I been giving more thought to the
kinds of questions I ask?   ____

Do pupils engage in some small-group
discussion or brainstorming each week?   ____

Are there opportunities for unstructured
investigation in science?   ____

Am I asking more open-ended questions
to which there are no "cut and dried"
answers?   ____

Do learning activities planned for the
children often turn out to be learning
experiences for me, too?   ____

HELPING CHILDREN DEVELOP A HIGHER LEVEL OF
SELF-CONTROL

Could I say, "It is now time for social
studies (or any subject)," and find the
class could take over from there?   ____

Are those who were formerly "problem
children" actively involved in room activities?   ____

If I left the room for half an hour,
would I return to find virtually every
child absorbed in learning tasks?   ____

Has the use of a variety of activities
eliminated much of the restlessness in
hyperactive pupils?   ____

Are my pupils more likely to make
suggestions on their own concerning room,
playground, or general school activities?   ____

If there is considerable difference between your topic score and the total score for questions in that section, you are thinking creatively, but not following through in classroom practice. If both scores are low, both thinking and classroom practices need some revamping. If both are high, keep up the good work! If the total score for the questions exceeds the topic score, you may be underestimating yourself!

selected references

INTRODUCTION: PORTRAIT OF A CHANGING FIELD

Berlyne, D. Curiosity and explanation. *Science,* 1966, 153:25–33.

Bloom, B. *Stability and change in human characteristics.* New York: Wiley, 1964.

Bowlby, J. Maternal care and mental health. *World Health Organization Monograph Series,* 1952, No. 2.

Dewey, J. *The child and the curriculum.* Chicago: University of Chicago Press, 1902.

Glass, D. C. (Ed.) *Environmental influences: Proceedings of a conference under the auspices of the Russell Sage Foundation and Rockefeller University.* New York: Rockefeller University Press, 1968.

Goldfarb, W. The effects of early institutional care on adolescent personality. *Journal of Experimental Education,* 1943, 12:106–129.

Gordon, I. J. *Reaching the child through parent education: The Florida approach.* Gainesville, Fla.: Institute for the Development of Human Resources, University of Florida, 1969.

Grotberg, E. Institutional responsibilities for early childhood education. In I. J. Gordon (Ed.), *Early childhood education: Seventy-first yearbook of the National Society for the Study of Education.* Chicago: University of Chicago Press, 1972.

Hamachek, D. Characteristics of good teachers and implications for teacher education. *Phi Delta Kappan,* 1969, 50:341–345.

Harlow, H., & Harlow, M. K. The effect of rearing conditions on behavior. *Bulletin of the Menninger Clinic,* 1962, 26:213–224.

Hunt, J. McV. *Intelligence and experience.* New York: Ronald Press, 1961.

Kayserling, M. *Windows on day care.* New York: National Council of Jewish Women, 1972.

Klaus, R., & Gray, S. The early training project for disadvantaged children: A report after five years. *Monographs of the Society for Research in Child Development*, 1968, 33(4, Serial No. 120).

Miller, D., & Swanson, G. *The changing American parent: A study in the Detroit area.* New York: Wiley, 1958.

Read, M. The biological bases: Malnutrition and behavioral development. In I. J. Gordon (Ed.), *Early childhood education: Seventy-first yearbook of the National Society for the Study of Education.* Chicago: University of Chicago Press, 1972.

Scott, J. P. The process of primary socialization in canine and human infants. *Monographs of the Society for Research in Child Development*, 1963, 28 (1, Serial No. 85).

Sears, R. R., Maccoby, E. E. & Levin, H. *Patterns of Child Rearing.* Chicago, Row, Peterson, 1957.

Simon, K., & Grant, W. V. *Digest of Educational Statistics.* Washington, D.C.: U.S. Department of Health, Education, and Welfare, 1972.

Skeels, H. M. Adult status of children with contrasting life experiences. *Monographs of the Society for Research in Child Development*, 1966, 31 (3, Serial No. 105).

Spitz, R. A. Hospitalism: An inquiry into the genesis of psychiatric conditions in early childhood. In *The psychoanalytic study of the child*, Pt. 1 (3rd ed.). New York: International Universities Press, 1945. Pp. 53–74.

Weikart, D. P.   Early childhood special education for intellectually subnormal and/or culturally different children. Paper, National Leadership Institute in Early Childhood Development, Washington, D.C., October 1971.

White House Conference on Children. Report of Forum 8. *Report to the President: White House conference on children, 1970.* Washington, D.C.: U.S. Government Printing Office, 1970.

White, R.   Motivation reconsidered: The concept of competence. *Psychological Review*, 1959, 66:297–333.

Whiting, J., & Child, I.   *Child training and personality: A cross cultural study.* New Haven: Yale University Press, 1953.

THE WHY OF EARLY CHILDHOOD EDUCATION

Association for Supervision and Curriculum Development. *Early childhood education today.* Washington, D.C.: National Education Association, 1968.

Bloom, B. S.   *Stability and change in human characteristics.* New York: Wiley, 1964.

Bruner, J. S.   *The process of education.* Cambridge: Harvard University Press, 1961.

Day Care and Child Development Council of America.   *Manual for community coordinated child care.* Washington, D.C., 1969.

Hunt, J. McV.   *Intelligence and experience.* New York: Ronald Press, 1966.

Hunt, J. McV.   *The challenge of incompetence and poverty: Papers on the role of early education.* Urbana, Ill.: University of Illinois Press, 1969.

Johnson, L. B.   Remarks on announcing plans to extend Head Start. In *Published papers of the President* (No. 467, Aug. 31, 1965), Book 2 (June 1–Dec. 1, 1965). Washington, D.C.: Government Printing Office, 1966.

Martin, W. E.   Rediscovering the mind of the child: A significant trend in research child development. *Merrill-Palmer Quarterly*, 1960, 6:67–76.

Miller, J. O.   Early childhood education as an intervention in the child's ecological system. Paper, annual meeting of the American Academy of Education, Chicago, 1969.

National Society for the Study of Education.   *Preschool and parental education: Twenty-eighth yearbook of the National Society for the Study of Education.* Bloomington, Ill.: Public School Publishing, 1929.

Office of Economic Opportunity.   *Head Start child development programs: A manual of policies and instructions.* Washington, D.C.: U.S. Government Printing Office, September 1967.

Omwake, E. B.   Letter from the president. *Young Children*, 1969, 24:3.

Seifert, K.   Comparison of verbal interaction in two preschool programs. *Young Children*, 1969, 24:350–355.

Zigler, E.   The environmental mystique: Training the intellect versus development of the child. *Childhood Education*, 1970, 46:402–412.

THE IMPACT OF THEORIES OF CHILD DEVELOPMENT

Erikson, E.   *Childhood and society.* New York: Norton, 1950.

Gesell, A.   Maturation and infant behavior patterns. *Psychological Review*, July 1929.

Gesell, A.   *Youth: The years from ten to sixteen.* New York: Harper, 1940.

Gesell, A., et al. *The first five years of life.* New York: Harper, 1940.

Gesell, A., & Ilg, F. L. *The child from five to ten.* New York: Harper, 1946.

Gesell, A., & Ilg, F. L. *Infant and child in the culture of today.* New York: Harper, 1943.

Knapp, P. *Expression of emotions in man.* Symposium, annual meeting of the American Association for the Advancement of Science, 1960.

Miller, N. E., & Dollard, J. *Social learning and imitation.* New Haven, Conn.: Yale University Press, 1953.

Richmond, J. B., & Caldwell, B. M. *Child rearing practices and their consequences.* In press.

Rotter, J. B. *Social learning and clinical psychology.* New York: Prentice-Hall, 1954.

Skinner, B. F. *Science and human behavior.* New York: Macmillan, 1953.

Spock, B. M. *The common sense book of baby and child care.* New York: Duell, Sloan, and Pearce, 1946.

Watson, J. B. *Psychological care of infant and child.* London: Allen & Unwin, 1928.

A PERSPECTIVE ON SOCIAL LEARNING

Almy, M. *Child development.* New York: Holt, 1955.

Erikson, E. H. *Childhood and society.* New York: Norton, 1950.

Giles, H. H. *Human dynamics and human relations.* New York: New York University Press, 1954.

Witmer, H. L., & Kotinsky, R. (Eds.) *Personality in the making.* New York: Harper, 1952.

SOCIETY AND EDUCATION

Bronfenbrenner, U. Freudian theories of identification and their derivatives. *Child Development*, 1960, 31:15–40.

Burton, R., & Whiting, J. The absent father and cross-sex identity. *Merrill-Palmer Quarterly*, 1961, 7:85–95.

Kagan, J. The concept of identification. *Psychological Review*, 1958, 65:296–305.

THE SPLIT-LEVEL AMERICAN FAMILY

Ainsworth, M. D. Patterns of attachment behavior shown by the infant in interaction with his mother. *Merrill-Palmer Quarterly*, 1964, 10:51–58.

Borke, H. A family over three generations: The transmission of interacting and relating patterns. *Journal of Marriage and the Family*, 1967, 29(4):196–213.

Minturn, L., & Lambert, W. W. *Mothers of six cultures.* New York: Wiley, 1964.

Radke-Yarrow, M. Problems of method in parent-child research. *Child Development*, 1963, 34:215–226.

Reiss, I. L. The universality of the family: A conceptual analysis. *Journal of Marriage and the Family*, 1965, 27(4):443–453.

Rodman, H. Talcott Parsons' view of the changing American family. *Merrill-Palmer Quarterly*, 1965, 11(3):229–237.

Rosen, B. C. Family structure and value transmission. *Merrill-Palmer Quarterly*, 1964, 10:1147–1153.

Sears, R., Maccoby, E. E., & Levin, H. *Patterns of child rearing.* Chicago: Row, Peterson, 1957.

Sears, R. R., Rau, L., & Alpert, R. *Identification and child rearing.* Stanford, Calif.: Stanford University Press, 1965.

Waters, E., & Crandall, V. J. Social class and observed maternal behavior from 1940–1960. *Child Development,* 1964, 35:1197–1210.

Yarrow, L. J. Research in dimensions of early maternal care. *Merrill-Palmer Quarterly,* 1963, 9(2):101–114.

CAN YOUNG CHILDREN HAVE A QUALITY LIFE IN DAY CARE?

Ainsworth, M. D. S. Object relations, dependency, and attachment: A theoretical review of the infant-mother relationship. *Child Development,* 1969, 40:969–1025.

Braun, S. J., & Caldwell, B. M. Social adjustment of children in day care who enrolled prior to or after the age of three. *Early Child Development and Care,* 1972.

Caldwell, B. M. Impact of interest in early cognitive stimulation. In R. Rie (Ed.), *Perspectives in psychopathology.* Chicago: Aldine-Atherton, 1971. Pp. 293–334.

Caldwell, B. M., & Richmond, J. B. The children's center: A microcosmic health, education, and welfare unit. In L. Dittman (Ed.), *Early child care: The new perspectives.* New York: Atherton, 1968. Pp. 326–358, 373–377.

Caldwell, B. M., Wright, C. M., Honig, A. S., & Tannenbaum, J. Infant day care and attachment. *American Journal of Orthopsychiatry,* 1970, 40:397–412.

Freud, A., & Dann, S. An experiment in group upbringing. *Psychoanalytic Study of the Child,* 1951, 6:127–168.

Glezen, W. P., et al. Epidemiologic patterns of acute lower respiratory diseases of children in a pediatric group practice. *Journal of Pediatrics,* March 1971.

Harrington, M. *The other America.* New York: Macmillan, 1962.

Kayserling, M. D. *Windows on day care.* New York: National Council of Jewish Women, 1972.

Keister, M. E. *The "good life" for infants and toddlers.* Washington, D.C.: National Association for the Education of Young Children, 1970.

Lay, M. Z., & Meyer, W. J. *Effects of early day care experience on subsequent observed program behaviors.* Final report, U.S. Office of Education, Subcontract No. 70-007, Syracuse, N.Y.: Syracuse University, 1971.

Prescott, E., Jones, E., & Kritchevsky, S. *Group day care as a child-rearing environment: An observational study of day care programs.* Pasadena, Calif: Pacific Oaks College, 1967.

Prescott, E., Jones, E., & Kritchevsky, S. *Day care as a child-rearing environment,* Vol. 2. Washington, D.C.: National Association for the Education of Young Children, 1972.

Robinson, H. B., & Robinson, N. M. Longitudinal development of very young children in a comprehensive day care program: The first two years. *Child Development,* 1971: 42(6):1673–1683.

Schaffer, H. R., & Emerson, P. E. The development of social attachments in infancy. *Monographs of the Society for Research in Child Development,* 1964, 29(3, Whole No. 94):1–77.

ON SELECTING MATERIALS FOR THE CLASSROOM

Association for Childhood Education International. *Equipment and supplies, ACEI.* Washington, D.C., 1967.

Churchill, E. H. E., & Leitman, A. *Approximations 1.* Newton, Mass.: The Elementary Science Study, 1966.

Education Development Center Follow Through Program. *Instructional aids, materials and supplies.* Newton, Mass., March 1969.

Hull. The Elementary Science Study: Leicestershire revisited. Unpublished manuscript, 1964.

Technology for Children Project. *Happenings.* Trenton, N.J.: New Jersey State Department of Education (Periodical.)

Yeomans, E. *Education for initiative and responsibility.* Boston: National Association of Independent Schools, 1967. Pp. 35–50.

TOWARD A CONTACT CURRICULUM

Harlem Youth Opportunities Unlimited. *Youth in the Ghetto: A study of the consequences of powerlessness and a blueprint for change.* New York, 1964.

BASIC IDEAS OF THE MONTESSORI METHOD

Bailey, C. S. *Montessori children.* New York: Holt, 1915.

Boyd. *From Locke to Montessori.* Pp. 172–268.

Culverwell. *The Montessori principles and practice.* Chaps. 4, 5, 7.

Fisher. *The Montessori manual.* Pp. 16–29, 107–123.

Montessori. *The Montessori system.* Chaps. 5–7, 10–13, 16, 17, 19, 20.

Smith, A. T. *The Montessori system in education.* No. 17. Washington, D.C.: U.S. Government Printing Office, 1912. Pp. 5–25.

Stevens. *A guide to the Montessori system.* Chaps. 1–3, 6, 8, 10.

White. *Montessori schools as seen in the summer of 1912.* Chaps. 1, 10, 11 or Chaps. 2, 7, 13.

PRESCHOOL ENRICHMENT AND LEARNING

Briggs, C. H. An experimental study of reflection-impulsivity in children. Doctoral dissertation, University of Minnesota, 1966.

Debus, R. L. Effects of brief observation of model behavior on conceptual tempo of impulsive children. Unpublished manuscript, 1968.

De Gourmont, R. Dust for sparrows. In E. Pound, *The translations of Ezra Pound.* New York: New Directions, 1953. Pp. 363–397.

Kagan, J., Pearson, L., & Welch, L. Modifiability of an impulsive tempo. *Journal of Educational Psychology,* 1966, 57:359–365.

Nelson, T. F. The effects of training in attention deployment on observing behavior in reflective and impulsive children. Doctoral dissertation, University of Minnesota, 1968.

Yando, R. M., & Kagan, J. The effect of teacher tempo on the child. *Child Development,* 1968, 39:27–34.

PSYCHOLOGICAL CONTROVERSIES IN THE TEACHING OF SCIENCE AND MATHEMATICS

Bruner, J. I. S. *The process of education.* Cambridge, Mass.: Harvard University Press, 1960.

Bruner, J. S. *Toward a theory of instruction.* Cambridge, Mass.: Belknap, 1966.

Gagné, R. M. *The conditions of learning.* New York: Holt, Rinehart, and Winston, 1965.

Gagné, R. M. Contributions of learning to human development. Address of the vice-president, Sec. I (Psychology). Washington, D.C.: American Association for the Advancement of Science, December 1966.

Gagné, R. M. Personal communication. May 1968.

Jennings, F. G. Jean Paiget: Notes on learning. *Saturday Review,* May 20, 1967, 82.

Pain and progress in discovery. *Time,* Dec. 8, 1967, 110ff.

Shulman, L. S., & Keislar, E. R., (Eds.) *Learning by discovery: A critical appraisal.* Chicago: Rand McNally, 1966.

Worthen, B. R. Discovery and expository task presentation in elementary mathematics. *Journal of Educational Psychology Monograph Supplement,* February 1968, 59(1, Pt. 2).

ASPECTS OF PIAGET'S THEORY THAT HAVE IMPLICATIONS FOR TEACHER EDUCATION

Dennis, W. Causes of retardation among institutional children. *Journal of Genetic Psychology,* 1960, 96:47–59.

Flavell, J. *The developmental psychology of Jean Piaget.* Princeton, N.J.: Van Nostrand, 1963.

Inhelder, B., & Piaget, J. *The growth of logical thinking from childhood to adolescence.* New York: Basic Books, 1958.

Inhelder, B., & Piaget, J. *The early growth of logic in the child.* New York: Harper & Row, 1964.

Kessen, W., & Kuhlman, C. (Eds.) Thought in the young child. *Monographs of the Society for Research in Child Development,* 1962, 27(2).

Moltz, H. Contemporary instinct theory and the fixed action pattern. *Psychological Review,* 1965, 72:27–47.

Morf, A. Apprentissage d'une structure logique concrete: Effets et limites. *Études d'Epistémologie Génétique,* 1959, 9:15–83.

Piaget, J. *The language and thought of the child.* New York: Harcourt, Brace, and World, 1926.

Piaget, J. *Judgment and reasoning in the child.* New York: Harcourt, Brace, and World, 1928.

Piaget, J. *The moral judgment of the child.* London: Kegan Paul, 1932.

Piaget, J. *The psychology of intelligence.* New York: Harcourt, Brace, and World, 1950.

Piaget, J. *The origins of intelligence in children.* New York: International Universities Press, 1952.

Piaget, J. *Les mécanismes perceptifs.* Paris: Presses Univ., 1961.

Ripple, R., & Rockcastle, V. Piaget rediscovered. Report, conference on cognitive studies and curriculum development, Cornell University, March 1964.

Sigel, I. The acquisition of conservation: A theoretical and empirical analysis, 1965. (Mimeographed.)

Smedslund, J. The acquisition of conservation of substances and weight in children: 3. Extinction of conservation of weight acquired normally and by means of empirical controls on a balance scale. *Scandinavian Journal of Psychology*, 1961, 2:85–87.

Smedslund, J. The acquisition of conservation of substance and weight in children: 5. Practice in conflict situations without external reinforcement. *Scandinavian Journal of Psychology*, 1961, 2:203–210.

COGNITIVE DEVELOPMENT AND LEARNING MATHEMATICS

Almy, M. *Young children's thinking.* New York: Teachers College Press, Columbia University, 1967.

Copeland, R. W. *How children learn mathematics: Teaching implications of Piaget's research.* New York: Macmillan, 1970. Chap. 2.

Duckworth, E. Piaget rediscovered. In E. Victor & M. Lerner (Eds.), *Readings in science education for the elementary school.* New York: Macmillan, 1967.

Elkind, D. Children's discovery of mass, weight and volume. In I. Sigel & F. Hooper (Eds.), *Logical thinking in children.* New York: Holt, Rinehart and Winston, 1968.

Piaget, J. *The child's conception of number.* New York: Humanities Press, 1964.

Philips, J. L. *The origins of intellect: Piaget's theory.* San Francisco: Freeman, 1969.

Voyat, G. Sioux children: A study of their cognitive development. Paper, annual meeting of the American Educational Research Association, Washington, D.C., 1970. (In *Abstracts/One*, 1970.)

MANIPULATIVES IN THE CLASSROOM

Dienes, Z. P. Some basic processes involved in mathematics learning. G. W. Schminke & W. R. Arnold (Eds.), *Mathematics is a verb.* Hinsdale, Ill.: Dryden, 1971.

Fennema, E. H. Models and mathematics. *Arithmetic Teacher*, December 1972, 18:635–640.

Hartung, M. L. The role of experience in the learning of mathematics. *Arithmetic Teacher*, May 1972, 18:279–284.

Kieren, T. E. Manipulative activity in mathematics learning. *Journal for Research in Mathematics Education*, May 1971, 2:228–234.

Neale, D. C. The role of attitudes in learning mathematics. *Arithmetic Teacher*, December 1969, 16:631–640.

Suydam, M. N., & Weaver, J. F. *Instructional Materials and Media.* University Park, Pa.: Pennsylvania State University, 1970.

Weaver, J. F. Seductive shibboleths. *Arithmetic Teacher*, April 1971, 18:263–264.

CONCEPT DEVELOPMENT IN SCIENCE

California State Department of Education. *Science curriculum development in the elementary school.* Sacramento, Calif., 1964. Pp. 12–13.

Fish, A. Doctoral dissertation, University of Maryland, 1965.

Strasser, B. A conceptual model of instruction evolves as a way to study interaction processes (Pts. 1–2). *Curriculum Exchange*, February–March 1966, 8(5–6).

LANGUAGE DEVELOPMENT IN DAY-CARE PROGRAMS

Baratz, S. S., & Baratz, J. C. Early childhood intervention: the social science base of institutional racism. *Harvard Educational Review*, 1970, 40:29–50.

Bellugi-Klima, U. H. The acquisition of the system of negation in children's speech. Doctoral dissertation, Harvard University, 1967.

Cazden, C. B. Evaluating language learning in early childhood education. In B. S. Bloom, T. Hastings, & G. Madaus (Eds.), *Formative and summative evaluation of student learning*. New York: McGraw-Hill, in press.

Gleason, J. B. Do children imitate? In *Proceedings of the International Conference on Oral Education of the Deaf*, June 1967, Vol. 2. Pp. 1441–1448.

Greenberg, P. *The devil has slippery shoes: A biased biography of the child development group of Mississippi*. New York: Macmillan, 1969.

Hawkins, D. I. Thou, it. Paper, primary teachers' residential course, Leicestershire, England, April 1967. Newton, Mass.: Educational Development Center.

John, W. P., & Horner, V. *Early childhood bilingual education*. New York: Modern Language Association, in press.

Labov, W. The logic of nonstandard English. In F. Williams (Ed.), *Language and poverty: Perspectives on a theme*. Chicago, Ill.: Markham, 1970. Pp. 153–189.

McAfee, O. The right words. *Young Children*. 1967, 23:74–78.

Palmer, F. H. Socioeconomic status and intellective performance among Negro preschool boys. *Developmental Psychology*, 1970, 3:1–9.

Smothergill, N. L. The effects of manipulation of teacher communication style in the preschool. Syracuse Center for Research and Development in Early Childhood Education. Paper, biennial meeting of the Society for Research on Child Development, Santa Monica, Calif., March 1969.

Stendler-Lavatelli, C. *Piaget's theory applied to an early childhood curriculum*. Boston, Mass.: American Science and Engineering, 1970.

Tizard, J. Child welfare research group: Report on work carried out 1967–1969. University of London Institute of Education, Department of Child Development, 1970.

VALUES AND ISSUES IN YOUNG CHILDREN'S LITERATURE

Children's reading interests as related to sex and grade and school. *The School Review*, 1932, 40:252–272.

Curriculum for English A. Lincoln, Nebr.: University of Nebraska Press, 1966.

Erikson, E. *Childhood and society*. New York: Norton, 1950.

Lipkind, W., & Duvoisin, R. (Illust.) *Nubber bear*. New York: Harcourt, Brace, 1966.

Piaget, J. *The moral judgement of the child*. Glencoe, Ill.: Free Press, 1932.

Pitcher, E. G., & Prelinger, E. *Children tell stories: An analysis of fantasy*. New York: International Universities Press, 1963.

Sendak, M. *Where the wild things are.* New York: Harper & Row, 1963.

The story reader as teacher. *NAEYC Journal,* October 1966.

CONFUSION AND MISCONCEPTIONS
IN THE CONTROVERSY ABOUT KINDERGARTEN READING

Brown, M. W. A study of reading ability in preschool children. Master's thesis, Stanford University, 1924.

Chall, I. What research says about beginning reading. In *Children can learn to read—but how? Proceedings of the Rhode Island College Reading Conference,* 1964, 17–25.

Davidson, H. P. An experimental study of bright, average, and dull children at the four-year mental level. *Genetic Psychology Monographs,* March 1931, 9:119–287.

Durkin, D. *Children who read early.* New York: Teachers College Press, Columbia University, 1966.

Gates, A. I., & Bond, G. Reading readiness: A study of factors determining success and failure in beginning reading. *Teachers College Record,* May 1936, 37:679–685.

Ilg, F. L., & Ames, L. B. *School readiness.* New York: Harper & Row, 1964.

Morphett, M. V., & Washburne, C. When should children begin to read? *Elementary School Journal,* March 1931, 31:496–503.

Olson, W. *Child development.* Boston: Heath, 1949.

Rudolph, M., & Cohen, D. H. *Kindergarten: a year of learning.* New York: Appleton-Century-Crofts, 1964.

Sutton, M. H. Children who learned to read in kindergarten: A longitudinal study. *Reading Teacher,* April 1969, 22:595–602.

Wilson, F. T. Reading progress in kindergarten and primary grades. *Elementary School Journal,* February 1938, 38:442–449.

A STRATEGY FOR DEVELOPING VALUES

Alexander, A. The gray flannel cover of the American history text. *Social Education,* 1960, 24:11.

Allport, G. *Becoming: Basic considerations for a psychology of personality.* New Haven, Conn.: Yale University Press, 1955.

Cousins, N. Hoffa, Hegel, and Hoffer. *Saturday Review,* April 23, 1963.

Dewey, J. *Moral principles in education.* Boston: Houghton Mifflin, 1909.

Educational Policies Commission. *Moral and spiritual values in the public schools.* Washington, D.C.: National Education Association, 1957.

Friedenberg, E. Z. *The vanishing adolescent.* New York: Dell, 1962.

Ginsburg, S. W. Values and the psychiatrist. *American Journal of Orthopsychiatry,* 1950, 20:466.

Jacob, P. E. *Changing values in college.* New York: Harper & Row, 1957.

Jonas, A. A study of the relationship of certain behaviors of children to emotional needs, values, and thinking. Doctoral dissertation, New York University, 1960.

Jones, V. Character education. In C. Harris (Ed.), *Encyclopedia of Educational Research.* New York: Macmillan, 1960.

Keevan, A.   An investigation of a methodology of value clarification: Its relationship to consistency of thinking, purposefulness, and human relations. Doctoral dissertation, New York University, 1958.

Kubic, L.   Are we educating for maturity? *NEA Journal*, January 1959.

Raths, J.   Underachievement and a search for values. *Journal of Educational Sociology*, May 1961, 34:2.

Raths, J.   Clarifying children's values. *National Elementary Principal*, 1962, 62:2.

Raths, L. E.   Values and teachers. *Educational Synopsis*, Spring 1957.

Raths, L. E.   Sociological knowledge and needed curriculum research. In J. B. Macdonald (Ed.), *Research frontiers in the study of children's learning.* Milwaukee: University of Wisconsin, Milwaukee, School of Education, 1960.

Raths, L. E.   Clarifying values. In R. S. Fleming (Ed.), *Curriculum for today's boys and girls.* Columbus, Ohio: Merrill, 1963.

MORAL EDUCATION IN THE SCHOOLS: A DEVELOPMENTAL VIEW

Dewey, J.   *Moral principles in education.* Boston: Houghton Mifflin, 1911.

Durkheim, E.   *Moral education.* Glencoe, Ill.: Free Press, 1961. (Originally published 1925.)

Freud, S.   *Civilization and its discontents.* London: Hogarth, 1955. (Originally published 1938.)

Fromm, E.   *Man for himself.* New York: Rinehart, 1949.

Hartshorne, H., & May, M. A.   *Studies in the nature of character.* New York: Macmillan, 1928–1930. 3 vols.

Havighurst, R. J., & Taba, H.   *Adolescent character and personality.* New York: Wiley, 1949.

Horney, K.   *The neurotic personality of our times.* New York: Norton, 1937.

Josselyn, I. M.   *Psychosocial development of children.* New York: Family Service Association, 1948.

Kohlberg, L.   Moral development and identification. In H. Stevenson (Ed.), *Child psychology.* Chicago: University of Chicago Press, 1963a.

Kohlberg, L.   The development of children's orientations toward a moral order: I. Sequence in the development of moral thought. *Vita Humana*, 1963b, 6:11–33.

Kohlberg, L.   The development of children's orientations toward a moral order: II. Social experience, social conduct, and the development of moral thought. *Vita Humana*, 1966, 9.

Kohlberg, L.   The development of moral character and ideology. In M. Hoffman & L. Hoffman (Eds.), *Review of child development research.* New York: Russell Sage Foundation, 1964.

Peck, R. F., & Havighurst, R. J.   *The psychology of character development.* New York: Wiley, 1960.

Piaget, J.   *The moral judgment of the child.* Glencoe, Ill.: Free Press, 1948. (Originally published 1932.)

THE ANTECEDENTS OF SELF-ESTEEM

Bandura, A., & Walters, R.   *Social learning and personality development.* New York: Holt, Rinehart and Winston, 1963.

Bateson, G. Cultural determinants of personality. In J. McV. Hunt (Ed.), *Personality and the behavior disorders*, Vol. 2. New York: Ronald Press, 1944.

Bowlby, J. Maternal care and mental health. *World Health Organization Monograph*, 1951, No. 2.

Goldfarb, W. Psychological privation in infancy and subsequent adjustment. *American Journal of Orthopsychiatry*, 1945, 15:247–255.

Levin, H. Permissive child rearing and adult role behavior in children. Paper, meeting of the Eastern Psychological Association, Atlantic City, N.J., March 1952.

Sears, R. R. Identification as a form of behavioral development. In D. B. Harris (Ed.), *The concept of development*. Minneapolis: University of Minnesota Press, 1954.

Whiting, J. W. [Symposium paper.] In J. M. Tanner & B. Inhelder (Eds.), *Discussions on child development* II. New York: International Universities Press, 1954.

EARLY PRESSURES IN CHILD DEVELOPMENT

Beller, E. K. Dependency and independence in young children. *Journal of Genetic Psychology*, 1955, 87:23–25.

Crandall, V. Achievement. In H. W. Stevenson (Ed.), *Child psychology: Sixty-second yearbook of the National society for the study of education*, Pt. 1. Chicago: University of Chicago Press, 1963.

Crandall, V. Achievement behavior in young children. *Young Children*, 1964, 20:76–90.

Crandall, V., Preston, A., & Ralson, A. Maternal reactions and the development of independence and achievement behavior in young children. *Child Development*, 1960, 31:243–251.

Fales, E. Genesis of level of aspiration in children from one and one-half to three years of age. Reported in K. Lewin et al., Level of aspiration. In J. McV. Hunt (Ed.), *Personality and the behavior disorders*, Vol. 1. New York: Ronald Press, 1944. Pp. 333–378.

Feld, S. Need achievement and test anxiety in children and maternal attitudes and behaviors toward independent accomplishments: A longitudinal study. Paper, convention of American Psychological Association, Cincinnati, 1959.

Festinger, L. *A theory of cognitive dissonance*. Stanford: Stanford University Press, 1957.

Gewirtz, J. L. Three determinants of attnetion-seeking in young children. *Monographs of the Society for Research in Child Development*, 1954, 19 (2, Serial No. 59).

Harris, F. R., Wolf, M. M., & Baer, D. M. Effects of adult social reinforcement on child behavior. *Young Children*, 1964, 20:8–17.

Hartup, W. W. Friendship status and the effectiveness of peers as reinforcing agents. *Journal of Experimental Child Psychology*, 1964, 1:154–162.

Heathers, G. Emotional dependence and independence in nursery-school play. *Journal of Genetic Psychology*, 1955, 87:37–58.

McClelland, D., Atkinson, J., Clark, R., & Lowell, E. *The achievement motive.* New York: Appleton-Century-Crofts, 1953.

McGraw, M. B. *Growth: a study of Johnny and Jimmy.* New York: Appleton-Century, 1935.

Moss, H. A., & Kagan, J. Maternal influences on early IQ scores. *Psychological Reports,* 1958, 4:655–661.

Rosen, B., & D'Andrade, R. The psychosocial origins of achievement motivation. *Sociometry,* 1959, 22:185–218.

Sears, R. R., Whiting, J. W. M., Nowlis, V., & Sears, P. S. Some child-rearing antecedents of dependency and aggression in young children. *Genetic Psychology Monographs,* 1953, 47:135–234.

Sonis, M. Controversy and conflict in child development. *Journal of Nursery Education,* 1963, 18:160–167.

Whiting, J. W. M., & Child, I. *Child training and personality.* New Haven: Yale University Press, 1953.

Winterbottom, M. The relation of need for achievement learning experiences in independence and mastery. In J. Atkinson (Ed.), *Motives in fantasy, action, and society.* Princeton: Van Nostrand, 1958. Pp. 453–478.

Wright, M. E. The influence of frustration upon the social relationships of young children. Doctoral dissertation, State University of Iowa, 1940.

AGGRESSION AND TIMIDITY IN YOUNG CHILDREN

Dawe, H. C. An analysis of two hundred quarrels of preschool children. *Child Development,* 1934, 5:139–157.

Green, E. H. Friendships and quarrels among preschool children. *Child Development,* 1933, 4:237–252.

Jersild, A. T., & Markey, F. V. *Conflicts between preschool children.* New York: Teachers College Press, Columbia University, 1935.

Muste, M. J., & Sharpe, D. F. Some influential factors in the determination of aggressive behavior in preschool children. *Child Development,* 1947, 18:11–28.

SEX ROLES IN EARLY READING TEXTBOOKS

Blom, G. E., et al. Content of first-grade reading books. *The Reading Teacher,* January 1968, 317–323.

Doely, S. B. Sex role stereotyping. In *Women's liberation and the church.* New York: Association Press, 1970. Pp. 119–124.

A feminist look at children's books. *School Library Journal,* January 1971, 19–24.

Harris, A. J., & Clark, M. K. *The Macmillan reading program: Primary grades.* New York: Macmillan, 1970.

Meade, M. Miss Muffett must go. *Woman's Day,* March 1971, 64–65ff.

Ousley, O., & Russell, D. H. The Ginn basic readers. Boston: Ginn, 1966.

Robinson, H. M., et al. The new basic readers. Glenview, Ill.: Scott, Foresman, 1962.

Seidenberg, R. *Marriage in life and literature.* New York: Philosophical Library, 1970.

Sheldon, W. D., et al. *Sheldon basic reading series*. Boston: Allyn & Bacon, 1968.

Stefflre, B. Run, mama, run: Women workers in elementary readers. *Vocational Guidance Quarterly*, December 1969, 99–102.

THE STUDENT'S WORLD

Santayna, G. The Latin school. In C. M. Fuess & E. S. Basford (Eds.), *Unseen harvests*. New York: Macmillan, 1947.

A SOCIAL REINFORCEMENT TECHNIQUE
FOR THE CLASSROOM MANAGEMENT OF BEHAVIOR DISORDERS

Azrin, N. H., & Lindsley, O. R. The reinforcement of cooperation between children. *The Journal of Abnormal and Social Psychology*, 1956, 52:100–102.

Golden grades. *Newsweek*, 1966, 67(14):62.

Hewett, F. M. A hierarchy of educational tasks for children with learning disorders. *Exceptional Children*, 1964, 31:207–214.

Hewett, F. M. The Tulare experimental class for educationally handicapped children. *California Education*, 1966, 3(6):6–8.

Lindsley, O. R. Experimental analysis of social reinforcement: terms and methods. *The American Journal of Orthopsychiatry*, 1963, 33:624–633.

ISSUES IN THE EDUCATION OF THE DISADVANTAGED

Ausubel, D. P. The influence of experience on the development of intelligence. In C. Bish & M. J. Aschner (Eds.), *Productive thinking in education*. Washington, D.C.: The National Education Association, 1965.

Bereiter, C., & Engelmann, S. *Teaching disadvantaged preschool children*. Englewood Cliffs, N.J.: Prentice-Hall, 1966.

Bronfenbrenner, U. The psychological costs of quality and equality in education. *Child Development*, 1967, 38:909–925.

Coleman, J. S., et al. Equality of educational opportunity. Washington, D.C.: U.S. Office of Education, Government Printing Office, 1966.

Harlem Youth Opportunities Unlimited (Haryou). *Youth in the ghetto*. New York, 1964.

Justman, J. Academic aptitude and reading test scores of disadvantaged children showing varying degrees of mobility. Bureau of Educational Program Research, N.Y.C. Board of Education, 1965. (Mimeographed.)

Lesser, G. S., Fifer, G., & Clark, D. H. *Mental abilities of children in different social and cultural groups*. Cooperative Research Project No. 1635. Washington, D.C.: U.S. Office of Education, 1964.

Moore, O. K. The responsive environments project and the deaf. *American Annals of the Deaf*, 1965, 110:604–614.

Rosenthal, R., & Jacobson, L. *Pygmalion in the classroom*. New York: Holt, Rinehart & Winston, 1968.

Sexton, P. C. *Education and income: inequalities of opportunity in our public schools*. New York: Viking, 1961.

Spache, G. D. Contributions of allied fields to the teaching of reading. In H. Robinson (Ed.), *Sixty-seventh yearbook of the National Society for the Study of Education*, Pt. 2, 1968.

Strodtbeck, F. L. The hidden curriculum of the middle-class home. In C. W. Hunnicut (Ed.), *Urban education and cultural deprivation.* Syracuse, N.Y.: Syracuse University Press, 1964. Pp. 15–31.

U.S. Bureau of Labor Statistics. Social and economic conditions of Negroes in the United States, BLS Report No. 332. *Current population reports,* Series P-23, No. 24. Washington, D.C.: U.S. Government Printing Office, October 1967.

Weikart, D. P. Preschool intervention: a preliminary report of the Perry preschool project. Ann Arbor, Mich.: Campus Publishers, 1967.

Wilson, A. B. Residential segregation of social classes and aspirations of high school boys. *American Sociological Review,* 1959, 24:836–845.

PREJUDICE AND YOUR CHILD

Berenda, R. W. *The influence of the group on the judgments of children.* New York: King's Crown Press, 1950.

Horowitz, E. L. The development of attitudes toward the Negro. *Archives of Psychology,* 1936, 194.

BEGINNING READING: A PERSONAL AFFAIR

Ashton-Warner, S. *Spinster.* New York: Simon & Schuster, 1958.

REQUIREMENTS FOR A VALID NEW CRITICISM

Epstein, J. The politics of school decentralization. *New York Review of Books,* June 6, 1968.

Goodman, P. Freedom and learning: The need for choice. *Saturday Review,* May 18, 1968a.

Goodman, P. In praise of populism. *Commentary,* June 1968b, 25–30.

PARENT INVOLVEMENT IN EARLY EDUCATION

Ainsworth, M. D. S. Object relations, dependency, and attachment: A theoretical review of the infant-mother relationship. *Child Development,* 1969, 40(4):969–1025.

Ainsworth, M. D. S., & Bell, S. M. Attachment, exploration, and separation: Illustrated by the behavior of one-year-olds in a strange situation. *Child Development,* 1970, 41(1):49–67.

Arsenian, J. M. Young children in an insecure situation. *Journal of Abnormal and Social Psychology,* 1943, 38:225–249.

Badger, E. Mothers' training program: Evaluation procedures. Unpublished manuscript, 1969.

Badger, E. Mothers' training program: A new identity for the poor. Unpublished manuscript, 1970.

Baumrind, D., & Black, A. Socialization practices associated with dimensions of competence in preschool boys and girls, *Child Development,* 1967, 38:291–327.

Bayley, N., & Schaefer, E. S. Correlations of maternal and child behavior with the development of mental abilities: Data from the Berkeley growth study. *Monographs of the Society for Research in Child Development,* 1964, 29(Serial No. 97).

Bee, H., et al.   Social class differences in maternal teaching strategies and speech patterns. *Developmental Psychology*, 1969, 1(6):726–734.

Bell, S. M.   The development of the concept of object as related to infant-mother attachment. *Child Development*, 1970, 41(2):291–311.

Bernstein, B.   Social class and linguistic development: A theory of social learning. In A. H. Halsey et al. (Eds.), *Economy, education and society*. Glencoe, Ill.: Free Press, 1961. Pp. 288–314.

Bing, E.   Effects of childrearing practices on development of differential cognitive abilities. *Child Development*, 1963, 34:631–648.

Bloom, B.   *Stability and change in human characteristics*. New York: Wiley, 1964.

Bowlby, J.   The nature of the child's tie to his mother. *International Journal of Psychoanalysis*, 1958, 39:350–372.

Bowlby, J.   *Attachment and loss*, Vol. 1: *Attachment*. London: Hogarth, 1969.

Bradshaw, C. E.   *Relationship between maternal behavior and infant performance in environmentally disadvantaged homes*. Doctoral dissertation, University of Florida, 1968.

Brody, G. F.   Maternal child-rearing attitudes and child behavior. *Developmental Psychology*, 1969, 1:66.

Bronfenbrenner, U.   Socialization and social class through time and space. In E. E. Maccoby, T. M. Newcomb, & E. L. Hartley (Eds.), *Readings in social psychology*, New York: Holt, 1958.

Bronfenbrenner, U.   *Two worlds of childhood: U.S. and U.S.S.R.* New York: Russell Sage Foundation, 1970.

Brophy, J. E.   Mothers as teachers of their own preschool children: The influence of socioeconomic status and task structure on teaching specificity. *Child Development*, 1970, 41(1):79–94.

Busse, T.   Child rearing correlates of flexible thinking. *Developmental Psychology*, 1969, 1:585–591.

Caldwell, B. M., Wright, C. M., Honig, A. B., & Tannenbaum, J.   Infant day-care and attachment. *American Journal of Orthopsychiatry*, 1970, 40(3):397–412.

Cazden, C. B.   The neglected situation in child language research and education. In F. Williams (Ed.), *Language and poverty, perspectives on a theme*. Chicago: Markham, 1970. Pp. 81–101.

Chance, J.   Independence training and first graders' achievements. *Journal of Consulting Psychology*, 1961, 25(2):149–154.

Coleman, J.   *Equality of educational opportunity*. Washington, D.C.: U.S. Government Printing Office, 1966.

Coopersmith, S.   *The antecedents of self-esteem*. San Francisco: Freeman, 1967.

Cox, F. N., & Campbell, D.   Young children in a new situation with and without their mothers. *Child Development*, 1968, 39:123–131.

Crandall, V. C., Preston, A., & Robson, A.   Maternal reactions and development of independence and achievement behavior in young children. *Child Development*, 1960, 31:243–251.

Crandall, V. C., Dewey, R., Katkovsky, W., & Preston, A.   Parents attitudes and behaviors and grade school children's academic achievements. *Journal of*

Davis, W. L., & Phares, E. J. Parental antecedents and internal control. *Psychological Reports*, 1969, 24:427–436.

Drews, E. M., & Teahan, J. E. Parental attitudes and academic achievement. *Journal of Clinical Psychology*, 1957, 13(4):328–332.

Freeberg, N. E., & Payne, D. T. Parental influence on cognitive development in early childhood: A review. *Child Development*, 1967, 111:245–261.

Gewirtz, J. L. Mechanisms of social learning. In D. A. Goslin (Ed.), *Handbook of socialization theory and research*. New York: Rand McNally, 1969, Pp. 57–212.

Goldberg, S., & Lewis, M. Play behavior in the year-old infant: Early sex differences. *Child Development*, 1969, 40:21–31.

Gordon, I. J. *Reaching the child through parent education: The Florida approach*. Gainesville, Fla.: Institute for the Development of Human Resources, University of Florida, 1969.

Gordon, I. J. Developing parent power. In E. Grotberg (Ed.), *Critical issues in research related to disadvantaged children*. Princeton, N.J.: Educational Testing Service, 1969.

Grotberg, E., (Ed.) *Critical issues in research related to Disadvantaged children*. Princeton, N.J.: Educational Testing Service, 1969.

Hanson, S., Stern, C., Kitano, H. L. Attitude differences related to economic status: The development of the ADRES scale. Unpublished manuscript, 1968.

Hess, R. D. Parental behavior and children's school achievement. Implications for Head Start. In E. Grotberg (Ed.), *Critical issues in research related to disadvantaged children*. Princeton, N.J.: Educational Testing Service, 1969.

Hess, R. D. Social class and ethnic influences upon socialization. In P. H. Mussen (Ed.), *Carmichael's manual of child psychology* (3rd ed.), Vol. 2. New York: Wiley, 1970.

Hess, R. D., & Shipman, V. Cognitive elements in maternal behavior. In J. P. Hill (Ed.), *Minnesota symposia on child psychology*, Vol. I. Minneapolis: University of Minnesota Press, 1967.

Hess, R. D., Shipman, V. C., Brophy, J., & Bear, R. B. *The Cognitive environments of urban preschool children*. Report to Children's Bureau, Social Security Administration, U.S. Department of Health, Education, and Welfare, 1968.

Hess, R. D., Shipman, V. C., Brophy, J., & Bear, R. B. (in collaboration with A. Adelberger) *The cognitive environment of urban preschool Negro children: Follow-up phase*. Report to Children's Bureau, Social Security Administration. Washington, D.C.: U.S. Department of Health, Education, and Welfare, 1969.

Herzog, E., & Sudia, C. E. *Boys in fatherless families*. Washington, D.C.: U.S. Department of Health, Education, and Welfare, Office of Child Development, Children's Bureau, 1970.

Hoffman, L. W. Effects of the employment of mothers on parental power relations and the division of household tasks. Unpublished manuscript, 1959.

Honzik, M. P. Environmental correlates of mental growth: Prediction from the family setting at 21 months. *Child Development*, 1967, 337–364.

Hubner, J. *Teaching styles of mothers of low income Spanish surname pre-school children.* Unpublished master's thesis, San Francisco State College, 1970.

Kagan, J., & Moss, H. A. *Birth to maturity.* New York: Wiley, 1962.

Kagan, J., & Freeman, M. Relation of childhood intelligence, maternal behaviors and social class to behavior during adolescence. *Child Development*, 1963, 34:899–911.

Kamii, C. K., & Radin, M. L. Class differences in the socialization practices of Negro mothers. *Journal of Marriage and the Family*, 1967, 29:302–310.

Karnes, M. B. *A new role for teachers: Involving the entire family in the education of preschool disadvantaged children.* Urbana: University of Illinois, 1969.

Karnes, M. B., Teska, J. A., Hodgins, A. A., & Badger, E. Educational intervention at home by mothers of disadvantaged infants. *Child Development*, 1970, in press.

Katkovsky, W., Preston, A., & Crandall, V. C. Parents' attitudes toward their personal achievements and toward the achievement behaviors of their children. *Journal of Genetic Psychology*, 1964, 104:105–121.

Katkovsky, W., Crandall, V. C., & Good, S. Parental antecedents of children's beliefs in internal-external control of reinforcements in intellectual achievement situations. *Child Development*, 1967, 38:765–776.

Klaus, R. A., & Gray, S. W. The educational training program for disadvantaged children. A report after five years. *Monographs of the Society for Research in Child Development.* 1965, 33(4).

Labov, W., et al. *A preliminary study of the sturcture of English used by Negro and Puerto Rican speakers in New York City.* Cooperative Research Project Report No. 3091, 1968.

Lane, M. *Nurseries in cross-cultural education.* Progress report, National Institute of Mental Health Grant MH-14782, June 1968.

Landy, F., Rosenberg, B. G., & Sutton-Smith, B. The effect of limited father absence on cognitive development. *Child Development*, 1969, 10(3):941–944.

Lesser, G. S., Fifer, G., & Clark, D. J. Mental abilities of children from different social class and cultural groups. *Monographs of the Society for Research in Child Development*, 1965, 30(Serial No. 102.)

Lesser, G. S. & Stodolsky, S. Learning patterns in the disadvantaged. *Harvard Education Review*, 1967, 37(4):546–593.

Levenstein, P. Fostering the mother's role in the cognitive growth of low income preschoolers: A new family agency function. Paper, National Conference of Social Welfare, 1969.

Levenstein, P. Cognitive growth in preschoolers through verbal interaction with mothers. *American Journal of Orthopsychiatry*, 1970, 40(3):426–432.

Lewis, H. Child rearing among low income families. In L. Ferman et al. (Eds.), *Poverty in America.* Ann Arbor, Mich.: University of Michigan Press, 1965. Pp. 342–353.

Lewis, M., & Goldberg, S. *Perceptual-cognitive development in infancy: A generalized expectancy model as a function of the mother-infant interaction.* ERIC Document File, 1968. ED 024 4170, 1968.

Maccoby, E. E., & Masters, J. C. Attachment and dependency. In P. Mussen (Ed.), *Carmichael's manual of child psychology* (3rd ed.), Vol. 2. New York: Wiley, 1970.

Mannino, F. V. Family factors related to school persistence. *Journal of Educational Sociology*, 1962, 35:193–202.

McCarthy, D. Language development in children. In L. Carmichael (Ed.), *Manual of child psychology* (2nd ed.). New York: Wiley, 1954.

Miller, J. O. *Diffusion of intervention effects in disadvantaged families.* Urbana, Ill.: University of Illinois Coordination Center, National Laboratory of Early Childhood Education, 1968.

Milner, E. A study of the relationship between reading readiness in grade one school children and patterns of parent-child interaction. *Child Development*, 1951, 22(2):95–112.

Moore, T. Language and intelligence: A longitudinal study of the first eight years. *Human Development*, 1968, 11:1–24.

Moss, H. A., & Robson, K. S. Maternal influences in early social visual behavior. *Child Development*, 1968, 39:401–408.

Piaget, J. *The origins of intelligence in children.* New York: Norton, 1952.

Rheingold, J. L., & Eckerman, C. D. The infant's free entry into a new environment. *Journal of Experimental Child Psychology*, 1969, 8:271–283.

Rosen, B. C., & D'Andrade, R. The psychosocial origins of achievement motivation. *Sociometry*, 1959, 22:185–218.

Rosenshine, B., & Furst, N. The effects of tutoring upon pupil achievement: A review of the research, 1969. (Available from Department of Psychology, Temple University, Philadelphia, Pa.)

Rotter, J. B. Generalized expectancies for internal versus external control of reinforcement. *Psychological Monographs*, 1966, 80(1):1–28.

Rubenstein, J. Maternal attentiveness and subsequent exploratory behavior on the infant. *Child Development*, 1967, 38:1089–1100.

Scheinfeld, D. On developing developmental families. In E. Grotberg (Ed.), *Critical issues in research related to disadvantaged children.* Princeton, N.J.: Educational Testing Service, 1969.

Scott, C. Recruiting low income families for family life education programs. Paper, annual forum National Conference on Social Welfare. New York: Child Study Association of America, 1964.

Sears, R. Relation of early socialization experiences to self-concepts and gender role in middle childhood. *Child Development*, 1970, 41(2):267–289.

Sears, R., Maccoby, E. E., & Levin, H. *Patterns of child-rearing.* Evanston, Ill.: Row, Peterson, 1957.

Shaw, M. C. Note on parent attitudes toward independence training and the academic achievement of their children. *Journal of Educational Psychology*, 1964, 55(6):371–374.

Slaughter, D. T. *Maternal antecedents of the academic achievement behavior of Negro Head Start children.* Doctoral dissertation, University of Chicago, 1968.

Slaughter, D. T. Parental potency and the achievements of inner-city black children. *American Journal of Orthopsychiatry*, 1970, 40(3):433–440.

478 *selected references*

Solomon, D., Parelious, R. K., & Busse, T. V.   Dimensions of achievement-related behavior among lower class Negro parents. *Genetic Psychology Monographs*, 1969, 79:163–190.

Spiro, M.   *Children of the kibbutz.* New York: Schocken, 1965.

Stern, C., Kitano, H. L., Gaal, A., Goetz, B., Davis, S., & Lockhart-Mummery, L.   Bridging the gaps. Unpublished manuscript, undated.

Stewart, R. S.   Personality maladjustment and reading achievement. *American Journal of Orthopsychiatry*, 1950, 20:410–417.

Tuck, S.   A model for working with black fathers. Paper, American Orthopsychiatric Association, San Francisco, 1969.

Weikart, D., & Lambie, D.   Preschool intervention through a home teaching program. In J. Hellmuth (Ed.), *The disadvantaged child*, Vol. 2. Seattle: Special Child Publications, 1967.

Weikart, D., & Lambie, D.   *Carnegie infant project.* Ypsilanti, Mich.: Public Schools, Department of Research and Development, 1969.

Westinghouse Learning Corporation.   *The impact of Project Head Start: An evaluation of the effects of Head Start on children's cognitive and affective development.* Athens, Ohio: Ohio University, June 1969.

Wolf, R. M.   *The identification and measurement of environmental process variables related to intelligence.* Doctoral dissertation, University of Chicago, 1964.

index